BECOMING NATIONAL

BECOMING NATIONAL

A READER

Edited by
Geoff Eley and Ronald Grigor Suny

New York   *Oxford*
OXFORD UNIVERSITY PRESS
1996

Oxford University Press

Oxford   New York

Athens   Auckland   Bangkok   Bombay
Calcutta   Cape Town   Dar es Salaam   Delhi
Florence   Hong Kong   Istanbul   Karachi
Kuala Lumpur   Madras   Madrid   Melbourne
Mexico City   Nairobi   Paris   Singapore
Taipei   Tokyo   Toronto

and associated companies in
Berlin   Ibadan

Published by Oxford University Press, Inc.
198 Madison Avenue, New York, New York 10016

Oxford is a registered trademark of Oxford University Press

Library of Congress Cataloging-in-Publication Data
Becoming national : a reader / edited by Geoff Eley and Ronald Grigor Suny.
p. cm.
Includes bibliographical references.
ISBN-13 978-0-19-509661-3 (pbk.)

1. Nationalism.   I. Eley, Geoff, 1949–   .   II. Suny, Ronald Grigor.
JC311.B4125   1996   320.5′4—dc20
95-34438

Printed in the United States of America
on acid-free paper

Contents

BECOMING NATIONAL

Introduction: From the Moment of Social History to the Work of Cultural Representation[1]

GEOFF ELEY AND RONALD GRIGOR SUNY

With the collapse of the Soviet Union and the end of Communism in Europe, a new specter has been haunting the globe. As Partha Chatterjee has written,

> Nationalism is now viewed as a dark, elemental, unpredictable force of primordial nature threatening the orderly calm of civilized life. What had once been banished to the outer peripheries of the earth is now seen picking its way back toward Europe, through the long-forgotten provinces of the Habsburg, the Czarist, and the Ottoman empires. Like drugs, terrorism, and illegal immigration, it is one more product of the Third World that the West dislikes but is powerless to stop.[2]

Taking the century as a whole, nationalism has come in waves, crashing across the ruins of empires. When the great multinational states of the nineteenth century fell apart, transforming the landscapes of eastern Europe, central Asia, and the Near East after 1917, not only were new nation-states formed in their debris, but nationalism itself became an object of academic study in the interwar years, conducted under the sign of a new validating norm, the self-determination of peoples. But this generally positive valence of nationalism in the first postwar decade dissipated rapidly before the rise of fascism, with its expansionist drives and attendant excess, its chauvinism and privileging of race. Something resembling the euphoria of national self-determination in 1917–18 then accompanied the end of the Second World War, as the European peoples cast off the Nazi occupation, while another wave of interest in nationalism and nation-forming rose from the slow collapse of the great European overseas empires in the decades after 1945. But liberalism's traditional support for national self-determination had now been shaken. The perverse extension of nationalism into racialized forms of political and cultural address, and their translation into violent action, including rampant anti-Semitism and the Nazis' genocidal ambitions, rendered nationalist beliefs deeply suspect. A far darker reading of nationalism's implications then combined with fear in the First World of the implications of nationalism's alliance with the anticolonialist Left. Allied with American power in the years of the cold war, the attack on nationalism and its legitimacy, a feature of European conservative thought long before Lord Acton, easily took on a new vigor. Still, the greatest ambivalence and suspicion of nationalism crested with the fall of the Soviet Union, which brought the third of our waves of nationalist activity into life, both within the former Soviet state and in eastern Europe. This most recent resurgence leaves the post-Communist world frighteningly vulnerable, confronted by new and seemingly incomprehensible threats.

The distance between popular and journalistic views of ethnic conflict and nationalism and the more recent academic thinking about nations and nationalities has been growing in recent years, as theorists and researchers have radically transformed our vision of these foundational categories of human organization. Decades ago, when we entered graduate school, the idealist and "organic" thinking about nations, deriving its long pedigree from Johann Gottfried von Herder, Johann Gottlieb Fichte, and the earliest initiators of the discourse of the nation, was still intact in the work of Hans Kohn and Carleton Hayes. The nation was seen as something natural and objective, even if the hard work of intellectuals was needed to convince large numbers of people that this was so. The world was inevitably and fatally divided into nations, based in cultural and linguistic diversity, and national self-realization was a legitimate and positive goal of political struggles, even wars. National spirits or essences, the irrepressible desire for "freedom," were the irreducible sources that ultimately would require national self-government, whether expressed in forms of national autonomy, independence, or statehood.

Carleton Hayes, the pioneer of serious academic work on the subject, treated nationalism largely as an intellectual tradition whose origins were to be uncovered in the writings of significant past intellectuals.[3] For many years the torch of straightforward intellectual history was borne by Hans Kohn, whose writings embraced virtually the entire European continent.[4] Kohn elaborated the idea that the history of nationalism represented a progressive degeneration from rationality into a kind of madness, best exemplified by National Socialism. Nationalism had consumed its own legitimacy in violence, war, and messianic authoritarianism— a view both Eurocentric in the extreme and also heavily focused on the special experience of Germany and Italy. Kohn distinguished between a political or voluntarist conception of nationality and an irrational or organic one. The former originates in the great constructive experience of the French Revolution and is linked to notions of citizenship and popular sovereignty, where the nation signifies a political category of freely associating individuals. The organic version, on the other hand, denies this implied contractual basis and insists instead on the inherited, historicist character of national identity. It originates with Herder and the German romantics, and has normally been associated with an intellectual and political reaction against the French Revolution. Hence it is thought to be deeply antipathetic to the ideas of liberal democracy usually derived from the first conception and marked a deep divide between German and Western political thought. As summarized by Anthony D. Smith, in the organic concept of the nation the individual has no meaning apart from the community of birth. Individuality is predicated of the group. The individual can realize himself through it alone. It has a life history, it is self-generating and self-sufficient, a seamless, mythic entity, ascertainable through objective characteristics—of history, religion, language and customs. Nations are "natural" wholes, they constitute the sole historical realities. Therefore the individual is primarily distinguishable in terms of his nationality, and only secondarily by social and personal traits. To opt out of the community is to risk the loss of a man's individuality.[5]

This binary opposition between a political and an organic conception of the nation—which in Kohn's case forms the basis of a simplistic distinction between "Western" and "Eastern" forms of nationalism—is also represented in much of the literature as a political contrast between left and right which is developmentally conceived, so that during the nineteenth and early twentieth centuries nationalism gradually sheds its "progressive" or democratic attributes and acquires a generally right-wing meaning. In the intellectual climate of the two postwar decades, with its stress on larger political communities, self-confessedly nationalist affiliations became somewhat disreputable and archaic, a symptom of regional backwardness eventually to be overcome.

Several points can be made about this syndrome. First, the political degeneration of nationalist ideology (the passage from left to right) is conceived as both a spatial and a temporal movement; as nationalism moves further to the east during the nineteenth century, embracing Germany and the territories of the Habsburg monarchy, the irrationalist and organicist elements increasingly prevail, while in the West specifically nationalist movements (those mobilizing exclusively or primarily around this or that aspect of the national idea) invariably fall prey to the same tendency. But, second, this homology of ideological, geographical, and chronological movement makes sense only in terms of a basically idealist mode of explanation, in which nationalism is seen as a global stream of ideas, with a common intellectual fount (the originating experience of the Enlightenment and the French Revolution) and several major tributaries (for example, the resurgence of economic protectionism during the nineteenth century, or the emergence of "integral" nationalism in the early twentieth). Broadly speaking, this was the approach of Hayes and his academic progeny. In principle it is scarcely conducive to a contextual analysis and in practice has seldom spawned a social history of nationalist ideas. Yet third, this has rarely prevented its exponents from venturing fairly strong generalizations about the social basis of nationalism's appeal. In this respect the degeneration was thought to coincide with the entry of the masses into politics, in situations where the mechanisms for integrating them (that is, parliamentary democracy, or a "developed" political culture) were inadequately formed. This has been a common analysis of Nazism, fascism, and other movements of the radical right, and clearly converges with important areas of discussion in political and developmental sociology. In intellectual history the symptomatic text was J. L. Talmon's *The Origins of Totalitarian Democracy* (1951).

Inspired by the conservative antinationalism of Lord Acton, Elie Kedourie's book *Nationalism*, which appeared in 1960, fired a first salvo in the process of deconstructing nationalism. "Nationalism," he proclaimed at the outset,

> is a doctrine invented in Europe at the beginning of the nineteenth century. It pretends to supply a criterion for the determination of the unit of population proper to enjoy a government exclusively its own, for the legitimate exercise of power in the state, and for the right organisation of a society of states. Briefly, the doctrine holds that humanity is naturally divided into nations, that nations are known by certain characteristics which can be ascertained, and that the only legitimate type of government is national self-government.[6]

But the most important interventions moving us from a primordialist, essentialist notion of the nation to the currently dominant view of the nation as constructed or invented (note here the move from nationalism to nation) were those of modernization theorists, like Ernest Gellner in the famous chapter 7 in *Thought and Change* (1964), and communications theorists, like Karl Deutsch, in his compelling work of social science, *Nationalism and Social Communication* (1953). Both connected the emergence of nationalism and, by implication, the nation to the "Great Transformation" of modern times—the rise of the modern, or what Marxists called the transition from feudalism to capitalism. In his typically iconoclastic prose, Gellner rejected any idea that nationality or nationalism was natural or primordial and pointed out that for much of history tribes, villages, city-states, feudal settlements, dynastic empires, or the "loose moral communities of a shared religion" were far more pervasive political units than nation-states. In modern societies the necessity of complex communication elevated the importance of "culture," the manner in which people communicate in the broadest sense. Culture replaced structure in modern societies, and identities derived more from culture than from one's place in a given, relatively fixed structure. Citizenship, that is "moral membership of a modern community," required literacy, which had to be produced by a nation-size education system in a chosen language. Nationalism, thus, was a sociological necessity in modern society, which created bounded language communities capable of sustaining an educational system. It became the "natural" form of political loyalty in a society in which "every man is a clerk" with knowledge of the common national language.

Marxists, too, for all their condescension toward nationalism and reductionism of the national to the material, ironically made major breakthroughs in reconceptualizing nationalism, whether in the pages of *New Left Review* or the groundlaying works of Eric Hobsbawm and Miroslav Hroch. In many ways, like so many other problems in politics and social science, the conversation about nationalism has been a dialogue with, within, or against the Marxist tradition. Marxists helped materialize and historicize the narrative of nationalism, and Hobsbawm and Terence Ranger's "invention of tradition" and Benedict Anderson's evocation of "imagined communities" moved the discussion beyond material and structural determinations into the realm of discourse and the generation of meaning.

In the last three decades an explosion of empirical studies of particular national movements has confirmed the artificial or manufactured character of nineteenth- and twentieth-century nationalities. The emergence of nations was no natural or logical development from a series of objective and empirically readily observable characteristics of human populations, like a common territory, language, or religion. A viable or successful nationalist movement bore a far more arbitrary and less predictable relationship to existing patterns of social organization than this familiar assumption might suggest. This is not to say that a common territory, language, or culture provided no basis for shared identity or consciousness, but for that consciousness to become *nationalist* in any true sense (rather than say regionalist, ethnic, religious, or peasant-populist) something else normally has to happen in the form of political intervention. In other words, creative political action is required to transform a segmented and disunited population into a coherent nationality, and though potential communities of this kind may clearly precede such interventions (so that they are rarely interventions into a vacuum), the interventions remain responsible for combining the materials into a larger collectivity.

One of the best examples of such creativity, because in the past it provided the commonest "objective" rationale for the existence of a nation, has been the adoption of national languages, which were very far from simply choosing themselves as the natural expression of majority usage. In one of the best-known instances, it has been calculated that in 1861 only 2.5 percent of the total Italian population could actually speak Italian, while the rest inhabited a "forest of dialect."[7] Much the same has been argued for France in the magisterial work of Eugen Weber.[8] In most new states the question of the official language became an object of much controversy, while during the period of "national awakening" great labor was expended in the selection, definition, and purification of an appropriate literary language. In Greece the argument raged over Koine, an extension of New Testament Greek preserved mainly through the Orthodox Church, and Katharevousa, a purified version of the demotic, with additional sniping from the advocates of ancient Greek. Among Armenians a cultural war was fought between "enlighteners" and "obscurantists" over the substitution of one or another dialects (Istanbul Armenian in the Ottoman Empire, Erevan dialect in the Russian) as standard literary languages in place of the classical fifth-century Armenian (Grabar) favored by the church. Examples of such conflicts can be multiplied. Typically the outcome was a compromise, a highly "artificial idiom discarding centuries of linguistic evolution in favor of 'false archaisms' and 'hypercorrect forms.' "[9]

Language is less a prior determinant of nationality than part of a complex process of cultural innovation, involving hard ideological labor, careful propaganda, and a creative imagination. Dictionaries and elementary primers are among the earliest and most important cultural artifacts of a national tradition. Much the same may be said of other aspects of the national culture, including literature, poetry, theater, music, opera, and painting; popular festivals; national dress; institutions of learning like academies or literary societies; or the invention of new rituals and insignia, like flags, anthems, and the commemoration of heroic events. A special case of this activity is the almost universal attempt to collect and adapt to new purposes the customary practices of the common people, like folk song and dance, or storytelling. Most fundamentally of all, we may mention the attempt to manufacture and manipulate a particular view of the past, invariably as a myth of origins which is meant to establish and legitimate the claim to cultural auton- omy and eventually to political independence. This was particularly important in the jumbled ethnic geography of central and eastern Europe and Transcaucasia, where the respective nationalities mobilized rival versions of the past, with special regard to patterns and sequences of settlement.

Thus, if politics is the ground upon which the category of the nation was first proposed, culture was the terrain where it was elaborated, and in this sense na- tionality is best conceived as a complex, uneven, and unpredictable process, forged from an interaction of cultural coalescence and specific political interven- tion, which cannot be reduced to static criteria of language, territory, ethnicity, or culture. Deutsch's early formulation can hardly be bettered:

> What counts is not the presence or absence of a single factor, but merely the presence
> of sufficient communication facilities with enough complementarity to produce the
> overall result. The Swiss may speak four different languages and still act as one
> people, for each of them has enough learned habits, preferences, symbols, memories,
> patterns of landholding and social stratification, events in history, and personal
> associations, all of which together permit him to communicate more effectively
> with other Swiss than with the speakers of his own language who belong to other
> peoples.''[10]

This need to constitute nations discursively, through processes of imaginative ideological labor—that is, the novelty of national culture, its manufactured or invented character, as opposed to its deep historical rootedness—is probably the most important point to emerge from the more recent literature. Moreover, in principle there is little difference in this respect between the "historic" nations (which enjoyed either the reality or the remembrance of autonomous statehood between the fifteenth and eighteenth centuries, like England, France, or Hungary) and the so-called history-less peoples (which did not). At one level the structural process of state formation clearly did facilitate a stronger sense of common be- longing or "patriotism" in the case of the former, particularly in England, France, or the Low Countries. Here we might say that the conditions of nationality arose in those processes of institutional development that enable a sense of shared loyalties to take shape—that is, the construction of "national" institutions as we now know them, whether centralized apparatuses of government (usually of a parliamentary kind), a "national public" (the press, a reading public, a cultural domain of theater and public spectacle, and so on), or a more comprehensive system of communications and transportation.

The most effective instance of such an institutional process is probably the development of centralized educational agencies. Lacking these advantages of political independence and prior institutional growth, the smaller nationalities of central and eastern Europe and Transcaucasia were more obviously an invention of enterprising intellectuals—of intellectuals, moreover, who aspired to emulate the histories they observed in the West, especially in France. But in either case the growth of national consciousness presumes an experience of cultural unification organized by some coherent ideology of nationhood. Without question the strongest version of the latter, where the "nation" becomes defined as a political category of citizens, draws its legitimacy and emotional resonance from the French Revolution, though arguably the combined experience of political revolution and militant Protestantism in late-sixteenth- and seventeenth-century England had a similar, if more localized, effect. But a fully developed national consciousness—one in which national identifications are strong enough to override regional, religious, and even class loyalties for most of the population most of the time, at least in certain kinds of situations—tends to require systematic propaganda or political education, normally but not invariably by a centralizing state and its agencies. As Weber and Theodore Zeldin have reminded us, in France this process occurred only with the early decades of the Third Republic, that is, well after the formation of the French state and well after the proclamation of a French nationality.[11] In Germany it began with unification but intensified in the 1890s. In Britain, arguably, the nationalization of culture only got properly under way with the experience of the First World War, though we may detect it more subtly from the revolutionary and Napoleonic wars onward.[12]

In effect, this leads to a threefold distinction in the overall periodization of nationalism: between structural processes of state formation (often referred to by social scientists as "nation-building"), located mainly in the countries of western and northern Europe between the fifteenth and late eighteenth centuries; the emergence of nationalism as a specific ideological and cultural innovation, particularly among peoples aspiring to a measure of political independence; and finally processes of cultural unification, extending over several generations and owing much to the widening penetration of a centralizing government (classically in the three areas of schooling, railway building, and conscription). On this basis nationalism becomes a clear instance of historical contingency, linked to political intervention, new ideologies, and cultural change, and expressing a transformation of social identity, initially on the part of individuals, but eventually for whole populations.

But does the stress on subjectivity and consciousness rule out any "objective" basis for the existence of nationality? Clearly, such a radically subjectivist view would be absurd. Most successful nationalisms presume some prior community of territory, language, or culture, which provide the raw materials for the intellectual project of nationality. Yet those prior communities should not be "naturalized," as if they have always existed in some essential way, or have simply prefigured a history yet to come. Religious, linguistic, ethnic, and regional communities are themselves always already in the process of historical formation and change. What looks from outside and from a distance as a bounded group appears much more divided and contested at closer range. Culture is more often not what people share, but what they choose to fight over.

Even as the terms *nation* and *nationality* have been destabilized, the word *ethnicity* has held on to much of its original fixity. Deep ethnic continuities, however, may also be unmasked as contingent historical creations or claims.

Though possessed of a long history, customary practices are rarely timeless or immune to symbolic modification and symbolic change.[13] Nationality, so often juxtaposed to ethnicity, is itself by no means free of ambiguity. For instance, it is now generally accepted that national movements may only be satisfied by what has come to be the standard but extreme solution of a totally independent, territorially and linguistically homogeneous, secular state for each people or nationality. Yet this is to do some violence to the expectations and behavior of many nationalist movements, certainly in the nineteenth century. It is perfectly possible to satisfy nationalist grievance within a variety of state forms or political arrangements, of which federal ones or those making careful allowance for cultural autonomies are the most familiar. Indeed, it was probably the First World War and the triumph of Wilsonian principles in 1917–19 that made full political sovereignty the leading demand of even the smallest national minority, whatever the realism or viability. Until then, the principle of nationality might be articulated just as well through the call for cultural autonomy, with special regard for matters of language, institutions of learning, and religious freedom.

Though premodern ethnic communities (what Anthony J. Smith calls "ethnies") and nationalities might be distinguished in any number of ways—size, attachment to territory, secular versus religious identity, "soft" versus "hard" boundaries—the most fundamental difference is not some objective characteristic internal to the group, but rather the discursive universe in which it operates and realizes itself. A modern nationality, with all its familiar qualities and political claims—popular sovereignty, ethnicity as a basis for political independence, and a claim on a particular piece of real estate—is only possible within the modern (roughly post–American Revolution) discourse of nationalism. Whatever Greeks in the classical period or Armenians in the fifth century were, they could not be nations in the same sense as they would be in the Age of Revolution. The discourses of politics of earlier times must be understood and respected in their own particularity and not submerged in understandings yet to be formed.

In many ways the reconceptualization over the last several decades of the rise of nationalism has paralleled the developments in thinking about other social categories, most importantly class and gender. Since the extraordinarily influential work of the late Edward Thompson on the English working class, there has been an advance over the immanentist view of interest and consciousness arising mysteriously from the material, and a more serious engagement with the specific ethnography of classes and the ways in which experience, always itself discursively framed and understood, creates identities of "interest," textures of identification, and architectures of community. Class consciousness, as well as national consciousness, to use one of Thompson's famous formulations, is the way in which experiences are handled in cultural terms, embodied in traditions, value systems, ideas, and institutional forms. Even more revolutionary in its effects on historical thinking, feminist theory has taken on the most naturalized of all categories, gender, and destabilized our understanding of the "natural" roles and capacities of women and men. The multiplicity, fluidity, contextual, and contested qualities of identities that studies of gender have highlighted have undermined any notion of a single all-embracing primary identity to which all others must be subordinated at all times and costs.

Just as protonationalities (ethnies, peoples) were constantly forming and re-producing in premodern times, so horizontal social formations (strata, estates, classes), related to particular regimes of production and legal structures, were similarly generated. They maintained a degree of demographic stability and cre-ated their own institutions and organizations in the context of the historical dis-courses that gave them sense, reason, and purpose. Yet, again, the long revolution of capitalism and the attendant formation of bureaucratic states provided the prin-cipal context for two opposing articulations of society and history, one based on horizontal affiliations (class), the other on vertical ones (nationality). As nation-alist intellectuals homogenized the differences within their ethnic populations and drew vertical lines of distinction between themselves and the "Others," a com-peting discourse based on new social differentiations and older traditions chal-lenged vertical allegiances and emphasized horizontal class solidarities.

Whatever the degree of cohesion and consciousness of classes and peoples before their mass mobilization, they represent authentic points of development. Rather than viewing them as premature, adolescent, or primitive, we should ap-preciate their full constellation of initiatives, influences, and responses. An eth-noreligious formation (such as the ancient Jews or the medieval Armenians) was not yet (nor could be) a modern nationality with its self-conscious sense of the value of ethnic and secular cultural (as opposed to religious) traditions, and with consequent political claims to territory, autonomy, or independence arising from a more modern discourse authorizing the claims of nationality to self-determi-nation. But earlier histories of classes and nations should be read not simply as prehistories, but as varied historical developments whose trajectories remained open.

Though a hundred years ago the claim of nationality to replace older ideas of legitimation was challenged by conservatives like Lord Acton, in our century it has become the hegemonic political discourse of sovereignty, the unavoidable—and unanswerable—language of self-determination, of those desiring the name of statehood. However artificial the doctrine may have appeared in the work of early intellectuals, with the material, social, cultural, and political transformations of the nineteenth and twentieth centuries, nationalism gained an enormous reso-nance—first among large numbers of educated people and then within the broad populace—until it promised to displace all rival forms of loyalty and identifica-tion. The languages of nationalism gave particular shape and meaning to historic social and cultural developments, and the modern representation of ethnicity in Europe became that associated with the nationalist discourse per se. Nationalism did not arise spontaneously from prior existing nationality, as most nationalists would have it, nor was it the "false consciousness" of the great transformation from precapitalism to postcapitalism, as some Marxists would say. Nationalism both contributed to the formation of nationality, which often in Europe (but not always) occurred on the basis of evolving ethnolinguistic or ethnoreligious com-munities, and evolved itself to become the political expression of mobilized na-tionalities.

Tragically, nationalist movements, which have used the universalist rhetoric of rights and the more antique claims to historical priority to claim their own privileged possession of territory and statehood, have rarely had many scruples about violating the rights of others. This was particularly true of the so-called historic nations like the Germans and Hungarians, but similar notions of cultural superiority and civilizing mission in relation to the smaller and "history-less" peoples (perfectly compatible in the nineteenth century with liberal or democratic ideas of progress) also appear among the Greeks and Romanians. Neither the Greek *Megale Idea* nor Greater Romania showed much respect for the principles of cultural autonomy, linguistic homogeneity, or ethnic self-determination within a separate state when it came to the claims of others. Nationalism's cultural and contingent origins have never prevented appeals to primordial roots or race. As the claims to nationhood metastasize into the evils of ethnic cleansing and genocide, the task of intellectuals to remind us all of the imaginary quality of much of the ideology and history that has gone into the making of nations becomes all the more acute.

I

The distinction between *ethnicity* and *nationality* requires some awareness of the dynamism that leads to political recognition. To move from practical conditions of cultural autonomy to forms of organized self-consciousness and the enunciating of political claims, and on to independent statehood, or at least to an advanced form of self-administration, always involves complex histories. To capture such transitions—for instance, from a fragmented and localized ethnic identity to a more coherent and unified national consciousness, or from cultural to political demands—a historical approach is needed, one that registers the inevitable complexity of social and political determinations. Before proceeding any further, therefore, it is worth building up a framework of general argumentation in this fashion, which can fill in some of the context that allowed the nineteenth-century nationalisms actually to emerge.

Taking the nineteenth century in the broadest of terms, Tom Nairn (following Gellner) linked the emergence of nationalism to the uneven diffusion of industrialization (or for Gellner, modernization), where "the advancing capitalism of the more bourgeois societies bore down upon the societies surrounding them—societies which predominantly appear until the 1790s as buried in feudal and absolutist slumber."

> The "tidal wave" invaded one zone after another, in concentric circles. First Germany and Italy, the areas of relatively advanced and unified culture adjacent to the Anglo-French center. It was in them that the main body of typically nationalist politics and culture was formulated. Almost at the same time, or shortly after, Central and Eastern Europe, and the more peripheral regions of Iberia, Ireland, and Scandinavia. Then Japan and, with the full development of imperialism, much of the rest of the globe.[14]

What Nairn calls "the 'nationalism-producing' dilemma" originated in the structured developmental handicaps which the unevenness of industrialization imposed on the more backward societies—in the awareness among the various national intelligentsias that the developmental gap could only be bridged by determined efforts to cast off the domination of the more advanced and exploitative cultures, whether British, French, German, Italian, or whatever. How exactly this affected individual societies depended very much on the particularities of the economies and social structures concerned, the nature of the political system, and the local complex of relations among the nationalities. As Nairn says again, "The dilemma of under-development becomes 'nationalism' only when it is (so to speak) refracted through a given society, perceived in a certain way, and then acted upon"; Nairn distinguishes the composition of the intelligentsia and the modalities of popular mobilization as the key variables in this respect.[15]

After this developmental context, we need to consider the international situation and the global ideological climate. For the Balkan nationalities in particular, the progress of the claim to statehood was closely bound to the demise of the Ottoman Empire and the complex alignments it produced among the Great Powers, from the winning of Greek independence in the 1820s to the crises of 1912–14. For the various "national awakenings" of the early nineteenth century, the impact of the French Revolution and the subsequent revolutionary tradition was paramount, though the nature of the influence varied. Thus the pioneers of Greek nationality—Rhigas Velestinlis and Adamantios Koraïs—were formed intellectually in the image of the Enlightenment and the Revolution's extreme radical democratic ideals; the Hungarian revival originated in the Jacobinism of the post-Josephian intelligentsia and the discussions around Napoleon's proclamation to the Hungarians of May 1809 ("I wish to see you a free and independent nation"), which the youthful Kossuth remembered learning by heart; while the South Slav movements, particularly Croatian Illyrism, were inspired by the more diffused radicalism after 1815.[16] As Hobsbawm has argued, the self-consciously nationalist movements of the 1830s and 1840s originated as offshoots of the post-1815 revolutionary tradition, with its conspiratorial forms and intellectual composition, and on the whole they sustained a genuine ideology of republicanism and radical democracy.[17] The year 1848 was at the same time the climax, further specification, and tragic fragmentation of this tradition: it both opened the way for impeccably democratic proclamations of nationality and dashed the ideal of fraternity on the rock of competing nationalist claims. But at all events, the experience of the French Revolution bequeathed a political vocabulary through which the new aspirations might be articulated, a structured ideological discourse into which the newly secularized intelligentsias of central and eastern Europe might naturally fit. This new amalgam of political claims based on cultural certainties might be called the "discourse of the nation." Even as it transcended its original limits as "state patriotism," this discourse linked the legitimation of polities to a preexisting cultural and (often) linguistic community which now was called "the nation." Political inspiration conjoined with cultural innovations to produce a new generation of visionaries. As Gwyn Williams puts it, "historians stamped nations out of the ground and wove new tricolours out of old legends."[18]

If the overall international situation or climate was one impetus toward a more politicized nationalism, another was supplied by a resistant and obstructive power structure, which proved unwilling to concede the more modest demands for cultural autonomy. This was true of both the particular imperial states concerned (the Austrian and Russian empires) and of the general period of the post-Napoleonic restoration. Thus after a brief honeymoon in the 1830s Habsburg intransigence gradually pushed the exponents of Illyrism or South Slav unity into the firmer advocacy of political independence. The Romanian nationalists had a similar experience between the 1830s and 1860s, as the supporters of "activity" (that is, participation in the institutions of the Austrian Empire) gradually lost ground to the partisans of "passivity" (noncooperation). In both cases, the argument for moderation foundered on a sustained counteroffensive of Magyarization and the superior influence of the Hungarians in the empire. Lacking the realistic option of a democratized multinational state, or even a more equitable corporative one, the national minorities were left little choice but the longer prospect of secessionist independence. This aspiration was powerfully encouraged later in the century by the foundation of the new Balkan states.

Moreover, the frustration experienced by the nationalist leaderships in their encounters with an inflexible Habsburg bureaucracy was radicalized by a third and fourth set of determinations, concerning (1) the changing composition of the intelligentsia, and (2) the possibility of new social coalitions. There is little disputing the primary role of the intelligentsia in the formative stages of nationalist movements—"the lower and middle professional, administrative and intellectual strata, in other words the *educated* classes," as Hobsbawm puts it.[19] Usually as an attempt to appropriate the experience of the French Revolution, nationalist doctrine materializes as the preoccupation of tiny intellectual elites, such as the 446 members of the Slovak Learned Society set up in 1792 and the 266 Slovak literary patriots identifiable between 1780 and 1820, or the 318 subscribers to the cultural monthly *Bibliotheca Romaneascu* in 1829 and the 500 or so subscribers to the only Romanian newspaper in Transylvania in 1838, *Gazeta de Transilvania*.[20] But this also occurred in a context of modestly expanding educational provision. As Hobsbawm again puts it:

> To be precise, the advance guard of middle-class nationalism fought its battle along the line which marked the educational progress of large numbers of "new men" into areas hitherto occupied by a small elite. The progress of schools and universities measures that of nationalism, just as schools and especially universities became its most conscious champions: the conflict of Germany and Denmark over Schleswig-Holstein in 1848 and again in 1864 was anticipated by the conflict of the universities of Kiel and Copenhagen on this issue in the middle 1840s.[21]

This has been documented mainly for the western part of the continent, but applies in principle to the east as well.[22] Moreover, the social composition of the intelligentsia underwent an important change, as education became less strictly tied to the recruiting needs of the church or the leisure pursuits of the aristocracy. Here the Napoleonic impact could be vital, as in the "Illyrian provinces," where the French occupation endowed the rudiments of a secularized educational system and helped crystallize the beginnings of a middle class. In Croatia, with its small and denationalized nobility (around 2–3 percent of the population at the turn of the century) opting for pragmatic Magyarization and closely bound to a conservative church hierarchy, this conjuncture of fresh educational opportunity with the inspiration of the French Revolution and the immobility of the Habsburg state could scarcely fail to have nationalist reverberations: between 1791–95 and 1826–30, the proportion of noble youths at the Zagreb Academy fell from 31 percent to 6.1 percent, while the representation of the bourgeoisie and peasantry rose to 62 percent and 25.6 percent respectively.[23]

Finally, in the very moment of their self-consciousness—the revolutionary conflagration of 1848–49, the "springtime of the peoples"—the Central and Eastern European nationalities found themselves faced with a Habsburg bureaucracy determined to reimpose its rule. This was especially poignant for those subject to Magyar domination, who had expected to benefit from the ruin of the Hungarian Revolution—Romanians, Croats, Slovaks, Rusyns—for instead of federalizing the monarchy into autonomous nationalities, Vienna eventually chose a course of renewed centralism borne by imported Germanized officials.[24] Though the subject nationalities salvaged some cultural autonomies (mainly under the aegis of their respective churches), these were rudely overridden by the later Austro-Hungarian compromise of 1867, which reinstated Magyar hegemony in the Hungarian territories in no uncertain terms. Thus the number of elementary schools with Slovak as the language of instruction was gradually reduced from its peak of 1,971 in 1874 down to an average of 1,300 in the 1880s, until by 1900 it fell to only 510. All higher education, state and private, was Magyar after 1874. This affected not only the training of the intelligentsia, but also their employment: in the Slovak districts only 345 elementary teachers gave Slovak as their language in 1914, as opposed to 129 with German and 4,257 with Magyar; in higher elementary schools the figures were 1, 16, and 425 respectively; in higher education, 10, 12, and 638.[25] In a backward and impoverished area like Subcarpathian Rus, this process virtually wiped out the native intelligentsia (thus in 1910 there were only 21 recorded Rusyn-speakers among 64,797 public employees and state teachers in Hungary), leaving only the church or emigration as realistic alternatives to some form of assimilation.[26] This closure of professional opportunity reemphasized the contribution of church autonomy to early nationalist movements in the east of the continent, because clerical employment tended to cushion the potential effects of linguistic and ethnic discrimination. By inaugurating new ideological conflicts and removing the clerical option, secularization helped radicalize the resentment of the native intelligentsia against the discriminatory practices of the Habsburg state.

This discussion of the intelligentsia already introduces a stronger social-historical dimension, because the overproduction of educated men created both a blockage of careerist mobility and a growing demand for the recognition of minority cultures, normally in the first instance through the language and its official currency. Potentially, this makes nationalism an expression of frustrated expression and intellectual underemployment, the ideological rebellion of "marginal men."[27] In its early stages nationalism was more a movement of intellectuals than of the masses. The generation of a nationalist discourse in colonial empires can almost without exception be traced back to displaced intellectuals. Yet it would be far too limiting to see nationalism as merely an elite protest against frustrated social mobility. Nationalism's power came from the resonance the discourse had beyond its first articulations. Consider, for example, Ireland, where the movement for Catholic emancipation took on a genuinely popular dimension in the 1820s, or Greece, where a unique combination of an educated administrative and clerical stratum, a cosmopolitan merchant class, and an independent popular force of brigands and insurgent peasantry became fused together under the special international circumstances of the 1820s into a successful nationalist rising.[28] But even for the period of wider popular agitation, which for most central and eastern European nationalities begins with a bang in 1848, there is still relatively little literature exploring the social bases of the mass patriotism that now started to emerge. This is what makes the work of Miroslav Hroch so important and exciting, all the more so because it still remains relatively little emulated.[29]

Briefly, Hroch tries to distinguish the social settings that proved especially fertile for the implantation of an active nationalist commitment. He does this by postulating three clear stages in the life of a nationalist movement: Phase A, when small groups of intellectuals first elaborate the category of the nation; Phase B, when wider networks of patriots begin to spread the word through concerted agitation; and Phase C, when serious popular mobilization begins. On this basis, he develops a careful sociology of the patriotic activists in Phase B (members of clubs and societies, collaborators and subscribers of patriotic journals and other projects, donors of money, and so on), concentrating in particular on three types of information, concerning intra- and intergenerational mobility and geographical location. From this analysis, there emerges an interesting pattern of uneven distribution. Geographically, the areas of strongest nationalist activity seem to have little correlation with either linguistic and administrative boundaries, linguistic and ethnic homogeneity, or crude measures of economic growth, like population density and the distribution of new industrial centers. Instead, they coincided with a mixture of cultural and more complex economic factors: on the one hand, areas with a denser school network and more extensive educational provision; on the other hand, areas of *intermediate* social change, including areas of petty commodity production with higher-than-average density of small handicrafts production for the market, even where industrialization was fairly well advanced; areas of high fertility, in both cereals and industrial crops; and areas of agricultural production for the market as opposed to mere subsistence, but where distribution occurred overwhelmingly through local rather than regional markets.

Socially speaking, the largest contingent of patriots came from the intelligentsia, where this is taken to mean those living from intellectual labor (that is, not just academics, journalists, and writers, but also teachers, small officials, and priests). The bourgeoisie proper, as a new class of owners and controllers of means of production, was poorly represented, with the partial exception of the Norwegian mercantile class. The role of the petty bourgeoisie was more important, though mainly for the later Phase C, and that of the peasantry rather variable. Residentially, patriots lived in towns, rather than the country. They came disproportionately from a younger generation (say, between eighteen and twenty-eight years). In Karl Deutsch's terms, they were firmly integrated into a developed system of communications, certainly by their attained social status; by origin, they came from groups like the artisanate and peasantry who were fairly poorly integrated, but were also raised in geographical locations where communications were well developed (for instance, with a high density of village schools). In summary, patriots came from literate strata intermediate between the masses and whatever local bourgeoisie and aristocracy might have existed: as Hobsbawm says, "teachers, the lower levels of the clergy, some urban shopkeepers and artisans, and the sort of men who had risen about as far as it was possible for the sons of a subordinate peasant people in a hierarchical society."[30]

While Hroch's comparative and materialist methodology pioneered a much needed social-historical approach to nationalist movements and their uneven spread and explicitly related the process of nation-forming to larger processes of social transformation, specifically those associated with the global, European-wide penetration of the unevenly expanding capitalist mode of production, it should not be misunderstood as economic reductionism. Quite the contrary, for the emergence of nationalist movements is no simple and unmediated consequence of industrialization in his account, but a rather complicated precipitate of the new social relations industrialization helped to establish. Specifically, Hroch sees the impact of industrialization as mediated by the processes of communication and mobility proposed by Karl Deutsch. Likewise, there is no simple equivalence between the growth of a national market and the coherence of a potential nation, and the optimal territorial extent of a national economy bears no necessary correspondence with the area the nation is thought to inhabit. Here Hroch argues for a basic distinction between the dominant or "large" nations (England, France, Holland, Sweden, Spain, and more ambiguously because of their later territorialized formation, Germany and Italy), whose sense of nationality was constituted in the course of the bourgeoisie's struggle against the aristocracy's social domination, and the "small" nations investigated in his book, whose independence could only be secured *against* the emerging domination of a foreign, metropolitan, or "de-nationalized" bourgeois-aristocratic coalition.

In other words, in the large nations the struggle *against* feudalism was also a struggle *for* the emancipation of the nation, in which the so-called third estate both installed itself at the head of society and self-consciously identified itself with the nation-in-general. In the small nations, by contrast, the dissolution of feudalism was accompanied by the predominance of a bourgeoisie whose culture evidently diverged from that of the "people." Such "small nations" had a very distinctive makeup: they lacked a native aristocracy and were subject to a landed class with an alien language and an already-formed nationality; they lacked a claim to historic statehood or political independence; they had no strong or continuous tradition of high culture in the native language; and they frequently lacked a strong native bourgeoisie. In these circumstances, the nationalist movement necessarily drew on a familiar popular coalition: a new secular intelligentsia as described above, eventually mobilizing larger numbers of the petty bourgeoisie (that is, in Hroch's Phase C).

In this way, Hroch's work has important bearing on questions of political development. Its model of a fully fledged public domain crystallizing gradually from the mosaic of parochial societies under the mediate impact of capitalist social transformation may be deployed in a variety of historiographical contexts not normally encountered in the literature on nationalism per se, from the varying regional configurations of politics in the English Civil War, or the uneven politicization of the countryside during the French Revolution and the nineteenth century, to the formation of territorialized political cultures in any developing society.[31] At this point, Hroch's approach conjoins not only with Deutsch's model of social communication and the literature on state-making, but also with Jürgen Habermas's concept of the public sphere, which has recently been enjoying some remarkable popularity in the English-speaking world.[32] In these terms, the problem of nationalism might be seen as a particular name for the general problematic of political development, or for the formation of territorialized political cultures in the era opened by the French Revolution, in all its rich and complex social and cultural dimensions. Here is John Womack, speaking from a Latin American context of history and discussion:

> Most broadly, the experience has served as a kind of liberal education for traditional individuals on the move out of tradition, justifying their repression of wistful longings for family, clan, village, province, promising them the excitement of exercising their wills like anyone else of "the people." It has felt to them like liberation. Nationalism has also served as a kind of professional education for individuals on the move into the bourgeoisie, justifying their repression of shame, promising them the excitement of imposing their wills in championing "the people." It has felt to them like responsibility. Usually, only fractions of any class have undergone either experience at a particular time. And usually, others entering as they leave, they have gone through it in two or three years. But like alumni, they have kept strong memories of it as they have settled into the routines of a new class.[33]

So far we have described the "moment of social history" in the historiography and theory of nationalism, a moment signaled by the influence of authors such as Gellner and Hobsbawm, and splendidly realized in the pathbreaking research of Hroch. In many ways, this moment is still very much in process, because the range of monographs situating nationalism in a strong and sophisticated context of social history as we have come to know it since the 1970s is still surprisingly small, and all the smaller in European history than in the analysis of non-Western societies, where the approach has been far more innovative.[34] Moreover, we have focused here on the early processes whereby the category of the nation has been proposed and elaborated as a foundation for the emergence of a coherent nationalist movement, whether expressed as the transition from ethnicity to nationality, by Hroch's three stages, or by some other developmental schema. Yet the statement by Womack already points us to a further set of questions, arising from the successful achievement of national independence.

Having stressed the element of conditioned subjectivity and cultural innovation in the early constitution of nationality, there is clearly a point at which nations begin existing independently of the political practices that originally formed them. With the attainment of independence or political self-determination at the latest, the nation starts to represent a discursive formation—ideologically, institutionally, culturally, practically in a thousand small ways—of immense power, which already determines the possible forms of political activity and belief. As Nairn has said, under these circumstances nationalism turns into "a name for the general condition of the modern body politic, more like the climate of political and social thought than just another doctrine."[35] Quite apart from anything else, the achievement of a nation-state immeasurably simplifies the cultural unification of the nation through systems of shared identification, and on this basis the transition to statehood marks a fundamental watershed in the life of a nationalist movement. The national ideal lends enormous legitimacy to the interventionist drives of a centralizing government, though the ability to contest such processes via alternative constructions of the national tradition is the necessary counterrecognition, we would argue, that should immediately follow. In fact, the field of negotiation inside the global framework of a common national identity, with all its powerful resonances, is where the most interesting discussions may now be found.

II

This issue of the transition to statehood, and the resulting pervasiveness of national identification, its inescapability for citizens and noncitizens of contemporary states, given the structured and structuring conditions of public and private life in the latter, particularly in the mass polities of the twentieth century, has encouraged a different set of analytical approaches from the social history of nation-forming explicated above.

As we have seen, the idea of the nation in its projective nineteenth-century sense imagined a desirable future of harmonious living and collective self-determination within the sovereign space of a well-integrated and solidaristic social and political order, increasingly with the accompanying ideal of a coherent and well-organized common culture. This utopia of modern nationality required a grounding of the national community in a specific and more definitively delineated territory, with harder boundaries, constitutionally regulated citizenship, and very demanding claims to legitimacy. It also meant the emphasizing of differences between one national community and another, and the effacing of differences within. Moreover, the project of the nation had a particular genealogy. It followed on the state-building histories of the old territorial states of Europe between the thirteenth and eighteenth centuries, which eliminated competing sovereignties inside a given territory, established permanent bureaucracies and standing armies, claimed radical powers of central taxation, and abolished rival jurisdictions, such as those of the church or locally based aristocracies. Then, with the French Revolution, ideas of the nation as the people, attaching to popular sovereignty and constitutional rule, with claims to a single national language and (eventually) an ethnically homogeneous population, inscribed this state-building process with their distinctive ideological content. To survive, dynastic and imperial states transmuted into nationalizing ones, usually under the impetus of capitalist industrialization and the associated politicocultural aspirations of the bourgeoisie, which the nineteenth century called "progress." Where empires failed to become nation-states, as in the Tsarist, Habsburg, and Ottoman cases, they were doomed to short lives in the era of Wilson and Lenin after 1917, where the international state system became organized around the principle of national self-determination. Indeed, the only twentieth-century survivor of the age of contiguous empires in Europe, the Soviet Union, justified its continuation through an ideology of internationalism, while simultaneously recognizing the presence of nations within its federation.

So "nations," sometimes a redescription of existing state-organized territorial populations, were sometimes an aspiration, a projection from emerging civil societies, movements seeking to reorder in terms of themselves the political and state-institutional landscapes they encountered. "National categories" or nationalities became announced and elaborated during the nineteenth century in ever-widening profusion, a process which in global terms during the twentieth century has shown few signs of contracting. While the effort at fashioning a "state" for every "nation" would surely be unrealistic, ultimately multiplying beyond the threshold of viability not only the numbers of states, but also the numbers of communities then aspiring to be nations, the modern discourse of nationhood has nonetheless conspired to eliminate other languages of legitimacy. This field of tension and creativity, of future-making and unfinished labor, between the political-institutional and state-territorial frameworks of politics and societal development (or the process of state formation and nation-building from our point of view) and the fashioning of collective identities where citizenries and otherwise divided populations may recognize themselves as "one" (the "nation" as a realm of consciousness and culture), is where cultural studies has chosen to focus.

As an interdisciplinary incitement, "cultural studies" has come to mean many things. Canonically speaking, we might begin with Richard Hoggart's *The Uses of Literacy* (1957) and Raymond Williams's *Culture and Society: 1780–1950* (1958), whose common aim was to "bring culture back" into the study of society, to link social life and individual lives, and to explore the "common meanings and directions" in the making of a society, but in the important recognition that any harmonious notion of culture as "a whole way of life" is necessarily compromised by the actualities of social fragmentation, class divisions, gender and ethnic exclusions, and hierarchies and relations of power.[36] But by now this very British founding moment is no longer sufficient for describing the possibilities, organized as it was around two rather specific studies, an elaborate ethnography of the respectable northern English working class (in the case of Hoggart), and a running debate with two hundred years of writing about high culture and popular culture (in the case of Williams). In Britain, such work became richly elaborated at the Birmingham Center for Contemporary Cultural Studies, focusing on questions of youth cultures and style, mass media and communications, public schooling, gender, race, popular memory, and the writing of history, all within frameworks of theories of ideology, signification, and subjectivity.[37] But the nature of that interdisciplinary conversation is also very specific to Britain, comprising mainly literary scholars, historians, and sociologists, together with the immediate progeny of the field itself now employed in departments of cultural studies in the newer universities. In the United States the constellation is tilted more toward literary studies, film studies, communications, anthropology, women's studies, American culture, and so on. Similarly, the range of theory varies, from Antonio Gramsci and psychoanalytic approaches in Britain, to reflexive anthropologies in the United States. On the other hand, feminist theory, postcolonial theories, the linguistic turn, and the fascination with postmodernism are all common to both.

How has the growth of cultural studies affected the study of nationalism? First, at a time when writers have been stressing the politically driven inventedness and novelty of national cultures, and the contingency, even the arbitrariness of the particular signs that make them up, cultural studies has allowed us to reinstate the centrality of culture in nation-forming without reattaching it to a misplaced notion of the primordial. Of course, *culture* is a notoriously mobile term, and in his many writings on the subject, Raymond Williams distinguished four strong clusters of meaning: (1) culture as ''a general process of intellectual, spiritual, and aesthetic development'' of individuals; (2) culture as ''a particular way of life, whether of a people, a period, a group, or humanity in general,'' in the anthropological sense; (3) culture as ''the works and practices of intellectual and especially artistic activity''; and (4) culture as ''the signifying system through which necessarily (though among other means) a social order is communicated, reproduced, experienced, and explored.''[38] Each of these meanings has its relevance to our theme, and together they make a useful template of distinctions as we proceed.

Second, culture in one anthropological sense, as an informal, practical, and unconscious territory of everydayness, corresponds closely to an important tradition of nationalist thinking descending from Herder, which stressed precisely these holistic principles of definition:

> Herder argued that each people—each society, each ethnic group, each linguistic community—could be distinguished by a ''whole way of life,'' by common customs, ways of thinking, and ways of being. He argued that each way of life is informed by a ''common spirit'': that the social activities, patterns of thought, and ways of being of a given group are produced in and through what we might call today a kind of ''grammar'' or ''syntax'' of everyday life, that is, by general values, categories, and so on, that guide and make sense of specific activities.[39]

If we freeze history in a particular moment, these features appear only too easily as unitary, essential, and fixed, whereas viewed over a period of time (as we argued above), such cultural coherence dissolves into indeterminacy, and appears far more as a process requiring explanation. Cultures of ethnicity are constructed via fields of difference which are also changeable and dynamic. Ethnicity arises in the interaction between groups. It exists in the boundaries constructed between them. Moreover, ''it is *in* history, the flow of past events, that emergence and variation appear, and only *through* history can we understand them.''[40] Boundaries are marked by symbols—''objects, acts, relationships or linguistic formations that stand *ambiguously* for a multiplicity of meanings, evoke emotions, and impel [people] to action.''[41] Such ''markers of difference,'' the differ-

ence between "Us" and "Them," are for most people experienced and reproduced during social transactions that are not consciously reflected or rationalized
in this way:

> These everyday experiences happen unconsciously; everyday awareness is naive.
> Such experiences are slang, nature and territory, social milieu, school socialization
> with its conveyance of historical myths, outer appearance and behavior, religion,
> customs, and habits. Individual elements of this everyday experience become evi-
> dent through the experience of strangeness. The experience of strangeness occurs
> constantly. Here elements of everyday experience are exaggerated and abstracted
> to become symbols, which define a community. These symbols are tangible, con-
> crete, and understandable everywhere on the basis of common everyday experience.
> Since everyday life in its totality is altogether naively experienced, this process
> leads to a diffuse and inexplicable combination of such symbols for the creation of
> ethnic boundaries and ethnic identity. This explains the paradox that individual
> ethnic symbols can be grasped concretely, while their combination as ethnicity
> remains indefinable.[42]

National identification is clearly a matter of sensibility in this sense—something transmitted from the past and secured as a collective belonging, something
reproduced in myriad imperceptible ways, grounded in everydayness and mundane experience. In trying to understand the fashioning of extremely disparate
populations into a nation, the passage from one kind of history (of dispersal,
heterogeneity, indeterminacy) to another (unification, instituted solidarity, se-
curely established community) is crucial, and the ability of leaderships—in existing national states or as aspiring nationalist movements—to work on this reservoir of cultural meanings is at the heart of the process of building the nation.
A common memory of belonging, borne by habits, customs, dialects, song, dance,
pastimes, shared geography, superstition, and so on, but also fears, anxieties,
antipathies, hurts, resentments, is the indistinct but indispensible condition of
possibility. For nationalism to do its work, ordinary people need to see themselves
as the bearers of an identity centered elsewhere, imagine themselves as an abstract
community. Securing the existence of the nation, mobilizing the nation politically,
presumes a long-accumulating identity in this way, one that that can be brought
to visibility both spontaneously and by concerted agitation. Here is the early
twentieth-century Irish nationalist politician Michael Collins describing one such
moment of collective self-recognition:

> I stand for an Irish civilization based on the people and embodying and maintaining
> the things—their habits, ways of thought, customs—that make them different—the
> sort of life I was brought up in. . . . Once, years ago, a crowd of us were going
> along the Shepherd's Bush Road [in Irish London] when out of a lane came a chap
> with a donkey—just the sort of donkey and just the sort of cart that they have at
> home. He came out quite suddenly and abruptly and we all cheered him. Nobody
> who has not been an exile will understand me, but I stand for that.[43]

Third, we need to move out from this territory of everydayness to culture in
the third of Raymond Williams's senses, as "the works and practices of intellectual and especially artistic activity," and consider the role of nationalist intelli-

gentsias, this time not as the agents of Hroch's social history of nation-forming, but as cultural producers and the authors of imaginative texts. Adapting a famous adage, we might say that nationalists make their own history, but not entirely as they please; not with cultures of their own choosing, but with cultures directly encountered, given, and transmitted from the past. Nonetheless, the fundamental insight of the "constructionists"—of the lineage of contemporary writers about nationalism since Kedourie—has lost none of its power: nationality is *not* a natural consequence or outgrowth of common culture of long antiquity; nations are not so much discovered or awakened, as they are created or invented by the labors of intellectuals. Thus, nationalist movements of the nineteenth and twentieth centuries depend on particular political histories and political ideals of citizenship and state organization far more than they arise spontaneously from preestablished cultural communities. Furthermore, the effort at continuity in national culture also requires hard, continuous, repeated, creative ideological and political labor on the part of intellectuals and nationalist leaderships. It does not occur by itself.

One of the most important contributions of cultural studies in this connection has concerned the formation of national publics. Here Habermas's work on the public sphere has provided one highly influential model, in which nineteenth-century liberal ideals of constitutional government, civil freedoms, and the rule of law were linked with wider processes of cultural innovation. In Habermas's argument, the public sphere—as an intermediary domain linking society and state, where the reasoning citizenry organizes itself as the bearer of public opinion—crystallized from the growth, in western Europe between the later eighteenth and later nineteenth centuries, of metropolitan and provincial urban cultures grounded in the novel structures of civil society and the associational arenas of a locally organized public life. This encompassed everything from the physical architecture of civic pride (meeting houses, concert halls, theaters, opera houses, lecture halls, museums), to a new infrastructure of social communication (the press, publishing houses, and other literary media; the rise of a reading public via literary and language societies; subscription publishing and lending libraries; improved transportation; and centers of sociability like coffeehouses, taverns, and clubs), and in general a new universe of voluntary association. This story of public-sphere formation redescribes the processes of social communication postulated by Deutsch and concretized by Hroch, elaborating in the process a compelling case for the centrality of cultural publics to the nation-building project. It can be extended easily to the formation of taste and the circulation of ideas.[44]

The study of national literatures has acquired greater and greater prominence in this respect. Given the claims made for the centrality of literary criticism, as opposed to other forms of academic knowledge such as sociology and social theory, in the dominant ideological structures of "Englishness" in the twentieth century, for example, literary studies have always been a key part of British cultural studies from the very beginning, with Raymond Williams taking the lead.[45] More generally, the importance of moral and aesthetic arguments in the founding discourse of nineteenth-century nationalisms, whether articulated around the novel and poetry, or the theater, or opera, is also very clear. For Friedrich Schiller, for instance, theater possessed the ethical power and sensuous force necessary to advance the rationalist and humanist values of the Enlightenment over the discredited claims of traditional religion, and thereby to create "Germany" as a public of educated men: "if we had a national theater, we would also become a nation."[46] The arts in this sense provided powerful languages of prestige and legitimation. As Brian Doyle puts it, " 'the English language' and the 'national literature,' in dominant definitions, represent ratifications of a selective sense of culture and history, or comfortable affirmations of a certain structure and forms of cultural authority."[47] On the other hand, fictional forms have also been media of contestation, lending themselves for oppositional and dissentient purposes as often as straightforwardly legitimatory ones, and at all events enacting the conflicts and uncertainties that occur in any actual, historical discourse of national self-determination and of proclaiming and instituting an official culture of the nation. National literatures, both constructively and symptomatically, provide a complex and challenging textual basis for exploring the languages of nationalism and national identification, not least because their authors and impresarios invariably saw them in this way, bringing a strategic intelligence to their creation. Latin American nationalisms, and the literatures of colonial revolt more generally, have been a rich context of analysis of this kind, and Julie Skurski's essay in this volume provides an excellent illustration of what can be done.[48]

How the nation is *represented*, how its aspirations are *authorized*, and how its origins and claims are *narrated* have become key themes of a growing cultural-studies literature. Benedict Anderson's *Imagined Communities* (1983) has become the emblematic text in this respect, marking the moment of transition in the literature from structural and materialist analyses of nationalism to an approach stressing the meanings and effects of a "sense of nationality" and the intimate connections between personhood and belonging to a nation. Anderson develops a complex argument from the macrohistorical changes proceeding during and around the Enlightenment and French Revolution, beginning in the Americas, in which people became able to reimagine the boundaries of their worlds, replacing allegiance to universal religions and divinely ordained dynasts with a new kind of community based on citizenship, conceived as a "fraternity of equals" and a "deep horizontal comradeship."[49] As he says, this formulation implies no juxtaposition of "truth" and "falseness" in the definition of nationalism: all communities are necessarily "imagined" in the sense that their fellow-members cannot possibly know each other directly, and so they "are to be distinguished, not by their falsity/genuineness, but by the style in which they are imagined."[50] Nations became idealized communities, which at one and the same time "recovered" the history they needed to bind diverse elements into a single whole, and yet concealed the actual inequalities, exploitations, and patterns of domination and exclusion inevitably involved. The power of national loyalty requires some transcendent appeal of this kind, invoking "the links between the dead and the yet unborn, the mystery of regeneration . . . a combined connectedness, fortuity, and fatality in a language of 'continuity.' "[51] This appeal to the past, what Lauren Berlant calls "this pseudo-genetic condition," which profoundly affects not only "the citizen's subjective experience of her/his political rights, but also of civil life, private life, the life of the body itself," is crucial to the utopia of nationality, to the nation's redemptive claims, its promise of wholeness, the abstract unity it desires to become.[52]

In exploring histories and processes of representation, fourth, cultural studies has focused not just on the characteristics of national literatures officially understood—on rereading the canon, so to speak—but even more on popular culture, both by writing social histories of its production, and by bringing established reading practices to these different kinds of texts. We are thinking here of work on the visual technologies of film, photography, television, and video; on commercial media like advertising, comic books, and magazines; on popular genres in books (romances, gothic novels, family sagas, crime fiction), television (soap operas, detective series, situation comedies), and film (film noir, horror, science fiction, melodrama); on the growth of new consumer economies, particularly in the mass-entertainment industries, but also affecting food, fashion and dress, domestic labor in households, leisure and play, and all manner of lifestyles; and last but not least, on sexualities, both mainstream and dissident. Moreover, such work is increasingly organized by a contemporary political agenda around questions of gender, race, and sexuality, bringing normative rhetorics of difference, diversity, and multiculturalism to an imposing practical dominance of the field.

There are perhaps two aspects of this turning to popular culture that deserve our attention here. On the one hand, it extends the analysis of national publics from the mainly literary model *Öffentlichkeit* (public sphere) in Habermas's classic account to the very different circumstances of the twentieth century and its mass-mediated structure of public communication. The rise of the cheap mass-circulation press and pulp literatures; the centrality of film, radio, and TV; the revolutionizing of transportation and spoken communications via the automobile, mass transit, and the telephone (not to speak of the late twentieth-century technologies of electronic communication); and the mass circulation of consumer goods—all of these developments transform the relationship of the local and the national, and the modalities of collective identification within a public sphere. On the other hand, cultural studies' validation of popular culture as an object of analysis—taking it seriously, as manifesting real needs and aspirations, and as something to be decoded imaginatively in that light, however apparently trivial the contents—reopens an older debate concerning the value of "high" and "low" culture and the possible meanings of the "mass." This not only allows for new readings of popular texts, getting inside the latter sympathetically to explore the workings of their appeal, and claiming "pleasure" and "desire" as categories of political understanding. It also highlights the ways in which national cultures are constructed discursively around systems of negative distinction, where the positivity of the nation presumes the existence of a variety of unassimilated (or unassimilable) "Others"—whether external, in the colonialist representation of non-Western peoples via racialized constructions of cultural superiority, or internal, in relation to differences of race, ethnicity, religion, and, of course, class. Cultural studies has allowed for an immeasurably richer understanding of this dialectic of national self-identification, of recognition and disavowal, which marks the imagined body of the nation in its twentieth-century massified guise.

In each of these regions of analysis—whether the polite domains of officially ratified national culture, or the rough and vulgar cultural productions of the objectified or disregarded mass—gender is an indispensible theoretical term. Although this figures formally here as our fifth point, it properly belongs as a dimension of them all. In the most familiar sense, the nation has invariably been imagined via metaphors of family, and has accordingly replicated the patriarchy of conventional familial forms. In one common chain of association, for instance, women might be the mothers of the nation, reproducing its biological future, nurturing the next generation, and teaching the "mother tongue," but as reproducers rather than producers, prized and revered objects of protection, rather than agents in their own right. Anxieties about the health of the nation, or its demographic future and productive efficiencies, or the stabilities of the social fabric, commonly translate into a politics directed to and against women, whether through systems of mother-and-child welfare, through rhetorics of family values, or by policy offensives around reproductive health, the regulation of sexuality, or the direct control of women's bodies. Maternalism has been a powerful and recurring discursive formation in this sense, specifying forms of welfare-state intervention, condensing programmatic political ambitions, resonating with popular aspirations and anxieties, and working with or against rival conceptions of citizenship. In twentieth-century contexts, especially, it is impossible to discuss nationalism without finding this explicit and systematic gendered dimension.[53] In these contexts, *woman* is at least a positive term of the national good, albeit in some disempowering and subordinating sense. In other situations of crisis, however, the feminine becomes demonized as corruption and threat. Misogynist constructions of the urban mass public as dangerously feminine are a pervasive instance of such discourse, orchestrating anxieties that are easily and brutally magnified apparently in times of social stress, of disorder, revolutionary insurgency, or wartime defeat. As the mass rapes of Bosnian women in the post-Yugoslavian civil war remind us, the performance of violence on the bodies of women can also be a national act.[54]

Membership in the nation is thus a highly gendered faculty. It is now a commonplace of feminist critique that modern political thought contains such partialities, not least in the double context of the Enlightenment and the French Revolution from which many of the key elements of democratic discourse first descended. This founding conjuncture of modern political understanding, which we have also identified with the origins of discourse about the nation, was itself shot through with binary orders of assumptions—some newly conceived, some rearranged—about woman and man, which found their way into constitutions, codes of law, and political mobilizations, as well the higher philosophical discourse around the universals of reason, law, and nature, grounding such talk in an ideologically constructed system of differences in gender.

In the most obvious manifestation, this translated into women's exclusion from citizenship, preeminently through lack of the franchise, but more extensively in a complex repertoire of silencings and disabilities, which barred them from property, education, profession, and politics—all those opportunities that qualified men for roles in the public sphere. It was not until the second quarter of the twentieth century and after, in fact, that women were allowed formal entry into the political process in most parts of the world.

If the fundamental terms of modern social and political identity—of class, citizenship, race, nationhood, religion, the very category of the self—have been constituted from dichotomous assumptions about what it means to be a woman or a man, whether the juridical definitions of citizenship and personhood concede formal equality or not, then two important consequences for our understanding of nationalism follow. For one, we finally need to consider the gendered dimensions and meanings of nationalist discourse more seriously, for this remains an astonishing absence in most of the scholarly literature, whether general or particular. The gendered text of international relations, of militarism, and of formally nationalist movements; the subtle, complex, and disguised dialectics of femininity and masculinity in the construction of national identity; the relationship between the politics of sexuality and the discourse of belonging in the nation; the field of reciprocity between languages of motherhood, family, and domesticity, and those of participation within the public sphere of the nation—all these require explicit recognition. Moreover, women are not exactly absent from the scene of nationalist grandiosity but figure as important supporting players—as ''conquerors' mistresses, wartime rape victims, military prostitutes, cinematic soldier-heroes, pin-up models on patriotic calenders,'' and, of course, as workers, wives, girlfriends, and daughters waiting dutifully at home—and this structure of meanings too needs to be unpacked.[55] But if nationalist discourse silences and marginalizes women from public roles, then we have to look elsewhere for the female presence and voice, in the family and household, in the education of children, in the unspectacular spaces of the everyday—in all those places which Berlant counterposes as ''the local'' to the national frame of abstracted citizenship and power.[56] It is this domain of not-political but highly political practice that cultural studies, with its emphasis on popular culture and representation, has become exceptionally valuable in addressing.

The definitional territory we began by mapping in this introduction tended to focus on nationalism's positivity, particularly in its relationship to the values of the Enlightenment tradition, and, as we are now seeing, this leaves it vulnerable to the now familiar critiques of the latter coming from a variety of poststructuralist, postmodernist, feminist, and postcolonialist positions. As our comments on gender have already acknowledged, the political theory of the Enlightenment was founded in one of its dimensions on systematic silences and suppressions. That is, the founding moments of democratic advance became predicated on the gendering of political capacities, on the social qualification and limitation of citizenship, and on the exploitative domination of some peoples over others. Social improvements and cultural goods (which are the goals of nationalism too) involved similar privilegings and exclusions, which may have brought the dream of a better life into the world, but did so as a result of others' pain. In Europe's Enlightenment traditions, we are now better able to see, certain constructions of value, agency, and interest were centered at the expense of others.

This is the sixth of our points. The Eurocentrism of the discussion needs to be signaled, because imperialism and colonialism as a set of exploitative power relations were inscribed in the Enlightenment tradition from the beginning. This is the dark side of nationalism's politics of citizenship and empowerment, which usually presumed disfranchisement and expropriation somewhere else. From a European historian's point of view, it is especially vital to see how the social relations, patterns of culture, and increasingly racialized discourse of national superiority produced in the colonies and the subordinated extra-European world became powerfully reinserted into the European metropolitan frame. "Colonial knowledge" in this sense had a crucial bearing on the structure of nationalist politics inside Europe. Forms of colonial representation through literature, museums, and exhibitions, entertainment, and popular culture have become especially fruitful fields of inquiry in this regard. The *gendering* of national identity, whether in militarism or warfare per se, or in the general ordering of nationalist representations around conceptions of masculinity and femininity, also had key colonialist roots—as, for instance, in discussions around colonial intermarriage, which generated complicated bodies of discourse around gender inequalities, sexual privilege, class priorities, and racial superiority, which in their turn became potently rearticulated into nationalist discourse at home.[57] Morever, while the complex dialectic between Europe and its Others has been constitutive for the experience of nationality since the late eighteenth century, such relations have also been replicated inside Europe itself—between metropolitan and peripheral cultures, between town and country, between high and low cultures, between dominant and subordinate nationalities ("historic nations" and "history-less peoples"), between West and East. This sensitivity to nationalism's negative codings, to the ways in which even the nation's most generous and inclusively democratic imaginings entail processes of protective and exclusionary positioning against others, often extraordinarily subtle, but including of course the most violent forms of direct colonial rule, is one of the most important gains of the last two decades.[58] Furthermore, in colonizing the world, metropolitan nations also create hegemonies of possible meanings. Even the most self-conscious and radical of oppositional, colonial, or minority nationalisms mount their emancipatory demands from a ground of identity which colonialism's power has already laid down.

From their own vantage points and particular experience with colonialism, anticolonial nationalism, Marxism, and postcolonial disillusionments, scholars from outside Europe have broken new ground in two important directions. First, they have insisted that the voices of the subalterns (here borrowing a term from Gramsci) be heard, even as their appreciation of the power of elite discourses seems to silence those voices. Coming out of Indian Marxism, with connections to the Maoist wing of the movement, the Subaltern Studies Group questioned the understanding of peasant movements of established Communist parties and nationalist scholars. Historians like Ranajit Guha and political scientists like Partha Chatterjee attempted to reinterpret the history of South Asia from the position of the inarticulate and the subordinated, only to turn their attention increasingly to the dominant structures and discourses in which the subaltern were forced to operate, particularly nationalism and colonialism.

This second direction, the exploration of dominant discourses and the ways in which they might be reworked, led Chatterjee to look at the ways in which "knowledge becomes the means to the domination of the world." Western ideas of rationality, he argued, relegate non-Western cultures "into the darkness of unscientific traditionalism." Likewise, the relativist approach, which holds that every culture is unique and autonomous, depends on an essentialist notion of culture that precludes understanding from outside. Both views are imbedded in power relations, but colonial nationalism in India, though a "derivative discourse," was never totally dominated by colonial discourses. More intriguingly, colonial nationalism doubly addressed the colonial powers and the people in a creative attempt to forge a new "historical bloc" for a "passive revolution" against the hegemon. Nationalism in the colonial world borrowed from European nationalism even as it attempted to liberate itself from the rationalist discourse of the colonizers. Without completely freeing themselves from the structure of power of imperialism, colonial nationalists nevertheless adapted the discourse to their own requirements, eventually even using nationalism as a new form of state ideology.

Chatterjee also asks the question, if nationalists have to choose their "imagined communities" from European models, as Benedict Anderson maintains, what do they have left to imagine? Is the postcolonial world only the consumer of modernity? He answers that postcolonial nationalism, in fact, has been based, not on an *identity* with the "modular" forms that Anderson proposes but on a *difference* with the modern West. Colonial nationalism created its own domain of sovereignty within colonial society even before it began its struggle with the imperial power by dividing the world into material and spiritual domains. While it granted that the West was dominant in the material realm, it claimed the spiritual, the space where the essential marks of cultural identity were to be found, as its own. Though this separation of the material and the spiritual between West and East might appear to be a replication of Orientalist dichotomies, Chatterjee sees the distinction as empowering postcolonial nationalism, which took over the spiritual domain and refused to allow the imperial power to penetrate its own inner world.[59]

This reference to *hegemony* brings us to a seventh and final major point, which concerns the forms of contestation inside nationalism's dominant frame. We ended the previous section of this introduction by highlighting the importance of the transition to statehood, and this third section explores some of the ways in which nationality or nation-ness—the complex, conscious, unspoken, and inescapable modalities of "being national"—provides the generic currency of political-identity formation in the public and everyday conditions of life of the twentieth century. Voting to exclude resident aliens from welfare benefits is not a particularly subtle but a pointedly cruel way of defining who is in and who is out of the national community. We are "national," when we vote, watch the six o'clock news, follow the national sport, observe (while barely noticing) the repeated iconographies of landscape and history in TV commercials, imbibe the visual archive of reference and citation in the movies, and define the nation day by day in our politics. As Berlant says, this is the sort of thing implied by the attribution of "a common national 'character,' " where "national subjects are taught to value certain abstract signs and stories as part of their intrinsic relation

to themselves, to all 'citizens,' and to the national terrain.'' This is the formation
and operation of the ''National Symbolic'':

> ... the order of discursive practices whose reign within a national space produces,
> and also refers to, the ''law'' in which the accident of birth within a geographic/
> political boundary transforms individuals into subjects of a collectively-held history.
> Its traditional icons, its metaphors, its heroes, its rituals, and its narratives, provide
> an alphabet for a collective consciousness or national subjectivity; through the Na-
> tional Symbolic the historical nation aspires to achieve the inevitability of the status
> of natural law, a birthright.[60]

In Berlant's usage, this describes ''the *political* space of the nation,'' which
is a ''tangled cluster'' of attributes—''juridical, territorial (*jus soli*), genetic (*jus
sanguinis*), linguistic, or experiential.'' Whereas ''law dominates the field of citizenship, constructing technical definitions of the citizen's rights, duties, and obligations,'' the National Symbolic aims for something more, ''to link regulation
to desire, harnessing affect to political life through the production of 'national
fantasy.' '' This is how the idea of the nation works, figuring a landscape of
complacency and promise, inciting memories of citizenship, but bringing its
claims and demands into the intimate and quotidian places of ordinary life: ''By
'fantasy' I mean to designate how national culture becomes local—through the
images, narratives, monuments, and sites that circulate through personal/collec-
tive consciousness.''[61]

There is an enormous amount that could still be said on this theme, about the
constructing and contesting of national hegemonies, using materials from a host
of places and literatures. The conflicts of left and right are one key to the changing
bases of nationalist discourse in the twentieth century, framed by the expansions
and transformations of the public sphere since the 1890s, and by the massive
enhancement of the state's relationship to society resulting from the two world
wars, with their complex relationship to the enlargement and regulation of citizenship. In the early twentieth century, we find a new discourse of the ''mass''
(the rise of the masses, mass society, mass culture), in which the dangerousness
of the people becomes pathologized via a new repertoire of ideologies—crowd
theories, theories of degeneration, claims about popular intelligence, programs of
eugenics and social engineering, theories of race, and so on—where the national
health turns into a kind of permanent emergency. Politically speaking, the rise of
socialist and labor movements, dramatized globally via the Russian Revolution
and the other popular insurgencies after 1917, reopened the question of democracy in national polities, but also provoked a new disciplinary discourse of nationalism on the right, in a complicated relation to earlier languages of national
freedom and the people's will. After 1918, this field of conflict changed the
valencies of nationalist appeals in already formed nation-states, making the authority of the-people-as-nation into the common referent of legitimacy. Fascism
and other forms of radical-right populisms have evacuated democracy per se, it
is true, but otherwise right-wing politics have successfully relocated to the formal
ground of popular sovereignty. Likewise, increasingly after 1918, and especially
since 1945, the Left simultaneously repositioned themselves inside the discursive

frame of the nation-state, which was no small development given the previous power of internationalist and class discourses in the formation of left-wing movements (and their exclusion from the legitimate nation by the dominant classes).

For around half a century, in developed capitalist countries, this consensual contest of national-popular projects provided forms of political intelligibility that persuasively marginalized more radical challenges from right and left. But since the 1980s for a variety of reasons—the crisis and collapse of the Soviet Union and state socialism, the dissolution of postwar social democracy and the Keynesian-welfare-state synthesis in the West, capitalist restructuring via globalization and the post-Fordist transition, the reconfiguring of national sovereignties via transnational regionalisms like the European Union, the changing social bases of politics and the decline of the traditional mass membership party, the dominance of mass-entertainment cultures in the public sphere, and so on—the reliable routines of organized collective identification are no longer there. How we recognize the forms of the National Symbolic and their operation, in an exercise of analysis, via the plenitude of cultural studies approaches now available, is perhaps still clear. How we take this as a basis for action is not. In the United States, for instance, there is now a disconcerting gap between on the one hand the forms of subcultural disidentification with official nationality, and the invention of localized alternatives to the latter in the molecular growth of dissident counterpublics (African-American, Hispanic, feminist, Gay-Lesbian, Queer, environmentalist, and so on), and on the other hand the persistence of a state-organized national political process which compels participation in practice, if legal protections, access to resources, and even the occasional reform are to be secured; in other words a gap "between a utopian politics of identity, difference, dispersion, and specificity, and a pluralist agenda in the liberal sense that imagines a 'gorgeous mosaic' of difference without a model of conflict."[62] And in the meantime, the Christian Right has its own forms of national identification which remain ever more intolerantly centered. The hegemony of the idea of the nation has a power all of its own:

> But the circle of dominant ideas *does* accumulate the symbolic power to map or classify the world for others; its classifications do acquire not only the constraining power of dominance over other modes of thought but also the inertial authority of habit and instinct. It becomes the horizon of the taken-for-granted: what the world is and how it works, for all practical purposes. Ruling ideas may dominate other conceptions of the social world by setting the limit to what will appear as rational, reasonable, credible, indeed sayable or thinkable, within the given vocabularies of motive and action available to us. Their dominance lies precisely in the power they have to contain within their limits, to frame within their circumference of thought, the reasoning and calculation of other social groups.[63]

In a rapidly changing and increasingly unknowable world, the nation is a refuge, a place to be at home with oneself and with one's own kind. This conservative inclusiveness reflects fear of the different, the alien, and the immigrant intruder. Here identity reveals its real power. As Stuart Hall explains, identity is a "guarantee that the world isn't falling apart as rapidly as it sometimes seems to be.'' For the nationalist or the racist, identity is a given, something stable and predictable, from which all kinds of information might be gleaned as common sense. Racial understanding, based on the notion that somatic features, skin color or nose size, are outward signs of inner qualities such as intelligence, morality, economic skills, or sexual prowess, looks for an elusive, illusory stability. But for the critic of racism or national or feminist essentialism, identities are accepted as relational, rather than absolute and fixed, existing always within discourse as the stories that are told about oneself or which one tells of oneself. Constructed in history and fatally dependent on difference, identity gives us a provisional place from which to speak.

Being national is the condition of our times, even as the nation is buffeted by the subnational rise of local, regional, and ethnic claims, and the transnational threats of globalization, hegemonic American culture, migration, diasporization, and new forms of political community. In one way nationalism, like racism, becomes the protective cover to resist the uncontrollable transformations of our time. In another, nationalism and belonging to a nation may be the kind of ''cultural recovery'' that could potentially lead—not to a politics of the blood—but to acceptance, even celebration, of difference.

NOTES

1. This essay is based on the exchanging of ideas and texts between the two authors, who cannibalized each other's works to arrive at a (hopefully) coherent presentation of their thinking on nationalism. They are grateful to the authors in this collection, other unnamed writers on nationalism, and colleagues and friends at their respective universities for their conversations and critiques that amplified their understanding.

2. Partha Chatterjee, *The Nation and Its Fragments: Colonial and Postcolonial Histories* (Princeton, N.J.: Princeton University Press, 1993), p. 4.

3. C. J. H. Hayes, *Essays on Nationalism* (New York: Macmillan, 1966); idem, *The Historical Evolution of Modern Nationalism* (New York: 1968).

4. Hans Kohn, *Nationalism, Its Meaning and History* (Princeton, N.J.: Princeton University Press, 1955); idem, *The Idea of Nationalism* (New York: Macmillan, 1967).

5. Anthony D. Smith, *Theories of Nationalism* (London: Duckworth, 1971, 1983), p. 198.

6. Elie Kedourie, *Nationalism* (London: Hutchinson, 1960), p. 1.

7. T. de Mauro, *Storia linguistica dell'Italia* (Bari, Italy, 1972), p. 43.

8. Eugen Weber, *Peasants into Frenchmen: The Modernization of Rural France, 1870–1914* (Stanford, Calif.: Stanford University Press, 1976). Weber emphasizes the agency of the state in creating common language and identity, while Peter Sahlins focuses on local issues and conflicts. See his ''The Nation in the Village: State-Building and Communal Struggles in the Catalan Borderland during the Eighteenth and Nineteenth Centuries,'' *Journal of Modern History*, 60, 2 (1988), pp. 234–63; idem, *Boundaries: The Making of France and Spain in the Pyrenees* (Berkeley and Los Angeles: University of California Press, 1989); and Herman Lebovics, *True France: The Wars Over Cultural Identity 1900–1945* (Ithaca, N.Y.: Cornell University Press, 1992).

9. Gerasimos Augustinos, *Consciousness and History: Nationalist Critics of Greek Society 1897–1914* (New York: Columbia University Press), p. 16 f.

10. Karl Deutsch, *Nationalism and Social Communication: An Inquiry into the Foundations of Nationality* (Cambridge, Mass.: MIT Press, 1966), p. 97.

11. Weber, *Peasants into Frenchmen*; Theodore Zeldin, *France 1848–1945. II: Intellect, Taste and Anxiety* (Oxford: Oxford University Press, 1977), pp. 3–85.

12. Nationalization of culture should be distinguished from the creation of a national identity. On the forging of British national identity in the eighteenth and early nineteenth centuries, see Linda Colley, *Britons: Forging the Nation, 1707–1837* (New Haven, Conn.: Yale University Press, 1992).

13. In this context see Lonsdale's excellent discussion of "tribalism" in western Kenya, where the social reality of the Gussii's developing existence as a tribe is located in specific historical processes of cultural redefinition, in which the people concerned seem to have "homogenized their own traditions" and achieved a "reworking of myth through time." At all events, "Gussii-ness," the quality of cultural belonging to the Gussii "tribe," was no timeless reality organically rooted in an ethnic essence, but a specific consequence of social change in processes of migration, settlement, and cultural cooperation. This is a good instance of how historians of European nations might usefully learn from their African colleagues. John M. Lonsdale, "When did the Gussii (or any other group) become a 'tribe'?" *Kenya Historical Review*, 5, 1 (1977), pp. 123–33.

14. See Tom Nairn, "Scotland and Europe," this volume.

15. Nairn, "Scotland and Europe."

16. H. Sundhausen, *Der Einfluss der Herderschen Ideen auf die Nationsbildung bei den Völkern der Habsburger Monarchie* (Munich: Oldenbourg, 1973); C. Koumarianou, "The Contribution of the Intelligentsia towards Greek Independence," in Richard Clogg (ed.), *The Struggle for Greek Independence* (London: Macmillan, 1973), pp. 67–86; D. Visvizi-Dontos, "The Idea of Nation in Relation to the Establishment of the Modern Greek State," in Theodor Schieder (ed.), *Staatsgründungen und Nationalitätsprinzip* (Munich: Oldenbourg, 1974), pp. 113–30; Bela K. Kiraly, "Napoleon's Proclamation of 1809 and Its Hungarian Echo," in S. B. Winters and J. Held (eds.), *Intellectual and Social Developments in the Habsburg Empire from Maria Theresa to World War I* (New York: Columbia University Press, 1975); Wayne S. Vucinich, "Croatian Illyrism: Its Background and Genesis," in ibid., pp. 55–114.

17. Eric Hobsbawm, *The Age of Revolution* (New York: New American Library, 1962), pp. 163 ff.

18. Gwyn A. Williams, *Madoc: The Making of a Myth* (London: Methuen, 1980). This quotation is taken from a review of the book in the *Times* (London), 8 March 1980.

19. Hobsbawm, *Age of Revolution*, p. 166. He quickly adds the observation "These are not, of course, distinct from the business classes, especially in backward countries where estate administrators, notaries, lawyers and the like are among the key accumulators of rural wealth."

20. Sundhausen, *Einfluss*, p. 102; Keith Hitchens, "The Sacred Cult of Nationality: Romanian Intellectuals and the Church in Transylvania, 1834–69," in Winters and Held (eds.), *Intellectual and Social Developments*, pp. 131–60.

21. Hobsbawm, *Age of Revolution*, p. 166.

22. Leonore O'Boyle, "The Problem of an Excess of Educated Men in Western Europe, 1800–1850," *Journal of Modern History*, 49 (1970), pp. 471–95; Fritz K. Ringer, *Education and Social Patterns in Modern Europe* (Bloomington: Indiana University Press, 1979); Miroslav Hroch, *Social Preconditions of National Revival in Europe: A Comparative Analysis of the Social Composition of Patriotic Groups among the Smaller European Nations* (Cambridge: Cambridge University Press, 1985).

23. Sundhausen, *Einfluss*, pp. 146 f., 164 ff.; Vucinich, "Croatian Illyrism," pp. 55

ff.; M. Gross, "Einfluss der sozialen Struktur auf den Charakter der Nationalbewegung in den kroatischen Ländern im 19. Jahrhundert," in Theodor Schieder (ed.), *Sozialstruktur und Organisation europäischer Nationalbewegungen* (Munich: Oldenbourg, 1971), pp. 67–96.

24. L. von Gogolak, *Beiträge zur Geschichte des slowakischen Volkes. III: Zwischen zwei Revolutionen (1848–1919)* (Munich, 1972), pp. 1–19; Keith Hitchins, *Orthodoxy and Nationality: Andrieu Saguna and the Rumanians of Transylvania 1846–1873* (Cambridge, Mass.: Harvard University Press, 1977), pp. 78 ff.

25. Charles A. Macartney, *Hungary and Her Successors* (Oxford: Oxford University Press, 1937), p. 90.

26. Ibid., p. 210 f.; Paul Robert Magocsi, *The Shaping of a National Identity: Subcarpathian Rus', 1848–1948* (Cambridge, Mass.: Harvard University Press, 1978), pp. 42–75.

27. There is much of this in Kedourie, *Nationalism*, pp. 43 ff., 99 ff. See also Elie Kedourie, *Afghani and Abduh: An Essay on Religious Unbelief and Political Activism in Modern Islam* (London: Cass, 1966); and for a critique, Bryan S. Turner, *Marx and the End of Orientalism* (London: Allen and Unwin, 1978), pp. 53–66.

28. This point is made by Hobsbawm, *Age of Revolution*, pp. 168–77. For Ireland, see J. A. Reynolds, *The Catholic Emancipation Crisis in Ireland 1823–1829* (New Haven, Conn., and London: Yale University Press, 1954); and Peter Alter, "Nationale Organisationen in Irland 1801–1921," in Theodor Schieder and Otto Dann (eds.), *Nationale Bewegung und soziale Organisation. I: Vergleichende Studien zur nationalen Vereinsbewegung des 19. Jahrhunderts in Europe* (Munich: Oldenbourg, 1978), pp. 1–130. For Greece, see Clogg (ed.), *Struggle for Greek Independence*; and Visvizi-Dontas, "Idea of Nation."

29. Hroch, *Social Preconditions of National Revival.*

30. Eric Hobsbawm, *The Age of Capital* (London: Weidenfeld, 1975), p. 90. There are some variations in Hroch's findings among the eight nationalities concerned. Thus about 50 percent of the Czech and Slovak patriots came from families of artisans and small traders, with a higher proportion of the Slovaks coming from the rural artisanate; by contrast, some 20 percent of the Norwegians came from the bourgeoisie (notably the merchant and shipping families), and a further 30 percent from the urban petty bourgeoisie. Finnish patriots came overwhelmingly from families of the intelligentsia (officials and priests), with some 20 percent from the bourgeoisie and urban petty bourgeoisie, and a mere 5 percent from the peasantry. Lithuanian, Estonian, and White Russian patriots came overwhelmingly from the villages, and in the Lithuanian case less than 5 percent came from the towns.

31. In many ways, Hroch's approach is reminiscent of Charles Tilly's classic analysis, *The Vendée* (Cambridge, Mass.: Harvard University Press, 1964).

32. See Jürgen Habermas, *The Structural Transformation of the Public Sphere: An Inquiry into a Category of Bourgeois Society* (Cambridge, Mass.: MIT Press, 1993; originally published in Germany 1962); and Craig Calhoun (ed.), *Habermas and the Public Sphere* (Cambridge, Mass.: MIT Press, 1992). For some reflections directly angled toward questions of the nation, see Geoff Eley, "Nations, Publics, and Political Cultures: Placing Habermas in the Nineteenth Century," in Calhoun (ed.), *Habermas and the Public Sphere*, pp. 289–339. For some examples of such an approach in a "practical state," see Gale Stokes, "The Social Origins of East European Politics," *East European Politics and Societies*, 1 (1987), pp. 30–74; Tom Garvin, "The Anatomy of a Nationalist Revolution: Ireland, 1858–1928," *Comparative Studies in Society and History*, 28 (1986), pp. 468–

501; Samuel Clark and James S. Donnelly (eds.), *Irish Peasants: Violence and Political Unrest, 1780–1914* (Madison: University of Wisconsin Press, 1983); and Rosalind Mitchison (ed.), *The Roots of Nationalism: Studies in Northern Europe* (Edinburgh: Edinburgh University Press, 1980).

33. John Womack, "Mariategui, Marxism, and Nationalism," *Marxist Perspectives*, 3 (1980), p. 172 f.

34. See for instance one of the best regarded of the more recent general books on nationalism, which seeks to present a synthesis of existing accounts by drawing on the monographic literature for a wide range of particular countries: John Breuilly, *Nationalism and the State* (Manchester, England: Manchester University Press, 1982; reissued in a new paperback edition, Chicago: University of Chicago Press, 1994). Though a social historian himself by immediate background, Breuilly adopts a somewhat narrow approach, which treats nationalism as a "form of politics." Peter Alter, *Nationalism* (London: Edward Arnold, 1989), provides a stronger context in the social-historical literature, but is far more essayistic as a book.

35. Nairn, "Scotland and Europe," this volume.

36. The best succinct statement of this view, movingly personal and restlessly eloquent, is Raymond Williams's 1958 essay, "Culture Is Ordinary," in *Resources of Hope: Culture, Democracy, Socialism* (London: Verso, 1989), pp. 3–18. Over the length of his career Williams was more sensitive to questions of power inequality and the silencing of voices within the common culture than Hoggart.

37. There are many introductions to the work of the Birmingham CCCS, but for an excellent guide and anthology, see Stuart Hall et al. (eds.), *Culture, Media, Language* (London: Hutchinson, 1980).

38. See Raymond Williams, *Keywords. A Vocabulary of Culture and Society*, rev. ed. (New York: Oxford University Press, 1983), p. 90; and *Culture* (London: Fontana, 1981), p. 13.

39. Glenn Jordan and Chris Weedon, *Cultural Politics: Class, Gender, Race and the Postmodern World* (Oxford: Blackwell, 1995), p. 565.

40. R. D. Grillo, "Introduction," in Grillo (ed.), *"Nation" and "State" in Europe: Anthropological Perspectives* (London: Academic Press, 1980), p. 11.

41. Abner Cohen, *Two Dimensional Man* (London, 1974), p. 23.

42. Jochen Blaschke, "Einleitung," in Blaschke (ed.), *Handbuch der europäischen Regionalbewegungen* (Frankfurt am Main: Syndikat, 1980), p. 17.

43. Kenneth Minogue, *Nationalism* (London: Batsford, 1967), p. 22 f.

44. For a full-scale presentation of this argument, see Eley, "Nations, Publics, and Political Cultures." See also Habermas, *Structural Transformation of the Public Sphere;* and Calhoun (ed.), *Habermas and the Public Sphere.*

45. See Raymond Williams, "Cambridge English, Past and Present," "Crisis in English Studies," and "Beyond Cambridge English," in Williams, *Writing in Society* (London: Verso, 1983), pp. 177–226; Chris Baldick, *The Social Mission of English Criticism, 1848–1932* (Oxford: Oxford University Press, 1983); Brian Doyle, *English and Englishness* (London: , 1989); Peter Widdowson (ed.), *Re-reading English* (London: Methuen, 1982); Francis Mulhearn, *The Moment of "Scrutiny"* (London: Verso, 1979); and Anthony Easthope, *Literary into Cultural Studies* (London: Routledge, 1991). For the classic text, originally published in 1964, see Perry Anderson, "Components of the National Culture," in *English Questions* (London: Verso, 1992), pp. 48–104.

46. Peter Jelavich, *Munich and Theatrical Modernism: Politics, Playwriting, and Performance, 1890–1914* (Cambridge, Mass.: Harvard University Press, 1985), p. 17.

47. Brian Doyle, "The Hidden History of English Studies," in Widdowson (ed.), *Rereading English*, p. 18.

48. See for instance, Doris Sommer, *Foundational Fictions: The National Romances of Latin America* (Berkeley: University of California Press, 1991); Ileana Rodríguez, *House/Garden/Nation: Space, Gender, and Ethnicity in Postcolonial Latin American Literatures by Women* (Durham, N.C.: Duke University Press, 1994). For an excellent compilation of such work, drawn from various parts of the world, see Homi K. Bhabha (ed.), *Nation and Narration* (London: Routledge, 1990). See also Lauren Berlant, *The Anatomy of National Fantasy: Hawthorne, Utopia, and Everyday Life* (Chicago: University of Chicago Press, 1991).

49. Benedict Anderson, *Imagined Communities: Reflections on the Origin and Spread of Nationalism,* rev. ed. (London: Verso, 1991), p. 7. As well as the factors already mentioned, Anderson also cites the growth of vernacular languages and the rise of "print capitalism," as well as changing conceptions of time. In some discussions of Anderson's book, there has developed recently an oversimplifying tendency to foreground the idea of print capitalism, to the neglect of these other key elements, and it is important to note the complexity of his overall argumentation.

50. Ibid., p. 6.

51. Ibid., p. 11.

52. Berlant, *Anatomy of National Fantasy,* p. 20.

53. See here Gisela Bock and Pat Thane (eds.), *Maternity and Gender Policies: Women and the Rise of the European Welfare States, 1880–1950s* (London: Routledge, 1991); and Seth Koven and Sonya Michel (eds.), *Mothers of a New World: Maternalist Politics and the Origins of Welfare States* (London: Routledge, 1993). Weimar and Nazi Germany are an especially fruitful context for exploring these connections. See Renate Bridenthal, Atina Grossmann, and Marion Kaplan (eds.), *When Biology Became Destiny: Women in Weimar and Nazi Germany* (New York: Monthly Review Press, 1984); Atina Grossmann, *Reforming Sex: The German Movement for Birth Control and Abortion Reform, 1920 to 1950* (New York: Oxford University Press, 1995); Cornelie Usborne, *The Politics of the Body in Weimar Germany: Women's Reproductive Rights and Duties* (Ann Arbor: University of Michigan Press, 1992); and Claudia Koonz, *Mothers in the Fatherland: Women, the Family, and Nazi Politics* (New York: St. Martin's Press, 1987). The wider literatures are enormous, but for France, see Karen Offen, "Depopulation, Nationalism, and Feminism in Fin de Siècle France," *American Historical Review,* 89 (1984), pp. 648–76; and Jane Jensen, "Gender and Reproduction or Babies and the State," *Studies in Political Economy,* 20 (1986), pp. 9–46. For Britain: Anna Davin, "Imperialism and Motherhood," *History Workshop Journal,* 5 (1978), pp. 9–65; and Susan Pedersen, "Gender, Welfare, and Citizenship in Britain during the Second World War," *American Historical Review,* 95 (1990), pp. 983–1006.

54. See especially Klaus Theweleit, *Male Fantasies,* 2 vols. (Minneapolis: University of Minnesota Press, 1987, 1989); George L. Mosse, *Nationalism and Sexuality: Middle-Class Morality and Sexual Norms in Modern Europe* (Madison: University of Wisconsin Press, 1985); Andrew Parker et al. (eds.), *Nationalisms and Sexualities* (New York: Routledge, 1992); and Judith R. Walkowitz, *City of Dreadful Delight: Narratives of Sexual Danger in Late-Victorian London* (Chicago: University of Chicago Press, 1992).

55. Cynthia Enloe, *The Morning After: Sexual Politics at the End of the Cold War* (Berkeley: University of California Press, 1993), p. 245.

56. See for instance, Berlant, *Anatomy of National Fantasy,* p. 216 f.

57. See Lora Wildenthal, " 'She Is the Victor': Bourgeois Women, Nationalist Identities, and the Ideal of the Independent Woman Farmer in German Southwest Africa,"

Social Analysis, 33 (1993), pp. 69–88; and the work of Anne L. Stoler, "Rethinking Colonial Categories: European Communities and the Boundaries of Rule," in Nicholas B. Dirks (ed.), *Colonialism and Culture* (Ann Arbor: University of Michigan Press, 1992), pp. 319–52, and "Sexual Affronts and Racial Frontiers," in this volume.

58. This discussion begins with Edward Said, *Orientalism* (New York: Pantheon, 1978). More recently, see Mary Louise Pratt, *Imperial Eyes: Travel Writing and Transculturalism* (London: Routledge, 1992); Dirks (ed.), *Colonialism and Culture*; Gyan Prakash (ed.), *After Colonialism: Imperial Histories and Postcolonial Displacements* (Princeton N.J.: Princeton University Press, 1995); idem, "Subaltern Studies as Postcolonial Criticism," *American Historical Review*, 99 (1994), pp. 1475–90; Florencia E. Mallon, "The Promise and Dilemma of Subaltern Studies: Perspectives from Latin American History," ibid., pp. 1491–1515; and Frederick Cooper, "Conflict and Connection: Rethinking Colonial African History," ibid. pp. 1516–45.

59. Partha Chatterjee, *Nationalist Thought and the Colonial World: A Derivative Discourse* (London: Zed Books, 1986); idem, *The Nation and Its Fragments: Colonial and Postcolonial Histories* (Princeton N.J.: Princeton University Press, 1993).

60. Berlant, *Anatomy of National Fantasy*, p. 20.

61. Ibid., p. 5.

62. Lauren Berlant and Elizabeth Freeman, "Queer Nationality," in Michael Warner (ed.), *Fear of a Queer Planet: Queer Politics and Social Theory* (Minneapolis: University of Minnesota Press, 1993), p. 197.

63. Stuart Hall, "The Toad in the Garden: Thatcherism among the Theorists," in Cary Nelson and Lawrence Grossberg (eds.), *Marxism and the Interpretation of Culture* (Urbana: University of Illinois Press, 1988), p. 44. For a brilliant reflection on the question of identity from a similar perspective, see Stuart Hall, "Cultural Identity and Diaspora," in Jonathan Rutherford (ed.), *Identity: Community, Culture, Difference* (London: Lawrence and Wishart, 1990), pp. 222–37. See also David Forgacs, "National-Popular: Genealogy of a Concept," in *Formations of Nation and People* (London: Routledge, 1984), pp. 83–98.

I

A CLASSICAL STATEMENT

Ernest Renan (1823–1892)

Born in a peasant family in France, Ernest Renan supported himself through his adult life from his voluminous philosophical and historical writings and the savings of his sister. Though he had planned to become a priest, he broke early with the Catholic Church and turned enthusiastically toward the revolutions of 1848. Politically he drifted from liberalism toward Bonapartism and authoritarianism. Intellectually he remained a skeptic and a critic of orthodox religion. In both his historical and dramatic works Renan promoted a positivist faith in science, and the church condemned his *La Vie de Jésus* (1863). In 1870 he was belatedly given the chair at the College de France from which he had earlier been suspended because of his atheism. Eight years later he was elected to the Academie Française.

Renan's famous essay "What Is a Nation?" [Qu'est-ce qu'une nation?] was first delivered as a lecture at the Sorbonne in 1882. Extraordinarily prescient in its disassembly of the usual characteristics of nationhood, the essay ends in a particularly Renanian fashion proclaiming the nation to be "a soul, a spiritual principle." His notions of solidarity constituted by sacrifice and the nation as an act of willful consent, "a daily plebiscite," resonate in recent writings. His insight that forgetting the actual past and reconstituting the nation in historical error is fundamental to the creation of nations was picked up a century later by Benedict Anderson as he developed the idea of the nation as an imagined political community.

What Is a Nation?

What I propose to do today is to analyse with you an idea which, though seem-ingly clear, lends itself to the most dangerous misunderstandings. [Consider] the vast agglomerations of men found in China, Egypt or ancient Babylonia, the tribes of the Hebrews and the Arabs, the city as it existed in Athens or Sparta, the assemblies of the various territories in the Carolingian Empire, those communities which are without a *patrie*[1] and are maintained by a religious bond alone, as is the case with the Israelites and the Parsees, nations, such as France, England and the majority of the modern European sovereign states, confederations, such as exist in Switzerland or in America, and ties, such as those that race, or rather language, establishes between the different branches of the German or Slav peo-ples. Each of these groupings exist, or have existed, and there would be the direst of consequences if one were to confuse any one of them with any other. At the time of the French Revolution, it was commonly believed that the institutions proper to small, independent cities, such as Sparta and Rome, might be applied to our large nations, which number some thirty or forty million souls. Nowadays, a far graver mistake is made: race is confused with nation and a sovereignty analogous to that of really existing peoples is attributed to ethnographic or, rather, linguistic groups.

I want now to try and make these difficult questions somewhat more precise, for the slightest confusion regarding the meaning of words, at the start of an argument, may in the end lead to the most fatal of errors. It is a delicate thing that I propose to do here, somewhat akin to vivisection; I am going to treat the living much as one ordinarily treats the dead. I shall adopt an absolutely cool and impartial attitude.

I

Since the fall of the Roman Empire or, rather, since the disintegration of Char-lemagne's empire, western Europe has seemed to us to be divided into nations,

Ernest Renan, "What Is a Nation?" translated and annotated by Martin Thom, from Homi K. Bhabha (ed.), *Nation and Narration* (London: Routledge, 1990), pp. 8–22.

Translator's note: ["What Is a Nation" was] a lecture delivered at the Sorbonne, 11 March 1882. "Qu'est-ce qu'une nation?" *Oeuvres Complètes* (Paris, 1947–61), vol. I, pp. 887–907. An earlier translation, which I have consulted, is in A. Zimmern (ed.), *Modern Political Doctrines* (London, 1939), pp. 186–205.

some of which, in certain epochs, have sought to wield a hegemony over the others, without ever enjoying any lasting success. It is hardly likely that anyone in the future will achieve what Charles V, Louis XIV and Napoleon I failed to do. The founding of a new Roman Empire or of a new Carolingian empire would now be impossible. Europe is so divided that any bid for universal domination would very rapidly give rise to a coalition, which would drive any too ambitious nation back to its natural frontiers.[2] A kind of equilibrium has long been established. France, England, Germany and Russia will, for centuries to come, no matter what may befall them, continue to be individual historical units, the crucial pieces on a chequerboard whose squares will forever vary in importance and size but will never be wholly confused with each other.

Nations, in this sense of the term, are something fairly new in history. Antiquity was unfamiliar with them; Egypt, China and ancient Chaldea were in no way nations. They were flocks led by a Son of the Sun or by a Son of Heaven. Neither in Egypt nor in China were there citizens as such. Classical antiquity had republics, municipal kingdoms, confederations of local republics and empires, yet it can hardly be said to have had nations in our understanding of the term. Athens, Sparta, Tyre and Sidon were small centres imbued with the most admirable patriotism, but they were [simply] cities with a relatively restricted territory. Gaul, Spain and Italy, prior to their absorption by the Roman Empire, were collections of clans, which were often allied among themselves but had no central institutions and no dynasties. The Assyrian Empire, the Persian Empire and the empire of Alexander the Great were not *patries* either. There never were any Assyrian patriots, and the Persian Empire was nothing but a vast feudal structure. No nation traces its origins back to Alexander the Great's momentous adventure, fertile though it was in consequences for the general history of civilization.

The Roman Empire was much more nearly a *patrie*. Roman domination, although at first so harsh, was soon loved, for it had brought about the great benefit of putting an end to war. The empire was a huge association, and a synonym for order, peace and civilization. In its closing stages, lofty souls, enlightened bishops, and the educated classes had a real sense of the *Pax Romana*, which withstood the threatening chaos of barbarism. But an empire twelve times larger than present-day France cannot be said to be a state in the modern sense of the term. The split between the eastern and western [empires] was inevitable, and attempts at founding an empire in Gaul, in the third century AD, did not succeed either. It was in fact the Germanic invasions which introduced into the world the principle which, later, was to serve as a basis for the existence of nationalities.

What in fact did the German peoples accomplish, from their great invasions in the fifth century AD up until the final Norman conquests in the tenth century? They effected little change in the racial stock, but they imposed dynasties and a military aristocracy upon the more or less extensive parts of the old empire of the west, which assumed the names of their invaders. This was the origin of France, Burgundy, and Lombardy, and, subsequently, Normandy. The Frankish Empire so rapidly extended its sway that, for a period, it re-established the unity of the west, but it was irreparably shattered around the middle of the ninth century; the partition of Verdun[3] outlined divisions which were in principle immutable and, from then on, France, Germany, England, Italy, and Spain made their way, by often circuitous paths and through a thousand and one vicissitudes, to their full national existence, such as we see it blossoming today.

What in fact is the defining feature of these different states? It is the fusion of their component populations. In the above mentioned countries, there is nothing analogous to what you will find in Turkey, where Turks, Slavs, Greeks, Armenians, Arabs, Syrians, and Kurds are as distinct today as they were upon the day that they were conquered. Two crucial circumstances helped to bring about this result. First, the fact that the Germanic peoples adopted Christianity as soon as they underwent any prolonged contact with the Greek or Latin peoples. When conqueror or conquered have the same religion or, rather, when the conqueror adopts the religion of the conquered, the Turkish system—that is, the absolute distinction between men in terms of their religion—can no longer arise. The second circumstance was the forgetting, by the conquerors, of their own language. The grandsons of Clovis, Alaric, Gundebald, Alboin, and Roland were already speaking the Roman tongue. This fact was itself the consequence of another important feature, namely, the fact that the Franks, Burgundians, Goths, Lombards, and Normans had very few women of their own race with them. For several generations, the chiefs only married German women; but their concubines were Latin, as were the wet-nurses of their children; the tribe as a whole married Latin women; which meant that, from the time the Franks and the Goths established themselves on Roman territory, the *lingua francica* and the *lingua gothica* did not last too long.

This was not how it was in England, for the invading Saxons undoubtedly brought women with them; the Celtic population took flight, and, besides, Latin was no longer, or rather had never been, dominant in Britain. If Old French had been generally spoken in Gaul in the fifth century Clovis and his people would not have abandoned German for Old French.

The crucial result of all this was that, in spite of the extreme violence of the customs of the German invaders, the mould which they imposed became, with the passing centuries, the actual mould of the nation. "France" became quite legitimately the name of a country to which only a virtually imperceptible minority of Franks had come. In the tenth century, in the first *chansons de geste*, which are such a perfect mirror of the spirit of the times, all the inhabitants of France are French. The idea, which had seemed so obvious to Gregory of Tours,[4] that the population of France was composed of different races, was in no way apparent to French writers and poets after Hugh Capet. The difference between noble and serf was as sharply drawn as possible, but it was in no sense presented as an ethnic difference; it was presented rather as a difference in courage, customs, and education, all of which were transmitted hereditarily; it did not occur to anyone that the origin of all this was a conquest. The spurious system according to which nobility owed its origin to a privilege conferred by the king for services rendered to the nation, so that every noble was an ennobled person, was established as a dogma as early as the thirteenth century. The same thing took place after almost all the Norman conquests. After one or two generations, the Norman invaders no longer distinguished themselves from the rest of the population, although their influence was not any less profound because of this fact; they had given the conquered country a nobility, military habits, and a patriotism that they had not known before.

Forgetting, I would even go so far as to say historical error, is a crucial factor in the creation of a nation, which is why progress in historical studies often constitutes a danger for [the principle of] nationality. Indeed, historical enquiry brings to light deeds of violence which took place at the origin of all political formations, even of those whose consequences have been altogether beneficial. Unity is always effected by means of brutality; the union of northern France with the Midi was the result of massacres and terror lasting for the best part of a century. Though the King of France was, if I may make so bold as to say, almost the perfect instance of an agent that crystallized [a nation] over a long period; though he established the most perfect national unity that there has ever been, too searching a scrutiny had destroyed his prestige. The nation which he had formed has cursed him, and, nowadays, it is only men of culture who know something of his former value and of his achievements.

It is [only] by contrast that these great laws of the history of western Europe become perceptible to us. Many countries failed to achieve what the King of France, partly through his tyranny, partly through his justice, so admirably brought to fruition. Under the Crown of Saint Stephen, the Magyars and the Slavs have remained as distinct as they were 800 years ago. Far from managing to fuse the diverse [ethnic] elements to be found in its domains, the House of Hapsburg has kept them distinct and often opposed the one to the other. In Bohemia [for instance], the Czech and German elements are superimposed, much like oil and water in a glass. The Turkish policy of separating nationalities according to their religion has had much graver consequences, for it brought about the downfall of the east. If you take a city such as Salonika or Smyrna, you will find there five or six communities each of which has its own memories and which have almost nothing in common. Yet the essence of a nation is that all individuals have many things in common, and also that they have forgotten many things. No French citizen knows whether he is a Burgundian, an Alan, a Taifale, or a Visigoth, yet every French citizen has to have forgotten the massacre of Saint Bartholomew,[5] or the massacres that took place in the Midi in the thirteenth century. There are not ten families in France that can supply proof of their Frankish origin, and any such proof would anyway be essentially flawed, as a consequence of countless unknown alliances which are liable to disrupt any genealogical system.

The modern nation is therefore a historical result brought about by a series of convergent facts. Sometimes unity has been effected by a dynasty, as was the case in France; sometimes it has been brought about by the direct will of provinces, as was the case with Holland, Switzerland, and Belgium; sometimes it has been the work of a general consciousness, belatedly victorious over the caprices of feudalism, as was the case in Italy and Germany. These formations always had a profound raison d'être. Principles, in such cases, always emerge through the most unexpected surprises. Thus, in our own day, we have seen Italy unified through its defeats and Turkey destroyed by its victories. Each defeat advanced the cause of Italy; each victory spelled doom for Turkey; for Italy is a nation, and

Turkey, outside of Asia Minor, is not one. France can claim the glory for having, through the French Revolution, proclaimed that a nation exists of itself. We should not be displeased if others imitate us in this. It was we who founded the principle of nationality. But what is a nation? Why is Holland a nation, when Hanover, or the Grand Duchy of Parma, not? How is it that France continues to be a nation, when the principle which created it has disappeared? How is it that Switzerland, which has three languages, two religions, and three or four races, is a nation, when Tuscany, which is so homogeneous, is not one? Why is Austria a state and not a nation? In what ways does the principle of nationality differ from that of races? These are points that a thoughtful person would wish to have settled, in order to put his mind at rest. The affairs of this world can hardly be said to be ruled by reasonings of this sort, yet diligent men are desirous of bringing some reason into these matters and of unraveling the confusions in which superficial intelligences are entangled.

II

If one were to believe some political theorists, a nation is above all a dynasty, representing an earlier conquest, one which was first of all accepted, and then forgotten by the mass of the people. According to the above-mentioned theorists, the grouping of provinces effected by a dynasty, by its wars, its marriages, and its treaties, ends with the dynasty which had established it. It is quite true that the majority of modern nations were made by a family of feudal origin, which had contracted a marriage with the soil and which was in some sense a nucleus of centralization. France's frontiers in 1789 had nothing either natural or necessary about them. The wide zone that the House of Capet had added to the narrow strip of land granted by the partition of Verdun was indeed the personal acquisition of this House. During the epoch when these acquisitions were made, there was no idea of natural frontiers, nor of the rights of nations, nor of the will of provinces. The union of England, Ireland, and Scotland was likewise a dynastic fact. Italy only tarried so long before becoming a nation because, among its numerous reigning houses, none, prior to the present century, constituted itself as the centre of [its] unity, Strangely enough, it was through the obscure island of Sardinia, a land that was scarcely Italian, that [the house of Savoy] assumed a royal title.[6] Holland, which—through an act of heroic resolution—created itself, has nevertheless contracted an intimate marriage with the House of Orange, and it will run real dangers the day this union is compromised.

Is such a law, however, absolute? It undoubtedly is not. Switzerland and the United States, which have formed themselves, like conglomerates, by successive additions, have no dynastic basis. I shall not discuss this question in relation to France, for I would need to be able to read the secrets of the future in order to do so. Let me simply say that so loftily national had this great French royal principle been that, on the morrow of its fall, the nation was able to stand without her. Furthermore, the eighteenth century had changed everything. Man had returned, after centuries of abasement, to the spirit of antiquity, to [a sense of] respect for himself, to the idea of his own rights. The words *patrie* and citizen had recovered their former meanings. Thus it was that the boldest operation ever yet put into effect in history was brought to completion, an operation which one might compare with the attempt, in physiology, to restore to its original identity a body from which one had removed the brain and the heart.

It must therefore be admitted that a nation can exist without a dynastic principle, and even that nations which have been formed by dynasties can be separated from them without therefore ceasing to exist. The old principle, which only takes account of the right of princes, could no longer be maintained; apart from dynastic right, there is also national right. Upon what criterion, however, should one base this national right? By what sign should one know it? From what tangible fact can one derive it?

Several confidently assert that it is derived from race. The artificial divisions, resulting from feudalism, from princely marriages, from diplomatic congresses are, [these authors assert], in a state of decay. It is a population's race which remains firm and fixed. This is what constitutes a right, a legitimacy. The Germanic family, according to the theory I am expounding here, has the right to reassemble the scattered limbs of the Germanic order, even when these limbs are not asking to be joined together again. The right of the Germanic order over such-and-such a province is stronger than the right of the inhabitants of that province over themselves. There is thus created a kind of primordial right analogous to the divine right of kings; an ethnographic principle is substituted for a national one. This is a very great error, which, if it were to become dominant, would destroy European civilization. The primordial right of races is as narrow and as perilous for genuine progress as the national principle is just and legitimate.

In the tribes and cities of antiquity, the fact of race was, I will allow, of very real importance. The tribe and the city were then merely extensions of the family. At Sparta and at Athens all the citizens were kin to a greater or lesser degree. The same was true of the Beni-Israelites; this is still the case with the Arab tribes. If we move now from Athens, Sparta, and the Israelite tribe to the Roman Empire the situation is a wholly different one. Established at first through violence but subsequently preserved through [common] interest, this great agglomeration of cities and provinces, wholly different from each other, dealt the gravest of blows to the idea of race. Christianity, with its universal and absolute character, worked still more effectively in the same direction; it formed an intimate alliance with the Roman Empire and, through the impact of these two incomparable unificatory agents, the ethnographic argument was debarred from the government of human affairs for centuries.

The barbarian invasions were, appearances notwithstanding, a further step along this same path. The carving out of the barbarian kingdoms had nothing ethnographic about them, their [shape] was determined by the might or whim of the invaders. They were utterly indifferent to the race of the populations which they had subdued. What Rome had fashioned, Charlemagne refashioned in his own way, namely, a single empire composed of the most diverse races; those responsible for the partition of Verdun, as they calmly drew their two long lines from north to south, were not in the slightest concerned with the race of the peoples to be found on the right or left of these lines. Frontier changes put into effect, as the Middle Ages wore on, likewise paid no heed to ethnographic divisions. If the policies pursued by the House of Capet by and large resulted in the grouping together, under the name of France, of the territories of ancient Gaul, this was only because these lands had a natural tendency to be joined together with their fellows. Dauphiné, Bresse, Provence, and Franche-Comté no longer recalled any common origin. All Gallic consciousness had perished by the second century AD, and it is only from a purely scholarly perspective that, in our own days, the individuality of the Gallic character has been retrospectively recovered.

Ethnographic considerations have therefore played no part in the constitution of modern nations. France is [at once] Celtic, Iberic, and Germanic. Germany is Germanic, Celtic and Slav. Italy is the country where the ethnographic argument is most confounded. Gauls, Etruscans, Pelasgians,[7] and Greeks, not to mention many other elements, intersect in an indecipherable mixture. The British isles, considered as a whole, present a mixture of Celtic and Germanic blood, the proportions of which are singularly difficult to define.

The truth is that there is no pure race and that to make politics depend upon ethnographic analysis is to surrender it to a chimera. The noblest countries, England, France, and Italy, are those where the blood is the most mixed. Is Germany an exception in this respect? Is it a purely Germanic country? This is a complete illusion. The whole of the south was once Gallic; the whole of the east, from the river Elbe on, is Slav. Even those parts which are claimed to be really pure, are they in fact so? We touch here on one of those problems in regard to which it is of the utmost importance that we equip ourselves with clear ideas and ward off misconceptions.

Discussions of race are interminable, because philologically-minded historians and physiologically-minded anthropologists interpret the term in two totally different ways.[8] For the anthropologists, race has the same meaning as in zoology; it serves to indicate real descent, a blood relation. However, the study of language and of history does not lead to the same divisions as does physiology. Words such as brachycephalic or dolichocephalic have no place in either history or philology. In the human group which created the Aryan languages and way of life, there were already [both] brachycephalics and dolichocephalics. The same is true of the primitive group which created the languages and institutions known as Semitic. In other words, the zoological origins of humanity are massively prior to the origins of culture, civilization, and language. The primitive Aryan, primitive Semitic, and primitive Touranian groups had no physiological unity. These groupings are historical facts, which took place in a particular epoch, perhaps 15,000 or 20,000 years ago, while the zoological origin of humanity is lost in impenetrable darkness. What is known philologically and historically as the Germanic race is no doubt a quite distinct family within the human species, but is it a family in the anthropological sense of the term? Certainly not. The emergence of an individual Germanic identity occurred only a few centuries prior to Jesus Christ. One may take it that the Germans did not emerge from the earth at this epoch. Prior to this, mingled with the Slavs in the huge indistinct mass of the Scythians, they did not have their own separate individuality. An Englishman is indeed a type within the whole of humanity. However, the type of what is quite improperly called the Anglo-Saxon race[9] is neither the Briton of Julius Caesar's time, nor the Anglo-Saxon of Hengist's time, nor the Dane of Canute's time, nor the Norman of William the Conqueror's time; it is rather the result of all these [elements]. A Frenchman is neither a Gaul, nor a Frank, nor a Burgundian. Rather, he is what has emerged out of the cauldron in which, presided over by the King of France, the most diverse elements have together been simmering. A native of Jersey or Guernsey differs in no way, as far as his origins are concerned, from the Norman population of the opposite coast. In the eleventh century, even the sharpest eye would have seen not the slightest difference in those living on either side of the Channel. Trifling circumstances meant that Philip Augustus did not seize these islands together with the rest of Normandy. Separated from each other for the best part of 700 years, the two populations have become not only strangers to each other but wholly dissimilar. Race, as we historians understand it, is therefore something which is made and unmade. The study of race is of crucial importance for the scholar concerned with the history of humanity. It has no applications, however, in politics. The instinctive consciousness which presided over the construction of the map of Europe took no account of race, and the leading nations of Europe are nations of essentially mixed blood.

The fact of race, which was originally crucial, thus becomes increasingly less important. Human history is essentially different from zoology, and race is not everything, as it is among the rodents or the felines, and one does not have the right to go through the world fingering people's skulls, and taking them by the throat saying: "You are of our blood; you belong to us!" Aside from anthropological characteristics, there are such things as reason, justice, the true, and the beautiful, which are the same for all. Be on your guard, for this ethnographic politics is in no way a stable thing and, if today you use it against others, tomorrow you may see it turned against yourselves. Can you be sure that the Germans, who have raised the banner of ethnography so high, will not see the Slavs in their turn analyse the names of villages in Saxony and Lusatia, search for any traces of the Wiltzes or of the Obotrites, and demand recompense for the massacres and the wholesale enslavements that the Ottoss inflicted upon their ancestors? It is good for everyone to know how to forget.

I am very fond of ethnography, for it is a science of rare interest; but, in so far as I would wish it to be free, I wish it to be without political application. In ethnography, as in all forms of study, systems change; this is the condition of progress. States' frontiers would then follow the fluctuations of science. Patriotism would depend upon a more or less paradoxical dissertation. One would come up to a patriot and say: "You were mistaken; you shed your blood for such-and-such a cause; you believed yourself to be a Celt; not at all, you are a German." Then, ten years later, you will be told that you are a Slav. If we are not to distort science, we should exempt it from the need to give an opinion on these problems, in which so many interests are involved. You can be sure that, if one obliges science to furnish diplomacy with its first principles, one will surprise her many times in *flagrant délit*. She has better things to do; let us simply ask her to tell the truth.

What we have just said of race applies to language too. Language invites people to unite, but it does not force them to do so. The United States and England, Latin America and Spain, speak the same languages yet do not form single nations. Conversely, Switzerland, so well made, since she was made with the consent of her different parts, numbers three or four languages. There is something in man which is superior to language, namely, the will. The will of Switzerland to be united, in spite of the diversity of her dialects, is a fact of far greater importance than a similitude often obtained by various vexatious measures.

An honourable fact about France is that she has never sought to win unity of language by coercive measures. Can one not have the same sentiments and the same thoughts, and love the same things in different languages? I was speaking just now of the disadvantages of making international politics depend upon ethnography; they would be no less if one were to make it depend upon comparative philology. Let us allow these intriguing studies full freedom of discussion; let us not mix them up with matters which would undermine their serenity. The political importance attaching to languages derives from their being regarded as signs of race. Nothing could be more false. Prussia, where only German is now spoken, spoke Slav a few centuries ago; in Wales, English is spoken; Gaul and Spain speak the primitive dialects of Alba Longa; Egypt speaks Arabic; there are countless other examples one could quote. Even if you go back to origins, similarity of language did not presuppose similarity of race. Consider, for example the proto-Aryan or proto-Semitic tribe: there one found slaves speaking the same language as their masters, and yet the slave was often enough a different race to that of his master. Let me repeat that these divisions of the Indo-European, Semitic, or other languages, created with such admirable sagacity by comparative philology, do not coincide with the divisions established by anthropology. Languages are historical formations, which tell us very little about the blood of those who speak them and which, in any case, could not shackle human liberty when it is a matter of deciding the family with which one unites oneself for life or for death.

This exclusive concern with language, like an excessive preoccupation with race, has its dangers and its drawbacks. Such exaggerations enclose one within a specific culture, considered as national; one limits oneself, one hems oneself in. One leaves the heady air that one breathes in the vast field of humanity in order to enclose oneself in a conventicle with one's compatriots. Nothing could be worse for the mind; nothing could be more disturbing for civilization. Let us not abandon the fundamental principle that man is a reasonable and moral being, before he is cooped up in such and such a language, before he is a member of such and such a race, before he belongs to such and such a culture. Before French, German, or Italian culture there is human culture. Consider the great men of the Renaissance; they were neither French, nor Italian, nor German. They had rediscovered, through their dealings with antiquity, the secret of the genuine education of the human spirit, and they devoted themselves to it body and soul. What an achievement theirs was!

Religion cannot supply an adequate basis for the constitution of a modern nationality either. Originally, religion had to do with the very existence of the social group, which was itself an extension of the family. Religion and the rites were family rites. The religion of Athens was the cult of Athens itself, of its mythical founders, of its laws and its customs; it implied no theological dogma. This religion was, in the strongest sense of the term, a state religion. One was not an Athenian if one refused to practise it. This religion was, fundamentally, the cult of the Acropolis personified. To swear on the altar of Aglauros[10] was to swear that one would die for the *patrie*. This religion was the equivalent of what the act of drawing lots [for military service], or the cult of the flag, is for us. Refusing to take part in such a cult would be the equivalent, in our modern societies, of refusing military service. It would be like declaring that one was not Athenian. From another angle, it is clear that such a cult had no meaning for someone who was not from Athens; there was also no attempt made to proselytize foreigners and to force them to accept it; the slaves of Athens did not practise it. Things were much the same in a number of small medieval republics. One was not considered a good Venetian if one did not swear by Saint Mark; nor a good Amalfitan if one did not set Saint Andrew higher than all the other saints in paradise. In these small societies, what subsequently was regarded as persecution or tyranny was legitimate and was of no more consequence than our custom of wishing the father of a family happy birthday or a Happy New Year.

The state of affairs in Sparta and in Athens already no longer existed in the kingdoms which emerged from Alexander's conquest, still less in the Roman Empire. The persecutions unleashed by Antiochus Epiphanes in order to win the east for the cult of Jupiter Olympus, those of the Roman Empire designed to maintain a supposed state religion were mistaken, criminal, and absurd. In our own time, the situation is perfectly clear. There are no longer masses that believe in a perfectly uniform manner. Each person believes and practises in his own fashion what he is able to and as he wishes. There is no longer a state religion; one can be French, English, or German, and be either Catholic, Protestant, or orthodox Jewish, or else practise no cult at all. Religion has become an individual matter; it concerns the conscience of each person. The division of nations into Catholics and Protestants no longer exists. Religion, which, fifty-two years ago, played so substantial a part in the formation of Belgium, preserves all of its [former] importance in the inner tribunal of each; but it has ceased almost entirely to be one of the elements which serve to define the frontiers of peoples.

A community of interest is assuredly a powerful bond between men. Do interests, however, suffice to make a nation? I do not think so. Community of interest brings about trade agreements, but nationality has a sentimental side to it; it is both soul and body at once; a *Zollverein*[11] is not a *patrie*.

Geography, or what are known as natural frontiers, undoubtedly plays a considerable part in the division of nations. Geography is one of the crucial factors in history. Rivers have led races on; mountains have brought them to a halt. The former have favoured movement in history, whereas the latter have restricted it. Can one say, however, that as some parties believe, a nation's frontiers are written on the map and that this nation has the right to judge what is necessary to round off certain contours, in order to reach such and such a mountain and such and such a river, which are thereby accorded a kind of a priori limiting faculty? I know of no doctrine which is more arbitrary or more fatal, for it allows one to justify any or every violence. First of all, is it the mountains or the rivers that we should regard as forming these so-called natural frontiers? It is indisputable that the mountains separate, but the rivers tend rather to unify. Moreover, all mountains cannot divide up states. Which serve to separate and which do not? From Biarritz to Tornea, there is no one estuary which is more suited than any other to serving as a boundary marker. Had history so decreed it, the Loire, the Seine, the Meuse, the Elbe, or the Oder could, just as easily as the Rhine, have had this quality of being a natural frontier, such as has caused so many infractions of the most fundamental right, which is men's will. People talk of strategic grounds. Nothing, however, is absolute; it is quite clear that many concessions should be made to necessity. But these concessions should not be taken too far. Otherwise, everybody would lay claim to their military conveniences, and one would have unceasing war. No, it is no more soil than it is race which makes a nation. The soil furnishes the substratum, the field of struggle and of labour; man furnishes the soul. Man is everything in the formation of this sacred thing which is called a people. Nothing [purely] material suffices for it. A nation is a spiritual principle, the outcome of the profound complications of history; it is a spiritual family not a group determined by the shape of the earth. We have now seen what things are not adequate for the creation of such a spiritual principle, namely, race, language, material interest, religious affinities, geography, and military necessity. What more then is required? As a consequence of what was said previously, I will not have to detain you very much longer.

III

A nation is a soul, a spiritual principle. Two things, which in truth are but one, constitute this soul or spiritual principle. One lies in the past, one in the present. One is the possession in common of a rich legacy of memories; the other is present-day consent, the desire to live together, the will to perpetuate the value of the heritage that one has received in an undivided form. Man, Gentlemen, does not improvise. The nation, like the individual, is the culmination of a long past of endeavours, sacrifice, and devotion. Of all cults, that of the ancestors is the most legitimate, for the ancestors have made us what we are. A heroic past, great men, glory (by which I understand genuine glory), this is the social capital upon which one bases a national idea. To have common glories in the past and to have a common will in the present; to have performed great deeds together, to wish to perform still more—these are the essential conditions for being a people. One loves in proportion to the sacrifices to which one has consented, and in proportion to the ills that one has suffered. One loves the house that one has built and that one has handed down. The Spartan song—"We are what you were; we will be what you are"[12]—is, in its simplicity, the abridged hymn of every *patrie*.

More valuable by far than common customs posts and frontiers conforming to strategic ideas is the fact of sharing, in the past, a glorious heritage and regrets, and of having, in the future, [a shared] programme to put into effect, or the fact of having suffered, enjoyed, and hoped together. These are the kinds of things that can be understood in spite of differences of race and language. I spoke just now of "having suffered together" and, indeed, suffering in common unifies more than joy does. Where national memories are concerned, griefs are of more value than triumphs, for they impose duties, and require a common effort.

A nation is therefore a large-scale solidarity, constituted by the feeling of the sacrifices that one has made in the past and of those that one is prepared to make in the future. It presupposes a past; it is summarized, however, in the present by a tangible fact, namely, consent, the clearly expressed desire to continue a common life. A nation's existence is, if you will pardon the metaphor, a daily plebiscite, just as an individual's existence is a perpetual affirmation of life. That, I know full well, is less metaphysical than divine right and less brutal than so-called historical right. According to the ideas that I am outlining to you, a nation has no more right than a king does to say to a province:"You belong to me, I am seizing you." A province, as far as I am concerned, is its inhabitants; if anyone has the right to be consulted in such an affair, it is the inhabitant. A nation never has any real interest in annexing or holding on to a country against its will. The wish of nations is, all in all, the sole legitimate criterion, the one to which one must always return.

We have driven metaphysical and theological abstractions out of politics. What then remains? Man, with his desires and his needs. The secession, you will say to me, and, in the long term, the disintegration of nations will be the outcome of a system which places these old organisms at the mercy of wills which are often none too enlightened. It is clear that, in such matters, no principle must be pushed too far. Truths of this order are only applicable as a whole in a very general fashion. Human wills change, but what is there here below that does not change? The nations are not something eternal. They had their beginnings and they will end. A European confederation will very probably replace them. But such is not the law of the century in which we are living. At the present time, the existence of nations is a good thing, a necessity even. Their existence is the guarantee of liberty, which would be lost if the world had only one law and only one master.

Through their various and often opposed powers, nations participate in the common work of civilization; each sounds a note in the great concert of humanity, which, after all, is the highest ideal reality that we are capable of attaining. Isolated, each has its weak point. I often tell myself that an individual who had those faults which in nations are taken for good qualities, who fed off vainglory, who was to that degree jealous, egotistical, and quarrelsome, and who would draw his sword on the smallest pretext, would be the most intolerable of men. Yet all these discordant details disappear in the overall context. Poor humanity, how you have suffered! How many trials still await you! May the spirit of wisdom guide you, in order to preserve you from the countless dangers with which your path is strewn!

Let me sum up, Gentlemen. Man is a slave neither of his race nor his language, nor of his religion, nor of the course of rivers nor of the direction taken by mountain chains. A large aggregate of men, healthy in mind and warm of heart, creates the kind of moral conscience which we call a nation. So long as this moral consciousness gives proof of its strength by the sacrifices which demand the abdication of the individual to the advantage of the community, it is legitimate and has the right to exist. If doubts arise regarding its frontiers, consult the populations in the areas under dispute. They undoubtedly have the right to a say in the matter. This recommendation will bring a smile to the lips of the transcendants of politics, these infallible beings who spend their lives deceiving themselves and who, from the height of their superior principles, take pity upon our mundane concerns. "Consult the populations, for heaven's sake! How naive! A fine example of those wretched French ideas which claim to replace diplomacy and war by childishly simple methods." Wait a while, Gentlemen; let the reign of the transcendants pass; bear the scorn of the powerful with patience. It may be that, after many fruitless gropings, people will revert to our more modest empirical solutions. The best way of being right in the future is, in certain periods, to know how to resign oneself to being out of fashion.

NOTES

(Notes followed by an asterisk are the translator's.)

1*. I have left *patrie* in the original French because it seems to me that to translate it into another European (or, indeed, non-European) language would be to eliminate the kinds of association the term had, in a very large number of countries, throughout the epoch of liberal-democratic nationalism. *Patrie* draws with it a whole cluster of complex and interlocking references to the values of the *patria* of classical republicanism. For an observer like Marx, these values were destroyed forever in the black farce of 1848. In another sense, as Marx's arguments in *The Eighteenth Brumaire* allow, they continued to influence the leaders of liberal, nationalist revolutions throughout the nineteenth century— although, obviously, if one were to phrase it in Italian terms, the Cavourian moderate rather than the Mazzinian or Garibaldian radical wing. It may be worth noting that, in the domain of scholarship, Fustel de Coulanges' *The Ancient City* (1864), a study which profoundly influenced Emile Durkheim and which Renan himself had very probably read, shattered the vision of classical republicanism which men such as Robespierre and Saint-Just had entertained.

2*. The doctrine of natural frontiers was given its definitive formulation in the course of the French Revolution, and was subsequently applied to other European countries, such as Germany or Italy; it was this doctrine that fuelled the irredentist movements of the second half of the nineteenth century. Justification of territorial claims often rested upon the interpretation of classical texts, such as Tacitus's *Germania* or Dante's *Commedia*.

3*. The partition of Verdun (AD 843) ended a period of civil war within the Frankish Empire, during which the grandsons of Charlemagne had fought each other. Two of the newly created kingdoms, that of Charles the Bald (843–77) and that of Louis the German (843–76), bear some resemblance, in territorial terms, to modern France and modern Germany. Furthermore, much has been made of the linguistic qualities of the Oaths of Strasbourg, sworn by Louis and Charles to each other's armies, in Old French and Old High German respectively. This has often been regarded as the first text in a Romance language (as distinct from Latin) and, by extension, as the first symbolic appearance of the French (and German) nations.

4*. Gregory of Tours (*c*. 539–94) was a Gallo-Roman and Bishop of Tours from 573 to 594. His *History of the Franks* is an account of life in Merovingian Gaul.

5*. Upon the occasion of the massacre of Saint Bartholomew, in 1572, many thousands of Huguenots were killed. This was an event with momentous repercussions for the history of France in general, and for the development of political theory in particular.

6. The House of Savoy owes its royal title to its acquisition of Sardinia (1720).

7*. The Pelasgians were believed, in the eighteenth and nineteenth centuries, to have been the original inhabitants of Italy.

8. I enlarged upon this point in a lecture, which is analysed in the Bulletin of the *Association scientifique de France*, 10 March 1878, "Des services rendus aux Sciences historiques par la Philologie."

9. Germanic elements are not more considerable in the United Kingdom than when they were in France, when she had possession of Alsace and Metz. If the Germanic language has dominated in the British isles, it was simply because Latin had not wholly replaced the Celtic languages, as it had done in Gaul.

10. Aglauros, who gave her life to save her *patrie*, represents the Acropolis itself.

11*. *Zollverein* is the German word for customs union. Both participants in bourgeois, national revolutions and later commentators emphasize the relation between the nationalist cause and free trade within a single territory. However, E. J. Hobsbawm's comments, on pp. 166–8 of *The Age of Revolution* (London, 1962), shed some light upon Renan's aphorism, in that the vanguard of European nationalism in the 1830s and 1840s was not so much the business class as "the lower and middle professional, administrative and intellectual strata, in other words, the educated classes." At another level, Renan's observation reflects his shock at the defeat of France by Prussia in the Franco-Prussian war, which is expressed in both major and occasional writings.

12*. Such epitaphs were part of the habitual repertoire of early-nineteenth-century nationalism, as Leopardi's "patriotic" *canzoni* make plain.

II

WHERE DO NATIONS COME FROM? THE SOCIAL CONSTRUCTION OF NATIONALITY

Miroslav Hroch

Influenced by the approach of Karl Deutsch in *Nationalism and Social Communication: An Inquiry into the Foundations of Nationality* (Cambridge, Mass.: MIT Press, 1953), and formed in the Marxist intellectual culture of central Europe, Miroslav Hroch pioneered the comparative social history of nation-forming in nineteenth-century Europe. In two books, *Die Vorkämpfer der nationalen Bewegungen bei den kleinen Völkern Europas. Eine vergleichende Analyse zur gesellschaftlichen Schichtung der patriotischen Gruppen* (Prague, 1969), and *Obrození malých evropských národu. I: Národy severní a východní Evropy* [The Revival of the Small European Nations. I: The Nations of Northern and Eastern Europe] (Prague, 1971), he sought to ground the study of national consciousness in a systematic comparison of patriotic activists and their resonance in eight cases (the Norwegians, Czechs, Finns, Estonians, Lithuanians, Slovaks, Flemish, and Schleswig Danes), whom he characterized as small nationalities, or "non-dominant ethnic groups," seeking national self-determination for themselves. He also proposed a three-stage periodization for the emergence of such national movements, charting the graduation of activity from purely intellectual work, through active proselytizing, to popular mobilization, and plotting its incidence by complex indicators of social change.

Hroch's approach was exciting in a number of ways. First, it undertook for the first time the quantitative social-historical study of nationalist movements in a systematic comparative frame, and brought the methods and concepts of social history into a field previously dominated by the historian of ideas. Second, he related the process of nation-forming explicitly to the larger processes of social transformation—those associated with capitalist industrialization and the spread of market relations in the countryside—but did so by carefully avoiding economistic forms of reductionism, stressing the mediating effects of greater social and geographical mobility, generational change, the commercialization of agriculture and small handicrafts production in the countryside, the spread of literacy, the founding of village schools and other institutions, and so on. Third, by combining the study of nationalism with a framework of social transformation, he delivered a socially and culturally grounded model of political development, allowing us to see concretely how the pre-1914 national political cultures took shape.

For many years Hroch's work was little known in English, and was made accessible mainly through the writings of Eric Hobsbawm (for example, "Some Reflections on Nationalism," in T. J. Nossiter et al. [eds.], *Imagination and Precision in the Social Sciences*, London: Faber and Faber, 1972, pp. 385–406), and later via the work of Tom Nairn (in the essay included in this collection). Finally his two books were translated as *Social Preconditions of National Revival in Europe: A Comparative Analysis of the Social Composition of Patriotic Groups among the Smaller European Nations* (Cambridge: Cambridge University Press, 1985). In the essay reprinted next, he summarizes and further elaborates his arguments while venturing reflections on the nature of nationalism in the present.

From National Movement to the Fully-Formed Nation: The Nation-Building Process in Europe

The nation has been an inseparable accompaniment of modern European history. It is not difficult to ironize over the record of "nationalism" in past and present, to criticize its role and to award good or bad marks to different groups, personalities or even nations, in the process. There is a public that finds this procedure to its taste, but it is not to be confused with a scientific approach to the subject. Historians are not judges; their task is to explain actual historical transformations. There has been a significant amount of new literature on nations and nationalism in recent years, much of it produced by social scientists developing theoretical frameworks, and then illustrating their generalizations with selected examples. Historians prefer to start with empirical research, and then move to broader conclusions. My own work has not sought to advance a theory of nation-building, but rather to develop effective methods for the classification and assessment of experiences of nation-building as a process set within a wider social and cultural history—treated not as so many singular and unrepeatable events, but as part of a broad transformation of society that is amenable to controlled generalizations.[1] But it is important to stress at the outset that we are very far from being able to explain all the major problems posed by the formation of modern nations. Every historian of national movements agrees there are numerous data gaps in our understanding of them. In this sense, all defensible conclusions still remain no more than partial findings, and all "theories" should be taken as projects for further research. Polemically, one might say that at the moment we have an over-production of theories and a stagnation of comparative research on the topic.

NATIONAL AND CIVIL SOCIETY

This misfortune is, I think, in part due to a widespread conceptual confusion. For today the process whereby nations were formed in Europe is typically represented

Miroslav Hroch, "From National Movement to the Fully-Formed Nation: The Nation-Building Process in Europe," *New Left Review*, 198 (March–April 1993), pp. 3–20.

as the unfolding or spread of the ideas of "nationalism." This is perhaps especially true of recent Anglo-Saxon literature.[2] In my view, this is a basically misleading way of looking at the subject. For the diffusion of national ideas could only occur in specific social settings. Nation-building was never a mere project of ambitious or narcissistic intellectuals, and ideas could not flow through Europe by their own inspirational force. Intellectuals can "invent" national communities only if certain objective preconditions for the formation of a nation already exist. Karl Deutsch long ago remarked that for national consciousness to arise, there must be something for it to become conscious of. Individual discoveries of national sentiment do not explain why such discoveries recurred in so many countries, independently of each other, under different conditions and in different epochs. Only an approach that looks for the underlying similarity of reasons why people accepted a new national identity, can shed light on this problem. These reasons may be verbalized, but below the level of "high politics" they are often unverbalized.

Now the "nation" is not, of course, an eternal category, but was the product of a long and complicated process of historical development in Europe. For our purposes, let us define it at the outset as a large social group integrated not by one but by a combination of several kinds of objective relationships (economic, political, linguistic, cultural, religious, geographical, historical), and their subjective reflection in collective consciousness. Many of these ties could be mutually substitutable—some playing a particularly important role in one nation-building process, and no more than a subsidiary part in others. But among them, three stand out as irreplaceable: (i) a "memory" of some common past, treated as a "destiny" of the group—or at least of its core constituents; (ii) a density of linguistic or cultural ties enabling a higher degree of social communication within the group than beyond it; (iii) a conception of the equality of all members of the group organized as a civil society.

The process whereby nations were built, around such central elements, was not preordained or irreversible. It could be interrupted, just as it could also be resumed after a long hiatus. Looking at Europe as a whole, it is clear that it went through two distinct stages, of unequal length. The first of these started during the Middle Ages, and led to two quite different outcomes, which provided contrasting starting-points for the second stage, of a transition to a capitalist economy and civil society. At that point the path to a modern nation in the full sense of the word proceeded from either one or the other of two contrasted socio-political situations (though, of course, there were transitional cases). Over much of Western Europe—England, France, Spain, Portugal, Sweden, the Netherlands—but also farther East in Poland, the early modern state developed under the domination of one ethnic culture, either in absolutist form or in a representative-estates system. In the majority of such cases, the late feudal regime was subsequently transformed, by reforms or revolution, into a modern civil society *in parallel* with the construction of a nation-state as a community of equal citizens. In most of Central and Eastern Europe, on the other hand, an "exogenous" ruling class dominated ethnic groups which occupied a compact territory but lacked "their own" nobility, political unit or continuous literary tradition. My own research has been concerned with this second type of situation. It is an error, however, to think that it never existed in Western Europe as well. The plight of the "non-dominant ethnic group" has come to be identified with lands in Eastern and South-Eastern Europe—as the fate of Estonians, Ukrainians, Slovenes, Serbs or others. But there were originally many similar communities in Western and South-Western Europe too. There, however, the medieval or early modern state assimilated most of them, although a significant number of distinctive ancient cultures persisted through such processes of integration—Irish, Catalan, Norwegian and others (in Eastern Europe, the Greeks perhaps form an analogy).[3] There was also an important set of transitional cases, in which ethnic communities possessed "their own" ruling class and literary traditions, but lacked any common statehood—the Germans and Italians, or later (after the loss of their commonwealth) the Poles.

Now in the second type of situation, on which my own work has concentrated, the onset of the modern stage of nation-building can be dated from the moment when selected groups within the non-dominant ethnic community started to discuss their own ethnicity and to conceive of it as a potential nation-to-be. Sooner or later, they observed certain deficits, which the future nation still lacked, and began efforts to overcome one or more of them, seeking to persuade their compatriots of the importance of consciously belonging to the nation. I term these organized endeavours to achieve all the attributes of a fully-fledged nation (which were not always and everywhere successful) *a national movement*. The current tendency to speak of them as "nationalist" leads to serious confusion. For nationalism *stricto sensu* is something else: namely, that outlook which gives an *absolute priority to the values of the nation over all other values and interests*. It was far from being the case that all the patriots in the national movements of Central and Eastern Europe in the nineteenth or early twentieth century were nationalists in this accurate sense of the word. The term can scarcely be applied to such representative figures as the Norwegian poet Wergeland, who tried to create a language for his country, the Polish writer Mickiewicz who longed for the liberation of his homeland, or even the Czech scholar Masaryk, who formulated and realized a programme of national independence after having fought all his life against Czech nationalists. Nationalism was only one of many forms of national consciousness to emerge in the course of these movements. Nationalism did, of course, often later become a significant force in this region, just as it did further west in the region of state-nations, as a type of power politics with irrationalist overtones. But the programme of the classic national movement was of another kind. Its goals covered three main groups of demands, which corresponded to felt deficits of national existence: (1) the development of a national culture based on the local language, and its normal use in education, administration and economic life; (2) the achievement of civil rights and political self-administration, initially in the form of autonomy and ultimately (usually quite late, as an express demand) of independence;[4] (3) the creation of a complete social structure from out of the ethnic group, including educated elites, an officialdom and an entrepreneurial class, but also—where necessary—free peasants and organized workers. The relative priority and timing of these three sets of demands varied in each case. But the trajectory of any national movement was only consumed when all were fulfilled.

Between the starting-point of any given national movement and its successful conclusion, three structural phases can be distinguished, according to the character and role of those active in it, and the degree of national consciousness emergent in the ethnic group at large. During an initial period, which I have called Phase A, the energies of the activists were above all devoted to scholarly enquiry into and dissemination of an awareness of the linguistic, cultural, social and sometimes historical attributes of the non-dominant group—but without, on the whole, pressing specifically national demands to remedy deficits (some did not even believe their group could develop into a nation). In a second period, or Phase B, a new range of activists emerged, who now sought to win over as many of their ethnic group as possible to the project of creating a future nation, by patriotic agitation to "awaken" national consciousness among them—at first usually without notable success (in one sub-stage), but later (in another sub-stage) finding a growing reception. Once the major part of the population came to set special store by their national identity, a mass movement was formed, which I have termed Phase C. It was only during this final phase that a full social structure could come into being, and that the movement differentiated out into conservative-clerical, liberal and democratic wings, each with their own programmes.

FOUR TYPES OF NATIONAL MOVEMENT

The purpose of this periodization, as I proposed it, was to permit meaningful comparisons between national movements—that is, something more than mere synchronic surveys of what was happening at the same time in different lands of Europe in the last century, namely the study of analogous forms and phases of historical development. Such comparison requires the selection of a limited set of specific dimensions in terms of which different national movements can be analysed. The more complex the phenomenon to be compared, the greater the number of such pertinent dimensions, of course. But it is normally advisable to proceed gradually, accumulating comparative results step by step, rather than introducing too many dimensions all at once. Here are some of the most significant markers, certain of which I or others have explored, while others remain topics for future research: the social profile and territorial distribution of leading patriots and activists; the role of language as symbol and vehicle of identification; the place of the theatre (also music and folklore) in national movements; the salience or otherwise of civil rights as a demand; the importance of historical awareness; the position of the school system and the spread of literacy; the participation of the churches and the influence of religion; the contribution of women as activists and as symbols. Above all, however, what emerged from my own work was the central significance for any typology of national movements in Central and Eastern Europe (but not only there) of the *relationship* between the transition to Phase B and then to Phase C, on the one hand, and the transition to

a constitutional society based on equality before the law, on the other hand—
what is often generically called the moment of "bourgeois revolution." Combining these two series of changes, we can distinguish four types of national movement in Europe:

1. In the first, the inception of national agitation (Phase B) occurred under the
   old regime of absolutism, but it acquired a mass character in a time of
   revolutionary changes in the political system, when an organized labour
   movement was also beginning to assert itself. The leaders of Phase B developed their national programmes in conditions of political upheaval. This
   was the case of Czech agitation in Bohemia, and of the Hungarian and
   Norwegian movements, all of which entered Phase B around 1800. The
   Norwegian patriots gained a liberal constitution and declaration of independence in 1814, while the Czechs and Magyars developed—albeit in very
   different fashion—their national programmes during the revolutions of
   1848.
2. In the second, national agitation likewise got under way under the old
   regime, but the transition to a mass movement, or Phase C, was delayed
   until after a constitutional revolution. This shift of sequence could be caused
   either by uneven economic development, as in Lithuania, Latvia, Slovenia
   or Croatia; or by foreign oppression, as in Slovakia or the Ukraine. Phase
   B can be said to have started in Croatia in the 1830s, in Slovenia in the
   1840s, in Latvia at the end of the 1850s, and in Lithuania not till the
   1870s—reaching Phase C in Croatia not before the 1880s, in Slovenia in
   the 1890s, and in Latvia and Lithuania only during the revolution of 1905.
   Forcible Magyarization checked the transition to Phase C in Slovakia after
   1867, as did oppressive Russification in the Ukraine.
3. In the third type, the national movement acquired a mass character already
   under the old regime, and so before the establishment of a civil society or
   constitutional order. This pattern produced armed insurrections, and was
   confined to lands of the Ottoman Empire in Europe—Serbia, Greece, and
   Bulgaria.
4. In the final type, national agitation first began under constitutional conditions, in a more developed capitalist setting, characteristic of Western Europe. In these cases, the national movement could reach Phase C quite early,
   as in the Basque lands and Catalonia, while in other cases it did so only
   after a very long Phase B, as in Flanders, or not at all—as in Wales, Scotland
   or Britanny.

None of the steps traced so far—from definition to periodization to typology—
is, of course, an end in itself. They do not explain the origins or outcomes of the
various national movements. They are no more than necessary starting-points for
the real task of every historical research: causal analysis. What explains the success of most of these movements in the epoch that ended at Versailles, and the
failure of others? What accounts for the variations in their evolution and upshot?
If the fashionable idea that nations in Europe were invented by nationalism is
clearly unfounded, mono-causal explanations fare little better. Any satisfactory

account will have to be multi-causal, and move between different levels of generalization; and it will have to extend across a chronologically lengthy span of uneven European development.

ANTECEDENTS TO NATION-BUILDING

Any such explanation must begin with the "prelude" to modern nation-building that lies in the late medieval and early modern epochs, which was of great moment not only for the state-nations of the West, but also for those ethnic groups that remained or became dominated by "external" ruling classes in the Centre and East of the continent, or elsewhere. In historical reality, of course, there were many transitional cases between these two ideal-types. A large number of medieval polities with their own written languages did not develop successfully into state-nations, but on the contrary lost their autonomy partly or completely, while their populations generally retained their ethnicity. This was true of the Czechs, Catalans, Norwegians, Croats, Bulgarians, Welsh, Irish and others. Even in cases of typologically rather "pure" non-dominant ethnic groups—for example, the Slovenes, Estonians or Slovaks—we cannot dismiss their common past as a mere myth. More generally, the legacy of the first stage of a nation-building process, even if aborted, often left significant resources for the second. These included, in particular, the following:

1. Very often, certain relics of an earlier political autonomy remained, though appropriated by members of estates belonging to the "ruling" nation, and generated tensions between the estates and absolutism that sometimes provided triggers for later national movements. This pattern could be observed in many parts of Europe during the late eighteenth century—for example, in the resistance of the Hungarian, Bohemian and Croatian estates to Josephine centralism, the reaction of the nobility in Finland to Gustav III's neo-absolutism, the opposition of the Protestant landowners in Ireland to English centralization, or the response of the local bureaucracy in Norway to Danish absolutism.

2. The "memory" of former independence or statehood, even situated far in the past, could play an important role in stimulating national historical consciousness and ethnic solidarity. This was the very first argument employed in Phase B by patriots in the Czech lands, Lithuania, Finland, Bulgaria, Catalonia and elsewhere.

3. In many cases, the medieval written language had more or less survived, making it easier to develop the norm of a modern language with its own literature, as proved to be the case with Czech, Finnish or Catalan, among others. However, the contrast between cases of this legacy and its absence was much exaggerated in the nineteenth century, when it was sometimes claimed it corresponded to a distinction between "historical" and "unhistorical" peoples, whereas in fact its salience was limited to the tempo at which historical consciousness of the nation now arose.

What is clear in all cases, however, is that the modern nation-building process started with the collection of information about the history, language and customs of the non-dominant ethnic group, which became the critical ingredient in the first phase of patriotic agitation. The learned researchers of Phase A "discovered" the ethnic group and laid a basis for the subsequent formation of a "national identity." Yet their intellectual activity cannot be called an organized social or political movement. Most of the patriots articulated no "national" demands as yet. The conversion of their aims into the objectives of a social movement seeking cultural and political changes was a product of Phase B, and the reasons why this occurred still remain in large measure an open question. Why did scholarly interests become emotional attachments? Why should affection or loyalty to a region pass into identification with an ethnic group as a nation-to-be?

THE ROLE OF SOCIAL MOBILITY AND COMMUNICATION

As a first approach, one might single out three processes as decisive for this transformation: (1) a social and/or political crisis of the old order, accompanied by new tensions and horizons; (2) the emergence of discontent among significant elements of the population; (3) loss of faith in traditional moral systems, above all a decline in religious legitimacy, even if this only affected small numbers of intellectuals (but not just those influenced by Enlightenment rationalism, also other dissenting currents). In general, it is clear that future research must pay more attention to these various facets of crisis, and to the competence or willingness of patriots to articulate responses to them in national—rather than simply social or political—terms. If certain groups of intellectuals now launched a true national agitation, this then initiated the critical Phase B. But this did not automatically mean the birth of a modern nation, which required further conditions for its emergence. For we must ask under what circumstances such agitation was ultimately successful, in passing over into a mass movement of Phase C capable of completing the national programme?

Various theories have been advanced by social scientists to explain this transformation, but it is difficult to be satisfied with them, because they do not correspond to the empirical facts. Ernest Gellner, for example, attributes the growth of "nationalism" essentially to the functional requirements of industrialization.[5] Yet most of the national movements in Europe emerged well before the arrival of modern industry, and usually completed the decisive Phase B of their development before they had any contact with it—many of them, indeed, in overwhelmingly agrarian conditions. But if such flaws are common to much of the sociological literature, we cannot, on the other hand, simply confine ourselves to inductive descriptions of the kind favoured by a traditionalist historiographer. Let us then look at two factors, designated by different terms by different authors, but in substance enjoying a certain consensus in the field. Adopting Karl Deutsch's vocabulary, we can term these social mobility and communication.[6] Here the situation seems on the surface relatively straightforward. We can confirm that in most cases members of patriotic groups belonged to professions with quite high vertical mobility, while in no case were they dominated by recruits from groups with low social mobility, like peasants. A high level of social mobility thus seems to have been a favourable condition for acceptance of patriotic programmes in Phase B. So far, so good. Unfortunately, however, we know that it often also facilitated successful upward assimilation of members of the same groups into the ranks of the ruling nation. Similarly, social communication as the transmission of information about reality, and of attitudes towards it, certainly played an important role in the advent of modern capitalist society—and if we analyze the occupations of the patriots, we will arrive at the conclusion that national agitation appealed most readily to those within the non-dominant ethnic group who enjoyed the best channels of such communication. A territorial analysis yields the same result: those regions with the densest networks of communication were most susceptible to such agitation. Thus far, Deutsch's view seems to be corroborated—that the growth of national movements (he spoke of nationalism) went hand in hand with the advance of social communication and mobility, themselves processes within a more general transformation of society.[7]

Yet it is still necessary to check this hypothesis against historical reality in at least two limiting cases. At one extreme, we have to hand the example of the district of Polesie in inter-war Poland, an area with minimal social mobility, very weak contacts with the market, and scant literacy. When its inhabitants were asked in the census of 1919 what was their nationality, most of them just replied: "from hereabouts."[8] The same pattern prevailed in Eastern Lithuania, West Prussia, Lower Lusatia, and various Balkan regions. But what of the opposite situation? Can an intensive growth of communication and a high rate of mobility be considered causes of a successful Phase B? By no means—the experience of such lands as Wales, Belgium, Britanny or Schleswig shows, on the contrary, that these could coexist with a weak response to national agitation, in conditions where a maturing constitutional order proved more important.

CRISIS AND CONFLICT

There must then have been another weighty factor, besides social change and high levels of mobility and communication, that typically helped to lend impetus to a national movement. I have termed this factor a nationally relevant conflict of interests—in other words a social tension or collision that could be mapped onto linguistic (and sometimes also religious) divisions. A common example in the nineteenth century was the conflict between new university graduates coming from a non-dominant ethnic group, and a closed elite from the ruling nation keeping a hereditary grip on leading positions in state and society.[9] But there were also clashes between peasants belonging to the subaltern group and landlords from the dominant one, between craftsmen from the former and large traders and manufacturers from the latter, and so on. It is important to stress that these conflicts of interest which bore on the fate of national movements cannot be reduced to class conflicts—for the national movements always recruited members from several classes and groups, so that their interests were determined by a broad spectrum of social relations (including among them, of course, class relations).

Why were social conflicts of this kind articulated in national terms more successfully in some parts of Europe than in others? Paradoxically, we may say that in the nineteenth century national agitation often started earlier and made more headway in those areas where the non-dominant ethnic groups as a whole, often including their leaders, had scant political education and all but no political experience, because of the absolutist oppression under which they had grown up. Bohemia or Estonia are two among many examples. In these circumstances, there was little room for the more developed forms of political discourse or argument. On both sides of a given conflict, it was easier to articulate social contradictions or hostilities in national categories—as dangers to a common culture, or particular language, or ethnic interest. This is the main reason why West European national movements reveal a typological deviance (see Type 4, above). It was the higher levels of political culture and experience that allowed conflicts of interest in most Western zones to be articulated in political terms. Thus Flemish patriots were from the outset of Phase B divided into two camps—liberal and clerical, and most Flemish electors expressed their political preferences by voting for the Liberal or Catholic parties, leaving only a small minority for the Flemish Party proper. The same phenomenon can be observed in Wales or Scotland today. In these conditions, the national programme could not easily win a mass following, and in some cases never achieved a transition to Phase C. The lesson is that it is not enough to consider only the formal level of social communication reached in a given society—one must also look at the complex of contents mediated through it (even if these are in part unconscious). If the national slogans and goals used by agitators to articulate social tensions do in fact correspond to the immediate daily experience, to the level of schooling, and the system of symbols and stereotypes current in the majority of the non-dominant ethnic group, Phase C can be attained in a relatively short time.

The pattern of a successful national movement thus invariably includes at least four elements: 1) a crisis of legitimacy, linked to social, moral and cultural strains; 2) a basic volume of vertical social mobility (some educated people must come from the non-dominant ethnic group); 3) a fairly high level of social communication, including literacy, schooling and market relations; and 4) nationally relevant conflicts of interest. Such a model does not pretend to explain everything in the long and complex history of national movements. Let me illustrate this with an indication of some of the problems that remain unsolved for us today, despite the plethora of new "theories of nationalism."

GAPS REVEALED BY THE MODEL

My own comparative research has focused on the range of social constellations at work in Phase B of the national movements of nineteenth-century Europe. So far, no analogous studies have been made of Phase C.[10] Here too comparative analysis is badly needed, not only of the social groups mobilized once the national programme acquired a mass appeal, but also of the relative importance of the three principal components of its own agenda. There was no single ideal combination of these. What we need to explore are the inter-relationships between the cultural, political and social aspirations in the national programmes of the time, as well as the inner structure of each, and the specific demands that issued from them. We already know these could vary widely. Furthermore, once political demands gained salience in the national programme, the movement itself inevitably became a battlefield for the pursuit of power, not only in struggle against the ruling nation, but within the leaderships of the national movement as well. Under these conditions, leadership of the national movements typically passed from intellectuals to professional strata in a wider sense.

Another vital field for comparative research is a social physiognomy of the leading patriots—above all, the national intelligentsias in the region. Some preliminary comparisons I have undertaken of Czech, Polish, Slovak and German intellectuals in this period suggest that there are so far unexploited opportunities here for interpretation of national stereotypes, of the political culture and social sentiments of the patriots. The striking differences in the social origins of German and Czech intelligentsias of the time cast a new light on the national movements of each group in Bohemia.[11] But we should also note that so far little work has been done on those intellectuals who, by reason of their education and ethnicity, could have participated in the national movement, but did not do so. We need to know more about these nationally unconcerned or assimilated intelligentsias as well.

A final and substantial lacuna in contemporary research on the national movements of the last century may seem unexpected. Much irony has been expended on the historical legends and fictive pasts purveyed by the patriots of the time.[12] But we do not in fact know very much about the real role of history in the emergence and growth of national movements. For, of course, there was a genuine fund of historical experience on which many of them could draw—all the materials deposited by the first, pre-modern stage of the nation-building process itself; and then there were the various forms in which these subsequently found reflection in the consciousness of the non-dominant ethnic group. Typically, the kind of historical thought that arose at the beginning of the national movement was very different from the sort that developed towards its end. Here comparisons between Western and Eastern Europe, ruling nations and ruled nations, are likely to be instructive. Setting German and Czech historical novels of this period side by side, as I have recently done, yields suggestive results: while most of the former take their heroes from the ranks of (mainly Prussian) rulers and nobles, the same social layer is only rarely represented in the latter.[13]

THE "NEW NATIONALISMS" RECAPITULATE THE OLD

To what extent is the model outlined so far, which was developed out of work on the national movements of nineteenth-century Europe, helpful for understanding the "new nationalisms" of Central and Eastern Europe today? The conventional view that current turmoil is the result of the release of irrational forces that were long suppressed—"deep-frozen" as it were—under Communism, and are now in full revival after a lapse of fifty years, is evidently superficial. Such a conception is extravagant—closer to the world of fairy-tales than of historical processes. It is much more plausible to see the forces reshaping Central and Eastern Europe during the last decade as "new national movements," whose goals offer many analogies with those of the nineteenth century, as well as some significant differences.

The most striking resemblance between the two lies in the contemporary reproduction of the same triptych of aspirations which composed the national programme a hundred years ago. The specific goals sought are naturally not identical to those of the earlier national movements, but the general thrust is closely related. Once again, linguistic and cultural demands have surfaced with force—above all, of course, in the territories of the former Soviet Union. There, official policy had never suppressed local languages in the way Tsarist rule often did—indeed it had helped to promote these in the inter-war period, when Ukrainian, Byelorussian, Caucasian and Central Asian vernaculars had become languages of school instruction and publication. But in the Western lands acquired after the war, no such policies were pursued, as Russian was increasingly imposed as a language of public life. Hence the importance of linguistic issues today in this zone, where Estonia has declared knowledge of its language to be a condition of civil rights, or Moldavia has reclaimed the Latin alphabet. In the countries to the west of the Bug and the Dniester, linguistic demands have been less salient. But here too among the first signs of the breakup of Yugoslavia was the campaign to separate Croat as a fully independent language from Serb, in the seventies and eighties; likewise the Institute of Slovak Literature (Matica) has led the way in pressing linguistic arguments for national independence in Slovakia.

If the significance of the linguistic component varies from region to region today, the political component is in every case central. The two main goals articulated here each have their parallel in the past. On the one hand, the call for democracy corresponds to the demand for civil rights in the programme of the "classical" movements. On the other hand, the desire for full independence recalls the drive for ethnic autonomy in the nineteenth century. In most cases, although not all (Slovenia, Croatia or Slovakia), the pre-war experience of independent statehood furnishes the decisive model here. By 1992, political independence has, of course, been fully reasserted over most of East-Central Europe; while in the former USSR, the constituent union republics are all now at least juridically sovereign states. In these conditions, energies turn to the direction now to be taken by the independence gained—that is, to questions of policies towards external neighbours, and to domestic minorities.

Finally, the new national movements exhibit a social programme of a distinct kind, in conditions where there is typically a rapid exchange of ruling classes. The leaders of these movements aim for a very specific goal: to complete the social structure of the nation by creating a capitalist class corresponding to that of Western states, in which they would come to enjoy a salient position themselves. Here too the formal analogies with the past are striking.

Beyond these, moreover, there are a series of further significant resemblances. In the nineteenth century, the transition to Phase B occurred at a time when the old regime and its social order were on the verge of disintegrating. As traditional ties weakened or dissolved, the need for a new collective identity brought together people from different social classes and then political currents into one national movement. In the same way today, after the breakdown of Communist rule and central planning, familiar ties have crumbled, leaving a generalized anxiety and insecurity in which the national idea takes over the role of collective integration. In conditions of acute stress, people characteristically tend to over-value the protective comfort of their own national group.

Identification with the national group in turn includes, as it also did in the last century, the construction of a personalized image of the nation. The glorious past of this personality comes to be lived as part of the individual memory of each citizen, and its defeats resented as failures that still touch them. One result of such personalization is that people will regard their nation—that is, themselves— as a single body in a more than metaphorical sense. If any distress befalls a small part of the nation, it can be felt throughout it, and if any branch of the ethnic group—even one living far from the "mother-nation"—is threatened with assimilation, the members of the personalized nation may treat it as an amputation of the national body.

The personalized national body needs, of course—as in the nineteenth century—its own distinct space. Now, as then, claims to such space tend to be based on appeals to two different criteria, whose relationship is often highly contentious: on the one hand, to the principle of an area defined by the ethnic homogeneity of its population, as a common linguistic-cultural group; and on the other hand, to the notion of a historic territory with its own traditional borders, that often include other ethnic groups with minority status. In the nineteenth century, the second criterion acquired especial importance for so-called "historical nations." Thus Czechs deemed all the lands inside the frontiers of Bohemia and Moravia as their national body; Croats viewed all three parts of the medieval kingdom as their property; Lithuanians regarded the Polish-Jewish city of Wilno as their true capital. Today, this pattern is potentially even more widespread, since besides those nations which were deemed "historical" in the past century, there are others that acquired the relevant kind of history before the war—when the Estonians or Latvians gained an independent state, or even during it—when Slovaks and Croats secured protectorates under a Nazi license. In these conditions, leaders of the new national movements are once again inclined to declare state borders to be national boundaries and to treat ethnic minorities in "their" territory as outsiders, whose identity can be neglected or whose members expelled. Psycho-geography is once more playing an important role in Europe, as children in elementary schools constantly contemplate official maps of their country.[14]

ETHNO-LINGUISTIC DEMANDS AND PROBLEMS
OF DEMOTION

Why, it may be asked, do ethnic and linguistic arguments so frequently become uppermost in the programme of many of the new national movements in Central and Eastern Europe—just at a time when the Western world is trying to bid farewell to ethnicity as an organizing principle of economic life? The experience of the classic national movements of the region suggests an explanation.[15] When their agitation first started in the nineteenth century, the members of the non-dominant ethnic group had no political education, or any experience of public activity in civil society. Appeals to the political discourse of civil or human rights could hardly be effective, in these conditions. To a Czech or an Estonian peasant, "freedom" meant the abolition of feudal exactions and the ability to use their own farmland without impediment, not a parliamentary regime. The reality of a common language and customs could be much more readily grasped than remote conceptions of constitutional liberty. Today, in a somewhat analogous fashion, after fifty years of dictatorial rule, an education in civil society is still largely missing, and linguistic and cultural appeals may once more act as substitutes for articulated political demands—we can see this in the former republics of Yugoslavia, in Romania, in the Baltic states. This can in practice happen even where official discourse resounds with talk of democracy and civil rights.

Linguistic and ethnic demands do not, of course, everywhere have the same importance. But in many of the republics of the former Soviet Union, in particular, the idiom of the dominant nation often remained a symbol of political oppression, whatever the formal position of the main local language. In the nineteenth century, much of the struggle waged by the national movements of the time against the German-speaking bureaucracy of the Habsburg Empire, or the Russian bureaucracy of the Tsarist Empire, or the officialdom of the Ottoman Empire, revolved around linguistic issues. Today too, the vernacular of any small nation fighting for its independence is automatically regarded as the language of liberty. At stake here, however, are more than questions of prestige and symbolism. The unwillingness of members of the dominant nation to accept real linguistic equality has always put the non-dominant ethnic group at a material disadvantage. German and Hungarian speakers under the Dual Monarchy refused to learn or use the languages of other ethnic groups living on "their" territory. Then, with the break-up of the Empire and the emergence of new independent states in 1918–19, many of them suddenly found themselves reduced to the status of official minorities. But they characteristically were still unwilling to accept the predominance of the language of the small—but now dominant—nations under whose rule they lived: Czechs, Romanians, Poles and others. This was an explosive situation, whose consequences became fateful with the advent of the Third Reich in Germany. Today a similar process of demotion is occurring, as—in particular—Russians in the outlying republics become minorities in the independent states under construction by national movements. The historical parallels between the position of the *Volksdeutsche* and that of—so to speak—the "*Volksrussen*" are striking and disquieting.

THE SPECIFICITY OF THE POST-COMMUNIST
CONJUNCTURE

What of the role of nationally relevant social conflicts in contemporary conditions? Theoretically, we might suppose that these would not arise where clashes
of interest can find straightforwardly political or social expression. Yet, although
our knowledge here remains quite limited, it is already clear that some such
conflicts are becoming nationally pointed. The cases where a local intelligentsia
confronts a nomenclatura elite of another ethnic origin, which refuses to learn the
local language—the paradigmatic Baltic situation—are in this respect not the most
widespread. In fact, the majority of social conflicts that are nationally relevant
today are quite distinct from the classic nineteenth-century situation, and bear
witness to the profound dissimilarity between the social structures of Central and
Eastern Europe of today and yesterday.

For the current situation in the region is in many respects a unique one in
European history. The old order, based on a planned economy and rule by a
nomenclatura, has suddenly disappeared, leaving a political and social vacuum.
In these conditions new elites, educated under the old regime, but now at the head
of the national movement, have rapidly occupied leading positions in society. The
educated strata of the non-dominant ethnic groups strove towards similar goals
in the nineteenth century, but they had to contend with the established elites of
the ruling nation for every position, and a condition of their success was acceptance of the traditional forms of life, moral codes and rules of the game of the
class above them. Today, by contrast, vertical social mobility into the highest
levels of wealth or power is subject to no traditional usages, but often appears to
be simply the resultant of individual or national egoisms. The vacuum at the top
of society has created the possibility of very swift careers, as a new ruling class
starts to take shape, recruited from a confluence of three principal streams—
apprentice politicians (some of them former dissidents), veteran bureaucrats (the
more skilful managers from the old command economy), and emergent entrepreneurs (sometimes with dubious capital resources). The fight within, and among,
these groups for positions of privilege has so far yielded the most intense conflicts
of interest in post-Communist society; and wherever members of different ethnic
groups live on the same territory, it generates the leading tensions of a nationally
relevant character today.

The hazards in this situation are significantly increased by another salient difference between the contemporary and the earlier constellation. In the nineteenth
century, nationally relevant conflicts of interest typically sprang from processes
of economic growth and social improvement—pitting traditionalist artisans
against modernizing industrialists, small peasants against large landlords, or modest entrepreneurs against big bankers, for respective shares of a cake that was
increasing in size. Today, however, conflicts of this sort are notoriously unfolding
against a background of economic depression and decline, in which the cake is
becoming smaller. In these circumstances, it is no surprise that the gamut of
conflicts within the national movement itself is notably wider than in the past.
One result is that the broad spectrum of political positions represented by the

programmes of even the (genuinely) "nationalist" parties of the hour, who can differ widely on methods and goals, make it more difficult to speak of a single national programme. At the same time, the qualitatively higher degree of social communication assured by the modern electronic media enables a much faster conversion of national agitation into mass sentiment. The possibilities for popular manipulation and invention of national interests where there are none become higher. Control of the mass media in Central and Eastern Europe is a vital stake in the struggle for power, for professional use of them confers extraordinary power on the controllers. We have by no means seen the full consequences here.

There is, however, a further difference in the present conjuncture that may work to counteracting effect. During the nineteenth century, the national movement and nation-building process, and nationalism too, were common to every part of Europe. The new national movements of Central and Eastern Europe, by contrast, appear on the scene at a time when the idea of European integration has become a historical reality in the Western part of the continent. The form it may take remains, of course, highly contested, as two opposite tendencies dispute the constitutional future of the EC—one seeking to make of Europe a continent of citizens irrespective of their ethnicity, the other holding fast to traditional ethnic identities and trying to construct Europe as a unity of separate nation-states. Whatever the outcome of this conflict, it cannot be ignored that the leaders of all the new national movements in the former Communist zone proclaim their desire to enter the field of a unified Europe. In this respect we can speak of two (subjectively) complementary processes of group identification in Central and Eastern Europe: the national, based on the historical experience of the different ethnic groups in the area and giving rise to the conflicts mentioned above, and the European, reflecting new horizons and hopes. Were we to apply the terms of our periodization of the classic national movement to the process of European integration itself, we would no doubt find a successful second stage of Phase B in Western Europe, while only the very beginning of Phase B is visible in Central and Eastern Europe—where it is in any case important to distinguish economically opportunist declarations of adherence to European ideals from cultural or political aspirations to them.

PROSPECTS OF CATASTROPHE?

What is likely to be the impact of the new national movements in the former Communist zone on the continent as a whole? The tragic processes under way in what was only yesterday Yugoslavia make the dangers of the conjuncture all too evident. Uncompromising concentration on the ethnic attributes of the nation leads quickly to nationalist politics in the true sense of the word. Once this dynamic is unleashed, moralist or humanist appeals typically prove vain—not because of any lack of talent among those who make them, but because once these new movements have acquired a mass character, they can neither be deflected by rational argument nor suppressed by political force (which may even provoke their radicalization), as the experience of their predecessors shows. How far do they thereby threaten, not only the integration, but the stability of Europe?

Everyone knows that the most disastrous consequence of the classic national movements of the region was their role in helping to precipitate the First World War. Today, critics of the "new nationalism" in Central and Eastern Europe warn of the dangers of a repetition of this fatal sequence. What they forget, however, is that it was the nationalist policies of the Great Powers which essentially brought about the War—the conflicts between small states and their nationalist politicians were little more than kindling used by these Powers. Contemporary "ethno-nationalism" is mainly a phenomenon of small ethnic groups or nations, which are far from possessing major international weight. The conflicts to which it gives rise are indeed factors of regional instability, but they do not endanger the peace of Europe in the same way as at the turn of the century—or at any rate, they will not do so as long as none of the Great Powers tries to profit from them. This seems a remote prospect at present, since all the major European states save Russia are now joined within the European Community. Nevertheless, it would be unwise to discount entirely the possibility of some interested politicians or parties in the leading Western states using certain of the new national movements to enlarge their own sphere of influence. German initiatives in Slovenia and Croatia have been interpreted by some in this light. There is, of course, a further problem now haunting the region, one that recalls the inter-war period rather than the last century. This is the position of minorities within the post-Communist states. Such minorities are of two types. The first comprises ethnic groups living in relatively compact areas within a state dominated by another nation, who at the same time belong to a nation on the other side of the frontier: for example, the Magyars in Slovakia or Transylvania, the Serbs in Croatia, the Poles in Moravia, the Russians in Estonia, the Albanians in Kosovo. The second numbers ethnic populations dispersed within a state that is not their own, such as the Slovaks or Germans in Hungary, the Romanians in Serbia, the Turks in Macedonia, the Gypsies everywhere. In either case, minority movements may arise similar in form to national movements, but with the critical difference that they cannot hope to achieve an independent nation state. The utmost goals of these movements can be political autonomy or border-revision. But such objectives may, of course, on occasion be more explosive than the aims of the new national movements themselves.

In conclusion, it may well be asked: on the basis of our knowledge of the classical national movements of nineteenth-century Europe, what could be thought alterable and what unalterable in the dynamic of the new movements? The basic precondition of all national movements—yesterday and today—is a deep crisis of the old order, with the breakdown of its legitimacy, and of the values and sentiments that sustained it. In the case of the current movements, this crisis is combined with economic depression and the threat of widespread social decline, generating increasing popular distress. But in both periods, a third crucial element of the situation is a low level of political culture and experience among the broad mass of the population. The coincidence of these three conditions—

societal crisis, economic recession, political inexperience—is specific to the contemporary conjuncture, when its effects have been intensified by the great increase in the density and speed of social communication. Once the ruling order—absolutism or Communism—underwent a certain liberalization, social or political movements against it were inevitable. These became national, if two further factors intervened: the existence of real deficits for a full national life, and of significant tensions that could be articulated as national conflicts, within a pattern of uneven development. Once such national movements acquire a mass character, whether in the past century or this one, they cannot be stopped by governmental ban or use of force. At most, they can today be inflected by civic education in schools and media, perhaps today in a putatively "European" direction, and by official measures to assure a reasonable ethnic balance in public employment. The limitations of such measures are only too evident. The one truly effective remedy against the dangers of the present situation is, alas, the most utopian: a resolution of the economic crisis of the region, and advent of a new prosperity.

NOTES

1. See, by this author, *Social Conditions of National Revival in Europe. A Comparative Analysis of the Social Composition of Patriotic Groups among the Smaller European Nations*, Cambridge 1985, and *Nardodni Hnuti v Europe 19. Stoleti*, Prague 1986.

2. The term "nationalism" itself entered into scholarly currency rather late—perhaps no earlier than the work of the American historian Carleton Hayes, above all with his *Historical Evolution of Modern Nationalism*, New York 1931. Its usage still remained fairly rare in inter-war Europe, as can be seen from A. Kemiläinen's survey *Nationalism. Problems concerning the Word, the Concept and the Classification*, Jyväskylä 1964. The first significant European scholar to deploy the notion for a systematic analysis was E. Lemberg, *Der Nationalismus* (two volumes), Hamburg 1964.

3. Thus if we compare the incidence of national movements in Western and Eastern Europe in the nineteenth century, the number is about the same. But the proportions change if we ask how many autonomous medieval cultures were either integrated or extinguished in each region. For in the West, only some of these cultures survived to form the basis of later national movements: others—Niederdeutsch, Arab, Provençal, etc.—did not. The Western monarchies generally proved much more capable of assimilating "non-state" cultures and communities than the Habsburg, Romanov or Ottoman Empires.

4. There were national movements which developed the goal of independence very early—for example, the Norwegian, Greek or Serb. But there were many more that came to it only rather late, and in the exceptional circumstances of the First World War—among them the Czech, Finnish, Estonian, Latvian, and Lithuanian movements; while others—the Slovene or Byelorussian—did not formulate it even then. The Catalan case provides a vivid example of the way in which even a powerful national movement need not pose the demand of an independent state.

5. See *Nations and Nationalism*, Oxford 1983, passim.

6. See Deutsch's work *Nationalism and Social Communication*, Cambridge, Mass., 1953. Other scholars have also stressed the importance of social communication for an understanding of national sentiment, without adopting Deutsch's perspective or terminol-

ogy. See, for example, Benedict Anderson, *Imagined Communities. Reflections on the Origins and Spread of Nationalism*, London 1983—enlarged edition 1991.

7. O. Bauer was the first to understand the relation of the nation-building process to the general capitalist transformation of the society; O. Bauer, *Die Nationalitätenfrage und die Sozialdemokratie*, Wien 1907.

8. This episode is not analyzed in Western literature; see J. Tomaszewski, *Zdziejów Polesia 1921–1939*, Warszawa 1963, p. 25, 32 ff.

9. I first pointed out the importance of this nationally relevant conflict in my book *Die Vorkämpfer der nationalen Bewegungen bei den kleinen Völkern Europas*, Prague 1968. For more detailed subsequent analysis of the problem of unemployed intellectuals see A. D. Smith, *The Ethnic Revival in the Modern World*, Cambridge 1981.

10. The shortage of case studies of this problem explains why E. J. Hobsbawm could not analyze the social structure of the Phase C in his latest work, *Nation and Nationalism 1789–1945*, Cambridge 1990.

11. Some partial results published in M. Hroch, *Das Bürgertum in den nationalen Bewegungen des 19. Jahrhunderts—ein europäischer Vergleich*, in Jürgen Kocka, ed., *Bürgertum in 19. Jahrhundert*, Bd. 3, Munich 1988, p. 345 ff

12. For a typical example of such a facile response, see W. Kolarz, *Myths and Realities in Eastern Europe*, London 1946.

13. *Die bürgerliche Belletristik als Vermittlerin des bürgerlichen Geschichtsbewusstsein: deutsches und tschechiches Geschichtsbild im Vergleich*, Bielefeld, ZIF, 1987.

14. On psycho-geography as a factor of national identity, see F. Barnes, ed., *Us and Them: the Psychology of Ethnonationalism*, New York 1987, p. 10 ff.

15. The present national movements of "East" and "West" are distinctly less comparable today than they were before 1918. Western national movements (for example, the Catalan, Basque, Welsh, Breton or Scots) are still typically engaged in a Phase C, or even a Phase B that started in the 19th century—whereas the majority of Eastern movements (for example the Czech, Estonian, Lithuanian or Polish) achieved national independence after the First World War, while others (for example the Byelorussian or Ukrainian) are now resuming an interrupted Phase B, or (like the Slovak or Croatian) Phase C.

Tom Nairn

Tom Nairn, a leading contemporary Scottish public intellectual, taught social science and philosophy at Birmingham University and then at Hornsey College of Art, where he was sacked in 1968 for participating in the student rebellion of that year. Since then, he has been an independent scholar and political writer, best-known recently for his brilliant extended polemic on the history and current meanings of the British monarchy, *The Enchanted Glass: Britain and Its Monarchy* (London: Hutchinson, 1988). His early writings were published mainly in *New Left Review* (whose board he joined in 1962), including a series of important essays on British history and its peculiarities. Together with similar essays by Perry Anderson (often referred to as the Anderson-Nairn theses), these became the main items in a major debate with Edward Thompson in the mid-1960s. In 1975 he published a book-length polemic against the British Left's opposition to the Common Market, initiating a long-term engagement with questions of nationalism, which resulted in *The Break-Up of Britain: Crisis and Neo-Nationalism* (London: Verso, 1977). This selection is an early piece of the latter.

In the first instance, Nairn's essay contains a complex argument about the effects of uneven and combined development, in which the more backward societies of the European periphery seek the benefits of progress they observe in a metropolitan core, whose economic dynamism is simultaneously the condition of their own socioeconomic and political subordination. Nairn chooses Scotland to exemplify this argument, precisely because in the heyday of romantic nationalisms in the early nineteenth century, when Scottish society possessed many of the features to qualify it for such a history (including the potential for industrialization, an exceptionally highly developed intelligentsia, and political subordination to England), a Scottish nationalist movement *failed* to develop. Instead, the Scottish bourgeoisie and intelligentsia proved satisfied with the opportunities their emplacement in the structures of an expanding English imperial state seemed to offer. When a Scottish nationalist movement *did* develop in the early twentieth century, as the English state entered its long-term structural decline, it belatedly drew upon the romantic model of cultural authenticity so prevalent in the drive of Europe's smaller peoples for self-determination. In building this argument, Nairn made use of the early work of three other writers, Ernest Gellner, Eric Hobsbawm, and Miroslav Hroch.

Nairn also pioneered the sympathetic rethinking of the subject of nationalism among contemporary Marxists of the New Left—a rethinking in which traditional nostrums of internationalism have been somewhat given up. In Nairn's case, this occurred partly under the influence of Antonio Gramsci, and partly through his experience in the Scottish nationalist milieu of the 1980s. For Nairn, Gramsci was a typical theorist of the dilemma of underdevelopment in its politico-cultural sense, who also theorized the priority for the Left of operating in and through the given structures and languages of the national political imagination.

Scotland and Europe

In a recent study of the present condition of the nation-state, Nicos Poulantzas wrote that we are seeing "ruptures in the national unity underlying existing national states, rather than the emergence of a new State over and above them: that is, the very important contemporary phenomenon of regionalism, as expressed particularly in the resurgence of nationalities, showing how the internationalization of capital leads rather to a fragmentation of the state as historically constituted than to a supra-national State . . ."[1] More recently, *Les Temps Modernes* has devoted a special issue to an extensive survey of national minorities in France, perhaps the most strongly unified of the "historically constituted" European nations at the state level.[2] In Italy, where regional self-government has become a question of practical politics, intellectual concern with the topic is also increasing. Perhaps the most valuable overview of repressed and resurgent nationalities in western Europe is provided by Sergio Salvi's *Le nazioni proibite: Guida a dieci colonie interne dell'Europa occidentale.*[3] Hence, it is indispensable to try and view Scottish or Welsh developments in a European perspective. This is the aim of the present paper. I would like to look at certain aspects of Scotland's nationalism and modern history in a wider, more comparative, and more objective way than has usually been done in the past.

THE THEORY OF NATIONALISM

What do the terms "objective" and "comparative" mean here? "Real understanding of one's own national history begins only where we can place it within the general historical process, where we dare to confront it within the general historical process, where we dare to confront it with European development as a whole," writes Miroslav Hroch in his own invaluable comparative study of the

Tom Nairn, "Scotland and Europe," *New Left Review*, 83 (January–February 1974), pp. 57–82.

Author's note: This paper was originally presented at a post-graduate seminar of the Glasgow University's Department of Politics, held in Helensburgh in October 1973. I would like to take this opportunity of thanking the students of the Department who asked me to speak there. As printed here it still largely consists of notes for a talk, with only minor changes and the addition of some quotations and references. Only the concluding section is mainly new, and has been influenced by working on the preparation of the International Conference on Minorities, due to be held in Trieste from 27 to 31 May 1974. This will be the largest forum so far for the expression and consideration of minority problems in Europe, including those of repressed or resurgent nationality.

genesis of nationalism in seven smaller European lands.[4] More generally still, it should be remarked that the history of theorizing about nationalism displays two dramatic faults. One is a tendency to treat the subject in a one-nation or one-state frame of reference: so that each nationalism has to be understood, in effect, mainly with reference to "its own" ethnic, economic, or other basis—rather than by comparison with the "general historical process." The second (and obviously related) tendency is to take nationalist ideology far too literally and seriously. What nationalists say about themselves and their movements must, of course, be given due weight. But it is fatal to treat such self-consciousness other than extremely cautiously. The subjectivity of nationalism must itself be approached with the utmost effort of objectivity. It should be treated as a psycho-analyst does the outpourings of a patient. Where—as is not infrequently the case with nationalism—the patient is a roaring drunk into the bargain, even greater patience is called for.

In short, the theory of nationalism has been inordinately influenced by nationalism itself. This is scarcely surprising. Nationalism is amongst other things a name for the general condition of the modern body politic, more like the climate of political and social thought than just another doctrine. It is correspondingly difficult to avoid being unconsciously influenced by it.[5]

So we must try and avoid the empiricism of the nation-by-nation approach, and the subjectivism involved in taking nationalist rhetoric at its face-value. What exactly should we compare to what, in circumventing such influences? Broadly speaking, what merits consideration here is, on the one hand, the characteristic general evolution of European nationalism, between say 1800 and the major nationalist settlement of 1918–22; and on the other, whatever ideas and movements in modern Scottish history can be held to correspond to that general development. I am aware of course that the general category begs a number of questions. Nationalism did not come to a stop in Europe in 1922 after the Versailles agreements. Everyone knows that nationalism is still extremely alive, if not exactly in good health, everywhere in present-day Europe. But that is not the point. It remains true nonetheless that by the time of the post-World War I settlement European nationalism had gone through the main arc of its historical development, over a century and more. And the main lines of that settlement have proved, in fact, remarkably tenacious and permanent. Hence it is the outline provided by that century's development which—without in any way minimizing Europe's remaining problems of *terre irredente*—should provide our principal model and reference point.

SCOTTISH BELATEDNESS

What corresponds to this now classical model of development in Scotland's case? Here, we encounter something very surprising right away. For what can reasonably be held to correspond to the mainstream of European nationalism is astonishingly recent in Scotland. As a matter of fact, it started in the 1920s—more or less at the moment when, after its prolonged gestation and maturation during the 19th century, European nationalism at last congealed into semi-permanent state forms. Thus it belongs to the last fifty years, and is the chronological companion of anti-imperialist revolt and Third World nationalism, rather than of those European movements which it superficially resembles. While the latter were growing, fighting their battles and winning them (sometimes), Scottish nationalism was simply absent.

I am aware that this assertion of Scottish belatedness also begs many questions. There is much to say about the precursors of nationalism in the 19th century, like the romantic movement of the 1850s and the successive Home Rule movements between 1880 and 1914. These are well described in H. J. Hanham's *Scottish Nationalism*. But all that need be said here is that they were quite distinctly precursors, not the thing itself, remarkable in any wider perspective for their feebleness and political ambiguity rather than their prophetic power. While in the 1920s we see by contrast the emergence of a permanent political movement with the formation of the National Party of Scotland (direct ancestor of the SNP) in 1928. And, just as important, the appearance of the epic poem of modern Scottish nationalism (a distinguishing badge of this, as of most other European nationalisms), MacDiarmid's *A Drunk Man Looks at the Thistle*, in 1926.

So, we have to start with a problem—a problem written into the very terms of any comparison one can make between Scotland and Europe, as it were. Why was Scottish nationalism so belated in its arrival on the European scene? Why was it absent for virtually the whole of the "founding period" of European nationalist struggle?

But we cannot immediately try to answer this. We must turn away from it and return to it later—for the simple reason that, as I hope to show, the belatedness in question is in no sense merely a chronological fact (as nationalists are likely to believe). It is intimately related to the essential historical character of Scottish nationalism. To understand the one is to understand the other. Hence to approach the problem correctly we must first make some progress at a more fundamental level.

THE TIDAL WAVE OF MODERNIZATION

Let us turn back to the general European model. How may we describe the general outlines of nationalist development, seen as "general historical process"? Here, by far the most important point is that nationalism is *as a whole* quite incomprehensible outside the context of that process's *uneven* development. The subjective point of nationalist ideology is, of course, always the suggestion that one nationality is as good as another. But the *real* point has always lain in the objective fact that, manifestly, one nationality has never been even remotely as good as, or equal to, the others which figure in its world-view. Indeed, the purpose of the subjectivity (nationalist myths) can never be anything but protest against the brutal fact; it is mobilization *against* the unpalatable, humanly unacceptable, truth of grossly uneven development.

Nationalism in general is (in Ernest Gellner's words) "a phenomenon connected not so much with industrialization or modernization as such, but with its uneven diffusion."[6] It first arose as a *general* fact (a determining general condition of the European body politic) after this "uneven diffusion" had made its first huge and irreversible impact upon the historical process. That is, after the combined shocks engendered by the French Revolution, the Napoleonic conquests, the English industrial revolution, and the war between the two super-states of the day, England and France. This English-French "dual revolution" impinged upon the rest of Europe like a tidal wave. What Gellner calls the "tidal wave of modernization." Through it the advancing capitalism of the more bourgeois societies bore down upon the societies surrounding them—societies which predominantly appear until the 1790s as buried in feudal and absolutist slumber.

Nationalism was one result of this rude awakening. For what did these societies—which now discovered themselves to be intolerably "backward"—awaken into? A situation where polite universalist visions of progress had turned into means of domination. The Universal Republic of Anacharsis Cloots had turned into a French empire; the spread of free commerce from which so much had been hoped was turning (as Friedrich List pointed out) into the domination of English manufactures—the tyranny of the English "City" over the European "Country." In short, there was a sort of imperialism built into "development." And it had become a prime necessity to resist *this* aspect of development.

Enlightenment thinkers had mostly failed to foresee this fatal antagonism. They had quite naturally assumed "a link between knowledge and the increase in happiness," so that (as Sidney Pollard writes) "Society and its rulers are increasingly able, because of greater knowledge, to combine the individual with the general interest, and the laws of nations will increasingly be changed to increase both. Thus the undoubted future progress of the human spirit will be accompanied by continuous social and individual amelioration."[7] They imagined continuous diffusion from centre to periphery, from the "leaders" to the regions still plunged in relative darkness. The metropolis would gradually elevate the rustic hinterland up to its level, as it were. It is, incidentally, worth noting that imperialists to this day always cling to some form or other of this pre-1800 ideology, at least partially.

In fact, progress invariably puts powerful, even deadly weapons in the hands of this or that particular "advanced" area. Since this is a particular place and people, not a disinterested centre of pure and numinous culture, the result is a gulf (far larger than hitherto, and likely to increase) between the leaders and the hinterland. In the latter, progress comes to seem a hammer-blow as well as (sometimes instead of) a prospectus for general uplift and improvement. It appears as double-edged, at least. So areas of the hinterland, even in order to "catch up" (to advance from "barbarism" to the condition of "civil society," as the Enlightenment put it), are *also* compelled to mobilize against progress. That is, they have to demand progress not as it is thrust upon them initially by the metropolitan centre, but "on their own terms." These "terms" are, of course, ones which reject the imperialist trappings: exploitation or control from abroad, discrimination, military or political domination, and so on.

"Nationalism" is in one sense only the label for the general unfolding of this vast struggle, since the end of the 18th century. Obviously no one would deny that nationalities, ethnic disputes and hatreds, or some nation-states, existed long before this. But this is not the point. The point is how such relatively timeless features of the human scene were transformed into the general condition of national*ism* after the bourgeois revolutions exploded fully into the world. Naturally, the new state of affairs made use of the "raw materials" provided by Europe's particularly rich variety of ethnic, cultural and linguistic contrasts. But—precisely—it also altered their meaning, and gave them a qualitatively distinct function, an altogether new dynamism for both good and evil.

In terms of broad political geography, the contours of the process are familiar. The "tidal wave" invaded one zone after another, in concentric circles. First Germany and Italy, the areas of relatively advanced and unified culture adjacent to the Anglo-French centre. It was in them that the main body of typically nationalist politics and culture was formulated. Almost at the same time, or shortly after, Central and Eastern Europe, and the more peripheral regions of Iberia, Ireland, and Scandinavia. Then Japan and, with the full development of imperialism, much of the rest of the globe. To locate at least some of the dimensions of the struggle today is simple. All one had to do was look around one in 1972 or 1973. Where were the storm-centres? Vietnam, Ireland, Bangladesh, the Middle East, Chile. Certain of these troubles may, or may not, have involved socialist revolutions and projected a non-national and Marxist image; there is no doubt that every one of them involved a *national* revolution quite comprehensible in the general historical terms of national*ism* (even without reference to other factors).

EUROPE'S BOURGEOISIES

The picture must be amplified and deepened in certain ways, however, to make it into a model applicable to a particular area like Scotland. We have glanced at the political geography of uneven development. What about its class basis and social content? Sociologically, the basis of the vital change we are concerned with obviously lay in the ascendancy of the bourgeoisie in both England and France: more exactly, in their joint rise and their fratricidal conflicts up to 1815. Their Janus-headed "modernity" was that of bourgeois society, and an emergent industrial capitalism.

And it was upon the same class that this advancing "civil society" everywhere had the principal impact. In the hinterland too there were "rising middle classes" impatient with absolutism and the motley assortment of *anciens régimes* which reigned over most of Europe. Naturally, these were far weaker and poorer than the world-bourgeoisies of the West. The gross advantages of the latter had been denied them by history's unequal development. Now they found themselves in a new dilemma. Previously they had hoped that the spread of civilized progress would get rid of feudalism and raise them to the grace of liberal, constitutional society. Now (e.g.) the German and Italian middle classes realised that only a determined effort of their own would prevent utopia from being marred by *Manchestertum* and French bayonets. Beyond them, in the still larger Europe east of Bohemia and Slovenia, the even weaker Slav middle classes realized that "progress'' would in itself only fasten German and Italian fetters upon their land and people more firmly. And so on.

This "dilemma" is indeed the characteristic product of capitalism's uneven development. One might call it the "nationalism-producing" dilemma. Given the premise of uneven growth, and the resultant impact of the more upon the less advanced, the dilemma is automatically transmitted outwards and onwards in this way. The result, nationalism, is basically no less necessary. Nationalism, unlike nationality or ethnic variety, cannot be considered a "natural" phenomenon. But of course it remains true that, as Gellner says, under these specific historical circumstances (those of a whole era in which we are still living) "nationalism does become a natural phenomenon, one flowing fairly inescapably from the general situation."

THE ROLE OF INTELLECTUALS

Equally naturally, nationalism was from the outset a "bourgeois" phenomenon in the sense indicated. But two farther qualifications are needed here, to understand the mechanism at work. The first concerns the intelligentsia, and the second concerns the masses whose emergence into history was—behind and beneath the more visible "rise of the bourgeoisie"—the truly decisive factor in the transformation we are dealing with. "The intelligentsia do, indeed, play a definitive part in the rise of nationalist movements—everywhere," remarks Anthony Smith.[8] In his history of the "dual revolution" and its impact Eric Hobsbawm is more specific: the motor rôle is provided by "The lesser landowners or gentry and the emergence of a national middle and even lower-middle class in numerous countries, the spokesmen for both being largely professional intellectuals . . . (above all) . . . the *educated* classes . . . the educational progress of large numbers of "new men" into areas hitherto occupied by a small élite. The progress of schools and universities measures that of nationalism, just as schools and especially universities become its most conspicuous champions."[9] The dilemma of underdevelopment becomes "nationalism" only when it is (so to speak) refracted into a given society, perceived in a certain way, and then acted upon. And the medium through which this occurs is invariably, in the first place, an intelligentsia—functioning, of course, as the most conscious and awakened part of the middle classes.

NATIONALISM AND THE MASSES

But if the intellectuals are all-important in one sense (spreading nationalism from the top downwards as it were), it is the masses—the ultimate recipients of the new message—that are all-important in another. As a matter of fact, they determine a lot of what the "message" is. Why this is can easily be seen, on the basis of the foregoing remarks.

These new middle classes, awakening to the grim dilemmas of backwardness, are confronted by a double challenge. They have (usually) to get rid of an anachronistic *ancien régime* as well as to beat "progress" into a shape that suits their own needs and class ambitions. They can only attempt this by radical political and social mobilization, by arousing and harnessing the latent energies of their own societies. But this means, by mobilizing people. People is all they have got: this is the essence of the under-development dilemma itself.

Consequently, the national or would-be national middle class is always compelled to "turn to the people." It is this compulsion that really determines the new political complex ("nationalism") which comes forth. For what are the implications of turning to the people, in this sense? First of all, speaking their language (or, over most of Europe, what had hitherto been viewed as their "brutish dialects"). Secondly, taking a kindlier view of their general "culture," that *ensemble* of customs and notions, pagan and religious, which the Enlightenment had relegated to the museum (if not to the dust-bin). Thirdly—and most decisively, when one looks at the process generally—coming to terms with the enormous and still irreconcilable *diversity* of popular and peasant life.

It is, of course, this primordial political compulsion which points the way to an understanding of the dominant contradiction of the era. Why did the spread of capitalism, as a rational and universal ordering of society, lead so remorselessly to extreme fragmentation, to the exaggeration of ethnic-cultural differences, and so to the *dementia* of "chauvinism" and war? Because that diffusion contained within itself (as it still does) the hopeless antagonism of its own unevenness, and a consequent imperialism; the latter forces mobilization against it, even on the part of those most anxious to catch up and imitate; such mobilization can only proceed, in practice, via a popular mass still located culturally upon a far anterior level of development, upon the level of feudal or pre-feudal peasant or "folk" life. That is, upon a level of (almost literally) "pre-historic" diversity in language, ethnic characteristics, social habits, and so on. This ancient and (in a more acceptable sense of the term) "natural" force imposes its own constraints upon the whole process, lending to it from the outset precisely that archaic and yet necessary colour, that primaeval-seeming or instinctive aspect which marks it so unmistakably.

If one now relates these two central features of the bourgeois dilemma to one another, what is the consequence? One perceives at once the true nerve of political nationalism. It is constituted by a distinctive relationship between the intelligentsia (acting for its class) and the people. There is no time here to explore this interesting general theme in detail. For our purposes it is sufficient to note the name, and some of the implications, of the relationship in question. Political nationalism of the classic sort was not necessarily democratic by nature, or revolutionary in a social sense (notoriously it could be inspired by fear of Jacobinism, as well as by Jacobinism). But it *was* necessarily "populist" by nature. The political and social variables to be observed in its development are anchored in this constant, which steadily expressed the class machinery of the process.

Thus, we can add to the "external" (or geo-political) co-ordinates of nationalism mentioned above, a set of "internal" or social-class co-ordinates. The former showed us the "tidal wave" of modernization (or bourgeois society) transforming one area after another, and soliciting the rise of nationalist awareness and movements. The latter shows us something of the mechanism behind the "rise": the bourgeois and intellectual populism which, in existing conditions of backwardness where the masses are beginning to enter history and political existence for the first time, is ineluctably driven towards ethnic particularism. Nationalism's forced "mobilization" is fundamentally conditioned, at least in the first instance, by its own mass basis.

But then, we are in a manner of speaking still living in this "first instance." Nationalism arose after the French and Industrial Revolutions, at the very beginning of the 19th century. But the *anciens régimes* which the new nationalist middle classes had to get rid of in Central and Eastern Europe lasted for more than a century after that. Absolutism was far more tenacious than most bourgeois intellectuals admitted. It learned to borrow from the new world elements of technology and populism, to help it survive. Even when killed at last by the First World War and the 1917 revolutions, its ruinous mass of unresolved "national questions" and fractured states was enough to poison history for another generation. And, of course, while this inheritance has become steadily less important in post-Second World War Europe, the expanding waves of extra-European nationalism are sufficient to hold us all still in this universe of discourse.

Let me now point out some important implications of this model of nationalism, before going on to consider the Scottish case. Its main virtue is a simple one. It enables us to decide upon a materialist, rather than an "idealist" explanation of the phenomenon. In the question of nationalism, this philosophical point is critical. This is so, because of the very character of the phenomenon. Quite obviously, nationalism is invariably characterized by a high degree of political and ideological voluntarism. Simply because it *is* forced mass-mobilization in a position of relative helplessness (or "under-development"), certain subjective factors play a prominent part in it. It is, in its immediate nature, idealistic. It always imagines an ideal "people" (propped up by folklore studies, antiquarianism, or some surrogate for these) and it always searches urgently for vital inner, untapped springs of energy both in the individual and the mass. Such idealism is inseparable both from its creative historical function and its typical delusions. Consequently a generally idealist mode of explanation has always been tempting for it. It lends itself rather to a Hegelian and romantic style of theorizing, than to a rationalist or Marxist one. This is one reason why Marxism has so often made heavy weather of it in the past.[10]

THE NATION AND ROMANTICISM

I pointed out earlier, indeed, that theories about nationalism have been overwhelmingly influenced by nationalism, as the prevailing universe of discourse. This is really the same point. For they have been overwhelmingly influenced in the sense of idealism—whether their bias is itself pro-nationalist, or anti-nationalist.[11] The question is, then, which can explain which? It is a fact that while idealist explanations of the phenomenon in terms of consciousness or *Zeitgeist* (however acute their observation may be, notably in German writers like Meinecke) never account for the material dynamic incorporated in the situation, a materialist explanation can perfectly well account for all the most "ideal" and cultural or ideological symptoms of nationalism (even at their most berserk). Start from the premise of capitalism's uneven development and its real class articulation, and one can come to grasp the point even of chauvinist lunacy, the "irrational" elements which have played a significant role in nationalism's unfolding from the outset to the end. Start from the lunacy itself and one will end there, after a number of gyrations—still believing, for instance, that (in Hegelian fashion) material development exists to serve the Idea of "spiritual development."

Perhaps this can be put in another way. The politico-cultural necessities of nationalism, as I outlined them briefly above, entail an intimate link between nationalist politics and *romanticism*. Romanticism was the cultural mode of the nationalist dynamic, the cultural "language" which alone made possible the formation of the new inter-class communities required by it. In that context, all romanticism's well-known features—the search for inwardness, the trust in feeling or instinct, the attitude to "nature," the cult of the particular and mistrust of the "abstract," etc.—make sense. But if one continues to adopt that language, then it becomes impossible to get back to the structural necessities which determined it historically. And of course, we *do* largely speak the language, for the same reason that we are still living in a world of nationalism.

Lastly let me point out an important limitation of the analysis. So far I have been concerned with the earlier or formative stages of nationalism. That is, with the nationalism which was originally (however much it has duplicated itself in later developments) that of Europe between 1800 and 1870. This is—for reasons which I hope will be clear—what primarily concerns us in approaching the Scottish case-history. But it is certainly true that after 1870, with the Franco-Prussian war and the birth of Imperialism (with a large "I"), there occurred farther sea-changes in nationalist development. These were related, in their external co-ordinates, to a new kind of great-power struggle for backward lands; and as regards their internal co-ordinates, to the quite different class-struggle provoked by the existence of large proletariats within the metropolitan centres themselves. I have no room here to consider this later phase so closely, but it is important to refer to it at least. Not only has it deeply influenced the development of Scotland (like everywhere else in the world). Also, where I have stated that we still live in a climate of nationalism, it would, of course, be more accurate to say we still inhabit the universe of late nationalism: that is, nationalism as modified by the successive, and decisive, mass experiences of imperialism and total war.

SCOTLAND'S ABSENT NATIONALISM

Let us now turn to Scotland. How exactly are we to set it over against this general model? I pointed out to begin with the very surprising fact which confronts anyone trying to do this: that is, that for virtually the whole century of nationalism's classical development there is no object of comparison at all. Between 1800 and 1870 for example, the dates just referred to, there simply *was* no Scottish nationalist movement of the usual sort.

It still may not be quite understood how disconcerting this absence is. To get it into perspective, one should compare certain aspects of Scotland's situation just prior to the age of nationalism with those of other European minor nationalities. With (e.g.) the Slav nationalities, Greece, Ireland, or Poland. In any such comparison, Scotland appears not as notably defective but, on the contrary, as almost uniquely *well* equipped for the nationalist battles ahead.

Nobody could, for example, claim that Scotland was a *geschichtloses Volk*.[12] It had only recently ceased being a wholly independent state. The century or so that had elapsed since 1707 is a fairly insignificant time-interval by the criteria which soon became common under nationalism. Many new "nations" had to think away millenia of oblivion, and invent almost entirely fictitious pasts.[13] Whereas the Scots not only remembered a reality of independence, they had actually preserved most of their own religious, cultural, and legal institutions intact. Their political state had gone, but their civil society was still there—still there and, in the later 18th century, thriving as never before. Most of backward, would-be nationalist Europe had neither the one nor the other.

Within this civil society Scotland also had at least two of the indispensable prerequisites for successful nationalism. It had a dynamic middle class, a "rising" bourgeoisie if ever there was one. And (above all) it had an intelligentsia. In fact, it had one of the most distinguished intellectual classes in the Europe of that time, a class whose achievements and fame far outshone that of any other minor nationality. Given the key importance of the intelligentsia in early formulations of the romantic populism associated with "nation-building," this was clearly a formidable advantage—at least in appearance.

As far as folklore and popular traditions went, Scotland was (needless to say) as well furnished for the struggle as anywhere else. Better than most, perhaps, since—as everybody knew then and knows now—one element in those traditions was an ancient, rankling hostility to the English, founded upon centuries of past conflict. These old conflicts gave Scotland a cast of national heroes and martyrs, popular tales and legends of oppression and resistance, as good as anything in *Mitteleuropa*. True, the Scots did not have a really separate majority language. But any comparative survey will show that, however important language becomes as a distinguishing mark in the subsequent advance of nationalism, it is rarely of primary importance in precipitating the movement. It is heavy artillery, but not the cause of the battle.

And in any case, the Scots had far heavier artillery to hand. They had—to consider only one thing—the enormously important factor of a clear religious difference. The Scottish Reformation had been a wholly different affair from the English one, and had given rise to a distinct social and popular ethos rooted in distinct institutions. There is no need to stress the potential of this factor in nationality-struggles today, looking across to Ireland (even in situations where both sides speak the same language). More important, and more generally, there was no doubt at the beginning of the 19th century—just as there is no doubt today— that "Scotland" was a distinct entity of some kind, felt to be such both by the people living in it and by all travellers who ventured into it from outside. It had (as it still has) a different "social ethic," in George Elder Davie's phrase. Analysis of the complex elements going into such a product, the recognizable and felt identity of a nationality-unit (whether state or province), may be difficult. But usually the fact is plain enough. And this is what counts most, as the potential fuel of nationalist struggle.

So why, in circumstances like these, was nationalism to be conspicuous only by its absence in Scotland? This question is interesting enough. But it is time to note that behind it there lies another, much more important in any general perspective, and even more fascinating. If, in a European land so strikingly marked out for nationalism, nationalism failed to materialize, then it can only be because the *real* precipitating factors of the nationalist response were not there. And one may therefore hope to discern, through this extraordinary "negative example," precisely what these factors were. To understand why Scotland did *not* "go nationalist" at the usual time and in the usual way is, in my opinion, to understand a great deal about European nationalism in general. I hope the claim does not sound too large (or even nationalist). But, as well as understanding Scotland better in relation to the general European model discussed above, one may also understand Europe better by focusing upon Scotland.

THREE KINDS OF NATION

To assist us in focusing on what is relevant, let me recall a basic point in the crudely materialist schema adopted previously. I suggested there that nationalism is in essence one kind of response to an enforced dilemma of "under-development." What we must do now is define the latter term more concretely, in relation to Europe at the critical period in question—that is, during the original formation of nationalism. European countries at the beginning of the 19th century can for this purpose conveniently be assigned to one or other of three categories. Firstly, there are the original, "historic" nation-states, the lands formed relatively early into relatively homogeneous entities, usually by absolute monarchy: England, France, Spain and Portugal, Sweden, Holland. Naturally, this category includes the "leaders," the two revolutionary nations whose impact was to be so great, as well as a number of formerly important ones which had now (for many different reasons) dropped out of the race. Then (secondly) there are the lands which have to try and catch up, under the impact of revolution: the German-speaking states, Italy, the Hapsburg domains, the Balkans, the countries of Tsardom, Ireland, Scandinavia apart from Sweden. These account for by far the greater part of Europe geographically, and in terms of population. They were all to attempt to redeem themselves through some form of nationalism, sooner or later: they were all (one might say) forced through the nationalist hoop.

Finally—thirdly—one needs another category. The two main groups of bourgeois-revolutionary lands and "under-developed" hinterland are easily classified at this point in time. But what about the countries which either had caught up, or were about to catch up? The countries on the move out of barbarism into culture, those on or near the point of (in today's terminology) "take-off"? Surely, in an age which thought so generally and confidently about progress of this sort, there were some examples of it?

This third group is a very odd one. It had, in fact, only one member. There was to be only one example of a land which—so to speak— "made it" before the onset of the new age of nationalism. The European Enlightenment had an immense general effect upon culture and society; but it had only one particular success-story, outside the great revolutionary centres. Only one society was in fact able to advance, more or less according to its precepts, from feudal and theological squalor to the stage of bourgeois civil society, polite culture, and so on. Only one land crossed the great divide *before* the whole condition of European politics and culture was decisively and permanently altered by the great awakening of nationalist consciousness.

NORTH BRITAIN

It was of course our own country, Scotland, which enjoyed (or suffered) this solitary fate. The intelligentsia at least had few doubts about what had happened. "The memory of our ancient state is not so much obliterated, but that, by comparing the past with the present, we may clearly see the superior advantages we now enjoy, and readily discern from what source they flow," ran the Preface to No. I of the original *Edinburgh Review* (1755). "The communication of trade has awakened industry; the equal administration of laws produced good manners . . . and a disposition to every species of improvement in the minds of a people naturally active and intelligent. If countries have their ages with respect to improvement, North Britain may be considered as in a state of early youth, guided and supported by the more mature strength of her kindred country."

A prodigy among the nations, indeed. It had progressed from fortified castles and witch-burning to Edinburgh New Town and Adam Smith, in only a generation or so. We cannot turn aside here to consider the reasons for this extraordinary success. Ordinarily it is no more than a sort of punch-bag in the old contest between nationalists and anti-nationalists: the former hold that Edinburgh's greatness sprang forth (like all true patriot flora) from indigenous sources, while the Unionists attribute it to the beneficent effects of 1707. It may be worth noting, however, that North Britain's intellectuals themselves normally thought of another factor as relevant. As the *Edinburgh Review* article mentioned above put it: "What the Revolution had begun, the Union rendered more complete." It was by no means the fact of union which had counted, but the fact that this unification had enabled the Scots to benefit from the great *revolution* in the neighbour kingdom. As the great Enlightenment historian William Robertson said, the 1707 agreement had "admitted the Scottish commons to a participation of all the privileges which the English had purchased at the expense of so much blood."[14] That is, the Scottish bourgeoisie had been able to exploit (by alliance) some of the consequences of the English bourgeois revolution. After the black, the unspeakable 17th century, Robertson notes, it was 1688 which marked the real dawn in Scotland.

But many other factors were involved too, clearly. The character of Scottish absolutism, for example, the feudalism which "collapsed as a vehicle for unity, and became instead the vehicle of faction," in T. C. Smout's words.[15] The character of the Scottish Reformation and its inheritance. I doubt if even the stoniest of Unionist stalwarts would deny that part of Scotland's 18th-century "improvement" was due to her own powers, and the retention of a large degree of institutional autonomy. But what matters most in the context of this discussion is that Scotland's situation was almost certainly unique. It was the only land which stood in *this* relationship to the *first* great national-scale bourgeois revolution: that is, to a revolutionary process which, because it was the first, proceeded both slowly and empirically, and therefore permitted in the course of its development things which were quite unthinkable later on. There was, there could not be, any situation like Scotland's within the enormously accelerated drive of 19th-century development. By then, the new inter-national competitiveness and political culture's new mass basis alike prohibited gentlemanly accords like 1707.[16]

We know at any rate that the success-story was never repeated quite like this anywhere else. There were a number of other zones of Europe where it clearly could have been, and would have been if "development" had gone on in the Enlightenment, rather than the nationalist, sense. Belgium and the Rhineland, for example, or Piedmont. In the earlier phases of the French Revolution these areas were indeed inducted for "improvement" into the ambit of the French Revolution, the Universal Republic. But as events quickly showed, this pattern could no longer be repeated.

ENLIGHTENMENT AND THE HIGHLANDS

The most remarkable comment upon Scotland's precocious improvement was provided by Scottish culture itself, during the Golden Age. The country not only "made it," in the generation before the great change (i.e. the generation between the failure of the Jacobite rebellion of 1745, and 1789)—it also produced the general formula for "making it." That is, it contributed proportionately far more than anywhere else in Europe to the development of social science. And it did so in the distinctive form of what was in essence a study *of* "development": a study of the "mechanics of transition," or how society in general can be expected to progress out of barbarism into refinement. Scottish Enlightenment thinkers were capable of this astonishing feat because, obviously, they had actually experienced much of the startling process they were trying to describe. Not only that: the old "barbaric" world was still there, close about them. The author of Scotland's sociological masterpiece, the *Essay on the History of Civil Society* (1767), had been brought up in the Highlands.[17]

Scotland's progress was all the more striking because there was this one large part of it which did not "improve" at all. Scotland beyond the Highland line

remained "under-developed." This fissure through Scottish society had been left
by the failure of later feudalism; now it was, if anything, aggravated by the swift
rise of Lowland culture in the 18th century. A "gulf" was formed which resembles in many ways the gulf that opened across Europe as a whole—that is, the
very gap I tried to describe previously, the development-gap with all its accompanying dilemmas and ambiguities. Highland Scotland, like most of Ireland, was
in effect a part of Central or Eastern Europe in the West. Therefore it was bound
to have a distinct development from the "successful" civil society south of it. It
had, as everyone knows, a distinct history of just this sort—one which painfully
resembles the history of Ireland or many of the weaker peoples of *Mitteleuropa*,
far more closely than it does that of the Scottish industrial belt. The Highlands
were to suffer the fate characteristic of many countries and regions which generated nationalist movements in order to resist. But (here unlike Ireland) Highland
society did not possess the prerequisites for *nationalist* resistance. Its position
was too marginal, its social structure was too archaic, and too much of its life
had been actually destroyed in the terrible reaction to 1745.

If this general analysis is right, then Scotland's precocious and pre-nationalist
development must clearly be reckoned the true "uniqueness" of its modern history. In European perspective, this emerges as much more striking than anything
else. Nationalists always perorate at length upon the unique charms and mission
of their object, I know: this is part of the structure of the nationalist thought-
world. So is the fact that, seen from a distance, these ineffable missions resemble
one another like a box of eggs. One has to be careful, consequently, before presenting a new candidate for the stakes. But I am comforted in doing so by one
thought. This is that my emphasis upon the Enlightenment has never in fact (to
the best of my knowledge) figured in such nationalist incantations in the past. On
the contrary—for reasons that may be clearer below—if Scottish nationalists have
ever been really united on one thing, it is their constant execration and denunciation of Enlightenment culture. In short, the real uniqueness of modern Scotland
is the one thing which does *not* (and indeed *cannot*) be admitted into nationalist
rhetoric.

There is logic behind this, of course. The same logic which drives one to the
following thought: it simply cannot be the case that there is *no* connection between
Scottish society's fulminating advance before 1800, and that society's subsequent
failure to produce a nationalism of its own. There must, surely, be some relation
between these two remarkable, peculiarly Scottish achievements. Let me now go
on to suggest what it may consist in.

There are two questions which cannot help dominating much of the cultural
debate upon nationalism in Scotland. One we have looked at already: it is the
problem of how and why the Scots emerged, so suddenly, from backwardness to
rise to the peaks of the Edinburgh Golden Age. The other is how and why—and
almost as suddenly—this florescence ended in the earlier decades of the 19th
century. So that, as far as the national culture is concerned—runs one typical
complaint—"The historian is left calling Victorian culture in Scotland 'strangely
rootless' . . . We have to recognize that there did not emerge along with modern
Scotland a mature, 'all-round' literature . . . In the mid-19th century the Scottish

literary tradition paused; from 1825 to 1880 there is next to nothing worth atten-tion.''[18] And, one might add, not much worth attention from 1880 to 1920 either.

It is inconceivable that the profoundest causes of this dramatic fall did not lie in Scottish society's general evolution. Yet where are these causes to be located? For, as Craig says, ''modern Scotland''—industrial Scotland, the economic Scot-land of the Glasgow–Edinburgh–Dundee axis—continued *its* startling progress unabated. In his history T. C. Smout situates the beginning of the movement towards take-off in midcentury, after the 'Forty-five: ''The ice began to break. Slow and unspectacular at first, the process of change then began to accelerate in the 1760s, until by the outbreak of the American War in 1775 practically all classes in Scottish society were conscious of a momentum which was carrying them towards a richer society . . .''[19] The momentum continued until by 1830 the country had ''come over a watershed.'' ''In 1828 J. B. Neilson's application of the hot-blast process to smelting the blackband ironstone of the Central Belt gave the Scottish economy the cue for its next major advance . . . it led to the birth of Scottish heavy industry with the swelling boom in iron towns and engineering in the 1830s and 1840s and the gigantic construction of shipyards on Clydeside in the last quarter of the century.''[20]

Thus, the economic ''structure'' continued its forward march, across the de-velopmental watershed and beyond, breeding new generations of Scottish entre-preneurs and a new and vast Scottish working class. But certain vital parts of the ''superstructure,'' far from sharing in this momentum, simply collapsed. On *that* level Scotland abruptly reverted to being a province again: a different sort of province, naturally, prosperous and imperial rather than theoretic and backward, but still (unmistakably) a very provincial *sort* of province. How is one to explain this remarkable disparity of development?

Let me relate it, first, to two other notable absences on the Scottish scene. One has already been several times referred to, since it is the main subject I am con-cerned with: that is, the absence of political nationalism. The other very striking absence is that of what one might call a developed or mature cultural romanticism. It is indeed the lack of this that constitutes the rootlessness, the ''void'' which cultural and literary historians so deplore.

I know that this may be thought a paradoxical assertion. We are all aware of the great significance of both Scotland and Sir Walter Scott in the general my-thology of European romanticism. And we are also conscious of the importance in Scotland itself of a kind of pervasive, second-rate, sentimental slop associated with tartan, nostalgia, Bonnie Prince Charlie, Dr. Finlay, and so on. Yet I would hold that both these phenomena are misleading, in different ways; and that the existence of neither of them is inconsistent with the absence I am referring to.

SIR WALTER SCOTT: VALEDICTORY REALIST

First of all Scott. In his essay on Scott in *The Historical Novel* (1962), Lukács points out that ''it is completely wrong to see Scott as a Romantic writer, unless one wishes to extend the concept of Romanticism to embrace all great literature in the first third of the 19th century." Indeed, what Scott expresses himself—in spite of the great importance of his historical themes for later romantic literature—is rather "a renunciation of Romanticism, a conquest of Romanticism, a higher development of the realist literary traditions of the Enlightenment." Thus, to describe Scott as a "romantic" is akin to describing Marx as a "Marxist": he undeniably gave rise to a great deal of this European "ism," but was not himself part of it. He was not, for example, a "Romantic" in the sense that his compatriot Thomas Carlyle was, in the next generation (even Carlyle's misunderstanding and denigration of Scott are typically romantic).[21]

Scott's imaginative world arose from the same "deeply felt experience of the contrast between two societies" mentioned above. That is, it belonged to the literary tradition of Scotland, as well as that of the Enlightenment in general. He brought to this an enormously heightened sense of the reality and values of the "backward" or pre-bourgeois past—a sense which is, of course, characteristic of the whole period of awakening nationalism. But the typical course of his own imagination is never consonant with what was to be the general tendency of that period. It ran precisely counter to that tendency. As Lukács observes, it continued to run upon the lines of what he calls Enlightenment "realism."

For Scott, the purpose of his unmatched evocation of a national past is never to revive it: that is, never to resuscitate it as part of political or social mobilization in the present, by a mythical emphasis upon continuity between (heroic) past and present. On the contrary: his essential point is always that the past really is gone, beyond recall. The heart may regret this, but never the head. As Scott's biographer J. G. Lockhart puts it, quite forcibly, his idea of nationalism was like his idea of witchcraft: "He delighted in letting his fancy run wild about ghosts and witches and horoscopes . . . (but) . . . no man would have been more certain to give juries sound direction in estimating the pretended evidence of supernatural occurrences of any sort; and I believe, in like manner, that had any anti-English faction, civil or religious, sprung up in his own time in Scotland, he would have done more than other living man could have hoped to do, for putting it down."[22] For all its splendour, his panorama of the Scottish past is valedictory in nature. When he returns to the present—in the *persona* of his typical prosaic hero-figure—the head is in charge. It speaks the language of Tory Unionism and "progress": the real interests of contemporary Scotland diverge from those of the auld sang.

But in nationalist Europe the entire purpose of romantic historicism was different. The whole point of cultural nationalism there *was* the mythical resuscitation of the past, to serve present and future ends. There, people learned the auld sangs in order to add new verses. Naturally, Scott was read and translated in those countries according to this spirit—and as we know, his contribution to the new rising tide of national romanticism was a great one. It was great everywhere but in his own nation. In his own national context, he pronounced, in effect, a great elegy. But the point of an elegy is that it *can* only be uttered once. Afterwards it may be echoed, but not really added to.

Consequently, Sir Walter's towering presence during the vital decades of the early 19th century is not only consistent with the absence of a subsequent romantic-national culture: to a large extent, it explains that absence. The very nature of his achievement—whether seen in terms of his own politics, or in terms of his typical plots and characters—cut off such a future from its own natural source of inspiration. It cut off the future from the past, the head from the "heart" (as romanticism now conceived this entity). As for the second phenomenon I referred to, popular or *Kitsch* Scotland, this is certainly a sort of "romanticism." And it is certainly important, and not to be dismissed with a shudder as most nationalist intellectuals tend to do. I shall have more to say about the great tartan monster below. For the moment, however, I think it is enough to point out that he is a sub-cultural creature rather than a performer in the elevated spheres we are concerned with. Whisky labels, the *Sunday Post*, Andy Stewart, the Scott Monument, the inebriate football patriots of International night: no-one will fail to compose his own lengthy list or discern its weighty role in the land. But this is a popular sub-romanticism, and not the vital national culture whose absence is so often lamented after Scott.

What we have therefore is the relatively sudden disintegration of a great national culture; an absence of political and cultural national*ism*; and an absence of any genuine, developing romanticism, of the kind which was to typify 19th-century cultural life. The three negative phenomena are, surely, closely connected. In fact, they are different facets of the same mutation. And if we now set this change over against the general explanatory model sketched out previously, we can begin to see what it consisted in.

If one views it as a disparity of development, as between the ongoing economic structure and a suddenly and inexplicably collapsed "super-structure," then the answer is contained in the very terms in which the problem is posed. That is, it is overwhelmingly likely that the cultural decline occurred *because* of the material development itself. Because Scotland had already advanced so far, so fast—to the watershed of development and beyond—it simply did not need the kind of cultural development we are concerned with. It had overleapt what was to be (over the greater part of Europe) the next "natural" phase of development. Its previous astonishing precocity led it, quite logically, to what appears as an equally singular "retardation" or incompleteness in the period which followed. This can only have happened because, at bottom, certain material levers were inoperative in the Scottish case; and they were inoperative during the usual formative era of romantic nationalism because they had already performed their function and produced their effect earlier, in the quite different culture-world of the 18th century.

THE ABSENT INTELLIGENTSIA

We have some clues as to how this actually worked. Normally nationalism arose out of a novel dilemma of under-development; but it did so through a quite specific mechanism, involving first the intelligentsia, then wider strata of the middle classes, then the masses. The process has been admirably described by Hroch in his comparative inquiry. Initially the property of a relatively tiny intellectual élite (usually reacting to the impact of the French Revolution), nationalism passed through "phase A" into "phase B" (approximately 1815–48) where it was generally diffused among the growing bourgeoisie. It was in the course of this prolonged process that the new cultural language of romanticism and the new credo of liberal nationalism were worked out. But even so 1848 was still mainly a "revolution of the intellectuals" (in Namier's phrase), and failed as such. It was only later that it turned into a mass movement proper ("phase C") with some roots in new working-class and peasant parties, and wide popular appeal. Thus, while the new *Weltanschauung* was (as we noticed) inherently populist in outlook, it took a long time to get to the people: that is, to the mystic source whence, in nationalist myth, it is supposed to spring.

Transfer this picture to the Scottish case: there was no real, material dilemma of under-development; hence the intelligentsia did not perceive it, and develop its perception in the normal way—it did *not* have to "turn to the people" and try to mobilize first the middle strata then the masses for the struggle; hence there was no call to create a new inter-class "community" of the sort invoked by nationalism, and no objective need for the cultural instrument which permitted this—"romanticism"; hence the intelligentsia in Scotland (its previous eminence notwithstanding) was deprived of the *normal* function of an intellectual class in the new, nationalist, European world.

But—it may be objected here—even given that this was so, and that the underlying situation decreed a different politico-cultural fate for the Scots, why did it have to take the sad form of this *collapse* into provinciality, this bewildering descent from great heights into the cultural "desert" of modern Scotland? Why could the Enlightenment not have continued there in some form, in a separate but still "national" development? This is another of those questions whose very formulation guides one towards an answer. It was, of course, *impossible* for any such development to take place. Impossible because no one intellectual class can ever follow such a separate path in Europe. Once the general intellectual and cultural climate had altered in the decisive way mentioned, in consort with the unfolding of nationalism, it has altered for everybody.

This was by no means just a question of fashion, or the fact that intellectuals heed what goes on abroad. Nationalism was a general, and a structural state of the whole body politic. Although it was born in the "fringe" lands under the impact of modernity, its subsequent impact transformed everyone—including the "source" countries of the bourgeois revolution themselves, France and England. The new, enormous, growing weight of masses in motion broke down the old hierarchies everywhere and forced more or less similar cultural adaptations everywhere. In this violent process of action and reaction, no one part of the wider area concerned could "escape" nationalism and its culture. It had either to evolve its own nationalist-type culture, or succumb to someone else's (becoming thereby "provincialized").

AGAINST THE FALL

Under these new conditions, what in fact happened to the great Scots intelligentsia? As an intellectual class it belonged, with all its virtues, *entirely* to the pre-

1789 universe. Both its patrician social character and its rationalist world-view were parts of that older, more stable, hierarchical world where the masses had scarcely begun to exist politically. Claims have been made for its "democratic" intellect. "Democratic" in the deeper sense which now became central it emphatically was not. It was pre-Jacobin, pre-populist, pre-romantic; and as a consequence, wholly pre-nationalist. In the drastically different geological epoch which now supervened, it could survive only for a short time, in somewhat fossil-like fashion. The sad tale is all there, in Lord Cockburn's *Memorials*. "We had wonderfully few proper Jacobins," he comments wryly upon the Scottish élite's wholesale slide into reaction, "but if Scotch Jacobinism did not exist, Scotch Toryism did, and with a vengeance. This party engrossed almost the whole wealth, and rank, and public office, of the country, and at least three-fourths of the population."[23] Sir Walter himself was, of course, in the front rank, battling (literally) to the death against the 1832 Reform Bill.

Elsewhere in Europe this suicide of former élites did not matter. They were displaced by what Eric Hobsbawm called the "large numbers of 'new men' " who *were* educated into nationalism and the other new rules of populist politics. These new men were awakened into radical dissatisfaction with their fate, and had the sense that without great collective efforts things would not improve much for them in a foreseeable future. They tended to come (as Hroch observes) from "regions of intermediate social change"—from small towns and rural zones whose old life had been undermined, but for whom industry and urbanization were still remote (and dubious) realities.[24] Out of such regions there arose a new and broader intelligentsia to take the place of the old: modern, romantic, populist, more mobile, mainly petit-bourgeois in background.

But—precisely—in Scotland it did not. No new intellectual class at once national in scope and basically disgruntled at its life-prospects arose, because the Scottish petty bourgeoisie had little reason to be discontented. In the overwhelming rush of the Scottish industrial revolution, even the regions of intermediate social change were quickly sucked in. Hence no new "intelligentsia" in the relevant sense developed, turning to the people to try and fight a way out of its intolerable dilemma. Hence Hroch's phases "A" and "B" were alike absent in Scottish development: there was, there could be, no nationalism or its associated romantic culture fully present in that development. There could only be the "void."

This kind of analysis will stick in a number of throats for two reasons: it is materialist in content, and rather complicated in form. How simple the old nationalist theory of the Fall appears, in contrast! It can be compressed into one word: treachery! The old Edinburgh élite was guilty of the (Romantic) original sin: cutting themselves off from the people. Second only to "community" in this value-vocabulary is the unpleasant term "roots." The Enlightenment intelligentsia sold out its birthright—its roots in the Scottish national-popular community—for the sake of its pottage of tedious abstractions.[25] Sir James Steuart may be forgiven, as he happened to be a Jacobite. The rest were cosmopolitan *vendus* to a man: they may have invented social science, but their attitude towards Scotticisms was unpardonable. It was this wilful rootlessness that started the rot. "The cultural sell-out of Scottish standards . . . the failure of Scotland's political and cultural leaders to be their Scottish selves has created the intellectual and cultural void which is at the centre of Scottish affairs," states Duncan Glen in *Whither Scotland*? (1971). As for David Hume and that band: "We should give the opposite answers to those of the great philosopher who failed to rise above the attitudes of his time. Since then, however, we have had two hundred years of the Scottish waste of the potential of the Scottish people and we should surely have learned the correct answers by now . . ."

The simple idealism and voluntarism of this diagnosis should need no further stressing. It amounts to saying, *if only* the intellectuals had behaved differently, then our national history might have left its banks, and changed its course. It is not explanation, but retrospective necromancy. But it has as a consequence that the Scottish Enlightenment (as I pointed out above) recedes into a curious limbo of non-recognition, in the nationalist perspective. That is, the country's one moment of genuine historical importance, its sole claim to imperishable fame, literally does not count in the saga of the Scottish national Self. The triumph of Reason produced a wasteland void, as still thriving Romantic clichés would have us believe; not for the first or last time, the nationalist and the romantic "theories" are really one.

THE REFORMATION AS SCAPEGOAT

Lest it be thought that I am treating romanticism too cursorily, and dismissing its view of Scotland too lightly, I shall turn briefly to the most influential study of this kind. Edwin Muir's *Scott and Scotland* appeared in 1936, and has never been reissued. This is a pity, and rather surprising, for it is a book which has reappeared in other people's books and articles ever since. The copies in the Scottish National Library and the Edinburgh City Library must be particularly well-thumbed. No-one who has spent any time in the archives of literary nationalism can have failed to notice how often Muir is quoted, nearly always with approval.

How did he diagnose what happened to Scotland in the time of Scott? Muir is impressed particularly by what he calls "a curious emptiness" behind Scott's imaginative richness. The void is already there, as it were, within the work of the Wizard of the North. What caused it? It reflects the fact that Sir Walter lived in "a country which was neither a nation nor a province and had, instead of a centre, a blank, an Edinburgh, in the middle of it . . . Scott, in other words, lived in a community which was not a community, and set himself to carry on a tradition which was not a tradition . . . (and) . . . his work was an exact reflection of his predicament." Scott's predicament was, of course, also one "for the Scottish people as a whole . . . for only a people can create a literature." England, by contrast, is "an organic society" with a genuine centre and true *Volksgemeinschaft*. The English author has something to sink his roots into, while his Scottish colleague cannot "root himself deliberately in Scotland" since there *is* no soil—

no "organic community to round off his conceptions," and not even any real wish for such a society (i.e. no real nationalism).

The mainspring of this, as of all similar arguments, is that it bestows eternal validity, or "natural" status, upon certain categories of 19th-century culture and politics. It is true that all 19th-century nation-states, and societies which aspired to this status through nationalism, had to foster what one may (although somewhat metaphorically) call "organic community." That is, for the specific motives mentioned previously their middle classes invented a type of inter-class culture, employing romantic culture and ideology. It is true also that Scotland was structurally unable to adapt to an age in which these categories and motives became the norm. What is not true—though it is the crux of Muir's position—is that this represented some sort of metaphysical disaster which one must despair over.

Muir then goes on to trace (again in very characteristic terms) the dimensions of both disaster and despair. One learns, with some surprise, that the trouble started in the middle ages. The Enlightenment and capitalism are only late symptoms; it was in fact the Reformation which "truly signalized the beginning of Scotland's decline as a civilized nation." The last of "coherent civilization" in Scotland was at the court of James IV (early 16th century). The metaphysical ailment of the Scots, a split between heart and head, began shortly thereafter, that ". . . simple irresponsible feeling side by side with arid intellect . . . for which Gregory Smith found the name of 'the Caledonian Antisyzygy.' "[26] So, after the Catholic "organic community" had ended there was no hope, and Scotland was simply preparing itself for "the peculiarly brutal form which the Industrial Revolution took in Scotland, where its chief agents are only conceivable as thoughtless or perverted children."

A markedly oneiric element has crept into the argument somehow, and one wants to rub one's eyes. Can anybody really think this? Not only somebody, but most literary nationalists: it should not be imagined that this position represents a personal vagary of the author. It does have a bizarre dream-logic to it. Muir himself took his pessimism so seriously that not even nationalism seemed a solution to him. But broadly speaking the dream in question is that of romantic nationalism, and the logic is as follows: modern Scottish society does not fit it, and one has to explain why; since the idea-world (roots, organs, and all) is all right, and has unchallengeable status, it has to be Scotland which is wrong; therefore Scottish society and history are monstrously misshapen in some way, blighted by an Original Sin; therefore one should look further back for whatever led to the frightful Enlightenment ("arid intellect," etc.) and the Industrial Revolution; the Reformation is the obvious candidate, so before that things were pretty sound (a safe hypothesis, given the extent of knowledge about the 15th century in modern Scotland).[27]

Start with Idealism and you end up embracing the Scarlet Woman of Rome. I do not wish to dwell longer on this paradox now (though I shall need to refer to it again below). The aura of madness surrounding it is surely plain enough. Farther exploration of the oddities of nationalist ideology in Scotland had better wait until we come to the formation of the nationalist movement itself, in this century.

Before I get to this, some more remarks have to be made about the consequences of the Scottish inability to generate a nationalism in the last century.

THE EMIGRÉ INTELLIGENTSIA

I suggested above that Scotland can be seen as a "negative image" of general European nationalist development, and one which tells us much about that development. There is a sense in which it tells us more than any "positive" example could: for, of course, in all actual case-histories of nationalism general and highly specific factors are fused together almost inextricably. Whereas in Scotland, where so many particular factors favoured nationalism so powerfully, it is easier to detect (simply by its absence) what the basic causative mechanism must have been. It is in this sense that one may argue that Scotland furnishes a remarkable confirmation of the materialist conception of development and nationalism outlined previously.

But so far the argument has been couched in over-negative terms. We have seen why the development of bourgeois society in Scotland did *not* decree a form of nationalism, and the various "absences" which followed from this peculiar evolutionary twist. The Scottish bourgeoisie was *not* compelled to frame its own pseudo-organic "community" of culture, in order to channel popular energies behind its separate interest. Hence there was no serious romanticism as a continuing "tradition," and the indigenous intellectual class became in a curious sense "unemployed" or functionless upon its home terrain. The new Scottish working class, in its turn, was deprived of the normal type of 19th-century cultural "nationalization": that is, such popular-national culture as there was (vulgar Scottishism, or tartanry) was necessarily unrelated to a higher romantic-national and intellectual culture.

One of the most striking single consequences of this overall pattern was massive intellectual emigration. The 19th century also witnessed great working-class and peasant emigration, of course, but these were common to England and Ireland as well. The Scottish cultural outflow was distinctive, although it had much in common with similar trends in Ireland and the Italian south. The reasons for it are clear enough. The country was well provided with educational institutions and its higher culture did not vanish overnight. However, it certainly changed direction, and assumed a markedly different pattern. Its achievements in the century that followed were to be largely in the areas of natural science, technology and medicine—not in the old 18th century ones of social science, philosophy, and general culture. And of course it was what happened to the latter that is most related to the problem of nationalism, and concerns us here. It is in *this* crucial zone that one may speak of "unemployment," and hence of the forced emigration of the sort of intellectual who elsewhere in Europe was forging a national or nationalist culture.

After the time of Sir Walter Scott, wrote the Victorian critic J. H. Robertson, "... we lost the culture-force of a local literary atmosphere; and defect superinduces defect, till it becomes almost a matter of course that our best men, unless tethered by professorships, go south."[28] In his *Scottish Literature and the Scottish People* the contemporary critic David Craig makes a similar point: "During the 19th century the country was emptied of the *majority* of its notable literary talents—men who, if they had stayed, might have thought to mediate their wisdom through the rendering of specifically Scottish experience. Of the leading British 'sages' of the time an astonishingly high proportion were of Scottish extraction—the Mills, Macaulay, Carlyle, Ruskin, Gladstone."[29] This last is an especially characteristic judgment, with its suggestion of retrospective voluntarism: *if only* the émigrés had chosen to stay at home, then it might all have been different. The point was that in reality they had no such "choice": "specifically Scottish experience" in the sense relevant here would have been a product of culture, not its natural, pre-existent basis—and since Scottish society did not demand the formation of that culture, there *was* no "experience" and nothing to be said. This phase of the country's history demonstrates, with exceptional vividness, both the social nature and the material basis of "culture" in the usual intellectuals' sense. It may look as if it could have simply come "out of people's heads," by free choice; in reality it could not.

There is no time here to say more about the fascinating history of the émigrés and their impact upon the neighbour kingdom. But in a broad sense there is no doubt what happened: unable, for the structural reasons described, to fulfill the "standard" 19th-century function of elaborating a romantic-national culture for their own people, they applied themselves with vigour to the unfortunate southerners. Our former intelligentsia lost its cohesion and unitary function (its nature *as* an élite) and the individual members poured their formidable energies into the authentically "organic community" centred on London. There, they played a very large part in formulating the new national and imperial culture-community. We must all be at times painfully aware of how England to this day languishes under the "tradition" created by the Carlyle-Ruskin school of mystification, as well as the brilliant political inheritance nurtured by Keir Hardie and J. Ramsay MacDonald.

In one way this can be considered a typical form of "provincialization" which went on in all the greater nation-states. Everywhere hungry and ambitious intellectuals were drawn out of their hinterlands and into the cultural service of their respective capitals. If there was a significant difference here, it lay surely in the higher level and stronger base from which the Scots started. These enabled them, perhaps, to make a contribution at once more important and more distinctive in character. They did not come from a province of an *ancien régime*, but from an advanced quasi-nation with a high (if now anachronistic) culture of its own, and so had a head-start on other backwoodsmen.

NOTES

1. "L'Internationalisation des rapports capitalistes et l'état-nation," *Les Temps Modernes*, no. 319, February 1973 pp. 1492–3.

2. *Les Temps Modernes*, nos. 324–6, August–September 1973.

3. Vallecchi, Florence 1973.

4. Miroslav Hroch, *Die Vorkämpfer der nationalen Bewegung bei den kleinen Völkern Europas*, Prague 1968, a study of the formation and early stages of nationalism in Bohemia, Slovakia, Norway, Finland, Estonia, Lithuania and Flanders.

5. There is no room to discuss this further. The reader will find useful surveys of nationalist theory in Aira Kemiläinen, *Nationalism: Problems Concerning the Word, the Concept and Classification*, London 1964, and in Anthony D. Smith, *Theories of Nationalism*, London 1971. One attempt to relate older theories of nationalism to contemporary developments is P. Fougeyrollas, *Pour une France Fédérale: vers l'unité européenne par la révolution régionale*, Paris 1968, especially Part I, chapters 1 and 2.

6. "Nationalism" in the volume *Thought and Change*, London 1964, the most important and influential recent study in English.

7. *The Idea of Progress*, London 1968, p. 46.

8. A. D. Smith, *Theories of Nationalism*, p. 83.

9. E. J. Hobsbawm, *The Age of Revolution: Europe 1789–1848*, London 1962, pp. 133–5.

10. I cannot refrain here from citing a criticism of the author made by the Scottish nationalist writer John Herdman, in his contribution to Duncan Glen's *Whither Scotland?* He castigates my unduly material conception of the purpose of development (in an earlier essay called "Three Dreams of Scottish Nationalism," *New Left Review* no. 49, May–June 1968, reprinted in Karl Miller's *Memoirs of a Modern Scotland*, 1970) and observes that: "To my mind both these (material) purposes are secondary and subservient to the mobilizing of populations for *spiritual* development. I dislike the word but cannot think of a better one . . ." (p. 109). And what does such spiritual development counter? The unacceptable face of "progress," as shown in "a nation which has become the very embodiment of anti-civilization, of an amorphous mass culture which is ignoble, ugly and debased." This is England of course. But it might equally well be France, as once seen by German nationalists; Germany, as once seen by Panslavism; America, as now seen by half the world; the USSR, as seen by the Chinese . . . and so on. By contrast Scotland's spiritual solution is (again very characteristically) "the difficult assumption of a cultural independence which will give a new dynamic to the country" (Duncan Glen, op. cit., p. 22).

11. Naturally, the anti-nationalist bias tends to be somewhat more revealing; yet this is to say little. The most interesting strain of bourgeois anti-nationalism is the conservative one deriving from Lord Acton's essay on "Nationality" (1862, reprinted in *Essays*, ed. G. Himmelfarb, 1949). But really very little has been added to it since, as one may see by consulting, e.g. Professor E. Kedourie's Actonian volume *Nationalism*, London 1960. It is significant in this connection that the first sensible progress in nationalism-theory was made after the First World War by scholars in America who had established a sufficient distance from Europe (the Hayes and Kohn schools). While with few exceptions further serious contributions have been made via the study of Third World "development" since the Second World War, especially by sociologists. All three stances (social conservatism, the vantage point of an—at that time—less nationalist USA, and Third Worldism) have permitted varying degrees of psychic detachment from the core of the nationalist thought-world.

12. The outstanding study of the problem of "historyless peoples" from a Marxist point of view is R. Rosdolsky, *Friedrich Engels und das Problem der "Geschichtslosen Völker,"* Hannover 1964, offprint from *Archiv für Socialgeschichte*, vol. 4, 1964.

13. Beginning with modern Greece, that first model and inspiration of nationalist re-

volts throughout Europe. There the gap between present realities and past history was so enormous that the new intellectuals had to create the new myths *de toutes pièces*. As one (notably pro-Greek) author says: "Those who spoke the Greek language . . . had no notion of classical Greece or of the Hellenistic civilization of Roman times . . . The classical ruins were quite unintelligible to early modern Greeks . . . From Roman times the Greeks had called themselves 'Romans' and continued to do so up to and during the War of Independence," D. Dakin, *The Greek Struggle for Independence 1821–1833*, London 1973, pp. 11–22.

14. William Robertson, *History of Scotland*, 1803, in *Works*, 1817, vol. 3, pp. 188–200.

15. T. C. Smout, *A History of the Scottish People 1560–1830*, 1969, p. 33.

16. Even more to the point perhaps, one need only think of the period just before 1707—that is, the period of the Scottish bourgeoisie's last attempt at separate and competitive development through the colonization of Darien. This was destroyed largely throu; h English pressures. Can anyone imagine that under 19th-century conditions this *débâc* e would have been forgiven and realistically forgotten? On the contrary, it would have een turned into a compelling popular reason for still more aggressive separate (i.e. natior list) development. As things were, in the pre-nationalist age this tailor-made nationalist tragedy led straight to the 1707 Union.

17. As the editor of the recent Edinburgh edition of the *Essay* states: "Adam Ferguson *was* a Highlander . . . and undoubtedly behind the *Essay* lies a deeply felt experience of the contrast between these two societies, and the question: what happens to man in the progress of society? Ferguson knew intimately, and from the inside, the two civilizations . . . which divided 18th-century Scotland: the *Gemeinschaft* of the clan, the *Gesellschaft* of the 'progressive,' commercial Lowlands." Duncan Forbes, Introduction pp. xxxviii–xxxix, 1966 edition.

18. David Craig, *Scottish Literature and the Scottish People, 1680–1830*, Edinburgh, 1961, pp. 13–14, 273.

19. T. C. Smout, op. cit., p. 226.

20. Ibid., pp. 484–5.

21. Lukács' essay is also reprinted in *Scott's Mind and Art*, ed. Jeffares, Edinburgh 1969. Thomas Carlyle's influential essay on Scott appeared in the *London and Westminster Review* (1838), and is partly reprinted in *Scott: the Critical Heritage*, ed. J. Hayden, London 1970.

22. J. G. Lockhart, *The Life of Sir Walter Scott* (1837–8), Everyman's abridged edition, 1906, p. 653.

23. *Memorials of His Time*, by Lord Cockburn (1856), abridged edition, 1946, pp. 64–5.

24. Hroch, op. cit., pp. 160–1; see also E. J. Hobsbawm, "Nationalism," in *Imagination and Precision in the Social Sciences*, London 1972, p. 399.

25. An interesting recent example of this was provided by the nationalist Stephen Maxwell, in censuring some favourable remarks I had made about the Scottish Enlightenment in *Scottish International* (April 1973). Replying in the following issue of the review he condemned their "intellectualism" as "a symptom of the schizophrenia in Scottish culture that eventually issued in the 'kailyard' and was partly responsible for obstructing an adequate radical response in Scotland to the problems of 19th-century industrialism . . ." Exactly: the 18th century is to blame for everything, even my own lamentable views!

26. This curious bacillus can be traced back to G. Gregory Smith, *Scottish Literature: Character and Influence* (1919). It explodes unpronounceably in the archives of literary

nationalism quite often after that—e.g. MacDiarmid: ''The Caledonian Antisyzygy . . . may be awaiting the exhaustion of the whole civilization of which English literature is a typical product in order to achieve its effective synthesis in a succeeding and very different civilization'' (*Albyn*, 1927, p. 34).

27. Edwin Muir, op. cit., pp. 22–4, 73–5.
28. J. H. Robertson, *Critiscisms*, vol. II (1885), p. 67.
29. Craig, op. cit., p. 276.

Anthony D. Smith

A reader in sociology at the London School of Economics and Political Science, Anthony D. Smith is the prolific producer of a series of theoretical and empirical investigations into nations and nationalism. From *Theories of Nationalism* (London: Duckworth, 1971) through *Nationalism in the Twentieth Century* (Oxford: Martin Robertson, 1979), *The Ethnic Revival* (Cambridge: Cambridge University Press, 1981), and *The Ethnic Origins of Nations* (Oxford: Basil Blackwell, 1986), Smith established himself as the foremost English-language proponent of what might be called the "ethnic continuationist" view of nations. His argument differs from both the "modernists," like Ernest Gellner, Tom Nairn, and Benedict Anderson, who contend that nations were uniquely the product of the post-eighteenth-century transformations of society and consciousness, and the "primordialists," who range from nationalists to sociobiologists and argue that ethnicity is a kind of kinship in which an essence of the nation is eternally present and ready to emerge under the right historical conditions. Influenced by John Armstrong's macrohistorical study, *Nations before Nationalism* (Chapel Hill: University of North Carolina, 1982), Smith locates the durability and special quality of the national in myths, memories, values, and symbols. For Smith, "there can be no identity without memory (albeit selective), no collective purpose without myth, and identity, and purpose or destiny are necessary elements of the very concept of a nation." Before there were nations in the modern sense, there were *ethnies*, communities with a collective name, a common myth of descent, a shared history, a distinctive shared culture, a sense of solidarity, and an association with a specific territory. However these ethnies may have coalesced, whether through interstate warfare, a shared religion, or nostalgia for a lost past, they provided a durable sense of identity that became the basis for the formation of modern territorialized nations. Though the modern nation is far more inclusive and far more able to mobilize its members than any ethnie, Smith constantly emphasizes the continuing elements between premodern and modern communities, rather than the novelty of the latter. "Put simply," he concludes, "modern nations are not as 'modern' as modernists would have us believe. If they were, they could not survive."

The Origins of Nations

Anyone exploring the shape and origins of the modern world must soon stumble on the power and ubiquity of nations. In a sense, nothing so clearly marks out the modern era and defines our attitudes and sentiments as national consciousness and nationalist ideology. Not only in everyday political and social life, but also in our underlying assumptions, the nation and its nationalism provide a stable framework for good or ill and define the goals and values of most collective activity. The modern world has become inconceivable and unintelligible without nations and nationalism; international relations, in particular, though they deal in the first place with the relations between states, are built around the premises of nationalism.

It follows that a fundamental way to grasp the nature and shape of the modern world is through an exploration of the nature and origins of nations. This is, of course, a vast subject whose investigation could fill several volumes. Here I can only look at the broad outlines of such an investigation. In particular, I shall be concerned with the "prehistory" of nations, the way in which collective identities in pre-modern eras helped to shape modern nations. Only in this way through an historical and sociological exploration of how pre-modern communities shaped our world of nations, can we really begin to grasp the power and significance of today's nations and nationalism.

THE "NATION" AND "NATIONALISM"

We can begin by narrowing down our enquiry to three questions. The first concerns the relationship between abstractions and realities. The "nation" is often seen as an abstraction, something that nationalists, and élites in general, have "constructed" to serve their partisan ends. On this reading, nations lack tangibility or any "primordial" character. They constitute mere ideals, or mere legitimations and political arguments (Breuilly 1982, pp. 1–41; Hobsbawm and Ranger 1983; Sathyamurthy 1983).

Against this fashionable view, the so-called "primordialists" argued for the "reality" of nations, and the almost "natural" quality of ethnic belonging. National sentiment is no construct, it has a real, tangible, mass base. At its root is a feeling of kinship, of the extended family, that distinguishes national from every other kind of group sentiment (Connor 1978; Fishman 1980; Smith 1981a, pp. 63–86; Horowitz 1985, pp. 55–92; Stack 1986, pp. 1–11).

Clearly, our investigation of the origins of nations cannot proceed far, until this fundamental question of whether the nation be viewed as construct or real historical process is resolved.

The second question is linked to the first. I have emphasized the importance, indeed the indispensability, of nations in the modern era and the modern world. The question arises whether it is fundamental in other eras and pre-modern worlds. Was there "nationalism" in antiquity? Can we find "nations" in medieval Europe or Asia? In part, of course, the answer will hinge on our definition of the nation; but equally, it will reflect our reading of the global historical process. If the "modernists" are right, if the nation is a fundamental feature only of the modern world, this will support, prima facie, the idea that nations are primarily abstractions and élite constructs. However, if the "perennialists" turn out to be nearer the mark, and we find nations and nationalism prior to the rise of the modern world from the sixteenth century (or the French Revolution) onwards, we may well have to change our view of the whole historical process. Nations might still be constructs, but ancient élites, or medieval ones, might be as adept at inventing them as their modern counterparts. This would inevitably devalue the importance attributed to specifically "modern" developments, like bureaucracy and capitalism, in the rise of nations, which "modernists" tend to emphasize (Nairn 1977, pp. 92–125; Anderson 1983; Gellner 1983).

The last question again concerns the nature of the concept of the nation. Should we view it as a largely political unit, or mainly a social and cultural entity? Can there be a cultural nationalism, which is not also ipso facto political? Or should we regard nations as operating on all these levels at once? These are important questions when it comes to looking at the political ramifications of the nation. Again, there are those who would downgrade its cultural importance for collective identity (Breuilly 1982); while others emphasize questions of cultural identity and social cohesion (Barnard 1965; Hutchinson 1987).

The answers to these three sets of questions will, I think, furnish important clues to our exploration of the processes by which nations were formed.

Let me start with a working definition of the nation. A nation is a named community of history and culture, possessing a unified territory, economy, mass education system and common legal rights. I take this definition from the ideals and blueprints of generations of nationalists and their followers. It sums up an "ideal type" of the nation that is fairly widely accepted today, even if given units of population aspiring to be full nations in this sense, lack one or other of these characteristics in lesser or greater degree. For example, in a unit of population aspiring to constitute a full nation, certain categories of the population may be excluded from the full exercise of the common legal rights. Or they may not enjoy equal access to the common system of education, or equal mobility in the territorial economy. Alternatively, they may enjoy all these attributes and rights, yet be treated by the majority as in some sense cultural aliens, standing outside the sense of history and much of the culture of the majority, as the Jews were felt to be at the time of Dreyfus, both in France and outside, or the Asians in East Africa after decolonization.

What this means is that the nation is not a once-for-all, all-or-nothing, concept; and that historical nations are ongoing processes, sometimes slow in their formation, at other times faster, often jagged and discontinuous, as some features emerge or are created, while others lag. In Europe, nations have been forming, I would argue, from the medieval period; in several other parts of the world, this process, or processes, have been more recent. It also means that both objective factors outside human control, and human will and action, go into the creation of nations. Geographical environment, and the political accidents of warfare, may provide a setting for a group to form into a nation; but, whether it will subsequently do so, may depend on how far the group, or its ruling classes, become conscious of their identity, and reinforce it through education, legal codes and administrative centralization (Tilly 1975, pp. 3–163).[1]

If this is accepted, it means in turn that nations can be seen as both constructs or visions of nationalist (or other) élites, but equally as real, historical formations that embody a number of analytically separable processes over long time-spans. It is these processes, as much as any visions, that form the object of our analysis.

Where does this leave "nationalism"? I should define nationalism as an ideological movement for attaining and maintaining the autonomy, unity and identity of an existing or potential "nation." I should also stress its often minority status as a movement. As a movement, nationalism often antedates, and seeks to create, the nation, even if it often pretends that the nation already exists (Smith 1973a; 1983a, pp. 153–81).

Of course, nationalists cannot, and do not, create nations *ex nihilo*. There must be, at least, some elements in the chosen population and its social environment who favour the aspirations and activities of the nationalist visionaries. To achieve their common goals—autonomy, unity, identity—there need to be some core networks of association and culture, around which and on which nations can be "built." Language groups are usually regarded as the basic network of nations; but religious sects, like the Druse, Sikhs or Maronites may also form the starting-point for "reconstructing" the nation. So may a certain kind of historic territory, for example, the mountain fastnesses of Switzerland or Kurdistan, or island homelands like Iceland or Japan.

Besides, not all nations are the product of nationalist political endeavour. The English or Castilian nations, for example, owed more to state centralization, warfare and cultural homogeneity than to any nationalist movement. Vital for any nation is the growth and spread of a "national sentiment" outwards from the centre and usually downwards through the strata of the population. It is in and through the myths and symbols of the common past that such a national sentiment finds its expression; and these too may develop over long periods.[2]

THE "ETHNIC CORE"

So much for initial definitions. Let us turn to the processes of nation-formation themselves.

At the turn of this century, it was quite common to argue that nations were immemorial. People talked of the ancient Greek, Persian and Egyptian nations, and even equated them with the present-day nations of those names. They certainly saw modern Bulgarian or French nations as the lineal descendants of their medieval counterparts. The familiar view was that nations were natural and perennial; people had a nationality much as they had speech or sight. Clearly, such a view of the nation is untenable. Nations are not perennial; they can be formed, and human will and effort play an important part in the process. People can also change their nationality, or at least their descendants can, over a period of time. Moreover, it is extremely doubtful, at the least, whether modern Greeks, Persians and Egyptians are lineal descendants of ancient Greeks, Persians and Egyptians. Are we not guilty here of a "retrospective nationalism" to epochs that lacked all sense of nationality (Levi 1965; Breuilly 1982)?

For these reasons, recent scholars have tended to emphasize the modernity of nations. The modernists argue that the nation is a modern construct of nationalists and other élites, and the product of peculiarly modern conditions like industrialism. They point out that ancient Egypt and even ancient Greece could boast no standardized, public, mass-education system, and that common legal rights, in so far as they existed, were restricted to particular classes. Because of its territorial unity, ancient Egypt did indeed enjoy more of a common economy than other ancient kingdoms, but it was unusual. In Assyria, Greece, Persia and China, local economies of different regions reflected a lack of territorial compactness of a kind unknown in the contemporary world.[3]

Clearly, in antiquity and much of the medieval era, nations in the sense that we have defined them, viz. named communities of history and culture, possessed of unified territories, economies, education systems and common legal rights, are rarely, if ever, to be found. Yet does this mean that there were no durable cultural communities in antiquity or the Middle Ages? Are we being retrospective nationalists in attributing some common history and culture to ancient Greeks and Persians or medieval Serbs and Irish? I think not. Despite the many changes that these cultures had undergone, they remained recognizably distinct to their own populations and to outsiders; and cultural differentiation was as vital a factor in social life then as now. The only difference then was that the scope and role of cultural diversity operated more at the social than the political level, but even this varied between peoples and eras.

Moreover, cultural differences, then as now, were not just a matter of outside observation. The people who possessed specific cultural attributes often formed a social network or series of networks, which over the generations became what we today designate "ethnic communities." These communities of history and culture generally display a syndrome of characteristics, by which they are usually recognized. These include:

1. a common name for the unit of population included;
2. a set of myths of common origins and descent for that population;

3. some common historical memories of things experienced together;
4. a common "historic territory" or "homeland," or an association with one;
5. one or more elements of common culture—language, customs, or religion;
6. a sense of solidarity among most members of the community.

I shall call the communities that manifest these characteristics (to a lesser or greater degree) *ethnies* (the French equivalent of the ancient Greek *ethnos*), as there is no single English-language equivalent. By no means all the cultural differences that scholars have distinguished in pre-modern or modern eras, are mirrored in such *ethnies*. Many remain as "ethnic categories"; certainly, in the past, the speakers of, say, Slovakian or Ukrainian dialects, were hardly conscious of their membership in any community. It had to wait for the rise of a romantic nationalism to build communities out of these and other differences (Brock 1976; Szporluk 1979).[4]

However, that still leaves a multitude of *ethnies* in the ancient and medieval worlds, which at first sight resemble, but are not, nations. For example, in Sassanid Persia between the third and seventh century A.D., we find a population group with a common name; a sense of a common homeland of "Iran" that the members opposed to another fabled land of enemies, "Turan"; some common historical memories and myths of descent related to Zoroaster and the Achaemenid kings; and a sense of solidarity, ever renewed by the protracted struggle with Byzantium (Frye 1966, pp. 235–62; *Cambridge History of Iran* 1983, vol. III/1, pp. 359–477).

Although it was divided, both into *poleis* and into sub-ethnic communities, ancient Greece could also be described as an *ethnie* in this sense. We find there, too, a common name, Hellas; a set of common-origin myths about the Greeks and their main divisions; common historical memories centered the Homeric canon; common Greek dialects and a common Greek pantheon of Olympic deities; an attachment to the Greek "homeland" around the Aegean; and, above all, a shared sense of being "Greek" and not "barbarian." This did not mean that many Greeks did not intermarry, that Greek *poleis* did not fight each other most of the time, that they did not form alliances with the Persians against each other, and so on. Yet all Greeks recognized their common Greek heritage and a common Greek cultural community (Fondation Hardt 1962; Andrewes 1965; Alty 1982; Finley 1986, pp. 120–33).

Perhaps the best-known of ancient and medieval *ethnie*, the Jews, managed to retain their distinctive identity, even when most of their members were scattered in diaspora communities. A common name, common myths of origin and descent, sedulously fostered, a whole canon of historical memories centred on charismatic heroes, a common liturgical language and script, an attachment to Eretz Israel wherever they might find themselves and especially to Jerusalem, all fed a strong bond of ethnic solidarity, which outside hostility renewed with almost monotonous regularity. Again, these bonds did not prevent apostasy, intermarriage or internal class and cultural divisions, particularly between Jews of the Ashkenazi and Sephardi rite (Hirschberg 1969; Barnett 1971; Raphael 1985).

One last example, this time from medieval western Europe, must suffice to illustrate the range of *ethnies*. Apart from their fame as builders of massive castles and cathedrals in the Romanesque style, the Normans evinced a common myth of origins and descent from Duke Rollo, a common name and historical memories of warfare and colonization, common customs and adopted language, along with an attachment to the duchy in northern France that they had conquered and settled. Above all, they maintained for nearly three centuries their *esprit de corps* as a warrior community, even when they conquered Ireland and Sicily (Jones 1973, pp. 204–40; Davis 1976).

"VERTICAL" AND "LATERAL" ETHNIES

What all these examples have in common is an underlying sense of historical and cultural community. This sense of community pervades and regulates their social life and culture, spilling over at times into the political and military realms. On the other hand, it rarely determines their economic conditions of existence. Generally speaking, economic localism and a subsistence economy fragment the community into a series of interlocking networks. What unites these networks, in so far as it does so, is the common fund of myths, symbols, memories and values that make up the distinctive traditions passed down the generations. Through common customs and rituals, languages, arts and liturgies, this complex of myths, symbols, values and memories ensures the survival of the sense of common ethnicity, of the sense of common descent and belonging, which characterizes a "community of fate."

Yet, the example of the Norman conquerors introduces a vital distinction. As with the Sassanid Persians, but even more so, it was really only the upper strata, especially around the Court and priesthoods that constituted the Norman *ethnie*. The myths of descent and the memories of battle clustered around the ruling house; it was their genealogies and their exploits that Dudo of St. Quentin and Orderic Vitalis were called on to record and extol. At the same time, the ruling house represented a whole upper stratum of warrior-aristocrats who had founded a *regnum* in Normandy, based on common customs and myths of descent. Other classes were simply subsumed under those customs and myths; and quite often, the latter were amalgams of the heritage of the conquerors and the conquered (Reynolds 1983).

Compared, however, to the community of Greeks or Jews, that of the Norman or Sassanid Persian ruling classes was rather limited. In one sense, it was wider. The sense of common ethnicity went wherever Normans sailed, and Persian arms conquered. In another sense, it was shallower. It never really reached far down the social scale. For all Kartir's attempts to institute Zoroastrian fire-worship as a state religion, many of the Persian peasants were untouched. Although Chosroes I (A.D. 531–79) attempted to revive ancient Persian culture, he was unable to stabilize the Persian state by extending a sense of common Persian ethnicity. As McNeill puts it: "As with other urban civilizations that lacked real roots in the countryside, the results were grand and artificial, in theology as in architecture;

and Moslem conquest cut off the entire tradition in the seventh century, just as Alexander's victories had earlier disrupted the high culture of the Achaemenids" (McNeill 1963, p. 400).

This is, perhaps, going too far. A sense of specifically Persian ethnicity remained beneath Islamization, after the Sassanid armies were defeated by the Arabs at Nihavand (642 A.D.). Islam even stimulated a Persian renaissance in poetry and the arts in the tenth and eleventh centuries, a renaissance that looked back for its inspiration to Chosroes and the Sassanids (*Cambridge History of Iran* 1975, vol. IV, pp. 595–632).

Yet the basic point remains. The Persian Sassanid *ethnie*, like the Norman, the Hittite or the Philistine, was socially limited. It was an aristocratic and "lateral" *ethnie*, as territorially wide as it was lacking in social depth. In contrast to this type, with its ragged boundaries and aristocratic culture, we find communities with much more compact boundaries, a more socially diffused culture and a greater degree of popular mobilization and fervour. This type of *ethnie* we may call "vertical" and "demotic." The Armenians, Greeks and Jews are classic examples, despite their territorial dispersion, because they lived in often segregated enclaves once they had left their clearly defined homelands. Other examples of "demotic" or "vertical" *ethnies* include the Irish, Basques, Welsh, Bretons, Czechs and Serbs, as well as the Druse, Sikhs and Maronites. Such *ethnies* are as stratified as any other, but the strata all share in a common heritage and culture, and in the common defence. Hence the ethnic bond is more exclusive and intensive, and the boundaries are more marked and more strongly upheld. Thus, in contrast to the looser ties that characterized the Philistine aristocratic pentapolis, the Israelite tribal confederation was from the outset marked by a greater ethnocentric zeal and communal mobilization for war, as well as greater ritual involvement of all strata (Kitchen 1973; Seltzer 1980, pp. 7–43).[5]

The distinction between "lateral" and "vertical" types of *ethnie* is important for a number of reasons. First, because it highlights a source of conflict between pre-modern ethnic communities, as aristocratic lateral *ethnie* attempted to incorporate and subdue different demotic vertical communities. It also suggests why many *ethnies*, especially of the more demotic variety, persisted over long periods, even when they experienced "character change." The Greek *ethnie*, for example, within the Eastern Roman empire was transformed in many ways by the influx of Slav immigrants. Yet they did not basically change the cultural and religious framework of Greek ethnicity, even though they grafted their customs and mores onto an existing Hellenic culture, especially in the countryside (Campbell and Sherrard 1968, pp. 19–49; Armstrong 1982, pp. 168–200). Similarly, a tenuous sense of Egyptian identity persisted even after the Arab conquest in the seventh century A.D., especially among Copts, despite the fact that any attempts to trace "descent" back to the inhabitants of ancient Egypt were bound to run into the sands. The point is that cultural forms and frameworks may outlive their physical bearers, and even the "character change" of cultural content that new immigrants and new religious movements bring with them (Atiya 1968, pp. 79–98).

One result of ethnic survival and coexistence over the long term is a patchwork or mosaic of *ethnies* in varying relationships of status and power. Quite often we find a dominant lateral *ethnie* of landowning aristocrats like the Magyar knights or Polish *szlachta* exploiting a peasantry of different culture, Croat or Ukrainian, and so helping to preserve these cultural differences as "ethno-classes." Wherever we find lateral *ethnies* attempting to expand into territories populated by demotic, vertical communities of culture, the opportunities for a "frozen" ethnic stratification to develop are greatly increased. This has occurred, not only in Eastern Europe, but in the Middle East, southeast Asia and parts of Africa. The overall result is to preserve ethnic difference and identity right up to the onset of the age of nationalism, and afford ready-made bases for political movements of autonomy (Seton-Watson 1977, pp. 15–142; Orridge 1982).

Already certain implications of the foregoing analysis can be clarified. Only in this modern era could we expect to find unified divisions of labour, mass, public education systems and equal legal rights, all of which have come to be part and parcel of a common understanding of what we mean by the concept of the nation. Moreover, the "modernists" are right when they speak of nations being "reconstructed" (but not "invented") out of pre-existing social networks and cultural elements, often by intellectuals.

The modernist definition of the nation omits important components. Even today, a nation qua nation must possess a common history and culture, that is to say, common myths of origin and descent, common memories and common symbols of culture. Otherwise, we should be speaking only of territorial states. It is the conjunction, and interpenetration, of these cultural or "ethnic" elements with the political, territorial, educational and economic ones, that we may term "civic," that produce a modern nation. Today's nations are as much in need of common myths, memories and symbols, as were yesterday's *ethnies*, for it is these former that help to create and preserve the networks of solidarity that underpin and characterize nations. They also endow nations with their individuality. So that, while nations can be read as reconstructions of intellectual and other élites, they are also legitimately viewed as configurations of historical processes, which can be analysed as real trends.[6]

Because nations embody ethnic as well as civic components, they tend to form around pre-existing "ethnic cores." The fact that pre-modern eras have been characterized by different types of *ethnie* is therefore vital to our understanding of the ways in which modern nations emerged. The number, location and durability of such *ethnies* are crucial for the formation of historical nations. The relations of power and exploitation between different kinds of *ethnie* also help to determine the bases for historical nations. It is this latter circumstance that provides an essential key to the processes of nation-formation in modern times.

BUREAUCRATIC "INCORPORATION"

The two basic kinds of ethnic core, the lateral and the vertical, also furnish the two main routes by which nations have been created.

Taking the lateral route first, we find that aristocratic *ethnies* have the potential for self-perpetuation, provided they can incorporate other strata of the population.

A good many of these lateral *ethnies* cannot do so. Hittites, Philistines, Mycenaeans, even Assyrians, failed to do so, and they and their cultures disappeared with the demise of their states (Burney and Lang 1971, pp. 86–126; Kitchen 1973; Saggs 1984, pp. 117–21). Other lateral *ethnies* survived by "changing their character," as we saw with Persians, Egyptians and Ottoman Turks, while preserving a sense of common descent and some dim collective memories.

Still others grafted new ethnic and cultural elements onto their common fund of myths, symbols and memories, and spread them out from the core area and down through the social scale. They did so, of course, in varying degrees. The efforts of the Amhara kings, for example, were rather limited in scope; yet they managed to retain their Monophysite Abyssinian identity in their heartlands (Atiya 1968; Ullendorff 1973, pp. 54–92). That of the Castilians was more successful. They managed to form the core of a Spanish state (and empire) that expelled the Muslim rulers and almost united the Iberian peninsula. Yet, even their success pales before that of their Frankish and Norman counterparts.

In fact, the latter three efforts at "bureaucratic incorporation" were to prove of seminal historical importance. In all three cases, lower strata and outlying regions were gradually incorporated in the state, which was grounded upon a dominant ethnic core. This was achieved by administrative and fiscal means, and by the mobilization of sections of the populations for inter-state warfare, as in the Anglo-French wars (Keeney 1972). An upper-class *ethnie*, in other words, managed to evolve a relatively strong and stable administrative apparatus, which could be used to provide cultural regulation and thereby define a new and wider cultural identity (Corrigan and Sayer 1985). In practice, this meant varying degrees of accommodation between the upper-class culture and those prevalent among the lower strata and peripheral regions; yet it was the upper-class culture that set its stamp on the state and on the evolving national identity.

Perhaps the most clear-cut example is afforded by British developments. As there had been an Anglo-Saxon kingdom based originally on Wessex before the Norman Conquest, the conquered populations could not be treated simply as a servile peasantry. As a result, we find considerable intermarriage, linguistic borrowing, élite mobility and finally a fusion of linguistic culture, within a common religio-political framework.

In other words, bureaucratic incorporation of subject *ethnies* entailed a considerable measure of cultural fusion and social intermingling between Anglo-Saxon, Danish and Norman elements, especially from the thirteenth century on. By the time of Edward III and the Anglo-French and Scottish wars, linguistic fusion had stabilized into Chaucerian English and a "British" myth served to weld the disparate ethnic communities together (Seton-Watson 1977, pp. 22–31; Smith 1985).

I am not arguing that an English nation was fully formed by the late fourteenth century. There was little economic unity as yet, despite growing fiscal and judicial intervention by the royal state. The boundaries of the kingdom, too, both with Scotland and in France, were often in dispute. In no sense can one speak of a public, mass-education system, even for the middle classes. As for legal rights, despite the assumptions behind Magna Carta, they were common to all only in the most minimal senses. For the full development of these civic elements of nationhood, one would have to wait for the Industrial Revolution and its effects (Reynolds 1984, pp. 250–331).

The ethnic elements of the nation, on the other hand, were well developed. By the fourteenth century or slightly later, a common name and myth of descent, promulgated originally by Geoffrey of Monmouth, were widely current, as were a variety of historical memories (MacDougall 1982, pp. 7–17). These were fed by the fortunes of wars in Scotland and France. Similarly, a sense of common culture based on language and ecclesiastical organization had emerged. So had a common strong attachment to the homeland of the island kingdom, which in turn bred a sense of solidarity, despite internal class-cleavages. The bases of both the unitary state and a compact nation had been laid, and laid by a lateral Norman-origin *ethnie* that was able to develop its regnal administration to incorporate the Anglo-Saxon population. Yet the full ideology of Englishness had to wait for late-sixteenth- and seventeenth-century developments, when the old British myth gave way to a more potent middle-class "Saxon" mythology of ancient liberties (MacDougall 1982, chs. 2–4).

A similar process of bureaucratic incorporation by an upper-class lateral *ethnie* can be discerned in France. Some fusion of upper-stratum Frankish with subject Romano-Gallic culture occurred under the Christianized Merovingians, but a regnal solidarity is really only apparent in northern France at the end of the twelfth century. It was in this era that earlier myths of Trojan descent, applied to the Franks, were resuscitated for all the people of northern France. At the same time, the *pays d'oc*, with its different language, customs and myths of descent, remained for some time outside the orbit of northern bureaucratic incorporation (Reynolds 1984, pp. 276–89; Bloch 1961, vol. II, pp. 431–7).

Of course, Capetian bureaucratic incorporation from Philip II onwards was able to draw on the glory and myths of the old Frankish kingdom and Charlemagne's heritage. This was partly because the kingdom of the Eastern Franks came to be known as the *regnum Teutonicorum*, with a separate identity. However, it was also due to the special link between French dynasties and the Church, notably the archbishopric of Rheims. The backing of the French clergy, and the ceremony of anointing at coronations, were probably more crucial to the prestige and survival of a French monarchy in northern France before the battle of Bouvines (1214) than the fame of the schools of Paris or even the military tenacity of the early Capetians. There was a sacred quality inhering in the dynastic *mythomoteur* of the Capetians and their territory that went back to the Papal coronation of Charlemagne and Papal legitimation of Pepin's usurpation in A.D. 754, which the Pope called a "new kingdom of David." The religious language is echoed centuries later, when at the end of the thirteenth century Pope Boniface declared: ". . . like the people of Israel . . . the kingdom of France [is] a peculiar people chosen by the Lord to carry out the orders of Heaven" (Davis 1958, pp. 298–313; Lewis 1974, pp. 57–70; Armstrong 1982, pp. 152–9).

Though there is much debate as to the "feudal" nature of the Capetian monarchy, the undoubted fact is that an originally Frankish ruling-class *ethnie* managed, after many vicissitudes, to establish a relatively efficient and centralized royal administration over north and central France (later southern France). So it became able to furnish those "civic" elements of compact territory, unified economy, and linguistic and legal standardization that from the seventeenth century onwards spurred the formation of a French nation as we know it. The process, however, was not completed until the end of the nineteenth century. Many regions retained their local character, even after the French Revolution. It required the application of Jacobin nationalism to mass education and conscription under the Third Republic to turn, in Eugen Weber's well-known phrase, "peasants into Frenchmen" (Kohn 1967; Weber 1979).[7]

An even more radical "change of character" occasioned by attempted bureaucratic incorporation by a "lateral" ethnic state is provided by Spain. Here it was the Castilian kingdom that formed the fulcrum of Christian resistance to Muslim power. Later, united with the kingdom of Aragon, it utilized religious community as an instrument of homogenization, expelling those who, like the Jews and Moriscos, could not be made to conform. Here, too, notions of *limpieza de sangre* bolstered the unity of the Spanish crown, which was beset by demands on several sides from those claiming ancient rights and manifesting ancient cultures. Quite apart from the Portuguese secession and the failed Catalan revolt, Basques, Galicians and Andalusians retained their separate identities into the modern era. The result is a less unified national community, and more polyethnic state, than either Britain or France. With the spread of ideological nationalism in the early nineteenth century, these ethnic communities felt justified in embarking on varying degrees of autonomous development, whose reverberations are still felt today. Yet, most members of these communities shared an overarching Spanish political sentiment and culture, over and beyond their often intense commitment to Basque, Catalan or Galician identity and culture (Atkinson 1960; Payne 1971; Greenwood 1977).

Historically, the formation of modern nations owes a profound legacy to the development of England, France and Spain. This is usually attributed to their possession of military and economic power at the relevant period, the period of burgeoning nationalism and nations. As the great powers of the period, they inevitably became models of the nation, the apparently successful format of population unit, for everyone else. Yet in the case of England and France, and to a lesser extent Spain, this was not accidental. It was the result of the early development of a particular kind of "rational" bureaucratic administration, aided by the development of merchant capital, wealthy urban centres and professional military forces and technology. The "state" formed the matrix of the new population-unit's format, the "nation." It aided the type of compact, unified, standardized and culturally homogenized unit and format that the nation exemplifies.

Some would say that the state actually "created" the nation, that royal administration, taxation and mobilization endowed the subjects within its jurisdiction with a sense of corporate loyalty and identity. Even in the West, this overstates the case. The state was certainly a necessary condition for the formation of the national loyalties we recognize today. However, its operations in turn owed much to earlier assumptions about kingdoms and peoples, and to the presence of core ethnic communities around which these states were built up. The process of ethnic fusion, particularly apparent in England and France, which their lateral *ethnies* encouraged through the channels of bureaucratic incorporation, was only possible because of a relatively homogeneous ethnic core. We are not here talking about actual descent, much less about "race," but about the *sense* of ancestry and identity that people possess. Hence the importance of myths and memories, symbols and values, embodied in customs and traditions and in artistic styles, legal codes and institutions. In *this* sense of "ethnicity," which is more about cultural perceptions than physical demography, albeit rooted perceptions and assumptions, England from an early date, and France somewhat later, came to form fairly homogeneous *ethnies*. These *ethnies* in turn facilitated the development of homogenizing states, extending the whole idea of an *ethnie* into realms and onto levels hitherto unknown, to form the relatively novel concept of the nation.

THE "REDISCOVERY" OF THE "ETHNIC PAST"

In contrast to the route of bureaucratic incorporation by lateral *ethnies*, the process by which demotic *ethnies* may become the bases for nations is only indirectly affected by the state and its administration. This was either because they were subject communities—the usual case—or because, as in Byzantium and Russia, the state represented interests partially outside its core *ethnie*. This subdivision also produces interesting variants on the constitutive political myth, or *mythomoteur*, of vertical *ethnies*.[8]

In all these communities, the fund of cultural myths, symbols, memories and values was transmitted not only from generation to generation, but also throughout the territory occupied by the community or its enclaves, and down the social scale. The chief mechanism of this persistence and diffusion was an organized religion with a sacred text, liturgy, rites and clergy, and sometimes a specialized secret lore and script. It is the social aspects of salvation religions, in particular, that have ensured the persistence and shaped the contours of demotic *ethnies*. Among Orthodox Greeks and Russians, Monophysite Copts and Ethiopians, Gregorian Armenians, Jews, Catholic Irish and Poles, myths and symbols of descent and election, and the ritual and sacred texts in which they were embodied, helped to perpetuate the traditions and social bonds of the community.

At the same time, the very hold of an ethnic religion posed grave problems for the formation of nations from such communities. It transpired that "religion-shaped" peoples, whose ethnicity owed so much to the symbols and organization of an ancient faith, were often constrained in their efforts to become "full" nations. Or rather, their intellectuals may find it harder to break out of the conceptual mould of a religio-ethnic community. So many members of such demotic *ethnies* simply assumed that theirs was already, and indeed always had been, a nation. Indeed, according to some definitions they were. They possessed in full measure, after all, the purely ethnic components of the nation. Arabs and Jews, for example, had common names, myths of descent, memories and religious cultures, as well as attachments to an original homeland and a persisting, if subdivided, sense of ethnic solidarity. Did this not suffice for nationhood? All that seemed to be necessary was to attain independence and a state for the community (Baron 1960, pp. 213–48; Carmichael 1967; Patai 1983).

Yet, as these examples demonstrate, matters were not so simple. Quite apart from adverse geo-political factors, social and cultural features internal to the Arab and Jewish communities made the transition from *ethnie* to nation difficult and problematic. The Arabs have been faced, of course, by their geographic extent, which flies in the face of the ideal of a "compact nation" in its clearly demarcated habitat. They have also had to contend with the varied histories of the sub-divisions of the "Arab nation," ranging from the Moroccan kingdoms to those of Egypt or Saudi Arabia. There is also the legacy of a divisive modern colonialism, which has often reinforced historical differences and shaped the modern Arab states with their varied economic patterns. Mass, public education has, in turn, like legal rights, been the product of the colonial and post-colonial states and their élites. Above all, however, the involvement of most Arabs and most Arab states with Islam, whose *umma* both underpins and challenges the circle and significance of an "Arab nation," creates an ambiguous unity and destiny, and overshadows efforts by Arab intelligentsia to rediscover an "Arab past" (Sharabi 1970; Smith 1973b).

The Jews were also faced with problems of geographic dispersion, accentuated by their lack of a recognized territory and exile from an ancient homeland. True, in the Pale of Settlement and earlier in Poland, something approaching a public religious education system and common legal rights (albeit restricted) had been encouraged by the *kahal* system and its successors. Yet, though Jews, like Armenians, were compelled to occupy certain niches in the European economy, we can hardly characterize their enclave communities as models of economic unity, let alone a territorial division of labour. Quite apart from these obstacles to national unity, there were also the ambivalent attitudes and self-definitions of Judaism and its rabbinical authorities. Only later, did some rabbis and one wing of Orthodoxy come to support Jewish nationalism and its Zionist project, despite the traditional hopes for messianic restoration to Zion of generations of the Orthodox. The concept of Jewish self-help had become alien to the medieval interpretation of Judaism; and the general notion that the Jews were a "nation in exile" actually strengthened this passivity (Hertzberg 1960; Vital 1975, pp. 3–20).

It was in these circumstances of popular resignation amid communal decline, set against Western national expansion, that a new stratum of secular intelligentsia emerged. Their fundamental role, as they came to see it, was to transform the relationship of a religious tradition to its primary bearers, the demotic *ethnies*. We must, of course, place this development in the larger context of a series of revolutions—socio-economic, political and cultural—which began in the early-modern period in the West. As we saw, the primary motor of these transformations was the formation of a new type of professionalized, bureaucratic state on the basis of a relatively homogeneous core *ethnie*. Attempts by older political formations to take over some of the dimensions of the Western "rational state" and so streamline their administrations and armies, upset the old accommodations of these empires to their constituent *ethnies*. In the Habsburg, Ottoman and Romanov empires, increasing state intervention, coupled with incipient urbanization and commerce, placed many demotic *ethnies* under renewed pressures. The spread of nationalist ideas from the late-eighteenth century on, carried with it new ideals of compact population-units, popular representation and cultural diversity, which affected the ruling classes of these empires and even more the educated stratum of their subject communities (see the essays in Sugar and Lederer 1969; more generally, Smith 1986a, pp. 129–52).

For the subject vertical *ethnie*, a secularizing intelligentsia led by educator-intellectuals supplied the motor of transformation, as well as the cultural framework, which among lateral *ethnie* had been largely provided by the incorporating bureaucratic state. It was this intelligentsia that furnished the new communal self-definitions and goals. These redefinitions were not simple "inventions," or wholesale applications of Western models. Rather, they were derived from a process of "rediscovery" of the ethnic past. The process tended to reverse the religious self-view: instead of "the people" acting as a passive but chosen vessel of salvation, subordinate to the divine message, that message and its salvation ethic became the supreme expression and creation of the people's genius as it developed in history (Haim 1962; Smith 1983a, pp. 230–56).[9]

At the centre of the self-appointed task of the intelligentsia stood the rediscovery and realization of the community. This entailed a moral and political revolution. In the place of a passive and subordinate minority, living precariously on the margins of the dominant ethnic society and its state, a new compact and politically active nation had to be created ("recreated" in nationalist terminology). From now on, the centre stage was to be occupied by the people, henceforth identified with "the masses," who would replace the aristocratic heroes of old. This was all part of the process of creating a unified, and preferably autarchic, community of legally equal members or "citizens," who would become the fount of legitimacy and state power. However, for this to occur, the people had to be purified of the dross of centuries—their lethargy, divisions, alien elements, ignorance and so on—and emancipate themselves. That was the primary task of the educator-intellectuals.

The transition, then, from demotic *ethnie* to civic nation carries with it several related processes and movements. These include:

1. a movement from subordinate accommodation and passivity of a peripheral minority to an active, assertive and politicized community with a unified policy;
2. a movement towards a universally recognized "homeland" for the community, a compact, clearly demarcated territory;
3. economic unification of all members of the territorially demarcated community, with control over its own resources, and movement towards economic autarchy in a competitive world of nations;
4. turning ethnic members into legal citizens by mobilizing them for political ends and conferring on each common civil, social and political rights and obligations;
5. placing the people at the centre of moral and political concern and cele-

brating the new role of the masses, by re-educating them in national values, myths and memories.

That traditional élites, especially the guardians of sacred texts which had so long defined the demotic *ethnie*, might resist these changes, was to be expected. This meant that the intellectuals had to undercut earlier definitions of the community by re-presenting their novel conceptions through ancient symbols and formats. These were in no sense mere manipulations (though there undoubtedly was individual manipulation, such as Tilak's use of the Kali cult in Bengal); there is no need to unmask what are so patently selective readings of an ethnic past. Yet selection can take place only within strict limits, limits set by the pre-existing myths, symbols, customs and memories of vertical *ethnies*. That still leaves considerable scope for choice of symbol or myth and understanding of history. Can we discern a pattern in the selective readings of educator-intellectuals?[10]

There were, I think, two main patterns by which educator-intellectuals could engage the community for their moral and political goals. Both had to be couched in the language and symbolism of the people, in the sense that any novelties must find an echo in popular historical traditions. The first pattern was the uses of landscape, or what we may call "poetic spaces." A nation, after all, needs before all else a national territory or homeland, and not just anywhere. The geographic terrain must be simultaneously an historic home. How do you create this sense of "homeland" for people who are either divided into small localities or scattered outside the chosen area? The answer is to endow the chosen home with poetic and historical connotations, or rather with an historical poetry. The aim is to integrate the homeland into a romantic drama of the progress of the nation. One way to do this, is to historicize natural features of the chosen area. This was, of course, a feature of older *ethnies*, with their myths of descent from gods who dwelt on great mountains like Ida, Olympus or Meru. A modern romantic historiography of the homeland turns lakes and mountains, rivers and valleys into the "authentic" repository of popular virtues and collective history. So the Jungfrau became a symbol of Swiss virtues of purity and naturalness, and the *Vierwaldstättersee* the national theatre of the historical drama of the foundation of the *Eidgenossenschaft* in 1291. In this poetic history, fact and legend become fused to produce a stirring symbol of purity and rectitude, and a dramatic myth of resistance to tyranny. Again, the English or Russian paeans to their respective landscapes, with rolling meadows or wide open spaces and birch trees, immortalized by painters and musicians like Constable and Elgar, or Levitan and Borodin, celebrate the community's involvement in its homeland habitat, turning bare nature into poetic history (Kohn 1957; Gray 1971, pp. 9–64; Crump 1986).

Another way to integrate the nation with its homeland is to naturalize historical features. Tells, temples, castles and stone circles are treated as natural components of an ethnic landscape, with an historical poetry of their own. The uses of Stonehenge are instructive in this respect. Interpreted in many ways, Stonehenge in the eighteenth- and ninteenth-century "historical revival" became so much a symbol of the antiquity of Britain and British ancestry, that it was difficult to erase so "natural" a part of the British scene from the ethnic consciousness of the nation

(Chippindale 1983, pp. 96–125). Similarly, the mysterious stone buildings of Great Zimbabwe, which seem to have grown out of their natural surroundings, despite the skill with which the Elliptical Temple was obviously constructed, suggest the rootedness of the modern nation of Zimbabwe in its natural habitat. By implying this close link between history and nature, the modern educator-intellectual is able to define the community in space and tell us "where we are" (Chamberlin 1979, pp. 27–35).

The other main pattern of involvement of the community in the national revolution was even more potent. If the uses of landscape define the communal homeland, the uses of history, or what I may call the cult of "golden ages," direct the communal destiny by telling us who we are, whence we came and why we are unique. The answers lie in those "myths of ethnic origins and descent" that form the groundwork of every nationalist mythology. Since the aims of nationalist educator-intellectuals are not academic, but social, i.e. the moral purification and political mobilization of the people, communal history must be taught as a series of foundation and liberation myths and as a cult of heroes. Together, these make up the vision of the golden age that must inspire present regeneration (Smith 1984a).

Typical of such uses of history is the Gaelic revival's vision of a Celtic, pre-Christian Irish golden age set in a half-mythical, half-historical time before the fifth-century conversion to Christianity by St. Patrick. When O'Grady and Lady Gregory rediscovered the Ulster Cycle with its legends of Cuchulain, they found a golden age of High Kings, *fianna* bands and *filid* guilds in a rural and free Celtic society that seemed the spiritual model for a modern Irish nation. The rediscovery of an early Celtic art and literature seemed to confirm the image of a once-great community, whose progress had been cut off by Norman, and later Protestant, English invasions. The cult of Celtic heroes in a free Gaelic Ireland suggested what was authentically "ours" and therefore what "we" must do to be "ourselves" once again, (Chadwick 1970, pp. 134–5, 268–71; Lyons 1979, pp. 57–83; Hutchinson 1987).

A similar process of ethnic reconstruction took place in Finland during the last century. In this case, a subordinate vertical *ethnie* differentiated from the Swedish élite and its Russian masters, formed a potential popular base for the reconstructions of nationalist educator-intellectuals like Lönnrot, Runeberg and Snellman from the 1830s on. Of course, the "Finns" and the "Finland" of their imaginations bore only a very partial resemblance to earlier Finnish society, particularly its pagan era in the later first millennium A.D. This appears to have been the epoch (to judge from its material remains) to which the later *Kalevala* songs and poems collected by Lönnrot in Karelia refer back. Nevertheless, the historicism of Lönnrot and his fellow-intellectuals, with their cults of a golden age of heroes like Väinämöinen and Lemminkainen, answered to a very real need to recover what was thought of as being an ancient but "lost" period of Finnish history and culture. Popularized by the paintings of Gallen-Kallela and the tone-poems and *Kullervo* symphony of Sibelius, this archaic golden age set in Finland's lakes and forests, provided an ideal self-definition and exemplar for the reconstruction of Finnish society and culture as a nation in its struggle against Swedish cultural and Russian political domination (Boulton Smith 1985; Branch 1985, pp. xi–xxxiv; Honko 1985).

The same patterns operated in other reconstructions from a demotic ethnic base. Historicist revivals of ancient Greek culture and heroes, of ancient Israelite archaeology and heroic examplars, of ancient Turkish steppe heroes, and of a Nordic pantheon of gods and heroes in a barbarian golden age among Germans, are some examples of nationalist attempts to recreate ethnic pasts that would define and guide modern nations (Barzilay 1959; Kohn 1965; Campbell and Sherrard 1968, pp. 19–49; Kushner 1976).

What they all had in common was their provision of "maps" of ethnic relations and history, and "moralities" of national endeavour. On the one hand, the educator-intellectuals furnished maps of the nature, descent and role of the community in the modern world; on the other hand, exemplary guides to collective action and models of "true" and authentic national behaviour. This is the purificatory and activist moral revolution which a "returning intelligentsia" in search of *its* roots performs and which, for demotic *ethnies*, is a prerequisite for constructing a civic nation.

Intellectuals and professionals, of course, also play a role in the transformation of lateral *ethnies*. Yet here their task is secondary. The bureaucratic state and its incorporating activities provide the framework and the motor of change. Among subordinate, demotic *ethnies*, the state is a target and a culturally alien one. It falls, therefore, to a returning intelligentsia to turn elements of an existing culture into a national grid and moral exemplar, if the civic nation is to be formed and its members mobilized for "nation-building." In the creation of a "community of history and destiny," the historicism of the educator-intellectuals provides the nation-to-be with its genealogy and purpose (Gella 1976; Smith 1986a, pp. 174–208).

I have concentrated on the role of historicist intelligentsia in creating nations from, and around, demotic *ethnies*. Such nations form a majority of all nations and aspirant nations today. Modern circumstances have encouraged vertical *ethnies* to proliferate, and their intelligentsia to put forward claims to national status, while at the same time eliminating "lateral" aristocratic *ethnies*, unless they could transform themselves through an incorporating bureaucratic state into a civic nation. This in turn means that intellectuals and professionals have assumed a disproportionate role in contemporary politics outside the West, often with fervently nationalistic outlooks and policies. This is true even where intelligentsias attempt to stem the tide of ethno-national claims and separatism, by attempting to use a Western-style bureaucratic state to incorporate competing *ethnies*, as in many sub-Saharan African states. They, too, must try to rediscover an ethnic past, but this time for a series of *ethnies* forcibly brought together by the colonial state. African practice suggests a combination of the two routes to nationhood, with one starting out from a lateral *ethnie* (especially if there is a dominant *ethnie* in the state) and operating through bureaucratic incorporation, the other from a vertical *ethnie* (often a core one) and reconstructing an ethno-national culture through the activities of educator-intellectuals like Senghor and Cheikh Anta Diop (Ajayi

1960; Geiss 1974). How successful such a combination is likely to prove remains to be seen (Smith 1983b, pp. 122–35).

"CULTURAL WARS"

In delineating the two main bases and routes of nation-formation, I have said nothing about the factors that determine which of the rival population-units are likely to achieve nationhood—except that they are most likely to stem from a pre-existing ethnic core. Yet, quite evidently, not all units that possess ethnic cores become nations in the sense of that term used here. There have been plenty of examples of ethnic cores that failed to move towards nationhood, like the Copts and Shan, the Sorbs and Frisians. This is not simply a matter of gaining independence or sovereign states of their own, though it may indicate a failure in the face of *force majeure*. More important is the inability to develop the cultural framework that can unite the chosen population-unit, and hence the political will and activism to resist encroachment and absorption by more powerful neighbours. This is where the relationship between conflict and cultural resources is crucial (Smith 1981b; Brass 1985).

Just as warfare acts as the agent of state-maintenance or state-extinction, so cultural conflict—for *ethnies* that lack states of their own—selects out potential nations from those destined to remain in various degrees of accommodation at the margins of other national societies. Clearly, in this competition the "strength" or "weakness" of the ethnic base itself is all-important. The "fuller," and more richly documented, the historical culture which a population-unit can claim, the better its chances of achieving political recognition and moving towards the status of a civic nation. Equally important, however, is the emergence of a relatively secularized intelligentsia, secular enough to promote auto-emancipation and political activism as a communal option. This in turn requires a cultural war with rival cultures, of the kind waged by German nationalists against French culture or Indian nationalists against British culture. However, it also entails an internal conflict of "sons against fathers," of the secular intelligentsia against the guardians of tradition, in the interests of moving a demotic *ethnie* along the road to nationhood. That may mean a judicious borrowing from external cultures, preferably distant ones, such as the Japanese under the Meiji Restoration utilized and assimilated to indigenous norms. Yet over-borrowing may undermine the strength of native traditions and attenuate an ethnic heritage. So a balance must be struck between archaism and syncretism, which is a function of culture conflict and cultural resources. Such balances and conflicts also place a premium on the control of the means of communication and socialization. The Meiji regime could sanction large-scale borrowings, not only because the foundations of a unique historical Japanese culture were so secure, but also because they controlled the means of communication and socialization (Kosaka 1959; Dore 1964; Mazrui 1985).

The ability to wage "cultural wars" by rejection or selective assimilation is, of course, a function of indigenous cultural resources and their availability for political ends in the hands of the intelligentsia. That is why the main battle of the nationalists is so often fought out within its chosen *ethnie* against the older self-definitions. However, we can only understand the significance of such internal struggles if we take the culture and history of the ethnic core seriously. This leads us back to our initial theses.[11]

CONCLUSIONS

Whatever the factors that make one bid for nationhood successful and another less so (and chance, too, plays a part here), the fundamental preconditions remain as before.

1. The nation, as we have defined it, is a modern phenomenon, and its civic features can only reach full flowering in the modern era, with its specific modes of domination, production and communication. At the same time, modern nations have their roots in pre-modern eras and pre-modern cultures. The origins of such nations must therefore be traced far back, since their ethnic features, though subject to considerable reconstructions, stem from often distant eras and ancient traditions. Modern nations are closely, if often indirectly, related to older, long-lived *ethnies*, which furnish the nation with much of its distinctive mythology, symbolism and culture, including its association with an ancient homeland. It is difficult to see a modern nation maintaining itself as a distinctive identity without such mythology, symbolism and culture. If it does not have them, it must appropriate them, or risk dissolution (Smith 1986b).

2. As we have seen, the nation that emerges in the modern era must be regarded as both construct and real process, and that in a dual sense. For the analyst, a "nation" represents an ideal-type combining elements in accentuated form, but equally needs to be broken down into the constituent dimensions of process to which the construct refers. For the nationalist, too, the nation represents an ideal to be striven for and reconstructed, particularly in the case of demotic *ethnies*, where educator-intellectuals' visions assume great importance. Equally, these visions must elicit a definite *praxis* in the context of real transformations that develop in partial independence of human design and nationalist action, transformations like increasing territorialization and economic unification, the rise of mobilized masses and more scientific communication systems. These transformations also force the cultural and political spheres more closely together, so that the emergent nation becomes both a cultural and a political community. Not surprisingly, their coincidence in time and space becomes one of the chief goals of nationalists everywhere (Gellner 1983, pp. 1–7).

3. The point of departure for any analysis of the modern cultural and political communities we call "nations" lies in the different kinds of pre-modern ethnic communities, the aristocratic lateral and the demotic vertical types. These form the main bases and "ethnic cores" from which the two main routes in the transition to nationhood set out. We can go further. Different types of ethnic base

largely determine the forms and mechanisms through which the nation is subsequently formed, in so far as this is achieved. Not only do they influence the role of the state, they also differentiate the social groups—aristocrats, bureaucrats, bourgeoisies, intelligentsia, lower clergy—that are likely to play leading roles in the movement towards nationhood. Even more important, they influence the forms and much of the content of the ensuing national culture, since it is from their myths of descent and the symbols, memories and values of different types of *ethnie*, that the modern mass culture of each nation and its modes of communication and socialization derive their distinctive identity and forms. That is why, in the fields of culture and socialization, there is greater continuity with the past of each *ethnie* than in such rapidly changing domains as science, technology and economics.[12]

4. In the case of nations formed on the basis of lateral *ethnies*, the influence of the state and its bureaucratic personnel is paramount. It is the culture of an aristocratic *ethnie* that an incorporating bureaucratic state purveys down the social scale and into the countryside and inner-city areas, displacing the hold of ecclesiastical authorities and local nobles (or using them for state ends). This is very much the route followed by those Western societies, in which cultural homogenization around an upper-stratum ethnic core proceeded *pari passu* with administrative incorporation.

In the case of nations formed on the basis of vertical *ethnies*, a returning intelligentsia with its ethnic historicism, provides the motor force and framework of an absent (because culturally alien) bureaucratic state. In this case, there is a more direct confrontation with the guardians of tradition. Often interwoven with a conflict of generations, the struggle of the intelligentsia is for the cultural resources of the community and their utilization for geo-cultural purposes, i.e. for their territorial and political expansion against rival geo-cultural centres. To these ends, the communal culture must be redefined and reconstituted through a national and civic appropriation of ethnic history, which will mobilize members on the basis of a rediscovered identity (Hobsbawm and Ranger 1983; Lowenthal 1985).

5. Finally, the continuity that such reconstructions encourage between many nations and their ethnic pasts, despite real transformations, implies a deeper need transcending individuals, generations and classes, a need for collective immortality through posterity, that will relativize and diminish the oblivion and futility of death. Through a community of history and destiny, memories may be kept alive and actions retain their glory. For only in the chain of generations of those who share an historic and quasi-familial bond, can individuals hope to achieve a sense of immortality in eras of purely terrestrial horizons. In this sense, the formation of nations and the rise of ethnic nationalisms appears more like the institutionalization of a "surrogate religion" than a political ideology, and therefore far more durable and potent than we may care to admit.

For we have to concede that, in the last analysis, there remain "non-rational" elements of explosive power and tenacity in the structure of nations and the outlook and myth of nationalism. These elements, I would contend, stem from the profound historical roots of the myths, symbols, memories and values that define the ethnic substratum of many modern nations. These are elements that many of us, including many social scientists, would prefer to ignore, but we do so at our peril. The conflicts that embitter the geo-politics of our planet often betray deeper roots than a clash of economic interests and political calculations would suggest, and many of these conflicts, and perhaps the most bitter and protracted, stem from just these underlying non-rational elements. Their persistence, and intensification, in the modern era suggest a long future for ethno-nationalism, and an increasingly violent one, if we fail to address the real issues in the formation of nations and the spread of nationalism.

NOTES

1. Further discussions of the subjective and objective features of nations, and of their dynamic and processual character, can be found in Rustow (1967) and Nettl and Robertson (1968).

2. For a general discussion, and an example from ancient Rome, see Tudor (1972).

3. For discussions of ancient empires and their economies, see Larsen (1979, especially the essays by Lattimore, Ekholm and Friedman, and Postgate).

4. The ancient Greek term *ethnos*, like the Latin *natio*, has a connotation of common origin, and so, being alike and acting together; but the emphasis is cultural rather than biological. As always, it is what people believe, rather than objective origins, that is important.

5. In many cases, the evidence from ancient and medieval records does not allow us to infer much about the degree of social penetration of élite culture and the range of ethnic ties, as the other essays in the volume by Wiseman (1973) make clear.

6. Of course, this conclusion owes much to the definition of the nation adopted here. Even so, one would have to distinguish in some way(s) between the types of cultural community in antiquity and the Middle Ages, and the very different kinds prevalent in the modern world. It is therefore better to make the distinctions explicit in the definitions themselves. Though there is a "before-and-after" model inherent in this conception, the argument advanced here suggests that the earlier components are *not* simply replaced by the later, modern ones; ethnic components do (and must) persist, if a nation is to be formed.

7. Again, the continuity is cultural, and indirect. It remained significant into the nineteenth century to claim descent from "Franks" and even "Gauls" for political purposes; the recovery of medieval French art and history also spurred this sense of ethnic identification. By the later Middle Ages, the claim to Frankish descent could hardly be substantiated; but again, it is claims within a cultural framework that count.

8. These are discussed by Smith (1986a, pp. 47–68); and see Armstrong (1982).

9. It is necessary to distinguish the educator-intellectuals proper from the wider stratum of the professional intelligentsia, on which see Gouldner (1979) and Smith (1981a, pp. 87–107).

10. For different readings of "manipulation" and "mass ethnic response" in Muslim India, see the essays by Brass and Robinson in Taylor and Yapp (1979).

11. That is why some recent devaluations of the role of "culture" in ethnic identification, particularly among anthropologists, seem beside the point. Of course, cultures change, and at the individual level change contextually, making ethnicity often "situational"; but at the collective level, and over the long term, cultural *forms* are relatively durable. Provided they are encoded in myths, symbols, traditions, artefacts and the like, they provide a delineated framework and repertoire for future generations, which influence

in often subtle ways the perceptions and attitudes of the majority of members of an *ethnie*; cf. the discussion of Armstrong and Gellner in Smith (1984b).

12. This vitally affects the issue of industrial "convergence" between societies of very different culture. It is in the ethnic heritage of different societies, above all, that divergences persist and spill over into the ideological and political spheres (cf. Goldthorpe [1964] for an early statement).

REFERENCES

Ajayi, Jacob F. A. 1960 "The place of African history and culture in the process of nation-building in Africa south of the Sahara," *Journal of Negro Education*, vol. 30, no. 3, pp. 206–13

Alty, J. H. M. 1982 "Dorians and Ionians," *Journal of Hellenic Studies*, vol. 102, no. 1, pp. 1–14

Anderson, Benedict 1983 *Imagined Communities: Reflections on the Origin and Spread of Nationalism*, London: Verso

Andrewes, Antony 1965 "The growth of the city-state," in Hugh Lloyd-Jones (ed.), *The Greek World*, Harmondsworth: Penguin, pp. 26–65

Armstrong, John 1982 *Nations before Nationalism*, Chapel Hill: University of North Carolina Press

Atiya, Aziz S. 1968 *A History of Eastern Christianity*, London: Methuen

Atkinson, William C. 1960 *A History of Spain and Portugal*, Harmondsworth: Penguin

Barnard, Frederik Mechner 1965 *Herder's Social and Political Thought*, Oxford: Clarendon Press

Barnett, Richard D. (ed.) 1971 *The Sephardi Heritage: Essays on the History and Cultural Contribution of the Jews of Spain and Portugal, vol. 1: The Jews in Spain and Portugal before and after the Expulsion of 1492*, London: Valentine, Mitchell & Co.

Baron, Salo W. 1960 *Modern Nationalism and Religion*, New York: Meridian Books

Bloch, Marc 1961 *Feudal Society*, 2 vols., London: Routledge & Kegan Paul

Boulton Smith, John 1985 "The *Kalevala* in Finnish art," *Books from Finland*, vol. 19, no. 1, pp. 48–55

Branch, Michael (ed.) 1985 *Kalevala: The Land of Heroes*, translated by William F. Kirby, London: The Athlone Press

Brass, Paul (ed.) 1985 *Ethnic Groups and the State*, London: Croom Helm

Breuilly, John 1982 *Nationalism and the State*, Manchester: Manchester University Press

Brock, Peter 1976 *The Slovak National Awakening*, Toronto: University of Toronto Press

Burney, Charles and Lang, David M. 1971 *The Peoples of the Hills: Ancient Ararat and Caucasus*, London: Weidenfeld & Nicolson

Cambridge History of Iran 1983 vol. III, *The Seleucid, Parthian and Sassanian Periods* (ed. Ehson Yarshater); 1975 vol. IV, *The Period from the Arab Invasion to the Saljuqs* (ed. Richard N. Frye), Cambridge: Cambridge University Press

Campbell, John and Sherrard, Philip 1968 *Modern Greece*, London: Benn

Carmichael, Joel 1967 *The Shaping of the Arabs*, New York: Macmillan Company

Chadwick, Nora 1970 *The Celts*, Harmondsworth: Penguin

Chamberlin, Eric R. 1979 *Preserving the Past*, London: J. M. Dent & Sons

Chippindale, Christopher 1983 *Stonehenge Complete*, London: Thames & Hudson

Connor, Walker 1978 "A nation is a nation, is a state, is an ethnic group, is a . . . ," *Ethnic and Racial Studies* vol. 1, no. 4, pp. 377–400

Corrigan, Philip and Sayer, Derek 1985 *The Great Arch: English State Formation as Cultural Revolution*, Oxford: Blackwell

Crump, Jeremy 1986 "The identity of English music: the reception of Elgar, 1898–1935," in Robert Colls and Philip Dodd (eds.), *Englishness, Politics and Culture, 1880–1920*, London: Croom Helm, pp. 164–90

Davis, R. H. C. 1958 *A History of Medieval Europe*, London: Longmans, Green and Co.
————1976 *The Normans and Their Myth*, London: Thames & Hudson

Dore, Ronald P. 1964 "Latin America and Japan compared," in John J. Johnson (ed.), *Continuity and Change in Latin America*, Stanford, CA: Stanford University Press

Eisenstein-Barzilay, Isaac 1959 "National and anti-national trends in the Berlin Haskalah," *Jewish Social Studies*, vol. 21, no. 3, pp. 165–92

Finley, M. I. 1986 "The Ancient Greeks and their nation," in his: *The Use and Abuse of History*, London: The Hogarth Press, pp. 120–33

Fishman, Joshua 1980 "Social theory and ethnography: neglected perspectives on language and ethnicity in eastern Europe," in Peter Sugar (ed.), *Ethnic Diversity and Conflict in Eastern Europe*, Santa Barbara: ABC-Clio, pp. 69–99

Fondation Hardt 1962 *Grecs et Barbares, Entretiens sur l'antiquité classique*, vol. VIII, Geneva

Frye, Richard N. 1966 *The Heritage of Persia*, New York: Mentor

Geiss, Immanuel 1974 *The PanAfrican Movement*, London: Methuen

Gella, Aleksander (ed.) 1976 *The Intelligentsia and the Intellectuals. Theory, Method and Case Study*, Sage Studies in International Sociology No. 5, Beverly Hills: Sage Publications

Gellner, Ernest 1983 *Nations and Nationalism*, Oxford: Blackwell

Goldthorpe, John 1964 "Social stratification in industrial society," in Paul Halmos (ed.), *The Development of Industrial Societies*, Sociological Review Monograph No. 8, pp. 97–122

Gouldner, Alvin 1979 *The Rise of the Intellectuals and the Future of the New Class*, London: Macmillan

Gray, Camilla 1971 *The Russian Experiment in Art, 1863–1922*, London: Thames & Hudson

Greenwood, Davydd 1977 "Continuity in change: Spanish Basque ethnicity as a historical process," in Milton Esman (ed.): *Ethnic Conflict in the Western World*, Ithaca: Cornell University Press, pp. 81–102

Haim, Sylvia (ed.) 1962 *Arab Nationalism: An Anthology*, Berkeley: University of California Press

Hertzberg, Arthur (ed.) 1960 *The Zionist Idea: A Reader*, New York: Meridian Books

Hirschberg, Hayyim Ze'ev (Joachim W.) 1969 "The Oriental Jewish communities," in Arthur J. Arberry (ed.), *Religion in the Middle East: Three Religions in Concord and Conflict*, vol. I, Judaism and Christianity, Cambridge: Cambridge University Press, pp. 119–225

Hobsbawm, Eric and Ranger, Terence (eds.) 1983 *The Invention of Tradition*, Cambridge: Cambridge University Press

Honko, Lauri 1985 "The *Kalevala* process," *Books from Finland*, vol. 19, no. 1, pp. 16–23

Horowitz, Donald L. 1985 *Ethnic Groups in Conflict*, Berkeley: University of California Press

Hutchinson, John 1987 *The Dynamics of Cultural Nationalism: The Gaelic Revival and the Creation of the Irish Nation State*, London: Allen & Unwin

Jones, Gwyn 1973 *A History of the Vikings*, London: Oxford University Press

Keeney, Barnaby C. 1972 "Military service and the development of nationalism in England, 1272–1327," in Leon Tipton (ed.), *Nationalism in the Middle Ages*, New York: Holt, Rinehart & Winston, pp. 87–97

Kitchen, K. A. 1973 "The Philistines," in D. J. Wiseman (ed.), *Peoples of the Old Testament*, Oxford: Oxford University Press, pp. 53–78

Kohn, Hans 1957 *Nationalism and Liberty: The Swiss Example*, New York: Macmillan

———1965 *The Mind of Germany*, London: Macmillan

———1967 *Prelude to Nation-States: the French and German Experience, 1789–1815*, New York: Van Nostrand

Kosaka, Masaaki 1959 "The Meiji era: the forces of rebirth," *Journal of World History*, vol. 5, no. 3, pp. 621–33

Kushner, David 1976 *The Rise of Turkish Nationalism*, London: Frank Cass

Larsen, Mogens T. (ed.) 1979 *Power and Propaganda: A Symposium on Ancient Empires*, Copenhagen: Akademisk Forlag

Levi, Mario Attilio 1965 *Political Power in the Ancient World* (translated by J. Costello), London: Weidenfeld & Nicolson

Lewis, Archibald 1974 *Knights and Samurai: Feudalism in Northern France and Japan*, London: Temple Smith

Lowenthal, David 1985 *The Past Is a Foreign Country*, Cambridge: Cambridge University Press

Lyons, Francis S. 1979 *Culture and Anarchy in Ireland, 1890–1930*, London: Oxford University Press

Macdougall, Hugh 1982 *Racial Myth in English History: Trojans, Teutons and Anglo-Saxons*, Montreal: Harvest House

Mazrui, Ali 1985 "African archives and oral tradition," *The Courier*, February 1985, UNESCO, Paris, pp. 13–15

McNeill, William H. 1963 *The Rise of the West: A History of the Human Community*, Chicago: University of Chicago Press

Nairn, Tom 1977 *The Break-up of Britain: Crisis and Neo-nationalism*, London: New Left Books

Nettl, J. P. and Robertson, Roland 1968 *International Systems and the Modernisation of Societies*, London: Faber

Orridge, Andrew 1982 "Separatist and autonomist nationalisms: the structure of regional loyalties in the modern state," in Colin H. Williams (ed.), *National Separatism*, Cardiff: University of Wales Press, pp. 43–74

Patai, Raphael 1983 *The Arab Mind*, rev. ed., New York: Charles Scribner's Sons

Payne, Stanley 1971 "Catalan and Basque nationalism," *Journal of Contemporary History*, vol. 6, no. 1, pp. 15–51

Raphael, Chaim 1985 *The Road from Babylon*, London: Weidenfeld & Nicolson

Reynolds, Susan 1983 "Medieval *origines gentium* and the Community of the Realm," *History*, vol. 68, pp. 375–90

———1984 *Kingdoms and Communities in Western Europe, 900–1300*, Oxford: Clarendon Press

Rustow, Dankwart 1967 *A World of Nations*, Washington DC: Brookings Institution

Saggs, Henry W. F. 1984 *The Might That Was Assyria*, London: Sidgwick & Jackson

Sathyamurthy, T. V. 1983 *Nationalism in the Contemporary World: Political and Sociological Perspectives*, London: Frances Pinter

Seltzer, Robert M. 1980 *Jewish People, Jewish Thought: The Jewish Experience in History*, New York: Macmillan

Seton-Watson, Hugh 1977 *Nations and States: An Enquiry into the Origins of Nations and the Politics of Nationalism*, London: Methuen.

Sharabi, Hisham 1970 *Arab Intellectuals and the West: The Formative Years, 1875–1914*, Baltimore: Johns Hopkins Press

Smith, Anthony D. 1973a Nationalism: A Trend Report and Annotated Bibliography, *Current Sociology*, vol. 21, no. 3, The Hague: Mouton

———1973b "Nationalism and religion: the role of religious reform in the genesis of Arab and Jewish nationalism," *Archives de Sociologie des Religions*, vol. 35, pp. 23–43

———1981a *The Ethnic Revival in the Modern World*, Cambridge: Cambridge University Press

———1981b "War and ethnicity: the role of warfare in the formation, self-images and cohesion of ethnic communities," *Ethnic and Racial Studies*, vol. 4, no. 4, pp. 375–97

———1983a *Theories of Nationalism*, 2nd ed., London: Duckworth, and New York: Holmes & Meier

———1983b *State and Nation in the Third World*, Brighton: Harvester

———1984a "National identity and myths of ethnic descent," *Research in Social Movements, Conflict and Change*, vol. 7, pp. 95–130

———1984b "Ethnic persistence and national transformation," *British Journal of Sociology*, vol. 35, no. 3, pp. 452–61

———1986a *The Ethnic Origins of Nations*, Oxford: Blackwell

———1986b "State-making and nation-building," in John A. Hall (ed.): *States in History*, Oxford: Blackwell, pp. 228–63

Smith, Leslie (ed.) 1985 *The Making of Britain: The Middle Ages*, London: Macmillan

Stack, John F. (ed.) 1986 *The Primordial Challenge: Ethnicity in the Contemporary World*, New York: Greenwood Press

Sugar, Peter and Lederer, Ivo (eds.) 1969 *Nationalism in Eastern Europe*, Seattle: University of Washington Press

Szporluk, Roman 1979 *Ukraine: A Brief History*, Detroit: Ukrainian Festival Committee

Taylor, David and Yapp, Malcolm (eds.) 1979 *Political Identity in South Asia*, Collected Papers on South Asia No. 2, Centre of South Asian Studies, School of Oriental and African Studies, University of London, London: Curzon Press

Tilly, Charles (ed.) 1975 *The Formation of National States in Western Europe*, Princeton NJ: Princeton University Press

Tudor, Henry 1972 *Political Myth*, London: Pall Mall Press

Ullendorff, Edward 1973 *The Ethiopians: An Introduction to Country and People*, 3rd ed., Oxford: Oxford University Press

Vital, David 1975 *The Origins of Zionism*, Oxford: Clarendon Press

Weber, Eugene 1979 *Peasants into Frenchmen: The Modernization of Rural France, 1870–1914*, London: Chatto and Windus

Wiseman, D. J. (ed.) 1973 *Peoples of the Old Testament*, Oxford: Oxford University Press

Etienne Balibar

Author of works on Marx and Marxism, Spinoza, and Foucault, Etienne Balibar has taught philosophy at the University of Paris and at Nanterre. He wrote *Reading Capital* (London: New Left Books, 1967), with the French Marxist theorist Louis Althusser and *Race, Nation: Class: Ambiguous Identities* (Paris: Editions la Découverte, 1988) with Immanuel Wallerstein. This latter book marked a transition in Balibar's work toward a deep concern with race and nation, themes he developed in *Masses, Classes, Ideas: Studies on Politics and Philosophy before and after Marx* (London: Verso, 1994).

Always interested in situating philosophical developments in social and political contexts, Balibar has been concerned with the specificity of contemporary racism and its relationship both to class division within capitalism and to the contradictions of the nation-state. Moving from a structuralist reading of modes of production toward a greater engagement with the politics and discourses of social formation, Balibar explores the tension between universalisms and particularisms, between attempts to create universalistic ideological constructions that harmonize the exploiter and the exploited and the always present pull of particular forms of domination, whether on the basis of class, sex, or race.

The nation form involves a historical narrative in which the nation is the subject moving continuously through time, fulfilling a project over many centuries of coming to self-awareness. This destiny of the nation is made possible by pre-national developments, like the ancient generation of linguistic, cultural, and religious communities, that produce a kind of "fictive ethnicity" that then gives content and substance to the nation form. "No modern nation possesses a given 'ethnic' basis, even when it arises out of a national independence struggle." Balibar's argument is a potent challenge to the essentializing nationalisms and racisms that promote an ethnic or racial origin for the nation and is quite congenial to Benedict Anderson's idea of an "imagined community." Balibar declares that "every social community reproduced by the functioning of institutions is imaginary," and that "in certain conditions, only imaginary communities are real."

The Nation Form: History and Ideology

> ... a "past" that has never been present, and which never will be.
>
> JACQUES DERRIDA, *Margins of Philosophy*

The history of nations, beginning with our own, is always already presented to us in the form of a narrative which attributes to these entities the continuity of a subject. The formation of the nation thus appears as the fulfillment of a "project" stretching over centuries, in which there are different stages and moments of coming to self-awareness, which the prejudices of the various historians will portray as more or less decisive—where, for example, are we to situate the origins of France? with our ancestors the Gauls? the Capetian monarchy? the revolution of 1789?—but which, in any case, all fit into an identical pattern: that of the self-manifestation of the national personality. Such a representation clearly constitutes a retrospective illusion, but it also expresses constraining institutional realities. The illusion is twofold. It consists in believing that the generations which succeed one another over centuries on a reasonably stable territory, under a reasonably univocal designation, have handed down to each other an invariant substance. And it consists in believing that the process of development from which we select aspects retrospectively, so as to see ourselves as the culmination of that process, was the only one possible, that is, it represented a destiny. Project and destiny are the two symmetrical figures of the illusion of national identity. The "French" of 1988—one in three of whom has at least one "foreign"[1] ancestor—are only collectively connected to the subjects of King Louis XIV (not to speak of the Gauls) by a succession of contingent events, the causes of which have nothing to do either with the destiny of "France," the project of "its kings" or the aspirations of "its people."

This critique should not, however, be allowed to prevent our perceiving the continuing power of myths of national origins. One perfectly conclusive example of this is the French Revolution, by the very fact of the contradictory appropriations to which it is continually subjected. It is possible to suggest (with Hegel and Marx) that, in the history of every modern nation, wherever the argument can apply, there is never more than one single founding revolutionary event (which explains both the permanent temptation to repeat its forms, to imitate its

Etienne Balibar, "The Nation Form: History and Ideology," from Etienne Balibar and Immanuel Wallerstein, *Race, Nation, Class: Ambiguous Identities* (London: Verso, 1991), pp. 86–106 episodes and characters, and the temptation found among the "extreme" parties to suppress it, either by proving that national identity derives from before the revolution or by awaiting the realization of that identity from a *new* revolution which would complete the work of the first). The myth of origins and national continuity, which we can easily see being set in place in the contemporary history of the "young" nations (such as India or Algeria) which emerged with the end of colonialism, but which we have a tendency to forget has also been fabricated over recent centuries in the case of the "old" nations, is therefore an effective ideological form, in which the imaginary singularity of national formations is constructed daily, by moving back from the present into the past.

FROM THE "PRE-NATIONAL" STATE TO THE NATION-STATE

How are we to take this distortion into account? The "origins" of the national formation go back to a multiplicity of institutions dating from widely differing periods. Some are in fact very old: the institution of state languages that were distinct both from the sacred languages of the clergy and from "local" idioms— initially for purely administrative purposes, but subsequently as aristocratic languages—goes back in Europe to the High Middle Ages. It is connected with the process by which monarchical power became autonomous and sacred. Similarly, the progressive formation of absolute monarchy brought with it effects of monetary monopoly, administrative and fiscal centralization and a relative degree of standardization of the legal system and internal "pacification." It thus revolutionized the institutions of the *frontier* and the *territory*. The Reformation and Counter-Reformation precipitated a transition from a situation in which church and state competed (rivalry between the ecclesiastical state and the secular one) to a situation in which the two were complementary (in the extreme case, in a state religion).

All these structures appear retrospectively to us as pre-national, because they made possible certain features of the nation-state, into which they were ultimately to be incorporated with varying degrees of modification. We can therefore acknowledge the fact that the national formation is the product of a long "prehistory." This pre-history, however, differs in essential features from the nationalist myth of a linear destiny. First, it consists of a multiplicity of qualitatively distinct events spread out over time, none of which implies any subsequent event. Second, these events do not of their nature belong to the history of *one* determinate nation. They have occurred within the framework of political units other than those which seem to us today endowed with an original ethical personality (this, just as in the twentieth century the state apparatuses of the "young nations" were prefigured in the apparatuses of the colonial period, so the European Middle Ages saw the outlines of the modern state emerge within the framework of "Sicily," "Catalonia" or "Burgundy"). And they do not even belong by nature to the history of the *nation*-state, but to other rival forms (for example, the "imperial" form). It is not a line of necessary evolution but a series of conjunctural relations which has inscribed them after the event into the pre-history of the nation form. It is the characteristic feature of states of all types to represent the order they institute as eternal, though practice shows that more or less the opposite is the case.

The fact remains that all these events, on condition they are repeated or integrated into new political structures, have effectively played a role in the genesis of national formations. This has precisely to do with their institutional character, with the fact that they cause the state to intervene in the form which it assumed at a particular moment. In other words, *non-national* state apparatuses aiming at quite other (for example, dynastic) objectives have progressively produced the elements of the nation-state or, if one prefers, they have been involuntarily "nationalized" and have begun to nationalize society—the resurrection of Roman law, mercantilism and the domestication of the feudal aristocracies are all examples of this. And the closer we come to the modern period, the greater the constraint imposed by the accumulation of these elements seems to be. Which raises the crucial question of the *threshold* of irreversibility.

At what moment and for what reasons has this threshold been crossed—an event which, on the one hand, caused the configuration of a *system* of sovereign states to emerge and, on the other, imposed the progressive diffusion of the nation form to almost all human societies over two centuries of violent conflict? I admit that this threshold (which it is obviously impossible to identify with a single date[2]) corresponds to the development of the market structures and class relations specific to modern capitalism (in particular, the proletarianization of the labour force, a process which gradually extracts its members from feudal and corporatist relations). Nevertheless this commonly accepted thesis needs qualifying in several ways.

It is quite impossible to "deduce" the nation form from capitalist relations of production. Monetary circulation and the exploitation of wage labour do not logically entail a single determinate form of state. Moreover, the realization space which is implied by accumulation—the world capitalist market—has within it an intrinsic tendency to transcend any national limitations that might be instituted by determinate fractions of social capital or imposed by "extra-economic" means. May we, in these conditions, continue to see the formation of the nation as a "bourgeois project"? It seems likely that this formulation—taken over by Marxism from liberal philosophies of history—constitutes in its turn a historical myth. It seems, however, that we might overcome this difficulty if we return to Braudel and Wallerstein's perspective—the view which sees the constitution of nations as being bound up not with the abstraction of the capitalist market, but with its concrete historical form: that of a "world-economy" which is always already hierarchically organized into a "core" and a "periphery," each of which have different methods of accumulation and exploitation of labour power, and between which relations of unequal exchange and domination are established.[3]

Beginning from the core, national units form out of the overall structure of the world-economy, as a function of the role they play in that structure in a given period. More exactly, they form against one another as competing instruments in the service of the core's domination of the periphery. This first qualification is a crucial one, because it substitutes for the "ideal" capitalism of Marx and, particularly, of the Marxist economists, a "historical capitalism" in which a decisive role is played by the early forms of imperialism and the articulation of wars with colonization. In a sense, every modern nation is a product of colonization: it has always been to some degree colonized or colonizing, and sometimes both at the same time.

However, a second qualification is necessary. One of the most important of Braudel and Wallerstein's contributions consists in their having shown that, in the history of capitalism, *state forms other than the national have emerged* and have for a time competed with it, before finally being repressed or instrumentalized: the form of empire and, most importantly, that of the transnational politico-commercial complex, centred on one or more cities.[4] This form shows us that there was not a single inherently "bourgeois" political form, but several (we could take the Hanseatic League as an example, but the history of the United Provinces in the seventeenth century is closely determined by this alternative which echoes through the whole of its social life, including religious and intellectual life). In other words, the nascent capitalist bourgeoisie seems to have "hesitated"—depending on circumstances—between several forms of hegemony. Or let us rather say that there existed *different bourgeoisies*, each connected to different sectors of exploitation of the resources of the world-economy. If the "national bourgeoisies" finally won out, even before the industrial revolution (though at the cost of "time-lags" and "compromises" and therefore of fusions with other dominant classes), this is probably both because they needed to use the armed forces of the existing states externally and internally, and because they had to subject the peasantry to the new economic order and penetrate the countryside, turning it into a market where there were consumers of manufactured goods and reserves of "free" labour power. In the last analysis, it is therefore the concrete configurations of the class struggle and not "pure" economic logic which explain the constitution of nation-states, each with its own history, and the corresponding transformation of social formations into national formations.

THE NATIONALIZATION OF SOCIETY

The world-economy is not a self-regulating, globally invariant system, whose social formations can be regarded as mere local effects; it is a system of constraints, subject to the unforeseeable dialectic of its internal contradictions. It is globally necessary that control of the capital circulating in the whole accumulation space should be exercised from the core; but there has always been struggle over the *form* in which this concentration has been effected. The privileged status of the nation form derives from the fact that, locally, that form made it possible (at least for an entire historical period) for struggles between heterogeneous classes to be controlled and for not only a "capitalist class" but the *bourgeoisies* proper to emerge from these—state bourgeoisies both capable of political, economic and cultural hegemony and *produced* by that hegemony. The dominant bourgeoisie and the bourgeois social formations formed one another reciprocally in a "process without a subject,'' by restructuring the state in the national form and by modifying the status of all the other classes. This explains the simultaneous genesis of nationalism and cosmopolitanism.

However simplified this hypothesis may be, it has one essential consequence for the analysis of the nation as a historical form: we have to renounce linear developmental schemas once and for all, not only where modes of production are concerned, but also in respect of political forms. There is, then, nothing to prevent us from examining whether in a new phase of the world-economy rival state structures to that of the nation-state are not tending to form once again. In reality, there is a close implicit connection between the illusion of a necessary unilinear evolution of social formations and the uncritical acceptance of the nation-state as the ''ultimate form'' of political institution, destined to be perpetuated for ever (having failed to give way to a hypothetical ''end of the state'').[5]

To bring out the relative indeterminacy of the process of constitution and development of the nation form, let us approach matters from the perspective of a consciously provocative question: *For whom today is it too late?* In other words, which are the social formations which, in spite of the global constraint of the world-economy and of the system of state to which it has given rise, can no longer completely effect their transformation into nations, except in a purely juridical sense and at the cost of interminable conflicts that produce no decisive result? An a priori answer, and even a general answer, is doubtless impossible, but it is obvious that the question arises not only in respect of the ''new nations'' created after decolonization, the transnationalization of capital and communications, the creation of planetary war machines and so on, but also in respect of ''old nations'' which are today affected by the same phenomena.

One might be tempted to say that it is too late for those independent states which are formally equal and represented in the institutions which are precisely styled ''international'' to become self-centred nations, each with its national language(s) of culture, administration and commerce, with its independent military forces, its protected internal market, its currency and its enterprises competing on a world scale and, particularly, with its ruling bourgeoisie (whether it be a private capitalist bourgeoisie or a state *nomenklatura*), since in one way or another every bourgeoisie is a state bourgeoisie. Yet one might also be tempted to say the opposite: the field of the reproduction of nations, of the deployment of the nation form is no longer open today except in the old peripheries and semiperipheries; so far as the old ''core'' is concerned, it has, to varying degrees, entered the phase of the decomposition of national structures which were connected with the old forms of its domination, even if the outcome of such a decomposition is both distant and uncertain. It clearly seems, however, if one accepts this hypothesis, that the nations of the future will not be like those of the past. The fact that we are today seeing a general upsurge of nationalism everywhere (North and South, East and West) does not enable us to resolve this kind of dilemma: it is part of the formal universality of the international system of states. Contemporary nationalism, whatever its language, tells us nothing of the real age of the nation form in relation to ''world time.''

In reality, if we are to cast a little more light on this question, we must take into account a further characteristic of the history of national formations. This is what I call the *delayed nationalization of society*, which first of all concerns the old nations themselves—so delayed is it, it ultimately appears as an endless task. A historian like Eugen Weber has shown (as have other subsequent studies) that, in the case of France, universal schooling and the unification of customs and beliefs by interregional labour migration and military service and the subordination of political and religious conflicts to patriotic ideology did not come about until the early years of the twentieth century.[6] His study suggests that the French peasantry was only finally "nationalized" at the point when it was about to disappear as the majority class (though this disappearance, as we know, was itself retarded by the protectionism that is an essential characteristic of national politics). The more recent work of Gérard Noiriel shows in its turn that, since the end of the nineteenth century, "French identity" has continually been dependent upon the capacity to integrate immigrant populations. The question arises as to whether that capacity is today reaching its limit or whether it can in fact continue to be exercised in the same form.[7]

In order completely to identify the reasons for the relative stability of the national formation, it is not sufficient, then, merely to refer to the initial threshold of its emergence. We must also ask how the problems of unequal development of town and countryside, colonization and decolonization, wars and the revolutions which they have sometimes sparked off, the constitution of supranational blocs and so on have in practice been surmounted, since these are all events and processes which involved at least a risk of class conflicts drifting beyond the limits within which they had been more or less easily confined by the "consensus" of the national state. We may say that in France as, *mutatis mutandis*, in the other old bourgeois formations, what made it possible to resolve the contradictions capitalism brought with it and to begin to remake the nation form at a point when it was not even completed (or to prevent it from coming apart before it was completed), was the institution of the *national-social state*, that is, of a state "intervening" in the very reproduction of the economy and particularly in the formation of individuals, in family structures, the structures of public health and, more generally, in the whole space of "private life." This is a tendency that was present from the very beginnings of the nation form—a point to which I return below—but one which has become dominant during the nineteenth and twentieth centuries, the result of which is entirely to subordinate the existence of the individuals of all classes to their status as citizens of the nation-state, to the fact of their being "nationals" that is.[8]

PRODUCING THE PEOPLE

A social formation only reproduces itself as a nation to the extent that, through a network of apparatuses and daily practices, the individual is instituted as *homo nationalis* from cradle to grave, at the same time as he or she is instituted as *homo oeconomicus, politicus, religiosus* . . . That is why the question of the nation form, if it is henceforth an open one, is, at bottom, the question of knowing under what historical conditions it is possible to institute such a thing: by virtue of what internal and external relations of force and also by virtue of what symbolic forms invested in elementary material practices? Asking this question is another way of asking oneself to what transition in civilization the nationalization of societies corresponds, and what are the figures of individuality between which nationality moves.

The crucial point is this: What makes the nation a "community"? Or rather in what way is the form of community instituted by the nation distinguished specifically from other historical communities?

Let us dispense right away with the antitheses traditionally attached to that notion, the first of which is the antithesis between the "real" and the "imaginary" community. *Every social community reproduced by the functioning of institutions is imaginary*, that is to say, it is based on the projection of individual existence into the weft of a collective narrative, on the recognition of a common name and on traditions lived as the trace of an immemorial past (even when they have been fabricated and inculcated in the recent past). But this comes down to accepting that, under certain conditions, *only* imaginary communities are real.

In the case of national formations, the imaginary which inscribes itself in the real in this way is that of the "people." It is that of a community which recognizes itself in advance in the institution of the state, which recognizes that state as "its own" in opposition to other states and, in particular, inscribes its political struggles within the horizon of that state—by, for example, formulating its aspirations for reform and social revolution as projects for the transformation of "its national state." Without this, there can be neither "monopoly of organized violence" (Max Weber), nor "national-popular will" (Gramsci). But such a people does not exist naturally, and even when it is tendentially constituted, it does not exist for all time. No modern nation possesses a given "ethnic" basis, even when it arises out of a national independence struggle. And, moreover, no modern nation, however "egalitarian" it may be, corresponds to the extinction of class conflicts. The fundamental problem is therefore to produce the people. More exactly, it is to make the people produce itself continually as national community. Or again, it is to produce the effect of unity by virtue of which the people will appear, in everyone's eyes, "as a people," that is, as the basis and origin of political power.

Rousseau was the first to have explicitly conceived the question in the terms "What makes a people a people?" Deep down, this question is no different from the one which arose a moment ago: How are individuals nationalized or, in other words, socialized in the dominant form of national belonging? Which enables us to put aside from the outset another artificial dilemma: it is not a question of setting a collective identity against individual identities. *All identity is individual*, but there is no individual identity that is not historical or, in other words, constructed within a field of social values, norms of behaviour and collective symbols. Individuals never identify with one another (not even in the "fusional" practices of mass movements or the "intimacy" of affective relations), nor, however, do they ever acquire an isolated identity, which is an intrinsically contradictory notion. The real question is how the dominant reference points of individual identity change over time and with the changing institutional environment.

To the question of the historical production of the people (or of national individuality) we cannot merely be content to rely with a description of conquests, population movements and administrative practices of "territorialization." The individuals destined to perceive themselves as the members of a single nation are either gathered together externally from diverse geographical origins, as in the nations formed by immigration (France, the USA) or else are brought mutually to recognize one another within a historical frontier which contained them all. The people is constituted out of various populations subject to a common law. In every case, however, a model of their unity must "anticipate" that constitution: the process of unification (the effectiveness of which can be measured, for example, in collective mobilization in wartime, that is, in the capacity to confront death collectively) presupposes the constitution of a specific ideological form. It must at one and the same time be a mass phenomenon and a phenomenon of individuation, must effect an "interpellation of individuals as subjects" (Althusser) which is much more potent than the mere inculcation of political values or rather one that integrates this inculcation into a more elementary process (which we may term "primary") of fixation of the affects of love and hate and representation of the "self." That ideological form must become an a priori condition of communication between individuals (the "citizens") and between social groups—not by suppressing all differences, but by relativizing them and subordinating them to itself in such a way that it is the symbolic difference between "ourselves" and "foreigners" which wins out and which is lived as irreducible. In other words, to use the terminology proposed by Fichte in his *Reden an die deutsche Nation* of 1808, the "external frontiers" of the state have to become "internal frontiers" or—which amounts to the same thing—external frontiers have to be imagined constantly as a projection and protection of an internal collective personality, which each of us carries within ourselves and enables us to inhabit the space of the state as a place where we have always been—and always will be—"at home."

What might that ideological form be? Depending on the particular circumstances, it will be called patriotism or nationalism, the events which promote its formation or which reveal its potency will be recorded and its origin will be traced back to political methods—the combination of "force" and "education" (as Machiavelli and Gramsci put it)—which enable the state to some extent to fabricate public consciousness. But this fabrication is merely an external aspect. To grasp the deepest reasons for its effectiveness, attention will turn then, as the attention of political philosophy and sociology have turned for three centuries, towards the analogy of *religion*, making nationalism and patriotism out to be a religion—if not indeed *the* religion—of modern times.

Inevitably, there is some truth in this—and not only because religions, formally, in so far as they start out from "souls" and individual identities, institute forms of community and prescribe a social "morality"; but also because theological discourse has provided models for the idealization of the nation and the sacralization of the state, which make it possible for a bond of sacrifice to be

created between individuals, and for the stamp of "truth" and "law" to be conferred upon the rules of the legal system.[9] Every national community must have
been represented at some point or another as a "chosen people." Nevertheless,
the political philosophies of the Classical Age had already recognized the inadequacy of this analogy, which is equally clearly demonstrated by the failure of
the attempts to constitute "civil religions," by the fact that the "state religion"
ultimately only constituted a transitory form of national ideology (even when this
transition lasted for a long time and produced important effects by superimposing
religious on national struggles) and by the interminable conflict between theological universality and the universality of nationalism.

In reality, the opposite argument is correct. Incontestably, national ideology
involves ideal signifiers (first and foremost the very *name* of the nation or "fatherland") on to which may be transferred the sense of the sacred and the affects
of love, respect, sacrifice and fear which have cemented religious communities;
but that transfer only takes place because *another type* of community is involved
here. The analogy is itself based on a deeper difference. If it were not, it would
be impossible to understand why national identity, more or less completely integrating the forms of religious identity, ends up tending to replace it, and forcing
it itself to become "nationalized."

FICTIVE ETHNICITY AND IDEAL NATION

I apply the term "fictive ethnicity" to the community instituted by the nation-
state. This is an intentionally complex expression in which the term fiction, in
keeping with my remarks above, should not be taken in the sense of a pure and
simple illusion without historical effects, but must, on the contrary, be understood
by analogy with the *persona ficta* of the juridical tradition in the sense of an
institutional effect, a "fabrication." No nation possesses an ethnic base naturally,
but as social formations are nationalized, the populations included within them,
divided up among them or dominated by them are ethnicized—that is, represented
in the past or in the future *as if* they formed a natural community, possessing of
itself an identity of origins, culture and interests which transcends individuals and
social conditions.[10]

Fictive ethnicity is not purely and simply identical with the *ideal nation* which
is the object of patriotism, but it is indispensable to it, for, without it, the nation
would appear precisely only as an idea or an arbitrary abstraction; patriotism's
appeal would be addressed to no one. It is fictive ethnicity which makes it possible
for the expression of a preexisting unity to be seen in the state, and continually
to measure the state against its "historic mission" in the service of the nation
and, as a consequence, to idealize politics. By constituting the people as a fictively
ethnic unity against the background of a universalistic representation which attributes to each individual one—and only one—ethnic identity and which thus
divides up the whole of humanity between different ethnic groups corresponding
potentially to so many nations, national ideology does much more than justify
the strategies employed by the state to control populations. It inscribes their de-

mands in advance in a sense of belonging in the double sense of the term—both what it is that makes one belong to oneself and also what makes one belong to other fellow human beings. Which means that one can be interpellated, as an individual, *in the name of* the collectivity whose name one bears. The naturalization of belonging and the sublimation of the ideal nation are two aspects of the same process.

How can ethnicity be produced? And how can it be produced in such a way that it does not appear as fiction, but as the most natural of origins? History shows us that there are two great competing routes to this: language and race. Most often the two operate together, for only their complementarity makes it possible for the "people" to be represented as an absolutely autonomous unit. Both express the idea that the national character (which might also be called its soul or its spirit) is immanent in the people. But both offer a means of transcending actual individuals and political relations. They constitute two ways of rooting historical populations in a fact of "nature" (the diversity of languages and the diversity of races appearing predestined), but also two ways of giving a meaning to their continued existence, of transcending its contingency. By force of circumstance, however, at times one or the other is dominant, for they are not based on the development of the same institutions and do not appeal to the same symbols or the same idealizations of the national identity. The fact of these different articulations of, on the one hand, a predominantly linguistic ethnicity and, on the other, an ethnicity that is predominantly racial has obvious political consequences. For this reason, and for the sake of clarity of analysis, we must begin by examining the two separately.

The language community seems the more abstract notion, but in reality it is the more concrete since it connects individuals up with an origin which may at any moment be actualized and which has as its content the *common act* of their own exchanges, of their discursive communication, using the instruments of spoken language and the whole, constantly self-renewing mass of written and recorded texts. This is not to say that that community is an immediate one, without internal limits, any more than communication is in reality "transparent" between all individuals. But these limits are always relative: even if it were the case that individuals whose social conditions were very distant from one another were never in direct communication, they would be bound together by an uninterrupted chain of intermediate discourses. They are not isolated—either *de jure* or *de facto*.

We should, however, certainly not allow ourselves to believe that this situation is as old as the world itself. It is, on the contrary, remarkably recent. The old empires and the *Ancien Régime* societies were still based on the juxtaposition of linguistically separate populations, on the superimposition of mutually incompatible "languages" for the dominant and the dominated and for the sacred and profane spheres. Between these there had to be a whole system of translations.[11] In modern national formations, the translators are writers, journalists and politicians, social actors who speak the language of the "people" in a way that seems all the more natural for the very degree of distinction they thereby bring to it. The translation process has become primarily one of internal translation between different "levels of language." Social differences are expressed and relativized as different ways of speaking the national language, which supposes a common code and even a common norm.[12] This latter is, as we know, inculcated by universal schooling, whose primary function it is to perform precisely this task.

That is why there is a close historical correlation between the national formation and the development of schools as "popular" institutions, not limited to specialized training or to elite culture, but serving to underpin the whole process of the socialization of individuals. That the school should also be the site of the inculcation of a nationalist ideology—and sometimes also the place where it is contested—is a secondary phenomenon, and is, strictly speaking, a less indispensable aspect. Let us simply say that schooling is the principal institution which produces ethnicity as linguistic community. It is not, however, the only one: the state, economic exchange and family life are also schools in a sense, organs of the ideal nation recognizable by a common language which belongs to them "as their own." For what is decisive here is not only that the national language should be recognized as the official language, but, much more fundamentally, that it should be able to appear as the very element of the life of a people, the *reality* which each person may appropriate in his or her own way, without thereby destroying its identity. There is no contradiction between the instituting of *one* national language and the daily discrepancy between—and clash of—"class languages" which precisely are not different languages. In fact , the two things are complementary. All linguistic practices feed into a single "love of the language" which is addressed not to the textbook norm nor to particular usage, but to the "mother tongue"—that is, to the ideal of a common origin projected back beyond learning processes and specialist forms of usage and which, by that very fact, becomes the metaphor for the love fellow nationals feel for one another.[13]

One might then ask oneself, quite apart from the precise historical questions which the history of national languages poses—from the difficulties of their unification or imposition, and from their elaboration into an idiom that is both "popular" and "cultivated" (a process which we know to be far from complete today in all nation-states, in spite of the labours of their intellectuals with the aid of various international bodies)—*why the language community is not sufficient* to produce ethnicity.

Perhaps this has to do with the paradoxical properties which, by virtue of its very structure, the linguistic signifier confers on individual identity. In a sense, it is always in the element of language that individuals are interpellated as subjects, for every interpellation is of the order of discourse. Every "personality" is constructed with words, in which law, genealogy, history, political choices, professional qualifications and psychology are set forth. But the linguistic construction of identity is by definition *open*. No individual "chooses" his or her mother tongue or can "change" it at will. Nevertheless, it is always possible to appropriate several languages and to turn oneself into a different kind of bearer of discourse and of the transformations of language. The linguistic community induces a terribly constraining ethnic memory (Roland Barthes once went so far as to call it "fascist"), but it is one which none the less possesses a strange plasticity: it immediately naturalizes new acquisitions. It does so *too quickly* in a sense. It is a collective memory which perpetuates itself at the cost of an individual forgetting of "origins." The "second generation" immigrant—a notion which in this context acquires a structural significance—inhabits the national language (and through it the nation itself) in a manner as spontaneous, as "hereditary" and as imperious, so far as affectivity and the imaginary are concerned, as the son of one of those native heaths which we think of as so very French (and most of which not so long ago did not even have the national language as their daily parlance). One's "mother" tongue is not necessarily the language of one's "real" mother. The language community is a community *in the present*, which produces the feeling that it has always existed, but which lays down no destiny for the successive generations. Ideally, it "assimilates" anyone, but holds no one. Finally, it affects all individuals in their innermost being (in the way in which they constitute themselves as subjects), but its historical particularity is bound only to interchangeable institutions. When circumstances permit, it may serve different nations (as English, Spanish and even French do) or survive the "physical" disappearance of the people who used it (like "ancient" Greek and Latin or "literary" Arabic). For it to be tied down to the frontiers of a particular people, it therefore needs an extra degree [*un supplément*] of particularity, or a principle of closure, of exclusion.

This principle is that of being part of a common race. But here we must be very careful not to give rise to misunderstandings. All kinds of somatic or psychological features, both visible and invisible, may lend themselves to creating the fiction of a racial identity and therefore to representing natural and hereditary differences between social groups either within the same nation or outside its frontiers. I have discussed elsewhere, as have others before me, the development of the marks of race and the relation they bear to different historical figures of social conflict. What we are solely concerned with here is the symbolic kernel which makes it possible to equate race and ethnicity ideally, and to represent unity of race to oneself as the origin or cause of the historical unity of a people. Now, unlike what applied in the case of the linguistic community, it cannot be a question here of a practice which is really common to *all* the individuals who form a political unit. We are not dealing with anything equivalent to communication. What we are speaking of is therefore a second-degree fiction. This fiction, however, also derives its effectiveness from everyday practices, relations which immediately structure the "life" of individuals. And, most importantly, whereas the language community can only create equality between individuals by simultaneously "naturalizing" the social inequality of linguistic practices, the race community dissolves social inequalities in an even more ambivalent "similarity"; it ethnicizes the social difference which is an expression of irreconcilable antagonisms by lending it the form of a division between the "genuinely" and the "falsely" national.

I think we may cast some light on this paradox in the following way. The symbolic kernel of the idea of race (and of its demographic and cultural equivalents) is the schema of genealogy, that is, quite simply the idea that the filiation of individuals transmits from generation to generation a substance both biological and spiritual and thereby inscribes them in a temporal community known as "kinship." That is why, *as soon as* national ideology enunciates the proposition

that the individuals belonging to the same people are interrelated (or, in the pre-
scriptive mode, that they should constitute a circle of extended kinship), we are
in the presence of this second mode of ethnicization.

The objection will no doubt be raised here that such a representation characterizes societies and communities which have nothing national about them. But,
it is precisely on this point that the particular innovation hinges by which the
nation form is articulated to the modern idea of race. This idea is correlative with
the tendency for "private" genealogies, as (still) codified by traditional systems
of preferential marriage and lineage, to disappear. The idea of a racial community
makes its appearance when the frontiers of kinship dissolve at the level of the
clan, the neighbourhood community and, theoretically at least, the social class,
to be imaginarily transferred to the threshold of nationality: that is to say, when
nothing prevents marriage with any of one's "fellow citizens" whatever, and
when, on the contrary, such a marriage seems the only one that is "normal" or
"natural." The racial community has a tendency to represent itself as one big
family or as the common envelope of family relations (the community of
"French," "American" or "Algerian" families).[14] From that point onward, each
individual has his/her family, whatever his/her social condition, but the family—
like property—becomes a contingent relation between individuals. In order to
consider this question further, we ought therefore to turn to a discussion of the
history of the family, an institution which here plays a role every bit as central
as that played by the school in the discussion above, and one that is ubiquitous
in the discourse of race.

THE FAMILY AND THE SCHOOL

We here run up against the lacunae in family history, a subject which remains
prey to the dominant perspective of laws relating to marriage on the one hand
and, on the other, of "private life" as a literary and anthropological subject. The
great theme of the recent history of the family is the emergence of the "nuclear"
or small family (constituted by the parental couple and their children), and here
discussion is focused on whether it is a specifically "modern" phenomenon (eighteenth and nineteenth centuries) connected with bourgeois forms of sociality (the
thesis of Ariès and Shorter) or whether it is the result of a development, the basis
of which was laid down a long time before by ecclesiastical law and the control
of marriage by the Christian authorities (Goody's thesis).[15] In fact, these positions
are not incompatible. But, most importantly, they tend to push into the shade what
is for us the most crucial question: the correlation which has gradually been
established since the institution of public registration and the codification of the
family (of which the Code Napoléon was the prototype) between the dissolution
of relations of "extended" kinship and the penetration of family relations by the
intervention of the nation-state, which runs from legislation in respect of inheritance to the organization of birth control. Let us note here that in contemporary
national societies, except for a few genealogy "fanatics" and a few who are
"nostalgic" for the days of the aristocracy, genealogy is no longer either a body

of th oretical knowledge or an object of oral memory, nor is it recorded and conserved *privately*: today *it is the state which draws up and keeps the archive of filiations and alliances.*

Here again we have to distinguish between a deep and a superficial level. The superficial level is familialist discourse (constitutive of conservative nationalism), which at a very early stage became linked with nationalism in political tradition— particularly within the French tradition. The deep level is the simultaneous emergence of "private life," the "intimate (small) family circle" *and* the family policy of the state, which projects into the public sphere the new notion of population and the demographic techniques for measuring it, of the supervision of its health and morals, of its reproduction. The result is that the modern family circle is quite the opposite of an autonomous sphere at the frontiers of which the structures of the state would halt. It is the sphere in which the relations between individuals are immediately charged with a "civic" function and made possible by constant state assistance, beginning with relations between the sexes which are aligned to procreation. This is also what enables us to understand the anarchistic tone that sexually "deviant" behaviour easily takes on in modern national formations, whereas in earlier societies it more usually took on a tone of religious heresy. Public health and social security have replaced the father confessor, not term for term, but by introducing both a new "freedom" and a new assistance, a new mission and therefore also a new demand. Thus, as lineal kinship, solidarity between generations and the economic functions of the extended family dissolve, what takes their place is neither a natural micro-society nor a purely "individualistic" contractual relation, but a nationalization of the family , which has as its counterpart the identification of the national community with a symbolic kinship, circumscribed by rules of pseudo-endogamy, and with a tendency not so much to project itself into a sense of having common antecedents as a feeling of having common descendants.

That is why the idea of eugenics is always latent in the reciprocal relation between the "bourgeois" family and a society which takes the nation form. That is why nationalism also has a secret affinity with sexism: not so much as a manifestation of the same authoritarian tradition but in so far as the inequality of sexual roles in conjugal love and child-rearing constitutes the anchoring point for the juridical, economic, educational and medical mediation of the state. Finally also, that is why the representation of nationalism as a "tribalism"—the sociologists' grand alternative to representing it as a religion—is both mystificatory and revealing. Mystificatory because it imagines nationalism as a regression to archaic forms of community which are in reality incompatible with the nation-state (this can be clearly seen from the incompleteness of the formation of a nation wherever powerful lineal or tribal solidarities still exist). But it is also revealing of the substitution of one imaginary of kinship for another, a substitution which the nation effects and which underpins the transformation of the family itself. It is also what forces us to ask ourselves to what extent the nation form can continue to reproduce itself indefinitely (at least as the dominant form) once the transformation of the family is "completed"—that is to say, once relations of sex and procreation are completely removed from the genealogical order. We would then reach the limit of the material possibilities of conceiving what human "races" are and of investing that particular representation in the process of producing ethnicity. But no doubt we have not reached that point yet.

Althusser was not wrong in his outline definition of the "Ideological State Apparatuses" to suggest that the kernel of the dominant ideology of bourgeois societies has passed from the family–church dyad to the family–school dyad.[16] I am, however, tempted to introduce two correctives to that formulation. First, I shall not say that a particular institution of this kind in itself constitutes *an* "Ideological State Apparatus": what such a formulation adequately designates is rather the combined functioning of *several* dominant institutions. I shall further propose that the contemporary importance of schooling and the family unit does not derive solely from the functional place they take in the reproduction of labour power, but from the fact that they subordinate that reproduction to the constitution of a fictive ethnicity—that is, to the articulation of a linguistic community and a community of race implicit in population policies (what Foucault called by a suggestive but ambiguous term the system of "bio-powers").[17] School and family perhaps have other aspects or deserve to be analysed from other points of view. Their history begins well before the appearance of the nation form and may continue beyond it. But what makes them together constitute the dominant ideological apparatus in bourgeois societies—which is expressed in their growing interdependence and in their tendency to divide up the time devoted to the training of individuals exhaustively between them—is their national importance, that is, their immediate importance for the production of ethnicity. In this sense, there is only *one* dominant "Ideological State Apparatus" in bourgeois social formations, using the school and family institutions for its own ends—together with other institutions grafted on to the school and the family—and the existence of that apparatus is at the root of the hegemony of nationalism.

We must add one remark in conclusion on this hypothesis. Articulation—even complementarity—does not mean harmony. Linguistic ethnicity and racial (or hereditary) ethnicity are in a sense mutually exclusive. I suggested above that the linguistic community is open, whereas the race community appears in principle closed (since it leads—theoretically—to maintaining indefinitely, until the end of the generations, outside the community or on its "inferior" "foreign" margins those who, by its criteria, are not authentically national). Both are ideal representations. Doubtless race symbolism combines the element of anthropological universality on which it is based (the chain of generations, the absolute of kinship extended to the whole of humanity) with an imaginary of segregation and prohibitions. But in practice migration and intermarriage are constantly transgressing the limits which are thus projected (even where coercive policies criminalize "interbreeding"). The real obstacle to the mixing of populations is constituted rather by class differences which tend to reconstitute caste phenomena. The hereditary substance of ethnicity constantly has to be redefined: yesterday it was "German-ness," "the French" or "Anglo-Saxon" race, today it is "European-ness" or "Western-ness," tomorrow perhaps the "Mediterranean race." Conversely, the openness of the linguistic community is an ideal openness, even though it has as its material support the possibility of translating from one language to another and therefore the capacity of individuals to increase the range of their linguistic competence.

Though formally egalitarian, belonging to the linguistic community—chiefly because of the fact that it is mediated by the institution of the school—immediately re-creates divisions, differential norms which also overlap with class differences to a very great degree. The greater the role taken on by the education system within bourgeois societies, the more do differences in linguistic (and therefore literary, "cultural" and technological) competence function as caste differences, assigning different "social destinies" to individuals. In these circumstances, it is not surprising that they should immediately be associated with forms of corporal *habitus* (to use Pierre Bourdieu's terminology) which confer on the act of speaking in its personal, non-universalizable traits the function of a racial or quasi-racial mark (and which still occupy a very important place in the formulation of "class racism"): "foreign" or "regional" accent, "popular" style of speech, language "errors" or, conversely, ostentatious "correctness" immediately designating a speaker's belonging to a particular population and spontaneously interpreted as reflecting a specific family origin and a hereditary disposition.[18] The production of ethnicity is also the racialization of language and the verbalization of race.

It is not an irrelevant matter—either from the immediate political point of view or from the point of view of the development of the nation form, or its future role in the instituting of social relations—that a particular representation of ethnicity should be dominant, since it leads to two radically different attitudes to the problem of integration and assimilation, two ways of grounding the juridical order and nationalizing institutions.[19]

The French "revolutionary nation" accorded a privileged place to the symbol of language in its own initial process of formation; it bound political unity closely to linguistic uniformity, the democratization of the state to the coercive repression of cultural "particularisms," local *patois* being the object on which it became fixated. For its part, the American "revolutionary nation" built its original ideals on a double repression: that of the extermination of the Amerindian "natives" and that of the difference between free "White" men and "Black" slaves. The linguistic community inherited from the Anglo-Saxon "mother country" did not pose a problem—at least apparently—until Hispanic immigration conferred upon it the significance of class symbol and racial feature. "Nativism" has always been implicit in the history of French national ideology until, at the end of the nineteenth century, colonization on the one hand, and an intensification of the importation of labour and the segregation of manual workers by means of their ethnic origin on the other, led to the constitution of the phantasm of the "French race." It was, by contrast, very quickly made explicit in the history of American national ideology, which represented the formation of the American people as the melting-pot of a new race, but also as a hierarchical combination of the different ethnic contributions, at the cost of difficult analogies between European or Asian immigration and the social inequalities inherited from slavery and reinforced by the economic exploitation of the Blacks.[20]

These historical differences in no sense impose any necessary outcome—they are rather the stuff of political struggles—but they deeply modify the conditions in which problems of assimilation, equality of rights, citizenship, nationalism and internationalism are posed. One might seriously wonder whether in regard to the production of fictive ethnicity, the "building of Europe"—to the extent that it will seek to transfer to the "Community" level functions and symbols of the nation-state—will orientate itself *predominantly* towards the institution of a "European co-lingualism" (and if so, adopting which language) or *predominantly* in the direction of the idealization of "European demographic identity" conceived mainly in opposition to the "southern populations" (Turks, Arabs, Blacks).[21] Every "people," which is the product of a national process of ethnicization, is forced today to find its own means of going beyond exclusivism or identitarian ideology in the world of transnational communications and global relations of force. Or rather: every individual is compelled to find in the transformation of the imaginary of "his" or "her" people the means to leave it, in order to communicate with the individuals of other peoples with which he or she shares the same interests and, to some extent, the same future.

NOTES

1. See Gérard Noiriel, *Le Creuset français. Histoire de l'immigration XIXe–XXe siècles*, Editions du Seuil, Paris 1988.

2. If one did, however, have to choose a date symbolically, one might point to the middle of the sixteenth century: the completion of the Spanish conquest of the New World, the break-up of the Habsburg Empire, the end of the dynastic wars in England and the beginning of the Dutch War of Independence.

3. Fernand Braudel, *Civilization and Capitalism*, vol. 2, *The Wheels of Commerce*, transl. Siân Reynolds, Collins, London 1982, and vol. 3, *The Perspective of the World*, transl. Siân Reynolds, Collins, London 1984; Immanuel Wallerstein, *The Modern World-System*, vol. 1, *Capitalist Agriculture and the Origin of the European World-Economy in the Sixteenth Century*, Academic Press, London 1974, and vol. 2, *Mercantilism and the Consolidation of the European World-Economy*, Academic Press, London 1980.

4. See Braudel, *The Perspective of the World*, pp. 97–105; Wallerstein, *Capitalist Agriculture*, pp. 165 et seq.

5. From this point of view, there is nothing surprising about the fact that the "orthodox" Marxist theory of the linear succession of modes of production became the official doctrine in the USSR at the point when nationalism triumphed there, particularly as it made it possible for the "first socialist state" to be represented as the new universal nation.

6. Eugen Weber, *Peasants into Frenchmen*, Stanford University Press, Stanford, CA 1976.

7. Gérard Noiriel, *Longwy, Immigrés et prolétaires, 1880–1980*, PUF, Paris 1984; *Le Creuset français*.

8. For some further remarks on this same point, see my study, "Propositions sur la citoyenneté," in C. Wihtol de Wenden, ed., *La Citoyenneté*, Edilig-Fondation Diderot, Paris 1988.

9. On all these points, the work of Kantorowicz is clearly of crucial significance: see *Mourir pour la patrie et autres textes*, PUF, Paris 1985.

10. I say "included within them," but I should also add "or excluded by them," since the ethnicization of the "others" occurs simultaneously with that of the "nationals": there are no longer any historical differences other than ethnic ones (thus the Jews also have to be a "people"). On the ethnicization of colonized populations, see J.-L. Amselle and E. M'Bokolo, *Au coeur de l'ethnie: ethnies, tribalisme et Etat en Afrique*, La Découverte, Paris 1985.

11. Ernest Gellner (*Nations and Nationalism*, Blackwell, Oxford 1983) and Benedict Anderson (*Imagined Communities*, Verso, London 1983), whose analyses are as opposed as "materialism" and "idealism," both rightly stress this point.

12. See Renée Balibar, *L'Institution du français. Essai sur le colingualisme des Carolingiens à la République*, PUF, Paris 1985.

13. Jean-Claude Milner offers some very stimulating suggestions on this point, though more in *Les Noms indistincts* (Seuil, Paris 1983), pp. 43 et seq. than in *L'Amour de la langue* (Seuil, Paris 1978). On the "class struggle"/"language struggle" alternative in the USSR at the point when the policy of "socialism in one country" became dominant, see F. Gadet, J.-M. Gaymann, Y. Mignot and E. Roudinesco, *Les Maîtres de la langue*, Maspero, Paris 1979.

14. Let us add that we have here a sure *criterion* for the commutation between racism and nationalism: every discourse on the fatherland or nation which associates these notions with the "defence of the family"— not to speak of the birth rate—is already ensconced in the universe of racism.

15. Philippe Ariès, *L'Enfant et la vie familiale sous l'Ancien Régime*, Plon, Paris 1960, revised edn. 1975 (*Centuries of Childhood*, transl. Robert Baldick, London, Cape 1962); Edward Shorter, *The Making of the Modern Family*, Basic Books, New York 1975; Jack Goody, *The Development of the Family and Marriage in Europe*, Cambridge University Press, Cambridge 1983.

16. See Louis Althusser, "Ideology and State Ideological Apparatuses," *Lenin and Philosophy and Other Essays*, New Left Books, London 1971.

17. Michel Foucault, *The History of Sexuality*, vol. 1, transl. Robert Hurley, Allen Lane, London 1977.

18. See P. Bourdieu, *Distinction*, transl. Richard Nice, Routledge & Kegan Paul, London 1984: *Ce que parler veut dire: l'économie des échanges linguistiques*, Fayard, Paris 1982; and the critique by the "Révoltes logiques" collective (*L'Empire du sociologue*, La Découverte, Paris 1984), which bears essentially on the way that Bourdieu *fixes* social roles as "destinies" and immediately attributes to the antagonism between them a function of reproducing the "totality" (the chapter on language is by Françoise Kerleroux).

19. See some most valuable remarks on this point in Françoise Gadet and Michel Pêcheux, *La Langue introuvable*, Maspero, Paris 1981, pp. 38 et seq. ("L'anthropologie linguistique entre le Droit et la Vie").

20. On American "nativism," see R. Ertel, G. Fabre and E. Marienstras, *En marge. Les minorités aux Etats-Unis*, Maspero, Paris 1974, pp. 25 et seq., and Michael Omi and Howard Winant, *Racial Formation in the United States. From the 1960s to the 1980s*, Routledge & Kegan Paul, London 1986, p. 120. It is interesting to see a movement developing today in the United States (directed against Latin American immigration) calling for English to be made the *official* language.

21. Right at the heart of this alternative lies the following truly crucial question: will the administrative and educational institutions of the future "United Europe" accept Arabic, Turkish or even certain Asian or African languages on an equal footing with French, German and Portuguese, or will those languages be regarded as "foreign"?

Prasenjit Duara

Born in Assam, India, Prasenjit Duara's educational and professional odyssey took him from undergraduate training at St. Stephens College in Delhi, to the doctoral program at Harvard, teaching at George Mason University and Stanford University, to his current position at the University of Chicago. A specialist in modern Chinese history, Duara's first book was the prizewinning *Culture, Power and the State: Rural North China, 1900–1942* (Stanford Calif.: Stanford University Press, 1988), which has been translated into both Chinese and Japanese. This essay reprises ideas from *Rescuing History from the Nation: Questioning Narratives of Modern China* (Chicago: University of Chicago Press, 1995). His current work, on the period of Japanese rule in Manchuria, the time of the "last emperor," attempts to illuminate the fatal embrace between Japanese colonialist discourse and Chinese nationalism. Duara explores the contesting discourses of the nation, particularly the intersections of language and the competing visions of political communites. Borrowing from the work of deconstructionists, he is concerned with the silences and repressions that occur in all acts of articulation.

Using the history of China, but also of South Asia and Japan, as his laboratory, Duara contends with the Gellner and Anderson theories of nationalism that locate the nation in modernity and posit a radical disjuncture with premodern political communities. Whatever the importance of print capitalism in European nation-making, in China an intimate relationship between the written and spoken word—the power of pan-Chinese myths, for example, and their incorporation in folk drama—provided a common cultural reservoir from which agrarian peoples gained a sense of identity with a broad cultural and political order. Without eliding the distinctions between modern identities and others, Duara emphasizes the multiplicity of identities at all times and the resemblances between more traditional and national identities.

Two particularly strong conceptualizations of the political community emerged in imperial Chinese society, one the ethnic self-description of the Han people, the other a community based on the cultural values of the elite. In the twentieth century modern discourses of the nation from outside influenced Chinese intellectuals and political actors, who combined them with selective use of existing Chinese ideas of political communality. The emergence of the modern nation-state system also powerfully determined the further elaboration of national discourses and identities as it promoted ethnic loyalty to territory. Rejecting any essentialist view of the nation, Duara proposes to look at national communities as relationships based on inclusions and exclusions and argues that "an incipient nationality is formed when the perception of the boundaries of community are transformed: when soft boundaries are transformed into hard ones." Hardening occurs when a community adopts a master narrative of descent, thus defining more exclusively who belongs and who is outside.

Historicizing National Identity,
or Who Imagines What and When

For a long time now nationalism and national identity have been understood within the assumptions of modernization theory. The effort to define nationalism as a quintessentially modern phenomenon in which citizens identify with the nation-state has done much to clarify nationalism. At the same time, however, this effort has tended to fix and objectify what is after all, a subjective, fluid and elusive phenomenon—the meanings of the nation to both citizens and nation-state.[1] In this essay I take a critical historical view of national identity and I explore the phenomenon less in its distinctiveness than in its changing relationships to other visions of political community, both historical and contemporary.

In the problematique of modernization theories, the nation is a unique and unprecedented form of community which finds its place in the oppositions between empire and nation, tradition and modernity, and center and periphery. As the new and sovereign subject of history, the nation embodies a moral force which supersedes dynasties and ruling clerisies, which are seen as merely partial subjects representing only themselves through history. By contrast, the nation is a collective subject—whose ideal periphery exists only outside itself—poised to realize its historical destiny in a modern future.[2] This narrative depicts not only the history of nationalism, but constitutes the master narrative of much modern history, allowing the nation-state to define the framework of its self-understanding. My goal is to take a step in extricating history from this framework and devise a perspective from which it can historicize the nation and national identity itself.

To see the nation as a collective subject of modernity obscures the nature of national identity. I propose instead that we view national identity as founded upon fluid relationships; it thus both resembles and is interchangeable with other political identities. If the dynamics of national identity lie within the same terrain as other political identities, we will need to break with two assumptions of mod-

---

Prasenjit Duara, "Historicizing National Identity, or Who Imagines What and When," unpublished essay outlining some ideas on the relationship between nationalism and history that are more fully developed in *Rescuing History from the Nation: Questioning Narratives of Modern China* (Chicago: University of Chicago Press, 1995).

Author's note: This essay outlines some ideas on the relationship between nationalism and history which are more fully developed in my book *Rescuing History from the Nation: Questioning Narratives of Modern China* Chicago: University of Chicago Press, 1995.

ernization theory. The first of these is that national identity is a radically novel form of consciousness. Below, we will develop a crucial distinction between the modern nation-state system and nationalism as a form of identification. National identification is never fully subsumed by it and is best considered in its complex relationships to other historical identities. The second assumption is the privileging of the grand narrative of the nation as a collective historical subject. Nationalism is rarely the nationalism of the nation, but rather represents the site where very different views of the nation contest and negotiate with each other. Through these two positions, we will seek to generate a historical understanding of the nation that is neither historically determinist nor essentialist, and through which we might try to recover history itself from the ideology of the nation-state.

The two most influential recent works on the subject of nationalism—by Benedict Anderson and Ernest Gellner—have stressed the radically novel form of consciousness represented by national identity. Both analysts identify national consciousness conventionally as the coextensiveness of politics and culture—an overriding identification of the individual with a culture that is protected by the state. Both also provide a sociological account of how it was only in the modern era that such a type of consciousness—where people from diverse locales could "imagine" themselves as part of a single community—was made possible. Gellner provides a full account of this discontinuity. Preindustrial society is formed of segmentary communities, each isolated from the other, with an inaccessible high culture jealously guarded by a clerisy—Gellner's general term for literati ruling elites. With the growth of industrialism, society requires a skilled, literate, and mobile work force. The segmentary form of communities is no longer adequate to create a homogenously educated work force in which the individual members are interchangeable. The state comes to be in charge of the nation, and through control of education creates the requisite interchangeability of individuals. The primary identification with segmentary communities is transferred to the nation-state (1983). In Anderson's view, the spread of print media through the capitalist market made possible a unity without the mediation of a clerisy. Print capitalism permitted an unprecedented mode of apprehending time that was "empty" and "homogenous"—expressed in an ability to imagine the simultaneous existence of one's co-nationals (1983).

I believe that this claim of a radical disjuncture is exaggerated. The long history of complex civilizations such as that of China does not fit the picture of isolated communities and a vertically separate but unified clerisy. Scholars have filled many pages writing about complex networks of trade, pilgrimage, migration, and sojourning that linked villages to wider communities and political structures. This was the case as well in Tokugawa Japan and eighteenth-century India (Bayly 1983; Habib 1963). Moreover, even if the reach of the bureaucratic state was limited, recently developed notions of the culture-state[3] indicate the widespread presence of common cultural ideas which linked the state to communities and sustained the polity.

It was not only, or perhaps even primarily, the print media that enabled Han Chinese to develop a sharp sense of the Other, and hence of themselves as a community, when they confronted other communities. The exclusive emphasis on print capitalism as enabling the imagining of a common destiny and the concept of simultaneity ignores the complex relationship between the written and spoken word. In agrarian civilizations this interrelationship furnishes an extremely rich and subtle context for communication across the culture. For instance, in pan-Chinese myths, such as that of Guandi, the god of war, not only were oral and written traditions thoroughly intertwined, but the myth provided a medium whereby different groups could announce their participation in a national culture even as they inscribed their own interpretation of the myth (through the written and other cultural media, such as folk drama and iconography) (Duara 1988b). As such, these groups were articulating their understanding of the wider cultural and political order from their own particular perspective. There were large numbers of people in agrarian societies who were conscious of their culture and identity at multiple levels, and in that sense were perhaps not nearly so different from their modern counterparts.

The point is not so much that national identity existed in premodern times; rather it is that the manner in which we have conceptualized political identities is fundamentally problematic. In privileging modern society as the only social form capable of generating political self-awareness, Gellner and Anderson regard national identity as a distinctive mode of consciousness: the nation as a whole imagining itself to be the unified subject of history. There is a special and restricted sense in which we can think of a unified subjectivity; we shall have occasion below to review it in our discussion of nationalism as a relational identity. But this restricted sense of unity is not unique to modern society.[4] The deeper error, however, lies in the general postulate of a cohesive subjectivity.

Individuals and groups in both modern and agrarian societies identify simultaneously with several communities that are all imagined; these identifications are historically changeable, and often conflicted internally and with each other. As we shall see in the following section, Chinese people historically identified with different types of communities, and when these identifications became politicized they came to resemble national identities. To be sure, this does not validate the claim of some nationalists that the nation had existed historically as a cohesive subject gathering self-awareness and poised to realize its destiny in the modern era. Premodern political identifications do not necessarily or teleologically develop into the national identifications of modern times. A new vocabulary and a political system selects, adapts, reorganizes and even re-creates these older identities. Nonetheless, the fact remains that modern societies are not the only ones capable of creating self-conscious political communities.

The dominant historiography of modern China in the West has also preferred to see nationalism in China as a purely modern phenomenon. Joseph Levenson observed a radical discontinuity between a nationalistic identity which he believed came to Chinese intellectuals around the turn of the twentieth century, and earlier forms of Chinese identity. The high culture, ideology and identification of the mandarin, he believed, were principally forms of cultural consciousness, an identification with the moral goals and values of a universalizing civilization. Thus the significant transition here is from a "culturalism" to a nationalism, to the awareness of the nation-state as the ultimate goal of the community (Levenson

1964). Culturalism referred to a natural conviction of cultural superiority that sought no legitimation or defense outside of the culture itself. Only when, according to Levenson, cultural values sought legitimation in the face of the challenge posed by the Other in the late nineteenth century, do we begin to see "decaying culturalism" and its rapid transformation to nationalism—or to a culture protected by the state (politicization of culture).

It is very hard to distinguish "culturalism" as a distinct form of identification from ethnic or national identification. In order for it to exist as a pure expression of cultural superiority, it would have to feel no threat from an Other seeking to obliterate these values. In fact, this threat arose historically on several occasions and produced several reactions from the Chinese literati and populace. First, there was a rejection of the universalist pretensions of Chinese culture and of the principle that separated culture from politics and the state. This manifested itself in a form of ethnocentrism that we will consider in a moment. A second, more subtle, response involved the transformation of cultural universalism from a set of substantive moral claims into a relatively abstract official doctrine. This doctrine was often used to conceal the compromises that the elite and the imperial state had to make in their ability to practice these values or to conceal their inability to make people who should have been participating in the cultural-moral order actually do so.

Consider the second reaction first. The Jin and Mongol invasions of North China during the twelfth century and their scant respect for Chinese culture produced an ideological defensiveness in the face of the relativization of the conception of the universal empire *(tianxia)*. In the twelfth and thirteenth centuries Confucian universalists could only maintain their universalism by performing two sleights of hand: connecting individuals to the infinite (severing theory from fact) and internalizing the determination of personal values, both of which represented a considerable departure from the traditional Confucian concern with an objective moral order (Trauzettel 1975). During the Ming dynasty, the Han Chinese dynasty that succeeded the Mongols, Chinese historians dealt with the lack of fit with the Chinese worldview simply by maintaining a silence (Wang 1968, 45–46). When we look at the tribute trade system which is often cited as the paradigmatic expression of its universalistic claims to moral superiority, the imperial state adapted readily to the practical power politics of the day. In the early nineteenth century, the tiny northwestern khanate of Kokand (like the Jesuits, the Russians, and several others before)successfully challenged the Qing tribute system and had established all but the formal declaration of equality with the Chinese empire. The Qing was forced into a negotiated settlement but it continued to use the language of universalism—civilizing values radiating from the son of heaven—to conceal the altered power relations between the two (Fletcher 1978b).

Thus the universalistic claims of Chinese imperial culture constantly adapted to alternative views of the world order which it tended to cover with the rhetoric of universalism: this was its defensive strategy. It seems evident that when the universalistic claims of this culture were repeatedly compromised and efforts were made to conceal these compromises, advocates of this universalism were operating within the tacit idea of a *Chinese* universalism—which is of course none

other than a hidden form of relativism. We have tended to accept Chinese declarations of universalism at face value far more readily than we do other official
doctrines (perhaps because it plays a crucial role as the Other in interpretations
of the encounter with the nation-states of the west).

Viewing "culturalism" (or universalism) as a "Chinese culturalism" is to see
it not as a form of cultural consciousness per se, but rather to see culture—a
specific culture of the imperial state and Confucian orthodoxy—as a criterion
defining a community. Membership in this community was defined by participation in a ritual order which embodied allegiance to Chinese ideas and ethics
centered on the Chinese emperor. While this conception of political community
may seem rather distant from nationalism, one should consider the fact that the
territorial boundaries and peoples of the contemporary Chinese nation correspond
roughly to the Qing empire that was held together ideologically precisely by these
ritual practices. A look at the ideas of Confucian modernizers writing in the late
nineteenth and early twentieth centuries, such as Kang Youwei and Zhang Zhi-
tong, reveal that the national community they had in mind was constituted by
Confucian cultural principles that would include ethnically non-Han peoples—
such as the Manchus—as long as they had accepted (Chinese) cultural principles.
This was, of course, challenged by the revolutionaries of 1911, who saw nationhood as based on inherited "racialist" (or ethnocentric), not cultural traits. However, it is important to note that after the 1911 revolution, the revolutionaries
themselves reverted to the boundaries of the Qing empire to bound their nation;
moreover, the Communist version of the nation builds upon a conception
grounded in the imperial idea of political community.

Just as significantly, during the Jin invasion of the twelfth century, segments
of the scholar class completely abandoned the concentric, radiant concept of universal empire for a circumscribed notion of the Han community and fatherland
(guo) in which the barbarians had no place. This ethnocentric notion of Chineseness was, of course, not new. Chinese authors typically trace it to a quotation
from the Zuo Zhuan: "the hearts of those who are not of our race must be different" (Li Guoqi 1970, 20; Dow 1982, 353). Others (Yang 1968; Langlois 1980,
362) find it still earlier in the concentric realm of inner and outer barbarians found
in the Shang Shu: pacific cultural activities were to prevail in the inner part, whose
inhabitants were not characterized as ethnically different, with militancy toward
the outer barbarians, who appeared to be unassimilable. Trauzettel believes that
in the Song dynasty, this ethnocentrism brought together state and people. The
state sought to cultivate the notion of loyalty to the fatherland downward into
peasant communities, from among whom arose resistance against the Jin in the
name of the Chinese culture and the Song dynasty (1975).

While we see the ethnic nation most clearly in the Song, its most explicit
advocate in the late Imperial period was Wang Fuzhi. Wang likened the differences between Manchus and Han to that between jade and snow, which are both
white but different in nature, or more ominously, between a horse and a man of
the same color whose natures are obviously different (Li Guoqi 1970, 22). To be
sure, it was the possession of civilization *(wen)* by the Han that distinguished
them from the barbarians, but it did not keep Wang from the view that "it is not

inhumane to annihilate [the barbarians] . . . because faithfulness and righteousness are the ways of human intercourse and are not to be extended to alien kinds *[i-lei (yilei)]"* (in Langlois 1980, 364). Although Wang may have espoused the most extreme view of his generation, several prominent scholars of the Ming–Qing transition era held on to the idea of the fundamental unassimilability of the *yi* (barbarian) by the *Hua* (Chinese) (see Onogawa 1970, 207–21; and Wu Wei-to 1970, 261–71).

Despite the undoubted success with which the Qing made themselves acceptable as the legitimate sons of heaven, they were unable to completely suppress the ethnocentric opposition to their rule either at a popular level or among the scholarly elite. The anti-Manchu writings of Wang Fuzhi, Huang Zongxi, and Gu Yanwu during the early period of Qing rule together with collections of stories of Manchu atrocities during the time (for example, Mingji Yeshi's *Unofficial History of the Late Ming*) were in circulation even before the middle of the nineteenth century (Wu Wei-to 1970, 263). Zhang Binglin, for instance, claims to having been nourished by a tradition both in his family and in wider Zhejiang society which held that the defense of the Han against the barbarians *(Yi Xia)* was as important as the righteousness of a ruler (Onogawa 1970, 216). Certainly Han ethnic consciousness seems to have reached a height by the late eighteenth century, when the dominant Han majority confronted the non-Han minorities of China in greater numbers than ever before over competition for increasingly scarce resources (Naquin and Rawski 1987). Thus it is hardly surprising to find that, from at least the time of resistance to the increased foreign presence in South China after the Opium Wars through to the Boxer Rebellion of 1898–1900, there existed a general expectation, not only among the elite, but also among the populace, that the state would protect the culture and the people of the empire (Wakeman 1966; Esherick 1987). Though this identification may not have affected every segment of the population, French peasants, too, had little conception of the nation until the end of the nineteenth century, as Eugen Weber has reminded us (Weber 1978).

We are able to discern at least two conceptualizations of the political community in imperial Chinese society: the exclusive ethnic-based one founded on a self-description of a people as Han, and a community based on the cultural values and doctrines of a Chinese elite. What has been described as culturalism is a statement of Chinese values as superior but, significantly, not exclusive. Through a process of education and imitation, barbarians could also become part of a community sharing common values and distinguishing themselves from yet other barbarians who did not share these values. In these terms, culturalism is not significantly different from ethnicity, because like ethnic groups, it defines the distinguishing marks and boundaries of a community. The difference lies in the criterion of admissibility: the ethnocentric conception refused to accept anyone not born into the community, despite their educability into Chinese values, as part of the political community; whereas, the cultural conception did.

During the years before the republican revolution of 1911, when modern nationalism took hold among the Chinese intelligentsia, the debates between them about the nature of the future Chinese nation were shaped as much by modern discourses of the nation-state (see below) as by the historical principles involved in defining community that we have traced above. The constitutional monarchists, represented by Kang Youwei, inherited the Confucian culturalist notion of community. Although Kang was influenced by modern Western ideas, the conception of political community that he retained drew on culturalist Confucian notions. We see this in his lifelong devotion to the emperor (Protect the Emperor Society), which in the political context of the time meant more than a nostalgia for monarchy. Since the monarchs were Manchu and not Han, it implied that he was convinced that community was composed of people with shared culture and not restricted to a race or ethnic group (imputed or otherwise).

The revolutionaries, such as Zhang Binglin and Wang Jingwei, articulated their opposition to this conception by drawing on the old ethnocentric tradition that acquired new meaning in the highly charged atmosphere of the 1900s. To be sure, Zhang was a complex figure whose thought can scarcely be reduced to any single strain. But he and his associate Zou Rong succeeded in articulating an image of the new community that was persuasive to many in his generation. At the base of this reformulation of the old ethnocentrism was a dialectical reading of Wang Fuzhi's notions of evolutionism plus a new Social Darwinist conception of the survival of the fittest races. The complex architecture of Zhang's ideas of the nation seems as much to use modern ideas to justify an ethnocentric celebration of the Han as it was a selective use of the past to ground the present. Modern nationalists like Kang and Zhang were each engaged in dialogues with disputed legacies which were, nonetheless, authentic and by no means completely assimilable by modern discourses.

NATIONS, NATION-STATES AND AMBIVALENCE TOWARD ANTIQUITY

What is novel about modern nationalism is not political self-consciousness, but the world *system* of nation-states. This system, which has become globalized in the last hundred years or so, sanctions the nation-state as the only legitimate form of polity. It is a political form with distinct territorial boundaries within which the sovereign state, "representing" the nation-people, has steadily expanded its role and power. The ideology of the nation-state system has sanctioned the penetration of state power into areas that were once dominated by local authority structures. For instance, "children" have come increasingly under the jurisdiction of the state as the institutional rules governing childhood were diffused to all types of nation-states over the last hundred years (Meyer and Boli-Bennet, 1978; Meyer 1980). The term *nationalism* is often confused with the ideology of the nation-state, which seeks to fix or privilege political identification at the level of the nation-state. The slippage in this relationship is a principal source of the instability of the meaning of the nation.

The lineage of the sovereign territorial conception may be traced to what William McNeill has characterized as the system of competitive European states. From as far back as A.D. 1000, each of these states was driven by the urge to increase its resources, population, and military technology over the others. In their competition, these states gradually became dependent on capital markets, both externally and internally, which further propelled the development of their economy and the competition between them (McNeill 1982). In time, the Church came to sanction some of these emergent regional states by endowing them with a theory of sovereignty without at the same time obliging them to achieve universalizing empire. This was possible because of the separation of spiritual and temporal authority, or, in other words, the source of legitimacy from actual exercise of power (Armstrong 1982). The culmination of this conception of the nation was first seen in the French Revolution and exemplified in the idea of citizenship for all within the territory (Eley 1981).

Elsewhere in the world, competition was never institutionalized in the same way. For instance, in China during the many periods of interdynastic struggles, the divisions of the empire were brought to an end by a victor who established a command polity that squelched the dynamic of competition among states. Similarly, although regional successor states emerged from the disintegration of the Mogul empire in eighteenth-century India, the competition between them was not institutionalized in the same way. Moreover, from the point of view of sovereignty, legitimacy in China necessarily resided in the imperial center, in the Son of Heaven, and thus regional states were never able to claim any durable sovereign status. Likewise, the most powerful successor state of the Moguls, the Hindu Marathas, strove not for territorial sovereignty but towards the Brahmin ideal of a universal ruler (Embree 1985, 32).

However, no contemporary state is a nation exclusively in this territorial sense. Even among the early modern European states, European dynasts had to combine the theory of territorial sovereignty with ethnicity to create modern nation-states (Armstrong 1982). While most historical nations, defined as self-aware and even politicized communities, lacked the conception of themselves as part of a system of territorially sovereign nation-states, modern nations embody both territorial and ethnic conceptions. Of course, it may legitimately be asked to what extent the (modern) nation-state system influences the political identities of its citizens. As Balibar (1990) points out, the nation-state has doubtless developed the ability to have territorial boundaries acquire a salience and have its citizens develop powerful attachments to these boundaries. Yet, even these territorial identifications have to come to terms with historical understandings as we have seen in China in the case of the republican revolutionaries. More generally, territorial identifications have to bear some relationship to an inherited sense of the "homeland"—even if this sense is a highly contested one.

Thus the shape and content of national identities in the modern era are a product of negotiation with historical identities within the framework of a modern nation-state system. From this vantage point the efforts by scholars—from Kedourie to Gellner—to vociferously debunk nationalist historiography for assuming an ancient history of the nation (the nation as a continuous subject gathering self-awareness) seems misdirected because it neglects the important fact that nationalists always have to engage with their many histories, even when they are manipulating them for their own purposes. It is also misplaced because it slights the strong contrary urge within nationalism to see itself as a modern phenomenon. While on the one hand, nationalist leaders and nation-states glorify the ancient or eternal character of the nation, they simultaneously seek to emphasize the unprecedented novelty of the nation-state, because it is only in this form that the people have been able to realize themselves as the subjects or masters of their history. The fact that the nation-state *represents* this subjecthood is, of course, maintained parenthetically.

There is thus a built-in ambivalence in modern nationalist ideology toward the historicality of the nation. This ambivalence presents us with a window to view history, not as something merely made up, but as the site of contestation and repression of different views of the nation. In the writings of Sun Yat-sen, the ambiguity is concealed through a political attack on his enemies. Sun argues that China, which for him is the Han nation, was the world's most perfectly formed nation because the people were bound together by all the five criteria that (for him) it took to form a nation: blood/race, language, custom, religion, and livelihood. At the same time, Sun is unclear on whether the nation is already fully awakened or whether national consciousness needs to be further aroused. He is torn between these options because on the one hand nationalists like himself could fulfill their mission only if the Han people still suffered from a "slave mentality" with no national consciousness. On the other hand, the preexisting fullness of China as a nation was necessary for the legitimacy of any nationalist rhetoric. Initially, Sun maintained both positions by arguing that the awakening was also a reawakening. There had been difficult historical periods when the Han people had risen to the occasion and revealed the fullness of their national being, as during Han resistance to the Jurchens or the Mongols. Ultimately, however, Sun concealed this ambiguity by transforming it into a problem inherent in Confucian cosmopolitanism: the original spirit of Han independence had been weakened by the cosmopolitanism which accepted alien rulers like the present Manchu regime as rulers of the Chinese people. This was, of course, precisely the cosmopolitanism advocated by his reformer enemies who advocated a China composed of all of the ethnic groups of the old empire. Sun and the republican revolutionaries sought to mobilize a particular history not only to serve as the foundation of the new nation-state, but to delegitimate the ideological core of the alternative territorial and culturalist conception of the nation (Sun 1986, 41–42).[5]

The ambivalence between the old and new is similarly contained by a narrative of a reawakening subject in Jawaharlal Nehru's history of India. Moreover, Nehru's historical narrative also embeds a challenge to the Hindu-dominated nationalist historiography of the time (Prakash 1990, 389). The historical unity of India for Nehru lay in the actual historical development of the nation. The high points of Indian history were the reigns of Asoka, the Guptas, the Muslim emperor Akbar and the Moguls—all of whom attempted to develop a political framework to unite the cultural diversity of the Subcontinent. Nehru saw civilizations and nations in the organic metaphor of growth and decline. The great heights of Indian thought, culture, and science had been reached as early as the eleventh century and subsequently entered a long dark period of rigidity and stagnation (Nehru 1960, 121–28). To be sure, there were short cycles of creativity thereafter, especially during the reign of Akbar, but the modern period had been dominated by the vigor and dynamism of the Europeans. It remained for the national movement in India to realize the greatness of the Indian nation once again. However, the purpose of Nehru's narrative is exactly the opposite of Sun's. Whereas Sun's political strategy (at least in the period before the 1911 revolution) involved a specification— a narrowing—of the Chinese nation to the Han, Nehru was striving to build an Indian nation that was not exclusively Hindu. In doing so, Nehru's history created the founding narrative of the secular modern nation-state. While this narrative has managed to withstand attacks in academic and official historiography, it is today being contested as never before in the realm of popular history—in the conflict over temples and mosques.

In Israel, as in India, the historical narrative is unable to contain the tension between those who would emphasize the ancient and pristine essence of the nation and those who stress the new and the modern. The conflict in Israel between the religious Right, for whom the meaning of the nation is embodied in the sacred books, and the more secular nationalists, who seek to project the nation along a progressive vision, can be traced to the founding moment of the nation. The Handelmans have examined the conflict over the choice of the emblem on the Israeli flag in the course of 1948. "The emerging national culture of Israeli Jews tended to be secular, yet rooted in ancient Israel, and so again intertwined with religion. Therefore the symbolism had to include the symbolism of the ancient that would be understood clearly as a source of secular culture"(Handelman and Shamgar-Handleman, 216). But this was a heavy ambiguity for the emblem to bear and it flared into an open conflict between the Zionist religious parties and the primarily secular ones. The religious parties wished to use the menorah, which is identified with the birth of the Israelites as a nation, the Temple cult, and statehood, blessed by the divine. The secularists wished to combine the symbolism of the menorah with that of the seven stars—the seven hours of the workday symbolizing the rationalization of labor and social benefits and, more widely, the values of the Enlightenment. This metaphor rapidly came under scathing attack by the religious parties and the resulting official emblem of Israel, the Titus menorah, "synthesized time (the last Jewish state), place (Jersualem, Israel), the Jewish people, and the qualities of the primordial and eternal. But the ratified emblem contained no motif of the innovative aspirations of modern Zionism for the future" (219–20).[6]

The ambivalence about the historicality of the nation reveals a fundamental aporia for nationalists: if the people-nation has always been present historically then on what grounds can the present nation-state make a special claim to legitimacy as the first embodiment of the people-nation? We have seen that nationalists have been able to address this ambiguity through a variety of rhetorical strategies, but they have not been able to fully control the meaning of the nation's history. The real signifigance of this aporia lie in the possibilities it generates for contested meanings of the nation. Modernist and postmodernist understandings of the nation tend to view history epiphenomenally—as the space for forgetting and re-creating in accordance with present needs. A more complex view of history suggests that if the past is shaped by the present, the present is also shaped by the past as inheritance, and the most fertile questions lie in understanding how this dialectic is articulated with the contest over the significance of national history.

IMAGINED NATIONS: WHO IMAGINES WHAT?

While the modern nation-state system clearly influences national identity—especially in its efforts to confine loyalty to a territory—the latter is by no means determined by the former. In order to understand national identity more fully, it needs to be studied in relation to other identities, as part of the generalized category of political identity; this is its true terrain. When considered in this terrain we can see how the ambiguities, the changeability, the fungibility and interplay of national identity with other forms of identification can be as subversive of the nation-state as it is supportive. And within this terrain we can ask if national identification is as privileged over others as the nation-state and nationalist leaders like to suggest.

Ever since Karl Deutsch, analysts of nationalism have emphasized how the nation-state, in the print era and after, has been able to avail of the proliferating mass media to facilitate the nation-building project. Few have emphasized how this same technology also enables rivals of the nascent nation-state to construct alternative forms of political and even national identity, whether in Breton, the Baltic states, Tibet or the Punjab. The state is never able to eliminate alternative constructions of the nation among both old and new communities. The most successful states are able to contain these conceptions within relatively depoliticized spaces; but even where such states are older, as in western Europe, there are overt challenges to the established national form in almost every nation. Walker Connor (1972) has shown us that there is scarcely a nation in the world— developed or underdeveloped—where ethnic mobilization has not challenged the nation-state. Defying the presumption of the nation-state to restrict the term "nationalism" to loyalty to itself, Connor insists on identifying these self-differentiating ethnic groups as in fact nations.

Connor's identification of nationalisms within the nation-state reveals the conflicted but isomorphic nature of political identities: ethnic mobilization develops into national identification identical to the one it opposes. But the relationship among different identities is more complex than this. Nationalism is often considered to override other forms of identification within a society, such as religious, racial, linguistic, class, gender, or even historical ones—to encompass these differences in a larger identity. I shall have more to say about the model of nested identities implicit in this understanding in the next section; here I would like to suggest that even when or where such an encompassment has been temporarily achieved, the way in which the nation is imagined, viewed, and voiced by different self-conscious groups can indeed be very different. Indeed we may speak of different "nation-views," as we do "world-views," which are not overridden by the nation, but actually define or constitute it. In place of the harmonized, monologic voice of the Nation, we find a polyphony of voices, overlapping and criss-crossing; contradictory and ambiguous; opposing, affirming, and negotiating their views of the nation.

Moreover, the shaping of identities is also historically changeable. The thesis that modernization leads to nationalism can hardly be sustained anymore. Developed nations have seen the birth of separatist identities where one might least expect to find them. Of the history of the relationship of the Ulster Irish, the Welsh, and the Scots to Britishness, historically the Scots may have had the weakest cultural basis for a separatist identity. Yet the circumstances of the 1960s and 1970s gave rise to a resurgent Scottish nationalism (Breuilly 1982, 280–90; Agnew 1987, 143–59). Areas of India are well known for separatist movements in recent years. What is less well known, however, is that the nationalist movement under Indian National Congress leadership against the British Raj was among the strongest in some of these same areas, such as Assam. Below, we will see how identities of groups in China, such as the Manchus, Hakka Chinese, and Subei folk in Shanghai, and their relationship to Chineseness fluctuated over the last two centuries.

National identities are unstable not only because they are susceptible to splits, whether by alternative criteria of identity formation (for example religion rather than language) or by the transference of loyalty to a subgroup (even where the identity of this subgroup is new), but also because all good nationalisms have a transnational vision—witness pan-Africanism, pan-Asianism, pan-Europeanism, pan-Islamism, Shiism, Judaism. To be sure, the manner in which territorial nationalism negotiates its relations with the wider identification takes many forms. Some arguments for national identification find their legitimation in the ultimate achievement of a transcendent order. For instance the reformist nationalism of Kang Youwei justified nationalism as a necessary stage in the ultimate achievement of the "great unity" of all peoples of the world *(datong)*. *Datong* was also an ideal that Sun Yat-sen would later celebrate when he linked the destiny of China to that of the oppressed peoples of the world. In Iran, the criterion that came to determine nationality historically had been the Persian language, first in the post-Hellenic Persian revival of Ardashir I in A.D. 224 and then in the flowering of Persian literature under the Arab conquests. The great achievement of the latter period was the Shahnamah of Firdawsi (A.D. 941–1020) in which the poet created an idealized history of pre-Islamic Iran by deliberately avoiding Arabic words as far as possible. Subsequently in the sixteenth century under the Safavis, Iranian distinctiveness came to be expressed through Shiism rather than language, as Iran became a "bastion of militant Shiism surrounded by hostile Sunni neighbors .... A fortress mentality, a we and they dichotomy, gradually developed ..." (Weryho 1986, 52). The nationalism of the present regime of the ayatollahs is composed of an exclusivist ideology formed by both Persian and Shiite myths, but it is clear that Shiism, while promoting national greatness, also obliges it to a transnational ideal (Bernard and Khalilzad, 1984).

Even in Japan, where one might most expect a perfect congruence between loyalty and territory and least expect any external sanctions for nationalist ideology, pan-Asianism and the idea that Japan derived its special position by protecting other Asian nations from the corrupting influence of Western capitalism bolstered Japanese national identity. To be sure, pan-Asianism also worked nicely to promote Japanese imperialism in Asia, but it would be wrong to see only this dimension. Marius Jansen has written persuasively of the pan-Asianism of Miyazaki Torazo, Oi Kentaro and others who inspired Sun Yat-sen and others with their zeal to destroy Western imperialism. "A re-birth for oppressed peasantries elsewhere in Asia was, for them, a necessary adjunct and stimulus to ameliorating the peasants' lot in Japan" (Jansen 1967, 219).

In Europe today, we see the contradictoriness of political identifications in full flower. Resurgent nationalism has surfaced in tandem with the near-realization of a transnational dream—often in a single country like Germany. Whatever the shape of the European community, it is likely that it will have to incorporate some of the functions and symbols of the nation-state. Etienne Balibar wonders whether in the building of the fictive ethnicity of Europe the tendency will be predominantly toward developing a European co-lingualism or in idealizing a "European demographic identity" conceived mainly in opposition to Turks, Arabs, blacks, and other "southern populations" (Balibar 1990, 359). Depending on how these boundaries are drawn, the consequences for the "Other" will be significantly different in each case.

The multiplicity of nation-views and the idea that political identity is not fixed but shifts between different loci introduces the idea that nationalism is best seen as a relational identity. In other words, the nation, even where it is manifestly not a recent invention, is hardly the realization of an original essence, but a historical configuration which is designed to include certain groups and exclude or marginalize others—often violently. (Linguistic definitions obviously exclude and marginalize different groups from those who seek to define nations by religious or racialist criteria or the criterion of common historical experience.) As a relationship among constituents, the national "self" is defined at any point in time by the Other. Depending on the nature and scale of the oppositional term, the national self contains various smaller "Others"—historical Others that have effected an often uneasy reconciliation among themselves and potential Others that are beginning to form their differences. And it is these potential Others that are most deserving of our attention because they reveal the performative principle that create nations—the willing into existence of a nation which will choose to privilege its difference and obscure all of the cultural bonds that had tied it to its sociological kin.

The most easily identifiable expressions of nationalism as a *relationship* are the antiimperialist movements the world over. Sun Yat-sen and other Chinese nationalists believed that it was in the self-interest of Chinese minorities to join with the Han majority against the imperialists during the war-ravaged republic because of the security in numbers. When the imperialist threat faded, it became easy for these minorities to perceive the threat from precisely the numbers of the Han majority. The pulling apart of eastern European nation-states in recent times represents the most dramatic indication that the conditions holding one type of nation together no longer prevail. What is just as important to note are the subnationalisms within Lithuania or Georgia as expressions of the great unraveling of our times. Canada is noteworthy not only because of Quebecois nationalism, but also because of the way in which the nation of Quebec might be challenged by a hidden Other, such as the Mohawks. The hidden Others are not only other groups but alternative principles of grouping as well. Consider the chameleonlike identities in western Asia, where a different configuration is invoked depending on whether the threat is directed against Arab nationalism, religious nationalism, or territorial nationalism.

I do not believe that the goal of the historian is simply to celebrate "difference." Rather, the fact that individuals and groups simultaneously recognize themselves in and respond to different ideologies and cultures suggests a critical power in society that is potentially resistant to totalizing ideologies. Historians have traditionally been concerned with the process whereby national identities are formed and have neglected to see that it is the same process whereby other identifications and nation-views are repressed and obscured. In the next segment I will try to show how the historian, by being able to take the long view, is uniquely situated to provide a complex accounting of the formation as well as the repression of nation-views and national identities.

THE ANALYTICS OF COMMUNITY CLOSURE

Identity and Meaning

While it is important to grasp nationalism as a contingent relationship, we also need to understand the mechanisms whereby this relationship or coalition endows itself with the mystique of a unitary or cohesive nation. Here we will attend to the procedures whereby a history is mobilized to produce "the national identity." It is important to recognize that while the discourses of the nation-state system importantly shape the meaning of the nation, the social process of community closure that we will examine here is hardly unique to the modern nation.

Social science explanations of political identity—ethnic and national—have centered on the debate over whether these are primordial or instrumentalist. Neither has much use for historical process since the primordialists simply assume an essential, unchanging identity whereas the instrumentalists, who usually attribute the creation of such identities to manipulation by interested elites or others, often find the past to be irrelevant. What remains unclear in the instrumentalist view is what it is that is being manipulated. More recently, the instrumentalist position is being revisited by scholars influenced by post-structuralism and discourse analysis who are extremely suspicous of historicist or even historical explanations, preferring to see identities as "constructed" by the discourses of the era. While I am partial to the view that discourses construct their subjects, yet this view, I believe, must be modified to acknowledge that there are multiple representations, including historical ones, which construct identities. Thus while a national identity may be invented, its formulators are typically able to build it around, or from among, preconstituted and resonant representations of community, as much as by destroying or obscuring other representations.

Consider the subtle relationship between identity and meaning in the processes by which nationalisms and nation-views are formed and repressed, negotiated and delegitimated. The argument is often made about nationalism that while one can have different ideas, or respond to different representations, of the nation, the sense of identification with the nation overrides the difference. It is doubtless true that there are times when one simply *feels* American or Chinese, and indeed, when faced with a common outside threat, differences about what it means to be an American or Chinese are often temporarily submerged. This is what we have meant by nationalism as a relational identity. But the strength of the feeling for the nation—which is also exactly what passionately divides fellow-nationals—derives from what it *means* to be American or Chinese. Identities are forged in a fluid complex of cultural signifiers: symbols, practices, and narratives. The process of community closure is the process of fixing certain signifiers within this fluid complex and authorizing them to mobilize the affective strength of the others.

For analytical purposes, I will separate "meaning"—what the nation means to the people—into two areas: (1) discursive meaning and (2) symbolic meaning. In the first realm, I include such subjects as language-as-rhetoric, narratives, and ideology—subjects that have traditionally fallen under the scope of the intellectual historian. In this sense, the nation is a product of the rhetoric and ideas of historians, nationalist intellectuals and pamphleteers. In the realm of symbolic meaning, I include the ensemble of cultural practices of a group such as rituals, festivals, kinship forms, culinary habits, etc.—subjects traditionally of the social historian or anthropologist. In this sense, the nation is an embodiment of the cultural marks of its distinctiveness. While, of course, the two realms are inseparable in the way the nation is imagined by the people, it is useful for the historian to be able to separate and subsequently recombine them in order to better conceive the formation/repression process.

In the discursive realm, the meanings of the nation are produced mainly through linguistic mechanisms. These are the narratives (Bhabha 1990), the signifying chains of metaphors, metonyms, and binary oppositions that give meaning to the nation.[7]

These include not only historical narratives of individual nations such as those of India by Jawaharlal Nehru and of China by Sun Yat-sen, but also global discourses with which these particular narratives have to engage. One such discourse by which early twentieth-century Chinese nationalists constructed their understanding of modern nations and the nation-state system was the language of evolutionary ranking and competition embodied in Social Darwinism. It was a discourse in which the meaning of a "civilized" nation derived from the model of Western nation-states. This discourse was both countered and intertwined with the language of "culture" as the irreducible core or essence of the nation. Redolent of Herder's romantic opposition to the inexorable evolutionism of "rational civilization," nationalist intellectuals in China, India, Japan, and elsewhere developed East-versus-West/spiritual-versus-material binaries in which they located an irreducible national essence which offered them limited space to resist History.

Even when Social Darwinism in China and elsewhere was overtaken in the 1920s by the antiimperialist rhetoric of victimization and redemption, the notion of culture continued its journey into this language of *ressentiment*. Thus the writings of Sun Yat-sen in the 1920s indicated that it was not enough for China to aspire to the goal of an industrial civilization. China would fulfill its "sacred mission" by supporting weak and small nations and resisting strong world powers. It would do so by transcending Western goals of materialism and violence and seek to realize its own cultural destiny in the way of the sage kings *(wanq dao)* of ancient China (Sun 1924, 631–36, 659). More than in China, perhaps more than anywhere else in the world, the language of redemption was developed in the hands of Gandhi, for whom the Western nation-states had no place among civilizations—which he believed were defined principally by their moral qualities. Only if the nation was able to fulfill spiritual and moral goals—and India, where according to him these goals had once emerged so brilliantly, was also his test case—could it truly aspire to be a civilized nation.

Whereas scholarship has posed class as the antithesis of nation (the two vying for the role of historical subject in the modern era), we can also see how, through a variety of rhetorical mechanisms, the trope of class and class struggle has given meaning to the nation. Li Dazhao imagined the nation in the language of a class on the international stage: the Chinese people were a national proletariat (within an international proletariat) oppressed by the Western capitalists (Meisner 1967, 188). Certainly, this is not unique to China. Abdullah Laroui speaks of a phase of nationalism which he calls "class nationalism":

> Where, in confrontation with Europe, the fundamentalists oppose a culture (Chinese, Indian, Islamic) and the liberal opposed a nation (Chinese, Turkish, Egyptian, Iranian), the revolutionary opposes a class—one that is often extended to include all the parts of the human race exploited by the European bourgeoisie. One may refer to it as class nationalism that nevertheless retains many of the motifs of political and cultural nationalisms; hence the difficulties experienced by many of the analysts who have attempted to define it. (quoted in Fitzgerald 1988, 10)

The class-nation of the international arena also has a domestic expression. In this conception, the supposed attributes of a class are extended to the nation, and the measure to which one fulfilled this criterion ideally governed admissibility to the national community. This is true in the case of Chinese Communism, especially during the Cultural Revolution, when the goal was to purge or disenfranchise undesirable classes in the nation and strive to shape the nation in the image of the idealized proletariat. Here the idea of the nation becomes the site of a tension between a revolutionary language with its transnational aspirations and the reality of national boundedness. Yet another means whereby the language of revolutionary class struggle comes to define the nation is the process of placing the "universal" theory of class struggle into a national context. The elevation of Mao to the role of supreme theorist (together with Lenin and Stalin) and the creation of the "Chinese model" of revolutionary transformation in the late 1930s

marks the sinification of Marxism in which national distinctiveness became embodied in the particular model of class struggle pioneered by the Chinese. Readers
will be reminded of Iranian Shiite clerics who further Iranian nationalism by
promoting it as the champion of true Islam.

That the nation is a linguistically *gendered* phenomenon is evident even from
the simple fact that its most common signifier is fatherland or motherland. The
master metaphor of the nation as family in turn yields a variety of strategies and
tactics for incorporating women into the nation. Historically in China, the purity
of the woman's body has served both as metaphor and metonymy of the purity
of the nation (see Schoppa 1989, for instance). The bodies of Chinese women
raped by foreign invaders—Mongol, Manchu, or Japanese—were both symbol
and part of the national body violated by these foreigners. However, as Lydia Liu
has recently shown, at least some women registered a strong ambivalence, and
in the case of the writer Xiao Hong, a rejection of nationalism's in-corporation
of women. In Liu's analysis of Xiao Hong's novel *Field of Life and Death*, set
in the period of the Japanese occupation of China, nationalism "comes across as
a profoundly patriarchal ideology that grants subject-positions to men who fight
over territory, possession and the right to dominate. The women in this novel,
being themselves possessed by men, do not automatically share the male-centred
sense of territory" (Liu 1994, 58). In a deliberate subversion of the trope of the
raped woman in nationalist discourse, Xiao Hong's protagonist turns out to have
been raped by a Chinese man. "The appropriation of the female body by nationalism is contested relentlessly throughout . . . . (and) raises poignant questions
about what it means to be Chinese/peasant/woman" (Liu 1994, 45).

In most modern nations the family was valorized as embodying national morality. The obligation to educate and "emancipate" women derived from the
imperative to produce more efficient mothers who in turn would reproduce, biologically and culturally, "superior" citizens (Yuval-Davis and Anthias 1989, 7–
9). Tani Barlow (1985) and Wendy Larsen have revealed that in China there
existed among the May 4th generation of cultural iconoclasts another strategy
whereby women were incorporated into the modern nation. These radicals sought
to absorb women directly as citizens of the nation *(guo)* and thus force them to
reject their kin-based gender roles in the family or *jia*. The vitriolic May 4th
attack on the family as site of the reproduction of hierarchy in society may have
been the reason why the radical intelligentsia found it almost impossible to "identify women's role within the *jia* as a position from which to initiate a positive re-
theorization of 'woman' " (Larsen 1991, 11). In doing so, they degendered
women (who were to be just like male citizens of the nation), and many important
women writers like Ding Ling ultimately abandoned writing about the problem
of gender. Nonetheless, Larsen observes a kind of resistance to this mode of
incorporation among some women writers as they began to reject " 'nation' as
an overarching concept within which to frame 'woman' " (Larsen 1991, 13).

These narratives and rhetorics of the nation—particularly historical narratives
that are able to speak to present needs—are only one means of articulating the
nation: the discursive means. Of course, for some individuals a historical narrative
itself may be sufficiently powerful to command identification even where no other

cultural commonalities exist. This is the case with nonpracticing, nonbelieving Jews who might nonetheless make great sacrifices for the historical narrative that legitimates the present nation-state of Israel. More commonly, the coming into being of a nation is a complex event in which an entire affective, cultural apparatus—the realm of symbolic meaning—is mobilized in the task of forming a distinctive political community. And this mobilization must be performed by, and in accordance with, the narratives we have outlined above. In turn, these narratives derive depth only when they are embodied in a culture. The intellectual historian must don the cap of the social historian.

Thus the manner in which a nation is created is not the result of a natural process of accumulating cultural commonalities. Rather the process reveals the imposition of a historical narrative of descent and/or dissent upon both heterogeneous and related cultural practices. I will permit myself a deconstructive excess and coin the word *discent* to suggest the porosity of these two signifiers. It reveals how the tracing of a history is frequently linked to differentiating the self from an Other. The narrative of *discent* serves as a template by which the cultural cloth will be cut and given shape and meaning. When this narrative is imposed upon cultural materials, the relevant community is formed not primarily by the creation of new cultural forms—or even the invention of tradition—but by transforming the perception of the boundaries of the community. However, this is not only a complex process, it is also fraught with danger. Narratives are necessarily selective processes which repress various historical and contemporary materials as they seek to define a community; these materials are fair game for the spokesmen of those on the outs or on the margins of this definition who will seek to organize them into a counternarrative of mobilization.

HARD AND SOFT BOUNDARIES

An incipient nationality is formed when the perception of the boundaries of community are transformed: when soft boundaries are transformed into hard ones. Every cultural practice or what I have called "symbolic meaning" is a potential boundary marking a community. These boundaries may be either soft or hard. One or more of the cultural practices of a group, such as rituals, language, dialect, music, kinship rules, or culinary habits, may be considered soft boundaries if they identify a group but do not prevent the group from sharing and even adopting, self-consciously or not, the practices of another. Groups with soft boundaries between each other are sometimes so unselfconscious about their differences that they do not view mutual boundary breach as a threat and could eventually even amalgamate into one community. Thus, differences in dietary and religious practices may not prevent the sharing of a range of practices between local Hui Muslim and Han communities. The important point is that they tolerate the sharing of some and the nonsharing of other boundaries.

When a master narrative of *discent*—a discursive meaning—seeks to define and mobilize a community, it usually does so by privileging a particular symbolic meaning (or a set of cultural practices) as the constitutive principle of the community—such as language, religion, or common historical experience—thereby heightening the self-consciousness of this community in relation to those around it. What occurs, then, is a hardening of boundaries. Not only do communities with hard boundaries privilege their differences, they tend to develop an intolerance and suspicion toward the adoption of the Other's practices and strive to distinguish, in some way or the other, practices that they share. Thus, communities with hard boundaries *will* the differences between them. It will be noted that the hardening of boundaries is by no means restricted to the nation or to the era of the nation-state, but the principle of national formation necessarily involves the closing off of a group whose self-consciousness is sharpened by the celebration of its distinctive culture.

Because the narrative's discursive meaning succeeds in privileging certain symbolic meanings as the constitutive principle of a community, it shapes the composition of the community: who belongs and who does not, who is privileged and who is not. Thus if common history is privileged over language and race (extended kinship), language and race always lie as potential mobilizers of an alternative nation that will distribute its marginals differently. Thus within the hard community there will always be other soft boundaries which may potentially transform into hard boundaries, or new soft boundaries may emerge and transform into hard ones. Moreover, boundaries between communities exist along a spectrum between hard and soft poles and are are always in flux. This is so as much in the modern nation as in premodern societies. Thus the growth of group self-consciousness does not entail the equal rejection of all others. A community may occupy a position on the harder side of the spectrum with respect to community A than to community B, and these positions may change over time as well. Not only do soft boundaries harden, but hard boundaries soften as well, as when a prolonged conflict against a common enemy submerges the differences between two erstwhile foes now united in their common opposition.

This mode of analysis challenges the notion of a stable community that gradually develops a national self-awareness like the evolution of a species. Rather it asserts a deliberate mobilization within a network of cultural representations toward a particular object of identification. Various social actors—often different groups of intellectuals and politicians—develop and deploy narratives to redefine the boundaries and identities of a collectivity with multiple identifications. But even when this closure is succesful, it will unravel in time; the privileged practices that organize this identification will also change.

Consider some examples of this process from modern Chinese history. The Qing dynasty (1644-1911) originated from a Manchu ethnic community which maintained an ambivalent attitude toward the dominant Han culture that it ruled. In the early stages of its rule it actively sought to maintain Manchu distinctiveness through a variety of means, including a ban on intermarriage and Han migration to Manchuria, and the fostering of different customs. In time, however, not only was the ban on migration and intermarriage ignored, but Manchu embrace of Chinese political institutions caused it to blur the distinctions between it and the communities it ruled. More importantly, and unlike the Mongols, the Manchus recognized early the roots of politics in culture and rapidly became the patrons not only of elite culture, but also of popular Han gods like Guandi and Mazu. Thus by the eighteenth century, in terms of their social and cultural relations, the Manchu communities resident in the hundreds of garrisons outside of their homeland in the northeast were losing their literacy in Manchu as well as contact with their folk traditions and melding into the general Han populace (Crossley 1990, 3, 30; Kuhn 1990, 68–70).

At the same time, however, powerful countertendencies worked to shore up— or reconstruct—a Manchu identity. Most noteworthy was the effort of the Qianlong emperor (1736–95) to introduce a classic narrative of *discent* of the Manchus—the "Researches of Manchu Origins" discussed by Crossley (1987). "Researches" traced the *descent* of the Manchu clans to the first attestable peoples of the northeast thereby demonstrating a "racial" distinctiveness which Crossley defines as "immutable identity based on ancestral descent" (1987, 762). Moreover, it celebrated the Manchus as inheritors of the imperial tradition of the region which was independent of (dissented from) the Han Chinese imperial tradition and most closely associated with the Jin empire of the twelfth century. To be sure, this narrative of *discent* played a part within a wider representation of power necessitated by the imperatives of ruling an empire which encompassed both Han Chinese and central Asian polities (Crossley 1987; Kuhn 1990, 69). Confucian universalism was offset by racial exclusivism, because, as Crossley says, every "racial" group—Manchus, Mongols, Tibetans, Han, and others—had their proper status according to their race. These races bore a relationship to the emperor set by the historical role of their ancestors in the creation and development of the state (Crossley 1987, 780). But this narrative which endorsed a conception of "race" as a constitutive principle of community, was also motivated by the fear on the part of the emperor of total cultural extinction of the Manchus. Thus, the Qianlong emperor took it upon himself to champion the Manchu language and values and punish those who forgot their roots (Kuhn 1990, 66–68).

Manchu identity flowered tragically in the late nineteenth century, both in response to Qianlong's efforts and also as a reaction to a Han ethnic exclusivism that became most evident during the years of the Taiping Rebellion (1850–64). As early as 1840, in the days before the British attack on the lower Yangzi city of Zhenjiang during the Opium War, the tension in the city led to hostility between the Manchu soldiers in the garrisons and the civilian Han populace in which countless Han were slaughtered by Manchu soldiers on the allegation that they were traitors. Elliot shows that the entire event was interpreted as ethnic conflict both by survivors and by local historians (Elliot 1990, 64). This simmering tension culminated in the horrifying massacre of Manchu bannermen and their families during the Taiping Rebellion and again in the republican revolution of 1911 (Crossley 1990, 130, 196–97). Manchus in the republican era sustained their identity only by hiding it from public view and by quietly teaching the oral traditions to their children and grandchildren within their homes. Today Manchu identity finds expression not only in their status as a national minority in the PRC, but, as Crossley observes, in such forms as the Manchu Association formed in Taipei in 1981 (Crossley 1990, 216).

My effort to link narratives of *discent* to the self-definition of a group is relevant not only for ethnic nationalisms such as those of the Manchu or Mongols,
but also for those less visible communities within. These include regional and
provincial groupings within the Han such as the Cantonese, the so-called sub-
ethnic groups such as the Tanka boat people, the Hùi and Subei people.[8] For
example, the mid-nineteenth-century Taiping Rebellion was built up by the Hakka
minority of South China who discovered a narrative of *discent* in a version of
Christianity which depicted them as a "chosen people." This narrative gave them
a mission as "god worshippers" in their protracted, dreary battle against the
earlier settlers in South China, whom they now saw as idolatrous, and caused
them to celebrate their own distinctive traditions over those of the larger Han
community of which they were a highly ambiguous part. As the movement developed imperial ambitions, the Hakka coupled their anti-idolatrous message with
appeals to an older rhetoric of the struggle of the Han against the Manchu (Kuhn
1977). The Taiping movement is instructive in showing how a community which
had been succesfully hardened by a redemptive narrative of *discent* was, in another political context, obliged to reopen the question of its identity, or rather,
identities.

CONCLUSION

Let me end this essay with an illustration of the complex process of nation-
formation from the history of the United States, namely Southern nationalism in
the American Civil War. It will, I hope, also reveal one dimension of the instability and repression involved in the idea of the American nation. Although the
Southern slaveholder's hierarchical society was different from Northern individualist and entrepreneurial society in the early 1830s, the two accommodated each
other quite comfortably within the nation. As Ellis and Wildavsky suggest, it was
only when radically egalitarian abolitionists with a powerful sense of their mission
and their refusal to "temporize with evil" began their agitation in midcentury
that a polarization appeared and Southerners were prompted to develop a counternarrative which infused slavery with value. "Slavery was transformed from an
instrumental tool into a symbol of the slave-holding community's aspirations and
sense of identity" (1990, 103). Justifying the master-slave relation as the foundation of a good society entailed, of course, a head-on clash with the individualist
culture of the North. In turn, this induced many in the north to articulate and
insist on the narrative celebrating the individualist way of life.

By turning inwards and privileging the social practice of slave ownership,
boundaries were hardened between the North and South. Nation-makers in the
South began the task of reordering cultural meanings. For instance, they came to
reject the Jeffersonian principle of equality of men and turned to concepts of
"hierarchy, rank and order." Boundary construction took on tangible expression
as mail from the North came to be closely monitored, those thought to be abolitionists expelled, and any relationship with northerners came to be suspect. Thus

the narrative of the abolitionists transformed what were two patterns of social relations in one nation into two self-conscious, exclusive nations.

And yet, the historical view persists that the North worked nationalistically to preserve the Union whereas the South was engaged in sectionalism and secessionism. David Morris Potter, a Southerner and a prominent historian of the 1950s and 1960s, has penetrated the nexus between historical practice and the ideology of the nation-state with unmatched clarity. What was being repressed when historians tended to accept the Northern view was not merely the ideology of the victorious establishment. He writes,

> Once the ethical question of the character of southern institutions becomes linked to the factual question of the nature of group loyalties in the South, it becomes very difficult for the historian to deal with the factual question purely on its own merits. If the finding that a majority of southern citizens wanted a nation of their own is inseparable from the conclusion that the institution of slavery enjoyed a democratic sanction, it is always possible to reverse the reasoning and to argue that since slavery could not have enjoyed a democratic sanction, therefore the Southern people must not have been a ''people'' in the sense that would entitle them to want a nation of their own. (Potter 1968, 64)

I began this essay by exploring the relations between our modern values, the ideology of the nation-state and historical scholarship. It is easy to see now how most of the central dichotomies of modernity—such as empire/nation, tradition/ modernity, center/periphery (or parochiality)—locate the nation-state in the morally privileged term. Historical writing has contributed the dynamic that links these terms in an epochal narrative of enlightenment and modernization and in doing so has secured the transparency of the nation-state's claim to historical subjecthood. Social historians and others, while sometimes defying this claim in practice, have not constructed a theoretical challenge to history as the History of the nation-state. The alternative I have proposed has emphasized the multiple sources of identity creation, the construction/repression of narratives of *discent* which often posture as eternal, essential or evolutionary history, and in place of a teleological movement toward a more cohesive ideal, a mobilization toward particular objects of identification. In this way, we may view the histories of nations as contingently as nations are themselves contingent. But this is no more than a beginning, for as David Potter suggests, we have as yet no response to the great challenge of writing a history from outside the ideology of the nation-state. That challenge is to come to grips with one's own ethical values as a historian, and the enormity of it derives from the fact that these values have themselves been intimately shaped by the nation-state.

NOTES

1. In fact, the effort to define nationalism, nation-state and related concepts is by no means over and turns out to have been a minor industry over the last century. See, for instance, Louis L. Snyder's ''Nationalism and the Flawed Concept of Ethnicity,'' in which he declared that his earlier attempt to clarify the meaning of nationalism yielded a definition

of no less than 208 pages (1983, 253). In general, the debates revolve around the more obvious factors such as the proportions and role of objective and subjective criteria and how to distinguish ethnicity from nationalism. Less obvious questions, such as the meaning of heterogeneity in a nation, how some collectivities come to be included and others excluded and how collectivities gain and lose national identification complicate the debate even further.

2. The *Oxford English Dictionary* defines the modern philosophical meaning of the "subject" as "More fully *conscious* or *thinking subject* . . . the thinking or cognizing agent; the self or ego." *The Compact Edition of the Oxford English Dictionary*, vol. 2, p. 3120. Oxford: Oxford University Press, 1971.

3. See for instance Burton Stein's concept of the segmentary state in India (1980) and Tambiah's galactic polity in the Thai kingdom of Ayutthaya (1985).

4. Even a premodern village, community has to be imagined. Etienne Balibar says about "imaginary" communities that *"Every social community reproduced by the functioning of institutions is imaginary*, that is, it is based on the projection of individual existence into the weft of a collective narrative, on the recognition of a collective *name* and on traditions lived as the trace of an immemorial past (even when they have been created and inculcated in the recent past). But this comes down to accepting that, in certain conditions, *only imaginary communities are real"* (346).

5. The discussion is reproduced in the third lecture of nationalism in Sun's Three People's Principles delivered in 1924. The attack against cosmopolitanism is also directed against the cosmopolitan strain in the May 4th "new culture" movement. Incidentally, the English version of this lecture contains yet another level of repression for it leaves out the vitriolic racialist language characteristic of the original Chinese text and omits many of Sun's references to his debates with the reformist cosmopolitans in the early years of the century.

6. In case it appears that the advocates of the ancient nation always win out over the advocates of the future nation, witness Maoist China during the Cultural Revolution. There is no question that Mao's radical utopianism was intensely nationalist in character and understood as a form of *Chinese* socialism. At the same time, its passionate utopianism anchored the foundations of the new community not in the historical past, but in the liberated future.

7. For a good example of a binary opposition defining the national identity of Australian settler culture see Wolfe (1991). Australian settlers adapted the anthropological notion of "dream time" and the Dreaming complex—the precontact idyll in which the aborigines lived—as timelessness and spacelessness, and they counterposed it to their own idea of "awakenment" embodied in the doctrine of progress and legitimation of colonization. By doing so, they were able to establish a claim to the land by romanticizing the "dreaming" aborigines and thus excluding them from any terrestrial claims.

8. Consider the way in which the hardening of boundaries between Chinese and Japanese during the Japanese occupation in Shanghai affected the internal contours of the Chinese nation. Emily Honig writes of the enduring prejudice against the underclass Subei people of northern Jiangsu in Shanghai, where a common curse is "Subei swine." After the 1932 Japanese attack on Shanghai, the Subei people became identified as Japanese collaborators and during the occupation of 1937–45, the expression "Jiangbei (Subei) traitor" and the accompanying hostility toward them became widespread. While there may have been an element of truth to the accusations of collaboration, Honig observes that other people who collaborated were not targeted in the same way. It was the intensified nationalist rhetoric in the context of previous prejudice against them that marked them as traitors. One Subei native complained in 1932, "When I walk on the street and hear people

making fun of us it feels worse than being a Chinese in a foreign country'' (quoted in Honig 1989, 269). The hardening of boundaries had excorporated the Subei folk from the nation.

REFERENCES

Agnew, John A. 1987. *Place and Politics: The Geographical Mediation of State and Society*. London: Allen & Unwin.

Anderson, Benedict. 1983. *Imagined Communities: Reflections on the Origins and Spread of Nationalism*. London: Verso Editions and NLB.

Armstrong, John A. 1982. *Nations before Nationalism*. Chapel Hill: University of North Carolina Press.

Balibar, Etienne. 1990. ''The Nation Form: History and Ideology.'' *Review* 13.3: 329–64.

Barlow, Tani. 1989. Introduction to Tani Barlow, with Gary J. Bjorge, *I Myself Am Woman: Selected Writings of Ding Ling*. Boston: Beacon Press.

Bayly, Chris. 1985. ''The Pre-history of 'Communalism': Religious Conflict in India, 1700–1850.'' *Modern Asian Studies* 19.2.

———. 1983. *Rulers, Townsmen and Bazaars: North Indian Society in the Age of British Expansion*. Cambridge: Cambridge University Press.

Benard, Cheryl, and Zalmay Khalilzad. 1984. *''The Government of God'': Iran's Islamic Republic*. New York: Columbia University Press.

Bhabha, Homi K., ed. 1990. *Nation and Narration*. London and New York: Routledge.

Boli-Bennet, John, and John W. Meyer. 1978. ''The Ideology of Childhood and the State: Rules Distinguishing Children in National Constitutions, 1870–1970.'' *American Sociological Review* 43:797–812.

Breuilly, John. 1982. *Nationalism and the State*. Chicago: University of Chicago Press.

Chatterjee, Partha. 1986. *Nationalist Thought and the Colonial World: A Derivative Discourse*. London: Zed Books.

Connor, Walker. 1972. ''Nation-Building or Nation-Destroying?'' *World Politics* 24:319–55.

Crossley, Pamela. 1990. *Orphan Warriors: Three Manchu Generations and the End of the Qing*. Princeton, N.J.: Princeton University Press.

———. 1990a. ''Thinking about Ethnicity in Early Modern China.'' *Late Imperial China* 11.1:1–35.

———. 1987. ''Manzhou yuanliu kao and the Formalization of the Manchu Heritage.'' *Journal of Asian Studies* 46.4:761–90.

Delyusin, Lev. 1985. ''Pan-Asiatic Ideas in Sun Yat-sen's Theory of Nationalism.'' In Lev Delyusin, ed., *China, State and Society*. Moscow: Social Sciences Today Editorial Board, USSR Academy of Sciences, 1985.

Deutsch, Karl W. 1961. ''Social Mobilization and Political Development.'' *American Political Science Review* 55.3:493–514.

Dow, Tsung-I. 1982. ''The Confucian Concept of a Nation and Its Historical Practice.'' *Asian Profile* 10.4:347–62.

Duara, Prasenjit. 1990. ''Provincial Narratives of the Nation: Centralism and Federalism in 20th-Century China.'' Forthcoming in Harumi Befu, ed. *Cultural Nationalism in East Asia*.

———. 1988a. *Culture, Power, and the State: Rural North China, 1900–1942*. Stanford, Calif.: Stanford University Press.

————. 1988b. "Superscribing Symbols: The Myth of Guandi, Chinese God of War." *Journal of Asian Studies* 47.4:778–95.

Eley, Geoff. 1981. "Nationalism and Social History." *Social History* 6.1:83–107.

Elliot, Mark. 1990. "Bannermen and Townsmen: Ethnic Tension in Nineteenth-Century Jiangnan." *Late Imperial China* 11.1:36–74.

Ellis, Richard, and Aaron Wildavsky. 1990. "A Cultural Analysis of the Role of Abolitionists in the Coming of the Civil War." *Comparative Studies in Society and History* 32.1:89–116.

Embree, Ainslee T. 1985. "Indian Civilization and Regional Cultures: The Two Realities." In Paul Wallace, ed., *Region and Nation in India*. New Delhi: Oxford University Press.

Esherick, Joseph W. 1987. *The Origins of the Boxer Uprising*. Berkeley: University of California Press.

Fischer, Michael M. J., and Mehdi Abedi. 1990. *Debating Muslims: Cultural Dialogues in Postmodernity and Tradition*. Madison: University of Wisconsin Press.

Fitzgerald, John. 1990. "The Misconceived Revolution: State and Society in China's Nationalist Revolution, 1923–1926." *Journal of Asian Studies* 49.2:323–43.

————. 1988. "Nation and Class in Chinese Nationalist Thought." Unpublished ms.

Fletcher, Joseph. 1978a. "Ch'ing Inner Asia c. 1800." In *The Cambridge History of China*, vol. 10, part 1, pp. 35–106. Cambridge: Cambridge University Press.

———— 1978b. "The Heyday of Ch'ing Order in Mongolia, Sinkiang, and Tibet." In *The Cambridge History of China*, vol. 10, part 1, pp. 351–408. Cambridge: Cambridge University Press.

Gellner, Ernest. 1983. *Nations and Nationalism*. Ithaca, N.Y.: Cornell University Press.

Gladney, D. C. 1988. *Hui-Wei Guanxi: Hui-Uigur Relations and Ethnoreligious Identity in the Political Economy of Xinj-iang*. Paper presented at the Association of Asian Studies Annual Meeting, San Francisco, March.

Grillo, R. D. 1980. Introduction to *"Nation" and "State" in Europe: Anthropological Perspectives*, ed. R. D. Grillo. London: Academic Press.

Habib, Irfan. 1963. *The Agrarian System of Moghul India, 1556–1701*. New York: Asia Publishing House.

Handelman, Don, and Lea Shamgar-Handelman. 1990. "Shaping Time: The Choice of the National Emblem in Israel." In Emiko Ohnuki-Tierney, ed. *Culture through Time: Anthropological Approaches*. Stanford, Calif.: Stanford University Press.

Honig, Emily. 1989. "Subei People in Republican-Era Shanghai." *Modern China* 15.3:243–74.

Jansen, Marius B. 1967. *The Japanese and Sun Yat-sen*. Cambridge, Mass.: Harvard University Press.

Kaiser, Robert John. 1989. "Homelands and National Solidarity in Modernized States." Unpublished ms.

Kuhn, Philip A. 1990. *Soulstealers: The Chinese Sorcery Scare of 1768*. Cambridge, Mass.: Harvard University Press.

————. 1977. "The Origins of the Taiping Vision: Cross-Cultural Dimensions of Chinese Rebellions." *Comparative Studies in Society and History* 19.3:350–66.

Langlois, John D., Jr. 1980. "Chinese Culturalism and the Yuan Analogy: Seventeenth-Century Perspectives." *Harvard Journal of Asiatic Studies* 40.2:355–98.

Laroui, Abdullah. 1976. *The Crisis of the Arab Intellectual: Traditionalism or Historicism?* Trans. from the French by Diarmid Cammell. Berkeley: University of California Press.

Larsen, Wendy. 1991. "Definition and Suppression: Women's Literature in Post–May 4th China." Paper presented at the Association of Asian Studies Annual Meeting, New Orleans, April 11–14.

Leong, S. T. 1985. "The Hakka Chinese of Lingnan: Ethnicity and Social Change in Modern Times." In David Pong and Edmund S. K. Fong, eds., *Ideal and Reality: Social and Political Change in Modern China, 1860–1947*. New York: University Press of America.

Levenson, Joseph. 1967. "The Province, the Nation, and the World: The Problem of Chinese Identity." In Rhodes Murphey et al., eds, *Approaches to Modern Chinese History*. Berkeley: University of California Press.

————. 1964. *Modern China and Its Confucian Past: The Problem of Intellectual Continuity*. New York: Anchor Books.

Li Guoqi. 1970. "Zhongguo jindai minzu sixiang" (Modern Chinese nationalist thought). In Li Guoqi, ed., *Minzuzhuyi*, 19–43. Taipei: Shibao Chuban Gongsi.

Liu, Lydia. 1994. "The Female Body and Nationalist Discourse: *The Field of Life and Death* Revisited." In Inderpal Grewal and Caren Kaplan, eds., *Scattered Hegemonies: Postmodernity and Transnational Feminist Practices*, 37–62. Minneapolis and London: University of Minnesota Press.

McNeill, William. 1982. *The Pursuit of Power*. Chicago: University of Chicago Press.

Meisner, Maurice. 1967. *Li Ta-Chao and the Origins of Chinese Marxism*. Cambridge, Mass.: Harvard University Press.

Meyer, John W. 1980. "The World Polity and the Authority of the Nation State." In *Studies of the Modern World System*, ed. Albert Bergesen. New York: Academic Press.

Meyer, John W., and John Boli-Bennet. 1978. "The Ideology of Childhood and the State: Rules Distinguishing Children in National Constitutions, 1870–1970." *American Sociological Review* 43:797–812.

Min Tu-ki. 1989. *National Polity and Local Power: The Transformation of Late Imperial China*. Ed. Philip A. Kuhn and Timothy Brook. Cambridge, Mass.: Council of East Asian Studies, Harvard University.

Nakami. 1984. "A Protest against the Concept of the 'Middle Kingdom': The Mongols and the 1911 Revolution." In Eto Shinkichi et al., eds., *The 1911 Revolution in China*. Tokyo: Tokyo University Press.

Naquin, Susan, and Evelyn S. Rawski. 1987. *Chinese Society in the Eighteenth Century*. New Haven, Conn.: Yale University Press.

Nehru, Jawaharlal. 1960. *The Discovery of India*. New York: Anchor Books.

Onogawa, Hidemi. 1970. "Zhang Binglinde paiman sixiang" (The anti-Manchu thought of Zhang Binglin). In Li Guoqi, ed., *Minzuzhuyi*, 207–60. Taipei: Shibao Chuban Gongsi.

Ou, Qujia. 1903. "Xin Guangdong" (New Guangdong). In Zhang Yufa, ed., *Wan Qing geming wenxue*. Taipei: Xinzhi zazhishe, 1971

Potter, David Morris. 1968. "The Historian's Use of Nationalism and Vice Versa." In *The South and the Sectional Conflict*, 34–83. Baton Rouge: Louisiana State University Press.

Prakash, Gyan. 1990. "Writing Post-Orientalist Histories of the Third World: Perspectives from Indian Historiography." *Comparative Studies in Society and History* 32.2:383–408.

Pusey, James Reeve. 1983. *China and Charles Darwin*. Cambridge, Mass.: Council on East Asian Studies, Harvard University.

Schoppa, R. Keith. 1989. *Xiang Lake: Nine Centuries of Chinese Life*. New Haven, Conn.: Yale University Press.

Smith, Anthony D. 1986. *The Ethnic Origins of Nations*. Oxford: Blackwell.

Snyder, Louis L. 1983. "Nationalism and the Flawed Concept of Ethnicity." *Canadian Review of Studies in Nationalism* 10.2.

Stein, Burton. 1980. *Peasant, State, and Society in Medieval South India*. Delhi and New York: Oxford University Press.

Sun Yat-sen. 1986 (reprint). *Sanminjuyi* (The three people's principles). Taipei: Zhongyang Wenwu Gongyingshe.

————. 1924. "Sanminzhuyi: Disanjiang" (The three people's principles: third lecture). In *Sun Zhongshan xuanji* (The selected works of Sun Yat-sen), 644–55. Beijing: Renmin Dabanshe, 1981.

Tambiah, Stanley Jeyaraja. 1985. *Culture, Thought, and Social Action*. Cambridge, Mass.: Harvard University Press.

Trauzettel, Rolf. 1975. "Sung Patriotism as a First Step toward Chinese Nationalism." In John W. Haeger, ed., *Crisis and Prosperity in Sung China*, 199–214. Tucson: University of Arizona Press.

Townsend, James R. 1990. "The Puzzle of Chinese Nationalism." Paper presented for the conference *East Asia: The Road Ahead*, Berkeley, California, March 29–31.

Wakeman, Frederic, Jr. 1966. *Strangers at the Gate: Social Disorder in South China, 1839–1861*. Berkeley and Los Angeles: University of California Press.

Wallerstein, Immanuel. 1974. *The Modern World-System*. New York: Academic Press.

Wang Gungwu. 1968. "Early Ming Relations with Southeast Asia: A Background Essay." In John K. Fairbank, ed., *The Chinese World Order: Traditional China's Foreign Relations*, 34–62. Cambridge, Mass.: Harvard University Press.

Watson, James. 1985. "Standardizing the Gods: The Promotion of T'ien Hou ('Empress of Heaven') along the South China Coast, 960–1960." In David Johnson et al., eds., *Popular Culture in Late Imperial China*, 292–324. Berkeley and Los Angeles: University of California Press.

Weber, Eugen. 1976. *Peasants into Frenchmen*. Stanford: Stanford University Press.

Weryho, Jan W. 1986. "The Persian Language and Shia as Nationalist Symbols: A Historical Survey." *Canadian Review of Studies in Nationalism* 13.1:49–55.

Wolfe, Patrick. 1991. "On Being Woken Up: The Dreamtime in Anthropology and in Australian Settler Culture." *Comparative Studies in Society and History* 33.2:197–224.

Wu Wei-to. 1970. "Zhang Taiyan zhi minzujuyi shixue" (Zhang Taiyan's historical studies of nationalism). In Li Guoqi, ed., *Minzuzhuyi*, 261–71. Taipei: Shibao Chuban Gongsi.

Yang Lien-sheng. 1968. "Historical Notes on the Chinese World Order." In John K. Fairbank, ed., *The Chinese World Order: Traditional China's Foreign Relations*, 20–33. Cambridge, Mass.: Harvard University Press.

Yuval-Davis, Nira, and Floya Anthias, eds. 1989. *Woman, Nation, State*. London: Macmillan.

Uffe Østergård

A professor of history at Århus University in Denmark, Uffe Østergård is the author of *Den materialistiske historieopfattelse i Danmark* (Århus: Modtryk, 1974) and other studies of Danish social history. His interest has been in the self-identity of the Danes, as well as larger questions of national and ethnic identity, as evidenced by his articles: "Was ist das Danische an den Danen?" in K. Schulte and W. Wucherpfennig (eds.), *Die Gegenwart der Vergangenheit* (Roskilde: Roskilde University Press, 1987); "Definitions of National Identity," *North Atlantic Studies*, no. 4, pp. 51–57; "What Is National and Ethnic Identity," in Jan Zahle (ed.), *Ethnicity in the Ptolemaic Kingdom* (Århus: Århus University Press, 1992); and " 'Denationalizing' National History: The Comparative Study of Nation-States," *Culture and History* (1992).

In the essay published here Østergård argues that Danish national identity is of relatively recent vintage, though it dates itself from the early thirteenth century. As late as the seventeenth century the kingdom of Denmark was centered in southern Sweden, not in the Jutland peninsula and the island of Zealand (on which Copenhagen is situated). Norway was lost in 1814 to Sweden, and Schleswig-Holstein in the 1860s to Prussia, leaving what became the Danish people with a truncated state on the edge of northern Europe. Rather than simply an elite invention, the new conceptualization of Denmark and the Danish people was deeply shaped by local peasant mentalities. The writings of Bergen-born Ludvig Holberg (1684–1754) and Nikolaj Federik Grundtvig (1783–1872) were important in giving content to a notion of Danishness, which included moderation and a democratic spirit as basic virtues and linked modern Danes back to Icelandic sagas and the Anglo-Saxon poem "Beowulf." Land, country, God, and people were united in a single Danish synthesis by the priest-poet Grundtvig. Østergård places both the history of ideas and the culture of smallholding peasants in the political and economic historical context of evolving Danish parliamentarianism and developing capitalism. By the twentieth century "communitarian peasant traditions of solidarity were transmitted from premodern village society to the Social Democracy" that attracted the new urban working class, "not directly but through the Grundtvigian synthesis." As a result of this particular mix of peasantism and democratic thought, the Danish welfare system, Østergård concludes, differs from the Swedish in its rejection of "state control and authoritarian benevolence" and promotion of a more "libertarian and anarchistic" model.

Peasants and Danes: The Danish National Identity and Political Culture

From a cultural and historical-sociological perspective, the Danish nation-state of today represents a rare situation of virtual identity between state, nation, and society, which is a more recent phenomenon than normally assumed in Denmark and abroad. Though one of the oldest European monarchies, whose flag came "tumbling down from heaven in 1219"—ironically enough an event that happened in present-day Estonia—Denmark's present national identity is of recent vintage. Until 1814 the word, Denmark, denominated a typical European, plurinational or multinational, absolutist state, second only to such powers as France, Great Britain, Austria, Russia, and perhaps Prussia. The state had succeeded in reforming itself in a revolution from above in the late eighteenth century and ended as one of the few really "enlightened absolutisms" of the day (Horstbøll and Østergård 1990; Østergård 1990). It consisted of four main parts and several subsidiaries in the North Atlantic Ocean, plus some colonies in Western Africa, India, and the West Indies. The main parts were the kingdoms of Denmark proper and Norway, plus the duchies of Schleswig and Holstein. How this particular state came about need not bother us here.

The only point worth mentioning from a comparative point of view is that the three provinces in the southern part of present-day Sweden, lost in 1660, originally constituted the central core of Denmark, if one can use such national terms for political entities in premodern times. From almost any cultural historical point of view the people of Scania, Halland, and Blekinge were more Danish than those of Jutland, not to speak of the island Bornholm in the Baltic, which was forgotten at the peace conference in 1660 and opted for Denmark in something close to a

Uffe Østergård, "Peasants and Danes: The Danish National Identity and Political Culture," *Comparative Studies in Society and History*, 34, 1 (January 1992), pp. 3–27. Copyright © 1992 Society for Comparative Study of Society and History.

Author's note: The paper has been presented for discussion at the Rutgers Center for Historical Analysis on March 15, 1990, and at the Interdisciplinary Workshop on The National Experience, University of Lund, Department of European Ethnology, October 18–20, 1990. I want to thank my friend and colleague, Steve Sampson, for his great help with the translation and a devastating critique of a previous version. Thanks as well to Jonathan Rée, who once again gave of his own valuable time in order to improve my English. More people than I can possibly mention in a brief footnote over the years have volunteered comments and observations on previous versions. Even more have helped indirectly by providing different aspects of their Danishness for observation.

popular referendum, a rare phenomenon in premodern times. Nowadays, however, the people of Southern Sweden speak an impeccable, though heavily accented, Swedish. How come? A closer investigation reveals one of the few instances in which an entire population successfully changed its national identity.

Although its intentions were comparable to those of the German Emperor, when he failed in the Czech lands of Bohemia and Moravia a few decades earlier, the Swedish government of Stockholm between 1660 and 1700 successfully changed the official language of the three provinces when the newly appointed parish ministers and a brand-new university established in Lund carried out a systematic indoctrination. These provinces nowadays still feel close to Denmark and more specifically to its capital Copenhagen and retain a certain distance from Stockholm, although they are undeniably Swedish. This came out clearly as early as the first decade of the eighteenth century. Whereas virtually the entire population supported the Danish armies during the first of the Swedish–Danish wars in 1685 to 1689, they demonstrated a completely different attitude in the Great Nordic War of 1700–21 (Fabricius 1906:58). This is the only known example of a successfully engineered switch of national identity of an entire population in the whole history of nation building. It therefore deserves closer inspection by comparative historians, which is not my aim in this article.

The problem I do want to address is the character of the Danish nation-state that resulted from the Napoleonic Wars and the German Unification. It lost Norway in 1814 because of some bad military and foreign policy dispositions, and Bismarck used the duchies of Schleswig and Holstein as a vehicle for bringing about German unification under the Prussian King between 1864 and 1866–71. This is all well-known diplomatic history. Probably less well-known are the internal repercussions of this catastrophe in foreign policy and the results in terms of a peasant ideological hegemony over the homogeneous political culture in the remaining Danish state, a type of ideological hegemony which to my knowledge is almost unique. This is not to say that peasant values are nonexistent in industrialized societies. Of course they do exist. But it is a far cry from the existence of some cultural traits to an ideological hegemony over all parts of society. And this latter seems to be the case in the Danish society of this century even after the industrialization of the country in the decades after the Second World War.

In contrast to the situation in most other emerging nation-states at the time, the sheer diminutiveness of the amputated state allowed a numerous class of relatively well-to-do peasants, who had become independent farmers through the reforms of the late eighteenth century, to take over, economically and politically. Gradually, throughout the latter part of the nineteenth century, though not without opposition, the middle peasant farmers took over from the despairing ruling elites. The latter were recruited from the tiny urban bourgeoisie, the officials of the state trained at German-style universities in Denmark and elsewhere, and the manorial class. They had lost faith in the survival of the state after the debacle of 1864 and the subsequent establishment of a strong united Germany next door. Some even played with the thought of joining this neighbouring state, which already dominated the culture of the upper-classes. But, in an outburst of popular energy an alternate rising elite proclaimed a strategy of winning internally what had been lost outside. This witticism turned into a literal strategy of retrieving the lost agrarian lands of Western Jutland. It also took the form of an opening of the so-called Dark Jutland in an attempt to turn the economy of the Jutland peninsula away from Hamburg and redirect it towards Copenhagen. This movement, sometimes nowadays provocatively called "the exploration of Jutland," refers to the exploitation of Jutland by its capital Copenhagen, which is situated on the far eastern rim of the country as a leftover from the former empire, rather like Vienna in present-day Austria. This battle is not yet over, as was amply demonstrated in the recent heated controversies about building a bridge between the islands of Fyn and Sjælland or about connecting Sweden and Copenhagen directly with Germany over the Fehmern Sund. The attempt to keep the Danish nation-state together and Jutland away from Hamburg won out, although by a narrow margin; and the decision to build the bridge will probably turn out to be economically unwise.

More important, though, is the cultural, economic and political awakening of the middle peasants who became farmers producing for an indefinite market precisely during this period. The reason for their success lies in the late industrialization and the relative weakness of the bourgeoisie in Denmark. The takeoff did not occur until the 1890s and the final breakthrough was as late as the 1950s (Hansen 1970). The middle peasants developed a consciousness of themselves as a class and understood themselves to be the real backbone of society. Their ideology supported free trade, which is no surprise as they were beginning to rely heavily on exporting food to the rapidly developing British market. Economically speaking, Denmark must indeed be considered part of the British empire from the mid-nineteenth to the mid-twentieth century. More surprising are the strong libertarian elements contained in the farmers' ideology because of their struggle with the existing urban and academic elites. The peasant movement won out basically because it succeeded in establishing an independent culture with educational institutions of its own. This again was possible because of the unique organization of the agrarian industries based on the cooperative.

The Danish case is unique, and I want to argue that it should be given more attention by students of comparative historical sociology. Barrington Moore argues in the introduction to his sweeping analysis of the main roads to political and economic modernity that the smaller countries, such as Switzerland, Scandinavia, and the Low Countries, should be left out of a systematic comparative treatment because of their small size and relative lack of importance. Barrington Moore addresses the question of the role of the smaller Western countries as follows:

> How is it possible to generalize about the growth of Western democracy or of communism while excluding them? Does not the exclusion of the smaller, Western democratic states produce a certain antipeasant basis throughout the whole book? To this objection there is, I think, an impersonal answer. This study concentrates on certain important stages in a prolonged social process which has worked itself out in several countries. As part of this process new social arrangements have grown up by violence and in other ways which have made certain countries political leaders at different points in time during the first half of the twentieth century. The focus

of interest is on innovation that has led to political power, not on the spread and reception of institutions that have been hammered out elsewhere, except where they have led to significant power in world politics. *The fact that the smaller countries depend economically and politically on big and powerful ones means that the decisive causes of their politics lie outside their own boundaries. It also means that their political problems are not really comparable to those of larger countries.* Therefore, a general statement about the historical preconditions of democracy or authoritarianism covering small countries as well as large would probably be so broad as to be abstractly platitudinous (Barrington Moore 1966: x–xi, emphases added).

I accept the latter part of Barrington Moore's argument as much as I disagree with the first part. Small countries are dependent, all right, but precisely because their relatively small size means that certain factors determining differences in political culture and nationality in nation-states come out in a more clear-cut way.

Danish historians and sociologists have hotly debated whether peasant ideological hegemony resulted from a particular class structure dating back to the 1780s or even to the early sixteenth century, when the number of farms was frozen by law, or whether this ideology created the particular class structure of Danish society in the nineteenth century. Putting the debate in such terms makes it almost impossible to resolve, as both of the protagonists' positions contain part of the truth. My contribution to the debate is an investigation of the important but virtually untranslated and untranslatable philosopher, priest, and poet Nikolaj Frederik Grundtvig, who lived from 1783 to 1872.

Grundtvig was a contemporary of Kierkegaard but has attracted much less attention outside Denmark. In Denmark on the other hand his influence is much greater. He wrote more than 1,500 songs, and his psalms take up almost half of the official psalmbook today. More than any other single person he is responsible for two most peculiarly Danish institutions, the folk high school and the church. The Lutheran church in Denmark is not a state church and does not have an official constitution; yet, still today it comprises almost 90 percent of the population. Although very few actively attend service nowadays, the huge majority has decided not to leave this institution and keeps paying an extra 1 percent in church taxes, even though everybody hates paying taxes and tax evasions and protests are perennial manifestations of Danish mentality and political culture. Such an aversion to taxation is surprising, as is the prevalence of a liberal free market economic policy in a country with a huge public sector dominated by an ethos of libertarianism and solidarity and with a Conservative party that is more socialist than most socialist parties in Europe.

Apparently these paradoxes date back a long time. In the year 1694 Robert Molesworth (1656–1725), former British ambassador to the king of Denmark, published *An Account of Denmark as It Was in the Year 1692*. Molesworth hated everything Danish, their petty peasant slyness and short-sighted scheming. He loathed every minute he had spent in the country. His conclusion runs as follows:

To conclude; I never knew any Country where the Minds of the People were more of one calibre and pitch than here; you shall meet with none of extraordinary Parts or Qualifications, or excellent in particular Studies and Trades; you see no Enthusiasts, Mad-men, Natural Fools, or fanciful Folks; but a certain equality of Understanding reigns among them: every one keeps the ordinary beaten road of Sence, which in this Country is neither the fairest nor the foulest, without deviating to the right or left: yet I will add this one Remark to their praise. That the Common People do generally write and read (Molesworth 1694:257).

The book is presented to the audience as a travel account, but the actual intention was to warn the English aristocracy which had recently expelled James II about the dangers of absolutism. Denmark, proclaimed an absolutist regime in 1660 after its disastrous military defeat by Sweden, became perhaps the most absolutist regime of all Europe, as its absolutism was actually put into writing in 1665 (''The King's Law,'' or *Lex Regia*). This had not happened in the France of Louis XIV, where absolutism was invented. Because Molesworth was aiming to warn his fellow countrymen about absolutism, one should perhaps treat his descriptions as comparable to those of his friend and contemporary, Jonathan Swift, when describing Lilliput or Brobdingnag. Yet his characterizations remind us of any number of subsequent descriptions of Danes. What varies are the valuations of the mediocrity and mundaneness of the society: Some see it as the utmost boredom, others as an egalitarian heaven on earth.

An early, premodern Danish national identity is often claimed to have been expressed in the writings of Ludvig Holberg. A famous playwright, historian, philosopher, and enlightenment moralist, he was born in Bergen on the West coast of Norway in 1684 and died in Copenhagen in 1754 after a highly successful career as a writer and university professor. His comedies equal those of Molière (1622–73) and Goldoni (1707–93); his history of Denmark and Norway measures up to the standards set by August Ludwig Schlözer (1735–1809) and Johann Christoph Gatterer (1727–99) of Göttingen; and his political philosophy rivalled that of Montesquieu. In 1753 he published a book in French intended to refute Montesquieu's *De L'esprit des lois* (1748). In his writings one can detect a realistic and pragmatic undercurrent resembling the values often attributed to a peasant culture. The German historian, Bernd Henningsen, sees Holberg as a typical embodiment of the nonauthoritarian, democratic political culture of Scandinavia. According to Henningsen, Holberg's thoughts were centered on common sense and limited by experience. Using narratives, fables, and the like, he forced people to recognize the truth. His philosophy was a philosophy of the concrete: He would always seek the truth in human experience, and never in a system (Henningsen 1980). In 1729, Holberg published *Description of Norway and Denmark*, which concluded:

> The Danes are nowadays considered to be a well-tempered and very civilized people
> .... The Danish nation is compliant and dependable, and curiously obedient to
> authority. There is no country where revolt has less place than in Denmark, nor
> where theft, robbery, and murder are less frequent (Holberg 1729, in Værker, 1:76).

Holberg, like Molesworth, emphasized the fundamentally moderate and mediating character of the Danish people. They are neither backward nor extremely clever. The middle way is considered a basic virtue. His Epistle no. 72, entitled *On Surprising Changes in the Danish National Character*, praises the Danes ''as a people who do not drift easily into extremes but take the middle way in all things" (Holberg 1729, in Værker, XI:79).

For him "virtue consists in mediocrity," i.e., harmony between the classes (Holberg 1729, in Værker, X:30). Politically Holberg argued in favour of the absolute power of the king, but he did this to forestall the undue influence of the aristocracy. His ultimate political goal was "an absolute monarchy guided by public opinion," an apparent contradiction in terms which was actually put into practice during the Danish-Norwegian monarchy for a short time in the 1780s and 1790s until the outbreak of the French Revolution made all talk of enlightened reform obsolete. The phrase "absolutism guided by the public opinion," invented by the Norwegian historian Seip (1958), is a political doctrine I recently investigated in a comparative context, primarily with the republican doctrines of the French Revolution (Horstbøll and Østergård 1990).

But is it correct to interpret Holberg as an early representative of a separate and particular Danishness, as it is done by Bernd Henningsen? A Danish literary historian and Marxist, Svend Møller Kristensen, has questioned the rather widespread assumption that Holberg is Danish. Skepticism and irony, keeping one's feet on the ground, shunning pathos, pomposity, and all sorts of affection and affected styles, may reflect a peasant or popular view of life, rather than a particularly Danish or Norwegian point of view. According to this well-known literary historian, Holberg should be understood as part of:

> a generalized reaction from below, partly defensive and partly an attack on the upper classes, their grandeur, pomposity, and splendour, their stiltedness and possible hypocrisy, known from hundreds of satires, comedies, parodies, and slapsticks, from jesters and storytellers, and popular anecdotes. This is the spirit which lives in Holberg. The critical spirit which ridicules the false skin, the empty shell, the imagined importance, and points to the real, the sensible, the natural instead . . . . It is not simply the bourgeois spirit which Holberg expresses, but a bourgeois "popular" spirit—ordinary, practical, and ironic. He incarnates simultaneously a "broader" and a "lower" mood (Møller Kristensen 1970:36–38).

There is a certain logic to the fact that it was Denmark and Norway, not neighbouring Sweden, which Holberg celebrated as Swedish, although Sweden's society and spiritual life reflected an aristocratic grandeur due to more than a hundred years as a leading European power. Elite culture in Denmark, on the other hand, appropriated many of the features of popular culture arising from the limited size of the country and the king's absolute dominance over the feudal nobility from 1660 onwards. The feudal nobility and later the bourgeoisie simply found it difficult to accumulate enough wealth to distinguish themselves from the other classes, which is why the relations between its elite culture and the common people follow a different pattern in Denmark than in most other European countries.

Nikolaj Frederik Grundtvig (1783–1872) expressed these thoughts. Depressed by Great Britain's defeat of Denmark in the war in 1807–14, the young priest took it upon himself to reestablish what he took to be the original Nordic or Danish mind. He translated the Icelandic Sagas, the twelfth-century history of

Saxo Grammaticus, the Anglo-Saxon Beowulf poem, and hundreds of other sources of what he considered the true but lost core of Danishness. His sermons attracted large crowds of enthusiastic students. His address on *The Light of the Holy Trinity*, delivered in 1814 to a band of student volunteers willing to fight the English, inspired a whole generation of young followers, including the priest, Jacob Christian Lindberg, who was later to become the organizer of the first Grundtvigian movement. When he embarked upon a sharp polemic with his superiors in the church on matters of theology, he was banned from all public appearances. This drove him into an inner exile in the 1830s during which he laid the foundations for a revival of the stagnant official religion. After the ban was lifted in 1839, he burst out in a massive production of sermons, psalms, and songs—a literary legacy that at least until a few years ago was the core of the socialization of most Danes. He created an all-embracing view of nature, language, and history. In 1848, after the outbreak of the war over Schleswig, he produced a refined definition of national identity that helped set the tone for a nationalism less chauvinistic than most in the nineteenth century. As is sometimes the case with prolific writers, his most precise theoretical expressions were to be found in the restricted form of verse:

> People! what is a people? what does popular mean?
> Is it the nose or the mouth that gives it away?
> Is there a people hidden from the average eye in burial hills and
> behind bushes, in every body, big and bony?
> They belong to a people who think they do,
> those who can hear the Mother tongue,
> those who love the Fatherland
> The rest are separated from the people, expel themselves,
> do not belong.
>
> *(Grundtvig 1848, author's translation)*

This definition, though produced in the heat of the battle with the German-speaking rebels in the duchies of Schleswig and Holstein, resembles the definition of national identity which the French orientalist, Ernest Renan, presented in a famous lecture at the Sorbonne on March 11, 1882. Now the standard formulation of the antiessentialist definition of national identity, this definition might be labelled voluntaristic and subjective, as it stresses the importance of the expressed will of people. The rival definition in modern European thinking could be called the objective and culturalist definition. It dates from Herder and has permeated all thinking in the nineteenth and twentieth centuries until fascism and Nazism (Østergård 1991b). It is surprising to find a Dane putting forward this democratic definition as early as 1848. Unlike France, no military defeat had preceded it in Denmark. Until 1870 French thinkers had defined nationality in terms no less essentialist than any German would after that date. It must be also remembered that Grundtvig wrote these lines in a highly explosive political situation that developed after the two predominantly German-speaking provinces of Schleswig and Holstein seceded. Admittedly Grundtvig left those who opted for the German language to their own choice as non-Danes, which in his opinion was a most deplorable fate. But he left them the choice and would never have dreamed of interfering with it.

There is a lot more to say about the thinking of Grundtvig, but it comes out badly in translation. Central to his thought was the assumption that culture and identity are embedded in the unity of life and language. Although this invites the label of chauvinism, Grundtvig, like his opposite number, Herder, did not assume that there was a hierarchy of nationalities. Cultural diversity, yes; cultural dominance, no. Whether these assumptions are really viable need not concern us here. Probably they are not, as completely incompatible cultures tend eventually to make war on each other. What does concern us, though, is the fact that his notions caught on among a class of people in the small state left over from the wars of the middle of that century.

His popularity began with the students immediately after 1814. The breakthrough only happened in 1838–40, when different religious and political movements decided to transform his thinking into practice. First, it influenced the revivalist religious movements; later, the more explicitly political movements; and eventually, his thinking served as the foundation for independent economic and educational institutions. Grundtvig himself did not seek such popular support. He delivered his message either in writing or orally and then stood aloof as others decided what to make out of it, which is why some of the guardians of his thoughts today say that the Grundtvigian movement took him prisoner by transforming his message into an ideology called "Grundtvigism." No doubt, there is some truth in this, as is always the case when an individual's thought is transformed into social practice, such as with Marx and Marxism. The only ones who do not suffer such a fate are those who, like the existentialist philosopher Søren Kierkegaard, formulate their ideas without reference to their relevance for society. Grundtvig's thinking, however, did strike a chord with some, only he did not care whether it did or not. He normally refused to meet people, and if he did, he talked incessantly and never listened. Consequently, the reasons for the influence of his thinking are not to be found in his personal behaviour but in the thought itself and its relevance for the surrounding society.

The revivalists came to Grundtvig of their own accord. This religious movement of the first half of the nineteenth century resembled many other Pietist movements throughout Europe. Because of the negative attitude of the official Lutheran state church, they chose to meet outside the churches, and were called *Forsamlingsbevægelsen* (the meeting movement). They were attracted by Grundtvig's independent interpretation of the Lutheran heritage. Grundtvig, however, succeeded in giving an optimistic tone to the normally rather gloomy Pietism of German origins. In their struggles with the officials of the absolutist state these revivalists learned an organizational lesson that they would soon put to political use. The leaders of the peasant movement of the 1840s were recruited from their ranks. Initially, working under the tutelage of the liberal intellectuals, the peasant party gradually broke away from the National Liberals, as they called themselves.

The liberal party initiated a debate over Schleswig with their fellow liberals in Kiel in 1842, hoping to attain popular backing in their bid for power. In 1847 they fused with the peasants in a party called *Bondevennerne* (Friends of the Peasants). After the death of the king and the subsequent peaceful revolution of 1848–49, the National Liberals came to power at the cost of a war with their opposites in Kiel, who had entered a similar alliance with some of their peasants. In Schleswig-Holstein, however, the liberals joined the all-German movement in the Paulskirche in Frankfurt and abandoned their peasant power base as fast as they could. The Danish National Liberals were completely dependent on the political support of the peasants (one reason why Marx denounced the Danish "counter-revolutionaries" along with the Slavs of Austria). The peasants did most of the actual fighting in Schleswig because there was no general conscription before the constitution of 1849. The peasant Danish armies went to war singing the verses of Grundtvig and other national songs (one of these, "When I Left [for War] My Girl Wanted to Come Along" is still very popular). This was how the peasants learned to be Danish, an abstraction that until then had never meant much to them. In the 1850s the National Liberals and the peasant party gradually fell apart over domestic policies. A proof of the estrangement are the utterings by a former National Liberal, Orla Lehmann (1810–70), at a mass meeting in Vejle on March 29, 1860. Disappointed by their apparent "lack of gratitude" and the deterioration of the political life, he declared that the political power should belong to "the Intelligent, the Educated and the Rich."

Such experiences led the various political factions of the peasant party to establish independent institutions, beginning with the church. Because the monarchy had been transformed from an absolutist to a constitutional regime, the church's organization had to be changed accordingly. These endeavours, though, differed in important ways from the otherwise comparable situation in the Lutheran monarchies of Sweden and Norway. In Denmark, a state church with a proper constitution, though envisaged in the constitution of 1849, never came into existence. This was a result of the influence of Grundtvig and the members of the revivalist movement, who wanted to guarantee religious freedom and avoid making the church the creature of the state or its agent of socialization, as it had been under absolutism.

Denmark has acquired a most peculiar mixture of freedom and state control in religious matters. There is a minister of religious affairs called the minister of the People's Church—a contradiction in terms that does not seem to bother Danes. He or she presides over church administration and the upkeep of church buildings, which is financed by a separate tax. However, individual priests and their congregations interpret the actual teachings of the church. Local councils, elected every four years, run these congregations. Nowadays the most influential groups are the fundamentalist Inner Mission and the Social Democrats! They often collaborate to control the free speech of the priests, who normally receive their academic training at the universities and represent an intellectually refined Lutheran theology that does not appeal to ordinary believers. Yet, as already mentioned, most of the apparently nonreligious Danish population belongs to this church in the sense that they pay the taxes, even if few attend service, except for Christmas, baptisms, burials, and weddings. Still, I think, the Lutheranism of the

People's Church plays an enormous and insufficiently recognised role in defining Denmark's political culture.

In the 1870s the ideological battle was carried into the educational field. The National Liberals, who now sided wholeheartedly with the conservative owners of the manors in a party called *Højre* (the Right), wanted a comprehensive school system under the supervision of the state. This, the majority of the farmers' party *Venstre* (the Left) resisted vehemently. They believed in the absolute freedom of education and attacked the "black" schools of learning in which Latin was still taught. They could do this because the peasant movement from 1844 had established a network of folk high schools throughout the country. Over the years Grundtvig had produced a series of programs for a new and more democratic educational system. Like most of his other thoughts, they did not constitute a coherent system but can be seen as an appeal for a practical schooling in democracy. However, what these schools lack in coherent programs, they make up for in flexibility. Today most of them are institutions of adult education catering mainly to the dropouts from the cities and to senior citizens.

In addition, Grundtvig's anti-institutional thinking permeated the Danish educational system so much that even today there is no enforced schooling, only enforced learning. How one is educated is a personal choice. This might not sound terribly surprising for an American audience, but taken in the context of the highly centralized European states with a Lutheran heritage, it is most surprising. What is more, these schools helped produce an alternative elite. Until very recently there were two or maybe three different ways of recruiting the political, cultural, and business elites. The university system was one, the workers movement, another—at least until the democratization of the official educational system in the sixties. Both are well-known in other countries. The third line of recruitment through the folk high schools, however, is a peculiarly Danish phenomenon. Grundtvig and his followers accomplished what amounts to a real cultural revolution. He hated the formal teachings of the official school system and favoured free learning with an emphasis on story telling—"the living word"—and discussion among peers. This program gave rise to a system of free schools for the children, plus folk high schools and agrarian schools for the farmers' sons and daughters in their late teens and early twenties.

A small but significant and highly articulate proportion of the population was educated within this alternative system, which has left its mark throughout educational practice in Denmark. Even in today's tightly controlled Danish society, there is no compulsory schooling, just compulsory learning. The present minister of education never had any formal education until he went to university. As a consequence of this freedom of choice in the school system, the state has for years supported an openly Marxist series of free schools, even though the explicit intention of these schools was to bring down the existing political and social order. As long as the parents come up with 10 percent of the funding, the state is compelled by law to provide the rest. This system also applies to the Danish schools in present-day Schleswig-Holstein in the Bundesrepublik. These schools have attracted a number of children from thoroughly German parents of the generation of the late sixties, who see them as an attractive alternative to the more authoritarian German schools. On the other hand, Danish children north of the border often attend German high schools in order to learn more and become more competitive.

It is difficult to estimate the importance of the Grundtvigian schools in precise quantitative terms, as their influence has been almost as great outside the schools as in them. There is no doubt, however, that the very existence of two competing elites has helped agrarian and libertarian values to make inroads into the mainstream of Danish political culture and has thus contributed heavily to defining Danishness. The informal and antisystematic character of Grundtvig's teachings was the reason why they always suited the peasant movement so well. They could provide inspiration without restricting innovation. It also helps to explain why Grundtvig has never been a favourite of academics: His thinking does not amount to a coherent theoretical system. His enmity toward all systems let him even deny that he himself was a Grundtvigian (much as Marx denied that he was a Marxist). Grundtvigians never used this term themselves. They talked of "Friends" and organized "meetings of Friends." This organizational informality also turned out to be a major advantage, at least in the beginning of the movement. Furthermore, it is the reason why the influence of this farmers' ideology was able to cross the boundaries of the class it originally served so well.

In the song "Far Whiter Mountains Shine Splendidly Forth" (or "Denmark's Consolation," its official name), Grundtvig expressed his version of the Danish virtues. The song, written in 1820 to commemorate the parting of a friend for the West Indies, has not been adopted as a national anthem but serves in many ways as the unofficial anthem. Its formulations are often taken as highlighting the real Danish peaceful and egalitarian national identity, in contrast to the aggressiveness expressed in other national anthems. It begins like this:

> Far whiter mountains shine splendidly forth
> Than the hills of our native islands,
> But, we Danish rejoice in the quiet North
> For our lowlands and rolling highlands.
> No peaks towered over our birth:
> It suits us best to remain on earth.

The song ends on a note of flat-hill self-satisfaction,

> Even more of the ore, so white and so red [the colours of the flag]
> Others might have gotten mountains in exchange
> For the Dane, however, the daily bread is found
> no less in the hut of the poor man;
> when few have too much and fewer too little
> then truly we have become wealthy.

> *(Grundtvig 1820, author's translation)*

This is the ultimate Danish discourse: Everyone is in the same boat. Yet, in the social reality of the nineteenth-century, it served as a class ideology for the struggling popular movements; first for the dissenters from the official church;

then for the political organizations; and, last but not least, for the cooperative movement in agriculture and the independent educational institutions such as the folk high schools. That a class ideology come to dominate the outlook and discourse of the other classes is nothing new. What is surprising is the peasant nature of this ideological hegemony. It has to be explained from the nature of the economy in the core lands of the Danish monarchy left over after the debacles of the Schleswig wars in 1848–50 and 1864.

The agrarian reforms of the 1780s created a unique form of agrarian capitalism based on approximately 60,000 tenant farms. The size and number of the farms date back to the sixteenth century, when the king, to protect his fiscal resources, succeeded in freezing the number and size of the existing farmsteads so as to save them from being swallowed up by the manors. Denmark proper switched from an East-Elbian model of serfdom to something closer to the norm in Western Europe (Anderson 1974; Blum 1978; Østergård 1982). The seigneurial class dominated the polity until 1660 and continued to dominate the administrative structure under the absolutist regime. Its inroad into the economy, though, remained restricted to the estates proper. The lands directly cultivated by the manors, the demesnes, were the highest yielding but only accounted for 8 to 12 percent of the arable land. The tenants belonged to the estates in the sense that the aristocrats administered the tenant farms and were responsible for paying their taxes. Serfdom in the German sense, however, was never introduced north of Holstein. The crown did not allow the manor owners to incorporate farms into the manors as was done in the Middle Ages. In the late eighteenth century most of the biggest aristocratic landowners realized they could get disposable capital for investments by selling off their unprofitable copyhold lands, which is why the reformers of the 1780s succeeded in transforming most of the 60,000 larger tenants into entrepreneurial independent farmers in a surprisingly short time (Horstbøll and Østergård 1990).

More than 30,000 tenants bought their farms on easy terms in the thirty years following the reforms of 1784–88, and the rest followed in a gradual process during the rest of the nineteenth century. The same reforms broke up the old system of common cultivation within the villages. The peasants left the secluded and restrictive life of the village community to live or die on their own as entrepreneurial farmers. Now they were free to succeed, to introduce new methods in farming, but also to go bankrupt and commit suicide if they failed. The last remnants of the feudal system were not abolished until 1919. In the period under review, 90 percent of the farmers owned their farms, 60,000 of these being middle peasants (*gårdmænd*) or peasant farmers. Their holdings ranged in size from about 30 to 120 hectares and accounted for 70 percent of the cultivated lands. In a population of a little more than 2 million, these 60,000 farmers became the economic, political, and cultural backbone of society through protracted political struggles in the sixty years following the introduction of parliamentary democracy in 1848–49; but it took more than sixty years of political struggles before the principle that the government should be based on the majority in parliament was recognised. Then, in 1901, Denmark had its first prime minister of peasant origins, J. C. Christensen, a former teacher from the westernmost town of Jutland, Ringkøbing. The departing members of the ruling elite proclaimed that they would never return to seats soiled by the manure of peasants. This turned out to be a sound prediction.

The economic basis of this unique political development was the cooperative organization of industrial processing of agricultural products. In 1882 the first cooperative dairy was set up in the westernmost periphery of the country. By 1903 cooperative dairies processed more than 80 percent of the country's total milk production. This does not mean that all production took place in middle-sized farms or that all agricultural processing was cooperatively organized. Large estates still cultivated 10 to 15 percent of the land and for a long time were the real innovators, helped in part by the capital they created by selling their copyhold lands. In the decades after 1882, however, the cooperatives gradually took the lead as the main technological innovators and providers of capital. This type of organization later spread to the newly created smaller cottagers known as *husmænd*, who mainly specialized in animal husbandry and dairy production, and who farmed the remaining 10 to 15 percent of the cultivated land. Basic agrarian production was still individual production on independent farms, although most of these were somewhat larger than the usual in most European countries. However, the processing of these products into exportable commodities took place in local farm industries run on a cooperative basis, where, as the farmers put it, the vote was cast by heads instead of heads of cattle (i.e., one man, one vote). This pun (in Danish *hoveder*, heads, and *høveder*, cattle) is less true when one starts investigating the realities of the cooperatives. Yet, the myth stuck and produced a sense of community which has become a dominant theme in Danish political culture through various political traditions.

The agricultural changes of the 1880s caused two modern economic spheres, a rural one and an urban one, to come into existence. They interacted in a complicated way, constituting what my colleague Vagn Wåhlin and I have labelled "the Danish road to agrarian capitalism" (Wåhlin and Østergård 1976; Wåhlin 1981). It is not a very precise notion, but it serves as a reminder that Danish society was thoroughly dominated by market exchange mechanisms long before the industrial revolution of the 1890s and 1950s and the emergence of an industrial working class. Most of the basic production in agriculture and the agricultural industries still took place in units with ten employees or less. But these units could cooperate on a fairly large scale and for this reason were able to compete in the world market. A fair number of employees would often belong to one family, and the employers themselves would normally participate in the work and life in the countryside as well as in the small towns. This lent a certain flavour not only of security but also of patriarchal oppression to life. One should not ignore, however, that this type of society accorded an equal though separate role to married women as heads of their part of the household. Contrary to the situation in Iceland, this important role was not reflected in separate surnames and independent economic status. In social reality, however, the relations between the sexes were more equal than the juridical abstractions suggest, at least within the class of middle farmers.

Grundtvig's teachings were permeated by a fundamental optimism with regard to people's capacities. He demanded economic and ideological freedom and the right of education for everybody. This program corresponded precisely with the needs of the large class of highly self-conscious and class-conscious farmers, men and women alike. In Danish literature and historiography, it has become a commonplace to interpret Grundtvigism narrowly as the religion of the well-to-do farmers. This identification of class and ideology dates back to the communist author, Hans Kirk (1888–1962). He contrasted the farmer religion of Grundtvigism with the more traditionally revivalist Inner Mission (*Indre Mission*) founded in 1853. This competing religious movement better suited the poorer farm hands and fishermen. The Grundtvigian farmers could reap their rewards in this life, but the lowly farm workers and fishermen would have to wait until the next. Kirk's interpretation originated in his own upbringing in northwestern Jutland, an area where wealthy farmers and fishermen lived geographically close but socially wide apart. He translated this interpretation into a very powerful novel in 1928 that has helped in the formation of the opinions of succeeding generations. In a later short story with autobiographical overtones, he expressed it as follows:

> My father and mother belonged to two clans with different gods, which a child quickly understands. In the well-off region of Thy, a fatherly old peasant God ruled, while in Harbøor Jesus ruled. He was severe and demanded prayer, repentence, and obedience. In rich Thy, one enters heaven after one's death as long as one has otherwise done something good among people. In poor Harbøor, it is terribly difficult to avoid Hell and Devil, and one must anoint oneself with the blood of the lamb . . . . I learned this from the farmers when we visited [his father was a country doctor.] . . . At home much good came without either God nor Jesus. We did not go to church. We did not have time for it. Neither were we afraid of the Devil, for he doesn't really exist (Kirk 1953:67–68).

In this very convincing description we are presented with three different social environments, each with a specific religion. A most satisfying materialist explanation has dominated Danish social history ever since, a good example being Lindhardt's overview (1959). This explanation, which has even caught on with the general public, as the 1928 novel was recently made into a popular television series, has only one problem: It is wrong. Research done at my home university has called into question the simplistic association between class position and religious belief (Thyssen 1960–75; Wåhlin 1987). Examinations of membership lists of Grundtvigian parishes, for example, show that they included more than just well-off farmers. The general pattern turns out to be that entire parishes were Grundtvigian, Inner Mission, or nothing at all. The determining factor seems to be the choice made by the parish's elite. In most parts of Denmark, despite openings toward other social classes, the well-off farmers were the core of both Inner Mission and the Free Grundtvigian churches but also dominated the great number of parishes which did not undergo any sort of revival, whether Grundtvigian or Inner Mission. These dead parishes accounted for one-half of the total votes in the first parish church council elections in 1909.

These results do not refute class-based explanations for religious beliefs but do force us to refine them. It turns out that Grundtvigism was not the only relevant ideological medium for the rising class of petty bourgeois entrepreneurs. What is important, however, is the function of both ideologies as a means of obtaining self-reliance. Both revivalist movements had their roots in and helped to express the needs of this class vis-à-vis government officials and influential businessmen. The difference lies in the content of the religious doctrines, whereas their function was similar. Apparently it did not matter what was said; what was important was that it was independent of the authorities. Most countries witnessed the spread of revivalist movements such as Inner Mission during the transition to industrialized modernity. The United States is full of them. What is particular for the Danish Grundtvigism is its underlining of the unity of land, country, God, and people (*folk*). It turned out to be virtually impossible to export this particular synthesis, which is why Grundtvigism has played a negligible role among Danish immigrants to the Midwest in the United States. Today it has almost vanished in those communities, mainly in Iowa and South Dakota, into which it was transported in the nineteenth century, whereas the Inner Mission is still thriving (Simonsen 1990). Grundtvigism is thus understood as a shorthand for all the revivalist ideologies of self-reliance thriving in Denmark at the time, regardless of their precise teachings.

Traditional business corporations could have conceivably managed the transformation of Danish society just as successfully as cooperative enterprises. However, this is difficult to know, as there are no comparable examples of such a massive and relatively smooth restructuring of an entire agrarian society. That something peculiar happened in Denmark between 1864 and 1914 is demonstrated by the fact that Northern Schleswig, whose agrarian structure resembled that of the rest of Denmark, did not undergo a similar modernization while it was part of the German Kaiserreich. This produced some despair among its inhabitants when it was reincorporated in 1920 after the German defeat in World War I. This province lagged behind in agricultural productivity and caught up only recently with the rest of the country.

The only comparable case to the Danish system of successful popular self-education and self-reliance among a farming population is in the Canadian province of Saskatchewan in the period immediately after World War II. The young political sociologist, Seymour Martin Lipset, did the research for his dissertation on the cooperative movement in this area, which had successfully staved off the economic crisis of the interwar period and still dominated cultural and political life during the period that Lipset was there. In the course of his fieldwork he encountered a society that ostensibly lived by Grundtvig's principles:

> Saskatchewan is a unique and rewarding place for a social scientist to do research, for the province contains a larger proportion of lay social scientists than any other area I have visited. The farmers are interested in their society and its relations to the rest of the world. Winter after winter, when the wheat crop is in, thousands of meetings are held throughout the province by political parties, churches, farmers' educational associations, and cooperatives. There are informal gatherings, also, in which farmers discuss economic and political problems. Not hedged in by the necessity of punching a time clock daily, these farmers, who have come from every part of Europe and North America, have frequent sessions in which they consider the ideas of Adam Smith, Karl Marx, William Morris, Henry George, James Keir Hardie, William Jennings Bryan, Thorstein Veblen, and others.

Almost every English-speaking farmer subscribes to three or four farm weeklies, which are veritable storehouses of economic and political debate. In their correspondence columns the more literate and vociferous farmers argue the merits of religion, systems of government, the Soviet Union, socialism, socialized medicine, Social Credit, and schemes for marketing wheat. In travelling about the province I soon learned not to be surprised when a farmer whom I was interviewing would open a book by Morris, Henry George, Veblen, Major C. H. Douglas or some technical social scientist (Lipset 1950:11–12).

However, this Jeffersonian Arcadia did not last. As explained in the introduction to the book's second edition, the cooperative movement, its political party, and its welfare system lost out to the larger corporations and banks in the 1950s exactly as had happened in other grain-producing areas in the states south of the border of the United States earlier in the century. And with the independent economy went the high level of consciousness. In Denmark, however, a climate of popular learning such as the one depicted by Lipset is still to be found. I encounter it every so often when lecturing in local meeting houses or at the still thriving folk high schools. Denmark seems unique—or at least it did until the early 1970s. Since then, the agriculture and the agricultural industries have been completely restructured and centralized, so I am probably addressing a vanishing phenomenon. It has, however, existed long enough that it has set its stamp on the national character, regardless of class, trade, region, sex, and age. I am very well aware that such an argument for Danish uniqueness or exceptionalism assumes an unprovable negative—that there are no other cases just like it. Historians traditionally mistrust arguments of that type, and it is in the search for the truth of my assumptions that I call attention to the Danish case in this essay's comparative context.

The libertarian values, though, were not originally meant to include all segments of the population. The agrarian system was based on the farmers' brutal exploitation of agricultural labourers. These, together with the urban elites, were often not even considered part of the people (*folk*) by the peasants. However, in an interesting and surprisingly original ideological maneuver, the rising Social Democracy adapted to the particular agrarian and industrial conditions in Denmark, developing a strategy very different from the Marxist orthodoxy of the German mother party. Danish Social Democracy even accepted the formation of a class of very small farmers called *husmænd*. In this way they reflected the aspirations of their landless members among the agricultural workers but simultaneously undermined their chances later on of obtaining an absolute majority in Parliament, as did their sister parties in Sweden and Norway.

This apparently suicidal strategy, including later compromises in housing policy, ruled out any possibility of monopoly of power similar to that in Norway and Sweden, by the Social Democrats (Esping-Andersen 1985). Yet, as far as we can judge today, the Social Democrats did it knowingly and on purpose. During World War I it became clear to the Social Democratic leadership that the party would never be able to achieve an absolute political majority. Under Thorvald Stauning's thirty-two years of charismatic leadership (1910–42), the party restructured its line from a class base to a more popular one. First openly formulated in

1923, the popular line was later expressed in such slogans as "The People Work Together to Rule" and, somewhat less clumsily, "Denmark for the People." The platform resulted in a stable governing coalition of the radical liberals (Det radikale Venstre) and the Social Democratic Party from 1929 to 1943. The Social Democratic leaders apparently accepted the ultimate check on the influence of their own movement in the interests of society at large or perhaps did not distinguish between the two. Many things might have turned out differently if the German Social Democratic Party in the 1920s had tried to appeal to the people as a whole and not just to the working class in the Marxist sense.

The eminent German socialist theoretician Karl Kautsky (1854–1938) never really understood the role of agriculture in modern societies. He saw it as something of the precapitalist past that would be better run according to the principles of mass-industrialization. The Danish Social Democrats had a better understanding of agriculture, though they failed to turn this into coherent theory. At the level of doctrine the party stuck to the formulations of the 1913 program. These reflected international debates in the Second International rather than Danish realities and the practical policy of the party. The fact that the program of 1913 was not changed until 1961 testifies to the low priority given to theory in this the most pragmatic of all reformist socialist parties. Danish Social Democracy never was strong on theory, but the labour movement produced an impressive number of capable administrators and politicians, at least until recently.

This lack of explicit strategy enabled remnants of the libertarian peasant ideology to take root early in the party and in the labour movement. The Social Democrats embarked as early as 1914 upon a policy for the people as such and not just for the working class (Finnemann 1985). This testifies to the importance of the liberal, popular ideological hegemony dating from the last third of the nineteenth century. This also proves that the leadership realized from an early date that they would never attain power on their own. Farmers constituted only a fragment of the population, but small-scale production permeated the whole society then, just as it still does today. In the early seventies I argued this in a book, and later and more comprehensive research seems to prove me right (Østergård 1974; Finnemann 1985; Lahme 1982; Grelle 1983).

Somewhat ironically it has to be admitted that Lenin was the Marxist who understood Denmark best. In his 1907 discussion, *The Agrarian Program of the Social Democracy*, he has a long section on the Danish cooperatives that he had studied (in the Royal Library in Copenhagen that is). He was quite favourable towards their strategy of self-reliance but refused to endorse it for Russia. Maybe this was one of his biggest mistakes. That a strategy directed towards the majority of the people would turn out more successful seems pretty obvious from today's point of view. Yet, a sophisticated socialist party like the German Social Democratic Party only embarked on such a strategy as late as 1959 in Bad Godesberg; the British Labour Party and the French Socialist Party still do not seem to have made up their minds; and what will happen in Eastern Europe remains to be seen.

What we have witnessed in nineteenth-century Danish society is how the urban and agrarian working classes took up the ideology of a class of very self-conscious capitalist farmers jealously guarding their newly won influence. We have also noticed how this same discourse undermined the class exclusiveness of these farmers, at times at least. Perhaps the farmers had not broken completely with their peasant traditions, although I doubt that this was the case. Or there was something libertarian in the discourse itself—something not restricted to its class origins, i.e., not purely functional—that can be demonstrated in the concept of *folkelighed*.

As we have seen, the farmers, much to the annoyance of the rest, originally monopolized the right to speak for the entire people. They tended to see themselves as heads of their households, their villages, their parishes, and ultimately of the entire country. This kind of monopolization, characteristic of all populist movements, is well demonstrated in the United States during the 1880s and 1890s, when American populist farmers in the Midwest and the South perceived themselves as the only real producers and so explicitly distanced themselves from the eastern plutocrats, whom they regarded as unproductive owners of capital (primarily railroads). These movements, however, had great difficulty in deciding whether the poor black petty farmers of the South belonged to the real (American) people. Southern farmers generally decided against including blacks (Canovan 1981:26–30). This ambiguity would have led to splits within the movement at a national level had the populists come to power in 1892 or 1896. In that case they would have had to confront the dilemma of all populists: Who does and who does not belong to the people?

Very few populists have had to confront this dilemma because they have hardly ever achieved power in a national state. Few Latin American populists have really tried, except Vargas and Peron, and have not fared well, if they have. The Nazi movement in Germany sets a frightening example. A *völkisch* definition of the real people led to the Nürnberg laws and the Holocaust. In Denmark, the populist farmers, represented by the Liberal Party (*Venstre*), came to dominate the parliament after 1870 and formed the government in 1901; yet this seemingly populist party did not exercise dictatorial powers, though for a short time it attained an absolute majority in both chambers of the parliament. I mainly attribute this to their Grundtvigian ideology, even though some pragmatic reasons may also have played a role. Somehow the majority of the farmers were able to free themselves from the potentially authoritarian outlook of their populism and maintain a genuinely open mind toward the rights of others, admittedly not all the time, but surprisingly often. One obvious explanation for this is the small size of the country and the homogeneous character of the population. The inherent libertarian qualities in the Grundtvigian discourse, though, also played a significant role as I see it. The secret is hidden in the concept of *folkelighed*.

The root of the word, *folkelig*, is folk. It is normally translated into German as *völkisch* and into English as *populist*. I would prefer using "popular" if it has to be translated, but basically the term seems to be untranslatable, as the connotations are so different in different languages. In English *popular* has the derogatory connotation of approval by the ignorant masses. The connotations of the word, folkelig, when used in a political context, however, suggest an informed, responsible, tolerant participation in the exercise of power. The German völkisch is often incorrectly rendered as "Nazi" in English and American textbooks, but it is undeniable that the radical nationalistic völkisch movements in Germany did lead to Nazism, whether directly or indirectly.

At a time when the overwhelming majority of intellectuals in a Europe of rising nation-states talked of the nationalization of the masses (Mosse 1975), Grundtvig developed an ideology centered on the concept of folkelighed that denominated the common feeling in the population. According to him this feeling originates in a historically developed national community and is manifested in actions of solidarity. His definition of national identity is closer to Anthony Smith's historicizing definition (1986) than to Ernest Gellner's purely functionalist (1983) but does not fall into the culturalistic-objective trap. At the level of ideological discourse Grundtvig succeeded in transforming the traditional amorphous peasant feelings of community and solidarity into symbols and words with relevance for a modern industrialized imagined community. It remains yet to be seen whether the resulting mentality can survive transplantation to entities larger than the Danish nation-state. Maybe it cannot. However, it was capable of influencing the majority of an industrial working class and establishing a welfare state. By means of easily remembered lyrics and bon mots, such as "Freedom for Loke as well as for Thor," (1832), Grundtvig influenced the mentality of a whole nation. Danes learned those concepts by heart at school and at home until the 1960s. Whether people live by them is of course another matter. Yet, at the level of discourse, in the political culture at least, they have had great impact by determining what can be expressed and what not, what does not have to be expressed at all, and which values are considered worth pursuing.

Peasant values do not normally resemble farmers' values—one important result of many years of comparative peasant studies (Shanin 1971). In my analysis though, communitarian peasant traditions of solidarity were transmitted from premodern village society to the Social Democracy of the twentieth century, not directly but through the intermediary of the Grundtvigian synthesis. A number of qualifications have to be made to this statement, though. The time period between 1870 to 1901, when Grundtvigism directly served as a farmers' class ideology, also witnessed the most intensive exploitation of landless agricultural workers in the history of Denmark. Although the farmers regarded the folk as only their own class and despised all others, they were gradually forced to take the interests of other groups into account. When the farmers' representatives began administrating local affairs in 1841 following a communal reform, they drastically cut back the provisioning for the poor. It remained at a very low level until after the turn of the century, when two political parties, the Social Democracy and the newly created smallholders, Det radikale Venstre (the radical left), gradually succeeded in pressuring the liberals in the farmers' party, Venstre, resulting in the origin of the Danish version of the welfare-state.

The actual outcome of Denmark's development of the welfare state resembles that in other Scandinavian countries and Western Germany fairly closely. Its ideological roots, however, are very different, which may help to explain the considerable differences between the Social Democracies and the different workings of the welfare states in the Scandinavian countries as analyzed by Gösta Esping-Andersen (1985). The Swedish welfare-state resulted from a long tradition of state control and authoritarian benevolence, whereas the Danish system has a libertarian and anarchistic tinge. This explains why it often works pretty badly, as does the economy, which is unable to regulate industrial development or to promote innovation in a systematic way. However, this is also the reason why Danish society, when left to itself, at times has been able to leap quite unexpectedly into a new structure. This happened in the 1880s, again in the 1950s, and apparently again today in the 1990s.

These are the peasant roots of Danish modernity. The peculiarity of the Danes probably helps explain why the folk high schools have not really struck roots in other countries. A few have been set up in India, one has functioned in France for more than thirty years because of the enthusiasm of its leader Erica Simon. Two or three still exist in the Midwest. The idea was introduced in Germany around the turn of the century but was rapidly coopted by the official educational system. They are to be found in fair numbers in Norway and Sweden but have not produced an alternative elite or an alternative political vocabulary.

Grundtvig and Grundtvigism have made a difference. Because of its influence, a certain pompously unpretentious and apparently self-ironic discourse has come to dominate the political culture and mentality of this nation-state. These national characteristics are hard for foreigners to detect, and sometimes for natives as well, because it is considered even worse to be a nationalist in Denmark than in most other industrialized countries. Nevertheless, the intrinsic nationalism surfaces immediately when foreigners start criticizing anything Danish. We love to criticize everything ourselves but go on the defensive as soon as a foreigner finds a fault with anything Danish. Luckily we are seldom confronted with such criticism, as Denmark has had a surprisingly good press in the international community—that is, when it is not mistaken for Sweden. This is mainly a reflection of the relative lack of importance attributed to this small country in world affairs. But, it has helped bring into existence a distinct attitude, which I baptized "humble assertiveness" a few years ago. We know we are the best, therefore we do not have to brag about it. So do not be deceived by apparent Danish or Scandinavian humility. It often hides a feeling of superiority. Over the last ten or fifteen years this security has been challenged by the arrival of a fairly small number of immigrants, some 100,000 foreigners out of a net total population of 5 million, little more than 2 percent. Many of these have been uncomfortable with the unspoken Danish way of life and have challenged it in ways never experienced before. That has produced a certain uneasiness. Perhaps the reason why there was no racism earlier on could be that there was nobody to discriminate against? An American friend of mine, a sociologist who has lived in Denmark for more than twenty years doing research on immigrants characterizes Danish culture in this way:

> Danish Academic culture, like agriculture, tends to be enclosed, fenced in and hedged. The *gård* (farm) likewise, is self-contained, and even the house is surrounded by protective trees and bushes. What is Danish in Denmark is so obvious to the foreigner here. *Hygge* (cosiness), *Tryghed* (security) and *Trivsel* (well-being) are the three Graces of Danish culture and socialization. Faces look towards a common *gård* (yard), or a table with candles and bottles on it. Hygge always has its backs turned on the others. Hygge is for the members, not the strangers. If you want

to know what is Danish about Denmark, ask first a Greenlander and then a guest-worker . . . .

An American asked me the difference between Denmark and America. I ventured an answer. In America there's one politics and fifteen ways to celebrate Christmas. In Denmark there are fifteen political parties and one way to celebrate Christmas . . . .

"Denmark is a little country." That's canon number one. A close second is "Danish is a difficult language." How many times have I been chastized for my foreign accent? (Schwartz 1985:124).

He tried to go back to the United States but returned to Denmark within half a year! Something seems to happen to even the most stalwart protagonists of the plurality and unlimited possibilities of bigger countries.

This blend of pettyness, libertarian values, prejudices, self-irony, and longing for warmer and bigger countries is well reflected in some of the popular songs. A recent hit runs like this:

There are other peoples than the Danes.
They live in caves and fight each other all day long.
This we Danes never ever have done.
The hot countries are a pile of shit.

(Shu-bi-dua 1978)

The Lilliputian chauvinism inherent in Danish national discourse is evident in the lyrics of the contemporary pop singer, Sebastian:

Denmark you are a dumb and delightful hussy,
tempting to take you while you sleep.
Denmark when you arise from your slumbers,
you will be screwed up by German dollars.

(Sebastian 1978)

This last song deplores the future of little Denmark in the Big Common European Market. There is a long tradition for such lamentations. The first and most famous explicit mention of the state of Denmark is the Latin poem *Planctus de Statu Regni* (Denmark's Complaint) from 1329. Whether the particularities of the Danish national identity will survive in the coming united Europe remains to be seen. The odds are, though, that they will given the unbroken continuity and exceptionally integrated character of this particular nation-state.

REFERENCES

Anderson, Perry. 1974. *Lineages of the Absolutist State*. London: NLB.

Bjørn, Claus. 1971. "Folkehøjskolen og andelsbevægelsen." *Årbog for dansk skolehistorie*, 7–28.

Blum, Jerome. 1978. *The End of the Old Order in Rural Europe*. Princeton: Princeton University Press.

Burke, Peter. 1978. *Popular Culture in Early Modern Europe*. London: Temple Smith.

Canovan, Margaret. 1981. *Populism*. London: Junction Books.

Christiansen, N. F. 1978. "Reformism within the Danish Social Democracy." *Scandinavian Journal of History*, 3:297–322.

Christiansen, Palle O. 1978. "Peasant Adaptation to Bourgeois Culture?" *Ethnologia Scandinavica*, 98–152.

Esping-Andersen, Gøsta. 1985. *Politics against Market*. Princeton: Princeton University Press.

Fabricius, Knud. 1906–58. *Skånes Overgang fra Danmark til Sverige*, I–IV. Copenhagen: Rosenkilde og Bagger.

Finnemann, N. O. 1985. *I broderskabets bånd*. Copenhagen: Gyldendal.

Gellner, Ernest. 1983. *Nations and Nationalism*. London: Blackwell.

Grelle, Henning. 1983. *Socialdemokratiet i det danske landbrugs samfund 1871–1903*. Copenhagen: Selskabet til forskning i arbejderbevægelsens historie.

Grundtvig, N. F. S. 1978 [1820]. "Langt højere bjerge så vide på jord." *Folkehøjskolens Sangbog*, 16th ed., Odense, 304–5.

————. 1832. *Nordens Mythologi*. Copenhagen.

————. 1978. [1848]. "Folkeligt skal alt nu være." *Folkehøjskolens Sangbog* 16th ed., Odense, 212–4.

Hansen, S. Aa. 1970. *Early Industrialization in Denmark*. Copenhagen: Gads Forlag.

Henningsen, Bernd. 1980. *Politik eller kaos*. Copenhagen: Berlingske Forlag.

Holberg, Ludvig. 1969–71. *Værker*, I–XII, F. Billeskov Jansen, ed. Copenhagen: Rosenkilde og Bagger.

————. 1729. *Dannemarks og Norges Beskrivelse*. Copenhagen.

————. 1753. *Remarques sur quelques positions qui se trouvent dans L'Esprit des Lois*. Copenhagen.

Horstbøll, H.; C. Løfting; and U. Østergård. 1989. "Les effets de la Révolution française au Danemark," in M. Vovelle, ed. *L'Image de la Revolution française*. I, 621–42. London: Pergamon Press.

Horstbøll, H.; and U. Østergård. 1990. "Reform or Revolution." *Scandinavian Journal of History*, 15:2, 155–79.

Kirk, Hans. 1928. *Fiskerne*. Copenhagen: Gyldendal.

Kjærgaard, Thorkild. 1985. "The Farmer's Interpretation of Danish History." *Scandinavian Journal of History*, 10:1, 97–118.

Lahme, Norbert. 1982. *Sozialdemokratie und Landarbeiter 1871–1901*. Odense: Odense University Press.

Lenin, V. I. 1907. "The Agrarian Program of the Social Democracy," in vol. 13 of *Works*. Moscow: Progress Publishers.

Lindhardt, P. G. 1959. *Vækkelse og kirkelige retninger*. Århus: Forlaget Aros.

Lipset, S. M. 1950. *Agrarian Socialism*. Berkeley: University of California Press and The Cooperative Commonwealth Federation in Saskatchewan.

Molesworth, Robert. 1694. *An Account of Denmark as It Was in the Year 1692*. London.

Møller Kristensen, S. 1970. *Litteratursociologiske Essays*. Copenhagen: Gyldendal.

Moore, Barrington, Jr. 1966. *The Social Origins of Dictatorship and Democracy*. Harmondsworth: Penguin Books.

Mosse, George L. 1975. *The Nationalization of the Masses*. New York: Howard Fertig.

Olesen, T.; N. Sørensen; U. Østergård. 1986. *Fascismen i Italien*. Århus: Århus University Press.

Østergård, Uffe. 1974. *Den materialistiske historieopfattelse i Danmark*. Århus: Modtryk.

————. 1982. "Socialhistoriens mange sider." *Den Jyske Historiker*, 23–24:183–98.

————. 1987. "Was ist das Dänische an den Dänen?," in K. Schulte und W. Wucherp-fennig, eds., *Die Gegenwart der Vergangenheit*. Roskilde: Roskilde University Press.

————. 1990. "Republican Revolution or Absolutist Reform? Enlightened Absolutism as a Political Regime and a Political Philosophy in 18th Century Denmark and France," in *17 Congreso Internacional de Ciencias Historicas*, vol. I, 74 ff. Madrid: Commité International des Sciences Historiques.

————. 1991. "Definitions of National Identity." *North Atlantic Studies*, 4, 51–57.

————. 1992. "What is National and Ethnic Identity," in Jan Zahle, ed., *Ethnicity in the Ptolemaic Kingdom*. Århus: Århus University Press, forthcoming.

Østerud, Øjvind. 1978. *Agrarian Structure and Peasant Politics in Scandinavia*. Oslo: Universitetsforlaget.

Renan, Ernest. 1947 [1882]. "Qu'est-ce-que une nation?," in *Oeuvres Complètes*, I. Paris: Calman Lévy.

Schwartz, J. 1985. "Letter to a Danish Historian." *Den Jyske Historiker*, 33:123–24.

Sebastian. 1978. "Danmark dum og dejlig," in *Ikke alene Danmark* Copenhagen: LP.

Seip, J. A. 1958. "Teorien om det opinionsstyrte enevelde" (Norwegian). *Historisk Tidskrift*, 38.

Shanin, T., ed. 1971. *Peasants and Peasant Societies*. Harmondsworth: Penguin Books.

Shu-bi-dua. 1978. "Danmark," in 78'eren. Copenhagen: LP.

Simon, Erica. 1960. *Réveil national et culture populaire en Scandinavie. La genèse de la Højskole nordique 1844–1878*. Copenhagen: Gyldendal.

Simonsen, Henrik Bredmose. 1990. *Kampen om danskheden. Tro og nationalitet i de danske kirkesamfund i Amerika*. Århus: Århus University Press.

Smith, Anthony. 1986. *The Ethnic Origins of Nations*. London: Blackwell.

Thyssen, Anders Pontoppidan. 1960–75. *Vækkelsernes frembrud i Danmark i første halvdel af det 19. århundrede*, vol. I–VII. Copenhagen: Gads Forlag.

Wåhlin, Vagn. 1981. *By og land*. Århus: Århus University Press.

————. 1987. "Popular Revivalism in Denmark." *Scandinavian Journal of History*, 11:4, 363–87.

Wåhlin, V.; and U. Østergård, 1976. *Klasse, demokrati og organisation. Politiseringsprocessen i Danmark 1830–70*, I–VI. Århus: University of Århus.

Weber, Eugen. 1976. *Peasants into Frenchmen. The Modernization of Modern France 1870–1914*. Stanford: Stanford University Press.

Yuri Slezkine

Born in the Soviet Union, Yuri Slezkine emigrated to the United States where he studied at the University of Texas and taught at Wake Forest University. He now teaches at the University of California, Berkeley, and has published a pioneering study of Russian imperial and Soviet policies toward the non-Russian peoples of their empires, *Arctic Mirrors: Russia and the Small Peoples of the North*. Slezkine is one of a number of recent historians who have investigated the way the Soviet state, through its policy of forming administrative units along ethnic lines and promoting ethnic cultures, particularly in the 1920s, helped foster ethnic distinctions and undercut its own stated policy goal of eventually eliminating nationalism.

For decades the study of the Soviet Union in the West was marred by an almost exclusive concentration on ethnic Russians, to the exclusion of the non-Russian half of the population, and on high politics, to the neglect of the study of society. The dominant paradigm through which westerners viewed the USSR, the theory of totalitarianism, depicted society as largely passive, atomized, and subject to the powerful, terror-driven initiatives of an all-powerful Soviet state. There was little room in this approach for appreciation of the ability of national cultures and local political elites to interpret, distort, shape, deflect, transform, and resist the policies from the center, particularly before and after the heyday of Stalinism. Despite the russifying drive of nationality policies in the period from the Great Purges through the 1950s, non-Russian nationalities managed in many cases to root themselves in local political institutions, maintain and promote their mother tongues, and preserve, even elaborate, ethnic culture. The very success of Soviet nationality policy in some areas, as well as its confusions and contradictions, according to Slezkine, contributed to the ultimate fate of the Soviet Union, when after seventy-four years the state founded by internationalist revolutionaries pulled apart along ethnic lines.

The USSR as a Communal Apartment, or How a Socialist State Promoted Ethnic Particularism

Soviet nationality policy was devised and carried out by nationalists. Lenin's acceptance of the reality of nations and "national rights" was one of the most uncompromising positions he ever took, his theory of good ("oppressed-nation") nationalism formed the conceptual foundation of the Soviet Union and his NEP-time policy of compensatory "nation-building" (*natsional'noe stroitel'stvo*) was a spectacularly successful attempt at a state-sponsored conflation of language, "culture," territory and quota-fed bureaucracy. The Lenin Guard duly brought up the rear (with Bukharin having completed his vertiginous leap from cosmo-politanism to non-Russian nationalism by 1923), but it was Stalin who became the true "father of nations" (albeit not all nations and not all the time). The "Great Transformation" of 1928–1932 turned into the most extravagant celebra-tion of ethnic diversity that any state had ever financed; the "Great Retreat" of the mid–1930s reduced the field of "blossoming nationalities" but called for an ever more intensive cultivation of those that bore fruit; and the Great Patriotic War was followed by an ex cathedra explanation that class was secondary to ethnicity and that support of nationalism in general (and not just Russian nation-alism or "national liberation" abroad) was a sacred principle of marxism-lenin-ism.

If this story sounds strange, it is because most historical accounts of Soviet nationality policy have been produced by scholars who shared Lenin's and Stal-in's assumptions about ontological nationalities endowed with special rights,

Yuri Slezkine, "The USSR as a Communal Apartment, or How a Socialist State Promoted Ethnic Particularism," *Slavic Review*, 53, 2 (Summer 1994), pp. 414–52.

Author's note: The first draft of this essay was written for a seminar organized by the Program for Comparative Studies in Ethnicity and Nationalism at the Henry M. Jackson School of International Studies, University of Washington. I am grateful to the Program's co-chairs, Charles Hirschman and Charles F. Keyes, for their hospitality and criticism, as well as for their permission to submit the piece to the *Slavic Review*. I also thank Peter Blitstein, Victoria Bonnell, George Breslauer, Daniel Brower, Michael Burawoy, Jane Burbank, Sheila Fitzpatrick, Bruce Grant, David Hollinger, Terry Martin, Nicholas V. Riasanovsky, Reggie Zelnik, the Berkeley Colloquium for the Study of Russia and Eastern Europe and the University of Chicago Russian History Workshop, for stimulating dis-cussions and helpful comments.

praised them for the vigorous promotion of national cultures and national cadres, chastized them for not living up to their own (let alone wilsonian) promises of national self-determination, and presumed that the "bourgeois nationalism" against which the bolsheviks were inveighing was indeed equal to the belief in linguistic/ cultural-therefore-political autonomy that the "bourgeois scholars" themselves understood to be nationalism. Non-Russian nationalism of all kinds appeared so natural and the Russian version of marxist universalism appeared so Russian or so universalist that most of these scholars failed to notice the chronic ethnophilia of the Soviet regime, took it for granted or explained it as a sign of deviousness, weakness or negligence. This essay is an attempt to recognize the earnestness of bolshevik efforts on behalf of ethnic particularism.[1] Uncompromisingly hostile to individual rights, they eagerly, deliberately and quite consistently promoted group rights that did not always coincide with those of the proletariat. "The world's first state of workers and peasants" was the world's first state to institutionalize ethnoterritorial federalism, classify all citizens according to their biological nationalities and formally prescribe preferential treatment of certain ethnically defined populations.[2] As I. Vareikis wrote in 1924, the USSR was a large communal apartment in which "national state units, various republics and autonomous provinces" represented "separate rooms."[3] Remarkably enough, the communist landlords went on to reinforce many of the partitions and never stopped celebrating separateness along with communalism.[4]

"A nation," wrote Stalin in his very first scholarly effort, "is a historically evolved, stable community based on a common language, territory, economic life and psychological make-up manifested in a community of culture."[5] On the eve of World War I this definition was not particularly controversial among socialists. There was disagreement about the origins of nations, the future fate of nationalism, the nature of pre-nation nationalities, the economic and political usefulness of nation states and the relative importance of nations' "characteristic features," but everyone seemed to assume that, for better or worse, humanity consisted of more or less stable *Sprachnationen* cemented by a common past.[6] Language and history (or *Schicksalgemeinschaft*/"community of fate," both the precondition and consequence of linguistic unity), were generally taken for granted; but even the more debatable items on Stalin's list were usually— if not always explicitly— considered legitimate. Otto Bauer, who attempted to detach nationality from territory, clearly assumed that the "community of fate" was ultimately the fate of a physical community. Rosa Luxemburg, who believed that the "principle of nationality" contradicted the logic of capitalism, saw large, "predatory" nation states as tools of economic expansion. And Lenin, who rejected the concept of "national culture," routinely spoke of "Georgians," "Ukrainians" and "Great Russians" as having national traits, interests and responsibilities. Nations might not be helpful and they might not last, but they were here and they were real.

As far as both Lenin and Stalin were concerned, this meant that nations had rights: "A nation can organize its life as it sees fit. It has the right to organize its life on the basis of autonomy. It has the right to enter into federal relations with other nations. It has the right to complete secession. Nations are sovereign and all nations are equal."[7] All nations were not equal in size: there were small nations and there were large (and hence "great-power") nations. All nations were not equal in their development: there were "backward" nations (an obvious oxymoron in Stalin's terms) and there were "civilized" nations. All nations were not equal in their economic (hence class hence moral) personae: some were "oppressor nations" and some were "oppressed."[8] But all nations—indeed all nationalities no matter how "backward"—were equal because they were equally sovereign, that is, because they all had the same rights.

What social class could demand self-determination and under what conditions it could do so were of course matters for vigorous and ultimately meaningless debate—all the more vigorous and meaningless because most of the peoples of the Russian Empire had not progressed very far along the road of capitalist development and thus were not nations in marxist terms.[9] Another acrimoniously fruitless affair was Lenin's insistence on the political meaning of "self-determination" and his deathbed dispute with Stalin over its practical implementation within the Soviet state. Much more significant in the long run was Lenin's and Stalin's common campaign for a strictly territorial definition of autonomy, a campaign they waged against Bund and Bauer but abandoned after 1917 because both sides won (Soviet federalism combined ethnicity with territory and—at least for the first twenty years—guaranteed the cultural rights of various leftover diasporas). The most remarkable aspect of that campaign was the assertion—rarely challenged either before or after 1917—that all territorial divisions could be described as either "medieval" or "modern," with modernity defined as democracy (borders "based on popular sympathies") and with democracy resulting in "the greatest possible homogeneity in the national composition of the population."[10] The borders of the socialist state would be "determined . . . according to the will and 'sympathies' of the population," and at least some of those sympathies would run along ethnic lines.[11] If this were to breed "national minorities," they, too, would have their equal status guaranteed.[12] And if equal status (and economic rationality) required the creation of countless "autonomous national districts" "of even the smallest size," then such districts would be created and probably combined "in a variety of ways with neighboring districts of various sizes."[13]

But why set up ethno-territorial autonomies under socialism if most socialists agreed that federalism was a "philistine ideal," that "national culture" was a bourgeois fiction and that assimilation was a progressive process that substituted a "mobile proletarian" for the "obtuse," "savage," "somnolent" peasant "glued to his pile of manure" and beloved for that very reason by conniving connoisseurs of national culture?[14] First of all, because Lenin's socialism did not grow on trees. To bring it about, Lenin's socialists had to "preach against [slogans of national culture] in all languages, 'adapting' themselves to all local and national requirements."[15] They needed native languages, native subjects and native teachers ("even for a single Georgian child") in order to "polemicize with 'their own' bourgeoisie, to spread anticlerical and antibourgeois ideas among 'their own' peasantry and burghers" and to banish the virus of nationalism from their proletarian disciples and their own minds.[16] This was a missionary project analogous to the so-called "Il'minskii system" formulated in the Kazan' of Lenin's youth.[17] "Only the mother tongue," claimed Il'minskii, "can truly, rather than only superficially, set the people on the path of Christianity.''[18] Only the mother tongue, wrote Stalin in 1913, can make possible ''a full development of the intellectual faculties of the Tatar or of the Jewish worker.''[19] Both theories of conversion assumed that ''native language'' was a totally transparent conduit for an apostle's message. Unlike more ''conservative'' missionaries, who saw culture as an integral system and argued that in order to defeat ''an alien faith'' one had to ''struggle against an alien nationality—against the mores, customs and the whole of the domestic arrangement of alien life,''[20] the Kazan' reformers and the fathers of the Soviet ethnic policy believed that nationality had nothing to do with faith. According to Lenin, marxist schools would have the same marxist curriculum irrespective of the linguistic medium.[21] Insofar as national culture was a reality, it was about language and a few ''domestic arrangements'': nationality was ''form.'' ''National form'' was acceptable because there was no such thing as national content.

Another reason for Lenin's and Stalin's early defense of nationalism (defining ''nationalism'' as a belief that ethnic boundaries are ontologically essential, essentially territorial and ideally political[22]) was the distinction that they drew between oppressor-nation nationalism and oppressed-nation nationalism. The first, sometimes glossed as ''great-power chauvinism,'' was gratuitously malevolent; the second was legitimate, albeit transitory. The first was the result of unfair size advantage; the second was a reaction to discrimination and persecution. The first could only be eliminated as a consequence of proletarian victory and subsequent self-discipline and self-purification; the second had to be assuaged through sensitivity and tact.[23] Accordingly, the slogans of national self-determination and ethno-territorial autonomy were gestures of contrition. They came easily and went a long way insofar as they dealt with ''form.'' ''A minority is discontented not because there is no [extraterritorial] national union but because it does not have the right to use its native language. Allow it to use its native language and the discontent will pass by itself.''[24] The more rights and opportunities a national minority would enjoy, the more ''trust'' (*doverie*) it would have in the proletarians of the former oppressor nation. Genuine equality of ''form'' would reveal the historically contingent nature of nationalism and the underlying unity of class content.

> Having transformed capitalism into socialism, the proletariat will create an *opportunity* for the total elimination of national oppression; this opportunity will become a *reality* ''only''—''only''!—after a total democratization of all spheres, including the establishment of state borders according to the ''sympathies'' of the population, and including complete freedom of secession. This, in turn, will lead *in practice* to a total abolition of all national tensions and all national distrust, to an accelerated drawing together and merger of nations which will result in the *withering away* of the state.[25]

The ''practice'' of the revolution and civil war did nothing to change this program. The earliest decrees of the new bolshevik government described the victorious masses as ''peoples'' and ''nations'' endowed with ''rights,''[26] proclaimed all peoples to be equal and sovereign, guaranteed their sovereignty through an ethnoterritorial federation and a right to secession, endorsed "the free development of national minorities and ethnic groups," and pledged to respect national beliefs, customs and institutions.[27] By the end of the war the need for local allies and the recognition of existing (and sometimes ethnically defined) entities combined with principle to produce an assortment of legally recognized (and increasingly ethnically defined) Soviet republics, autonomous republics, autonomous regions and toilers' communes. Some autonomies appeared more autonomous than others but "nationality" reigned supreme. "Many of these peoples have nothing in common except the fact that before they were all parts of the Russian Empire and now they have all been liberated by the revolution, but there are no internal connections among them."[28] According to Lenin's paradox, the surest way to unity in content was diversity in form. By "fostering national cultures [*nasazhdat' natsional'nuiu kul'turu*]" and creating national autonomies, national schools, national languages and national cadres, the bolsheviks would overcome national distrust and reach national audiences. "We are going to help you develop your Buriat, Votiak, etc. language and culture, because in this way you will join the universal culture [*obshchechelovecheskaia kul'tura*], revolution and communism sooner."[29]

To many communists this sounded strange. Did nations not consist of different classes? Should not proletarian interests prevail over those of the national(ist) bourgeoisie? Were not the proletarians of all countries supposed to unite? And were not the toilers of the besieged Soviet state supposed to unite with all the more determination? In spring 1918 M. I. Latsis attacked the "absurdity of federalism" and warned that the endless "breeding of republics," particularly in the case of "undeveloped ethnic groups" such as the Tatars or the Belorussians, was as dangerous as it was ludicrous.[30] In winter 1919 A. A. Ioffe cautioned against growing nationalist appetites and appealed for the "end of separatism" on the part of the "buffer republics."[31] And in spring 1919, at the VIII Party Congress, N. I. Bukharin and G. L. Piatakov launched an all-out assault against the slogan of national self-determination and the resulting primacy of ethnicity over class in non-Russian areas.[32]

Lenin's response was as adamant as it was familiar. First, nations existed "objectively." "If we say that we do not recognize the Finnish nation but only the toiling masses, it would be a ridiculous thing to say. Not to recognize something that is out there is impossible: it will force us to recognize it."[33] Second, former oppressor nations needed to gain the trust of the former oppressed nations.

> The Bashkirs do not trust the Great Russians because the Great Russians are more cultured and used to take advantage of their culture to rob the Bashkirs. So in those remote places the name "Great Russian" stands for "oppressor" and "cheat." We should take this into account. We should fight against this. But it is a long-term thing. It cannot be abolished by decree. We should be very careful here. And a nation like the Great Russians should be particularly careful because they have provoked such bitter hatred in all the other nations.[34]

Finally, backward nations had not developed a "differentiation of the proletariat from bourgeois elements" and thus could not be expected to have revolutionary classes consistently hostile "to their mullahs."[35] Taken as a whole and compared to more "cultured" nations, however, they were legitimate proletarians by virtue of having been cheated and oppressed. Under imperialism ("as the highest and final stage of capitalism") colonial peoples had become the global equivalents of the western working class. Under the dictatorship of the (Russian) proletariat, they were entitled to special treatment until the economic and psychological wounds of colonialism had been cured. Meanwhile, nations equaled classes.

Lenin lost the argument but won the vote because, as Tomskii put it, while "not a single person in this room would say that national self-determination or national movements were either normal or desirable," most people seemed to believe that they were a "necessary evil" that had to be tolerated.[36] Accordingly, the scramble for national status and ethnoterritorial recognition continued unimpeded. The Kriashen were different from the Tatars in customs, alphabet and vocabulary, and thus needed a special administrative unit.[37] The Chuvash were poor and did not speak Russian, and thus needed a special administrative unit.[38] The Iakut deserved their own government because they lived compactly and were ready to "organize their lives through their own efforts."[39] The "primitive tribes" who lived next to the Iakut deserved a special government because they lived in widely dispersed communities and were not ready to run their own affairs.[40] The Estonian settlers in Siberia had a literary tradition and needed a special bureaucracy to provide them with newspapers.[41] The Ugrian natives of Siberia had no literary tradition and needed "an independent government" to "direct at the dark masses a ray of enlightenment and to cultivate their way of life [kul'tivirovat' ikh byt zhizni]."[42] Local intellectuals, Commissariat of Nationalities officials, "native conferences" and Petrograd ethnographers all demanded institutional autonomy, offices and funding (for themselves or their protégés). Having received autonomy, they demanded more offices and more funding.

Funding was scarce, but autonomous areas and offices were becoming ever more plentiful. In addition to ethnoterritorial units, complete with their own bureaucracies and (in theory, at least) "mother-tongue" education, there were national units within national units, national sections in party cells and local soviets, and national quotas in colleges. In 1921 Poles received 154,000 newly published books in their language while the half-recognized Kriashen received 10; the Azerbaijani Communist Party had Iranian, German, Greek and Jewish sections; the Comissariat of Enlightenment in Moscow had 14 national bureaus; and 103 local party organizations in Russia were supposed to transact their business in Estonian.[43]

Some doubts persisted. According to one Commissariat of Nationalities official, linguistic self-assertion might not work for those nationalities that were "weak, backward and dispersed in the sea of some advanced culture." Therefore, "the tendency to preserve and develop one's native language at all costs and ad infinitum, with the sole purpose of creating a symmetrical, geometrically complete system of education in a single language, does not have a future and does not take into account all the complexity and diversity of the socio-cultural composition of our age."[44] Others argued that the age was primarily about economic rationality and that ethnic units should be superceded, or at least complemented, by scientifically defined economic entities based on environmental, industrial and commercial affinity. If military districts could cut across national borders, so should economic ones.[45]

Such arguments were not simply rejected. Starting in 1922 they became ideologically unacceptable. Lenin's passion, Stalin's Narkomnats bureaucracy, the tradition of party decisions and the vested interests of proliferating ethnic institutions had congealed into a "nationality question" that could no longer be questioned, so that when the X Party Congress legitimized the policy of institutionalized ethnicity, no one called it a "necessary evil," let alone bourgeois nationalism. What the X Congress (and specifically Stalin) did was to conflate Lenin's themes of national oppression and colonial liberation, equate the "nationality question" with the question of backwardness and present the whole issue as a neat opposition between "Great Russians" and "non-Great Russians." The Great Russians belonged to an advanced, formerly dominant nation possessed of a secure tradition of national statehood and frequently guilty of ethnic arrogance and insensitivity known as "great-power chauvinism." All the other nationalities, defined negatively and collectively as "non-Great Russians," were victims of tsarist-imposed statelessness, backwardness and "culturelessness [nekul'turnost']," which made it difficult for them to take advantage of new revolutionary opportunities and sometimes tempted them to engage in "local nationalism."[46] In Stalin's formulation, "the essence of the nationality question in the RSFSR consists of the need to eliminate the backwardness (economic, political and cultural) that the nationalities have inherited from the past, to allow the backward peoples to catch up with central Russia."[47] To accomplish this goal, the Party was to help them

> a) develop and strengthen their own Soviet statehood in a form that would correspond to the national physiognomy of these peoples; b) introduce their own courts and agencies of government that would function in native languages and consist of local people familiar with the life and mentality of the local population; c) develop their own press, schools, theaters, local clubs and other cultural and educational institutions in native languages.[48]

There were to be as many nation states with varying degrees of autonomy as there were nationalities (not nations!) in the RSFSR. Nomads would receive lands lost to the Cossacks and "national minorities" scattered among compact ethnic groups would be guaranteed "free national development" (which called for the creation of territorial units).[49] Perhaps most remarkably, this triumph of ethnicity was presented by Stalin as both the cause and the consequence of progress. On the one hand, "free national development" was the only way to defeat non-Russian backwardness. On the other,

> You cannot go against history. Even though the Russian element still predominates in Ukrainian cities, it is clear that as time goes on these cities will inevitably become Ukrainianized. About forty years ago Riga was a German city, but as cities grow at the expense of villages, and villages are the keepers of nationality, Riga is now a purely Latvian city. About fifty years ago all cities of Hungary were German in

character, but now they have been Magyarized. The same will happen to Belorussia, in whose cities non-Belorussians currently predominate.[50]

Once this had happened, the Party would redouble its efforts at nation building because, "in order to conduct communist work in the cities, it will be necessary to reach the new proletarian-Belorussian in his native language."[51]

However "dialectical" the logic of the official policy, its practice was unequivocal and, by 1921, fairly well established. In a sense, the introduction of the New Economic Policy at the X Congress was tantamount to the "lowering" of all other pursuits to the level of the already "NEP-like" nationality policy. NEP constituted a temporary but deliberate reconciliation with "backwardness"—backwardness represented by peasants, traders, women, all non-Russian peoples in general and various "primitive tribes" in particular. There was a special women's department, a Jewish section and the Committee for Assistance to the Peoples of the Northern Borderlands, among others. Backwardness endlessly multiplied itself and each remnant of the past required an individual approach based on "specific peculiarities" and characterized by sensitivity and paternal benevolence. The ultimate goal was the abolition of all backwardness and thus all difference, but the fulfillment of that goal was postponed indefinitely. Attempts to force it through would be "dangerous" and "utopian"—as was the impatience of those otherwise "mature and politically aware comrades" in central Asia who asked, "What on earth is going on? How much longer are we going to keep breeding separate autonomies?"[52] The Party's answer was the vague but emphatic: "For as long as it takes." For as long as it takes to overcome "economic and cultural backwardness ... , economic differences, differences in customs (particularly important among nations that have not yet reached the capitalist stage) and linguistic differences."[53] Meanwhile, nation building appeared to be a praiseworthy goal in its own right. There was beauty in difference.

With one exception. One particular remnant of the past had few redeeming qualities and was to be tolerated but not celebrated, used but not welcomed. This was the Russian peasant. The NEP alliance (*smychka*) between the peasantry and the working class seemed to mirror similar arrangements with other "underdeveloped" groups but its official rationale was quite different. The "peasant element" was aggressive, contagious and menacing. No one assumed that its brand of savagery would dialectically dissolve itself through further development because the stubbornly "somnolent" Russian peasant was incapable of development *as a peasant* (his was a difference "in content"). By equating ethnicity with development and dividing the population of the country into Russians and non-Russians, the X Congress recognized and reinforced this distinction. The Russian nationality was developed, dominant and thus irrelevant. The Russian territory was "unmarked" and, in effect, consisted of those lands that had not been claimed by the non-Russians known as "nationals [*natsionaly*]." Mikoyan's objection that this was too neat, that Azerbaijan was culturally and economically "ahead of many Russian provinces" and that the Armenian bourgeoisie was as imperialistic as any was dismissed by Stalin and by the congress.[54]

"Lenin's last struggle" with the nationality question did not change the official line.[55] Upset by the alleged "Great-Russian chauvinism" of Stalin, Dzerzhinskii and Ordzhonikidze ("Russians" by behavior and profession, if not by national origin), the ailing leader recommended more of the same medicine. Internationalism on the part of the Russians "should consist not only in the formal equality of nations, but also in the kind of inequality at the expense of the big oppressor nation that would compensate for the de facto inequality that exists in life."[56] This called for more—much more—"caution, deference and concessions" with regard to the " 'offended' nationals," more conscious (and hence non-chauvinist) proletarians in the Russian apparatus, and more emphasis on the wide and consistent use of non-Russian languages.[57] In April 1923 the XII Party Congress duly reaffirmed this view without questioning either the old strategy or the new urgency (the only delegate to challenge the national development orthodoxy was a self-described "rank-and-file worker" who timidly mentioned Marx's cosmopolitan proletarians and was chided by Zinov'ev[58]). At the two extremes of expert opinion, Stalin argued that Russian chauvinism constituted "the main danger" ("nine tenths of the problem"), while Bukharin insisted that it was the only danger.[59] Solutions to the problems of national representation and ethnoterritorial federation varied but the principles of the "leninist nationality policy" remained the same. (Stalin's "autonomization plan" called for greater centralization in "everything essential" but took it for granted that such nonessential matters as "language" and "culture" were to be left to the "genuine internal autonomy of the republics."[60]) Even the noisy discussion of the Georgian affair had little to add to the issue, with the "offended nationals" complaining of insensitivity and the "great-power chauvinists" pointing to the dominance of the Georgian language and the remarkable successes of nationality-based preferential promotion (according to Ordzhonikidze, Georgians made up 25% of the overall population of Tiflis but 43% of the city soviet, 75% of the city executive committee 91% of the presidium of the executive committee, and 100% of both the republican *Sovnarkom* and the Central Committee of the Party).[61] The only truly theoretical innovation introduced at the congress was not discussed as such and proved shortlived: defending himself against Lenin's epistolary accusations, Stalin took up Mikoyan's old position and attempted to deprive the Russians of their monopoly on imperialism and to redefine "local nationalism" as great-power chauvinism writ small. Georgians oppressed Abkhazians and Ossetians, Azeris bullied Armenians, Uzbeks ignored the Turkmen and so on. In fact, Stalin's main argument against Georgia's secession from the Transcaucasian Federation was the alleged campaign by Georgian officials to deport local Armenians and "transform Tiflis into a real Georgian capital."[62] This meant that the Ukrainization of Kiev and the Belorussification of Minsk might not be such a good idea after all, but the majority at the congress either did not get Stalin's meaning or chose to ignore it. "Great-power chauvinism" was clearly reserved for the Russians, "local nationalism" had to be anti-Russian to be a danger (not the "main danger" perhaps but dangerous enough to the perpetrators) and national territories belonged to those nationalities whose names they bore.

But what was "nationality"? At the time of the February revolution, the only characteristic ascribed to all imperial subjects was "religious confession," with both the Russian national identity and the tsar's dynastic legitimacy largely associated with Orthodoxy. Not all of the tsar's subjects and not all Orthodox believers were Russians, but all Russians were expected to be Orthodox subjects of their Orthodox tsar. The non-Orthodox could serve the tsar in his capacity as emperor, but they had no immunity from occasional conversion campaigns and were legally handicapped in cases of mixed marriages. Some non-Orthodox were legally designated as "aliens" (*inorodtsy*), a term whose etymology ("non-kin," "non-native") suggested genetic difference but which was usually interpreted to mean "non-Christian" or "backward." These two concepts reflected the Muscovite ("premodern") and petrine ("modern") notions of otherness and were now used interchangeably. Some baptized communities were too backward to be "real Christians" and all aliens were formally classified according to their religion ("Muslim," "Lamaist") or "way of life" understood as degree of development ("settled," "nomadic," "wandering"). With the spread of state-sponsored education and the attendant effort to reach the "eastern aliens"[63] and to control (and Russify) the autonomous educational institutions of western non-Russians, "native language" also became a politically meaningful category. The names of languages, however, did not always coincide with the collective names that variously defined communities used to refer to themselves and to others. On the eve of the revolution, Russia had census nationalities, nationalist parties and national "questions," but it had no official view of what constituted nationality.

On the eve of the February revolution (exactly one day before Nicholas II left for Mogilev and the locked-out Putilov workers poured into the streets of Petrograd), President of the Russian Academy of Sciences S. F. Ol'denburg wrote to Minister of Foreign Affairs N. N. Pokrovskii that, moved by a "sense of patriotic duty," he and his colleagues would like to propose the formation of a Commission for the Study of the Tribal Composition of the Russian Borderlands.

> The most thorough determination of the tribal composition of the areas lying on both sides of Russia's borders with hostile states is of extraordinary importance at the present moment because a world war is being waged to a considerable extent over the national question. The determination of the validity of various territorial claims by various nationalities will become particularly important at the time of peace negotiations because, even if new borders are drawn in accordance with certain strategic and political considerations, the national factor will still play an enormously important role.[64]

Under the Provisional Government the nationality question moved farther inland and the new commission was charged with the study of the whole population of Russia, not just the borderlands. Under the bolsheviks "the essence of Soviet nationality policy" came to consist in the "coincidence of ethnographic and administrative borders,"[65] which meant that most of the imperial territory would have to be divided into borderlands and that professional ethnographers would have to play an important role in the endeavor.

There was no time to discuss terminology. Aliens and Christians were replaced by an undifferentiated collection of *narody* (peoples), *narodnosti* (peoples sometimes understood to be small or underdeveloped), *natsional'nosti* (nationalities),

natsii (nations) and *plemena* (tribes). There was no agreement as to how durable
(and hence territorially viable) these entities were. In what seems to have been a
common attitude, the head of the commission's Caucasian section, N. Ia. Marr,
considered nationality to be too "transitory" and too complex to be pinned down
by "primitive territorial demarcation," but worked hard (a lot harder than most,
in fact) to uncover "primeval ethnicity [*etnicheskaia pervobytnost'*]" and "true
tribal composition."[66] The most commonly used "marker of tribal composition"
was language. Party ideologues championed "native-language education" as the
basis for their nationality policy; education officials proceeded from a "linguistic
definition of national culture";[67] and ethnographers tended to fall back on language as the most dependable, albeit not universal, indicator of ethnicity. Thus,
E. F. Karskii, the author of *Ethnographic Map of the Belorussian Tribe*, adopted
mother tongue as "the exclusive criterion" of national difference and claimed,
in a characteristic non sequitur, that Lithuanians who spoke Belorussian should
be considered Belorussians.[68] More controversially, the central Asian Sart (usually defined as settled Muslims) were decreed out of existence, the various Pamir
communities became "Tajiks" and the Uzbeks were radically redefined to include most of the Turkic speakers of Samarkand, Tashkent and Bukhara.[69] Yet
language was still perceived to be insufficient and the 1926 census included two
unequal categories of "language" and "nationality," revealing large numbers of
people who did not speak "their own language." Such communities were considered "denationalized" by ethnographers[70] and not entirely legitimate by party
officials and local elites: Russian-speaking Ukrainians or Ukrainian-speaking
Moldavians were expected, and sometimes forced, to learn their mother tongue
irrespective of whether their mothers knew how to speak it.

What made "denationalized" Ruritanians Ruritanians? More often than not,
it was the various combinations of "material life," "customs" and "traditions"
jointly known as "culture." Thus, when dealing with areas where "Russian"
and "Belorussian" dialects blend into each other, Karskii distinguished between
the two nationalities by referring to differences in clothing and architecture.[71]
Similarly, Marr classified Iranian-speaking Ossetians and Talysh as north Caucasians (Japhetids) on the basis of their "ethnic culture," "genuine popular religion," "way of life [*byt*]" and "emotional attachment to the Caucasus."[72]
Sometimes religion-as-culture outweighed language and became a crucial ethnic
marker in its own right, as when the Kriashen (Tatar-speaking Christians) received
their own "department" and the Adzhar (Georgian-speaking Muslims) received
their own republic (a similar appeal by Marr on behalf of Muslim, Armenian-
speaking Khemshil proved unsuccessful[73]). Cultures, religions and indeed languages could be reinforced by topography (highland versus valley Caucasians)
and chronological primacy (in the Caucasian case, a native-versus-settler distinction did not necessarily coincide with a dichotomy based on progress, as it did in
Siberia[74]). Physical ("racial," "somatic") type was never used independently
but sometimes—particularly in Siberia—was used to support other distinguishing features.[75] Finally, none of these features could be decisive in the case
of the steppe nomads, whose "national awareness" or "tribal self-identity"
were considered so strong as to make any other criteria practically use-

less. Linguistic, cultural and religious differences among the Kazakh, Kirgiz and Turkmen might be negligible, but their clan geneologies were so clearly drawn and so vigorously upheld that most ethnographers had no choice but to follow.[76]

To be sure, the actual borders of new ethnic units did not always correspond to those suggested by scholars. Kazakh authorities demanded Tashkent, Uzbek authorities wanted autonomy for the Osh district and the Central Committee in Moscow formed special arbitration commissions.

> Subsequently the Kirgiz [i.e., Kazakh] abandoned their claims on Tashkent but became all the more insistent i.i their demand that three *volosts* . . . of the Tashkent *uezd* be included in Kazakhstan. If this demand had been fully satisfied, the portions of the canals . . . that feed Tashkent would have wound up on Kirgiz territory . . . Besides, the adoption of the Kirgiz variant would have cut the central Asian railway line by a Kirgiz wedge 17 versts south of Tashkent.[77]

Such odd strategic or "national interest" considerations (as in Kazakh versus Uzbek), as well as more conventional political and economic priorities at various levels affected the final shape of ethnoterritorial units, but there is no doubt that the dominant criterion was indeed ethnic. "Nationality" meant different things in different areas but the borders of most areas were seen as truly "national" and were, indeed, remarkably similar to ethnographic maps drawn up by the Commission for the Study of Tribal Composition. Bolshevik officials in Moscow saw the legitimation of ethnicity as a concession to ethnic grievances and developmental constraints, not as a brilliant divide-and-rule stratagem, and confidently asserted, after Lenin and Stalin, that the more genuine the "national demarcation" the more successful the drive to internationalism.

In the short run, national demarcation resulted in a puzzling and apparently limitless collection of ethnic nesting dolls. All non-Russians were "nationals" entitled to their own territorial units and all nationally defined groups living in "somebody else's" units were national minorities entitled to their own units. By 1928, various republics contained national *okrugs*, national *raions*, national soviets, native executive committees (*tuzriki*), native soviets (*tuzemnye sovety*), *aul* (*aul'nye*) soviets, clan (*rodovye*) soviets, nomadic (*kochevye*) soviets and encampment committees (*lagerkomy*).[78] Secure within their borders, all Soviet nationalities were encouraged to develop and, if necessary, create their own autonomous cultures. The key to this effort was the widest possible use of native languages—"native language as a means of social discipline, as a social unifier of nations and as a necessary and most important condition of successful economic and cultural development."[79] Both the main reason for creating a national autonomy and the principal means of making that autonomy truly national, "native language" could refer to the official language of a given republic (almost always indicated by the republic's name[80]), to the official language of a given minority unit or to the mother tongue of particular individuals. The proliferation of territorial units seemed to suggest that eventually there would be an official language for most individuals, even if it resulted in state-sponsored trilingualism (in 1926 Abkhaz-speaking Abkhazia, itself a part of Georgian-speaking Georgia, had 43 Armenian, 41 Greek, 27 Russian, 2 Estonian and 2 German schools[81]). To put it differently, all 192 languages identified during the 1920s would sooner or later become official.

To become official, however, a language had to be "modernized." This involved the creation or further codification of a literary standard based on "live popular speech," rendered through a "rational" phonetic alphabet (all Arabic and some Cyrillic writing systems were abandoned in favor of Latin) and "purged of alien ballast."[82] A purge—or institutionalized linguistic purism—was important because if nationalities were by definition culturally different (in form) and if language was "the most important characteristic that distinguished one nationality from another," then languages had to become as different as possible.[83] Local intellectuals encouraged by central authorities (or, when these were unavailable, metropolitan scholars jealous for "their peoples") set out to draw linguistic borders. The inventors of literary Uzbek and Tatar declared war on "Arabisms and Farsisms," the framers of standard Ukrainian and Belorussian campaigned against "Russisms," and the protectors of the eliteless "small peoples" liberated the newly codified Chukchi language from English borrowings.[84] The first two of the five theses adopted by Tatar writers and journalists read as follows:

> I. The principal material of the Tatar literary language should consist of elements taken from the native language. If a needed word exists in the Tatar language, it can under no circumstances be replaced by a foreign equivalent.
>
> II. If a word does not exist in the Tatar language, it should, whenever possible, be replaced
>
> a) by a new artificial word composed of stems (roots) that exist in our language;
>
> b) by a borrowing from among old-Turkish words that are no longer in use or from the vocabularies of related Turkish tribes that reside on Russian territory provided they will be accepted and easily assimilated.[85]

Duly codified and apparently insulated from each other (not least by means of dictionaries[86]), the various official languages could be used to reach the "toiling nationals." By 1928, books were being published in 66 languages (as compared to 40 in 1913) and newspapers in 47 (205 non-Russian titles in all[87]). How many people were actually reading them was not of immediate importance: as in other Soviet campaigns, supply was supposed to generate demand (or suppliers would engineer it). Much more ambitious was the requirement that all official business including education be conducted in native languages (the languages of the eponymous republics as well as the languages of local communities).[88] This was necessary because Lenin and Stalin kept saying it was necessary, because it was the only way to overcome national mistrust, because "speech reactions in native languages occur more quickly,"[89] because socialist content was only accessible to nationals in national form, because "developed" nations consisted of individuals whose native language equaled the official language equaled the nation's name, and because the adoption of rigid literary standards had created large numbers of people who either spoke non-languages or spoke their native languages "incorrectly."[90] By 1927, 93.7 percent of Ukrainian and 90.2 percent of Belorussian elementary-school students were taught in their "native" languages (that is, the language implied by the name of their "nationality").[91] High schools, vocational schools and colleges lagged behind, but everyone seemed to agree that the ultimate goal was a total coincidence of national and linguistic identity. Theoretically at least, a Jew from a shtetl was to be educated in Yiddish even if his parents preferred Ukrainian (Hebrew not being an option), while a Ukrainian from Kuban' was to be taught in Ukrainian if scholars and administrators decided that her parents' vernacular was a dialect of Ukrainian rather than a dialect of Russian (or a Kuban' language in its own right).[92] As one official put it, "We cannot take the desires of parents into account. We must teach the child in the language he speaks at home."[93] In many parts of the USSR such an approach could not be implemented or even seriously argued, but the validity of the final goal (total ethnolinguistic consistency under socialism rather than total ethnolinguistic transparency under communism) was usually taken for granted.

Finally and most dramatically, the promotion of native languages was accompanied by the promotion of the speakers of those languages. According to the official policy of *korenizatsiia* (literally, "taking root" or indigenization), the affairs of all ethnic groups at all levels—from union republics to clan soviets—were to be run by the representatives of those ethnic groups. This involved the preferential recruitment of "nationals" to party, government, judicial, trade union and educational institutions, as well as the preferential "proletarianization" of mostly rural non-Russian populations.[94] The specific goals were not clear, however. On the one hand, an ethnic group's share of the total population in a given territory was to be equal to its share in all high-status occupations, which in effect meant all occupations with the exception of traditional rural ones (precisely those that, according to ethnographers, made most nationalities "national").[95] On the other hand, not all territories were equal or equally self-contained, with the "republican" identity frequently dominating over all others. Indeed, most indigenization campaigns assumed republic-controlling (non-Russian) nationalities to be more indigenous than others, so that if the share of Armenian office-holders actually exceeded the share of Armenians in the total population of "their own" republic, no one seemed to allege a violation of the Soviet nationality policy (the Kurds were to control their own village soviets; their proportionate representation on the republican level was not a clearly stated priority).[96] No other union republic could equal Armenia's success but most of them tried (with Georgia making particularly great strides). Nationality was an asset and there were no nationally defined entities above the union republic.

Yet even though administrative hierarchy tended to interfere with the principle of national equality, the idea of a formal ranking of ethnic groups was absent from the NEP nationality policy. No one bothered with Stalin's distinction between nations and nationalities, least of all Stalin himself. The dictatorship of the proletariat consisted of countless national groups (languages, cultures, institutions) endowed with apparently limitless national—that is, "nonessential"—rights (to develop their languages, cultures, institutions). The key themes were "national diversity [*raznoobrazie*]" and "national uniqueness [*svoeobrazie*]," both useful as paradoxical prerequisites for ultimate unity but also as values in their own right. The symbolic representation of the USSR at the Agricultural Exhibit of 1923 included

> The majestic ancient mosques of Samarkand . . . ; the white minarets of Azerbaijan; a colorful Armenian tower; a strikingly Oriental building from Kirghizia; a solid Tatar house covered with grillwork; some picturesque chinoiserie from the far east; and further on the yurts and *chums* from Bashkiria, Mongol-Buriatia, Kalmykia, Oiratia, Iakutia, the Khakass, the Ostiak and the Samoed; all of it surrounded by the artificially created mountains and villages of Dagestan, Caucasian Highland [*Gorskaia*] Republic, and Chechnia . . . They each have *their own* flag; signs in *their own* language; maps of *their own* expanses and borders; diagrams of *their own* riches. Nationality, individuality and uniqueness are forcefully emphasized everywhere.[97]

If the USSR was a communal apartment, then every family that inhabited it was entitled to a room of its own. "Only through free national self-determination could we arrive in this apartment," argued Vareikis, "for only because of this self-determination can any formerly oppressed nation shed its legitimate mistrust of larger nations."[98]

Not all mistrust was legitimate, of course. The failure to recognize Moscow as "the citadel of the international revolutionary movement and leninism"[99] (and thus the only true center of democratic centralism) was a nationalist deviation, as Sultan-Galiev and Shums'kyi, among others, had a chance to find out. National rights were matters of cultural "form" as distinct from political and economic "content"; but ultimately all form was derived from content and it was up to party leaders in Moscow to decide where the line should be drawn in each case. One thing was clear, however: the distinction itself remained obligatory, albeit temporary, and the share of form remained significant, although theoretically negligible. Even as he attacked Mykola Khvyl'ovyi in 1926 for turning "away from Moscow," Stalin reiterated his support for the further development of Ukrainian culture and repeated his 1923 prediction that eventually (as opposed to right now) "the Ukrainian proletariat would be Ukrainianized in the same way in which the proletariat of, say, Latvia and Hungary, which used to be German, had been Latvianized and Magyarized."[100]

But what about the Russians? In the center of the Soviet apartment there was a large and amorphous space not clearly defined as a room, unmarked by national paraphernalia, unclaimed by "its own" nation and inhabited by a very large number of austere but increasingly sensitive proletarians. The Russians, indeed, remained in a special position. They could be bona fide national minorities in areas assigned to somebody else, but in Russia proper they had no national rights and no national opportunities (because they had possessed and misused them before). The war against Russian huts and Russian churches was the Party's raison d'être, and the heavy burden of that war was the reason it needed the support of the yurts, *chums* and minarets. In fact, ethnicity-based affirmative action in the national territories was an exact replica of class-based affirmative action in Russia. A Russian could benefit from being a proletarian; a non-Russian could benefit from being a non-Russian. "Udmurt" and "Uzbek" were meaningful concepts because they substituted for class; "Russian" was a politically empty category unless it referred to the source of great-power chauvinism (which meant arrogant bureaucratic statism, not excessive national self-assertion) or to the history of relentless imperialist oppression (which meant that the tsarist state was a prison for non-Russian peoples). In Trotsky's March 1923 formulation of Lenin's policy,

> The relationship between the Great Russian proletariat and the Great-Russian peasantry is one thing. Here the question is one of class, pure and simple, which makes the solution of the problem easier. The relationship between the Great Russian proletariat, which plays first fiddle in our federal state, and the Azerbaijani, Turkestani, Georgian and Ukrainian peasantry is something else entirely.[101]

The Russians were not the only non-nation in the Soviet Union. The Soviets were not a nation either (the apartment was not larger than the sum total of its rooms). This is all the more remarkable because after March 1925 the citizens of the USSR were building socialism "in one country"—a country with a central state, a centralized economy, a definite territory and a monolithic Party. Some people ("great-power chauvinists") associated that country with Russia[102] but as far as the party line was concerned, the USSR had no national identity, no official language and no national culture. The USSR was like Russia insofar as both represented pure "socialist content" completely devoid of "national form."

One could not criticize socialist content, of course, but the campaign to foster national forms had numerous, though mostly inarticulate, detractors. While almost none of the delegates to the XII Congress spoke out against the Lenin/Stalin indigenization (korenizatsiia) program, the greatest applause was reserved for the few attacks on "local nationalism," not for the Party's crusade against great-power chauvinism.[103] Meanwhile, in the Tatar Republic great-power chauvinism consisted in complaints "that 'all the power is in Tatar hands these days'; that 'Russians are badly off now'; that 'Russians are being oppressed'; that 'Russians are being fired from their jobs, not hired anywhere, and not admitted to colleges'; that 'all Russians should leave Tataria as soon as possible,' etc."[104] In Povolzh'e, Siberia and central Asia, "non-native" settlers, teachers and administrators resented official pressure to learn languages they considered useless, hire "nationals" they deemed incompetent, teach children they called "savage" and waste scarce resources on projects they regarded as unfair tokenism.[105] Ukrainian peasants were not enthusiastic about the arrival of Jewish agricultural colonists, while the "overrepresented" Jewish officials objected to wholesale Ukrainianization.[106] The presumed beneficiaries were not always grateful, either. "Politically immature" parents, students and teachers exhibited an "abnormal attitude" towards native language education and had to be forced along the path of "Yiddishization" and "Belorussification" (for technical reasons, this path rarely stretched beyond middle school and thus appeared to be an educational dead end).[107] "Backward" Belorussian settlers in Siberia preferred instruction in Russian, while "particularly backward" indigenous peoples of Siberia argued that insofar as literacy was of any value in the tundra, it was to get to know the Russian ways and learn the skills that could not be mastered at home.[108]

While NEP lasted, these arguments fell on deaf ears because the correct way out of backwardness lay through exuberant and uncompromising nation building (*natsional'noe stroitel'stvo*)—that is, in official terminology, through more backwardness. But in 1928 NEP came to an end and so did the toleration of all "survivals." The "revolutionaries from above" restored the original bolshevik equation of "otherness" with "backwardness" and vowed to destroy it within ten years. Collectivization would take care of rural barbarians, industrialization would bring about urban progress and the cultural revolution would "liquidate illiteracy" (and thus all deviance). According to the apostles of the Great Transformation, "socialism in one country" meant that the difference between self and other would soon coincide with the borders of that country: all internal boundaries would presently disappear, schools would merge with production, writers with readers, minds with bodies. But did any of this apply to nationalities? Did this mean that national territories were a concession to backwardness that had to be withdrawn? That nations were to be eliminated like NEP men or collectivized like peasants? Some serious signs pointed in that direction. Just as legal scholars anticipated the withering away of law and teachers predicted the imminent obsolescence of formal education, linguists and ethnographers expected—and tried to bring about—the fusion and consequent disappearance of linguistic and ethnic communities.[109] According to N. Ia. Marr's allegedly marxist and hence obligatory "Japhetic theory," language belonged to a social superstructure and thus reflected the cyclical changes of the economic base. Language families were remnants of evolutionary stages united by the inexorable process of global "glottogony" and were destined to become merged under communism.[110] Similarly, the speakers of those languages ("nationalities") constituted historically "unstable" communities that rose and fell with socio-economic formations:[111] "By freeing itself from its bourgeois aspect, national culture will become fused into one human culture . . . The nation is a historic, transitional category that does not represent anything primeval or eternal. Indeed, the process of the evolution of the nation essentially repeats the history of the development of social forms."[112] In the meantime, the need to speed up the study of marxism-leninism and "master technology" seemed to require both the abandonment of the "preposterous" practice of linguistic indigenization among mostly "assimilated" groups and the encouragement of the widest possible use of the Russian language.[113]

This was not to be, however. Linguistic purism did come under attack from the marrists and later the Party,[114] but the issue was not officially resolved until 1933–1934 and the principle of ethnocultural autonomy was never put into question. As Stalin declared to the XVI Party Congress in July 1930,

> The theory of the fusion of all nations of . . . the USSR into one common *Great Russian* nation with one common *Great Russian* language is a nationalist-chauvinist and anti-leninist theory that contradicts the main thesis of leninism, according to which national differences cannot disappear in the near future but will remain in existence for a long time, even after the victory of the proletarian revolution *on a world scale*.[115]

Accordingly, for as long (very long) as "national differences, language, culture, ways of life, etc." remained in existence, the ethnoterritorial entities would have to be preserved and reinforced.[116] The Great Transformation in nationality policy consisted in a dramatic escalation of the NEP nation-building drive. The champions of the Russian language were forced to recant[117] and all of Soviet life was to become as "national" as possible as quickly as possible. If there were no fortresses that the bolsheviks could not storm, no plan that they could not over-fulfill and no fairy tale that they could not turn into reality, then surely it would not take more than a few months to master Uzbek, let alone the "mere 600 to 700 everyday words" that made up the Nenets language.[118] On 1 March 1928 the Central Asian Bureau of the Party, the Central Committee of the Communist Party of Uzbekistan and the Uzbek Executive Committee formally decided to become fully "Uzbekified" by 1 September 1930.[119] On 28 December 1929 the Uzbek government required that all officials of the Central Committee, Supreme Court and commissariats of labor, enlightenment, justice and social welfare learn the Uzbek language within two months (the other commissariats were given nine months and "everyone else" a year).[120] On 6 April 1931 the Central Executive Committee of the Crimean Autonomous Republic decreed that the share of in-digenous government officials be raised from 29 to 50 percent by the end of the year.[121] And on 31 August 1929 the predominantly Russian-speaking residents of Odessa woke up to discover that their daily *Izvestiia* had been transformed into the Ukrainian-language *Chornomors'ka komuna*.[122]

Only cities, however, were expected to become fully Ukrainianized or Kazak-hified. The most spectacular aspect of the Stalin revolution among nationalities was the vastly increased support for the cultural autonomy of all "national mi-norities" (non-titular nationalities), however small. "The essence of indigeniza-tion does not fully coincide with such concepts as Ukrainianization, Kazakhiza-tion, Tatarization, etc . . . . Indigenization cannot be limited to issues relating only to the indigenous nationality of a given republic or province."[123] By 1932 Ukraine could boast of Russian, German, Polish, Jewish, Moldavian, Chechen, Bulgarian, Greek, Belorussian and Albanian village soviets, while Kazakhstan hosted Russian, Ukrainian, "Russo-Cossack," Uzbek, Uigur, German, Tajik, Dungan, Tatar, Chuvash, Bulgarian, Moldavian and Mordvinian rural soviets, not counting 140 that were "mixed."[124] It was a feast of ethnic fertility, an exuberant national carnival sponsored by the Party and apparently reaffirmed by Stalin's attack on Rosa Luxemburg in his letter to *Proletarskaia revoliutsiia*.[125] It turned out that the Chechen and Ingush were different nationalities (and not all Vainakh speakers), that Mingrelians were different from Georgians, that Karels were dif-ferent from Finns, that the "Pontus Greeks" were different from the "Ellas Greeks," that the Jews and Gypsies were different (but not *that* different) from everybody else and that therefore all of them urgently needed their own literary languages, presses and education systems.[126] Between 1928 and 1938 the number of non-Russian newspapers increased from 205 titles in 47 languages to 2,188 titles in 66 languages.[127] It was considered a scandal if north Caucasians of Ukrai-nian origin did not have their own theaters, libraries and literary organizations, if the peoples of Dagestan had a Turkic lingua franca (as opposed to several dozen separate standards), or if the cultural needs of the Donbass workers were being served "only in the Russian, Ukrainian and Tatar languages."[128] Most official positions and school admissions in the Soviet Union were subject to complex ethnic quotas that aimed at a precise correspondence between demography and promotion—an almost impossibly confusing task given the number of administrative levels at which demography and promotion could be measured.[129] The dictatorship of the proletariat was a Tower of Babel in which all tongues on all floors would have a proportionate share of all jobs. Even shock-worker detachments at individual factories and construction sites were to be organized along ethnic lines if at all possible (the famous female Stakhanovite, Pasha Angelina, was a proud member of the "Greek brigade").[130]

The Great Transformation was not just NEP gone berserk, however. In nationalities policies as much as any other, it represented the last war against backwardness-as-exploitation, a permanent escape from social (and hence all?) difference, and the final leap into timelessness conceived as classlessness. Great Transformation goals and identities were valid only if they were obstructed by villains. Starting in 1928, real or imaginary non-Russian elites could no longer claim nationwide backwardness or nationwide rights. Collectivization presupposed the existence of classes and that meant that all nationalities without exception had to produce their own exploiters, heretics, and anti-Soviet conspirators.[131] (If classes could not be found, gender and age sufficed.[132]) Life consisted of "fronts" and fronts—including the national one—separated warring classes. "If in the case of the Russian nationality the internal class struggle has been extremely acute from the very first days of October . . . , the various nationalities are only now beginning to engage in [it] . . . ."[133] Indeed, sometimes the social corrective to the ethnic principle seemed to dissolve that principle altogether, as when a prominent party spokesman declared that "the intensification of class conflicts reveal[ed] the class essence of many national peculiarities,"[134] or when a young ethnographer/collectivizer concluded that the whole "system that impress[ed] the superficial and usually naive observer as a national peculiarity . . . turn[ed] out to be a system of ideological defense of private property."[135]

Not all national peculiarities could be dissolved by class analysis, however. The rhetoric of ethnic diversity and the practice of ethnic quotas remained obligatory, and most local officials purged during the first five-year plan were replaced by their social betters from the same nationality.[136] What did change was the amount of room allowed for "national form." The ethnic identity of the Great Transformation was the ethnic identity of NEP minus "backwardness" as represented and defended by the exploiting classes. The members of the so-called Union for the Liberation of Ukraine were accused of nationalism not because they insisted on Ukraine's separate identity, administrative autonomy or ethnolinguistic rights—that was the official Soviet policy. They were accused of nationalism because the Ukraine they allegedly defined and celebrated was a rural Utopia from the remote but recoverable past, not an urban Utopia from the near but ethnically fragmented future.

They remained emotionally attached to the old Ukraine dotted with farmsteads and manor houses, a predominantly agrarian country with a solid base for the private ownership of land . . . . They were hostile to the industrialization of Ukraine and to

the Soviet five-year plan, which was transforming the republic and endowing it with
an independent industrial base. They sneered [*glumilis'*] at the Dnieper Hydroelec-
tric Dam and at Soviet Ukrainianization. They did not trust its sincerity and seri-
ousness. They were convinced that without them, without the old Ukrainian intelligentsia, no genuine Ukrainianization was possible. But more than anything else
they were afraid that their monopoly on culture, literature, science, art and the
theater would be wrested from them.[137]

The continued existence of nationally defined communities and the legitimacy
of their claims to particular cultural, territorial, economic and political identities
(which Stalin regarded as the principle of national rights and which I call "nationalism") was never in doubt. The crime of "bourgeois nationalism" consisted
in attempts by some "bourgeois intellectuals" to lead such communities away
from the party line—in the same way as the crime of wrecking consisted in the
attempts by some "bourgeois specialists" to derail Soviet industry. To engage
in "bourgeois nationalism" was to sabotage a nation, not to "build" it.

In 1931 the "socialist offensive" began to wane and in 1934 it was effectively
halted for lack of an adversary. Addressing the "Congress of Victors," Stalin
declared that the USSR had finally "divested itself of everything backward and
medieval" and become an industrialized society based on a solid socialist foundation.[138] For purposes of official representation, time had been conquered and
the future had become present. All essential differences had been overcome, all
scholarly pursuits had become marxist and all non-marxist pursuits had disappeared. In the absence of backwardness, there was no need for the institutions
that had been created to deal with its various manifestations: the Women's Department, the Jewish Section, and the Committee for the Assistance to the Peoples
of the Northern Borderlands had all been closed down. The science of pedology
had been banned because it claimed that women, minorities and the socially
disadvantaged might need special assistance along the path to modernity. The
science of ethnology had been banned because it assumed that some contemporary
cultures might still be primitive or traditional. And all non-socialist-realist art had
been banned because all art reflected reality and all Soviet reality was socialist.

According to the X Congress's equation of nationality with backwardness,
nationality would have had to be banned, too. Once again, however, it weathered
the storm and re-emerged chastened but vigorous. "High stalinism" did not reverse the policy of nation building, as most authors on the subject would have us
believe.[139] It changed the shape of ethnicity but it never abandoned the "leninist
principle" of unity through diversity. It drastically cut down on the number of
national units but it never questioned the national essence of those units. The
abolition of the Central Asian Bureau was no more a call for ethnic assimilation
than the abolition of the Women's Department was a prelude to an attack on
gender differences. In fact, just as the newly emancipated Soviet women were
expected to become more "feminine," the fully modernized Soviet nationalities
were supposed to become more national. Class was the only legitimate kind of
"content" and by the late 1930s class-based quotas, polls and identity cards had
been discontinued.[140] Differences "in form" remained acceptable, however, and

nationality (the most venerable and certifiably hollow form of "form") was allowed to develop, regroup and perhaps even acquire a little content.

The most striking innovation of the early 1930s was the emergence of the
Russians as an ethnic group in their own right. As class criteria became irrelevant,
the former default nationality became almost as saturated with ethnicity as all
others. The noun "national" was criticized and later killed because there were
no "non-nationals" left.[141] First cautiously but then more and more forcefully as
the decade progressed, the Party began to endow Russians with a national past,
national language and an increasingly familiar national iconography, headed principally by Alexander Pushkin—progressive and "freedom-loving" to be sure,
but clearly celebrated as a great Russian, not a great revolutionary. By 1934,
"derussifying" Russian proletarians and deliberately pulling away from Moscow
in the course "cultural construction" had become a serious crime, not a "mistake" born of well intentioned impatience.[142] And yet, the Russians never became
a nationality like any other. On the one hand, they did not have a clearly defined
national territory (RSFSR remained an amorphous "everything else" republic
and was never identified with an ethnic or historic "Russia"), they did not have
their own Party and they never acquired a national Academy. On the other hand—
and this, of course, explains the lacunae—the Russians were increasingly identified with the Soviet Union as a whole. Between 1937 and 1939 Cyrillic replaced
Latin in all the literary standards created in the 1920s, and in 1938, after a three-
year campaign, Russian became an obligatory second language in all non-Russian
schools. The Soviet past was becoming progressively more Russian and so were
the upper echelons of the Party and state.[143] "Internationalism," defined as close
ties among Soviet nationalities, and later "friendship of the peoples," defined as
even closer ties among Soviet nationalities, became official dogmas[144] and both
could only be expressed in Russian, the Soviet lingua franca. Still, no one ever
suggested that there existed a "Soviet nation" (natsiia, that is, as opposed to the
ethnically non-specific narod) or that Russian should become the first language
in all national areas or institutions. Even in Karelia, where in 1938 the local
Finnish standard was discovered to be "fascist," the orphaned Finnic-speakers
were forced to switch to the newly-codified "Karelian" rather than Russian,
which had already become "the language of interethnic communication."[145] The
Russians began to bully their neighbors and decorate their part of the communal
apartment (which included the enormous hall, corridor and the kitchen where all
the major decisions were made), but they did not claim that the whole apartment
was theirs or that the other (large) families were not entitled to their own rooms.
The tenants were increasingly unequal but reassuringly separate.

The culture of the Great Transformation had been, by definition, rootless, fluid
and carnivalesque. Old people acted like adolescents, children acted up, women
dressed like men (although not vice versa), classes changed places and words lost
meaning. People, buildings, languages and nationalities endlessly multiplied, migrated and spread evenly and thinly over a leveled, decentered landscape. But
this proletarian postmodernism proved premature. The Great Retreat of the 1930s
was the revenge of the literal—the triumph of real korenizatsiia, as in "taking

root'' or ''radicalization.'' The forces of gravity (in both senses) pinned buildings
to the ground, peasants to the land, workers to factories, women to men and
Soviets to the USSR.[146] At the same time and in the same basic way, each individual got stuck with a nationality and most nationalities got stuck with their
borders. In the early 1930s, at the time of the reappearance of college admissions
tests and shortly before the introduction of student files (*lichnye dela*), employee
cards (*trudovye knizhki*) and the death penalty for attempted flight abroad, all
Soviet citizens received internal passports that formally defined them in terms of
name, time and place of birth, authorized domicile (*propiska*) and nationality.
One's name and *propiska* could be changed, nationality could not. By the end of
the decade every Soviet child inherited his nationality at birth: individual ethnicity
had become a biological category impervious to cultural, linguistic or geographical change.[147] Meanwhile, collective ethnicity was becoming more and more
territorial. The administrative units created just a few years before in order to
accommodate pre-existing nationalities were now the most important defining
feature of those nationalities. To cite a typical and perfectly circular argument,
''The fact that an ethnic group has its own national territory—a republic, province, district or village soviet—is proof that the ethnic group in question is an
officially recognized nationality . . . . For example, the existence, in Cheliabinsk
province, of a Nagaibak national district makes it imperative that a special nationality, the Nagaibak, be distinguished from the Tatars.''[148]

In the same way, the Jews became a true nation after the creation of the Jewish
Autonomous district in Birobidzhan.

> By acquiring their own territory, their own statehood, the toiling Jews of the USSR
> received a crucial element that they had lacked before and that had made it impos-
> sible for them to be considered a nation in the scientific sense of the term. And so
> it happened that, like many other Soviet nationalities completing the process of
> national consolidation, the Jewish national minority became a nation as a result of
> receiving its own national administrative entity in the Soviet Union.[149]

This view refers to two important innovations. First, the formal ethnic hierarchy was back for the first time since 1913. Different ethnoterritorial units (republics, provinces, districts) had always had different statuses, but no serious
attempt had been made to relate this bureaucratic arrangement to an objective and
rigidly evolutionary hierarchy of ethnicity. After the mid-1930s students, writers
and shockworkers could be formally ranked—and so could nationalities. Second,
if the legitimacy of an ethnic community depended on the government's grant of
territory, then the withdrawal of that grant would automatically ''denationalize''
that community (though not necessarily its individual passport-carrying members!). This was crucial because by the second half of the decade the government
had obviously decided that presiding over 192 languages and potentially 192
bureaucracies was not a very good idea after all. The production of textbooks,
teachers and indeed students could not keep up with formal ''nationalization,''
the fully bureaucratized command economy and the newly centralized education
system required manageable and streamlined communication channels, and the
self-consciously Russian ''promotees'' who filled the top jobs in Moscow after

the Great Terror were probably sympathetic to complaints of anti-Russian discrimination (they themselves were beneficiaries of *class*-based quotas). By the end of the decade most ethnically defined soviets, villages, districts and other small units had been disbanded, some autonomous republics forgotten and most "national minority" schools and institutions closed down.[150]

However—and this is the most important "however" of this essay—the ethnic groups that already had their own republics and their own extensive bureaucracies were actually told to redouble their efforts at building distinct national cultures. Just as the "reconstruction of Moscow" was changing from grandiose visions of refashioning the whole cityscape to a focused attempt to create several perfect artifacts,[151] so the nationality policy had abandoned the pursuit of countless rootless nationalities in order to concentrate on a few full-fledged, fully equipped "nations." While the curtailment of ethnic quotas and the new emphasis on Soviet meritocracy ("quality of cadres") slowed down and sometimes reversed the indigenization process in party and managerial bureaucracies, the celebration of national cultures and the production of native intelligentsias intensified dramatically. Uzbek communities outside Uzbekistan were left to their own devices but Uzbekistan as a quasi-nation-state remained in place, got rid of most alien enclaves on its territory and concentrated on its history and literature. The Soviet apartment as a whole was to have fewer rooms but the ones that remained were to be lavishly decorated with hometown memorabilia, grandfather clocks and lovingly preserved family portraits.

Indeed, the 1934 Congress of Soviet Writers, which in many ways inaugurated high stalinism as a cultural paradigm, was a curiously solemn parade of old-fashioned romantic nationalisms. Pushkin, Tolstoy and other officially restored Russian icons were not the only national giants of international stature—all Soviet peoples possessed, or would shortly acquire, their own classics, their own founding fathers and their own folkloric riches. The Ukrainian delegate said that Taras Shevchenko was a "genius" and a "colossus" "whose role in the creation of the Ukrainian literary language was no less important than Pushkin's role in the creation of the Russian literary language, and perhaps even greater."[152] The Armenian delegate pointed out that his nation's culture was "one of the most ancient cultures of the orient," that the Armenian national alphabet predated Christianity and that the Armenian national epic was "one of the best examples of world epic literature" because of "the lifelike realism of its imagery, its elegance, the profundity and simplicity of its popular wisdom and the democratic nature of its plot."[153] The Azerbaijani delegate insisted that the Persian poet Nizami was actually a classic of Azerbaijani literature because he was a "Turk from Giandzha," and that Mirza Fath Ali Akhundov was not a gentry writer, as some proletarian critics had charged, but a "great philosopher-playwright" whose "characters [were] as colorful, diverse and realistic as the characters of Griboedov, Gogol' and Ostrovskii."[154] The Turkmen delegate told the Congress about the eighteenth century "coryphaeus of Turkmen poetry," Makhtum-Kuli; the Tajik delegate explained that Tajik literature had descended from Rudaki, Firdousi, Omar Khayyam and "other brilliant craftsmen of the word"; while the Georgian delegate delivered an extraordinarily lengthy address in which he claimed that Shot'ha

Rust'haveli's *The Man in the Panther's Skin* was "centuries ahead of west European intellectual movements," infinitely superior to Dante and generally "the greatest literary monument of the whole ... so-called medieval Christian world."[155]

According to the new party line, all officially recognized Soviet nationalities were supposed to have their own nationally defined "Great Traditions" that needed to be protected, perfected and, if need be, invented by specially trained professionals in specially designated institutions. A culture's "greatness" depended on its administrative status (from the Union republics at the top to the non-territorial nationalities who had but a tenuous hold on "culture"), but within a given category all national traditions except for the Russian were supposed to be of equal value. Rhetorically this was not always the case (Ukraine was sometimes mentioned as second-in-command while central Asia was often described as backward), but institutionally all national territories were supposed to be perfectly symmetrical—from the party apparatus to the school system. This was an old Soviet policy but the contribution of the 1930s consisted in the vigorous leveling of remaining uneven surfaces and the equally vigorous manufacturing of special—and also identical—culture-producing institutions. By the end of the decade all Union republics had their own writers' unions, theaters, opera companies and national academies that specialized primarily in national history, literature and language.[156] Republican plans approved by Moscow called for the production of ever larger numbers of textbooks, plays, novels, ballets and short stories, all of them national in form (which, in the case of dictionaries, folklore editions and the "classics" series came dangerously close to being in content as well).

If some republics had a hard time keeping up with others, Moscow tried to oblige. In 1935 and 1936, for example, the new State Institute of Theater Art was in the process of training or had already released eleven national theater companies complete with all actors and full repertoires.[157] If a national repertoire was still incomplete, translations from mostly nineteenth century Russian and west European literatures were actively encouraged or provided (the first productions of the new Bashkir Opera in 1936 were *Prince Igor* and *The Marriage of Figaro*[158]). In fact, in the late 1930s translation became one of the major Soviet industries as well as the main source of sustenance for hundreds of professional writers. The "friendship of the peoples" thesis required that all Soviet nationalities be deeply moved by the art of other Soviet nationalities. As Gorky put it, "We need to share our knowledge of the past. It is important for all Union republics that a Belorussian know what a Georgian or a Turk is like, etc."[159] This resulted not only in frenzied translation activity but also in histories of the USSR that were supposed to include all the Soviet peoples, radio shows that introduced Soviet listeners to "Georgian polyphony and Belorussian folk songs," tours by hundreds of regulation "song and dance ensembles," decades of Azerbaijani art in Ukraine, evenings of Armenian poetry in Moscow, exhibits of Turkmen carpets in Kazan' and festivals of national choirs, athletes and Young Pioneers all over the country. From the mid-1930s through the 1980s, this activity was one of the most visible (and apparently least popular) aspects of Soviet official culture.

The pursuit and propagation of national cultures were far from uneventful, of course. Within ten years of the First Writers' Congress most of the founding fathers of the new cultural institutions had perished; large areas had been annexed, lost and reannexed; numerous small ethnic units had been abolished as "unpromising"; and several nations and former "national minorities" had been forcibly deported from their territories. At the same time, the Russians had been transformed from a revolutionary people recovering a national past into "the most outstanding of all nations comprising the Soviet Union"[160] and the focus of world history. Once again, however, the legitimacy of non-Russian "Great Traditions" was not questioned. The main enemies of Russia-as-progress were "bourgeois nationalism," which now referred to insufficient admiration for Russia, and "rootless cosmopolitanism," which represented the opposite of *korenizatsiia*-as-rootedness. Even in 1936–1939, when hundreds of alleged nationalists were being sentenced to death, "the whole Soviet country" was noisily celebrating the 1000th anniversary of Firdousi, claimed by the Tajiks as one of the founders of their (and not Persian) literature; the 500th anniversary of Mir Ali Shir Nawaiy (Alisher Navoi), appropriated by the Uzbeks as the great classic of their (and not Chaghatay) culture; and the 125th anniversary of Taras Shevchenko, described by *Pravda* as "a great son of the Ukrainian people" who "carried Ukrainian literature to a height worthy of a people with a rich historical past."[161] The few national icons that suffered during this period were attacked for being anti-Russian, not for being national icons.[162] Similarly, when the Ukrainian poet Volodymyr Sosiura was castigated by *Pravda* in 1951 for his poem "Love Ukraine," the alleged sin consisted not in loving Ukraine too much but in not thanking the elder brother enough.[163] A major reason for gratitude was the recent Soviet annexation of west Ukraine and the subsequent "reunification" of the Ukrainian nation state, a Soviet/Russian achievement widely advertised as a fulfillment of Ukrainian national aspirations.

In fact, it was in this period of Russian delusions of grandeur that the theoretical justification for non-Russian national aspirations was clearly formulated. On 7 April 1948 Stalin said something that closely resembled his 1913 statement on national rights:

> Every nation, whether large or small, has its own specific qualities and its own peculiarities, which are unique to it and which other nations do not have. These peculiarities form a contribution that each nation makes to the common treasury of world culture, adding to it and enriching it. In this sense all nations, both small and large, are in the same position and each nation is equal to any other nation.[164]

This seemed to suggest that ethnicity was universal, irreducible and inherently moral. But this was only an overture. In summer 1950 Stalin put his pen to paper in order to exorcize the spirit of N. Ia. Marr, one of the last saints of the Great Transformation whose theories and students had somehow escaped the fate of the other "simplifiers and vulgarizers of marxism."[165] According to Stalin, language was not part of the superstructure—or, indeed, of the base. It "belonged to the whole nation" and was "common to the whole society" across social classes and throughout history. "Societies" represented ethnic communities and ethnic communities had "essences" that existed "incomparably longer than any base or any superstructure."[166] In short, it was official: classes and their "ideologies" came and went, but nationalities remained. In a country free from social conflict, ethnicity was the only meaningful identity.

This was the legacy that Stalin bequeathed to *his* successors and that survived 1984 to haunt Gorbachev and *his* successors. Khrushchev balked, of course: in his struggle for local initiative he strengthened the position of the entrenched national elites, while in his struggle against the entrenched national elites he tried to promote an ethnicity-blind personnel policy and even scared some people by resurrecting the "fusion of nations" doctrine. The fusion was to occur under communism, however, and communism was to occur too soon to be taken seriously. The only practical step in this direction was the 1959 school reform that allowed parents the freedom to choose between Russian and non-Russian schools and made "another" language optional. Theoretically, a Kazakh could now forego Russian; practically, a Russian was no longer forced to take Kazakh.[167] The self-confidently homogeneous establishments of Armenia and Lithuania expressed relatively little concern, the "numerically small" ethnic bureaucracies within the RSFSR prepared for the inevitable and the linguistically threatened but politically vigorous elites in Latvia, Ukraine and Azerbaijan put up a desperate fight. Their argument was summed up by Oles' Honchar thirty years later: "To learn or not to learn a native language in school—this question cannot arise in any civilized country."[168] A civilized country, in other words, was an ethnonational state in which the official language was by definition "native." The stalinist nationality policy had obviously borne fruit.

Civilized stalinism ("developed socialism") was the credo of the "collective leadership" that presided over the twilight years of the Soviet Union. Deriving its legitimacy from the "really existing" ethnoterritorial welfare state rather than future communism and past revolution, the new official discourse retained the language of class as window dressing and relied on nationality to prop up the system.[169] Every Soviet citizen was born into a certain nationality, took it to day care and through high school, had it officially confirmed at the age of sixteen and then carried it to the grave through thousands of application forms, certificates, questionnaires and reception desks. It made a difference in school admissions and it could be crucial in employment, promotions and draft assignments.[170] Soviet anthropologists, brought back to life in the late 1930s and provided with a raison d'être after the banishment of marrism, were not supposed to study "culture": their job was to define, dissect and delight in the primordial "ethnos." Even abroad, in a world dominated by capitalism, the most visible virtue was "national liberation."

All nationalities were ranked—theoretically along the evolutionary scale from tribe to nation, and practically by territorial or social status. The status of a given nationality could vary a great deal but the continuing use of ethnic quotas made sure that most practical advantages accrued to the members of titular nationalities residing in "their own" republics. Sixty years of remarkable consistency on this score had resulted in almost total "native" control over most Union republics:

large ethnic elites owed their initial promotions and their current legitimacy (such as it was) to the fact of being ethnic.[171] Dependent on Moscow for funds, the political and cultural entrepreneurs owed their allegiance to "their own people" and their own national symbols. But if the politicians were structurally constrained within the apparatus, the intellectuals were specifically trained and employed to produce national cultures. Limits were set by the censor but the goal was seen as legitimate both by party sponsors and by national consumers. A very large proportion of national intellectuals were professional historians, philologists and novelists, and most of them wrote for and about their own ethnic group.[172] They produced multi-volume national histories, invented national genealogies, purified national languages, preserved national treasures and bemoaned the loss of a national past.[173] In other words, they acted like good patriots—when they were not acting like bad nationalists. As time went on, however, it became increasingly difficult to distinguish between the two because the national form seemed to have become the content and because nationalism did not seem to have any content other than the cult of form. More ominously, the country's leaders found it harder and harder to explain what their "socialist content" stood for and, when Gorbachev finally discarded the worn-out marxist verbiage, the only language that remained was the well honed and long practiced language of nationalism.

The Soviet regime's contribution to the nationalist cause was not limited to "constructive measures," of course. It forced the high priests of national cultures to be part-time worshipers of other national cultures, it instituted an administrative hierarchy that privileged some ethnic groups over others, it interfered in the selection and maintenance of national pantheons, it isolated ethnic communities from their relatives and sympathizers abroad, and it encouraged massive migrations that resulted in competition for scarce resources, diluted the consumer base of the national elites and provoked friction over ethnic quotas. Finally and most fatefully, it deprived the various nations of the right to political independence—a right that was the culmination of all nationalist doctrines, including the one that lay at the foundation of the Soviet Union.

This points to another great tension in Soviet nationality policy: the coexistence of republican statehood and passport nationality.[174] The former assumed that territorial states made nations, the latter suggested that primordial nations might be entitled to their own states. The former presupposed that all residents of Belorussia would (and should) some day become Belorussian, the latter provided the non-Belorussian residents with arguments against it. The Soviet government endorsed both definitions without ever attempting to construct an ethnically meaningful Soviet nation or turn the USSR into a Russian nation state, so that when the non-national Soviet state had lost its Soviet meaning, the national non-states were the only possible heirs. Except for the Russian Republic, that is. Its borders were blurred, its identity was not clearly ethnic and its "titular" residents had trouble distinguishing between the RSFSR and the USSR.[175] Seventy years after the X Party Congress the policy of indigenization reached its logical conclusion: the tenants of various rooms barricaded their doors and started using the windows, while the befuddled residents of the enormous hall and kitchen stood in the center scratching the backs of their heads. Should they try to recover their belongings? Should they knock down the walls? Should they cut off the gas? Should they convert their "living area" into a proper apartment?

NOTES

1. Not the first such attempt, of course, but sufficiently different from the previous ones to make it worth the effort, I hope. My greatest debt is to the work of Ronald Grigor Suny, most recently summarized in his *The Revenge of the Past: Nationalism, Revolution, and the Collapse of the Soviet Union* (Stanford: Stanford University Press, 1993). On the last three decades, see also Kenneth C. Farmer, *Ukrainian Nationalism in the Post-Stalin Era* (The Hague: Martinus Nijhoff, 1980); Gail Warshofsky Lapidus, "Ethnonationalism and Political Stability: The Soviet Case," *World Politics* 36, no. 4 (July 1984): 355–80; Philip G. Roeder, "Soviet Federalism and Ethnic Mobilization," *World Politics* 23, no. 2 (January 1991): 196–233; Teresa Rakowska-Harmstone, "The Dialectics of Nationalism in the USSR," *Problems of Communism* XXIII (May–June 1974), 1–22; and Victor Zaslavsky, "Nationalism and Democratic Transition in Postcommunist Societies," *Daedalus* 121, no. 2 (Spring 1992): 97–121. On the promotion of "national languages" and bilingualism, see the work of Barbara A. Anderson and Brian D. Silver, especially "Equality, Efficiency, and Politics in Soviet Bilingual Education Policy, 1934–1980," *American Political Science Review* 78, No. 4 (October 1984): 1019–39; and "Some Factors in the Linguistic and Ethnic Russification of Soviet Nationalities: Is Everyone Becoming Russian?" in Lubomyr Hajda and Mark Beissinger, eds., *The Nationalities Factor in Soviet Politics and Society* (Boulder: Westview Press, 1990). For a fascinating analysis of state-sponsored nationalism in a non-federal communist state, see Katherine Verdery, *National Ideology under Socialism: Identity and Cultural Politics in Ceausescu's Romania* (Berkeley: University of California Press, 1991).

2. For an excellent overview of recent debates on the ethnic boundaries of political communities, see David A. Hollinger, "How Wide the Circle of the 'We'? American Intellectuals and the Problem of Ethnos since World War Two." *American Historical Review* 98, no. 2 (April 1993): 317–37.

3. I. Vareikis and I. Zelenskii, *Natsional'no-gosudarstvennoe razmezhevanie Srednei Azii* (Tashkent: Sredne-Aziatskoe gosudarstvennoe izdatel'stvo, 1924). 59.

4. For a witty elaboration of the reverse metaphor (the communal apartment as the USSR), see Svetlana Boym, "The Archeology of Banality: The Soviet Home," *Public Culture* 6, no. 2 (1994): 263–92.

5. I. V. Stalin, *Marksizm i natsional'nyi vopros* (Moscow: Politizdat, 1950), 51.

6. For early marxist debates on nationalism, see Walker Connor, *The National Question in Marxist-Leninist Theory and Strategy* (Princeton: Princeton University Press, 1984); Hélène Carrère d'Encausse, *The Great Challenge: Nationalities and the Bolshevik State, 1917–1930* (New York: Holmes and Meier, 1992); Helmut Konrad, "Between 'Little International' and Great Power Politics: Austro-Marxism and Stalinism on the National Question," in Richard L. Rudolph and David F. Good, eds., *Nationalism and Empire: The Habsburg Empire and the Soviet Union* (New York: St. Martin's Press, 1992); Richard Pipes, *The Formation of the Soviet Union: Communism and Nationalism, 1917–1923* (Cambridge: Harvard University Press, 1964); Roman Szporluk, *Communism and Nationalism: Karl Marx versus Friedrich List* (New York: Oxford University Press, 1988).

7. Stalin, *Marksizm i natsional'nyi vopros*, 51. See also V. I. Lenin, *Voprosy natsional'noi politiki i proletarskogo internatsionalizma* (Moscow: Politizdat, 1965), passim.

8. The "oppressor" was not always "civilized," as in most marxist analyses of Russia vis-à-vis Poland or Finland.

9. Stalin, *Marksizm*, 37. The view of a nation (as opposed to a nationality) as a "historical category belonging to a particular epoch, the epoch of rising capitalism" became something of a truism and was reconfirmed without debate at the X Party Congress.

10. Lenin, "Kriticheskie zametki po natsional'nomu voprosu" (1913), in *Voprosy*, 32–34.

11. Ibid., 33; and Lenin, "Itogi diskussii o samoopredelenii" (1916), in *Voprosy*, 128.

12. Lenin, "Kriticheskie zametki," 26.

13. Ibid., 33–34.

14. Ibid., 15, 16; and Lenin, "O prave natsii na samoopredelenie" (1914), in *Voprosy*, 81 (footnote), and "O natsional'noi gordosti velikorossov" (1914), in *Voprosy*, 107.

15. Lenin, "Kriticheskie zametki," 9.

16. Ibid., 9, 28; and "O prave," 61, 83–84.

17. Isabelle Kreindler, "A Neglected Source of Lenin's Nationality Policy," *Slavic Review* 36, no. 1 (March 1977): 86–100.

18. Quoted in Isabelle Kreindler, "Educational Policies toward the Eastern Nationalities in Tsarist Russia: A Study of the Il'minskii System," Ph.D. Diss., Columbia University, 1969, 75–76.

19. Stalin, *Marksizm*, 21.

20. Veniamin, Arkhiepiskop Irkutskii i Nerchinskii, *Zhiznennye voprosy pravoslavnoi missii v Sibiri* (St. Petersburg: A. M. Kotomin, 1885), 7. For a discussion of the controversy, see Yuri Slezkine, "Savage Christians or Unorthodox Russians? The Missionary Dilemma in Siberia," in Galya Diment and Yuri Slezkine, eds., *Between Heaven and Hell: The Myth of Siberia in Russian Culture* (New York: St. Martin's Press, 1993), 18–27.

21. Lenin, "Kriticheskie zametki," 7.

22. Cf. Ernest Gellner, *Nations and Nationalism* (Ithaca: Cornell University Press, 1983), 1; E. J. Hobsbawm, *Nations and Nationalism since 1780: Programme, Myth, Reality* (New York: Cambridge University Press, 1991), 9; John Breuilly, *Nationalism and the State* (Chicago: University of Chicago Press. 1985), 3.

23. Lenin, "O natsional'noi programme RSDRP" (1913), in *Voprosy*, 41; idem, "O prave," 61–62, 102; idem, "Sotsialisticheskaia revoliutsiia i pravo natsii na samoopredelenie" (1916), in *Voprosy*, 113–14.

24. Stalin, *Marksizm*, 163. The same applied to national schools, freedom of religion, freedom of movement and so on.

25. Lenin, "Itogi diskussii o samoopredelenii" (1916), in *Voprosy*, 129.

26. "Peoples" and "nations" were used interchangeably.

27. *Dekrety Sovetskoi vlasti* (Moscow: Gospolitizdat. 1957), 1: 39–41, 113–15, 168–70, 195–96, 340–44, 351, 367.

28. S. Dimanshtein, "Narodnyi komissariat po delam natsional'nostei," *Zhizn' natsional'nostei* 41 (49) (26 October 1919).

29. S. Dimanshtein, "Sovetskaia vlast' i melkie natsional'nosti," *Zhizn' natsional'nostei* 46 (54) (7 December 1919). See also S. Pestkovskii, "Natsional'naia kul'tura," *Zhizn' natsional'nostei* 21 (29) (8 June 1919).

30. A. P. Nenarokov, *K edinstvu ravnykh: Kul'turnye faktory ob''edinitel'nogo dvizheniia sovetskikh narodov, 1917–1924* (Moscow: Nauka, 1991), 91–92.

31. Ibid., 92–93.

32. *Vos'moi s'' ezd RKP(b): Protokoly* (Moscow: Gospolitizdat, 1959), 46–48, 77–81.

33. Ibid., 55.

34. Ibid., 106.

35. Ibid., 53. In the same speech, Lenin argued that even the most "advanced" western countries were hopelessly behind Soviet Russia in terms of social differentiation (which meant that they could—and sometimes should—be regarded as integral nations rather than as temporarily isolated class battlefields). By being Soviet, Russia was more advanced than the advanced west.

36. Ibid., 82.

37. Fedor Kriuchkov, "O Kriashenakh," *Zhizn' natsional'nostei* 27 (84) (2 September 1920).

38. R. El'mets, "K voprosu o vydelenii chuvash v osobuiu administrativnuiu edinitsu," *Zhizn' natsional'nostei* 2 (59) (11 January 1920).

39. V. Vilenskii (Sibiriakov), "Samoopredelenie iakutov," *Zhizn' natsional'nostei* 3 (101) (2 February 1921).

40. V. G. Bogoraz-Tan, "O pervobytnykh plemenakh," *Zhizn' natsional'nostei* 1 (130) (10 January 1922); idem, "Ob izuchenii i okhrane okrainnykh narodov," *Zhizn' natsional'nostei* 3–4 (1923): 168–77; Dan. Ianovich, "Zapovedniki dlia gibnushchikh tuzemnykh plemen," *Zhizn' natsional'nostei* 4 (133) (31 January 1922); TsGAOR, f. 1377, op. 1, d. 8, ll. 126–27, d. 45, ll. 53, 77, 81.

41. "Chetyre goda raboty sredi estontsev Sovetskoi Rossii," *Zhizn' natsional'nostei* 24 (122) (5 November 1921).

42. TsGAOR, f. 1318, op. 1, d. 994, l. 100.

43. See *Zhizn' natsional'nostei* (1921) and TsGAOR, f. 1318.

44. L. Segal', "Vserossiiskoe soveshchanie rabotnikov po prosveshcheniiu narodov ne-russkogo iazyka," *Zhizn' natsional'nostei* 33 (41) (31 August 1919).

45. I. Trainin, "Ekonomicheskoe raionirovanie i natsional'naia politika," *Zhizn' natsional'nostei* 21 (119) (10 October 1921); S. K., "Ekonomicheskoe raionirovanie i problemy avtonomno-federativnogo stroitel'stva," *Zhizn' natsional'nostei* 25 (123) (12 November 1921).

46. *Desiatyi s'' ezd Rossiiskoi Kommunisticheskoi partii: Stenograficheskii otchet* (Moscow: Gosudarstvennoe izdatel'stvo, 1921), 101.

47. Ibid.

48. Ibid., 371.

49. Ibid., 372.

50. Ibid., 115.

51. "Belorusskii natsional'nyi vopros i kommunisticheskaia partiia," *Zhizn' natsional'nostei* 2 (131) (17 January 1922).

52. Vareikis and Zelenskii, *Natsional'no-gosudarstvennoe razmezhevanie*, 57.

53. Ibid., 60. "Nations that have not yet reached the capitalist stage" were not nations according to Stalin's definition.

54. *Desiatyi s'' ezd*, 112, 114.

55. For two different interpretations, see Moshe Lewin, *Lenin's Last Struggle* (New York: Pantheon, 1968); and Richard Pipes, *The Formation of the Soviet Union: Communism and Nationalism, 1917–1923* (Cambridge: Harvard University Press, 1954).

56. V. I. Lenin, "K voprosu o natsional'nostiakh ili ob 'avtonomizatsii,' " in *Voprosy*, 167.

57. Ibid., 168–70.

58. *Dvenadtsatyi s'' ezd Rossiiskoi Kommunisticheskoi partii (bol'shevikov). Steno-grafcheskii otchet* (Moscow: Glavpolitprosvet, 1923), 462, 552.

59. Ibid., 439–54, 561–65.

60. Quoted in Nenarokov, *K edinstvu*, 116–17.

61. *Dvenadtsatyi s'' ezd*, 543–45.

62. Ibid., 449.

63. See, for example, "S'' ezd po narodnomu obrazovaniiu," *Zhurnal Ministerstva narodnago prosvieshcheniia* L (March–April 1914): 195, 242–44.

64. *Ob uchrezhdenii Komissii po izucheniiu plemennogo sostava naseleniia Rossii. Izvestiia Komissii po izucheniiu plemennogo sostava naseleniia Rossii* (Petrograd: Rossiiskaia Akademiia Nauk, 1917), 1: 8.

65. I. Gertsenberg, "Natsional'nyi printsip v novom administrativnom delenii RSFSR," *Zhizn' natsional'nostei* 37 (94) (25 November 1920).

66. N. Ia. Marr, *Plemennoi sostav naseleniia Kavkaza: Trudy Komissii po izucheniiu plemennogo sostava naseleniia Rossii* (Petrograd: Rossiiskaia Akademiia nauk, 1920), 3: 9, 21–22. See also N. Ia. Marr, "Ob iaffeticheskoi teorii," *Novyi vostok* 5 (1924): 303–9.

67. "The richest associations and the strongest perceptions are those acquired through the mother tongue" (Segal', "Vserossiiskoe soveshchanie").

68. E. F. Karskii, *Etnograficheskaia karta Bielorusskago plemeni: Trudy Komissii po izucheniiu plemennogo sostava naseleniia Rossii*, vol. 2 (Petrograd: Rossiiskaia Akademiia nauk, 1917).

69. I. I. Zarubin, *Spisok narodnostei Turkestanskogo kraia: Trudy Komissii po izucheniiu plemennogo sostava naseleniia Rossii*, vol. 9 (Leningrad: Rossiiskaia Akademiia nauk, 1925); I. I. Zarubin, *Naselenie Samarkandskoi oblasti: Trudy Komissii po izucheniiu plemennogo sostava naseleniia Rossii*, vol. 10 (Leningrad: AN SSSR, 1926); Edward A. Allworth, *The Modern Uzbeks: From the Fourteenth Century to the Present* (Stanford: Hoover Institution Press, 1990), 181; Alexandre Bennigsen and Chantal Lemercier-Quelquejay, *Islam in the Soviet Union* (New York: Praeger, 1967), 131–33; Teresa Rakowska-Harmstone, *Russia and Nationalism in Central Asia: The Case of Tadzhikistan* (Baltimore: Johns Hopkins University Press, 1970), 78.

70. *Instruktsiia k sostavleniiu plemennykh kart, izdavaemykh Komissieiu po izucheniiu plemennogo sostava naseleniia Rossii* (Petrograd: Rossiiskaia Akademiia nauk, 1917), 1: 11.

71. Karskii, *Etnograficheskaia karta.* 19

72. N. Ia. Marr, *Plemennoi sostav naseleniia Kavkasa: Trudy Komissii po izucheniiu plemennogo sostava naseleniia Rossii* (Petrograd: Rossiiskaia Akademiia nauk, 1920), 9: 24–25; N. Ia. Marr, *Talyshi: Trudy Komissii po izucheniiu plemennogo sostava naseleniia Rossii* (Petrograd: Rossiiskaia Akademiia nauk, 1922), 4: 3–5, 22.

73. Marr, *Plemennoi sostav*, 9.

74. Ibid., 59–61. Cf. S. K. Patkanov, *Spisok narodnostei Sibiri: Trudy Komissii po izucheniiu plemennogo sostava naseleniia Rossii* (Petrograd: Rossiiskaia Akademiia nauk, 1923), 7: 3.

75. See, for example, Patkanov on "Paleoasiatics" in Patkanov, *Spisok*, 8.

76. Vl. Kun, "Izuchenie etnicheskogo sostava Turkestana," *Novyi vostok* 6 (1924): 351–53; Zarubin, *Spisok*, 10.

77. I. Khodorov, "Natsional'noe razmezhevanie Srednei Azii," *Novyi vostok* 8–9 (1926): 69.

78. See, for example, S. Dimanshtein, "Desiat' let natsional'noi politiki partii i so-vvlasti," *Novyi vostok* 19 (1927): vi; "Vremennoe polozhenie ob upravlenii tuzemnykh

narodnostei i plemen Severnykh okrain." *Severnaia Aziia* 2 (1927): 85–91; N. I. Leonov, "Tuzemnye sovety v taige i tundrakh," *Sovetskii Sever: Pervyi sbornik statei* (Moscow: Komitet Severa, 1929), 225–30; Zvi Y. Gitelman, *Jewish Nationality and Soviet Politics: The Jewish Sections of the CPSU, 1917–1930* (Princeton: Princeton University Press, 1972), 289; Gerhard Simon, *Nationalism and Policy toward the Nationalities in the Soviet Union: From Totalitarian Dictatorship to Post-Stalinist Society* (Boulder: Westview Press, 1991), 58.

79. I. Davydov, "O probleme iazykov v prosvetitel'noi rabote sredi natsional' nostei," *Prosveshchenie natsional'nostei* 1 (1929): 18.

80. After the abolition of the "Highland" (*Gorskaia*) republic, the only autonomous republic that had no ethnic "landlord" and hence no obvious official language was Dagestan, one of the most linguistically diverse places on earth (see A. TakhoGodi, "Problema iazyka v Dagestane," *Revoliutsiia i natsional'nosti* 2 [1930]: 68–75).

81. V. A. Gurko-Kriazhin, "Abkhaziia." *Novyi vostok* 13–14 (1926): 115.

82. See, in particular, William Fierman, *Language Planning and National Development: The Uzbek Experience* (Berlin: Mouton de Gruyter, 1991); and Simon Crisp, "Soviet Language Planning since 1917–53." in Michael Kirkwood, ed., *Language Planning in the Soviet Union* (New York: St. Martin's Press, 1989), 23–45. The quote is from Agamalyogly, "K predstoiashchemu tiurkologicheskomu s" ezdu v Azerbaidzhane," *Novyi vostok* 10–11 (1925): 216.

83. Davydov, "O probleme iazykov," 18.

84. See, for example, Fierman, *Language Planning*, 149–63; James Dingley, "Ukrainian and Belorussian—A Testing Ground," in Kirkwood, ed., *Language Planning*, 180–83; V. G. Bogoraz-Tan, "Chukotskii bukvar'," *Sovetskii Sever* 10 (1931): 126.

85. I. Borozdin, "Sovremennyi Tatarstan," *Novyi vostok* 10–11 (1925): 132.

86. M. Pavlovich, "Kul'turnye dostizheniia tiurko-tatarskikh narodnostei so vremeni Oktiabr'skoi revoliutsii," *Novyi vostok* 12 (1926): viii.

87. Simon, *Nationalism*, 46. The number of Yiddish books and brochures, for example, rose from 76 in 1924 to 531 in 1930 (see Gitelman, *Jewish Nationality*, 332–33).

88. See, for example, Fierman, *Language Planning*, 170–76; Gitelman, *Jewish Nationality*, 351–65; James E. Mace, *Communism and the Dilemmas of National Liberation: National Communism in Soviet Ukraine, 1918–1933* (Cambridge: Harvard Ukrainian Research Institute, 1983), 96; Simon, *Nationalism*, 42.

89. Davydov, "O probleme iazykov," 23.

90. The Ukrainian Commissar of Education, Mykola Skrypnyk, defined the Donbass vernacular as a "neither Russian nor Ukrainian" patois in need of proper Ukrainianization (see Mace, *Communism and the Dilemmas*, 213).

91. Simon, *Nationalism*, 49.

92. I. Bulatnikov, "Ob ukrainizatsii na Severnom Kavkaze," *Prosveshchenie natsional'nostei* 1 (1929): 94–99; Gitelman, *Jewish Nationality*, 341–44.

93. Gitelman, *Jewish Nationality*, 342.

94. For a survey, see Simon, *Nationalism*, 20–70.

95. See, for instance, Borozdin, "Sovremennyi Tatarstan," 118–19; 122–23: Dimanshtein, "Desiat' let," v–vi, xvii.

96. Simon, *Nationalism*, 32–33, 37.

97. A. Skachko, "Vostochnye respubliki na S.-Kh. Vystavke SSSR v 1923 godu," *Novyi vostok* 4 (1923): 482–84. Emphasis in the original.

98. Vareikis and Zelenskii, *Natsional'no-gosudarstvennoe razmezhevanie*, 59.

99. Stalin, *Sochineniia*, 8: 153.

100. Ibid., 151.

101. Quoted in Nenarokov, *K edinstvu ravnykh*, 132.

102. See, in particular, M. Agurskii, *Ideologiia natsional-bol'shevizma* (Paris: YMCA Press, 1980).

103. *Dvenadtsatyi s'' ezd*, 554, 556, 564.

104. N. Konoplev, "Shire front internatsional'nogo vospitaniia," *Prosveshchenie natsional'nostei* 2 (1931): 49. See also N. Konoplev, "Za vospitanie internatsional'nykh boitsov," *Prosveshchenie natsional'nostei* 4–5 (1930): 55–61.

105. TsGAOR, f. 1377, op. 1, d. 224, ll. 8, 32; N. Amyl'skii, "Kogda zatsvetaiut zharkie tsvety," *Severnaia Aziia* 3 (1928): 57–58; Fierman, *Language Planning*, 177–85; N. I. Leonov, "Tuzemnye shkoly na Severe," *Sovetskii Sever: Peruyi sbornik statei* (Moscow: Komitet Severa, 1929), 200–4; Leonov, "Tuzemnye sovety," 242, 247–48; D. F. Medvedev, "Ukrepim sovety na Krainem Severe i ozhivim ikh rabotu," *Sovetskii Sever* 1 (1933): 6–8; P. Rysakov, "Praktika shovinizma i mestnogo natsionalizma," *Revoliutsiia i natsional'nosti* 8–9 (1930): 28; T. Semushkin. *Chukotka* (Moscow: Sovetskii pisatel', 1941), 48; I. Sergeev, "Usilit' provedenie natspolitiki v Kalmykii," *Revoliutsiia i natsional'nosti* 7 (1930): 66; Simon, *Nationalism*, 25, 41, 73–74.

106. Gitelman, *Jewish Nationality*, 386, 398, 402–3.

107. Davydov, "O probleme iazykov," 22: Konoplev, "Shire front," 50; A. Valitov, "Protiv opportunisticheskogo otnosheniia k stroitel'stvu natsshkoly," *Prosveshchenie natsional'nostei* 5–6 (1932): 68.

108. I. Skachkov, "Prosveshchenie sredi belorusov RSFSR," *Prosveshchenie natsional'nostei* 3 (1931): 76; P. Kovalevskii, "V shkole-iurte," *Sovetskii Sever* 2 (1934): 105–6; I. Nesterenok, "Smotr natsional'nykh shkol na Taimyre," *Sovetskii Sever* 6 (1932): 84; G. N. Prokof'ev, "Tri goda v samoedskoi shkole," *Sovetskii Sever* 7–8 (1931): 144; S. Stebnitskii, "Iz opyta raboty v shkole Severa," *Prosveshchenie natsional'nostei* 8–9 (1932): 49–51.

109. For professional abolitionism during the first five-year plan, see Sheila Fitzpatrick, ᵊd., *Cultural Revolution in Russia, 1928–1931* (Bloomington: Indiana University Press. 1978). On linguistics and ethnography, see Yuri Slezkine, "The Fall of Soviet Ethno graphy, 1928–38," *Current Anthropology* 32, no. 4 (1991): 476–84.

110. Slezkine, "The Fall," 478.

111. N. Ia. Marr, "K zadacham nauki na sovetskom vostoke," *Prosveshchenie natsional'nostei* 2 (1930): 12; S. Asfendiarov, "Problema natsii i novoe uchenie o iazyke," *Novyi vostok* 22 (1928): 174.

112. Asfendiarov, "Problema natsii," 174.

113. I. Davydov, "Ocherednye zadachi prosveshcheniia natsional'nostei," *Prosveshchenie natsional'nostei* 4–5 (1930): 30–34; M. Vanne, "Russkii iazyk v stroitel'stve natsional'nykh kul'tur," *Prosveshchenie natsional'nostei* 2 (1930): 31–40.

114. I. Kusik'ian, "Ocherednye zadachi marksistov-iazykovedov v stroitel'stve iazykov narodov SSSR," *Prosveshchenie natsional'nostei* 11–12 (1931): 75; E. Krotevich, "Vypravit' nedochety v stroitel'stve Kazakhskoi terminologii," *Prosveshchenie natsional'nostei* 8–9 (1932): 94–96; Fierman, *Language Planning*, 126–129; Mace, *Communism*, 277–79; Roman Smal-Stocki, *The Nationality Problem of the Soviet Union and Russian Communist Imperialism* (Milwaukee: The Bruce Publishing Company, 1952), 106–41.

115. I. V. Stalin, *Sochineniia* (Moscow: Politizdat, 1952), 13: 4. Emphasis in the original.

116. Ibid., 12: 365–66.

117. See, for example, *Prosveshchenie natsional'nostei* 11–12 (1931): 102–6.

118. Fierman, *Language Planning*, 177; Evgen'ev and Bergavinov, "Nachal'niku

Obdorskogo politotdela Glavsevmorputi t. Mikhailovu," *Sovetskaia Arktika* 4 (1936): 65–67.

119. P. Rysakov, "Praktika shovinizma i mestnogo natsionalizma," *Revoliutsiia i natsional'nosti* 8–9 (1930): 29.

120. S. Akopov, "K voprosu ob uzbekizatsii apparata i sozdanii mestnykh rabochikh kadrov promyshlennosti Uzbekistana," *Revoliutsiia i natsional'nosti* 12 (1931): 22–23.

121. B. Rodnevich, "Korenizatsiia apparata v avtonomiiakh i raionakh natsmen'shinstv RSFSR," *Revoliutsiia i natsional'nosti* 12 (1931): 19–20.

122. Mace, *Communism*, 212. See also Simon, *Nationalism*, 39–40.

123. A. Oshirov, "Korenizatsiia v sovetskoi strane," *Revoliutsiia i natsional'notsi* 4–5 (1930): 111.

124. A. Gitlianskii, "Leninskaia natsional'naia politika v deistvii (natsional'nye men'shinstva na Ukraine)," *Revoliutsiia i natsional'nosti* 9 (1931): 37; A. Zuev, "Natsmeny Kazakhstana," *Revoliutsiia i natsional'nosti* 4 (1932): 48.

125. Or so most people thought. Cf. Stalin, *Sochineniia* 13: 91–92 and *Revoliutsiia i natsional'nosti* 1 (1932); and Iiul'skii, "Pis'mo t. Stalina—orudie vospitaniia Bol'shevistskikh kadrov," *Prosveshchenie natsional'nostei* 2–3 (1932): 9.

126. See for example I. K., "Indoevropeistika v deistvii," *Prosveshchenie natsional'nostei* 11–12 (1931): 97–102; I. Kusik'ian, "Protiv burzhuaznogo kavkazovedeniia," *Prosveshchenie natsional'nostei* 1 (1932): 45–47; I. Zhvaniia, "Zadachi sovetskogo i natsional'nogo stroitel'stva v Mingrelii," *Revoliutsiia i natsional'nosti* 7 (1930): 66–72; D. Savvov, "Za podlinno rodnoi iazyk grekov Sovetskogo Soiuza," *Proveshchenie natsional'nostei* 4 (1932): 64–74; M. Bril', "Trudiashchiesia tsygane v riady stroitelei sotsializma," *Revoliutsiia i natsional'nosti* 7 (1932): 60–66; S. D., "Evreiskaia avtonomnaia oblast'—detishche Oktiabr'skoi revoliutsii," *Revoliutsiia i natsional'nosti* 6 (1934): 13–25.

127. Simon, *Nationalism*, 46.

128. *Revoliutsiia i natsional'nosti* 1 (1930): 117; A. Takho-Godi, "Problema iazyka v Dagestane," *Revoliutsiia i natsional'nosti* 2 (1930): 68–75; Gitlianskii, "Leninskaia natsional'naia politika," 77.

129. See, for example, G. Akopov, "Podgotovka natsional'nykh kadrov," *Revoliutsiia i natsional'nosti* 4 (1934): 54–60; A. Polianskaia, "Natsional'nye kadry Belorussii," *Revoliutsiia i natsional'nosti* 8–9 (1930): 79–88; Rodnevich, "Korenizatsiia apparata"; Zuev, "Natsmeny"; E. Popova, "Korenizatsiia apparata—na vysshuiu stupen'," *Revoliutsiia i natsional'nosti* 7 (1932): 50–55; I. Iuabov, "Natsmeny Uzbekskoi SSR," *Revoliutsiia i natsional'nosti* 9 (1932): 74–78; P. S-ch, "Partorganizatsii natsional'nykh raionov," *Revoliutsiia i natsional'nosti* 10–11 (1932): 143–48; I. Karneev, "Nekotorye tsifry po podgotovke inzhenerno-tekhnicheskikh kadrov iz korennykh natsional'nostei," *Revoliutsiia i natsional'nosti* 3 (1933): 86–92.

130. Kh. Khazanskii, I. Gazeliridi, "Kul'tmassovaia rabota sredi natsional'nykh men'shinstv na novostroikakh," *Revoliutsiia i natsional'nosti* 9 (1931): 86–91; A. Kachanov, "Kul'turnoe obsluzhivanie rabochikh-natsmen Moskovskoi oblasti," *Revoliutsiia i natsional'nosti* 6 (1932): 54–58; I. Sabirzianov, "Natsmenrabota profsoiuzov Moskvy," *Revoliutsiia i natsional'nosti* 9 (1932): 69–74.

131. A. Mitrofanov, "K itogam partchistki v natsrespublikakh i oblastiakh," *Revoliutsiia i natsional'nosti* 1 (1930): 29–36; Martha Brill Olcott, *The Kazakhs* (Stanford: Hoover Institution Press, 1987), 216–20; Mace, *Communism*, 264–80; Rakowska-Harmstone, *Russia and Nationalism*, 39–41; Azade-Ayse Rorlich, *The Volga Tatars: A Profile in National Resilience* (Stanford: Hoover Institution Press, 1986), 155–56.

132. In other words, women and children could become default proletarians. See Greg-

ory Massell, *The Surrogate Proletariat: Moslem Women and Revolutionary Strategies in Soviet Central Asia*, 1919–1929 (Princeton: Princeton University Press, 1974); Yuri Slezkine, "From Savages to Citizens: The Cultural Revolution in the Soviet Far North, 1928–1938," *Slavic Review* 51, no. 1 (Spring 1992): 52–76.

133. "*Vskrytie klassovoi rozni.*" See N. Krupskaia, "O zadachakh natsional'-nokul'turnogo stroitel'stva v sviazi s obostreniem klassovoi bor'by," *Prosveshchenie natsional'nostei* 4–5 (1930): 19.

134. S. Dimanshtein, "Za klassovuiu chetkost' v prosveshchenii natsional'nostei," *Prosveshchenie natsional'nostei* 1 (1929): 9.

135. N. Bilibin, "U zapadnykh koriakov," *Sovetskii Sever* 1–2 (1932): 207.

136. See, for example, Olcott, *The Kazakhs*, 219; Rakowska-Harmstone, *Russia and Nationalism*, 100–1.

137. D. Zaslavskii, "Na protsesse 'vyzvolentsev,' " *Prosveshchenie natsional'nostei* 6 (1930): 13.

138. Stalin, *Sochineniia*, 13: 306, 309.

139. For two remarkable exceptions, see Barbara A. Anderson and Brian D. Silver, "Equality, Efficiency, and Politics in Soviet Bilingual Education Policy, 1934–1980," *American Political Science Review* 78, no. 4 (October 1984): 1019–39; and Ronald Grigor Suny, "The Soviet South: Nationalism and the Outside World," in Michael Mandelbaum, ed., *The Rise of Nations in the Soviet Union* (New York: Council of Foreign Relations Press, 1991): 69.

140. Sheila Fitzpatrick, *Education and Social Mobility in the Soviet Union, 1921–1934* (Cambridge: Cambridge University Press, 1979). 235.

141. *Pervyi vsesoiuznyi s'' ezd sovetskikh pisatelei. Stenograficheskii otchet* (Moscow: Khudozhestvennaia literatura, 1934), 625.

142. Compare, for example, Stalin, *Sochineniia*, 8: 149–54; and S. Dimanshtein, "Bol'shevistskii otpor natsionalizmu," *Revoliutsiia i natsional'nosti* 4 (1933): 1–13; S. D., "Bor'ba s natsionalizmom i uroki Ukrainy," *Revoliutsiia i natsional'nosti* 1 (1934): 15–22.

143. Simon, *Nationalism*, 148–55.

144. After Stalin's speeches at the XVII Party Congress and at the Conference of the Leading Collective Farmers of Tajikistan and Turkmenistan (see Stalin, *Sochineniia*, 13: 361; 14 [1]: 114–15).

145. Paul M. Austin, "Soviet Karelian: The Language That Failed," *Slavic Review* 51, no. 1 (Spring 1992), esp. 22–23.

146. This is, in effect, a crude summary of Vladimir Papernyi's delightful *Kul'tura Dva* (Ann Arbor: Ardis, 1985).

147. On the "passport system," see Victor Zaslavsky, *The Neo-Stalinist State* (Armonk, N.Y.: M. E. Sharpe, 1982), 92 ff.

148. L. Krasovskii, "Chem nado rukovodstvovat'sia pri sostavlenii spiska narodnostei SSSR," *Revoliutsiia i natsional'prnosti* 4 (1936): 70–71.

149. S. Dimanshtein, "Otvet na vopros, sostavliaiut li soboi evrei v nauchnom smysle natsiiu," *Revoliutsiia i natsional'nosti* 10 (1935): 77.

150. Simon, *Nationalism*, 61.

151. Greg Castillo, "Gorki Street and the Design of the Stalin Revolution," in Zeynep Celik, Diane G. Favro and Richard Ingersoll, eds. *Streets: Critical Perspectives on Public Space* (Berkeley: University of California Press, 1994).

152. *Pervyi vsesoiuznyi s'' ezd*, 43, 49.

153. Ibid., 104.

154. Ibid., 116–17.

155. Ibid., 136, 142, 77.

156. Zaslavsky, "Nationalism and Democratic Transition," 102.

157. North Ossetian, Iakut, Kazakh, Kirghiz, Kara-Kalpak, Kabarda, Balkar, Turkmen, Tajik, Adyge and Kalmyk (see A. Furmanova, "Podgotovka natsional'nykh kadrov dlia teatra," *Revoliutsiia i natsional'nosti* 5 [1936]: 29–30).

158. A. Chanyshev, "V bor'be za izuchenie i sozdanie natsional'noi kul'tury," *Revoliutsiia i natsional'nosti* 9 (1935): 61.

159. Pervyi vsesoiuznyi s'' ezd, 43. "Turk" stands for "Azerbaijani."

160. Stalin, *Sochineniia* 2 (XV): 204.

161. "Khronika," *Revoliutsiia i natsional'nosti* 8 (1936): 80; Rakowska-Harmstone, *Russia and Nationalism*, 250–59; Allworth, *The Modern Uzbeks*, 229–30; Yaroslav Bilinsky, *The Second Soviet Republic: The Ukraine after World War II* (New Brunswick: Rutgers University Press, 1964), 191.

162. Lowell Tillett, *The Great Friendship: Soviet Historians on the Non-Russian Nationalities* (Chapel Hill: University of North Carolina Press, 1969), passim.

163. Bilinsky, *The Second Soviet Republic*, 15–16: Robert Conquest, *Soviet Nationalities Policy in Practice* (New York: Praeger, 1967), 65–66.

164. Stalin, *Sochineniia* 3 (XVI): 100.

165. Ibid., 146.

166. Ibid., 117, 119, 138.

167. See Yaroslav Bilinsky, "The Soviet Education Laws of 1958–9 and Soviet Nationality Policy," *Soviet Studies* 14, no. 2 (October 1962): 138–57.

168. Quoted in Isabelle T. Kreindler, "Soviet Language Planning since 1953," in Kirkwood, ed., *Language Planning*, 49. See also Bilinsky, *The Second Soviet Republic*, 20–35; Farmer, *Ukrainian Nationalism*, 134–43; Grey Hodnett, "The Debate over Soviet Federalism," *Soviet Studies* 28, no. 4 (April 1967): 458–81; Simon, *Nationalism*, 233–64.

169. See, in particular, Lapidus. "Ethnonationalism and Political Stability," 355–80; Zaslavsky, "Nationalism and Democratic Transition"; Farmer, *Ukrainian Nationalism*, 61–73.

170. Rasma Karklins, *Ethnic Relations in the USSR: The Perspective from Below* (Boston: Unwin Hyman, 1986).

171. See Roeder, "Soviet Federalism," 196–233.

172. Rakowska-Harmstone, "The Dialectics," 10–15. Cf. Miroslav Hroch, *Social Preconditions of National Revival in Europe* (New York: Cambridge University Press, 1985).

173. See, in particular, Farmer, *Ukrainian Nationalism*, 85–121. Also Allworth, *The Modern Uzbeks*, 258–59; Simon, *Nationalism*, 281–82.

174. For a remarkably elegant interpretation of this tension, see Rogers Brubaker, "Nationhood and the National Question in the Soviet Union and Post-Soviet Eurasia: An Institutionalist Account," forthcoming in *Theory and Society*.

175. Victor Zaslavsky, "The Evolution of Separatism in Soviet Society under Gorbachev," in Gail W. Lapidus and Victor Zaslavsky, with Philip Goldman, eds., *From Union to Commonwealth: Nationalism and Separatism in the Soviet Republics* (New York: Cambridge University Press, 1992), 83; Leokadiia Drobizheva, "Perestroika and the Ethnic Consciousness of the Russians," in ibid., 98–111.

III

COLONIALISM, RACE, AND IDENTITY

Benedict Anderson

Few books have had the transformative influence of Benedict Anderson's *Imagined Communities: Reflections on the Origins and Spread of Nationalism* (London: Verso, 1983). A political scientist and anthropologist who had done field work in Indonesia, Anderson was intrigued by the observation that "every successful revolution has defined itself in national terms" and sought to explain how earlier cultural systems, like universalist religious communities and dynastic realisms, were replaced by societies based on nationality beginning in the late eighteenth century. He begins by defining the nation as "an imagined political community—and imagined as both inherently limited and sovereign." In order for the modern nation to emerge, three ancient cultural conceptions had to fall away. The premodern understanding of time conceived as all events occurring simultaneously, without progression and development. A new understanding of time— "the steady onward clocking of homogeneous empty time"—had to emerge, which allowed a chronological story of the nation to be told. The unselfconscious coherence of supranational religious communities and their attendent script-languages, like Latin, that offered privileged access to ontological truth in time were replaced by the use of a vernacular language and its diffusion through print-capitalism. And the belief that society was naturally organized around high centers, divinely ordained monarchs, gave way to new communities based on popular sovereignty and common citizenships.

For Anderson the nation is neither natural nor eternal but a modern historical construction with its origins in the Creole nationalisms of the New World. He argues that nationalism was a modular phenomenon that spread to Europe and then across the globe. "By the second decade of the nineteenth century, if not earlier, a 'model' of 'the' independent national state was available for pirating." Once popular nationalisms revealed their mobilizing power, dynastic states responded by forging "official nationalisms," which attempted to merge the dynastic realm with a "nation." These state-driven nationalisms often gravitated into imperialism. Finally, colonial nationalisms, generated by bilingual intelligentsias and a shared European discourse of freedom and independence, arose as a response to global imperialism and to the intellectuals' own exclusion from the highest centers of power.

Though Anderson is the key figure in the shift in thinking about nationalism from the material, broadly understood, to the cultural, his close examination of the history of initial nationalisms grounds his theory in macrohistorical social and technological transformations. "What, in a positive sense, made the new communities imaginable was a half-fortuitous, but explosive, interaction between a system of production and productive relations (capitalism), a technology of communications (print), and the fatality of human linguistic diversity." But he moves beyond any simple reduction of nationality to the needs of modernization and, unlike Gellner, refuses to see nationalism as merely a masquerade or a fabrication. Rather he develops the insight of Renan and explores how misremembering the past, memory and imagination, were the acts of initiation that created new forms of human community. The nation is never what its nationalist defenders believe it to be: "It is imagined as a *community*, because, regardless of the actual inequality and exploitation that may prevail in each, the nation is always conceived as a deep, horizontal comradeship. Ultimately it is this fraternity that makes it possible, over the past two centuries, for so many millions of people, not so much to kill, as willingly to die for such limited imaginings."

Census, Map, Museum

In the original edition of *Imagined Communities* I wrote that "so often in the 'nation-building' policies of the new states one sees both a genuine, popular nationalist enthusiasm, and a systematic, even Machiavellian, instilling of nationalist ideology through the mass media, the educational system, administrative regulations, and so forth."[1] My short-sighted assumption then was that official nationalism in the colonized worlds of Asia and Africa was modelled directly on that of the dynastic states of nineteenth-century Europe. Subsequent reflection has persuaded me that this view was hasty and superficial, and that the immediate genealogy should be traced to the imaginings of the colonial state. At first sight, this conclusion may seem surprising, since colonial states were typically *anti*-nationalist, and often violently so. But if one looks beneath colonial ideologies and policies to the grammar in which, from the mid nineteenth century, they were deployed, the lineage becomes decidedly more clear.

Few things bring this grammar into more visible relief than three institutions of power which, although invented before the mid nineteenth century, changed their form and function as the colonized zones entered the age of mechanical reproduction. These three institutions were the census, the map, and the museum: together, they profoundly shaped the way in which the colonial state imagined its dominion—the nature of the human beings it ruled, the geography of its domain, and the legitimacy of its ancestry. To explore the character of this nexus I shall, in this chapter, confine my attention to Southeast Asia, since my conclusions are tentative, and my claims to serious specialization limited to that region. Southeast Asia does, however, offer those with comparative historical interests special advantages, since it includes territories colonized by almost all the "white" imperial powers—Britain, France, Spain, Portugal, The Netherlands, and the United States—as well as uncolonized Siam. Readers with greater knowledge of other parts of Asia and Africa than mine will be better positioned to judge if my argument is sustainable on a wider historical and geographical stage.

Benedict Anderson, "Census, Map, Museum," from *Imagined Communities: Reflections on the Origin and Spread of Nationalism*, revised edition (London: Verso, 1991), pp. 163–85.

THE CENSUS

In two valuable recent papers the sociologist Charles Hirschman has begun the study of the *mentalités* of the British colonial census-makers for the Straits Settlements and peninsular Malaya, and their successors working for the independent conglomerate state of Malaysia.[2] Hirschman's facsimiles of the "identity categories" of successive censuses from the late nineteenth century up to the recent present show an extraordinarily rapid, superficially arbitrary, series of changes, in which categories are continuously agglomerated, disaggregated, recombined, intermixed, and reordered (but the politically powerful identity categories always lead the list). From these censuses he draws two principal conclusions. The first is that, as the colonial period wore on, the census categories became more visibly and exclusively racial.[3] Religious identity, on the other hand, gradually disappeared as a primary census classification. "Hindoos"—ranked alongside "Klings," and "Bengalees"—vanished after the first census of 1871. "Parsees" lasted until the census of 1901, where they still appeared—packed in with "Bengalis," "Burmese," and "Tamils"—under the broad category "Tamils and Other Natives of India." His second conclusion is that, on the whole, the large racial categories were retained and even concentrated after independence, but now redesignated and reranked as "Malaysian," "Chinese," "Indian," and "Other." Yet anomalies continued up into the 1980s. In the 1980 census "Sikh" still appeared nervously as a pseudoethnic subcategory—alongside "Malayali" and "Telegu," "Pakistani" and "Bangladeshi," "Sri Lankan Tamil," and "Other Sri Lankan,"—under the general heading "Indian."

But Hirschman's wonderful facsimiles encourage one to go beyond his immediate analytical concerns. Take, for example, the 1911 Federated Malay States Census, which lists under "Malay Population by Race" the following: "Malay," "Javanese," "Sakai," "Banjarese," "Boyanese," "Mendeling" (sic), "Krinchi" (sic), "Jambi," "Achinese," "Bugis," and "Other." Of these "groups" all but (most) "Malay" and "Sakai" originated from the islands of Sumatra, Java, Southern Borneo, and the Celebes, all parts of the huge neighboring colony of the Netherlands East Indies. But these extra-FMS origins receive no recognition from the census-makers who, in constructing their "Malays," keep their eyes modestly lowered to their own colonial borders. (Needless to say, across the waters, Dutch census-makers were constructing a different imagining of "Malays," as a minor ethnicity alongside, not above, "Achinese," "Javanese," and the like.) "Jambi" and "Krinchi" refer to places, rather than to anything remotely identifiable as ethnolinguistic. It is extremely unlikely that, in 1911, more than a tiny fraction of those categorized and subcategorized would have recognized themselves under such labels. These "identities," imagined by the (confusedly) classifying mind of the colonial state, still awaited a reification which imperial administrative penetration would soon make possible. One notices, in addition, the census-makers' passion for completeness and unambiguity. Hence their intolerance of multiple, politically "transvestite," blurred, or changing identifications. Hence the weird subcategory, under each racial group, of "Others"—who, nonetheless, are absolutely not to be confused with *other* "Others." The fiction of the census is that everyone is in it, and that everyone has one—and only one—extremely clear place. No fractions.

This mode of imagining by the colonial state had origins much older than the censuses of the 1870s, so that, in order fully to understand why the late-nineteenth-century censuses are yet profoundly novel, it is useful to look back to the earliest days of European penetration of Southeast Asia. Two examples, drawn from the Philippine and Indonesian archipelagoes, are instructive. In an important recent book, William Henry Scott has attempted meticulously to reconstruct the class structure of the pre-Hispanic Philippines, on the basis of the earliest Spanish records.[4] As a professional historian Scott is perfectly aware that the Philippines owes its name to Felipe II of "Spain," and that, but for mischance or luck, the archipelago might have fallen into Dutch or English hands, become politically segmented, or been recombined with further conquests.[5] It is tempting therefore to attribute his curious choice of topic to his long residence in the Philippines and his strong sympathy with a Filipino nationalism that has been, for a century now, on the trail of an aboriginal Eden. But the chances are good that the deeper basis for the shaping of his imagination was the sources on which he was compelled to rely. For the fact is that wherever in the islands the earliest clerics and conquistadors ventured they espied, on shore, *principales, hidalgos, pecheros,* and *esclavos* (princes, noblemen, commoners and slaves)—quasi-estates adapted from the social classifications of late medieval Iberia. The documents they left behind offer plenty of incidental evidence that the "*hidalgos*" were mostly unaware of one another's existence in the huge, scattered, and sparsely populated archipelago, and, were aware, usually saw one another not as *hidalgos,* but as enemies or potential slaves. But the power of the grid is so great that such evidence is marginalized in Scott's imagination, and therefore it is hard for him to see that the "class structure" of the precolonial period is a "census" imagining created from the poops of Spanish galleons. Wherever *they* went, *hidalgos* and *esclavos* loomed up, who could only be aggregated as such, that is "structurally," by an incipient colonial state.

For Indonesia we have, thanks to the research of Mason Hoadley, a detailed account of an important judicial case decided in the coastal port of Cirebon, Java, at the end of the seventeenth century.[6] By luck, the Dutch (VOC) and local Cirebonese records are still available. If the Cirebonese account only had survived, we would know the accused murderer as a high official of the Cirebonese court, and only by his title Ki Aria Marta Ningrat, not a personal name. The VOC records, however, angrily identify him as a *Chinees*—indeed that is the single most important piece of information about him that they convey. It is clear then that the Cirebonese court classified people by rank and status, while the Company did so by something like "race." There is no reason whatever to think that the accused murderer—whose high status attests to his and his ancestors' long integration into Cirebonese society, no matter what their origins—thought of himself as "a" *Chinees.* How then did the VOC arrive at this classification? From what poops was it possible to imagine *Chinees*? Surely only those ferociously mercantile poops which, under centralized command, roved ceaselessly from port to port between the Gulf of Mergui and the mouth of the Yangtze-kiang. Oblivious of

the heterogeneous populations of the Middle Kingdom; of the mutual incompre-
hensibility of many of their spoken languages; and of the peculiar social and
geographic origins of their diaspora across coastal Southeast Asia, the Company
imagined, with its trans-oceanic eye, an endless series of *Chinezen*, as the conquistadors had seen an endless series of *hidalgos*. And on the basis of this inventive census it began to insist that those under its control whom it categorized as
Chinezen dress, reside, marry, be buried, and bequeath property according to that
census. It is striking that the much less far-faring and commercially minded Iberians in the Philippines imagined a quite different census category: what they
called *sangley*. *Sangley* was an incorporation into Spanish of the Hokkien *sen-
gli*—meaning "trader."[7] One can imagine Spanish proto-census men asking the
traders drawn to Manila by the galleon trade: "Who are you?," and being sensibly
told: "We are traders."[8] Not sailing the seven Asian seas, for two centuries the
Iberians remained in a comfortably provincial conceptual fog. Only very slowly
did the *sangley* turn into "Chinese"—until the word disappeared in the early
nineteenth century to make way for a VOC-style *chino*.

The real innovation of the census-takers of the 1870s was, therefore, not in
the *construction* of ethnic-racial classifications, but rather in their systematic
quantification. Precolonial rulers in the Malayo-Javanese world had attempted
enumerations of the populations under their control, but these took the form of
tax-rolls and levy-lists. Their purposes were concrete and specific: to keep track
of those on whom taxes and military conscription could effectively be imposed—
for these rulers were interested solely in economic surplus and armable man-
power. Early European regimes in the region did not, in this respect, differ markedly from their predecessors. But after 1850 colonial authorities were using
increasingly sophisticated administrative means to enumerate populations, including the women and children (whom the ancient rulers had always ignored),
according to a maze of grids which had no immediate financial or military purpose. In the old days, those subjects liable for taxes and conscription were usually
well aware of their numerability; ruler and ruled understood each other very well,
if antagonistically, on the matter. But by 1870, a non-taxpaying, unlevyable "Cochin-Chinese" woman could live out her life, happily or unhappily, in the Straits
Settlements, without the slightest awareness that this was how she was being
mapped from on high. Here the peculiarity of the new census becomes apparent.
It tried carefully to count the objects of its feverish imagining. Given the exclusive
nature of the classificatory system, and the logic of quantification itself, a "Cochin-Chinese" had to be understood as one digit in an aggregable series of replicable "Cochin-Chinese"—within, of course, the state's domain. The new demographic topography put down deep social and institutional roots as the colonial
state multiplied its size and functions. Guided by its imagined map it organized
the new educational, juridical, public-health, police, and immigration bureaucracies it was building on the principle of ethno-racial hierarchies which were, however, always understood in terms of parallel series. The flow of subject populations through the mesh of differential schools, courts, clinics, police stations and
immigration offices created "traffic-habits" which in time gave real social life
to the state's earlier fantasies.

Needless to say, it was not always plain sailing, and the state frequently bumped into discomforting realities. Far and away the most important of these was religious affiliation, which served as the basis of very old, very stable imagined communities not in the least aligned with the secular state's authoritarian grid-map. To different degrees, in different Southeast Asian colonies, the rulers were compelled to make messy accommodations, especially to Islam and Buddhism. In particular, religious shrines, schools, and courts—access to which was determined by individual popular self-choice, not the census—continued to flourish. The state could rarely do more than try to regulate, constrict, count, standardize, and hierarchically subordinate these institutions to its own.[9] It was precisely because temples, mosques, schools and courts were topographically anomalous that they were understood as zones of freedom and—in time—for tresses from which religious, later nationalist, anticolonials could go forth to battle. At the same time, there were frequent endeavours to force a better alignment of census with religious communities by—so far as was possible—politically and juridically ethnicizing the latter. In the Federated States of colonial Malaya, this task was relatively easy. Those whom the regime regarded as being in the series "Malay" were hustled off to the courts of "their" castrated Sultans, which were in substantial part administered according to Islamic law.[10] "Islamic" was thus treated as really just another name for "Malay." (Only after independence in 1957 were efforts made by certain political groups to reverse this logic by reading "Malay" as really another name for "Islamic"). In the vast, heterogeneous Netherlands Indies, where by the end of the colonial era an array of quarrelling missionary organizations had made substantial conversions in widely scattered zones, a parallel drive faced much more substantial obstacles. Yet even there, the 1920s and 1930s saw the growth of "ethnic" Christianities (the Batak Church, the Karo Church, later the Dayak Church, and so on) which developed in part because the state allocated proselytizing zones to different missionary groups according to its own census-topography. With Islam Batavia had no comparable success. It did not dare to prohibit the pilgrimage to Mecca, though it tried to inhibit the growth of the pilgrims' numbers, policed their travels, and spied on them from an outpost at Jiddah set up just for this purpose. None of these measures sufficed to prevent the intensification of Indies Muslim contacts with the vast world of Islam outside, and especially the new currents of thought emanating from Cairo.[11]

THE MAP

In the meantime, however, Cairo and Mecca were beginning to be visualized in a strange new way, no longer simply as sites in a sacred Muslim geography, but also as dots on paper sheets which included dots for Paris, Moscow, Manila and Caracas; and the plane relationship between these indifferently profane and sacred dots was determined by nothing beyond the mathematically calculated flight of the crow. The Mercatorian map, brought in by the European colonizers, was beginning, via print, to shape the imagination of Southeast Asians.

In a recent, brilliant thesis the Thai historian Thongchai Winichakul has traced the complex processes by which a bordered "Siam" came into being between 1850 and 1910.[12] His account is instructive precisely because Siam was not colonized, though what, in the end, came to be its borders were colonially determined. In the Thai case, therefore, one can see unusually clearly the emergence of a new state-mind within a "traditional" structure of political power.

Up until the accession, in 1851, of the intelligent Rama IV (the Mongkut of *The King and I*), only two types of map existed in Siam, and both were handmade: the age of mechanical reproduction had not yet there dawned. One was what could be called a "cosmograph," a formal, symbolic representation of the Three Worlds of traditional Buddhist cosmology. The cosmograph was not organized horizontally, like our own maps; rather a series of supraterrestrial heavens and subterrestrial hells wedged in the visible world along a single vertical axis. It was useless for any journey save that in search of merit and salvation. The second type, wholly profane, consisted of diagrammatic guides for military campaigns and coastal shipping. Organized roughly by the quadrant, their main features were written-in notes on marching and sailing times, required because the mapmakers had no technical conception of scale. Covering only terrestrial, profane space, they were usually drawn in a queer oblique perspective or mixture of perspectives, as if the drawers' eyes, accustomed from daily life to see the landscape horizontally, at eye-level, nonetheless were influenced subliminally by the verticality of the cosmograph. Thongchai points out that these guide-maps, always local, were never situated in a larger, stable geographic context, and that the bird's-eye view convention of modern maps was wholly foreign to them.

Neither type of map marked borders. Their makers would have found incomprehensible the following elegant formulation of Richard Muir:[13]

> Located at the interfaces between adjacent state territories, international boundaries have a special significance in determining the limits of sovereign authority and defining the spatial form of the contained political regions . . . . Boundaries . . . occur where the vertical interfaces between state sovereignties intersect the surface of the earth . . . . As vertical interfaces, boundaries have no horizontal extent . . . .

Boundary-stones and similar markers did exist, and indeed multiplied along the western fringes of the realm as the British pressed in from Lower Burma. But these stones were set up discontinuously at strategic mountain passes and fords, and were often substantial distances from corresponding stones set up by the adversary. They were understood horizontally, at eye level, as extension points of royal power; not "from the air." Only in the 1870s did Thai leaders begin thinking of boundaries as segments of a continuous map-line corresponding to nothing visible on the ground, but demarcating an exclusive sovereignty wedged between other sovereignties. In 1874 appeared the first geographical textbook, by the American missionary J. W. Van Dyke—an early product of the print-capitalism that was by then sweeping into Siam. In 1882, Rama V established a special mapping school in Bangkok. In 1892, Minister of Education Prince Damrong Rajanuphab, inaugurating a modern-style school system for the country, made geography a compulsory subject at the junior secondary level. In 1900, or thereabouts, was published *Phumisat Sayam* [Geography of Siam] by W. G. Johnson, the model for all printed geographies of the country from that time onwards.[14] Thongchai notes that the vectoral convergence of print-capitalism with the new conception of spatial reality presented by these maps had an immediate impact on the vocabulary of Thai politics. Between 1900 and 1915, the traditional words *krung* and *muang* largely disappeared, because they imaged dominion in terms of sacred capitals and visible, discontinuous population centers.[15] In their place came *prathet*, "country," which imaged it in the invisible terms of bounded territorial space.[16]

Like censuses, European-style maps worked on the basis of a totalizing classification, and led their bureaucratic producers and consumers towards policies with revolutionary consequences. Ever since John Harrison's 1761 invention of the chronometer, which made possible the precise calculation of longitudes, the entire planet's curved surface had been subjected to a geometrical grid which squared off empty seas and unexplored regions in measured boxes.[17] The task of, as it were, "filling in" the boxes was to be accomplished by explorers, surveyors, and military forces. In Southeast Asia, the second half of the nineteenth century was the golden age of military surveyors—colonial and, a little later, Thai. They were on the march to put space under the same surveillance which the census-makers were trying to impose on persons. Triangulation by triangulation, war by war, treaty by treaty, the alignment of map and power proceeded. In the apt words of Thongchai:[18]

> In terms of most communication theories and common sense, a map is a scientific abstraction of reality. A map merely represents something which already exists objectively "there." In the history I have described, this relationship was reversed. A map anticipated spatial reality, not vice versa. In other words, a map was a model for, rather than a model of, what it purported to represent . . . . It had become a real instrument to concretize projections on the earth's surface. A map was now necessary for the new administrative mesbanisms and for the troops to back up their claims . . . . The discourse of mapping was the paradigm which both administrative and military operations worked within and served.

By the turn of the century, with Prince Damrong's reforms at the Ministry of the Interior (a fine mapping name), the administration of the realm was finally put on a wholly territorial-cartographic basis, following earlier practice in the neighboring colonies.

It would be unwise to overlook the crucial intersection between map and census. For the new map served firmly to break off the infinite series of "Hakkas," "Non-Tamil Sri Lankans," and "Javanese" that the formal apparatus of the census conjured up, by delimiting territorially where, for political purposes, they ended. Conversely, by a sort of demographic triangulation, the census filled in politically the formal topography of the map.

Out of these changes emerged two final avatars of the map (both instituted by the late colonial state) which directly prefigure the official nationalisms of twentieth century Southeast Asia. Fully aware of their interloper status in the distant tropics, but arriving from a civilization in which the legal inheritance and the legal transferability of geographic space had long been established,[19] the Europeans frequently attempted to legitimize the spread of their power by quasi-legal methods. Among the more popular of these was their "inheritance" of the putative sovereignties of native rulers whom the Europeans had eliminated or subjected. Either way, the usurpers were in the business, especially vis-à-vis other Europeans, of reconstructing the property-history of their new possessions. Hence the appearance, late in the nineteenth century especially, of "historical maps," designed to demonstrate, in the new cartographic discourse, the antiquity of specific, tightly bounded territorial units. Through chronologically arranged sequences of such maps, a sort of political-biographical narrative of the realm came into being, sometimes with vast historical depth.[20] In turn, this narrative was adopted, if often adapted, by the nation-states which, in the twentieth century, became the colonial states' legatees.'[21]

The second avatar was the map-as-logo. Its origins were reasonably innocent— the practice of the imperial states of coloring their colonies on maps with an imperial dye. In London's imperial maps, British colonies were usually pink-red. French purple-blue, Dutch yellow-brown, and so on. Dyed this way, each colony appeared like a detachable piece of a jigsaw puzzle. As this "jigsaw" effect became normal, each "piece" could be wholly detached from its geographic context. In its final form all explanatory glosses could be summarily removed: lines of longitude and latitude, place names, signs for rivers, seas, and mountains, *neighbours*. Pure sign, no longer compass to the world. In this shape, the map entered an infinitely reproducible series, available for transfer to posters, official seals, letterheads, magazine and textbook covers, tablecloths, and hotel walls. Instantly recognizable, everywhere visible, the logo-map penetrated deep into the popular imagination, forming a powerful emblem for the anticolonial nationalisms being born.[22]

Modern Indonesia offers us a fine, painful example of this process. In 1828 the first fever-ridden Dutch settlement was made on the island of New Guinea. Although the settlement had to be abandoned in 1836, the Dutch Crown proclaimed sovereignty over that part of the island lying west of 141 degrees longitude (an invisible line which corresponded to nothing on the ground, but boxed in Conrad's diminishing white spaces), with the exception of some coastal stretches regarded as under the sovereignty of the Sultan of Tidore. Only in 1901 did The Hague buy out the Sultan, and incorporate West New Guinea into the Netherlands Indies—just in time for logoization. Large parts of the region remained Conrad-white until after World War II; the handful of Dutchmen there were mostly missionaries, mineral-prospectors—and wardens of special prison-camps for die-hard radical Indonesian nationalists. The swamps north of Merauke, at the extreme southeastern edge of Dutch New Guinea, were selected as the site of these facilities precisely because the region was regarded as utterly remote from the rest of the colony, and the "stone-age" local population as wholly uncontaminated by nationalist thinking.[23]

The internment, and often interment, there of nationalist martyrs gave West New Guinea a central place in the folklore of the anticolonial struggle, and made it a sacred site in the national imagining: Indonesia Free, from Sabang (at the northwestern tip of Sumatra) to—where else but?—Merauke. It made no difference at all that, aside from the few hundred internees, no nationalists ever saw New Guinea with their own eyes until the 1960s. But Dutch colonial logo-maps sped across in the colony, showing a West New Guinea *with nothing to its East*, unconsciously reinforced the developing imagined ties. When, in the aftermath of the bitter anticolonial wars of 1945–49, the Dutch were forced to cede sovereignty of the archipelago to a United States of Indonesia, they attempted (for reasons that need not detain us here) to separate West New Guinea once again, keep it temporarily under colonial rule, and prepare it for independent nationhood. Not until 1963 was this enterprise abandoned, as a result of heavy American diplomatic pressure and Indonesian military raids. Only then did President Sukarno visit for the first time, at the age of sixty-two, a region about which he had tirelessly orated for four decades. The subsequent painful relations between the populations of West New Guinea and the emissaries of the independent Indonesian state can be attributed to the fact that Indonesians more or less sincerely regard these populations as "brothers and sisters," while the populations themselves, for the most part, see things very differently.[24]

This difference owes much to census and map. New Guinea's remoteness and rugged terrain created over the millennia an extraordinary linguistic fragmentation. When the Dutch left the region in 1963 they estimated that within the 700,000 population there existed well over 200 mostly mutually unintelligible languages.[25] Many of the remoter "tribal" groups were not even aware of one another's existence. But, especially after 1950, Dutch missionaries and Dutch officials for the first time made serious efforts to "unify" them by taking censuses, expanding communications networks, establishing schools, and erecting supra-"tribal" governmental structures. This effort was launched by a colonial state which, as we noted earlier, was unique in that it had governed the Indies, not primarily via a European language, but through "administrative Malay."[26] Hence West New Guinea was "brought up" in the same language in which Indonesia had earlier been raised (and which became the national language in due course). The irony is that *bahasa Indonesia* thus became the lingua franca of a burgeoning West New Guinean, West Papuan nationalism.[27]

But what brought the often quarrelling young West Papuan nationalists together, especially after 1963, was the map. Though the Indonesian state changed the region's name from West New Guinea, first to Irian Barat (West Irian) and then to Irian Jaya, it read its local reality from the colonial-era bird's-eye atlas. A scattering of anthropologists, missionaries and local officials might know and think about the Ndanis, the Asmats, and the Baudis. But the state itself, and through it the Indonesian population as a whole, saw only a phantom "Irianese" (*orang Irian*) named *after the map*; because phantom, to be imagined in quasi-logo form: "negroid" features, penis-sheaths, and so on. In a way that reminds us how Indonesia came first to be imagined within the racist structures of the early-twentieth-century Netherlands East Indies, an embryo "Irianese" national community, bounded by Meridian 141 and the neighboring provinces of North and South Moluccas, emerged. At the time when its most prominent and attractive spokesman, Arnold Ap, was murdered by the state in 1984, he was curator of a state-built museum devoted to "Irianese" (provincial) culture.

THE MUSEUM

The link between Ap's occupation and assassination is not at all accidental. For museums, and the museumizing imagination, are both profoundly political. That his museum was instituted by a distant Jakarta shows us how the new nation-state of Indonesia learned from its immediate ancestor, the colonial Netherlands East Indies. The present proliferation of museums around Southeast Asia suggests a general process of political inheriting at work. Any understanding of this process requires a consideration of the novel nineteenth-century colonial archaeology that made such museums possible.

Up until the early nineteenth century the colonial rulers in Southeast Asia exhibited very little interest in the antique monuments of the civilizations they had subjected. Thomas Stamford Raffles, ominous emissary from William Jones's Calcutta, was the first prominent colonial official not merely to amass a large personal collection of local *objets d'art*, but systematically to study their history.[28] Thereafter, with increasing speed, the grandeurs of the Borobudur, of Angkor, of Pagan, and of other ancient sites were successively disinterred, unjungled, measured, photographed, reconstructed, fenced off, analysed, and displayed.[29] Colonial Archaeological Services became powerful and prestigious institutions, calling on the services of some exceptionally capable scholar-officials.[30]

To explore fully why this happened, when it happened, would take us too far afield. It may be enough here to suggest that the change was associated with the eclipse of the commercial-colonial regimes of the two great East India Companies, and the rise of the true modern colony, directly attached to the metropole.[31] The prestige of the colonial state was accordingly now intimately linked to that of its homeland superior. It is noticeable how heavily concentrated archaeological efforts were on the restoration of imposing monuments (and how these monuments began to be plotted on maps for public distribution and edification: a kind of necrological census was under way). No doubt this emphasis reflected general Orientalist fashions. But the substantial funds invested allow us to suspect that the state had its own, non-scientific reasons. Three immediately suggest themselves, of which the last is surely the most important.

In the first place, the timing of the archaeological push coincided with the first political struggle over the state's education policies.[32] "Progressives"—colonials as well as natives—were urging major investments in modern schooling. Against them were arrayed conservatives who feared the long-term consequences of such schooling, and preferred the natives to stay native. In this light, archaeological restorations—soon followed by state-sponsored printed editions of traditional literary texts—can be seen as a sort of conservative educational program, which also served as a pretext for resisting the pressure of the progressives. Second, the formal ideological programme of the reconstructions always placed the builders of the monuments and the colonial natives in a certain hierarchy. In some cases, as in the Dutch East Indies up until the 1930s, the idea was entertained that the builders were actually not of the same "race" as the natives (they were "really" Indian immigrants).[33] In other cases, as in Burma, what was imagined was a secular decadence, such that contemporary natives were no longer capable of their putative ancestors' achievements. Seen in this light, the reconstructed monuments, juxtaposed with the surrounding rural poverty, said to the natives: Our very presence shows that you have always been, or have long become, incapable of either greatness or self-rule.

The third reason takes us deeper, and closer to the map. We have seen earlier, in our discussion of the "historical map," how colonial regimes began attaching themselves to antiquity as much as conquest, originally for quite straightforward Machiavellian-legalistic reasons. As time passed, however, there was less and less openly brutal talk about right of conquest, and more and more effort to create alternative legitimacies. More and more Europeans were being born in Southeast Asia, and being tempted to make it their home. Monumental archaeology, increasingly linked to tourism, allowed the state to appear as the guardian of a generalized, but also local, Tradition. The old sacred sites were to be incorporated into the map of the colony, and their ancient prestige (which, if this had disappeared, as it often had, the state would attempt to revive) draped around the mappers. This paradoxical situation is nicely illustrated by the fact that the reconstructed monuments often had smartly laid-out lawns around them, and always explanatory tablets, complete with datings, planted here and there. Moreover, they were to be kept empty of people, except for perambulatory tourists (no religious ceremonies or pilgrimages, so far as possible). Museumized this way, they were repositioned as regalia for a *secular* colonial state.

But, as noted above, a characteristic feature of the instrumentalities of this profane state was infinite reproducibility, a reproducibility made technically possible by print and photography, but politico-culturally by the disbelief of the rulers themselves in the real sacredness of local sites. A sort of progression is detectable everywhere: (1) massive, technically sophisticated archaeological reports, complete with dozens of photographs, recording the process of reconstruction of particular, distinct ruins; (2) Lavishly illustrated books for public consumption, including exemplary plates of all the major sites reconstructed *within the colony* (so much the better if, as in the Netherlands Indies, Hindu-Buddhist shrines could be juxtaposed to restored Islamic mosques).[34] Thanks to print-capitalism, a sort of pictorial census of the state's patrimony becomes available, even if at high cost, to the state's subjects; (3) A general logoization, made possible by the profaning processes outlined above. Postage stamps, with their characteristic series—tropical birds, fruits, fauna, why not monuments as well?—are exemplary of this stage. But postcards and schoolroom textbooks follow the same logic. From there it is only a step into the market: Hotel Pagan, Borobudur Fried Chicken, and so on.

While this kind of archaeology, maturing in the age of mechanical reproduction, was profoundly political, it was political at such a deep level that almost everyone, including the personnel of the colonial state (who, by the 1930s, were in most of Southeast Asia 90 per cent native) was unconscious of the fact. It had all become normal and everyday. It was precisely the infinite quotidian reproducibility of its regalia that revealed the real power of the state.

It is probably not too surprising that post-independence states, which exhibited marked continuities with their colonial predecessors, inherited this form of political museumizing. For example, on 9 November 1968, as part of the celebrations commemorating the 15th anniversary of Cambodia's independence, Norodom Sihanouk had a large wood and papier-mâché replica of the great Bayon temple of Angkor displayed in the national sports stadium in Phnom Penh.[35] The replica was exceptionally coarse and crude, but it served its purpose—instant recognizability via a history of colonial-era logoization. "Ah, our Bayon"—but with the memory of French colonial restorers wholly banished. French-reconstructed Angkor Wat, again in "jigsaw" form, became . . . the central symbol of the successive flags of Sihanouk's royalist, Lon Nol's militarist, and Pol Pot's Jacobin regimes.

More striking still is evidence of inheritance at a more popular level. One revealing example is a series of paintings of episodes in the national history commissioned by Indonesia's Ministry of Education in the 1950s. The paintings were to be mass-produced and distributed throughout the primary-school system; young Indonesians were to have on the walls of their classrooms—everywhere— visual representations of their country's past. Most of the backgrounds were done in the predictable sentimental-naturalist style of early-twentieth-century commercial art, and the human figures taken either from colonial-era museum dioramas or from the popular *wayang orang* pseudohistorical folk-drama. The most interesting of the series, however, offered children a representation of the Borobudur. In reality, this colossal monument, with its 504 Buddha images, 1,460 pictorial and 1,212 decorative stone panels, is a fantastic storehouse of ancient Javanese sculpture. But the well-regarded artist imagines the marvel in its ninth century A.D. heyday with instructive perversity. The Borobudur is painted completely white, with not a trace of sculpture visible. Surrounded by well-trimmed lawns and tidy tree-lined avenues, *not a single human being is in sight.*[36] One might argue that this emptiness reflects the unease of a contemporary Muslim painter in the face of an ancient Buddhist reality. But I suspect that what we are really seeing is an unselfconscious lineal descendant of colonial archaeology: the Borobudur as state regalia, and as "of course, that's it" logo. A Borobudur all the more powerful as a sign for national identity because of everyone's awareness of its location in an infinite series of identical Borobudurs.

Interlinked with one another, then, the census, the map and the museum illuminate the late colonial state's style of thinking about its domain. The "warp" of this thinking was a totalizing classificatory grid, which could be applied with endless flexibility to anything under the state's real or contemplated control: peoples, regions, religions, languages, products, monuments, and so forth. The effect of the grid was always to be able to say of anything that it was this, not that; it belonged here, not there. It was bounded, determinate, and therefore—in principle—countable. (The comic classificatory and subclassificatory census boxes entitled "Other" concealed all real-life anomalies by a splendid bureaucratic *trompe l'oeil*). The "weft" was what one could call serialization: the assumption that the world was made up of replicable plurals. The particular always stood as a provisional representative of a series, and was to be handled in this light. This is why the colonial state imagined a Chinese series before any Chinese, and a nationalist series before the appearance of any nationalists.

No one has found a better metaphor for this frame of mind than the great Indonesian novelist Pramoedya Ananta Toer, who entitled the final volume of his tetralogy on the colonial period *Rumah Kaca*—the Glass House. It is an image, as powerful as Bentham's Panopticon, of total surveyability. For the colonial state did not merely aspire to create, under its control, a human landscape of perfect visibility; the condition of this "visibility" was that everyone, everything, had (as it were) a serial number.[37] This style of imagining did not come out of thin air. It was the product of the technologies of navigation, astronomy, horology, surveying, photography and print, to say nothing of the deep driving power of capitalism.

Map and census thus shaped the grammar which would in due course make possible "Burma" and "Burmese," "Indonesia" and "Indonesians." But the concretization of these possibilities—concretizations which have a powerful life today, long after the colonial state has disappeared—owed much to the colonial state's peculiar imagining of history and power. Archaeology was an unimaginable enterprise in precolonial Southeast Asia; it was adopted in uncolonized Siam late in the game, and after the colonial state's manner. It created the series "ancient monuments," segmented within the classificatory, geographic-demographic box "Netherlands Indies," and "British Burma." Conceived within this profane series, each ruin became available for surveillance and infinite replication. As the colonial state's archaeological service made it technically possible to assemble the series in mapped and photographed form, the state itself could regard the series, up historical time, as an album of its ancestors. The key thing was never the specific Borobudur, nor the specific Pagan, in which the state had no substantial interest and with which it had only archaeological connections. The replicable *series*, however, created a historical depth of field which was easily inherited by the state's postcolonial successor. The final logical outcome was the logo—of "Pagan" or "The Philippines," it made little difference—which by its emptiness, contextlessness, visual memorableness, and infinite reproducibility in every direction brought census and map, warp and woof, into an inerasable embrace.

NOTES

1. See Benedict Anderson, *Imagined Communities: Reflections on the Origin and Spread of Nationalism*, rev. ed. (London: Verso, 1991), pp. 113–14.

2. Charles Hirschman, "The Meaning and Measurement of Ethnicity in Malaysia: An Analysis of Census Classifications," *J. of Asian Studies*, 46:3 (August 1987), pp. 552–82; and "The Making of Race in Colonial Malaya: Political Economy and Racial Ideology" *Sociological Forum*, 1:2 (Spring 1986), pp. 330–62.

3. An astonishing variety of "Europeans" were enumerated right through the colonial era. But whereas in 1881 they were still grouped primarily under the headings "resident," "floating," and "prisoners," by 1911 they were fraternizing as members of a (white) race.

It is agreeable that up to the end, the census-makers were visibly uneasy about where to place those they marked as "Jews."

4. William Henry Scott, *Cracks in the Parchment Curtain*, chapter 7, "Filipino Class Structure in the Sixteenth Century."

5. In first half of the seventeenth century, Spanish settlements in the archipelago came under repeated attack from the forces of the Vereenigde Oost-Indische Compagnie, the greatest "transnational" corporation of the era. For their survival, the pious Catholic settlers owed a great debt to the arch-heretical Protector, who kept Amsterdam's back to the wall for much of his rule. Had the VOC been successful, Manila, rather than Batavia [Jakarta], might have become the centre of the "Dutch" imperium in Southeast Asia. In 1762, London seized Manila from Spain, and held it for almost two years. It is entertaining to note that Madrid only got it back in exchange for, of all places, Florida, and the other "Spanish" possessions east of the Mississippi. Had the negotiations proceeded differently, the archipelago could have been politically linked with Malaya and Singapore during the nineteenth century.

6. Mason C. Hoadley, "State vs. Ki Aria Marta Ningrat (1696) and Tian Siangko (1720–21)" (unpublished ms., 1982).

7. See, e.g., Edgar Wickberg, *The Chinese in Philippine Life, 1850–1898*, chapters 1 and 2.

8. The galleon trade—for which Manila was, for over two centuries, the *entrepôt*—exchanged Chinese silks and porcelain for Mexican silver.

9. See chapter 7 of *Imagined Communities* (p. 125) for mention of French colonialism's struggle to sever Buddhism in Cambodia from its old links with Siam.

10. See William Roff, *The Origins of Malay Nationalism*, pp. 72–4.

11. See Harry J. Benda, *The Crescent and the Rising Sun*, chapters 1–2.

12. Thongchai Winichakul, "Siam Mapped: A History of the Geo-Body of Siam" (Ph.D. Thesis, University of Sydney, 1988).

13. Richard Muir, *Modern Political Geography*, p. 119.

14. Thongchai, "Siam Mapped," pp. 105–10, 286.

15. For a full discussion of old conceptions of power in Java (which, with minor differences, corresponded to that existing in Old Siam), see my *Language and Power*, chapter 1.

16. Thongchai, "Siam Mapped," p. 110.

17. David S. Landes, *Revolution in Time: Clocks and the Making of the Modern World*, chapter 9.

18. "Siam Mapped," p. 310.

19. I do not mean merely the inheritance and sale of private property in land in the usual sense. More important was the European practice of political transfers of lands, with their populations, via dynastic marriages. Princesses, on marriage, brought their husbands duchies and petty principalities, and these transfers were formally negotiated and "signed." The tag *Bella gerant alii, tu, felix Austria, nube*! would have been inconceivable for any state in precolonial Asia.

20. See Thongchai, "Siam Mapped," p. 387, on Thai ruling class absorption of this style of imagining. "According to these historical maps, moreover, the geobody is not a modern particularity but is pushed back more than a thousand years. Historical maps thus help reject any suggestion that nationhood emerged only in the recent past, and the perspective that the present Siam was a result of ruptures is precluded. So is any idea that intercourse between Siam and the European powers was the parent of Siam."

21. This adoption was by no means a Machiavellian ruse. The early nationalists in all the Southeast Asian colonies had their consciousnesses profoundly shaped by the "format" of the colonial state and its institutions. See chapter 7 of *Imagined Communities*.

22. In the writings of Nick Joaquín, the contemporary Philippines' preeminent man of letters—and an indubitable patriot—one can see how powerfully the emblem works on the most sophisticated intelligence. Of General Antonio Luna, tragic hero of the anti-American struggle of 1898–99, Joaquín writes that he hurried to "perform the role that had been instinctive in the Creole for three centuries: the defense of *the form* of the Philippines from a foreign disrupter." *A Question of Heroes*, p. 164 (italics added). Elsewhere he observes, astonishingly, that Spain's "Filipino allies, converts, mercenaries sent against the Filipino rebel may have kept the archipelago Spanish and Christian, but they also kept it from falling apart"; and that they "were fighting (whatever the Spaniards may have intended) to keep the Filipino one." Ibid., p. 58.

23. See Robin Osborne, *Indonesia's Secret War, The Guerrilla Struggle in Irian Jaya*, pp. 8–9.

24. Since 1963 there have been many bloody episodes in West New Guinea (now called Irian Jaya–Great Irian), partly as a result of the militarization of the Indonesian state since 1965, partly because of the intermittently effective guerrilla activities of the so-called OPM (Organization for a Free Papua). But these brutalities pale by comparison with Jakarta's savagery in ex-Portuguese East Timor, where in the first three years after the 1976 invasion an estimated one-third of the population of 600,000 died from war, famine, disease and "resettlement." I do not think it a mistake to suggest that the difference derives in part from East Timor's absence from the logos of the Netherlands East Indies and, until 1976, of Indonesia's.

25. Osborne, *Indonesia's Secret War*, p. 2.

26. See *Imagined Communities*, p. 110.

27. The best sign for this is that the anti-Indonesian nationalist guerrilla organization's name, Organisasi Papua Merdeka (OPM), is composed of Indonesian words.

28. In 1811, the East India Company's forces seized all the Dutch possessions in the Indies (Napoléon had absorbed the Netherlands into France the previous year). Raffles ruled in Java till 1815. His monumental *History of Java* appeared in 1817, two years prior to his founding of Singapore.

29. The museumizing of the Borobudur, the largest Buddhist stupa in the world, exemplifies this process. In 1814, the Raffles regime "discovered" it, and had it unjungled. In 1845, the self-promoting German artist-adventurer Schaefer persuaded the Dutch authorities in Batavia to pay him to make the first daguerrotypes. In 1851, Batavia sent a team of state employees, led by civil engineer F. C. Wilsen, to make a systematic survey of the bas-reliefs and to produce a complete, "scientific" set of lithographs. In 1874, Dr. C. Leemans, Director of the Museum of Antiquities in Leiden, published, at the behest of the Minister of Colonies, the first major scholarly monograph; he relied heavily on Wilsen's lithographs, never having visited the site himself. In the 1880s, the professional photographer Cephas produced a thorough modern-style photographic survey. In 1901, the colonial regime established an Oudheidkundige Commissie (Commission on Antiquities). Between 1907 and 1911, the Commission oversaw the complete restoration of the stupa, carried out at state expense by a team under the civil engineer Van Erp. Doubtless in recognition of this success, the Commission was promoted, in 1913, to an Oudheidkundigen Dienst (Antiquities Service), which kept the monument spick and span until the end of the colonial period. See C. Leemans, *Boro-Boudour*, pp. ii–lv; and N. J. Krom, *Inleiding tot de Hindoe-Javaansche Kunst*, I, chapter 1.

30. Viceroy Curzon (1899–1905), an antiquities buff who, writes Groslier, "energized" the Archaeological Survey of India, put things very nicely: "It is . . . equally our duty to dig and discover, to classify, reproduce and describe, to copy and decipher, and to cherish and conserve." (Foucault could not have said it better). In 1899, the Archaeological Department of Burma—then part of British India—was founded, and soon began

the restoration of Pagan. The previous year, the École Française d'Extrême-Orient was established in Saigon, followed almost at once by a Directorate of Museums and Historical Monuments of Indochina. Immediately after the French seizure of Siemreap and Battambang from Siam in 1907, an Angkor Conservancy was established to Curzonize Southeast Asia's most awe-inspiring ancient monuments. See Bernard Philippe Groslier, *Indochina*, pp. 155–7, 174–7. As noted above, the Dutch colonial Antiquities Commission was founded in 1901. The coincidence in dates—1899, 1898, 1901—shows not only the keenness with which the rival colonial powers observed one another, but sea-changes in imperialism under way by the turn of the century. As was to be expected, independent Siam ambled along more slowly. Its Archaeological Service was only set up in 1924, its National Museum in 1926. See Charles Higham, *The Archaeology of Mainland Southeast Asia*, p. 25.

31. The VOC was liquidated, in bankruptcy, in 1799. The colony of the Netherlands Indies, however, dates from 1815, when the independence of The Netherlands was restored by the Holy Alliance, and Willem I of Orange put on a Dutch throne first invented in 1806 by Napoléon and his kindly brother Louis. The British East India Company survived till the great Indian Mutiny of 1857.

32. The Oudheidkundige Commissie was established by the same government that (in 1901) inaugurated the new "Ethical Policy" for the Indies, a policy that for the first time aimed to establish a Western-style system of education for substantial numbers of the colonized. Governor-General Paul Doumer (1897–1902) created both the Directorate of Museums and Historical Monuments of Indochina and the colony's modern educational apparatus. In Burma, the huge expansion of higher education—which between 1900 and 1940 increased the number of secondary-school students eightfold, from 27,401 to 233,543, and of college students twentyfold, from 115 to 2,365—began just as the Archaeological Department of Burma swung into action. See Robert H. Taylor, *The State in Burma*, p. 114.

33. Influenced in part by this kind of thinking, conservative Thai intellectuals, archaeologists, and officials persist to this day in attributing Angkor to the mysterious Khom, who vanished without a trace, and certainly have no connection with today's despised Cambodians.

34. A fine late-blooming example is *Ancient Indonesian Art*, by the Dutch scholar, A. J. Bernet Kempers, self-described as "former Director of Archaeology in Indonesia [sic]." On pages 24–5 one finds maps showing the location of the ancient sites. The first is especially instructive, since its rectangular shape (framed on the east by the 141st Meridian) willy-nilly includes Philippine Mindanao as well as British-Malaysian north Borneo, peninsular Malaya, and Singapore. All are blank of sites, indeed of any naming whatsoever, except for a single, inexplicable "Kedah." The switch from Hindu-Buddhism to Islam occurs after Plate 340.

35. See *Kambuja*, 45 (15 December 1968), for some curious photographs.

36. The discussion here draws on material analysed more fully in *Language and Power*, chapter 5.

37. An exemplary policy-outcome of Glass House imaginings—an outcome of which ex-political prisoner Pramoedya is painfully aware—is the classificatory ID card that all adult Indonesians must now carry at all times. This ID is isomorphic with the census—it represents a sort of political census, with special punchings for those in the sub-series "subversives" and "traitors." It is notable that this style of census was only perfected after the achievement of national independence.

Anne McClintock

Gender and sexuality have not figured prominently in the general literature on nationalism, we may say without fear of contradiction. As the editors of *Nationalisms and Sexualities* rightly observe, neither the relationship between eros and nationalism (love of country) nor the nation's place for women has entered the discussion, and most scholars have tacitly bracketed such questions from their accounts, tending "simply [to] conflate the national with 'public' identity, the sexual with 'private' behavior" (Andrew Parker et al. [eds.], *Nationalisms and Sexualities* [New York: Routledge, 1992], p. 2). The contemporary classics of writing about nationalism—for instance, Gellner, Smith, Hroch, Anderson—maintain a silence regarding the gendered dimension of their subject, and as McClintock says, "theories of nationalism have tended to ignore gender as a category constitutive of nationalism itself." The maleness of the nation's profile is seldom brought to full theorization, and even Anderson's formulation of the nation as a "fraternity" and "a deep, horizontal comradeship" leads to no explicit discussion of the gendered meanings. But just as the homosocial affinities of nationalism become easier to see or discuss, given the readier availability of analytical languages from gay and lesbian studies, so one of the commonest tropes of femininity in nationalist discourse—as the "mother of the nation"—should be easy enough to identify after the last three decades of intensive feminist work in women's history and women's studies. Family has supplied both metaphorical languages and practical objects of policy for nationalist movements and the nation-state, with motherhood constructed as national duty or service. Nationalist movements have made little space for specifically women's interests and demands, either regarding them as secondary concerns and diversions, or maintaining women's place in private and domestic roles, conceding at best the familiar auxiliary activities beyond the edge of politics itself. It is only with great difficulty that women's activism forces the discriminations and inequalities concealed by nationalism's solidarities out into an open arena.

Our own volume reflects this existing lack, as it is only here, well into the book, that such questions are foregrounded in the selected readings. At the same time, part of our intention, in this and in other ways, is to destabilize the classical approaches by presenting a range of further perspectives for their attention. Anne McClintock teaches gender and cultural studies at Columbia University and is the author of *Imperial Leather: Race, Gender, and Sexuality in the Colonial Contest* (London: Routledge, 1994). In this essay, she not only demonstrates the centrality of gender as an analytical term, but by juxtaposing the histories of Afrikaaner nationalism and African nationalism in South Africa she also presents an important diversity in women's relation to nationalist movements, reemphasizing in both cases the invented character of the nationalist discourses concerned.

"No Longer in a Future Heaven": Nationalism, Gender, and Race

> The tribes of the Blackfoot confederacy, living along what is now known as the United States/Canadian border, fleeing northward after a raiding attack, watched with growing amazement as the soldiers of the United States army came to a sudden, magical stop. Fleeing southwards, they saw the same thing happen, as the Canadian mounties reined to an abrupt halt. They came to call this invisible demarcation the "medicine line."
>
> SHARON O'BRIEN

All nationalisms are gendered, all are invented and all are dangerous—dangerous, not in Eric Hobsbawm's sense of having to be opposed but in the sense that they represent relations to political power and to the technologies of violence.[1] Nationalisms are not simply phantasmagoria of the mind; as systems of cultural representation whereby people come to imagine a shared experience of identification with an extended community, they are historical practices through which social difference is both invented and performed.[2] Nationalism becomes in this way radically constitutive of people's identities, through social contests that are frequently violent and always gendered. Yet, if the invented nature of nationalism has found wide theoretical currency, explorations of the gendering of the national imagery have been conspicuously paltry.

Nations are contested systems of cultural representation that limit and legitimize people's access to the resources of the nation-state. But despite many nationalists' investment in the idea of popular unity, nations have historically amounted to the sanctioned institutionalization of gender difference. No nation in the world grants women and men the same access to the rights and resources of the nation-state. Yet, with the notable exception of Frantz Fanon, male theorists have seldom felt moved to explore how nationalism is implicated in gender power. As a result, as Cynthia Enloe remarks, nationalisms have "typically sprung from masculinized memory, masculinized humiliation and masculinized hope."[3] Not

Anne McClintock, " 'No Longer in a Future Heaven': Women and Nationalism in South Africa," *Transition*, 51 (1991), pp. 104–23.

only are the needs of the nation here identified with the frustrations and aspirations of men, but the representation of male national power depends on the prior construction of gender difference. All too often in male nationalisms, gender difference between women and men serves to define symbolically the limits of national difference and power between men. Even Fanon, who at other moments knew better, writes: "The look that the native turns on the settler town is a look of lust . . . to sit at the settler's table, to sleep in the settler's bed, with his wife if possible. The colonized man is an envious man."[4] For Fanon, both colonizer and colonized are here unthinkingly male and the Manichean agon of decolonization is waged over the territoriality of female, domestic space.

Excluded from direct action as national citizens, women are subsumed symbolically into the national body politic as its boundary and metaphoric limit: "Singapore girl, you're a great way to fly." Women are typically constructed as the symbolic bearers of the nation, but are denied any direct relation to national agency. As Elleke Boehmer notes in her fine essay, the "motherland" of male nationalism thus may "not signify 'home' and 'source' to women."[5] Boehmer notes that the male role in the nationalist scenario is typically "metonymic"; that is, men are contiguous with each other and with the national whole. Women, by contrast, appear "in a metaphoric or symbolic role."[6] Yet it is also crucial to note that not all men enjoy the privilege of political contiguity with each other in the national community.

In an important intervention, Nira Yuval-Davis and Floya Anthias identify five major ways in which women have been implicated in nationalism:

- as biological reproducers of the members of national collectivities
- as reproducers of the boundaries of national groups (through restrictions on sexual or marital relations)
- as active transmitters and producers of the national culture
- as symbolic signifiers of national difference
- as active participants in national struggles[7]

Nationalism is thus constituted from the very beginning as a gendered discourse and cannot be understood without a theory of gender power. Nonetheless, theories of nationalism reveal a double disavowal. If male theorists are typically indifferent to the gendering of nations, feminist analyses of nationalism have been lamentably few and far between. White feminists, in particular, have been slow to recognize nationalism as a feminist issue. In much Western, socialist feminism, as Yuval-Davis and Anthias point out, "Issues of ethnicity and nationality have tended to be ignored."[8]

A feminist theory of nationalism might thus be strategically fourfold: (1) investigating the gendered formation of sanctioned male theories; (2) bringing into historical visibility women's active cultural and political participation in national formations; (3) bringing nationalist institutions into critical relation with other social structures and institutions; and (4) at the same time paying scrupulous attention to the structures of racial, ethnic and class power that continue to bedevil privileged forms of feminism.

THE NATIONAL FAMILY OF MAN: A DOMESTIC GENEALOGY

A paradox lies at the heart of most national narratives. Nations are frequently figured through the iconography of familial and domestic space. The term nation derives from *natio*: to be born. We speak of nations as "motherlands" and "fatherlands." Foreigners "adopt" countries that are not their native homes and are naturalized into the national "family." We talk of the "Family of Nations," of "homelands" and "native" lands. In Britain, immigration matters are dealt with at the Home Office; in the United States, the president and his wife are called the First Family. Winnie Mandela was, until her recent fall from grace, honored as South Africa's "Mother of the Nation." In this way, despite their myriad differences, nations are symbolically figured as domestic genealogies. Yet since the midnineteenth century in the West at least, the family itself has been figured as the antithesis of history.

The family trope is important for nationalism in at least two ways. First, it offers a "natural" figure for sanctioning national *hierarchy* within a putative organic *unity* of interests. Second, it offers a "natural" trope for figuring national time. After 1859 and the advent of social Darwinism, Britain's emergent national narrative took increasing shape around the image of the evolutionary Family of Man. The family offered an indispensable metaphoric figure by which national difference could be shaped into a single historical genesis narrative. Yet a curious paradox emerged. The family as a *metaphor* offered a single genesis narrative for national history while, at the same time, the family as an *institution* became void of history and excluded from national power. The family became, at one and the same time, both the organizing figure for national history and its *antithesis*.

In the course of the nineteenth century, the social function of the great service families was displaced onto the national bureaucracies, while the image of the family was projected onto these nationalisms as their shadowy, naturalized form. Since the subordination of woman to man and child to adult was deemed a natural fact, hierarchies within the nation could be depicted in familial terms to guarantee social difference as a category of nature. The metaphoric depiction of social hierarchy as natural and familial—the "national family," the global "family of nations," the colony as a "family of black children ruled over by a white father"—depended in this way on the prior naturalizing of the social subordination of women and children within the domestic sphere.

In modern Europe, citizenship is the legal representation of a person's relationship to the rights and resources of the nation-state. But the putatively universalist concept of national citizenship becomes unstable when seen from the position of women. In post–French revolution Europe, women were incorporated directly into the nation-state not directly as citizens, but only indirectly, through men, as dependent members of the family in private and public law. The Code Napoléon was the first modern statute to decree that the wife's nationality should follow her husband's, an example other European countries briskly followed. A woman's *political* relation to the nation was thus submerged as a *social* relation to a man through marriage. For women, citizenship in the nation was mediated by the marriage relation within the family. This chapter is directly concerned with the consequences for women of this uneven gendering of the national citizen.

THE GENDERING OF NATION TIME

A number of critics have followed Tom Nairn in naming the nation "the modern Janus."[9] For Nairn, the nation takes shape as a contradictory figure of time: one face gazing back into the primordial mists of the past, the other into an infinite future. Deniz Kandiyoti expresses the temporal contradiction with clarity: "[Nationalism] presents itself both as a modern project that melts and transforms traditional attachments in favour of new identities and as a reflection of authentic cultural values culled from the depths of a presumed communal past."[10] Bhabha, following Nairn and Anderson, writes: "Nations, like narratives, lose their origins in the myths of time and only fully realize their horizons in the mind's eye."[11] Bhabha and Anderson borrow here from Walter Benjamin's crucial insight into the temporal paradox of modernity. For Benjamin, a central feature of nineteenth-century industrial capitalism was the "use of archaic images to identify what was historically new about the 'nature' of commodities."[12] In Benjamin's insight, the mapping of Progress depends on systematically inventing images of archaic time to identify what is historically new about enlightened, national progress. Anderson can thus ask: "Supposing 'antiquity' were, at a certain historical juncture, the *necessary consequence* of 'novelty'?"[13]

What is less often noticed, however, is that the temporal anomaly within nationalism—veering between nostalgia for the past and the impatient, progressive sloughing off of the past—is typically resolved by figuring the contradiction in the representation of time as a natural division of gender. Women are represented as the atavistic and authentic body of national tradition (inert, backward-looking and natural), embodying nationalism's conservative principle of continuity. Men, by contrast, represent the progressive agent of national modernity (forward-thrusting, potent and historic), embodying nationalism's progressive, or revolutionary, principle of discontinuity. Nationalism's anomalous relation to time is thus managed as a natural relation to gender.

In the nineteenth century, the social evolutionists secularized time and placed it at the disposal of the national, imperial project. The axis of time was projected onto the axis of space and history became global. Now not only natural space but also historical time was collected, measured and mapped onto a global science of the surface. In the process history, especially national and imperial history, took on the character of a spectacle.

Secularizing time has a threefold significance for nationalism. First figured in the evolutionists' global Family Tree, the world's discontinuous nations appear to be marshaled within a single, hierarchical European Ur-narrative. Second, national history is imaged as naturally teleological, an organic process of upward growth, with the European nation as the apogee of world progress. Third, inconvenient discontinuities are ranked and subordinated into a hierarchical structure of branching time—the progress of "racially" different nations mapped against the tree's self-evident boughs, with "lesser nations" destined, by nature, to perch on its lower branches.

National time is thus not only *secularized*, it is also *domesticated*. Social evolutionism and anthropology gave to national politics a concept of natural time as familial. In the image of the Family Tree, evolutionary progress was represented as a series of anatomically distinct family types, organized into a linear procession, from the "childhood" of "primitive" races to the enlightened "adulthood" of European imperial nationalism. Violent national change takes on the character of an evolving spectacle under the organizing rubric of the family. The merging of the racial evolutionary Tree and the gendered family into the Family Tree of Man provided scientific racism with a simultaneously gendered and racial image through which it could popularize the idea of linear national Progress.

Britain's emerging national narrative gendered time by figuring women (like the colonized and the working class) as inherently atavistic—the conservative repository of the national archaic. Women were not seen as inhabiting history proper but existing, like colonized peoples, in a permanently anterior time within the modern nation. White, middle-class men, by contrast, were seen to embody the forward-thrusting agency of national progress. Thus the figure of the national Family of Man reveals a persistent paradox. National Progress (conventionally the invented domain of male, public space) was figured as familial, while the family itself (conventionally the domain of private, female space) was figured as beyond history.

One can safely say, at this point, that there is no single narrative of the nation. Different groups (genders, classes, ethnicities, generations and so on) do not experience the myriad national formations in the same way. Nationalisms are invented, performed and consumed in ways that do not follow a universal blueprint. At the very least, the breathtaking Eurocentricism of Hobsbawm's dismissal of Third World nationalisms warrants sustained criticism. In a gesture of sweeping condescension, Hobsbawm nominates Europe as nationalism's "original home," while "all the anti-imperial movements of any significance" are unceremoniously dumped into three categories: mimicry of Europe, anti-Western xenophobia and the "natural high spirits of martial tribes."[14] By way of contrast, it might be useful to turn at this point to Frantz Fanon's quite different, if also problematic, analysis of the gendering of the national formation.

FANON AND GENDER AGENCY

As male theorists of nationalism go, Frantz Fanon is exemplary, not only for recognizing gender as a formative dimension of nationalism but also for recognizing—and immediately rejecting—the Western metaphor of the nation as a family. "There are close connections," he observes in *Black Skin, White Masks*, "between the structure of the family and the structure of the nation."[15] Refusing, however, to collude with the notion of the familial metaphor as natural and normative, Fanon instead understands it as a cultural projection ("the characteristics of the family are projected onto the social environment'') that has very different consequences for families placed discrepantly within the colonial hierarchy.[16] "A normal Negro child, having grown up within a normal family, will become abnormal on the slightest contact with the white world."[17]

The challenge of Fanon's insight is threefold. He throws radically into question the naturalness of nationalism as a domestic genealogy. At the same time, he reads familial normality as a product of social power—indeed, of social violence. Fanon is remarkable for recognizing, in this early text, how military violence and the authority of a centralized state borrow on and enlarge the domestication of gender power within the family: "Militarization and the centralization of authority in a country automatically entail a resurgence of the authority of the father."[18]

Perhaps one of Fanon's most provocative ideas is his challenge to any easy relation of identity between the psychodynamics of the unconscious and the psychodynamics of political life. The audacity of his insight is that it allows one to ask whether the psychodynamics of colonial power and of anti-colonial subversion can be interpreted by deploying (without mediation) the same concepts and techniques used to interpret the psychodynamics of the unconscious. If the family is not "a miniature of the nation," are metaphoric projections from family life (the Lacanian "Law of the Father," say) adequate for an understanding of colonial or anticolonial power? Fanon himself seems to say no. Relations between the individual unconscious and political life are, I argue, neither separable from each other nor reducible to each other. Instead, they comprise crisscrossing and dynamic mediations, reciprocally and untidily transforming each other, rather than duplicating a relation of structural analogy.

Even in *Black Skin, White Masks,* the most psychological of Fanon's texts, he insists that racial alienation is a "double process."[19] First, it "entails an immediate recognition of social and economic realities." Then, it entails the "internalization" of inferiority. Racial alienation, in other words, is not only an "individual question" but also involves what Fanon calls a "sociodiagnostic."[20] Reducing Fanon to a purely formal psychoanalysis, or a purely structural Marxism, risks foreclosing precisely those suggestive tensions that animate, in my view, the most subversive elements of his work. These tensions are nowhere more marked than in his tentative exploration of the gendering of national agency.

Gender runs like a multiple fissure through Fanon's work, splitting and displacing the "Manichean delirium" to which he repeatedly returns. For Fanon, the colonial agon appears, at first, to be fundamentally Manichean. In *Black Skin, White Masks,* he sees colonial space as divided into "two camps: the white and the black."[21] Nearly a decade later, writing from the crucible of the Algerian resistance in *The Wretched of the Earth,* Fanon once again sees anticolonial nationalism as erupting from the violent Manicheanism of a colonial world "cut in two," its boundaries walled by barracks and police stations.[22] Colonial space is split by a pathological geography of power, separating the bright, well-fed settler's town from the hungry, crouching casbah: "This world ... cut in two is inhabited by two different species."[23] As Edward Said puts it: "From this Manichean and physically grounded statement Fanon's entire work follows, set in motion, so to speak, by the native's violence, a force intended to bridge the gap between white and non-white."[24] Yet the fateful chiaroscuro of race is at almost every turn disrupted by the criss-crossings of gender.

Fanon's Manichean agon appears at first to be fundamentally male: "There can be no further doubt that the real Other for the white man is and will continue to be the black man." As Homi Bhabha writes: "It is always in relation to the place of the Other that colonial desire is articulated."[25] But Fanon's anguished musings on race and sexuality disclose that "colonial desire" is not the same for men and women: "Since he is the master and more simply the male, the white man can allow himself the luxury of sleeping with many women .... But when a white woman accepts a black man there is automatically a romantic aspect. It is a giving, not a seizing."[26] Leaving aside, for the moment, Fanon's complicity with the stereotype of women as romantically rather than sexually inclined, as giving rather than taking, Fanon opens race to a problematics of sexuality that reveals far more intricate entanglements than a mere doubling of "the Otherness of the Self." The psychological Manicheanism of *Black Skin, White Masks* and the more political Manicheanism of *The Wretched of the Earth* are persistently inflected by gender in such a way as to radically disrupt the binary dialectic.

For Fanon, the envy of the black man takes the form of a fantasy of territorial displacement: "The fantasy of the native is precisely to occupy the master's place."[27] This fantasy can be called a *politics of substitution*. Fanon knows, however, that the relation to the white woman is altogether different: "When my restless hands caress those white breasts, they grasp white civilization and dignity and make them mine."[28] The white woman is seized, possessed and taken hold of, not as an act of *substitution*, but as an act of *appropriation*. However, Fanon does not bring this critical distinction between a politics of substitution and a politics of appropriation into explicit elaboration as a theory of gender power.

As Bhabha astutely observes, Fanon's *Black Skin, White Masks* is inflected by a "palpable pressure of division and displacement"—though gender is a form of self-division that Bhabha himself fastidiously declines to explore.[29] Bhabha would have us believe that "Fanon's use of the word 'man' usually connotes a phenomenological quality of humanness, inclusive of man and woman."[30] But this claim is not borne out by Fanon's texts. Potentially generic terms like "the Negro" or "the Native"—syntactically unmarked for gender—are almost everywhere immediately contextually marked as male: "Sometimes people wonder that the native, rather than giving his wife a dress, buys instead a transistor radio"[31] ". . . the Negro who wants to go to bed with a white woman"[32] ". . . the Negro who is viewed as a penis symbol."[33] The generic category "native" does not include women; women are merely possessed by the (male) native as an appendage: "When the native is tortured, when his wife is killed or raped, he complains to no one."[34]

For Fanon, colonized men inhabit "two places at once." If so, how many places do colonized women inhabit? Certainly, Bhabha's text is not one of them. Except for a cursory appearance in one paragraph, women haunt Bhabha's analysis as an elided shadow—deferred, displaced and dis-remembered. Bhabha concludes his eloquent meditation on Fanon with the overarching question: "How can the human world live its difference? how can a human being live Otherwise?"[35] Yet immediately appended to his foreword appears a peculiar Note. In it Bhabha announces, without apology, that the "crucial issue" of the woman of color "goes well beyond the scope" of his foreword. Yet its scope, as he himself insists, is bounded by nothing less than the question of humanity: "How can the human world live its difference? how can a human being live Other-wise?" Apparently, the question of the woman of color falls beyond the question of human difference, and Bhabha is content simply to "note the importance of the problem" and leave it at that. Bhabha's belated note on gender appears after his authorial signature, after the time and date of his essay. Women are thus effectively deferred to a nowhere land, beyond time and place, outside theory. If, indeed, "the state of emergency is also a state of emergence," the question remains whether the national state of emergency turns out to be a state of emergence for women at all.[36]

To ask "the question of the subject" ("What does a man want? What does the black man want?"), while postponing a theory of gender, presumes that subjectivity itself is neutral with respect to gender.[37] From the limbo of the male afterthought, however, gender returns to challenge the male question not as women's "lack," but as that excess that the masculine "Otherness" of the Self can neither admit nor fully elide. This presumption is perhaps nowhere more evident than in Fanon's remarkable meditations on the gendering of the national revolution.

At least two concepts of national agency shape Fanon's vision. His anticolonial project is split between a Hegelian vision of colonizer and colonized locked in a life-and-death conflict and an altogether more complex and unsteady view of agency. These paradigms slide discrepantly against each other throughout his work, giving rise to a number of internal fissures. These fissures appear most visibly in his analysis of gender as a category of social power.

On the one hand, Fanon draws on a Hegelian metaphysics of agency inherited, by and large, through Jean-Paul Sartre and the French academy. In this view, anticolonial nationalism irrupts violently and irrevocably into history as the logical counterpart to colonial power. This nationalism is, as Edward Said puts it, "cadenced and stressed from beginning to end with the accents and inflections of liberation."[38] It is a liberation, moreover, that is structurally guaranteed, immanent in the binary logic of the Manichean dialectic. This metaphysics speaks, as Terry Eagleton nicely phrases it, "of the entry into full self-realization of a unitary subject known as the people."[39] Nonetheless, the privileged national agents are urban, male, vanguardist and violent. The progressive nature of the violence is preordained and sanctioned by the structural logic of Hegelian progress.

This kind of nationalism can be called an anticipatory nationalism. Eagleton calls it nationalism "in the subjunctive mood," a premature utopianism that "grabs instinctively for a future, projecting itself by an act of will or imagination beyond the compromised political structures of the present."[40] Yet, ironically, anticipatory nationalism often claims legitimacy by appealing precisely to the august figure of inevitable progress inherited from the Western societies it seeks to dismantle.

Alongside this Manichean, mechanical nationalism, however, appears an altogether more open-ended and strategically difficult view of national agency. This nationalism stems not from the inexorable machinery of Hegelian dialectics but from the messy and disobliging circumstances of Fanon's own activism, as well as from the often dispiriting lessons of the anticolonial revolutions that preceded him. In this view, agency is multiple rather than unitary, unpredictable rather than immanent, bereft of dialectical guarantees and animated by an unsteady and nonlinear relation to time. There is no preordained rendezvous with victory; no single, undivided national subject; no immanent historical logic. The national project must be laboriously and sometimes catastrophically invented, with unforeseen results. Time is dispersed and agency is heterogeneous. Here, in the unsteady, sliding interstices between conflicting national narratives, women's national agency makes its uncertain appearance.

In "Algeria Unveiled," Fanon ventriloquizes—only to refute—the long Western dream of colonial conquest as an erotics of ravishment. Under the hallucinations of empire, the Algerian woman is seen as the living flesh of the national body, unveiled and laid bare for the colonials' lascivious grip, revealing "piece by piece, the flesh of Algeria laid bare."[41] In this remarkable essay, Fanon recognizes the colonial gendering of women as symbolic mediators, the boundary markers of an agon that is fundamentally male. The Algerian woman is "an intermediary between obscure forces and the group."[42] "The young Algerian woman . . . establishes a link," he writes.[43]

Fanon understands brilliantly how colonialism inflicts itself as a domestication of the colony, a reordering of the labor and sexual economy of the people, so as to divert female power into colonial hands and disrupt the patriarchal power of colonized men. Fanon ventriloquizes colonial thinking: "If we want to destroy the structure of Algerian society, its capacity for resistance, we must first of all conquer the women."[44] His insight here is that the dynamics of colonial power are fundamentally, though not solely, the dynamics of gender: "It is the situation of women that was accordingly taken as the theme of action."[45] Yet, in his work as a whole, Fanon fails to bring these insights into theoretical focus.

Long before Anderson, Fanon recognizes the inventedness of national community. He also recognizes the power of nationalism as a scopic politics, most visibly embodied in the power of sumptuary customs to fabricate a sense of national unity: "It is by their apparel that types of society first become known."[46] Fanon perceives, moreover, that nationalism, as a politics of visibility, implicates women and men in different ways. Because, for male nationalists, women serve as the visible markers of national homogeneity, they become subjected to especially vigilant and violent discipline. Hence the intense emotive politics of dress.

Yet a curious rupture opens in Fanon's text over the question of women's agency. At first, Fanon recognizes the historical meaning of the veil as open to the subtlest shifts and subversions. From the outset, colonials tried to grant Algerian women a traitorous agency, affecting to rescue them from the sadistic thrall of Algerian men. But, as Fanon knows, the colonial masquerade of giving women power by unveiling them was merely a ruse for achieving "a real power over the man."[47] Mimicking the colonial masquerade, militant Algerian women deliberately began to unveil themselves. Believing their own ruse, colonials at first misread the unveiled Algerian women as pieces of "sound currency" circulating between the casbah and the white city, mistaking them for the visible coinage of cultural conversion.[48] For the *Fidaï*, however, the militant woman was "his arsenal," a technique of counterinfiltration, duplicitously penetrating the body of the enemy with the armaments of death.

So eager is Fanon to deny the colonial rescue fantasy that he refuses to grant the veil any prior role at all in the gender dynamics of Algerian society. Having refused the colonial's desire to invest the veil with an essentialist meaning (the sign of women's servitude), he bends over backward to insist on the veil's semiotic innocence in Algerian society. The veil, Fanon writes, was no more than "a formerly inert element of the native cultural configuration."[49] At once the veil loses its historic mutability and becomes a fixed, "inert" element in Algerian culture: "an undifferentiated element in a homogeneous whole."[50] Fanon denies the "historic dynamism of the veil" and banishes its intricate history to a footnote, from where, however, it displaces the main text with the insistent force of selfdivision and denial.[51]

Fanon's thoughts on women's agency proceed through a series of contradictions. Where, for Fanon, does women's agency begin? He takes pains to point out that women's militancy does not precede the national revolution. Algerian women are not self-motivating agents, nor do they have prior histories or consciousness of revolt from which to draw. Their initiation in the revolution is learned, but it is not learned from other women or from other societies, nor is it transferred analogously from local feminist grievances. The revolutionary mission is "without apprenticeship, without briefing."[52] The Algerian woman learns her "revolutionary mission instinctively."[53] This theory is not, however, a theory of feminist spontaneity, for women learn their militancy only at men's invitation. Theirs is a *designated agency*—an agency by invitation only. Before the national uprising, women's agency was null, void, inert as the veil. Here Fanon colludes not only with the stereotype of women as bereft of historical motivation, but he also resorts, uncharacteristically, to a reproductive image of natural birthing: "It is an authentic birth in a pure state."[54]

Why were women invited into the revolution? Fanon resorts immediately to a mechanistic determinism. The ferocity of the war was such, the urgency so great, that sheer structural necessity dictated the move: "The revolutionary wheels had assumed such proportions; the mechanism was running at a given rate. The machine would have to be complicated."[55] Female militancy, in short, is simply a passive offspring of male agency and the structural necessity of the war. The problem of women's agency, so brilliantly raised as a question, is abruptly foreclosed.

Women's agency for Fanon is thus agency by designation. It makes its appearance not as a direct political relation to the revolution but as a mediated, domestic relation to a man: "At the beginning, it was the married women who were contacted. Later, widows or divorced women were designated."[56] Women's first relation to the revolution is constituted as a domestic one. But domesticity, here, also constitutes a relation of possession. The militant was, in the beginning, obliged to keep "his woman" in "absolute ignorance."[57] As designated agents, moreover, women do not commit themselves: "It is relatively easy to commit oneself . . . . The matter is a little more difficult when it involves designating someone."[58] Fanon does not consider the possibility of women committing themselves to action. He thus manages women's agency by resorting to contradictory frames: the authentic, instinctive birth of nationalist fervor; the mechanical logic of revolutionary necessity; male designation. In this way, the possibility of a distinctive feminist agency is never broached.

Once he has contained women's militancy in this way, Fanon applauds women for their "exemplary constancy, self-mastery and success."[59] Nonetheless, his descriptions of women teem with instrumentalist similes and metaphors. Women are not women, they are "fish"; they are "the group's lighthouse and barometer," the *Fidaï's* "women-arsenal."[60] Most tellingly, Fanon resorts to a curiously eroticized image of militarized sexuality. Carrying the men's pistols, guns and grenades beneath her skirts, "the Algerian woman penetrates a little further into the flesh of the Revolution."[61] Here, the Algerian woman is not a victim of rape but a masculinized rapist. As if to contain the unmanning threat of armed women—in their dangerous crossings—Fanon masculinizes the female militant, turning her into a phallic substitute, detached from the male body but remaining, still, the man's "woman-arsenal." Most tellingly, however, Fanon describes the phallic woman as penetrating the flesh of the "revolution," not the flesh of the colonials. This odd image suggests an unbidden fear of emasculation, a dread that the arming of women might entail a fatal unmanning of Algerian men. A curious instability of gender power is here effected as the women are figured as masculinized and the male revolution is penetrated.

Fanon's vision of the political role of the Algerian family in the national uprising likewise proceeds through contradiction. Having brilliantly shown how the family constitutes the first ground of the colonial onslaught, Fanon seeks to reappropriate it as an arena of nationalist resistance. Yet the broader implications of the politicizing of family life are resolutely naturalized after the revolution. Having recognized that women "constituted for a long time the fundamental strength of the occupied," Fanon is reluctant to acknowledge any gender conflict or feminist grievance within the family prior to the anticolonial struggle, or after the national revolution.[62] Although, on the one hand, he admits that in "the Algerian family, the girl is always a notch behind the boy," he quickly insists that she is assigned to this position "without being humiliated or neglected."[63] Although the men's words are "Law," women "voluntarily" submit themselves to "a form of existence limited in scope."[64]

The revolution shakes the "old paternal assurance" so that the father no longer knows "how to keep his balance," and the woman "ceased to be a complement for man."[65] It is telling, moreover, that in his analysis of the family, the category of mother does not exist. Women's liberation is credited entirely to national liberation and it is only with nationalism that women "enter into history." Prior to nationalism, women have no history, no resistance, no independent agency.[66] And since the national revolution automatically revolutionizes the family, gender conflict naturally vanishes after the revolution. Feminist agency, then, is contained by and subordinated to national agency, and the heterosexual family is preserved as the "truth" of society—its organic, authentic form. The family is revolutionalized, taken to a higher plane through a Hegelian vision of transcendence, but the rupturing force of gender is firmly foreclosed: "The family emerges strengthened from this ordeal."[67] Women's militancy is contained within the postrevolutionary frame of the reformed, heterosexual family, as the natural image of national life.

In the postrevolutionary period, moreover, the tenacity of the father's "unchallengeable and massive authority" is not raised as one of the "pitfalls" of the national consciousness.[68] The Manichean dialectic—as generating an inherently resistant agency—does not, it seems, apply to gender. Deeply reluctant as he is to see women's agency apart from national agency, Fanon does not foresee the degree to which the Algerian National Liberation Front (FLN) will seek to co-opt and control women, subordinating them unequivocally once the revolution is won.

A feminist investigation of national difference might, by contrast, take into account the dynamic social and historical contexts of national struggles; their strategic mobilizing of popular forces; their myriad, varied trajectories; and their relation to other social institutions. We might do well to develop a more theoretically complex and strategically subtle genealogy of nationalisms.

With these theoretical remarks in mind, I wish now to turn to the paradoxical relation between the invented constructions of family and nation as they have taken shape within South Africa in both black and white women's contradictory relations to the competing national genealogies. In South Africa, certainly, the competing Afrikaner and African nationalisms have had both distinct and overlapping trajectories, with very different consequences for women.

NATIONALISM AS FETISH SPECTACLE

Until the 1860s, Britain had scant interest in its unpromising colony at the southern tip of Africa. Only upon the discovery of diamonds (1867) and gold (1886) were the Union Jack and the redcoats shipped out with any real sense of imperial mission. But very quickly, mining needs for cheap labor and a centralized state collided with traditional farming interests and out of these contradictions, in the conflict for control over African land and labor, exploded the Anglo-Boer War of 1899–1902.

Afrikaner nationalism was a doctrine of crisis. After their defeat by the British, the bloodied remnants of the scattered Boer communities had to forge a new counterculture if they were to survive in the emergent capitalist state. From the outset, this counterculture had a clear class component. When the Boer generals and the British capitalists swore blood-brotherhood in the Union of 1910, the ragtag legion of "poor whites" with few or no prospects, the modest clerks and shopkeepers, the small farmers and poor teachers, the intellectuals and petite bourgeoisie, all precarious in the new state, began to identify themselves as the vanguard of a new Afrikanerdom, the chosen emissaries of the national volk.[69]

However, Afrikaners had no monolithic identity to begin with, no common historic purpose and no single unifying language. They were a disunited, scattered people, speaking a medley of High Dutch and local dialects, with smatterings of the slave, Nguni and Khoisan languages—scorned as the kombuistaal (kitchen-language) of house-servants, slaves and women. Afrikaners therefore had, quite literally, to invent themselves. The new, invented community of the volk required the conscious creation of a single print-language, a popular press and a literate populace. At the same time, the invention of tradition required a class of cultural brokers and image-makers to do the inventing. The "language movement" of the early twentieth century, in a flurry of poems, magazines, newspapers, novels and countless cultural events, provided just such an invention, fashioning the myriad Boer vernaculars into a single identifiable Afrikaans language. In the early decades of the twentieth century, as Isabel Hofmeyer has brilliantly shown, an elaborate labor of "regeneration" was undertaken as the despised Hotnotstaal (Hottentot's language) was revamped and purged of its rural, "degenerate" associations and elevated to the status of the august mother-tongue of the Afrikaner people. In 1918, Afrikaans achieved legal recognition as a language.[70]

At the same time, the invention of Afrikaner tradition had a clear gender component. In 1918 a small, clandestine clique of Afrikaner men launched a secret society with the express mission of capturing the loyalties of dispirited Afrikaners and fostering white male business power. The tiny, white brotherhood swiftly burgeoned into a secret countrywide mafia that came to exert enormous power over all aspects of Nationalist policy.[71] The gender bias of the society, as of Afrikanerdom as a whole, is neatly summed up in its name: the Broederbond (the Brotherhood). Henceforth, Afrikaner nationalism would be synonymous with white male interests, white male aspirations and white male politics. Indeed, in a recent effort to shore up its waning power, the Broederbond has decided to admit so-called colored Afrikaans speakers into the brotherhood. All women will, however, continue to be barred.

In the voluminous Afrikaner historiography, the history of the volk is organized around a male national narrative figured as an imperial journey into empty lands . . . [T]he myth of the empty land is simultaneously the myth of the virgin land—effecting a double erasure. But the empty lands are in fact peopled, so the contradiction is contained by the invention, once more, of anachronistic space. The colonial journey is figured as proceeding forward in geographical space, but backward in racial and gender time, to a prehistoric zone of linguistic, racial and gender degeneration. At the heart of the continent, a historic agon is staged as degenerate Africans "falsely" claim entitlement to the land. A divinely organized military conflict baptizes the nation in a male birthing ritual, which grants to white men the patrimony of land and history. The white nation emerges as the progeny of male history through the motor of military might. Nonetheless, at the center of the imperial gospel stands the contradictory figure of the volksmoeder, the mother of the nation.

INVENTING THE ARCHAIC: THE TWEEDE (SECOND) TREK

The animating emblem of Afrikaner historiography is the Great Trek, and each trek is figured as a family presided over by a single, epic male patriarch. In 1938, two decades after the recognition of Afrikaans as a language, an epic extravaganza of invented tradition enflamed Afrikanerdom into a delirium of nationalist passion. Dubbed the *Tweede Trek* (second trek), or the *Eeufees* (centenary), the event celebrated the Boers' first mutinous Great Trek in 1838 away from British laws and the effrontery of slave emancipation. The Centenary also commemorated the Boer massacre of the Zulus at the Battle of Blood River. Nine replicas of Voortrekker wagons were built in a vivid example of the reinvention of the archaic to sanction modernity. Each wagon was literally baptized and named after a male Voortrekker hero. No wagon was named after an adult woman, although one was called, generically, *Vrou en Moeder* (wife and mother). This wagon, creaking across the country, symbolized woman's relation to the nation as indirect, mediated through her social relation to men, her national identity lying in her unpaid services and sacrifices, through husband and family, to the *volk*.

Each wagon became the microcosm of colonial society at large: the whip-wielding white patriarch prancing on horseback, black servants toiling alongside, white mother and children sequestered in the wagon—the women's starched white bonnets signifying the purity of the race, the decorous surrender of their sexuality to the patriarch and the invisibility of white female labor.

The wagons rumbled along different routes from Cape Town to Pretoria, sparking along the way an orgy of national pageantry and engulfing the country in a four-month spectacle of invented tradition and fetish ritual. Along the way, white men grew beards and white women donned the ancestral bonnets. Huge crowds gathered to greet the trekkers. As the wagons passed through the towns, babies were named after trekker heroes, as were roads and public buildings. Not a few girls were baptized with the improbable but popular favorites: *Eeufesia* (Centenaria) or *Ossewania* (from *ossewa*, ox wagon). Children scrambled to rub grease from the wagon axles onto their handkerchiefs. The affair climaxed in Pretoria in a spectacular marathon with Third Reich overtones, led by thousands of Afrikaner boy scouts bearing flaming torches.

The first point about the *Tweede Trek* is that it invented white nationalist traditions and celebrated unity where none had existed before, creating the illusion of a collective identity through the political staging of vicarious spectacle. The second point is that the Nationalists adopted this ploy from the Nazis. The *Tweede Trek* was inspired not only by the Nazi creed of *Blut und Boden* but by a new political style: the Nürenberg politics of fetish symbol and cultural persuasion.

In our time, national collectivity is experienced preeminently through spectacle. Here I depart from Anderson, who sees nationalism as emerging primarily from the Gutenberg technology of print capitalism. Anderson neglects the fact that print capital has, until recently, been accessible to a relatively small literate elite. Indeed, the singular power of nationalism since the late nineteenth century, I suggest, has been its capacity to organize a sense of popular, collective unity through the management of mass national *commodity spectacle*.

In this respect, I argue, nationalism inhabits the realm of fetishism. Despite the commitment of European nationalism to the idea of the nation-state as the embodiment of rational progress, nationalism has been experienced and transmitted primarily through fetishism—precisely the cultural form that the Enlightenment denigrated as the antithesis of Reason. More often than not, nationalism takes shape through the visible, ritual organization of fetish objects—flags, uniforms, airplane logos, maps, anthems, national flowers, national cuisines and architectures as well as through the organization of collective fetish spectacle—in team sports, military displays, mass rallies, the myriad forms of popular culture and so on. Far from being purely phallic icons, fetishes embody crises in social value, which are projected onto and embodied in what can be called impassioned objects. Considerable work remains to be done on the ways in which women consume, refuse or negotiate the male fetish rituals of national spectacle.

The *Eeufees* was, by anyone's standards, a triumph of fetish management, from the spectacular regalia of flags, flaming torches and patriotic songs to incendiary speeches, archaic costumes and the choreographing of crowd spectacle and everywhere visible the unifying fetish of the wagon. More than anything, the *Eeufees* revealed the extent to which nationalism is a theatrical performance of invented community: the *Eeufees* was a calculated and self-conscious effort by the *Broederbond* to paper over the myriad regional, gender and class tensions that threatened it. As a fetishistic displacement of difference, it succeeded famously, for the *Tweede Trek's* success in mobilizing a sense of white Afrikaner collectivity where none before existed was a major reason, though certainly not the only one, for the Nationalists' triumphant sweep to power in 1948.[72]

Yet, as Albert Grundlingh and Hilary Sapire note, historians have shown scant interest in explaining the overwhelming emotional euphoria elicited by the celebrations, tending instead to collude with the mythologizing of Afrikaners as inherently atavistic and temperamentally given to quaint anthropological rituals.[73] Certainly, as Grundlingh and Sapire suggest, "it was economic insecurity . . . that made Afrikaners susceptible to the cultural and political blandishments of the 'second Trek.' "[74] The idea of the symbolic trek had originated amongst the recently urbanized Afrikaner railway workers, who had very good reason to feel that their position was precarious in the new English-dominated state. Very quickly, moreover, the insecure scattering of Afrikaans-speaking petit bourgois professionals and intellectuals—teachers, civil servants, lawyers, members of the clergy, writers and academics—eagerly embraced their vocation of choreographing the symbolic trek, with all the renewed prominence and prestige that attended their status as cultural brokers imbued with the mission of unifying the *volk*.

Nonetheless, the *Tweede Trek* was not simply the lurid, melodramatic offspring of ethnic insecurity and class fission. Grundlingh and Sapire point out that there were rival mythologies—socialism and "South Africanism" being the most prominent—that were as eager to capture the loyalties of the poor whites. The *Tweede Trek*, however, enjoyed a number of stunning advantages. For those dispirited and disoriented Afrikaners, who had so recently trekked from the rural areas to the mines, railyards and sweatshops of urban South Africa, the *Tweede Trek* offered a potent symbolic amalgam of disjointed times, capturing in a single fetish spectacle the impossible confluence of the modern and the archaic, the recent displacement and the ancestral migration.

Rather than enacting a backward-looking, atavistic ceremony of ancestral cult worship, the *Tweede Trek* can rather be read as an exemplary act of modernity: a theatrical performance of Benjamin's insight into the evocation of archaic images to identify what is new about modernity. Photographs of the *Eeufees* vividly capture the doubling of time consequent upon this evocation of the archaic, as anachronistic ox-wagons jostle amongst the motorcars and women in white *kappies* mingle with the modern urban crowd. Unlike socialism, then, the *Tweede Trek* could evoke a resonant archive of popular memory and a spectacular iconography of historical travail and fortitude, providing not only the historical dimension necessary for national invention but also a theatrical stage for the collective acting out of the traumas and privations of industrial dislocation.

The *Tweede Trek* also dramatized a crisis in the poetics of historical time. The ox-wagon embodied two distinct notions of time. First, it represented the linear time of imperial progress, figured as a forward-thrusting journey traced across the space of the landscape, obedient to the unfolding telos of racial advance and the rational mapping of measurable space. Second, it embodied in the same fetish object of the wagon a quite different notion of recurring, nonlinear time: the divinely preordained event rehearsed once more in the zone of historical nature. For recently urbanized Afrikaners, these two overlapping, but conflictual, figures of time: pastoral, cyclical time (the time of rural nostalgia) and modern, industrial time (the time of mechanical simulacrum and repetition) were marvelously embodied in the single icon of the ox-wagon.

As they passed through towns, the wagons were driven through wet concrete to immemorialize their tracks, petrifying history as an urban fossil—exemplifying the modern compulsion to collect time in the form of an object; history as palimpsest: "in such a way," as Theodor Adorno put it, "that what is natural emerges as a sign for history and history, where it appears most historical, appears as a sign for nature."[75]

The *Tweede Trek* had another advantage. Tom Nairn has pointed out, in the British context: "Mobilization had to be in terms of what was there; and the whole point of the dilemma was that there was nothing there—none of the economic and political institutions of modernity. The middle-classes, therefore, had to function through a sentimental culture sufficiently accessible to the lower strata now being called to battle."[76] Lacking control of the institutions of modernity, Afrikaners mobilized through the one institution with which they were intimate and over which they still held precarious control: the family. Not only was much of the folk-memory and sentimental culture of the Great Trek fostered through the family, but its centralizing iconography and the epic social unit was familial. Perhaps this also goes some way toward explaining the zest with which Afrikaner women participated in the national pageantry that would soon write them out of power.

From the outset, as the *Eeufees* bore witness, Afrikaner nationalism was dependent not only on powerful constructions of racial difference but also on powerful constructions of gender difference. A racial and gendered division of national creation prevailed whereby white men were seen to embody the political and economic agency of the *volk*, while women were the (unpaid) keepers of tradition and the volk's moral and spiritual mission. This gendered division of labor is summed up in the colonial gospel of the family and the presiding icon of the *volksmoeder* (mother of the nation). In photographs in the Gedenkboek, women serve as boundary markers visibly upholding the fetish signs of national difference and visibly embodying the iconography of race and gender purity. Their starched white bonnets and white dresses set a stark chiaroscuro of gender difference against the somber black of the men's clothes. Photographic captions hail women in the Victorian iconography of cleanliness, purity and maternal fecundity as the gatekeepers of the nation.

The *volksmoeder*, however, is less a biological fact than a social category. Nor is it an ideology imposed willy-nilly on hapless female victims. Rather, it is a changing, dynamic ideology rife with paradox, under constant contest by men and women and adapted constantly to the pressures arising from African resistance and the conflict between Afrikaner colonialists and British imperialists.

THE INVENTION OF THE *VOLKSMOEDER*

The Anglo-Boer War (fundamentally a war over African land and labor) was in many respects waged as a war on Boer women. In an effort to break Boer resistance, the British torched the farms and lands and herded thousands of women and children into concentration camps, where twenty-five thousand women and children perished of hunger, desolation and disease. Yet after the Anglo-Boer War, the political power of the fierce Boer women was muted and transformed. In 1913, three years after Union, the *Vrouemonument* (women's monument) was erected in homage to the female victims of the war. The monument took the form of a circular domestic enclosure, where women stand weeping with their children.

Here, women's martial role as fighters and farmers was purged of its indecorously militant potential and replaced by the figure of the lamenting mother with babe in arms. The monument enshrined Afrikaner womanhood as neither militant nor political, but as suffering, stoical and self-sacrificing.[77] Women's disempowerment was figured not as expressive of the politics of gender difference, stemming from colonial women's ambiguous relation to imperial domination, but as emblematic of national (that is, male) disempowerment. By portraying the Afrikaner *nation* symbolically as a weeping woman, the mighty male embarrassment of military defeat could be overlooked and the memory of women's vital efforts during the war washed away in images of feminine tears and maternal loss.

The icon of the *volksmoeder* is paradoxical. On the one hand, it recognizes the power of (white) motherhood; on the other hand, it is a retrospective iconography of gender containment, containing women's mutinous power within an iconography of domestic service. Defined as weeping victims, white women's activism is overlooked and their disempowerment thereby ratified.

Yet, in the early decades of this century, as Hofmeyer shows, women played a crucial role in the invention of Afrikanerdom. The family household was seen as the last bastion beyond British control and the cultural power of Afrikaner motherhood was mobilized in the service of white nation-building. Afrikaans was a language fashioned very profoundly by women's labors, within the economy of the domestic household. "Not for nothing," as Hofmeyer notes, "was it called the 'mother tongue.' "

In Afrikaner nationalism, motherhood is a political concept under constant contest. It is important to emphasize this for two reasons. Erasing Afrikaner women's historic agency also erases their historic complicity in the annals of apartheid. White women were not the weeping bystanders of apartheid history but active, if decidedly disempowered, participants in the invention of Afrikaner identity. As such they were complicit in deploying the power of motherhood in the exercise and legitimation of white domination. Certainly, white women were jealously and brut lly denied any formal political power but were compensated by their limited auth rity in the household. Clutching this small power, they became implicated in th : racism that suffuses Afrikaner nationalism. For this reason, black South African women have been justly suspicious of any easy assumption of a universal, essential sisterhood in suffering. White women are both colonized and colonizers, ambiguously complicit in the history of African dispossession.

"NO LONGER IN A FUTURE HEAVEN": GENDER AND THE ANC

African nationalism has roughly the same historical vintage as Afrikaner nationalism. Forged in the crucible of imperial thuggery, mining capitalism and rapid industrialization, African nationalism was, like its Afrikaner counterpart, the product of conscious reinvention, the enactment of a new political collectivity by specific cultural and political agents. But its racial and gender components were very different, and African nationalism would describe its own distinct trajectory across the century.

In 1910, the Union of South Africa was formed, uniting the four squabbling provinces under a single legislature. Yet at the "national" convention, not a single black South African was present. For Africans the Union was an act of profound betrayal. A color bar banished Africans from skilled labor and the franchise was denied to all but a handful. And so, in 1912, African men descended on Bloemfontein from all over South Africa to protest a Union in which no black person had a voice. At this gathering, the South African Natives National Congress (SANNC) was launched, soon to become the African National Congress.

At the outset the ANC, like Afrikaner nationalism, had a narrow class base. Drawn from the tiny urban intelligentsia and petite bourgeoisie, its members were mostly mission-educated teachers and clerks, small businessmen and traders, the mimic-men whom Fanon described as "dusted over with colonial culture." As Tom Lodge shows, they were urban, antitribal and assimilationist, demanding full civic participation in the great British empire rather than confrontation and radical change.[78] Although Lodge does not mention this fact, they were also solidly male.

For the first thirty years of the ANC, black women's relation to nationalism was structured around a contradiction: their exclusion from full political membership within the ANC contrasted with their increasing grassroots activism. As

Frene Ginwala has argued, women's resistance was shaped from below.[79] While the language of the ANC was the inclusive language of national unity, the Congress was in fact exclusive and hierarchical, ranked by an upper house of chiefs (which protected traditional patriarchal authority through descent and filiation), a lower house of elected representatives (all male) and an executive (always male). Indians and so-called coloreds were excluded from full membership. Wives of male members could join as "auxiliary members" but were denied formal political representation as well as the power to vote. Their subordinate, service role to nationalism was summed up in the draft constitution of the SANNC (later the ANC), which presented women's political role within nationalism as mediated by the marriage relation and as replicating wives' domestic roles within marriage: "All the wives of the members . . . shall ipso facto become auxiliary members . . . . It shall be the duty of all auxiliary members to provide suitable shelter and entertainment for delegates to the Congress."

In 1913, the white state saw fit to impose passes on women in an effort to preempt their migration to the cities. In outraged response, hundreds of women marched mutinously on Bloemfontein to fling back their passes and for their temerity met the full brunt of state wrath in a barrage of arrests, imprisonment and hard labor. Women's insurgence alarmed both the state and not a few African men. Nonetheless, the climate of militancy gave birth to the Bantu Women's League of the African National Congress, which was launched in 1918, drawing by and large, but not solely, on the tiny, educated, Christian elite. Thus, from the outset, women's organized participation in African nationalism stemmed less from the invitation of men than from their own politicization in resisting the violence of state decree.

At this time, however, women's potential militancy was muted and their political agency domesticated by the language of familial service and subordination. Women's volunteer work was approved insofar as it served the interests of the (male) "nation," and women's political identity was figured as merely supportive and auxiliary. As President Seme said: "No national movement can be strong unless the women volunteers come forward and offer their services to the nation." Nonetheless, women's national mission was still trivialized and domesticated, defined as providing "suitable shelter and entertainment for members or delegates." At women's own insistence, the ANC granted women full membership and voting rights in 1943. It had taken thirty-one years.

After the Urban Areas Act of 1937, which severely curtailed women's movements, new insistence began to be voiced for a more militant and explicitly political national women's organization: "We women can no longer remain in the background or concern ourselves only with domestic and sports affairs. The time has arrived for women to enter the political field and stand shoulder to shoulder with their men in the struggle."[80] In 1943, the ANC decided that a Women's League should be formed, yet tensions would persist between women's calls for greater autonomy and men's anxieties about losing control.

During the turbulent 1950s, however, the ANC Women's League thrived. This was the decade of the Defiance Campaign, the Freedom Charter, the Congress Alliance and the Federation of South African Women. In 1956 thousands of women marched on Pretoria to once more protest passes for women and the Women's Charter was formed, calling for land redistribution; worker benefits and union rights; housing and food subsidies; the abolition of child labor; universal education; the right to vote; and equal rights with men in property, marriage and child custody. It is seldom noted that this charter preceded the Freedom Charter and inspired much of its substance.

Within African nationalism, as in its Afrikaans counterpart, women's political agency has been couched in the presiding ideology of motherhood. Winnie Mandela has long been hailed as "Mother of the Nation," and the singer Miriam Makeba is reverently addressed as "Ma Africa." The ideologies of motherhood in Afrikaner and ANC nationalism differ, however, in important respects.[81] Motherhood is less the universal and biological quintessence of womanhood than it is a social category under constant contest. African women have embraced, transmuted and transformed the ideology in a variety of ways, working strategically within traditional ideology to justify untraditional public militancy. Unlike Afrikaner women, moreover, African women appealed to a racially inclusive image of motherhood in their campaigns to fashion a nonracial alliance with white women. A Federation of South African Women pamphlet of 1958 exhorted white women: "In the name of humanity, can you as a woman, as a mother, tolerate this?" In 1986, Albertina Sisulu appealed impatiently to white women: "A mother is a mother, black or white. Stand up and be counted with other women."

Over the decades, African women nationalists, unlike their Afrikaner counterparts, have transformed and infused the ideology of motherhood with an increasingly insurrectionary cast, identifying themselves more and more as the "mothers of revolution." Since the 1970s, women's local rites of defiance have been mirrored on a national scale in rent and bus boycotts, organized squatter camps, strikes, antirape protests and community activism of myriad kinds. Even under the State of Emergency, women have everywhere enlarged their militancy, insisting not only on their right to political agency but also on their right of access to the technologies of violence. Black women's relation to nationalism has thus undergone significant historical changes over the years. At the outset, women were denied formal representation; then their volunteer work was put at the service of the national revolution, still largely male. Gradually, as a result of women's own insistence, the need for women's full participation in the national liberation movement was granted, but their emancipation was still figured as the handmaiden of national revolution. Only recently has women's empowerment been recognized in its own right as distinct from the national, democratic and socialist revolution. Nonetheless, the degree to which this rhetorical recognition will find political and institutional form remains to be seen.

FEMINISM AND NATIONALISM

For many decades, African women have been loath to talk of women's emancipation outside the terms of the national liberation movement.[82] During the 1960s and 1970s, black women were understandably wary of the middle-class feminism that was sputtering fitfully to life in the white universities and suburbs. African women raised justifiably skeptical eyebrows at a white feminism that vaunted itself as giving tongue to a universal sisterhood in suffering. At the same time, women's position within the nationalist movement was still precarious and women could ill afford to antagonize men so embattled, who were already reluctant to surrender whatever patriarchal power they still enjoyed.

In recent years, however, a transformed African discourse on feminism has emerged, with black women demanding the right to fashion the terms of nationalist feminism to meet their own needs and situations.[83] On May 2, 1990, the National Executive of the ANC issued a historic ''Statement on the Emancipation of Women,'' which forthrightly proclaimed: ''The experience of other societies has shown that the emancipation of women is not a by-product of a struggle for democracy, national liberation or socialism. It has to be addressed within our own organisation, the mass democratic movement and in the society as a whole.'' The document is unprecedented in placing South African women's resistance in an international context; in granting feminism independent historic agency; and in declaring, into the bargain, that all ''laws, customs, traditions and practices which discriminate against women shall be held to be unconstitutional.'' If the ANC remains faithful to this document, virtually all existing practices in South Africa's legal, political and social life will be rendered unconstitutional.

A few months later, on June 17, 1990, the leaders of the ANC Women's Section, recently returned to South Africa from exile, insisted on the strategic validity of the term feminism: ''Feminism has been misinterpreted in most third world countries . . . there is nothing wrong with feminism. It is as progressive or reactionary as nationalism. Nationalism can be reactionary or progressive. We have not got rid of the term nationalism. And with feminism it is the same.'' Feminism, they believed, should be tailored to meet local needs and concerns.

Yet very real uncertainties for women remain. So far, theoretical and strategic analyses of South Africa's gender imbalances have not run deep. There has been little strategic rethinking of how, in particular, to transform labor relations within the household and women are not given the same political visibility as men. At a Congress of South African Trade Unions (COSATU) convention, trade union women called for attention to sexual harrassment in the unions, but their demand was brusquely flicked aside by male unionists as a decadent symptom of ''bourgeois imperialist feminism.'' Lesbian and gay activists have been similarly condemned as supporting life-styles that are no more than invidious imports of empire.[84]

There is not only one feminism, nor is there only one patriarchy. Feminism is imperialist when it puts the interests and needs of privileged women in imperialist countries above the local needs of disempowered women and men, borrowing from patriarchal privilege. In the last decade, women of color have been vehement in challenging privileged feminists who don't recognize their own racial and class power. In an important article, Chandra Mohanty challenges the appropriation of women of color's struggles by white women, specifically through the use of the category ''Third World Woman'' as a singular, monolithic and paradigmatically victimized subject.[85]

Denouncing all feminisms as imperialist, however, erases from memory the long histories of women's resistance to local and imperialist patriarchies. As Kumari Jayawardena notes, many women's mutinies around the world predated Western feminism or occurred without any contact with Western feminists.[86] Moreover, if all feminisms are derided as a pathology of the West, there is a very real danger that Western, white feminists will remain hegemonic, for the simple reason that such women have comparatively privileged access to publishing, the international media, education and money.

A good deal of this kind of feminism may well be inappropriate to women living under very different situations. Instead, women of color are calling for the right to fashion feminism to suit their own worlds. The singular contribution of nationalist feminism has been its insistence on relating feminist struggles to other liberation movements.

All too frequently, male nationalists have condemned feminism as divisive, bidding women hold their tongues until after the revolution. Yet feminism is a political response to gender conflict, not its cause. To insist on silence about gender conflict when it already exists is to cover and thereby ratify women's disempowerment. Asking women to wait until after the revolution serves merely as a strategic tactic to defer women's demands. Not only does it conceal the fact that nationalisms are from the outset constituted in gender power, but, as the lessons of international history portend, women who are not empowered to organize during the struggle will not be empowered to organize after the struggle. If nationalism is not transformed by an analysis of gender power, the nation-state will remain a repository of male hopes, male aspirations and male privilege.

All too often, the doors of tradition are slammed in women's faces. Yet traditions are both the outcome and the record of past political contests as well as the sites of present contest. In a nationalist revolution, both women and men should be empowered to decide which traditions are outmoded, which should be transformed and which should be preserved. Male nationalists frequently argue that colonialism or capitalism has been women's ruin, with patriarchy merely a nasty second cousin destined to wither away when the real villain expires. Yet nowhere has a national or socialist revolution brought a full feminist revolution in its train. In many nationalist or socialist countries, women's concerns are at best paid lip service, at worst greeted with hilarity. If women have come to do men's work, men have not come to share women's work. Nowhere has feminism in its own right been allowed to be more than the maidservant to nationalism.

A question thus remains for progressive nationalism: Can the iconography of the family be retained as the figure for national unity, or must an alternative, radical iconography be developed? In South Africa currently, critical questions for women remain. The Freedom Charter promises that the land will be given to those that work it. Since, in South Africa, women do much of the farming, will the land be given to them? Or, as in so many other postindependence countries, will the property rights, the technology, the loans and aid, be given to men? Will men become the principal beneficiaries of the rights and resources of the new South Africa?

Frantz Fanon's prescient warnings against the pitfalls of the national consciousness were never more urgent than now. For Fanon, nationalism gives vital expression to popular memory and is strategically essential for mobilizing the populace. At the same time, no one was more aware than Fanon of the attendant risks of projecting a fetishistic denial of difference onto a conveniently abstracted "collective will." In South Africa, to borrow Fanon's phrase, national transformation is "no longer in a future heaven." Yet the current situation gives sober poignancy, especially for women, to the lines from Giles Pontecorvo's famous film on the Algerian national war of liberation, *The Battle of Algiers*: "It is difficult to start a revolution, more difficult to sustain it. But it's later, when we've won, that the real difficulties will begin."

NOTES

1. See Eric Hobsbawm's critique of nationalism in *Nations and Nationalism Since 1780* (Cambridge: Cambridge University Press, 1990).

2. Benedict Anderson, *Imagined Communities* (London: Verso, 1983, 1991), p. 6.

3. Cynthia Enloe, *Bananas, Beaches and Bases: Making Feminist Sense of International Politics* (Berkeley: University of California Press, 1989), p. 44.

4. Fanon, *The Wretched of the Earth*, trans. Constance Farrington (London: Penguin, 1963), p. 30.

5. Elleke Boehmer, "Stories of Women and Mothers: Gender and Nationalism in the Early Fiction of Flora Nwapa," in Susheila Nasta, ed., *Motherlands: Black Women's Writing from Africa, the Caribbean and South Asia* (London: The Women's Press, 1991), p. 5.

6. Boehmer, "Stories of Women and Mothers," p. 6.

7. Nira Yuval-Davis and Floya Anthias, eds., *Women-Nation-State* (London: Macmillan, 1989), p. 7.

8. Yuval-Davis and Anthias, *Women-Nation-State*, p. 1.

9. Tom Nairn, *The Break-up of Britain* (London: New Left Books, 1977).

10. Deniz Kandiyoti, "Identity and Its Discontents: Women and the Nation" *Millennium: Journal of International Studies* 20, 3 (1991): 431.

11. Homi K. Bhabha, ed., *Nation and Narration* (London: Routledge, 1991), p. 1.

12. Susan Buck-Morss, *The Dialectics of Seeing: Walter Benjamin and the Arcades Project* (Cambridge, Mass.: MIT Press, 1990), p. 67.

13. Buck-Morss, *The Dialectics of Seeing*, xiv.

14. Hobsbawm, *Nations and Nationalism*, p. 151.

15. Frantz Fanon, *Black Skin, White Masks*, trans. Charles Lam Markmann (London: Pluto Press, 1986), p. 141.

16. Fanon, *Black Skin, White Masks*, p. 142.

17. Fanon, *Black Skin, White Masks*, p. 143.

18. Fanon, *Black Skin, White Masks*, pp. 141–42.

19. Fanon, *Black Skin, White Masks*, p./008193/

20. Fanon, *Black Skin, White Masks*, p./008193/

21. Fanon, *Black Skin, White Masks*, p. 10.

22. Fanon, *The Wretched of the Earth*, p. 29.

23. Fanon, *The Wretched of the Earth*, p. 30.

24. Edward Said, *Culture and Imperialism* (London: Chatto and Windus, 1993), p. 326.

25. Bhabha, introduction to Fanon, *Black Skin, White Masks*, p. ix.

26. Fanon, *Black Skin, White Masks*, p. 46.

27. Fanon, *Black Skin, White Masks*, p. 46.

28. Fanon, *Black Skin, White Masks*, p. 63.

29. Bhabha, intro. to Fanon, *Black Skin, White Masks*, p. ix.

30. Bhabha, intro. to Fanon, *Black Skin, White Masks*, p. xxvi.

31. Fanon, *Black Skin, White Masks*, p. 81.

32. Fanon, *Black Skin, White Masks*, p./008193/

33. Fanon, *Black Skin, White Masks*, p. 159.

34. Fanon, *Black Skin, White Masks*, p. 92.

35. Bhabha, intro. to Fanon, *Black Skin, White Masks*, p. xxv.

36. Bhabha, intro. to Fanon, *Black Skin, White Masks*, p. xi.

37. Bhabha, intro. to Fanon, *Black Skin, White Masks*, p. xi.

38. Said, *Culture and Imperialism*, p. 89.

39. Terry Eagleton, "Nationalism: Irony and Commitment," in Terry Eagleton, Fredric Jameson and Edward Said, *Nationalism, Colonialism and Literature* (Minneapolis: University of Minnesota Press, 1990), p. 28.

40. Eagleton, "Nationalism," p. 25.

41. Frantz Fanon, "Algeria Unveiled," in *A Dying Colonialism*, trans. Haakon Chevalier (New York: Grove Press, 1965), p. 42.

42. Fanon, "Algeria Unveiled," p. 37.

43. Fanon, "Algeria Unveiled," p. 53.

44. Fanon, "Algeria Unveiled," pp. 37–38.

45. Fanon, "Algeria Unveiled," p. 38.

46. Fanon, "Algeria Unveiled," p. 35.

47. Fanon, "Algeria Unveiled," p. 39.

48. Fanon, "Algeria Unveiled," p. 42.

49. Fanon, "Algeria Unveiled," p. 46.

50. Fanon, "Algeria Unveiled," p. 47.

51. Fanon, "Algeria Unveiled," p. 63.

52. Fanon, "Algeria Unveiled," p. 50.

53. Fanon, "Algeria Unveiled," p. 50.

54. Fanon, "Algeria Unveiled," p. 50.

55. Fanon, "Algeria Unveiled," p. 48.

56. Fanon, "Algeria Unveiled," p. 51.

57. Fanon, "Algeria Unveiled," p. 48.

58. Fanon, "Algeria Unveiled," p. 49.

59. Fanon, "Algeria Unveiled," p. 54.

60. Fanon, "Algeria Unveiled," pp. 54, 58.

61. Fanon, "Algeria Unveiled," p. 54.

62. Fanon, "Algeria Unveiled," p. 66.

63. Fanon, "Algeria Unveiled," p. 105.

64. Fanon, "Algeria Unveiled," p. 66.

65. Fanon, "Algeria Unveiled," p. 109.

66. Fanon, "Algeria Unveiled," p. 107.

67. Fanon, "Algeria Unveiled," p. 116.

68. Fanon, "Algeria Unveiled," p. 115.

69. For accounts of the rise of Afrikanerdom, see Dunbar T. Moodie, *The Rise of*

Afrikanerdom: Power, Apartheid, and the Afrikaner Civil Religion (Berkeley: University of California Press, 1975), and Dan O'Meara, *Volkskapitalisme: Class, Capital and Ideology in the Development of Afrikaner Nationalism 1934–1948* (Cambridge: Cambridge University Press, 1983).

70. Isabel Hofmeyer, " 'Building a Nation from Words: Afrikaans Language, Literature and Ethnic Identity, 1902–1924," in Shula Marks and Stanley Trapido, eds., *The Politics of Race, Class and Nationalism in Twentieth Century South Africa* (London: Longmans, 1987), p. 105.

71. See Dunbar Moodie, *The Rise of Afrikanerdom*, and Dan O'Meara, *Volkskapitalisme*.

72. The degree to which the *Eeufees* papered over fatal divisions within the white populace became most manifest in 1988, when during the height of the State of Emergency two competing Treks set out to reenact the reenactment, each sponsored by two bitterly rivalrous white nationalist parties.

73. Albert Grundlingh and Hilary Sapire, "From Feverish Festival to Repetitive Ritual? The Changing Fortunes of the Great Trek Mythology in an Industrializing South Africa, 1938–1988," *South African Historical Journal* 21 (1989): 19–37.

74. Grundlingh and Sapire, "From Feverish Festival," p. 24.

75. Theodor Adorno, *Gesammelte Schriften*, vol. 1. pp. 360–61. Quoted in Susan Buck-Morss, *The Dialectics of Seeing*, p. 59.

76. Tom Nairn, *The Break-up of Britain*, p. 340.

77. See Elsabie Brink, "Man-made Women: Gender, Class and the Ideology of the Volksmoeder," in C. Walker, ed., *Women and Gender in Southern Africa to 1945* (London: James Currey, 1990), pp. 273–92.

78. See Tom Lodge, "Charters from the Past: The African National Congress and Its Historiographical Traditions," *Radical History Review* 46/7 (1990): 161–89.

79. Frene Ginwala, *Agenda* 8 (1990): 77–93.

80. J. Mpama, *Umsebenzi*, June 26, 1937.

81. See Deborah Gaitskell and Elaine Unterhalter, "Mothers of the Nation: A Comparative Analysis of Nation, Race and Motherhood in Afrikaner Nationalism and the African National Congress," in Nira Yuval-Davis and Floya Anthias, *Women-Nation-State*.

82. The ANC delegation to the Nairobi Conference on Women in 1985 declared: "It would be suicidal for us to adopt feminist ideas. Our enemy is the system and we cannot exhaust our energies on women's issues."

83. At a seminar titled "Feminism and National Liberation," convened by the Woman's Section of the ANC in London in 1989, a representative from the South African Youth Congress (SAYCO) exclaimed: "How good it feels that feminism is finally accepted as a legitimate school of thought in our struggles and is not seen as a foreign ideology."

84. For a groundbreaking book on the history, politics and culture of lesbian and gay life in South Africa, see Edwin Cameron and Mark Gevisser, eds., *Defiant Desire: Gay and Lesbian Lives in South Africa* (New York: Routledge, 1994).

85. Chandra T. Mohanty, "Under Western Eyes: Feminist Scholarship and Colonial Discourses" in Chandra T. Mohanty, Ann Russo, and Lourdes Torres, eds. *Third World Women and the Politics of Feminism* (Bloomington: Indiana University Press, 1991), p. 52.

86. Kumari Jayawardena, *Feminism and Nationalism in the Third World* (London: Zed Press, 1986).

Ann Stoler

Bridging the fields of history and anthropology, Ann Stoler has investigated the complex ways in which race, class, and gender have structured inequality, first in Javanese and Sumatran society and more broadly in the colonial world. Author of *Capitalism and Confrontation in Sumatra's Plantation Belt* (New Haven: Yale University Press, 1985) and *Race and the Education of Desire: A Colonial Reading of Foucault's History of Sexuality* (Durham: Duke University Press, 1995), Stoler has also co-authored a collection on *Tensions of Empire: Colonial Cultures in a Bourgeois World* with Frederick Cooper (1995). Stoler has taught at the University of Wisconsin and the University of Michigan. Her interest in how citizenship has been constituted in the colonial setting has led her to deal with the discourses and structures of feeling of both the colonizer and the colonized. Foregrounding the sexual politics of colonialism and the intimate injuries of empire, Stoler shows how certain kinds of citizens have been shaped in the domestic environment, how race and nation are intimately tied together, and every apparently inclusive category, like citizenship or nation, has all kinds of exclusions written into it.

Her technique has been to look at the borders of categories, at mixed racial figures, like the *métis,* and how cultural competence functioned to distinguish who could be Dutch and who had to be ''native.'' Stoler dissects the contradiction between the ''new humanitarian liberalism'' institutionalized in mass education and political representation with the maintenance of separate spheres for Europeans and colonials. She demonstrates how women particularly were the site at which these contests over inclusion and exclusion were fought.

Sexual Affronts and Racial Frontiers: European Identities and the Cultural Politics of Exclusion in Colonial Southeast Asia

This essay is concerned with the construction of colonial categories and national identities and with those people who ambiguously straddled, crossed, and threatened these imperial divides. It begins with a story about *métissage* (interracial unions) and the sorts of progeny to which it gave rise (referred to as *métis*, mixed bloods) in French Indochina at the turn of the century. It is a story with multiple versions about people whose cultural sensibilities, physical being, and political sentiments called into question the distinctions of difference which maintained the neat boundaries of colonial rule. Its plot and resolution defy the treatment of European nationalist impulses and colonial racist policies as discrete projects, since here it was in the conflation of racial category, sexual morality, cultural competence and national identity that the case was contested and politically charged. In a broader sense, it allows me to address one of the tensions of empire which this essay only begins to sketch: the relationship between the discourses of inclusion, humanitarianism, and equality which informed liberal policy at the turn of the century in colonial Southeast Asia and the exclusionary, discriminatory practices which were reactive to, coexistent with, and perhaps inherent in liberalism itself.[1]

Nowhere is this relationship between inclusionary impulses and exclusionary practices more evident than in how métissage was legally handled, culturally inscribed, and politically treated in the contrasting colonial cultures of French

Ann Stoler, "Sexual Affronts and Racial Frontiers: National Identity, 'Mixed Bloods' and the Cultural Genealogies of Europeans in Colonial Southeast Asia," *Comparative Studies in Society and History*, 34, 3 (July 1992), pp. 514–51. Copyright © 1992 Society for Comparative Study of Society and History.

Author's note: Earlier versions of this essay were presented at the American Anthropological Association meetings, "Papers in Honor of Eric Wolf," in New Orleans, December 1990, and at the TNI Conference, "The Decolonization of Imagination: The New Europe and Its Others," Amsterdam, May 1991. I thank Talal Asad, Val Daniel, Geoff Eley, Lawrence Hirschfeld, Barbara Laslett, Jeffrey Weeks, Luise White, and fellows of the Histories of Sexuality Seminar at the Institute of the Humanities, the University of Michigan, for their comments.

Indochina and the Netherlands Indies. French Indochina was a colony of commerce occupied by the military in the 1860s and settled by *colons* in the 1870s with a métis population which numbered no more than several hundred by the turn of the century.[2] The Netherlands Indies by contrast, had been settled since the early 1600s with those of mixed descent or born in the Indies numbering in the tens of thousands in 1900. They made up nearly three-quarters of those legally designated as European. Their *Indische* mestizo culture shaped the contours of colonial society for its first two hundred years.[3] Although conventional historiography defines sharp contrasts between French, British, and Dutch colonial racial policy and the particular national metropolitan agendas from which they derived, what is more striking is that similar discourses were mapped onto such vastly different social and political landscapes.[4]

In both the Indies and Indochina, with their distinct demographics and internal rhythms, métissage was a focal point of political, legal, and social debate. Conceived as a dangerous source of subversion, it was seen as a threat to white prestige, an embodiment of European degeneration and moral decay.[5] This is not to suggest that the so-called mixed-blood problem was of the same intensity in both places nor resolved in precisely the same ways. However, the issues which resonated in these different colonies reveal a patterned set of transgressions that have not been sufficiently explored. I would suggest that both situations were so charged, in part because such mixing called into question the very criteria by which Europeanness could be identified, citizenship should be accorded, and nationality assigned. Métissage represented not the dangers of foreign enemies at national borders, but the more pressing affront for European nation-states, what the German philosopher Fichte so aptly defined as the essence of the nation, its "interior frontiers."[6]

The concept of an interior frontier is compelling precisely because of its contradictory connotations. As Etienne Balibar has noted, a frontier locates both a site of enclosure and contact, of observed passage and exchange. When coupled with the word interior, frontier carries the sense of internal distinctions within a territory (or empire); at the level of the individual, frontier marks the moral predicates by which a subject retains his or her national identity despite location outside the national frontier and despite heterogeneity within the nation-state. As Fichte deployed it, an interior frontier entails two dilemmas: the purity of the community is prone to penetration on its interior and exterior borders, and the essence of the community is an intangible "moral attitude," "a multiplicity of invisible ties."[7]

Viewing late nineteenth-century representations of a national essence in these terms, we can trace how métissage emerges as a powerful trope for internal contamination and challenge conceived morally, politically, and sexually.[8] The changing density and intensity of métissage's discursive field outlines the fault lines of colonial authority: In linking domestic arrangements to the public order, family to the state, sex to subversion, and psychological essence to racial type, métissage might be read as a metonym for the biopolitics of the empire at large.

In both Indochina and the Netherlands Indies, the rejection of métis as a distinct legal category only intensified how the politics of cultural difference were played out in other domains.[9] In both colonies, the *métis-indo* problem produced a discourse in which facile theories of racial hierarchy were rejected, while confirming the practical predicates of European superiority at the same time. The early Vietnamese and Indonesian nationalist movements created new sources of colonial vulnerability, and some of the debates over the nature and definition of Dutch and French national identity must be seen in that light. The resurgence of European nationalist rhetoric may partly have been a response to nationalist resistance in the colonies, but it cannot be accounted for in these terms alone.[10] For French Indochina, discourses about the dangers of métissage were sustained in periods of quiescence and cannot be viewed as rhetorics of reaction *tout court*. This is not to suggest that there was no correspondence between them.[11] But anticolonial challenges in Indochina, contrary to the discourse which characterized the métis as a potential subversive vanguard, were never predominantly led nor peopled by them. And in the Indies, where persons of mixed descent made up a potentially powerful constituency, the bids they made for economic, social, and political reform were more often made in contradistinction to the demands of the native population, not in alliance with them.

Although the content of the métis problem was partially in response to popular threats to colonial rule, the particular form that the securing of European privilege took was not shaped in the colonies alone. The focus on moral unity, cultural genealogy, and language joined the imagining of European colonial communities and metropolitan national entities in fundamental ways. Both visions embraced a moral rearmament, centering on the domestic domain and the family as sites in which state authority could be secured or irreparably undermined.[12]

At the turn of the century, in both metropole and colony, the liberal impulse for social welfare, representation, and protective legislation focused enormous energy on the preparatory environment for civic responsibility: on domestic arrangements, sexual morality, parenting, and more specifically on the moral milieu of home and school in which children lived.[13] Both education and upbringing emerged as national projects, but not as we might expect, with a firm sense of national identity imported to the periphery from the metropolitan core. As Eugen Weber has argued for late nineteenth-century France, "patriotic feelings on the national level, far from instinctive, had to be learned."[14] As late as 1901, six out of every ten French army recruits had not heard of the Franco-Prussian war.[15] Thus the Gallicization of France and its colonies through compulsory education, moral instruction, and language was not a one-way process with a consensual template for that identity forged in the metropole and later transported by new metropolitan recruits to colonial citizens. Between 1871 and 1914, French authorities were preoccupied with the threat of national diminishment and decline, with the study of national character a "veritable industry in France."[16]

French anxieties over national identity are commonly attributed to the loss of Alsace-Lorraine in 1870, but of perhaps equal import was the collective assimilation of over 100,000 Algerian Jews under the Crémieux Decree of the same year.[17] Debates over who was really French and who was not intensified over the next twenty years as increasing numbers of working-class Italians, Spanish, and Maltese in Algeria were accorded French citizenship. A declining birth rate (accelerating in the 1880s) placed a premium on expanded membership in the French national community but prompted a fear of internal aliens and pseudo-compatriots at the same time.[18] The Dreyfus affair coupled with concerns over the suspect loyalties of the new French of Algeria gave particular urgency to debates about the cultural contours of what it meant to be French.[19]

Heightened debates over the mixed-blood question in the Dutch context converged with domestic and colonial social reform, crystallizing in a civilizing offensive of a somewhat different order. It targeted the "dangerous classes" in both locales—Holland's paupered residuum (as distinguished from its respectable working class) and the Indies' growing population of impoverished (Indo) Europeans, the majority of whom were of mixed descent but legally classified as European. The domestic project joined liberals and conservatives, Protestants, and Catholics in a shared mission, with middle-class energies concentrated around the "uplifting" of the working-class family and its moral reform. This "civilizing offensive" focused in large part on child welfare and particularly on those "neglected" and "delinquent" children whose "upbringing" ill-prepared them for "their future place in the social system" and thus marked them as a danger to the state.[20]

Although national anxieties were not at the same pitch as in France, there is evidence that, at the turn of the century, Dutch national feeling—what Maarten Kuitenbrouwer has called an "extreme nationalism"—"underwent something of a revival," then later subsided again.[21] In tandem with the domestic offensive was also an imperial one that spanned concerns about Dutch paupers in the Indies and "vagabond Hollanders" in South Africa both. Efforts to counter "the perils of educational failure" and the increased mixing, marrying, and interaction of poor whites with colonized populations in the two locales gave rise to increased investments in the education of poor white children and assaults on the parenting styles those children were subject to at home.[22] The securing of Dutch influence in South Africa on the eve of the Boer War centered on strategies to instill a cultural belonging that was to mark the new boundaries of a "Greater Netherlands" embracing Flanders, South Africa, and the Indies.[23] In both metropolitan class and imperial projects, questions of national identity, childrearing, and education were on the public agenda and intimately tied.

Thus, the question of who might be considered truly French or Dutch resonated from core to colony and from colony to core.[24] In the Indies and Indochina, cultural milieu, represented by both upbringing and education, was seen to demarcate which métis children would turn into revolutionaries, patricides, loyal subjects, or full-fledged citizens of the nation-state. As T. H. Marshall has argued, "when the State guarantees that all children shall be educated, it has the requirements and the nature of citizenship definitely in mind."[25] Métis education raised issues about retaining colonial boundaries and regenerating the nation. At issue were the means by which European *beschaving* (civilization or culture) would be disseminated without undercutting the criteria by which European claims to privilege were made.

As such, the discourses about métissage expressed more pervasive, if inchoate, dilemmas of colonial rule and a fundamental contradiction of imperial domination: the tension between a form of domination simultaneously predicated on both incorporation and distancing.[26] This tension expressed itself in the so-called métis problem in quintessential form. Some métis were candidates for incorporation, but others were categorically denied. In either case, the decision to grant citizenship or subject status to a métis could not be made on the basis of race alone, because all métis shared some degree of European descent by definition. How then could the state mark some candidates so they would be excluded from the national community while retaining the possibility that other individuals would be granted the rights of inclusion because French and Dutch "blood prevailed in their veins"? I explore that question here by working off of a seemingly disparate set of texts and contexts: a criminal court proceeding in Haiphong in 1898; the Hanoi campaign against child abandonment in the early 1900s; the protracted debate on mixed marriage legislation in the Indies between 1887 and 1898; and finally, the confused and failed efforts of the Indo-European movement itself in the Indies to articulate its opposition to "pure-blood" Dutch by calling upon race, place, and cultural genealogy to make its demands.

In each of these texts, class, gender, and cultural markers deny and designate exclusionary practices at the same time. We cannot determine which of these categories is privileged at any given moment by sorting out the fixed primacy of race over gender or gender over class. On the contrary, I trace an unstable and uneven set of discourses in which different institutional authorities claimed primacy for one over another in relationship to how other authorities attempted to designate how political boundaries were to be protected and assigned. For mid-Victorian England, Mary Poovey argues that discourses about gender identity were gradually displaced in the 1850s by the issue of national identity.[27] However, the contestations over métissage suggest nothing linear about these developments. Rather, class distinctions, gender prescriptions, cultural knowledge, and racial membership were simultaneously invoked and strategically filled with different meanings for varied projects.

Patriarchal principles were not always applied to shore up government priorities. Colonial authorities with competing agendas agreed on two premises: Children had to be taught both their place and race, and the family was the crucial site in which future subjects and loyal citizens were to be made. These concerns framed the fact that the domestic life of individuals was increasingly subject to public scrutiny by a wide range of private and government organizations that charged themselves with the task of policing the moral borderlands of the European community and the psychological sensibilities of its marginal, as well as supposedly full-fledged, members.

At the heart of this tension between inclusionary rhetorics and exclusionary practices was a search for essences that joined formulations of national and racial identity—what Benedict Anderson has contrasted as the contrary dreams of "historical destinies" and "eternal contaminations."[28] Racism is commonly understood as a visual ideology in which somatic features are thought to provide the crucial criteria of membership. But racism is not really a visual ideology at all; physiological attributes only signal the non-visual and more salient distinctions of exclusion on which racism rests. Racism is not to biology as nationalism is to culture. Cultural attributions in both provide the observable conduits, the indices of psychological propensities and moral susceptibilities seen to shape which individuals are suitable for inclusion in the national community and whether those of ambiguous racial membership are to be classified as subjects or citizens within it. If we are to trace the epidemiologies of racist and nationalist thinking, then it is the cultural logics that underwrite the relationship between fixed, visual representations and invisible protean essences to which we must attend. This convergence between national and racial thinking achieves particular clarity when we turn to the legal and social debates in the colonies that linked observable cultural styles of parenting and domestic arrangement to the hidden psychological requirements for access to French and Dutch citizenship in this period.

CULTURAL COMPETENCE, NATIONAL IDENTITY, AND MÉTISSAGE

In 1898 in the French Indochinese city of Haiphong, the nineteen-year-old son of a French minor naval employee, Sieur Icard, was charged with assaulting without provocation a German naval mechanic, striking his temple with a whip, and attempting to crush his eye. The boy was sentenced by the tribunal court to six months in prison.[29] Spurred by the father's efforts to make an appeal for an attenuated prison term, some higher officials subsequently questioned whether the penalty was unduly severe. Clemency was not accorded by the Governor-General, and the boy, referred to by the court as "Nguyen van Thinh *dit* Lucien" (called Lucien) was sentenced to bear out his full term. The case might have been less easily dismissed if it were not for the fact that the son was métis, the child of a man who was a French citizen and a woman who was a colonial subject, his concubine and Vietnamese.

The granting of a pardon rested on two assessments: whether the boy's cultural identity and his display of French cultural competence supported his claim to French citizenship rights. Because the Governor-General's letters listed the boy as Nguyen van Thinh dit Lucien, they thereby invoked not only the double naming of the son, privileging first Nguyen van Thinh over Lucien, but suggested the dubious nature of his cultural affinities, giving the impression that his real name was Nguyen van Thinh, although he answered to the name Lucien. The father, Sieur Icard, attempted to affirm the Frenchness of his son by referring to him as Lucien and eliminated reference to Nguyen. But the angry president of Haiphong's tribunal court used only the boy's Vietnamese name, dropping Lucien altogether and put the very kinship between the father and son in question by naming Icard as the "alleged" father.

Icard's plea for pardon, which invoked his own patriotic sentiments as well as those of his son, was carefully conceived. Icard protested that the court had wrongly treated the boy as a "*vulgaire annamite*" (a common Annamite) and not as the legally recognized son of a French citizen. Icard held that his son had been provoked and only then struck the German in retaliation. But more important, Lucien had been raised in a French patriotic milieu, in a household in which

Germans were held in "contempt and disdain." He pointed out that their home was full of drawings of the 1870 (Franco-Prussian) War and that like any impressionable [French] boy of his age, Lucien and his imagination were excited by these images.

The tribunal's refusal to accept the appeal confronted and countered Icard's claims. At issue was whether Nguyen van Thinh dit Lucien could really be considered culturally and politically French and whether he was inculcated with the patriotic feelings and nationalist sentiments which might have prompted such a loyal response. The tribunal argued that Icard was away sailing too much of the time to impart such a love of *patrie* to his son and that Icard's "hate of Germans must have been of very recent origin since he had spent so much time sailing with foreigners."[30] The non-French inclinations of the boy were firmly established with the court's observation that Lucien was illiterate and knew but a few French words. Icard's argument was thus further undermined since Icard himself "spoke no annamite" and therefore shared no common language with his offspring.

Although these counter-arguments may have been sufficient to convince the Governor-General not to grant leniency, another unclarified but damning reason was invoked to deny the son's case and the father's appeal: namely, the "immoral relations which could have existed between the detainee and the one who declared himself his father."[31] Or as put by Villeminot, the city attorney in Haiphong charged with further investigating Icard's appeal, the boy deserved no leniency because "his morality was always detestable" and the police reports permitted one "to entertain the most serious suspicions concerning the nature of the relations which Nguyen van Thinh maintained with his alleged father."[32]

Whether these were coded allegations of homosexuality or referred to a possibly illegal recognition of the boy by Icard (pretending to be his father) is unclear. Icard's case came up at a time when acts of "fraudulent recognition" of native children were said to be swelling the French citizenry with a bastard population of native poor.[33] Perversion and immorality and patriotism and nationalist sentiments were clearly considered mutually exclusive categories. As in nineteenth-century Germany, adherence to middle-class European sexual morality was one implicit requisite for full-fledged citizenship in the European nation-state.[34]

But with all these allusions to suspect and duplicitous behavior perhaps what was more unsettling in this case was another unspeakable element in this story: Namely, that Icard felt such a powerful sentiment between himself and his son and that he not only recognized his Eurasian son but went so far as to plead the case of a boy who had virtually none of the exterior qualities (skin tone, language, or cultural literacy), and therefore could have none of the interior attributes of being French at all. What the court seemed to have condemned was a relationship in which Icard could have shown such dedication and love for a child who was illiterate, ignorant of the French language, and who spent most of his time in a cultural milieu that was much less French than Vietnamese. Under such circumstances, Icard's concern for Lucien was inappropriate and improper; his fatherly efforts to excuse his son's misdeeds were neither lauded by the lower courts nor the Governor-General. On the contrary, paternal love and responsibility were not to be disseminated arbitrarily as Icard had obviously done by recognizing his progeny but allowing him to grow up Indochinese. In denying the father's plea, the court passed sentence both on Icard and his son: Both were guilty of transgressing the boundaries of race, culture, sex, and patrie. If Icard (whose misspellings and profession belied his lower-class origins) was not able to bring his son up in a proper French milieu, then he should have abandoned him all together.

What was perhaps most duplicitous in the relationship was that the boy could both be Nguyen van Thinh in cultural sensibilities and Lucien to his father, or, from a slightly different perspective, that Lucien's physical and cultural non-French affinities did not stand in the way of the father's love. Like the relationship with the boy's mother, which was easily attributed to carnal lust, Icard's choice to stand up for his son was reduced to a motive of base desires, sexual or otherwise. Neither father nor son had demonstrated a proper commitment to and identification with those invisible moral bonds by which racist pedigrees and colonial divides were marked and maintained.

CULTURAL NEGLECT, NATIVE MOTHERS, AND THE RACIAL POLITICS OF ABANDONMENT

The story invokes the multiple tensions of colonial cultures in Southeast Asia and would be of interest for that alone. But it is all the more startling because it so boldly contradicts the dominant formulation of the "métis question" at the turn of the century as a problem of "abandonment," of children culturally on the loose, sexually abused, economically impoverished, morally neglected, and politically dangerous. European feminists took up the protection of abandoned mixed-blood children as their cause, condemning the irresponsibility and double standards of European men, but so too did colonial officials who argued that these concubinary relations were producing a new underclass of European paupers, of rootless children who could not be counted among the proper European citizenry, whose sartorial trappings merely masked their cultural incompetence, who did not know what it meant to be Dutch or French. The consequences of mixed unions were thus collapsed into a singular moral trajectory, which, without state intervention, would lead to a future generation of Eurasian paupers and prostitutes, an affront to European prestige and a contribution to national decay.

If we look more closely at what was identified as abandonment, the cultural and historical peculiarities of this definition become more apparent. In his comprehensive history of child abandonment in western Europe, John Boswell commonly uses "abandonment" to refer to "the *voluntary* relinquishing of control over children by their natal parents or guardians" and to children who were exposed at the doors of churches or in other public spaces and less frequently for those intentionally exposed to death.[35] Boswell argues that ancient and contemporary commentators have conflated abandonment with infanticide far more than the evidence suggests. Nevertheless, perceptions and policies on abandonment were integrally tied to issues of child mortality. Jacques Donzelot argues that in nineteenth-century France abandonment often led to high rates of child mortality and that the intensified policing of families was morally justified for those reasons among others.[36] This does not suggest that abandonment always led to death nor that this was always its intent. The point is that in the colonial context, in contrast, discussions of abandonment rarely raise a similar concern for infanticide or even obliquely address this eventuality.

The abandonment of métis children invoked, in the colonial context, not a biological but a social death—a severing from European society, a banishment of "innocents" from the European cultural milieu in which they could potentially thrive and where some reformers contended they rightfully belonged.[37] Those officials who wrote about métis children argued that exposure in the colonial context was to the native milieu, not the natural elements, and to the immoral influence of native women whose debased characters inclined them to succumb to such illicit unions in the first place. Moreover, abandonment, as we shall see, was not necessarily voluntary, nor did both parents, despite the implication in Boswell's definition, participate in it. The statutes of the Society for the Protection and Education of Young French Métis of Cochinchine and Cambodia defined the issue of abandonment in the following way:

> Left to themselves, having no other guide than their instincts and their passions, these unfortunates will always give free rein to their bad inclinations; the boys will increase the ranks of vagabonds, the girls those of prostitution.
>
> Left to their mothers and lost in the milieu of Annamites, they will not become less depraved. It must not be forgotten that in most cases, the indigenous woman who consents to live with a European is a veritable prostitute and that she will never reform. When, after several years of free union with Frenchmen, the latter disappear or abandon her, she fatally returns to the vice from which she came and she nearly always sets an example of debauchery, sloth, and immorality for her children. She takes care of them with the sole purpose of later profiting from their labor and especially from their vices.
>
> For her métis son, she seeks out a scholarship in a school with the certainty that when her child obtains a minor administrative post, she will profit from it. But, in many cases, the child, ill-advised and ill-directed, does not work and when he leaves school, abandons himself to idleness and then to vagabondage; he procures his means of existence by extortion and theft.
>
> Abandoned métisse girls are no better off; from the cradle, their mothers adorn them with bracelets and necklaces and maintain in them a love of luxury innate in the Annamites. Arriving at the age of puberty, deprived of any skills which would help them survive, and pushed into a life by their mothers that they have a natural tendency to imitate, they will take to prostitution in its diverse forms to procure the means necessary to keep themselves in luxury.[38]

Here, abandonment has specific race, cultural, and gender coordinates. Most frequently, it referred to the abandonment of métis children by European fathers and their abandonment of the children's native mothers with whom these men lived outside of marriage. The gaze of the colonial state was not directed at children abandoned by native men but only at the progeny of mixed unions. Most significantly, the child, considered abandoned whether he or she remained in the care of the mother, was most frequently classified that way precisely because the child was left to a native mother and to the cultural surroundings in which she lived. But the term abandonment was also used freely in another context to condemn those socially *déclassé* European men who chose to reside with their mixed-blood children in the supposedly immoral and degraded native milieu. In designating cultural rather than physical neglect, abandonment connoted at least two things: that a proper French father would never allow his offspring prolonged contact nor identification with such a milieu and that the native mother of lower class origins would only choose to keep her own children for mercenary purposes.

If abandonment of métis offspring by European men was considered morally reprehensible, the depraved motives of colonized women who refused to give up their children to the superior environment of state institutions were considered worse. Thus the president of The Hanoi Society for the Protection of Métis Youths in 1904 noted that "numerous mothers refuse to confer their children to us . . . under the *pretext* of not wanting to be apart from them, despite the fact that they may periodically visit them at school."[39] But if maternal love obscured more mercenary quests to exploit their young for profits and pleasure, as was often claimed, why did so many women not only refuse to hand over their children but reject any form of financial assistance for them? Cases of such refusal were not uncommon. In 1903 the Haiphong court admonished a métisse mother who was herself "raised with all the exterior signs of a European education" for withdrawing her daughter from a government school "for motives which could not be but base given the mother's character."[40] Resistance also came from the children themselves: In 1904, the seventeen-year-old métisse daughter of an Annamite woman cohabited with the French employer of her mother's Annamite lover, declaring that she *volontairement* accepted and preferred her own situation over what the Society for the Protection of Métis Youths could offer.[41] Numerous reports are cited of métisse girls forced into prostitution by *concubin*, that is, by native men who were the subsequent lovers of the girls' native mothers. These cases expressed another sexual and cultural transgression that metropolitan social reformers and colonial authorities both feared: namely, a "traffic in *filles françaises*" for the Chinese and Annamite market, not for Europeans.[42]

The portrait of abandonment and charitable rescue is seriously flawed, for it misses the fact that the channeling of abandoned métis children into special state institutions was part of a larger (but failed) imperial vision. These children were to be molded into very special colonial citizens; in one scenario, they were to be the bulwark of a future white settler population, acclimatized to the tropics but loyal to the state.[43] As proposed by the French Feminist caucus at the National Colonial Exposition of 1931, métisse young women could

> marry with Frenchmen, would accept living in the bush where young women from the metropole would be hesitant to follow their husbands, . . . [and would form] the foundation of a bourgeoisie, attached at one and the same time to their native land and to the France of Europe.[44]

This perspective on mixed marriages was more optimistic than some, but echoes the commonly held view that if métisse girls were rescued in time, they could be effectively educated to become *bonnes menageres* (good housekeepers) of a settled Indochina, wives or domestics in the service of France. Similar proposals, as we shall see, were entertained in the Indies in the same period and there too met with little success. However, in both contexts, the vision of fortifying the colonial project with a mixed-blood yeomanry was informed by a fundamental concern: What could be done with this mixed population, whose ambiguous positioning and identifications could make them either dangerous adversaries or effective partisans of the colonial state?

FRAUDULENT RECOGNITIONS AND OTHER DANGERS OF MÉTISSAGE

The question of what to do with the métis population prompted a number of different responses, but each hinged on whether métis should be classified as a distinct legal category subject to special education or so thoroughly assimilated into French culture that they would pose no threat. In French Indochina, the model treatment of métis in the Netherlands Indies was invoked at every turn. In 1901, Joseph Chailley-Bert, director of the *Union Colonial Française*, was sent on a government mission to Java to report on the status of métis in the Indies and on the efficacy of Dutch policy towards them. Chailley-Bert came away from Batavia immensely impressed and convinced that segregation was not the answer. He was overwhelmed by the sheer numbers of persons of mixed descent who occupied high station in the Indies, with wealth and cultivation rivaling those of many ''full-blooded'' Europeans. He argued that the Dutch policy not to segregate those of mixed descent nor distinguish between illegitimate and legitimate children was the only humane and politically safe course to pursue. He urged the government to adopt several Dutch practices: that abandoned métis youth be assigned European status until proof of filiation was made, that private organizations in each legal grouping (i.e., European and native) be charged with poor relief rather than the government; and that European standing not be confined to those with the proper ''dosage of blood'' alone. In the Indies he noted that such a ruling would be impossible because the entire society was in large part métis and such a distinction ''would allow a distance between the aryan without mix and the asiatic hybrids.''[45]

Monsieur A. July, writing from Hanoi in 1905, similarly applauded ''the remarkably successful results'' of the Indies government policy rejecting the legal designation of métis as a caste apart. He argued that France's abolition of slavery and call for universal suffrage had made a tabula rasa of racial prejudice; however, he was less sanguine that France's political system could permit a similar scale of naturalization as that practiced by the Dutch, since not all young métis could be recognized as *citoyen français* for reasons he thought better not to discuss. Firmin Jacques Montagne, a head conductor in the Department of Roads and Bridges also urged that French Indochina follow the Indies path, where the Dutch had not only ''safeguarded their prestige, but also profited from a force that if badly directed, could turn against Dutch domination.''[46] Based on the account of a friend who administered a plantation on Java, he urged that métis boys in

Indochina, as in the Indies, should be educated in special institutions to prepare them to be soldiers and later for modest employment in commerce or on the estates.

These appeals to Dutch wisdom are so curious because they reflected neither the treatment of the poor Indo-European population in the Indies, nor what administrative quandaries were actually facing Dutch officials there. In the very year of Chailley-Bert's visit to Batavia, the Indies government began a massive investigation of the recent proliferation of European pauperism and its causes. Between 1901 and 1903 several thousands of pages of government reports outlined the precarious economic conditions and political dangers of a population legally classified as European but riddled with impoverished widows, beggars, vagrants, and abandoned children who were mostly Indo-Europeans.[47] The pauperism commission identified an "alarming increase" of poor Europeans born in the Indies or of mixed parentage, who could neither compete for civil service positions with the influx of "full-blooded" Dutch educated in Europe nor with the growing number of better-educated Indonesians now qualified for the same jobs.[48]

The Dutch did investigate Indo-European adult life and labor, but the focus of the commissions' concern was on children and their upbringing in the parental home (opvoeding in de ouderlijkewoning).[49] Among the more than 70,000 legally classified Europeans in the Indies in 1900, nearly 70 percent knew little Dutch or none at all. Perhaps the more disturbing finding was that many of them were living on the borderlands of respectable bourgeois European society in styles that indicated not a failed version of European culture but an outright rejection of it.[50]

The causes of the situation were found in the continued prevalence of concubinage, not only among subaltern European military barred from legal marriage but also among civil servants and European estate supervisors for whom marriage to European women was either formally prohibited or made an economically untenable option. Although government and private company policies significantly relaxed the restrictions imposed on the entry of women from Europe after the turn of the century, non-conjugal mixed unions, along with the gendered and racist assumptions on which they were based, were not about to disappear by government fiat. In Indochina, French officials had to issue repeated warnings against concubinage from 1893 to 1911 (just when the societies for protection of métis youth were most active), suggesting the formation of another generation that threatened not to know where they belonged.[51] The pauperism commission condemned the general moral environment of the Indies, targeting concubinage as the source of a transient "rough and dangerous pauper element" that lived off the native population when they could disgracing European prestige and creating a financial burden for the state.[52]

But Indo-European pauperism in the Indies could not be accounted for by concubinage alone. The pauperism commission's enquiry revealed a highly stratified educational system in which European youths educated in the Indies were categorically barred from high-level administrative posts and in which middling Indo-Europeans were offered only a rudimentary training in Dutch, a basic requisite for any white collar job.[53] European public (free) schools in the Indies, like those in Indochina, were largely schools for the poor (*armenscholen*) attended by and really only designed for a lower-class of indigent and mixed-blood Europeans.[54]

A concrete set of reforms did form a response, to some extent, to concubinage and educational inequities, but European pauperism was located in a more unsettling problem: It was seen to have deeper and more tenacious roots in the surreptitious penetration of inlanders into the legal category of European.[55] Because the European legal standing exempted men both from labor service and from the harsher penal code applied to those of native status, officials argued that an underclass of European soldiers and civilians was allegedly engaged in a profitable racket of falsely recognizing native children who were not their own for an attractive fee. Thus, the state commission argued, European impoverishment was far more limited than the statistics indicated: The European civil registers were inflated by lowlife mercenaries and, as in Indochina, by *des sans-travail* (the unemployed), who might register as many as thirty to forty children who did not have proper rights to Dutch or French citizenship at all.[56]

The issue of fraudulent recognition, like concubinage, hinged on the fear that children were being raised in cultural fashions that blurred the distinctions between ruler and ruled and on the fear that uneducated native young men were acquiring access to Dutch and French nationality by channels, such as false filiation, that circumvented state control. Such practices were allegedly contingent on a nefarious class of European men who were willing to facilitate the efforts of native mothers who sought such arrangements. Whether there were as many fraudulent recognitions of métis children in Indochina, or *kunstmatig gefabriceerde Europeanen* (artificially fabricated Europeans) in the Indies as authorities claimed is really not the point. The repeated reference to fictitious, fraudulent, and fabricated Europeans expressed an underlying preoccupation of colonial authorities, shared by many in the European community at large, that illicit incursions into the Dutch and French citizenry extended beyond those cases labelled fraudulent recognition by name. We should remember that Nguyen van Thinh dit Lucien's condemnation was never explicitly argued on the basis of his suspect parentage, but on the more general contention that his behavior had to be understood as that of an *indigene* in disguise, not as a citizen of France. Annamite women who had lived in concubinage were accused of clothing their métisse daughters in European attire, while ensuring them that their souls and sentiments remained deeply native.[57]

Colonial officials wrestled with the belief that the Europeanness of métis children could never be assured, despite a rhetoric affirming that education and upbringing were transformative processes. Authorities spoke of abandoned métisse daughters as *les filles françaises* when arguing for their redemption, but when supporting segregated education, these same authorities recast these youths as physically marked and morally marred with "the faults and mediocre qualities of their [native] mothers" as "the fruits of a regrettable weakness."[58] Thus, abandoned métis children not only represented the sexual excesses and indiscretions of European men but the dangers of a subaltern class, degenerate (*verwild-*

eren) and lacking paternal discipline (*gemis aan vaderlijke tucht*), a world in which mothers took charge.[59] To what extent the concern over neglected métis children was not only about the negative influence of the native milieu but about the threat of single-mother families as in Europe and America in the same period is difficult to discern.[60] The absence of patriarchal authority in households of widows and native women who had exited from concubinary domestic arrangements was clearly seen as a threat to the proper moral upbringing of children and sanctioned the intervention of the state. Métis children undermined the inherent principles upon which national identity thrived—those *liens invisibles* (invisible bonds) that all men shared and that so clearly and comfortably marked off *pursang* French and Dutch from those of the generic colonized.

The option of making métis a legal category was actively debated in international colonial fora through the 1930s but was rejected on explicitly political grounds. French jurists persuasively argued that such a legal segregation would infest the colonies with a destructive virus, with a "class of *déraciné*, déclassé," "our most dangerous enemies," "insurgents, irreconcilable enemies of our domination."[61] The legal rejection of difference in no way diminished the concern about them. On the contrary, it produced an intensified discourse in which racial thinking remained the bedrock on which cultural markers of difference were honed and more carefully defined.

This was nowhere clearer than in the legal discussion about whether and by what criteria children of unknown parents should be assigned French or native nationality.[62] Under a 1928 *décret*, all persons born in Indochina (that is, on French soil) of unknown parents of which one was presumed to be French could obtain recognition of "*la qualité de français.*"[63] Presumed Frenchness rested on two sorts of certainty: the evaluation of the child's "physical features or race" by a "medico-legal expert" and a "moral certainty" derived from the fact that the child "has a French name, lived in a European milieu and was considered by all as being of French descent."[64] Thus, French citizenship was not open to all métis but restricted by a "scientific" and moral judgment that the child was decidedly non-indigene.[65] As we have seen in the case of Nguyen van Thinh dit Lucien, however, the name Lucien, the acknowledged paternity by Icard, and the patriotic ambiance of the household were only sufficient for the child to be legally classified as French, not for him to be treated as French by a court of law. Inclusionary laws left ample room for an implementation based on exclusionary principles and practices.

The moral outrage and crusade against abandonment attended to another underlying dilemma for those who ruled. Métis youth not only had to be protected from the "demoralisation of the special milieu" in which they were raised but, as important, educated in a way that would not produce unreasonable expectations nor encourage them to harbor desires for privilege above their station simply because French or Dutch blood flowed in their veins. The aim of the Hanoi society for the protection of métis youth was "to inculcate them with our sense of honor and integrity, while only suggesting to them modest tastes and humble aspirations."[66] Similarly, in the Indies, Indo-European pauperism was commonly at-

tributed to the "false sense of pride" of Indos who refused to do manual labor
or take on menial jobs, who did not know that "real Dutchmen" in the Netherlands worked with their hands. The assault was double-edged. It blamed those
impoverished for their condition but also suggested more subtly that if they were
really Dutch in spirit and drive, such problems of pauperism would not have
arisen.

THE CULTURAL FRONTIERS OF THE NATIONAL COMMUNITY

Fears of white impoverishment in the colonies were held by many different constituencies: by social reformers concerned with child welfare, by European feminists opposed to the double-standard of European men, and by colonial officials
who fiercely debated whether increased education would diffuse the discontents
of the European poor or, as with the peasants of France, turn them into empowered
enemies of the state.[67] However, none of these fears were very far removed from
the more general concern that European men living with native women would
themselves lose their Dutch or French identity and would become degenerate and
décivilisé. Internal to this logic was a notion of cultural, physical, and moral
contamination, the fear that those Europeans who did not subscribe to Dutch
middle-class conventions of respectability would not only compromise the cultural distinctions of empire, but waver in their allegiances to metropolitan rule.

Such fears were centered on mixed bloods but not on them alone. In the Indies,
at the height of the liberal Ethical Policy, a prominent doctor warned that those
Europeans born and bred in the colonies, the blijvers (those who remained), lived
in surroundings that stripped them of their zuivere (pure) European sensibilities,
which "could easily lead them to metamorphize into Javanese."[68] A discourse
on degeneracy with respect to the creole Dutch was not new in the Indies but in
this moment of liberal reform took on a new force with specific moral coordinates.
This discourse was directed at poor whites living on the cultural borderlands of
the echte (true) European community, at some European men who married native
women, at all European women who chose to marry native men, and at both
European and Indo-European women who cohabited with, but chose not to marry,
men of other nationalities.

These specific fears may have been intensified by the surge of political activity
at the turn of the century, coalescing around an Indisch population of "mixed-
blood" and "pure-blood" Dutch of Indies origin. Their distinct economic interests, cultural style, and legal positioning produced equivocal loyalties to the colonial state. The Indische voice, evident in a range of new publications and
associations, identified itself in two ways: by its cultural rooting in the Indies
rather than the Netherlands and by an ambiguous appeal to the notion of race. At
a time when the native nationalist project was not yet underway, this Indische
press articulated a new notion of a fatherland loyal to, but distinct from, the Dutch
fatherland and firmly opposed to the Dutch-born elite who managed the state.

Between 1898 and 1903 various Indische groups rose, fell, and reassembled as they each sought viable programs to promote the "uplifting" of the Indo-European poor without linking their own fate to them. To do so, they resorted to principles of racial hierarchy that accorded those of a certain upbringing, sexual morality, and cultural sensibility a right to privilege and to rule.[69]

What underwrites this common discourse is a new collusion between race and culture: As race dropped out of certain legal discriminations, it reemerged, marked out by specific cultural criteria in other domains. The contemporary discourse on the new racism in Europe situates "cultural racism" as a relatively recent and nuanced phenomenon, replacing the physiological distinctions on which earlier racisms had so strongly relied.[70] The "novelty" of the new racism is often located in its strong cultural inflection, embedded in wider structures of domination, based in the family, and tied to nationalist sentiments in ways that make it more relevant to a wider constituency and therefore more pervasive and insidious to weed out.[71] But are these features of the "new racism" really new at all? I would argue, on the contrary, that they are firmly rooted in a much earlier discourse that linked race, culture, and national identity, a discourse elaborated at the turn of the century in Europe's "laboratories of modernity"—the colonies—not at home.[72]

It is striking how critical the concept of cultural surroundings (*milieu* in French, *omgeving* in Dutch) in this period was to the new legal stipulations on which racial distinctions and national identity were derived. Paul Rabinow makes a strong case that the concern about milieu permeating French colonial thinking on education, health, labor, and sex in the late nineteenth century can only be understood in terms of the scientific *episteme* on which it relied.[73] Medical guides to the acclimatization of Europeans in tropical regions frequently warned that Europeans would lose their physical health and cultural bearings if they stayed in the tropics too long. Debates over whether European children should be schooled in France or the Netherlands were prompted by efforts to create the social habitus in which sentiments and sensibilities would be shaped.[74] These debates drew not so much on Darwin as on a popular neo-Lamarckian understanding of environment in which racial and national essences could be secured or altered by the physical, psychological, climatic, and moral surroundings in which one lived. The issue of omgeving and the linkages between national, racial and cultural identity were, however, most thoroughly thought out in the colonial legal discourse on the criteria for European status and inscribed, not in the laws themselves, which self-consciously disclaimed racial difference, but in the cultural logic and racist assumptions underpinning the legal arguments. What is apparent in these documents is a tension between a belief in the immutability and fixity of racial essence and a discomforting awareness that these racial categories are porous and protean at the same time. More unsettling still was the cultural perception that the essences embodied by the colonized and colonizer were asymmetric. Thus Javanese or Vietnamese might at any moment revert to their natural indigenous affiliations, while a Dutch essence was so fragile that it could unwittingly transform into something Javanese.

JUS SOL, JUS SANGUINIS, AND NATIONALITY

In the civilized world, no one may be without a relationship to the state.[75]

J. A. Nederburgh, one of the principal architects of Indies colonial law in 1898, engaged the question of national identity and membership more directly than many of his contemporaries. He argued that in destroying racial purity, colonialism had made obsolete the criteria of *jus soli* (place of birth) and *jus sanguinis* (blood descent) for determining nationality. Colonial *vermenging* (mixing or blending), he contended, had produced a new category of "wavering classes," large groups of people whose place of birth and mixed genealogies called into the question the earlier criteria by which rights to metropolitan citizenship and designations of colonial subject had once been assigned. Taking the nation to be those who shared "morals, culture, and perceptions, feelings that unite us without one being able to say what they are." Nederburgh concluded that one could not differentiate who had these sensibilities by knowing birthplace and kinship alone. He pointed to those of "pure European blood" who

> for years remained almost entirely in native surroundings [*omgeving*] and became so entirely nativized [*verinlandschen*] that they no longer felt at ease among their own kind [*rasgenooten*] and found it difficult to defend themselves against *Indische* morals and points of view.[76]

He concluded that surroundings had an "overwhelming influence," with "the power to almost entirely neutralise the effects of descent and blood."[77] Although Nederburgh's claim may seem to suggest a firm dismissal of racial supremacy, we should note that he was among the most staunchly conservative legalists of his time, a firm defender of the superiority of Western logic and law.[78] By Nederburgh's cultural account, Europeans, especially children "who because of their age are most susceptible and often the most exposed" to native influence in school and native servants at home, who remained too long in the Indies "could only remain *echte-Europeesch* (truly European) in thought and deed with much exertion."[79] While Nederburgh insisted that he was not "against *Indische* influence per se," he recommended that the state allocate funds to bring up European children in Holland.[80] Some eight years later, at the height of the Ethical Policy, another prominent member of the colonial elite made a similar but more radical recommendation to close all schools of higher education in Batavia and to replace them with state-subsidized education in Holland to improve the quality of the colored (*kleuringen*) in the civil servant ranks.[81] Both proposals derived from the same assumption: that it was "impossible for persons raised and educated in the Indies to be bearers [*dragers*] of Western culture and civilization."[82]

Attention to upbringing, surroundings, and milieu did not disengage personal potential from the physiological fixities of race. Distinctions made on the basis of *opvoeding* (upbringing) merely recoded race in the quotidian circumstances that enabled acquisition of certain cultural competencies and not others. The focus on milieu naturalized cultural difference, sexual essence, and moral fiber of Europeanness in new kinds of ways. I have discussed elsewhere how the shift in the colonies to white endogamy and away from concubinage at the turn of the century, an intensified surveillance of native servants, and a sharper delineation of the social space in which European children could be brought up and where and with whom they might play marked out not only the cultural borders of the European community but indicated how much political security was seen to reside in the choices of residence, language, and cultural style that individuals made. Personal prescriptions for inclusion as citizens of the Dutch state were as stringent and intimate as those that defined the exclusion of its subjects.[83] The wide gap between prescription and practice suggests why the prescriptions were so insistently reiterated, updated, and reapplied. Among those classified as European, there was little agreement on these prescriptions, which were contested, if not openly defied.

In 1884, legal access to European equivalent status in the Indies required a "complete suitability [*geschiktheid*] for European society," defined as a belief in Christianity, fluency in spoken and written Dutch, and training in European morals and ideas.[84] In the absence of an upbringing in Europe, district authorities were charged with evaluating whether the concerned party was "brought up in European surroundings as a European."[85] But European equivalence was not granted simply on the display of a competence and comfort in European norms. It required that the candidate "no longer feel at home" (*niet meer thuis voelt*) in native society and have already "distanced" himself from his native being (*Inlander-zijn*). In short the candidate could neither identify nor retain inappropriate senses of belonging or longings for the milieu from which she or he came.[86] The mental states of potential citizens were at issue, not their material assets alone. Who were to be the arbitrators? Suitability to which European society and to which Europeans? The questions are disingenuous because the coding is clear: cultural competence, family form, and a middle-class morality became the salient new criteria for marking subjects, nationals, citizens, and different kinds of citizens in the nation-state. As European legal status and its equivalent became accessible to an ever broader population, the cultural criteria of privilege was more carefully defined. European women who subscribed to the social prescription of white endogamy were made the custodians of a new morality—not, as we shall see, those "fictive" European women who rejected those norms.

Colonial practice contradicted the moral designations for European national and racial identity in blatant ways: which European morality was to be iconized? That embraced by those European men who cohabited with native women, became nativized, and supported their offspring? Or the morality of European men who retained their cultural trappings as they lived with native women who bore métis children, then departed for Europe unencumbered when their contracts were done? Or was it the morality of colonial officials who barred the filing of paternity suits against European men by native women or the morality of those who argued for it on the grounds that it would hinder fraudulent acknowledgments and easy recognitions by lower-class European men? What can we make of the ruling on European equivalence for non-native residents that stipulated that candidates must be from regions or states that subscribed to a monogamous family law?[87] How did this speak to the thousands of Indisch Dutch men for whom concubinage was the most frequently chosen option? And finally, if national identity was, as often stated, "an indescribable set of invisible bonds," what did it mean when a European woman upon marriage to a native man was legally reclassified to follow his nationality? As we shall see, these invisible bonds, in which women only had a conjugal share by proxy to their husbands, were those enjoyed by some but not all men. The paradox is that native women married to European men were charged with the upbringing of children, with the formative making of Dutch citizens, and with culturally encoding the markers of race. Colonial cultures created problematic contexts in which patriarchal principles and criteria for citizenship seemed to be at fundamental odds. At a time when European feminists were turning to motherhood as a claim to citizenship, this notion of "mothers of citizens" meant something different in colonial politics, where definitions of proper motherhood served to clarify the blurred boundaries of nation and race.[88]

THE MIXED-MARRIAGE LAW OF 1898

The mixed-marriage law of 1898 and the legal arguments which surrounded it are of special interest on several counts. Nowhere in the Dutch colonial record is the relationship between gender prescription, class membership, and racial category so contentiously debated and so clearly defined; nowhere is the danger of certain kinds of mixing so directly linked to national image while references to race are denied.[89] This is a liberal discourse ostensibly about the protection of native (men's) rights and later viewed as the paragon of ethical intent to equalize and synchronize colonial and metropolitan law. But, as Willem Wertheim noted nearly forty years ago, it did far more to buttress racial distinctions than to break them down.[90]

Legal attention to mixed marriages was not new in the Indies but had never been formalized as it was to be now.[91] Mixed marriages had been regulated by government decree and church decretals soon after the East Indies Company established a settlement in Batavia in the early seventeenth century. The decree of 1617 forbidding marriages between Christian and non-Christian remained intact for over 200 years. With the new Civil Code of 1848, the religious criteria were replaced with the ruling that marriage partners of European and native standing would both be subject to European law.

The legislation on mixed marriages prior to 1898 was designed to address one kind of union but not others. The 1848 ruling allowed European men already living in concubinage with non-Christian native women to legalize those unions and the children borne from them. Although the civil law of 1848 was derived from the Napoleonic civil code, a dominant principle of it had been curiously ignored: that upon marriage a woman's legal status was made that of her husband. As Dutch jurists were to argue a half-century later, because mixed marriages had then been overwhelmingly between European men and native women, the latter's legal incorporation could be easily assumed. This, however, was no longer the case in the 1880s when Indies colonial officials noted two troubling phenomena: First, more women classified as European were choosing to marry non-European men; and second, concubinage continued to remain the domestic arrangement of choice over legal marriage.[92] Legal specialists argued that concubinage was a primary cause of Indo-European impoverishment and had to be discouraged. However, the mixed-marriage rulings, as they stood, were so complicated and costly that people continued to choose cohabitation over legal marriage. Perhaps more disturbing still, some European, Indo-European, and native women opted to retain their own legal standing (thereby protecting their own material assets and those they could bestow on their children), thus rejecting marriage altogether.[93]

Colonial lawyers were thus faced with a conundrum: How could they implement a ruling that would facilitate certain kinds of mixed marriages (over concubinage) and condemn others. Two basic premises were accepted on all sides: that the family was the bulwark of state authority and that the unity of the family could only be assured by its unity in law.[94] Thus, legitimate children could not be subject to one law and their father to another, nor could women hold native status while their husbands retained that of a European.[95] Given this agreement there were two possible solutions: either the "superior European standing" of either spouse would determine the legal status (and nationality) of the other; or, alternately, the patriarchal principle—that is, a woman follows the legal status of her husband (regardless of his origin)—would be applied. Principles of cultural and male supremacy seem to be opposed. Let us look at why they were not.

Those who argued that a European woman should retain her European standing in a mixed marriage did so on the grounds, among others, that European prestige would be seriously compromised. The liberal lawyer J. H. Abendanon cogently argued that European women would be placed in a "highly unfavorable and insecure position"; by being subject to adat, she risked becoming no more than a concubine if her native husband took a second wife, as polygamy under Islamic law was not justification for divorce. Others pointed out that she would be subject to the penal code applied to those of native status. Should she commit a crime, she would be treated to "humiliating physical and psychological punishment," for which her "physical constitution" was unsuited. Her relegation to native status would thus cause an "outrageous scandal" in the European community at large.[96]

The argument above rested on one central but contested assumption: that all women classified as European deserved the protection and privilege of European law. However, those who made the countercase that the patriarchal principle be applied regardless of origin, argued that the quality of women with European standing was not the same. Although the state commission noted that mixed marriages between European women and native men were relatively few, it underlined their marked and "steady increase among certain classes of the inhabitants."[97] Such mixed marriages, all but unthinkable in 1848 but now on the rise among Indo-European and even full-blooded European women with native men, were attributed to the increasing impoverishment and declining welfare of these women on the one hand and of the "intellectual and social development" among certain classes of native men on the other.[98] The latter issue, however, was rarely addressed because the gender hierarchy of the argument was contingent on assuming that women who made such conjugal choices were neither well-bred nor deserving of European standing.

One lawyer, Taco Henny, argued that the category, European, was a legal fiction not indicative of those who actually participated in the cultural and moral life of the European community and that the majority of women who made such choices were "outwardly and inwardly indistinguishable from natives." Because these women tended to be of lower-class origin or mixed racial descent, he held that they were already native in culture and inclination and needed no protection from that cultural milieu in which they rightly belonged. Similarly, their subjection to the native penal code was no reason for scandal because it was appropriate to their actual station. They were already so far removed from Dutch society proper that it would cause no alarm.

If Taco Henny's argument was not convincing enough, Pastor van Santen made the case in even bolder terms:

> The European woman who wants to enter into such a marriage has already sunk so deep socially and morally that it does not result in ruin, either in her own eyes or those of society. It merely serves to consolidate her situation.[99]

Such arguments rested on an interior distinction between echte Dutch women and those in whom "very little European blood actually flowed in their veins" within the category of those classified as European. Pastor van Santen's claim that this latter group had already fallen from cultural and racial grace had its "proof" in yet another observation: "that if she was still European in thought and feeling, she would never take a step that was so clearly humiliating and debasing in the eyes of actual (*werkelijk*) European women."[100] This reasoning (which won in the end) marshaled the patriarchal tenets of the civil code to exclude women of a certain class and cultural milieu from Dutch citizenship rights without directly invoking race in the legal argument.

But this gendered principle did more work still and could be justified on wider grounds. First, such legislation defined a "true" European woman in accepted cultural terms: first, by her spousal choice, and, second, by her maternal sentiments. She was to demonstrate that she put her children's interests first by guarding their European standing, which would be lost to her future progeny if she married a non-European under the new law. As such, it strongly dissuaded "true" European women from choosing to marry native men. This was its implicit and, according to some advocates, its explicit intent. In addition, it spoke on the behalf of well-to-do native men, arguing that they would otherwise lose their access to agricultural land and other privileges passed from fathers to sons under adat law.[101] Finally, the new legislation claimed to discourage concubinage, as native men could thus retain their customary rights and would not be tempted to live with Indo-European and "full-blooded" European women outside of marriage. But perhaps most important, this appeal to patriarchy prevented the infiltration of increasing numbers of native men into the Dutch citizenry, particularly those of the middling classes, who were considered to have little to lose and much to gain by acquiring a Dutch nationality. Those who supported "uplifting" native men to European status through marriage would in effect encourage marriages of convenience at the expense of both European women who were drawn to such unions and those who prided themselves on the cultural distinctions that defined them as European.[102] Here again, as in the fraudulent recognitions of métis children, at issue was the undesirability of an increase in "the number of persons who would only be European in name."[103]

In the end, the mixed-marriage ruling and the debates surrounding it were more an index than a cause of profound changes in thinking about sexual practice, national identity, and colonial morality. Mixed marriages increased between native women and European men between 1900 and 1920. This was evident in the declining number of acknowledgments of children born out of wedlock and in an increased number of single European men who now married their *huishoudster* (housekeeper or sexual companion or both).[104] Condemnation of concubinage came simultaneously from several sources. The Pauperism Commission had provided new evidence that concubinage was producing an underclass of Indos that had to be curbed. By treating prostitution and the huishoudster system in the colonies as similar phenomena, the *Nederlandschen Vrouwenbond* (Dutch Women's Association) conflated the distinct options such arrangements afforded women and rallied against both.[105] The *Sarekat Islam*, one of the strongest native nationalist organizations, also campaigned against concubinage on religious grounds that may have discouraged some native women from such unions.[106] Still, in 1920 half the métis children of a European father and native mother were born outside of marriage. After 1925 the number of mixed marriages fell off again as the number of Dutch-born women coming to the Indies increased fourfold.

Hailed as exemplary liberal legislation, the mixed-marriage ruling was applied selectively on the basis of class, gender, and race. By reinvoking the Napoleonic civil code, European men were assured that their "invisible bonds" of nationality remained intact regardless of their legal partner. European women, on the other hand, were summarily (but temporarily) disenfranchised from their national community on the basis of conjugal choice alone.[107] Those mixed marriages which derived from earlier cohabitations between European men and native women were not the unions most in question, and jurists of different persuasions stated as much throughout the debate. These marriages were considered unproblematic on the assumption that a native woman would be grateful for, and proud of, her elevated European status and content with legal dependence on a European man. Were native women easily granted European legal standing and Dutch citizenship because there was no danger that they could or would fully exercise their rights? The point is never discussed because racial and gender privileges were in line.

But what about the next generation of métis? Although the new ruling effectively blocked the naturalization of native adult men through marriage, it granted a new generation of métis children a European standing by affixing their nationality to their father's. Would this generation be so assuredly cut from their mother's roots as well? The persistent vigilance with which concern for omgeving, upbringing, class, and education were discussed in the 1920s and 1930s suggests that there were resounding doubts. The Netherlands Indies Eugenics Society designed studies to test whether children of Europeans born in the Indies might display different "racial markers" than their parents.[108] Eugenicist logic consolidated discussions about national identity and cultural difference in a discourse of "fitness" that specified the interior frontiers of the nation, reaffirming yet again that upbringing and parenting were critical in deciding who would be marked as a fictive compatriot or true citizen.

Although the race criterion was finally removed from the Indies constitution in 1918 under native nationalist pressure, debates over the psychological, physical, and moral make-up of Indo-Europeans intensified in the 1920s and 1930s more than they had before. A 1936 doctoral dissertation at the University of Amsterdam could still "explain the lack of energy" of Indo-Europeans by the influence of a sapping and warm, dank climate; by the bad influence of the "energy-less Javanese race" on Indo-Europeans; and by the fact that "halfbloods" were not descended from the "average European" and the "average Javanese."[109] In the 1920s, the European-born Dutch population was visibly closing its ranks, creating new cultural boundaries while shoring up its old ones. Racial hate (*rassenhaat*) and representation were watchwords of the times. A renewed disdain for Indos permeated a discourse that heightened in the Depression as the nationalist movement grew stronger and as unemployed "full-blooded" Europeans found "roaming around" in native villages blurred with the ranks of the Indo poor. How the colonial state distinguished these two groups from one another and from "natives" on issues of unemployment insurance and poor relief underscored how crucial these interior frontiers were to the strategies of the emerging welfare state.[110]

INDO-EUROPEANS AND THE QUEST FOR A FATHERLAND

The slippage between race and culture, as well the intensified discussions of racial membership and national identity, were not invoked by the echte-Europeesche population alone. We have seen that the moral geography of the colonies had a metonymic quality: Despite the huge numbers of Europeans of mixed parentage and substantial economic means, the term Indo was usually reserved for that segment who were *verindische* (indianized) and poor. Less clear are the cultural, political, and racial criteria by which those of mixed descent identified themselves. The contradictory and changing criteria used by the various segments of the Indo-European movement at the turn of the century highlight how contentious and politically contingent these deliberations were.

It is not accidental that the term Indo-European is difficult to define. In the Indies it applied to those of *mengbloeden* (mixed blood) of European and native origin, to Europeans born in the Indies of Dutch nationality and not of native origin, and to those pur-sang Europeans born elsewhere who referred to the Indies as a "second fatherland."[111] The semantics of mixing thus related to blood, place, and belonging to different degrees and at different times. *Soeria Soemirat*, one of the earliest publications of the Indo-European constituency in the late 1890s, included among its members all Indies-born Europeans and took as its central goal the uplifting of the (Indo)-European poor. The *Indisch Bond*, formed in 1898, was led by an Indies-born European constituency that spoke for the Indo poor but whose numbers were rarely represented in their ranks. At the heart of both organizations was the push for an *Indisch vaderland*, contesting both the popular terms of Indonesian nationalism and the exclusionary practices of the Dutch-born (*totok*) society.[112]

The Indo-European movement never developed as a nationalist movement. As "socially thin" as Benedict Anderson suggests its creole counterpart was in the Americas, it could neither enlist a popular constituency nor dissociate from its strong identification with the European-born Dutch elite. The Indisch movement often made its bids for political and economic power by invoking Eurasian racial superiority to inlanders while concurrently denying a racial criteria for judging their status vis-à-vis European-born Dutch. The subsequent effort in 1912 to form an *Indische Partij* (with the motto "Indies for the Indiers") was stridently anti-government, with a platform that addressed native as well as poor Indo welfare. Despite an inclusionary rhetoric, its native and poor Indo constituency were categorically marginalized and could find no common political ground.[113] By 1919, when native nationalist mobilization was gaining strength, the need for a specifically *Indo-Bond* took on new urgency and meaning. As its founder argued, it would be a *class-verbond* (class-based association) to support the interests of the larger Indo-group.[114] This organization, eventually called the Indo-Europeesch Verbond (IEV), with more than 10,000 members in 1924, continued to plead the cause of the Indo poor while remaining unequivocally loyal to the Dutch colonial state. This truncated version of a much more complicated story, nevertheless, illustrates the unsettling point that the poor Indo constituency never achieved a political voice. However large their numbers, they were silently rejected from the early Indonesian nationalist movement and could only make their demands based on claims to a cultural and racial alliance with those Dutch who ruled.[115]

Questions of cultural, racial, and national identity were particularly charged around proposals for Indo-European agricultural settlements. This utopian project for white settler colonies peopled with those of mixed descent joined persons of widely disparate political persuasions in curious ways. In 1874 and 1902 state commissions on European pauperism had begun to explore the agricultural possibilities for the Indo poor. Their proposals focused on beggar-colonies, self-sufficient rural confinements in which (Indo)European paupers would be housed, fed, and kept out of sight. Other, more ambitious schemes advocated intensive horticultural and small-scale estates that would neither compete with native peasant production nor the agribusiness industry. These rural solutions to the mixed-blood problem, entertained in both the Indies and Indochina, were based on a common set of premises: that native blood ties would make them more easily acclimatized to tropical agriculture, while their European heritage would provide them with the reason and drive for success. Thus brawn and brains, tropical know-how and European science, and government assistance and private initiative were to come together to produce an economically self-sustaining, morally principled, and loyal *volk*. The Indische Bond first, and the IEV later, made land rights and agricultural settlements for needy Indos one of its principal platforms. Conservative and fascist-linked organizations concerned with European unemployment in Holland and European prestige in the colonies also proposed a New Guinea settled by white people that would serve their imperial plan. As a province of a *Groter Nederland*, New Guinea might absorb an economically weak underclass in the metropole, alleviate Dutch unemployment, and foster a settler colonialism in the Indies for continued rule.[116]

The vision of turning potential patricides into pastoral patriots never worked, but its discussion raised critical national issues for different constituencies. The state viewed the poor Indo population as déraciné, rootless and therefore dangerous. The Indisch movement clearly could not claim a fatherland without territorial rights and roots within it (since many Indo-Europeans had European standing, they could not own land). The movement's appeal to an *Indisch* nationalism lacked a proper mass-based constituency, a volk, and a homeland to make its claims. For the conservative Vaderlandse Club, rural settler colonies in the 1930s were part of a wider effort to ward off a Japanese invasion while reducing overpopulation in the Netherlands. The Fatherlands' Club and the IEV joined in a short-lived alliance to support the settler schemes, to oppose the *ontblanking* (unwhitening) of the Indies, and to attack the ethical policy that had fostered the increased entry of educated Javanese into subaltern civil service jobs. However, as the IEV became increasingly anti-Totok, their conflicting images of the future fatherland became difficult to deny.[117]

For the Indo-European movement, their *vaderland* was an Indisch fatherland independent of Holland. For the Indies fascists, who defined their task as the self purification of the nation (*zelfzuivering der natie*), their notion of the vaderland juxtaposed images of "a tropical Netherlands," uniting the Netherlands and Indies into a single state.[118] Neither of these imaginings concurred with that of the native nationalists who were to oppose them both.

ROOTLESSNESS AND CULTURAL RACISM

With rootedness at the center state of nationalist discourse, the notion of rootlessness captured a range of dangers about métissage.[119] Abandoned métis youths were generically viewed as vagrants in Indochina, as child delinquents in the Indies, as de facto stateless subversives without a patrie.[120] In times of economic crisis "free-roaming European bastards" were rounded up for charity and goodwill in efforts to avert a racial disgrace. Liberal colonial projects spent decades creating a barrage of institutions to incorporate, inculcate, and insulate abandoned métis youths. But the image of rootlessness was not only applied to those who were abandoned.

In 1938, government officials in Hanoi conducted a colony-wide enquiry to monitor the physical and political movements of métis. The Resident of Tonkin recommended a comprehensive state-sponsored social rehabilitation program to give métis youths the means to function as real *citoyens* on the argument that with "French blood prevailing in their veins," they already "manifested an instinctive attachment to France."[121] But many French in Indochina must have been more equivocal about their instinctive patriotic attachments. The fear that métis might revert to their natural inclinations persisted, as did a continuing discourse on their susceptibility to the native milieu, where they might relapse to the immoral and subversive states of their mothers.

Fears of métissage were not confined to colonial locales. We need only read the 1942 treatise, *Les Métis*, of René Martial who combined his appointment on the faculty of medicine in Paris with eugenic research on the *anthrobiologie des races*. For him, métis were categorically persons of physical and mental deformity. He saw métis descent as a frequent cause both of birth defects in individuals and of the contaminated body politic of France. As he put it,

> Instability, the dominant characteristic of métis, . . . is contagious, it stands in opposition to the spirit of order and method, it generates indeterminable and futile discussion and paralyzes action. It is this state of mind that makes democracies fail that live with this chimera of racial equality, one of the most dangerous errors of our times, defended with piety by pseudo-French who have found in it a convenient means to insinuate themselves everywhere.[122]

That Martial's spirit continues to thrive in contemporary France in the rhetoric of LePen is not coincidental. The discourses on métissage in the early twentieth century and in LePen's rhetoric on immigrant foreigners today are both about external boundaries and interior frontiers. Both discourses are permeated with images of purity, contamination, infiltration, and national decay. For both Martial and LePen, cultural identities refer to human natures and psychological propensities inimical to the identity of the French nation and a drain on the welfare state.[123]

ON CULTURAL HYBRIDITY AND DOMESTIC SUBVERSIONS

These historically disparate discourses are striking in how similarly they encode métissage as a political danger predicated on the psychological liminality, mental instability, and economic vulnerability of culturally hybrid minorities.[124] But could we not re-present these discourses by turning them on their heads, by unpacking what the weakness of métissage was supposed to entail? Recast, these discourses may be more about the fear of empowerment, not about marginality at all; about groups that straddled and disrupted cleanly marked social divides and whose diverse membership exposed the arbitrary logic by which the categories of control were made.[125] These discourses are not unlike those about Indische women that, in disparaging their impoverished and hybrid Dutch and non-European tastes, eclipsed the more compelling reality that they could "sometimes pass between ethnic communities, cross lines drawn by color and caste and enter slots for which they had no birthright, depending on their alliance with men."[126] The final clause is critical because through these varied sexual contracts citizenship rights were accorded and métis identities were contested and remade.[127] The management of sexuality, parenting, and morality were at the heart of the late imperial project. Cohabitation, prostitution, and legally recognized mixed marriages slotted women, men, and their progeny differently on the social and moral landscape of colonial society. These sexual contracts were buttressed by pedagogic, medical, and legal evaluations that shaped the boundaries of European membership and the interior frontiers of the colonial state.

Métissage was first a name and then made a thing. It was so heavily politicized because it threatened both to destabilize national identity and the Manichean categories of ruler and ruled. The cultural identity of class, gender, and national issues that it invoked converged in a grid of transgressions which tapped into metropolitan and colonial politics at the same time. The sexual affront that it represented challenged middle-class family order and racial frontiers, norms of childrearing and conjugal patriarchy, and made it increasingly difficult to distinguish between true nationals and their sullied, pseudo-compatriots. The issue of fraudulent recognition could be viewed in a similar light. Poor white men and native women who arranged legal recognition of their own children or those of others, defied the authority of the state by using the legal system to grant Dutch and French citizenship to a younger generation.[128]

The turn of the century represents one major break point in the nature of colonial morality and in national projects. In both the Indies and Indochina, a new humanitarian liberal concern for mass education and representation was coupled with newly recast social prescriptions for maintaining separatist and exclusionary cultural conventions regarding how, where, and with whom European colonials should live. Virtually all of these differentiating practices were worked through a psychologizing and naturalizing impulse that embedded gender inequalities, sexual privilege, class priorities, and racial superiority in a tangled political field. Colonial liberalism in its nationalist cast opened the possibilities of representation for some while it set out moral prescriptions and affixed psychological attributes which partially closed those possibilities down.

But the exclusionary strategies of the colonial state were not meted out to a passive population, nor is it clear that many of those who inhabited the borderlands of European colonial communities sought inclusion within them. At the core of the métis problem were cultural contestations of gender and class that made these "laboratories of modernity" unwieldy sites of engineering.[129] The experiments were reworked by their subjects, not least of all by women who refused to give "up" their children to charitable institutions for European training and by others who chose cohabitation (not concubinage) over marriage. Women and men who lived culturally hybrid lifestyles intercepted nationalist and racist visions. Without romanticizing their impoverishment, we might consider the possibility that their choices expressed a domestic subversion, a rejection of the terms of the civilizing mission. For those who did not adhere to European bourgeois prescripts, cultural hybridity may have affirmed their own new measures of civility.

NOTES

1. Uday Mehta outlines some features of this relationship in "Liberal Strategies of Exclusion," *Politics and Society*, 18:4 (1990), 427–54. He cogently argues for the more radical claim that the theoretical underpinnings of liberalism are exclusionary and cannot be explained as "an episodic compromise with the practical constraints of implementation" (p. 429).

2. Cochinchine's European population only increased from 594 in 1864 to 3,000 by 1900 (Charles Meyer, *De Francais en Indochine, 1860–1910*, 70 [Paris: Hachette, 1985]). By 1914 only 149 planters qualified as electors in the Chamber of Agriculture of Tonkin and Annam; on Java alone there were several thousand (John Laffey, "Racism in Tonkin before 1914," *French Colonial Studies*, no. 1 [1977], 65–81). In 1900 approximately 91,000 persons were classified as European in the Indies. As late as 1931 there were just under 10,500 French civilians in Indochina, when the Indies census counted 244,000 Europeans for the same year (see A. van Marle, "De groep der Europeanen in Nederlands-Indie, iets over ontstaan en groei," *Indonesie*, 5:5 [1952], 490; and Gilles de Gante, *La population française au Tonkin entre 1931 et 1938*, 23 [Mémoire de Maitrise, Université de Provence], 1981).

3. See Jean Taylor's subtle gendered analysis of the mestizo features of colonial culture in the Netherlands Indies (*The Social World of Batavia* [Madison: University of Wisconsin Press, 1983]). The term *Indisch* is difficult to translate. According to Taylor, it is a cultural marker of a person who "partook of Mestizo culture in marriage, practice, habit and loyalty" (p. xx). It is most often used in contrast to the life style and values of the Dutch *totok* population comprised of Hollanders born and bred in Europe who refused such cultural accommodations and retained a distinct distance from inlander (native) customs and social practice. Thus, for example, the European *blivjers* (those who stayed in the Indies) were commonly referred to as *Indisch* as opposed to *vertrekkers* (those Europeans who treated their residence in the Indies as a temporary assignment away from their native metropolitan homes).

4. See Martin Lewis, "One Hundred Million Frenchmen: The 'Assimilation' Theory in French Colonial Policy," *Comparative Studies in Society and History*, 3:4 (1961), 129–51. While the social positioning of Eurasians in India is often contrasted to that in the Indies, there are striking similarities in their changing and contradictory legal and social status in the late nineteenth century. See Mark Naidis, "British Attitudes toward the Anglo-Indians," *South Atlantic Quarterly*, LXII:3 (Summer 1963), 407–22; and Noel Gist and Roy Wright, *Marginality and Identity: Anglo-Indians as a Racially-Mixed Minority in India*, especially 7–20 (Leiden, 1973).

5. For an extended discussion of the politics of degeneracy and the eugenics of empire, see my "Carnal Knowledge and Imperial Power: The Politics of Race and Sexual Morality in Colonial Asia," in *Gender at the Crossroads: Feminist Anthropology in the Post-Modern Era*, 51–101, Micaela di Leonardo, ed. (University of California Press, 1991).

6. In the following section I draw on Etienne Balibar's discussion of this concept in "Fichte et la Frontière Intérieure: A propos des *Discours a la nation allemande*," *Les Cahiers de Fontenay*, 58/59 (June 1990).

7. Fichte quoted in Balibar, "Fichte et la Frontière Intérieure," 4.

8. See my "Carnal Knowledge and Imperial Power" on métissage and contamination. Also see Andre-Pierre Taguieff's *La Force du Préjugé* (1987), in which he discusses "la hantise du métissage" and argues that the métis problem is not a question of mixed-blood but a question of the indeterminate "social identity" which métissage implies (p. 345).

9. This is not to suggest that the French and Dutch rejection of métis as a legal category followed the same trajectory or occurred in the same way. As I later show, the legal status of métis children with unknown parents was still a subject of French juridical debate in the 1930s in a discourse in which race and upbringing were offered as two alternative criteria for judging whether a métis child should be granted the rights of a *citoyen*. See Jacques Mazet, *La condition juridique des métis dans les possession françaises* (Paris: Domat-Montchresiten, 1932).

10. Paul Rich, *Race and Empire in British Politics* (Cambridge: Cambridge University Press, 1986), argues that the anti-black riots in Liverpool and Cardiff in 1919 represented "the extension of rising colonial nationalism into the heart of the British metropolis itself at a time when nationalist ferment was being expressed in many parts of the empire" (p. 122).

11. The profusion of French juridical tracts in the 1930s debating whether métis should be made a separate legal category (distinct from European and *indigene*) and what were the political effects of doing so were forged in the tense environment in which Vietnamese nationalists were making their opposition most strongly felt. See David Marr's two important studies of the Vietnamese nationalist movements, *Vietnamese Anticolonialism, 1885–1925* (Berkeley: California Press, 1971) and *Vietnamese Tradition on Trial, 1920–1945* (Berkeley: California Press, 1981). It is noteworthy that Marr makes no reference to the métis problem (generally or as it related to citizenship, immigration and education) in either text.

12. This is not to suggest, however, that the battles for legal reform regarding, for example, paternity suits, illegitimate children, and family law waged by jurists, feminists, and religious organizations in the Netherlands and the Indies at the turn of the century were animated by the same political projects or fears; on the contrary, in the colonies, the social menace of illegitimate children, as we shall see, was not only about future criminals and prostitutes but also about mixed-blood criminals and prostitutes, about European paternity, and native mothers—and thus about the moral landscape of race and the protection of European men by the Dutch colonial state. For contrasting discourses on paternity suits in the Indies and Holland, compare Selma Sevenhuijsen's comprehensive study of this political debate (*De Orde van het Vaderschap: Politieke debatten over ongehuwd moederschap, afstamming en huwelijk in Nederland 1870–1900* [Amsterdam: Stichting Beheer HSG, 1987]) to R. Kleyn's "Onderzoek naar het vaderschap" (*Het Recht in Nederlandsch-Indie*, 67 [1896], 130–50).

13. On the relationship between racial supremacy and new conceptions of British motherhood at the turn of the century, see Anna Davin's "Imperialism and Motherhood," *History Workshop*, no. 5 (1978), 9–57, and Lucy Bland's " 'Guardians of the Race' or 'Vampires upon the Nation's Health'?: Female Sexuality and Its Regulations in Early Twentieth-Century Britain," in *The Changing Experience of Women*, 373–88, Elizabeth Whitelegg, et al., eds. (Oxford: Oxford University Press, 1982). On the European maternalist discourse of the emerging welfare states, see Seth Koven and Sonya Michel's "Womanly Duties: Maternalist Politics and the Origins of the Welfare States in France, Germany, Great Britain, and the United States, 1880–1920," *American Historical Review*, 95 (October 1990), 1076–1108.

14. See Eugen Weber's *Peasants into Frenchmen*, 114 (Stanford: Stanford University Press, 1976). Although Weber's argument that much of France's rural population neither considered itself French nor embraced a national identity has been refuted by some scholars, for my purposes his ancillary argument holds: Debates over the nature of French citizenship and identity were heavily contested at the time.

15. Weber, *Peasants into Frenchmen*, 110.

16. Raoul Girardet, *Le nationalisme français*, 30–31 (Paris: Seuil, 1983); and Robert Nye, *Crime, Madness and Politics in Modern France: The Medical Concept of National Decline*, 140 (Princeton: Princeton University Press, 1984).

17. See Pierre Nora, *Les Français d'Algerie* (Paris: R. Julliard, 1961).

18. French fertility rates began to decline in the late eighteenth century, much earlier than in other European countries, but then they decreased most sharply after 1881 (see Claire Goldberg Moses, *French Feminism in the 19th Century*, 20–24 [Binghamton: SUNY, 1984]).

19. Thus, of the 200,000 *"Française d'Algerie,"* more than half were of non-French origin. Coupled with the 20,000 Parisian political undesirables deported there by the Second Republic in 1851 (commonly referred to as *"les sans-travail," "les révoltés," "les déracinés"*), the equivocal national loyalties of Algeria's French colonial population were reopened to question. See Pierre Nora's *Les Français d'Algerie* (Paris: René Julliard, 1961). Also see Stephen Wilson's comprehensive study of French antisemitism at the turn of the century, in which he suggests that violent cultural racism in the colonies against Jews provided a "model" for antisemitism at home (in *Ideology and Experience: Antisemitism in France at the Time of the Dreyfus Affair*, especially 230–42 [Teaneck: Fairleigh Dickinson University Press, 1982]).

20. See Ali de Regt's "De vorming van een opvoedings-tradite: arbiederskinderen rond 1900" in *Geschiedenis van opvoeding en onderwijs*, B. Kruithof, J. Nordman, Piet de Rooy, eds. (Nijmegen: Sun, 1982). On the relationship between the development of the modern Dutch state and the new focus on family morality and motherhood at the turn of the century, see Siep Stuurman's *Verzuiling, Kapitalisme en Patriarchaat: aspecten van de ontwiddeling van de moderne staat in Nederland* (1987). For France, see Jacques Donzelot's *The Policing of Families* (New York: Pantheon, 1979) which traces state interventions in family life and childrearing practices to a half-century earlier.

21. See I. Schoffer's "Dutch 'Expansion' and Indonesian Reactions: Some Dilemmas of Modern Colonial Rule (1900–1942)," in *Expansion and Reaction*, H. Wesseling, ed., 80 (Leiden: Leiden University Press, 1978); and Maarten Kuitenbrouwer's *The Netherlands and the Rise of Modern Imperialism: Colonies and Foreign Policy, 1870–1902*, 220 (New York: Berg, 1991).

22. See Colin Bundy's "Vagabond Hollanders and Runaway Englishmen: White Poverty in the Cape before Poor Whiteism," in *Putting a Plough to the Ground: Accumulation and Dispossession in Rural South Africa, 1850–1930*, 101–28. William Beinart, Peter Delius, and Stanley Trapido, eds. (Johannesburg: Raven Press, 1987). On the colonial state's concern about Dutch paupers in the Indies, see *Rapport der Pauperisme-Commissie* (Batavia: Landsdrukkerij, 1902) I discuss these issues at more length in "Children on the Imperial Divide: Sentiments and Citizenship in Colonial Southeast Asia" (Paper prepared for the conference on "Power: Working Through the Disciplines" held by Comparative Study of Social Transformations at the University of Michigan in January 1992).

23. See Kuitenbrouwer, *The Netherlands*, 223.

24. For the Netherlands, compulsory education was only instituted in 1900, about the same time it was introduced to the Indies (see Jan Romein, *The Watershed of Two Eras: Europe in 1900*, 278 [Middletown, Conn.: Wesleyan University Press, 1978]).

25. See T. H. Marshall, *Class, Citizenship and Social Development*, 81 (Westport, Conn.: Greenwood, 1963, reprint 1973).

26. See Gerard Sider, "When Parrots Learn to Talk, and Why They Can't: Domination, Deception, and Self-Deception in Indian-White Relations," *Comparative Studies in Society and History*, 27:1 (1987), 3–23.

27. See Mary Poovey's *Uneven Developments: The Ideological Work of Gender in Mid-Victorian England* (Chicago: Chicago University Press, 1988).

28. Benedict Anderson, *Imagined Communities*, 136 (London: Verso, 1983).

29. Archives of d'Outre-Mer, Protectorat de l'Annam et du Tonkin, no. 1506, 17 December 1898

30. See Archives d'Outre Mer, December 1898, No. 39127, Report from Monsieur E. Issaud, Procureur-Général to the Résident Superieure in Tonkon at Hanoi.

31. "Relations immorales qui ont pu exister entre le détenue et celui qui s'est declaré son père" (Archives d'Outre Mer [hereafter, AOM], Fonds Amiraux, No. 1792, 12 December 1898).

32. AOM, Aix-en Provence, No. 1792, 12 December 1898. Report of M. Villemont, Procureur in Haiphong, to the Procureur-Général, Head of the Judicial Service in Hanoi.

33. According to the procureur-general, Raoul Abor, these fraudulent achknowledgments were threatening to submerge the French element by a deluge of naturalized natives (see Raoul Abor, *Des Reconnaisances Frauduleuses d'Enfants Naturels en Indochine*, 25 [Hanoi: Imprimerie Tonkinoise, 1917]).

34. George Mosse, *Nationalism and Sexuality* (Madison: University of Wisconsin Press, 1985).

35. John Boswell's *The Kindness of Strangers: The Abandonment of Children in Western Europe from Late Antiquity to the Renaissance* (New York: Pantheon, 1988). According to Boswell, this relinquishment might occur by "leaving them somewhere, selling them, or legally consigning authority to some other person or institution" (p. 24). As we shall see, abandonment in colonial practice did not fit this definition at all.

36. See Jacques Donzelot's *The Policing of Families*, 29.

37. I do not use this term in the sense employed by Orlando Patterson with regard to slavery but to suggest the definitive exile from European society which abandonment implied.

38. AOM, Amiraux 7701, 1899, Statute of the "Société de protection et d'education des Jeunes Métis Français de la Cohcinchine et du Cambodge."

39. AOM, No. 164, 11 May 1904 (my emphasis).

40. AOM, 13 November 1903.

41. Letter from the Administrative Resident in Bac-giang to the Résident Superieure in Hanoi.

42. AOM, Letter (No. 151) to the Governor-General in Hanoi from Monsieur Paris, the President of the Société de Protection et d'Education des Jeunes Métis Français abandonnés, 29 February 1904. This concern over the entrapment of European young women in the colonies coincides with the concurrent campaigns against the white slave trade in Europe (see Frank Mort, *Dangerous Sexualities: Medico-Moral Politics in England Since 1830*, 126–7 [London: Routledge and Kegan Paul, 1987]).

43. For such recommendations, see A. Brou, "Le métis franco annamite," *Revue Indochinois* (July 1907), 897–908; Douchet, *Métis et congaies d'Indochine* (Hanoi, 1928); Jacques Mazet, *La conditions juridique des métis* (Paris: Domat-Montchrestien, 1932); Philippe Gossard, *Études sur le métissage principalement en A.O.F.* (Paris: Les Presses Modernes, 1934).

44. Etats-Generaux du Feminisme, *Exposition Coloniale Internationale de Paris 1931, rapport général présenté par le Gouverneur Général Olivier*, 139 (Paris: Imprimerie Nationale, 1931).

45. AOM, Amiraux 7701, *Report on Métis in the Dutch East Indies* (1901).

46. "Courte notice sur les métis d'Extreme Orient et an particulier sur ceux de l'Indochine," Firmin Jacques Montagne, AOM, Amiraux 1669 (1903), 1896–1909.

47. The fact that the issue of poor whites loomed large on a diverse number of colonial landscapes at this time, in part, may derive from the fact that white poverty itself was coming to be perceived in metropole and colony in new ways. In Calcutta nearly one-fourth of the Anglo-Indian community of the Anglo-Indian community in the late nineteenth century was on poor relief (N. Gist and R. Wright, *Marginality and Identity: Anglo-Indians as a Racially Mixed Minority in India*, 16 [Leiden: Brill, 1973]). Colin Bundy argues for South Africa that white poverty was redefined "as a social problem to be tackled by state action rather than as a phenomenon of individual failure to be assuaged by charity" (p. 104). In the Indies, this reassignment of poor relief from civic to state responsibility was hotly contested and never really made.

48. *Rapport der Pauperisme-Commissie* (Batavia: Landsdrukkerij, 1902); *Uitkomsten der Pauperisme-Enquete: Algemeen Verslag* (Batavia: Landsdrukkerij, 1902); *Het Pauperisme onder de Europeanen in Nederlandsch-Indie*, Parts 3, 5 (Batavia: Landsdrukkerij, 1901); *Uitkomsten der Pauperisme-Enquete: Gewestelijke Verslagen* (Batavia: Landsdrukkerij, 1901); *De Staatsarmenzorg voor Europeanen in Nederlandsch-Indie* (Batavia: Landsdrukkerij, 1901).

49. See Petrus Blumberger's *De Indo-Europeesche Beweging in Nederlandsch-Indie*, 26 (Haarlem: Tjeenk Willink, 1939).

50. See J. M. Coetzee, *White Writing: On the Culture of Letters in South Africa* (New Haven Yale University Press, 1988), in which he argues that the British railed against Boer idleness precisely because they refused the possibility that an alternative, native milieu may have been preferred by some European men and have held a real attraction.

51. AOM, Archives Centrales de l'Indochine, nos. 9147, 9273, 7770, 4680.

52. *Encyclopedie van Nederlandsch-Indie* (1919), 367.

53. In 1900, an educational survey carried out in Dutch elementary schools in the Indies among 1,500 students found that only 29 percent of those with European legal standing knew some Dutch and more than 40 percent did not know any (Paul van der Veur, "Cultural Aspects of the Eurasian Community in Indonesian Colonial Society," *Indonesia*, no. 6 (1968), 45.

54. See Dr. I. J. Brugmans, *Geschiedenis van het onderwijs in Nederlandsch-Indie* (Batavia: Wolters, 1938).

55. See J. F. Kohlbrugge, "Prostitutie in Nederlandsch-Indie," *Indisch Genootschap*, 19 February 1901, 26–28.

56. See n.a., "Ons Pauperisme," *Mededeelingen der Vereeniging "Soeria Soemirat*," no. 2 (1892), 8. One proof of the falsity of the claim was that these fathers often conferred upon these children "repulsive and obscene" names frequently enough that a government ruling stipulated that no family name could be given that "could humiliate the child" (G. H. Koster, "Aangenomen Kinderen en Staatsblad Europeanen," *De Amsterdammer*, 15 July 1922).

57. Letter from the Administrative Resident in Bac-giang to the Resident Superieure, Hanoi, AOM, No. 164, 11 May 1904.

58. See Jacques Mazet, *La Condition Juridique de Métis* (Paris: Domat-Montchrestien, 1932) and Douchet *Métis et congaies d'Indochine*.

59. Kohlbrugge, "Prostitutie in Nederlandsch-Indie," 23.

60. See Linda Gordon's discussion of this issue for early twentieth-century America in *Heroes of Their Own Lives: The Politics and History of Family Violence* (New York: Vintage, 1988)

61. See Mazet, *La Condition Juridique de Métis*, 37, 42.

62. Questions about the legal status of métis and the political consequences of that decision were not confined to the French alone. The International Colonial Institute in

Brussels created by Joseph Chailley-Bert in 1893 engaged this question in at least three of its international meetings in 1911, 1920, and 1924. See *Comptes Rendus de l'Institut Colonial International* (Bruxelles: Bibliotheque Coloniale Internationale, 1911, 1920, 1924).

63. Mazet, *La Condition Jurdique de Métis*, 114.

64. Ibid., 80.

65. Ibid., 90.

66. Statute of the "Societé de protection des enfants métis," 18 May 1904, Article 37.

67. Similar debates occurred at the International Colonial Congress of 1889, in which scholars and administrators compared and contrasted pedagogic strategies for natives in the colonies to those for the peasants of France. See Martin Lewis, "One Hundred Million Frenchmen: The 'Assimilation' Theory in French Colonial Policy," *Comparative Studies in Society and History*, 34, 140.

68. J. Kohlbrugge, "Het Indische kind en zijne karaktervorming," in *Blikken in het zielenleven van den Javaan en zijner overheerschers* (Leiden: Brill, 1907).

69. Michel Foucault's discussion of the historical shift from a "symbolics of blood" to an "analytics of sexuality" in the mid- and late- nineteenth century would be interesting to explore in this colonial context, where the mixed-blood problem invoked both of these principles in resolving issues of paternity and citizenship rights (*An Introduction*, vol. 1 of *The History of Sexuality*, especially 147–50 [New York: Pantheon Books, 1978]). Although a discussion of race and sexuality is notably absent from all but the very end of *The History of Sexuality*, Foucault once remarked that it was "the fundamental part of the book" (*Power/Knowledge: Selected Interviews and Other Writings, 1972–1977*, 222 (New York: Pantheon, 1980).

70. See, for example, the contributions of those in British cultural studies, such as by Stuart Hall and Paul Gilroy; also compare the discussion of nationalism and racism in France by Etienne Balibar, who does not mark cultural racism as a recent phenomenon but does argue for a new intensification of the force of cultural difference in marking the interior frontiers of the modern nation-state. See *Race, Nation, Class: Ambiguous Identities*, Etienne Balibar and Immanuel Wallerstein (New York: Verso, 1991).

71. Thus Paul Gilroy (*There Ain't No Black in the Union Jack*, 43 (London: Hutchinson, 1987), for example, argues that the "novelty" of the new racism "lies in the capacity to link discourses of patriotism, nationalism, xenophobia, Englishness, Britishness, militarism, and gender differences into a complex system which gives 'race' its contemporary meaning. These themes combine to provide a definition of 'race' in terms of culture and identity . . . . 'Race' differences are displayed in culture which is reproduced in educational institutions and, above all, in family life. Families are therefore not only the nation in microcosm, its key components, but act as the means to turn social processes into natural, instinctive ones."

72. It is not coincidental that this is precisely the period in which George Stocking identifies a shift in the meaning of culture in the social sciences from its singular humanistic sense of refinement to the plural anthropological notion of cultures as shared values of specific human groups. Although Stocking argues that Franz Boas made the analytic leap from culture to cultures as an anti-racist response, it is clear that these two connotations joined to shape the exclusionary tenets of nationalist and racist projects (*Race, Culture, and Evolution: Essays in the History of Anthropology*, especially 200–04 [New York: Free Press, 1968]).

73. See Paul Rabinow's *French Modern: Norms and Forms of the Social Environment*, especially 126–67 (Cambridge: MIT Press, 1989), where he traces the effects of

neo-Lamarckian thinking on colonial pacification policies. I am more concerned here with how this attention to milieu fixed the boundaries of the European community and identified threats to it. On the contaminating influences of milieu, see my "Carnal Knowledge and Imperial Power," 51–101.

74. The similarity to Pierre Bourdieu's notion of "habitus" as a stylization of life, an unconsciously embodied set of rules of behavior that engenders durable schemes of thought and perception, is striking. These colonial discussions of milieu denote not only a social ecology of acquired competencies but a psychological environment in which certain dispositions are promoted and affective sensibilities are shaped (Pierre Bourdieu, *Outline of a Theory of Practice* (Cambridge: Cambridge University Press, 1977), 82.

75. "In de beschaafd wereld, niemand zonder staatsverband mag zijn" (K. H. Beyen, *Het Nederlanderschap in verband met het international recht* [Utrecht, 1890]), quoted in J. A. Nederburgh, *Wet en Adat*, 83 [Batavia: Kolff and Co., 1898]). The word *staatsverband* literally means "relationship to the state." Nederburgh distinguishes it from nationality and defines it as "the tie that exists between the state and each of its members, the membership of the state" (p. 91). Dutch scholars of colonial history say the term is rarely used but connotes citizenship.

76. Ibid., 87–88.

77. Ibid., 87.

78. See Willem Wertheim's incisive review of Prof. R. D. Kollewijn's *Intergentiel Recht, Indonesie*, 19 (1956), 169–73. Nederburgh's name comes up in this critique of Kollewijn, whose liberal rhetoric and opposition to such conservatives as Nederburgh belied that fact that he praised the virtues of the Indies mixed-marriage legislation of 1898, despite the racist principles that underwrote it.

79. Nederburgh, *Wet en Adat*, 88.

80. Ibid., 90.

81. Kooreman 1906.

82. Ibid.

83. See my "Rethinking Colonial Categories: European Communities and the Boundaries of Rule," *Comparative Studies in Society and History*, 31:1 (1989), 134–61; and "Carnal Knowledge and Imperial Power."

84. W. E. van Mastenbroek, *De Historische Ontwikkeling van de Staatsrechtelijke Indeeling der Bevolking van Nederlandsch-Indie*, 70 (Wageningen: Veenam, 1934).

85. See W. F. Prins, "De Bevolkingsgroepen in het Nederlandsch-Indische Recht," *Koloniale Studien*, 17 (1933), 652–88, especially 677.

86. Ibid., 677; Van Marle, "De groep der Europeanen in Nederlands," *Indonesie*, 5:2 (1951). 110.

87. See William Mastenbroek, *De Historische Ontwikkeling van de Staatsrechtelijke Indeeling der Bevolking van Nederlandsch-Indie*, 87.

88. See Karen Offen's "Depopulation, Nationalism and Feminism in Fin-de-Siècle France," *American Historical Review*, 89:3 (1984), 648–76.

89. The following discussion is based on several documents that I will abbreviate in referring to in the section below as follows: *Verslag van het Verhandelde in de Bijeenkomsten der Nederlandsch-Indische Juristen-Vereeniging* on 25, 27, and 29 June 1887 in Batavia [hereafter, JV]; "Voldoet de wetgeving betreffende huwelijken tusschen personen behoorende tot de beide staatkundige categorien der Nederlandsch Indische bevolking (die der Europeanen en met hen, en die der Inlanders en met hen gelijkgestelden) aan de maatschappelijke behoefte? Zoo neen, welke wijzigingen zijn noodig?" (1887) [hereafter, VW]; J. A. Nederburgh, *Gemengde Huwelijken, Staatsblad 1898, No. 158: Officiele Bescheiden met Eenige Aanteekeningen* [hereafter, GH].

90. Werthein, *Intergentiel Recht.*

91. The term mixed marriages (*gemengde huwelijken*) had two distinct but overlapping meanings in the Indies at the turn of the century. Common usage defined it as referring to contracts between a man and a woman of different racial origin; the state defined it as "a marriage between persons who were subject to different laws in the Netherlands Indies" with no reference to race. The distinction is significant for at least two reasons: (1) because the designations of legal standing as inlander versus European cut across the racial spectrum, with generations of mixed bloods falling on different sides of this divide and (2) because adat (customary) and Dutch law followed different rulings with respect to the marriage contract, divorce, inheritance, and child custody.

92. Although the hierarchies of gender and race of Indies colonial society in part account for the fact that in 1895 more than half of the European men in the Indies still lived with native women outside of marriage, this may only tell one part of the story. The juridical debates on legal reform of mixed marriages suggest that there were women who chose cohabitation over legal marriage. At the very least, this suggests that concubinage may not have been an appropriate term for some of these arrangements, nor does it necessarily reflect what options women may have perceived in these arrangements.

93. W. F. Prins, "De bevolkingsgroepen in het Nederlandsch-Indische recht," *Koloniale Studien*, 17, 665. That some women chose cohabitation over legal mixed marriages is rarely addressed in the colonial or secondary literature on the assumption that all forms of cohabitation could be subsumed by the term concubinage, signaling the moral degradation of a "kept woman" that the later term implies. References in these legal debates to the fact that some women chose not to marry suggests that this issue needs further investigation.

94. Nederburgh, *GH*, 17.

95. As the chairman of the commission poignantly illustrated, a woman with native legal standing could be arrested for wearing European attire at the very moment she emerged from the building in which she had just married a European. Nor could a European man and his wife of native standing take the short boat trip from Soerabaya to Madura without prior permission of the authorities since sea passage for natives was forbidden by law (*JV*, 29–30).

96. Nederburgh, *GH*, 20.

97. Ibid., 13.

98. Ibid., 13.

99. *JV*, 39.

100. Idem.

101. Ibid., 51.

102. Ibid., 40. The arguments presented over the mixed-marriage ruling are much more numerous and elaborate than this short account suggests. There were indeed those such as Abendanon (the lawyer friend of Kartini), whose proposals raised yet a whole different set of options than those offered in these accounts. He argued that both man and woman should be given European status, except in those cases in which a native man preferred to retain his rights under adat law. Abendanon also singlehandedly countered the claim that any European woman who chose to marry a native man was already debased, arguing that there were many Dutch girls in the Netherlands for whom this was not the case. But these arguments were incidental to the main thrust of the debate and had little sway in the final analysis.

103. Nederburgh, *GM*, 64.

104. See A. van Marle's "De Groep der Europeanen in Nederlands-Indie, iets over ontstaan en groei," *Indonesie*, 5:3 (1952), 322, 328. Van Marle suggests that the much

larger number of illiterate women of European standing in central Java and the Moluccas compared to the rest of the Indies indicates that the number of mixed marriages in these regions was particularly high (p. 330). But this was not the case everywhere. In East Java, European men acknowledged more of their métis children but continued to cohabit with the native mothers of their children outside of marriage (p. 495).

105. Mevrouw Douaire Klerck, *Eenige Beschouwingen over Oost-Indische Toestanden*, 3–19 (Amsterdam: Versluys, 1898).

106. S. S. J. Ratu-Langie, *Sarekat Islam*, 21 (Baarn: Hollandia Drukkerij, 1913).

107. A woman who had contracted a mixed marriage could, upon divorce or death of her husband, declare her desire to reinstate her original nationality as long as she did so within a certain time. However, a native woman who married a European man and subsequently married and divorced a man of non-European status could not recoup her European status.

108. Ernest Rodenwalt, "Eugenetische Problemen in Nederlandsch-Indie," *Ons Nageslacht*, 1–8 (1928).

109. Johan Winsemius, *Nieuw-Guinee als kolonisatie-gebied voor Europeanen en var. IndoEuropeanen*, 227 (Ph.D. Disser., Faculty of Medicine, University of Amsterdam, 1936).

110. Jacques van Doorn emphasizes the dualistic policy on poverty in the 1930s in "Armoede en Dualistisch Beleid" (unpublished); I would refer to it as a three-tiered policy, not a dualistic one.

111. J. Th. Petrus Blumberger, *De Indo-Europeesche Beweging in Nederlandsch-Indie*, 5 (Haarlem: Tjeenk Willink, 1939).

112. See Paul van der Veur's "The Eurasians of Indonesia: A Problem and Challenge in Colonial History," *Journal of Southeast Asian History*, 9:2 (September 1966), 191–207, and his "Cultural Aspects of the Eurasian Community in Indonesian Colonial Society," *Indonesia*, 6 (October 1968), 38–53.

113. On the various currents of Eurasian political activity, see Paul W. van der Veur's "The Eurasians of Indonesia: A Problem and Challenge in Colonial History." On the importance of Indo individuals in the early Malay press and nationalist movement, see Takashi Shiraishi's *An Age in Motion: Popular Radicalism in Java*, 1912–1926, especially 37, 58–59 (Ithaca: Cornell University Press, 1990). Neither account addresses the class differences within Eurasian groups and where their distinct allegiances lay.

114. Blumberger, *De Indo-Europeesche Beweging*, 50.

115. According to the historian, Rudolph Mrazek, the early silent rejection of the Indo-European community from the Indonesian nationalist project turned explicit under Soekarno in the mid-1920s, when Indo-Europeans were categorically barred from membership in nationalist political organizations. Mrazek suggests that this silence among Dutch-educated nationalist leaders on the Indo question should be understood as a response from their own cultural formation and identification as cultural hybrids themselves (personal communication).

116. See P. J. Drooglever's discussion of this failed effort in *De Vaderlandse Club*, 193–208 (Franeker: T. Wever, 1980).

117. P. J. Drooglever, *De Vaderlandse Club, 1929–1942: Totoks en de Indische Politiek*, 285 (Franeker: T. Wever, 1980).

118. *Verbond Nederland en Indie*, no. 3, September 1926, 3. In the late 1920s, this publication appended the subtitle to the name above of "A Fascist Monthly."

119. This issue of rootlessness is most subtly analyzed in contemporary contexts. Liisa Malkki explores the meanings attached to displacement and uprootedness in the national order of things ("National Geographic: The Rooting of Peoples and the Territorialization

of National Identity among Scholars and Refugees," *Cultural Anthropology* (1992). André-Pierre Taguieff examines LePen's nationalist rhetoric on the dangers of the rootlessness of immigrant workers in France. See Pierre-André Taguieff's excellent analysis of LePen's rhetoric in "The Doctrine of the National Front in France (1972–1989)," in *New Political Science*, no. 16/17, 29–70.

120. See A. Braconier, "Het Pauperisme onder de in Ned. Oost-Indie levende Europeanen," *Nederlandsch-Indie*, no. 1 (1917), 291–300, at 293.

121. Enquete sur Métissage, AOM, Amiraux 53.50.6.

122. René Martial, *Les Métis*, 58 (Paris: Flammarion, 1942).

123. See Taguieff, "The Doctrine of the National Front."

124. On the recent British discourse on Britishness and the cultural threat of Islam to that identity, see Talal Asad's rich analysis in "Multiculturalism and British Identity in the Wake of the Rushdie Affair," *Politics and Society*, 18:4 (December 1990), 455–80.

125. Hazel Carby ("Lynching, Empire and Sexuality," *Critical Enquiry*, 12:1 (1985), 262–77) argues that Afro-American women intellectuals at the turn of the century focused on the métis figure because it both enabled an exploration and expressed the relations between the races, because it demythologized concepts of pure blood and pure race while debunking any proposition of degeneracy through amalgamation. Such black women writers as Pauline Hopkins embraced the mulatto to counter the official script that miscegenation was not the inmost desire of the nonwhite peoples but the result of white rape (p. 274). In both the Indies and the United States at the same time, the figure of the Indo-mulatto looms large in both dominant and subaltern literary production, serving to convey strategic social dilemmas and political messages. It is not surprising, then, that the portrayal of the Indo in fiction was widely discussed in the Indies and metropolitan press by many more than those who were interested in literary style alone.

126. Taylor, *The Social World of Batavia*, 155.

127. Carole Pateman argues that the sexual contract is fundamental to the functioning of European civil society, in that the principle of patriarchal right defines the social contract between men, and the individual and citizen as male (*The Sexual Contract* [Stanford: Stanford University Press, 1988]).

128. I thank Luise White for pressing me to think out this point.

129. Gwendolyn Wright, "Tradition in the Service of Modernity: Architecture and Urbanism in French Colonial Policy, 1900–1930," *Journal of Modern History*, 59 (June 1987), 291–316, at 297.

Marianne Heiberg

Marianne Heiberg, an anthropologist at the Norwegian Institute of International Affairs, provides an excellent case study of the process by which a particular people became transformed into a nationality, namely, the Basque people inhabiting a relatively small territory in the north of Spain. On the one hand, this history lends itself very much to the framework provided by Hroch, in which intellectuals first propose and elaborate a particular national category, mobilizing the available materials of customary practice and cultural difference, combined with certain institutional autonomies of the region and the physical facts of its topography, to form a distinctive claim to collective identity. The relationship of this process to the complex sociocultural dynamics of industrialization and demographic change also fits quite well with the argument of Nairn about "the 'nationalism-producing' dilemma" of uneven development and its consequences. On the other hand, the exact forms of the identity fashioned by Basque nationalists were certainly not given in the existing continuities of the region's culture, but emerged from a more mobile and inventive history of "imagining" (to use Anderson's term). Whereas "Basqueness" was "traditionally" associated with the rugged and independent, but illiterate and unsophisticated, culture of an upland peasantry, despised by the polite society of the towns, in the late nineteenth century it was reinvented as a positive territorialized ethnicity once the new nationalist intellectuals set to work. Under the available political languages of the time, the construction of such a regional identity became inevitably "national," although the range of variation and the element of contingency should still not be underestimated, for the Basque lands were also (for instance) one of the major bastions of the Spanish Socialist Party in the 1920s and 1930s. Heiberg illustrates the "constructionist" case regarding the origins and formation of nations beautifully, not least because the argument is finely modulated by careful knowledge of the social, economic, and political histories involved. More recently, she has published a book-length study, *The Making of the Basque Nation* (Cambridge: Cambridge University Press, 1989).

Beyond this general character of the argument, several particular points are worth highlighting. First, the "invented" qualities of the Basque national identity—both as a description of the concrete processes entailed and in relation to the earlier "prenationalist" understandings of "Basque" cultural attributes—cannot be emphasized too strongly. The "Basques" (namely, the people who lived in this land) had to be specifically interpellated as such. The Basque nation had to be constructed via labors of imagination and political argument, had to be fashioned in language and cultural practice, shaped discursively via a new system of meanings, with credible markers of difference. Secondly, this process of construction—the cultural formation of a new Basque nationality—was empowered and constrained by a set of contingent political histories too, from the late nineteenth century (beginning with the suppression of the region's historical administrative autonomies in 1876) to the Spanish Civil War of 1936–39 and its Francoist outcome. Thirdly, in the ideological system of Basque nationalism elaborated by Sabino de Arana and other nationalist intellectuals at the end of the nineteenth century, race and racialized understandings of national difference were also key, and in this sense Basque nationalism participated fully in the prevailing ideological climate in Europe as a whole during this time.

Basques, Anti-Basques, and the Moral Community

Social boundaries provide the interfaces for the necessary process of social classification and ordering. They are the means by which those who are perceived as "similar" are separated from those who are perceived as significantly "different." Without such boundaries social life would have little, if any, coherent shape. A system of social boundaries is as complex, fluid and, at points, contradictory as the social structure of which it forms part.

Those boundaries which are emphasized or, occasionally, newly erected—be they boundaries of class, ethnicity, religion, kinship and so forth—are responses to specific social circumstances (Mitchell, 1965; Barth, 1969). They reflect and affect the distribution of political, economic and social resources in a particular society at a particular historical moment. As such, the generation and maintenance of social boundaries implies the competition for and/or the reproduction of power (Barth, 1969; Cohen, 1969, 1974). Therefore, as the wider economic and political environment changes, the social grid of boundaries shifts accordingly although not necessarily in a direct relation. As importantly, the categories enclosed within the boundaries may radically alter in meaning and value.

This paper will deal with Basque identity and its changing function and meaning in the formation of social boundaries in the Spanish Basque country. The social boundary defined by cultural differentiation is an active, explicit feature of all realms of social life in the Basque region and most political and economic behaviour is viewed in terms of it. (However, the nature of this boundary and the cultures which it marks and separates have altered radically over the last 100 years or so. This alteration can only be understood in reference to equally radical changes that have occurred in Basque economic and political life.)

The mountainous and verdant Basque region lies in the north-west corner of Spain and is one of the most industrialized, advanced parts of the country. Its inhabitants enjoy a standard of living some 60% above the Spanish average (figure from "Renta Nacional de Espana," Banco de Bilbao). Of the approximately 2.5

Marianne Heiberg, "Basques, Anti-Basques, and the Moral Community," in R. D. Grillo (ed.), *"Nation" and "State" in Europe: Anthropological Perspectives* (London: Academic Press, 1980), pp. 45–59.

Author's note: This paper is based on research originally funded by the Social Science Research Council. I should like to thank Ms. Gill Shephard for her valuable comments.

million people who live in the region only around one half are Basque by descent. The remaining half came to the region as immigrants from the more impoverished rural areas of Spain attracted by Basque expanding industrial prosperity. Many of these Spanish immigrants have now lived in the Basque country for three to five generations. The vast majority of those who are Basque by descent are totally fluent in Spanish and less than 50% have a working knowledge of the Basque language, Euskera. Partly because of Euskera's legendary difficulty—it is unrelated to any Indo-European language—few of the immigrants have learnt the language.

There is a rather elaborate stereotype as to what constitutes the typical Basque. The ideal Basque should be of medium height, broad-shouldered with a triangular head and long, narrow nose. He (or she) should be born in the Basque country, have four Basque surnames (showing purity of descent for at least two generations), have his family roots in the countryside rather than the cities and, most importantly, speak Euskera. However, only a very few Basques fit into this image. Particularly in the urban centers where the large majority of Basques live, in terms of education, religion, general physical appearance and life style most Basques are—broadly speaking—indistinguishable from other Spanish citizens. Nevertheless, the inhabitants of the Basque country have been severely polarized into two ethnically differentiated, socially separated and mutually exclusive categories of people. Following the terminology of the Basques themselves, I have labelled these categories "Basque" and "anti-Basque."

This cleavage between "Basque" and "anti-Basque" must be distinguished from another boundary which divides Basques from immigrants or non-Basques. Although a deep social division does exist between the Basque and immigrant populations—in the more rural communities the two groups tend to lead completely separate social lives—this is not the *operationally* important cleavage. One of the Basques' most revered martyrs, Juan Paredes Manot, who cried, "*Gora Euskadi askatuta!*" (Long live free Euskadi) as he was executed by Franco's police, was an immigrant who spoke no Euskera. Equally, Basque descent is not in itself sufficient to be considered by others as truly "Basque." To achieve and maintain "Basque" status requires continual and strict obedience to a certain type of social behaviour and political ideology.

BOUNDARY AND BASQUE CULTURE: PRE-INDUSTRIAL BASQUE SOCIETY

The value placed on Basque identity—which is now a highly esteemed and sought-after commodity—and its role in dividing the social universe of the Basque country, has undergone a radical change. This change is intimately linked to a fundamental transformation of Basque society as a whole. Historically the most significant social boundary which regulated an individual's general public identity divided urbanites, *kaletara* (people from the *kalea*, or street) from the rural population, *baserritara* (people from the *baserri*, or farm). This division has far-reaching roots.

The Basque country has enjoyed three major economic assets that have profoundly patterned its entire economic and social history. These are (1) its abundant
and readily available reserves of iron and lumber, the bases for the Basque iron
and steel industry as well as ship-building, (2) natural, protected harbours in the
Bay of Biscay and, (3) an advantageous geographical setting. The Basque country
was a cross-roads between two important economic areas—England and Flanders
to the north and the Castillian meseta rich in wool and grain to the south (Monreal,
1977:358). In the main, these resources were economically capitalized by the
urban centers, called *villas*, which were dedicated to commerce, administrative
and military activities and which linked wool and grain exporting Castilla to her
external markets.

Against the advantages enjoyed by the *villas* the Basque rural hinterland has
been burdened with a steep, arduous terrain and infertile soil in addition to chronic
overpopulation. The poverty and high demographical density of the rural areas,
together with the Basque inheritance system which transmits the *baserri* (farmstead) intact to only one heir, has induced a constant flow of people into the
towns.

Economically, politically and culturally town and country in the Basque region
have represented two discrete and frequently opposed social orders. The interpenetration between these two orders was minimal (Caro Baroja, 1974). Economically the compact, walled towns dedicated to administration and international
commerce were set in stark relief to the dispersed and isolated farmsteads founded
on domestic self-sufficiency. Politically the *villas* and the rural areas were circumscribed into different legal frameworks called *fueros*. In the main the *villas*
had been established by the kings of Castilla (and later Spain) for political and
military purposes and were directly tied into the Spanish monarchy. However,
the rural areas were governed by elected assemblies, the *Juntas Generales*, and
were only marginally integrated into the wider Spanish political apparatus.

Culturally the opposition between the two orders was as striking. Partly because of their successful participation in an international economy, the Basque
mercantile classes viewed themselves as modern, cosmopolitan and illustrious.
From the sixteenth century onward the Basque urban bourgeoisie were quick to
adopt intellectual and technological innovations radiating out from other European countries. Vigorous, industrious, reform-minded and thoroughly Hispanized,
the Basque bourgeoisie were the main agents for the introduction and diffusion
of the ideas of the Enlightenment into Spain. In contrast the austere life of the
euskaldun (Basque-speaking) rural areas was confined largely to the closed world
of the rural neighbourhood, the *auzo*. The means for long-distance communication—roads, rivers, literacy, etc.—were in general lacking and contact between
auzoak (-ak = plural) was restricted.

This duality of the Basque-speaking countryside against the Hispanized towns
(although Euskera was often used as a domestic language, Spanish was the preferred public language) was frequently marked by armed confrontation. From the
fifteenth century onward the Basque country was the scene of numerous peasant
uprisings against urban political and economic encroachment. This process of
political opposition reached its pinnacle in the nineteenth century. Throughout

the major part of this century, the centralizing tendencies of the various Madrid governments combined with the aspirations of the Basque urban bourgeoisie to attack frontally the traditional Basque political order based on the *fueros*. The foral institutions (i.e. those founded on *fueros*) protected, by and large, a rural mode of life and the advantaged position of the rural elites within it. The tensions between the anti-*fuero* urban centres and the pro-*fuero* rural areas erupted twice into bitterly fought and prolonged war. These Carlist Wars (1833–39, 1873–76) are complicated affairs, but a few features should be noted.

The military defeat of the rural Basques in the Carlist Wars resulted in the abolition of the *fueros*. And foral abolition was crucial for the development of Basque industry. Under the *fueros* the Basque country was a duty-free zone. Customs lines were drawn along the boundary separating the Basque country from Castilla. Therefore, incipient Basque industry was strangled since it was cut off from Spanish markets by heavy tariff barriers while simultaneously subject to the uninhibited influx of competing industrial goods from abroad. Moreover, under the foral regime the cornerstone of Basque industrial potential—the supremely rich iron mines near Bilbao—was communal rather than private property. After 1876 and the suppression of the Basque *fueros*, the Basque country rapidly developed into the second most important industrial area in Spain (the first being Catalonia).

The modern Basque country was created by the defeat of Carlism and the victory of liberalism and it emerged deeply divided. Foral abolition meant the political alienation of the peasantry. It also meant the political, economic and cultural ascendancy of the expanding urban centres.

In this context, then, how was "Basqueness" perceived in the cities before the impact of Basque nationalism? What was the value placed on Basque identity? Although the vast majority of the population of the cities prior to 1876 was Basque by descent, in Bilbao—the birthplace of Basque industry and Basque nationalism—Euskera had become a rarity as a spoken language already by the early nineteenth century. The language together with other aspects of Basque traditional culture—all part of a rural mode of life—were considered largely irrelevant to the contingencies of modern Basque society. Miguel de Unamuno, one of the major Basque contributions to the famous Spanish literary generation of '98, reflected widely held attitudes when he argued in 1901 that a Bilbao speaking the Basque language was a contradiction in terms. According to Unamuno, it could be scientifically demonstrated that Euskera was not adaptable to modern thought. In the main, Euskera was dismissed as the language of the stables, the language of unsophisticated rustics, in contrast to Spanish, the language of refinement, culture, education and urban success. Whereas Spanish historical and artistic achievements were lauded and admired, Euskera—like rural life in general—was linked to the contemptuous image of the uncultured, brutish peasant—a stigma deeply felt by rural Basques.

Euskera was mainly an oral language and its vulnerability was in part due to its lack of a literary production. In the late nineteenth century when Spanish primary schools were established throughout the Basque region, the rise of literacy and the regression of Euskera became parallel processes.

Whereas the value placed on Basque identity by the Basque urbanites was by-and-large scornful, for the rural Basques, usually illiterate and monolingual, Basque identity was accepted with mixed feelings. Their perception of the opposition between the *euskaldun baserritar* (Basque-speaking peasant) and the Hispanized *kaletar* (urbanite) was strong. On one hand the *baserritar* was regarded as a more rugged, noble being. His social code which stressed the notions of honour, social harmony and egalitarianism was perceived as a model of moral rectitude. On his isolated farmstead the *baserittar* was an independent, sovereign and virtuous individual. In contrast, the *kaletar* was viewed as delicate, dependent, tamed, manipulated and corrupt.

This vision of the moral, hard-working peasant in confrontation with the immoral, effete urbanite has had a long history in the Basque country. It has frequently been used by the Basque peasantry as a language to protest the growing power of urban elites. The ideology of peasant nobility and noble equality was given its most complete expression by Manuel de Larramendi, a Jesuit priest, in his *Corografía de Guipúzcoa* written in 1754. For Larramendi, nobility was an attribute of the land and those who worked it. The *baserritar* cultivating the land and governed by traditional rural values was the original Basque in a state of grace. It was this state of grace that had been shattered by the cities and their easy, luxurious life style. From this decadent, outside world came all inequalities and improbity.

However, the life of the street, of the urban centres, held irresistible attractions. It represented an ordered, comfortable world of regular work days, cash salaries, new housing, bars, shops, leisure and cultural excellence. It was also the world of power—of state bureaucracies, political leaders, courts, lawyers and large landlords in front of which the *baserritar*, lacking the basic skills of literacy and Spanish, was insignificant and impotent. Although the *baserritar* was perceived as more spiritually majestic, the status of *kaletar* was more desirable and prestigious. This status was an important requirement for access to political and economic resources.

To escape the drudgery and poverty of the farms, young men and women came down to the towns, hid their rural awkwardness and learnt Spanish in order through urban employment or marriage to achieve full participation in fashionable city life. From the latter part of the nineteenth century up to the present the rural sector has shrunk dramatically from some 90% of the Basque total population to less than 10%. Until the full impact of Basque nationalism made itself felt, the Basque language as well as Basque traditional culture faced extinction.

One further point: although inside the Basque country, reflecting urban ascendancy, Basque culture and identity were relegated to an inferior position, in their relations with other Spanish citizens and the Madrid political centre the Basque urbanites stressed their claims to a distinct history and culture—i.e. their Basqueness. The core of the Basque argument lay in the notion of Basque collective nobility. Against an intricate background of civil war in the Basque country and the wider military and bureaucratic ambitions of the Basque elites, during the sixteenth century all Basques were extended the legal status of *hidalguía*, nobility (see Otazu, 1973; Greenwood, 1977 for discussion). Collective nobility and the mistaken belief that Basque blood was uncontaminated by either Jewish or Moorish influences combined to create a general feeling of Basque superiority. The advantages conferred by this grant of collective nobility were immense. Noble status was an essential first step for achieving military and administrative position in the Spanish state. Noble status was an important factor in the Basques' successful economic penetration of the Americas. But, as importantly, the notion of collective nobility and hence, the special status of Basques inside Spain, were the central instruments used to maintain Basque fiscal privileges—the Basque region was exempt from all Spanish taxation—when these privileges came into conflict with the designs of the Madrid government. In short, the meaning and function of Basque status varied in accordance to the socio political boundary it served to define and defend.

BOUNDARY AND BASQUE ETHNICITY: INDUSTRIAL BASQUE SOCIETY

Basque nationalism has been a dominant force in the region for some 80 years now. Although the urban centres are still the loci for the mainsprings of political, economic and social power and the rural areas are faced with a deepening crisis, the concept of Basque identity was changed drastically. Previously inside the Basque country Basqueness was essentially a descriptive term referring to cultural form judged to be of little consequence. Now the ascription of Basque status corresponds to Basque cultural content only by coincidence. In general, Basqueness has become a political category. Basque nationalism, an urban product, created Basque ethnicity and defined the rules for membership, and Basque ethnicity has created a new boundary based on the symbols of an old culture.

The general nineteenth century background for the emergence of Basque nationalism in Bilbao in the 1890s can be briefly sketched as follows. First, Spanish nationalism had shown itself to be a failed nationalism. It was incapable of overriding intense local and regional loyalties. Because of the failure of nineteenth century liberal reforms, an economically stagnant and politically corrupt centre was unable either to inspire or control Spain's more vigorous peripheries. Secondly, the Basque country had never been a "regular" part of Spain in the same sense as Extremadura or Andalucia, for example. It had enjoyed administrative autonomy considerably longer than any other Spanish region. Also, parts of the Basque country were characterized by a culture in marked relief to other Iberian cultures. This "fact" of political and cultural differentiation provided the raw material upon which Basque nationalism drew to construct its arguments. Thirdly, the last quarter of the nineteenth century in the Spanish Basque country was a period of radical social change. The old, traditional Basque country governed by *fueros* and dedicated to commercial and agricultural enterprise was superseded by a new Basque society founded on a unified Spanish constitution and heavy, rapidly expanding industry.

In Bilbao—the Basque industrial heartland—industrialization generated extremely high social costs. Its uncontrolled and intense pace placed intolerable strains upon the social fabric of Bilbao and the whole nature of social life deteriorated noticeably. The problems of urban congestion, pollution, inflation and disease became severe. Moreover, the Basque industrial take-off created two new and politically powerful social classes. One was the Basque financial oligarchy which by the turn of the twentieth century probably formed the single most important vested-interest group in Spain. The second was the large industrial proletariat composed mainly of unskilled Spanish immigrant workers who were militant and, at times, violent advocates of socialism. Caught between these two prime movers of Basque industrialization were the economically threatened and politically encircled Basque middle and petty bourgeoisie. It was from this latter grouping that Basque nationalism arose and would recruit its following.

Basque nationalism was inspired by a condemnation of capitalistic industrialization and led to an exaltation of traditional rural society. Although bedecked in the emotive symbols of rural society, it was an ideology constructed by urbanites to deal with urban problems. Unlike most nationalist movements, the principal attack of the early Basque nationalists was not focused on the political centre, Madrid. Its main concern was with social relationships inside the modernizing Basque country. In general, Basque nationalism has been confined to the industrial and industrializing parts of the region. Its arguments were basically aimed at two targets—first and foremost, the Spanish immigrant proletariat and secondly, the Basque financial elite. The main task of Basque nationalism—a task now successfully completed—was to transfer political and economic power away from these two social classes to those entrapped urban classes which had been peripheral to the main thrust of industrialization.

The Basque ideology is based on two fundamental assumptions:

1. The Basques and, therefore, the Basque country, constitute a sovereign nation.
2. By natural right, this Basque nation must be governed solely by Basques for the sole benefit of Basques.

However, the creation and maintenance of boundaries which would define and delimit "Basque" as a discrete and exclusive category was not a straightforward matter. A clear-cut opposition between Basques as "nationals" and Spaniards as "non-nationals" could not serve. One of the chief targets of Basque nationalism—the financial oligarchy—was Basque by descent and many of the early nationalists, as William Douglass (1971:180) has pointed out, had themselves only "shaky geneological claims" to Basque status. Moreover, for Basque nationalism to have its desired effects "Basque" had to become a politically operative category and not a static matter of once-and-for-all biological inclusion or exclusion. The opposition between Basque speakers and Spanish speakers was even less useful. Few of the nationalists spoke Euskera.

The problem was resolved through the construction of an elaborate and largely symbolic nationalist ideology. The overt historical and cultural arguments upon which this ideology rested were less important than the covert political functions these arguments were meant to perform.

The ideology can be broken down into two inter-related sets of symbols. (Cohen's definition of symbols as, "objects, acts, relationships or linguistic formations that stand *ambiguously* for a multiplicity of meanings, evoke emotions and impel men to action," (1974:23) is relevant here.) One set defined the elements of Basque cohesion and exclusiveness and consisted of Euskera, religion, traditional Basque customs and Basque character. These four elements represented the Basque mode of being in diametrical opposition to the Spanish one. Derived from Basque preindustrial society, these elements as symbols functioned to differentiate one sector of urban society defined as "Basque" opposed to other sectors rejected as "anti-Basque." Despite the nationalists' claims to the contrary, Basque customs, Euskera and so forth were not ultimately things valued in and of themselves. These symbols demarcated the battle-lines and provided "national" legitimacy in the struggle for economic and political precedence inside the Basque country.

The nationalists' view of Euskera is illustrative of the symbolic nature of the Basque ideology.

The nationalists expended considerable efforts in studying and attempting to preserve the Basque language. Among other reasons, Euskera was seen as a vehicle for the virtues of the Basque people.

> Euskera cannot be considered merely as a beautiful language worth being cultivated in literature: it is the support of our race and the buttress of the religiosity and morality of our people. (Sabino de Arana, Epílogo, "Collected Works," p. 432)

Nonetheless, the language was not itself important.

> What is the national language, considered by itself except a simple sign by which members of a nation communicate their ideas and emotions? If it is repressed and replaced by another, the nation will continue exactly as before. (Sabino de Arana, Efectos de la invasión, "Collected Works," p. 1327)

For the early nationalists the principal value of Euskera lay in its ability to differentiate Basques, in particular *bizcainos* (Basques from the province of Vizcaya of which Bilbao is the capital) from Latins, in particular *maketos* (the nationalists' derogatory term for Spanish immigrants). Symbolically Euskera placed a barrier of linguistic distance between Basques and their enemies.

> If we had to chose between a Vizcaya populated by *maketos* who spoke only Euskera and a Vizcaya populated by *bizcainos* who spoke only Spanish, without doubt we would select the latter . . . . *Bizcainos* are as obliged to speak their national language as they are not to teach it to the *maketos* or Spaniards. Speaking one language or another is not important. Rather the difference between languages is the means of preserving us from the contagion of Spaniards and avoiding the mixing of the two races. If our invaders learnt Euskera, we would have to abandon it . . . and dedicate ourselves to speaking Russian, Norwegian or some other language unknown to them. (Sabino de Arana, Errores Catalanistas, "Collected Works," p. 404)

The main role of Euskera—like the nationalists' conception of Basque customs, religion and so forth—was as part of the defensive armament to be used against "foreign infiltrators." In addition the nationalists also viewed these elements as underlining the opposition of the moral Basque and the immoral Spaniard. Whereas, Basque religion was a true reflection of sacred beliefs, Spanish religiosity was a mask for superstition and fanaticism. Euskera was the oldest and purest language in Europe. Spanish was *erdera*, a half-language and "bastardized degeneration." In short, the nationalists' conception of Euskera, religion, Basque customs and character provided symbols of exclusion, distance and moral differentiation which yielded ethnically and ethically separated groupings inside the Basque country. The boundary created was both a political and a moral one. In nationalist ideology the Spanish immigrant proletariat—like all things Spanish or Hispanized—was not only excluded from Basque and, hence, "national" status; it was also ejected from the moral universe.

The second set of symbols consisted of the elements of Basque history, *fueros* and the notion of Basque "original sovereignity." These elements served to separate the Basque country as a whole from the process of state unification and centralization. They provided legitimacy in the struggle over the allocation of political and economic resources between the Basque country and Madrid. Whereas, the first set of symbols demonstrated that the Basques were both culturally and morally distinct from Spaniards, the second set demonstrated that the Basque country could never either historically nor politically be regarded as part of Spain.

Standing over both these two sets of symbols and linking them together was a supreme symbol—the Basque race. The Basque race was a totally exclusive category. Race was a God-given condition that could never be achieved. Assimilation was impossible. Moreover, historic races, like the Basque, had a natural right to self-government. They were the *sine qua non* of nations.

Although race was an intrinsic attribute, nevertheless it was an attribute that could easily be lost. In nationalist ideology it was not sufficient to be Basque in terms of surnames, language or character. Ultimately it was not cultural markers that determined nationality. It was the attribute of *abertzalismo*, patriotism. The over-riding feature of the nationalist stress on race was a concern about political loyalties. Political loyalty meant unquestioned public fidelity to the political goal of Basque differentiation, exclusiveness and preference. The Basque ethnic community was viewed as a moral community. The moral duty of all "Basques" was the economic and political defence of this community. In other words, a *real* Basque—a Basque with full national rights—could only be a Basque nationalist.

Clearly the Basque financial oligarchy whose economic behaviour had brought with it the massive inflow of Spanish immigrants and whose political behaviour depended on strong links with Madrid were placed firmly and irrevocably into the camp of the "anti-Basques." For the Basque nationalists the Basque industrialists were responsible for "all the immorality, blasphemy, crime, free-thought, socialism, anarchism . . . that is corrupting the Vizcayan soul."

Whereas, in the rest of Spain political life has broadly operated in terms of the left versus the right, Basque politics has been determined by the complex interactions of three discrete political options—the non-nationalist right, the nationalists and the non-nationalist left.

By the outbreak of the Spanish Civil War in 1936 the Basque nationalists commanded one-third of the electoral vote. The remaining two-thirds was evenly divided between the nationalists' two traditional opponents—the socialists, supported by the immigrant workers and sectors of the Basque working class and the right-wing parties, supported by the Basque economic elite. Both these latter two political forces each from their own vantage point viewed the nationalists with undisguised hostility. The socialists were appalled at the nationalists' arch-conservatism, ethnic exclusiveness and frantic religiosity. The Basque right-wing parties ridiculed the nationalist claim to a monopoly over Basque status and, therefore, Basque "national" resources. If the nationalists were Basques, by all geneological evidence so were the Basque financial oligarchy.

The repression the nationalists in particular and the Basques in general suffered under the Franco regime was brutal. Thousands were imprisoned or forced into exile. Many were executed. Moreover, Franco viewed Basque culture largely as an excuse for and sign of separatism. Therefore, the regime unleashed a thorough campaign of cultural repression. The public use of Basque greetings, traditional garments, folklore, names, publications and the teaching of Euskera were strictly forbidden. These measures were enforced by a vast array of new pro-Franco officials who exercised a stringent control over all aspects of public life. Under the force of the Franco regime Basque nationalism was paralysed into dormancy.

ABERTZALES AND ESPAÑOLISTAS: THE RENOVATION OF THE BASQUE MORAL COMMUNITY

When Basque nationalism slowly resurfaced in the 1960s, its ideology in certain aspects had shifted dramatically. Previously the nationalists had declared Social-ism and Socialists to be anti-Basque and anti-Christ. However, the young nation-alists who emerged with ETA (*Euzkadi'Ta Askatasuna*) proclaimed themselves Socialists as well as nationalists. This conversion was in part inspired by the model of Third World anti-colonial struggles and the European student move-ments. On the non-nationalist side of the political divide attitudes had also changed. Due to the increasing visibility of minority nationalisms in Europe and the deeply hated centralism of the Franco period, the idea that the Basques formed a distinct nationality and had an inherent right to some sort of sovereignty—i.e. to be governed by Basques only—became profoundly acknowledged by the non-nationalists. As a reflection of this attitude most residents of the Basque region claimed Basque status. Such a claim was regarded a moral obligation and a po-litical necessity. Thus, at Franco's death in 1975 the nationalists and the left-wing non-nationalists appeared to be united in a broad agreement concerning the de-sired relationship with Madrid and in a common front against the various Basque right-wing parties.

However, Basque nationalism was and is not just a struggle for territory, for Basque autonomy. More importantly, Basque nationalism supports arguments for a *differential* relationship between certain sectors of the population and others inside the Basque country. It is a struggle for power within a territory occupied by two different political orientations. When competitive politics again became possible in Spain, this struggle for precedence—for exclusive political ownership over economic and social resources—erupted in full force. But Basque nation-alism implies a very special form of competition. It is strictly non-oecumenical.

In nationalist doctrine, the "national"—or nationalist—community should have control over the resources of the "national" territory by natural right.

The symbols of Basque nationalism had been transformed to accord with new European intellectual doctrines. The concept of Basque culture replaced the Basque race as the central symbol of Basque identity and exclusiveness. Basque Socialism substituted Basque Catholicism as the defining element of Basque morality and innate social justice. (see Sarrailh de Ihartza, 1973 for fullest exposition of this view.) But the covert political functions behind these new symbols remained unchanged. The nationalist conception of Basque culture, language, Socialism and so forth, continued to be subordinate to an exclusive political loyalty summed up in the term *abertzalismo* (patriotism). For the Basque nationalists only an *abertsale* (patriot) could be a true "Basque" and only a Basque nationalist could be an *abertzale*.

Despite the apparent agreement in political platforms—both nationalists and non-nationalists demanded Basque autonomy, amnesty for Basque political prisoners, sweeping social reform, official bilingualism and measures to revive Basque culture—the social logic of nationalism bitterly polarized Basque society into *abertzales* and *españolistas*. All aspects of public life—newspapers, schools, popular festivals, academic research, publishing houses, artistic production, amnesty organizations, labour unions as well as political parties were categorized into *abertzale—españolista*, Basque–anti-Basque, national–non-national.

A fuller consideration of Basque politics, which are exceedingly complex, falls outside the confines of this paper. However, one aspect should be noted. The "Basque" side of this cleavage is replete with internal conflicts and tension. Politically it ranges from the Christian democratic Basque Nationalist Party, by far the most important party in the Basque country, to the Marxist–Leninist ETA. Despite political fragmentation and disparities, however, the nationalists perceive themselves as forming a political family bonded by a shared moral cause. On the level of political action the unity forged by nationalism is much stronger than the disunity generated by political conflict.

In contrast the "anti-Basque" side of this boundary does not have a separate, coherent existence. It is a category created by nationalism into which a wide range of disparate groupings are placed. These groupings—which include the Spanish police, the Communist and Socialist parties of Euskadi, Basque industrialists and so forth—have no shared interests, ideology, identity or political ambitions. On no level do they combine for the purpose of political action. Moreover, with the exception of the Spanish police, these groupings fiercely reject their "anti-Basque" label.

The boundary created by this division between *abertzales* and *españolistas*, or anti-Basques, is currently successfully being used to establish the lines of a differential access to public resources. A Basque home-rule statute was granted in 1979 and at present all key public positions in both the political and economic spheres are occupied by nationalists. Many Basque non-nationalists are beginning to fear that this structural inequality of access to public resources may eventually generate tensions in the Spanish Basque country similar to those experienced in Northern Ireland, with equally tragic consequences.

REFERENCES

Arana-Goiri, S. de. "Obras Completas," Sabindiaf-Batza, Buenos Aires.

Barth, F. (1969). "Ethnic Groups and Boundaries," Universtetsforlaget, Oslo.

Caro Baroja, J. (1974). "Introducción a la Historia Social y Económica del Pueblo Vasco," Txertoa, San Sebastian.

Cohen, A. (1969). "Custom and Politics in Urban Africa," Routledge and Kegan Paul, London.

Cohen, A. (1974). "Two-dimensional Man," Routledge and Kegan Paul, London.

Douglass, W. (1971). "Basque Nationalism," Pi-Sunyer (Ed.), *The Limits of Integration: Ethnicity and Nationalism in Modern Europe.* Research Reports nr. 9, Dept. of Anthropology, University of Massachusetts.

Greenwood, D. (1977). Continuity in change: Spanish Basque ethnicity as a historical process. (Ed. D. Esman), "Ethnic Conflict in the Western World," Cornell University Press, Ithaca, New York.

Larramendi, M. de (1754). *Corografía de Guipúzcoa.*

Mitchell, J. C. (1956). "The Kalela dance," Manchester University Press for the Rhodes-Livingstone Institute, Manchester.

Monreal, G. (1977). Las instituciones vascas. "Cultura Vasca I." Erein, San Sebastian.

Otazu y Llana, A. (1973). "El 'Igualitarirismo' Vasco: Mito y Realidad," Txertoa, San Sebastian.

Sarrailh de Ihartza, F. (pseud.) (1973). "Vasconia," Norbait, Buenos Aires.

Stuart Hall

One of the biggest influences in discussions of questions of race and nation in the contemporary English-speaking world has been the now-defunct Centre for Contemporary Cultural Studies (CCCS) at the University of Birmingham, where Stuart Hall (now professor of sociology at the Open University, London) was director from 1972 to 1979. During the 1970s, CCCS became the site of an intensive encounter between indigenous British traditions of cultural criticism and social history (mainly but not only Marxist) with continental European theory of diverse kinds, in which the successive influences of Louis Althusser, Antonio Gramsci, and Michel Foucault were probably the most salient. In the later part of this process feminist theory also entered the picture, while the Centre also engaged head on the issues of race. Initially through a series of stenciled working papers and an occasional journal, and then through a number of thematic volumes, CCCS became enormously influential in the new interdisciplinary field of cultural studies then taking shape in Britain, Australia, and the United States. From our point of view, the key publication of the Centre was a collectively written analysis of the law-and-order issue in British politics, focused on the moral panic surrounding a particular mugging in Handsworth, Birmingham, in August 1972, and developing an argument about the British state and its legitimacy going back over two centuries, in which the authors saw the state as losing its capacity for organizing popular democratic consent. This was *Policing the Crisis: Mugging, the State, and Law and Order* (London: Hutchinson, 1978), authored by Stuart Hall, Chas Critcher, Tony Jefferson, John Clarke, and Brian Roberts. Moreover, while ''race'' as such did not appear in the terms of the title, racism was seen as a central figure of the crisis. Several years later, the Centre explicitly foregrounded this question in another key book: CCCS (eds.), *The Empire Strikes Back: Race and Racism in 70s Britain* (London: Hutchinson, 1982).

The reading included here by Hall combines a theoretical argument about identity, which draws on the post-structuralist perspectives uppermost in the CCCS collective outlook by the 1980s, with a historicized commentary on the politics of the British present, in which a racialized construction of national identity has come increasingly to the fore. Hall argues that older notions of identity as secure, coherent, unitary, and fixed have been fundamentally destabilized both by movements of ideas (the post-structuralist critique of Enlightenment models of the rational actor, but extending much further back through Marx, Freud, and Saussure), and by changes in the world (summarizable as the postmodern condition). The indeterminacies of identity open new horizons of politics for constructing new forms of solidarity. But at the same time, old forms of identification retain their power, particularly those defining themselves negatively via the Other, which in Britain means primarily those who are black, from the Caribbean, Africa, and South Asia. The contemporary discourse of identity in Britain, therefore, is structured around a violent dialectic: on the one hand, the emergence of self-conscious subcultural identities around British blackness; on the other hand, the efforts of conservatives to recenter national identity around an extremely narrow and exclusive notion of Englishness, in which race is the key. In a variety of writings since the late 1970s, Hall has worked this argument into a theory of "Thatcherism," a new form of authoritarian populism built on the ruins of the postwar social-democratic consensus, which established itself during the 1980s (and three election victories) as a hegemonic project. A virulent discourse of the nation, sharpened via the Falklands-Malvinas War in 1982, and turned against the striking coalminers during 1984–85 as the "enemy within," was vital to the cementing of this history. Constant evocations of "Englishness" are crucial, drawing on older imperial memories, as well as the racist antagonisms of the postimperial present. (See *The Hard Road to Renewal: Thatcherism and the Crisis of the Left* [London: Verso, 1988]).

Ethnicity: Identity and Difference

I've chosen to talk about questions of identity and ethnicity, first because questions about identity and ethnicity have suddenly surfaced again in English intellectual and critical discussion and debate. And secondly, because the relationship between cultural identities and ethnicities is a question that is also on the *political* agenda in Britain at the moment. I'll try to say in the course of my talk why I think questions of identity are once again in play conceptually and politically.

THE RETURN OF IDENTITY

I'm concerned with what is sometimes called the "return of the question of identity,"—not that the question of identity ever went away, but it has come back with a particular kind of force. That return has something to do with the fact that the question of identity focuses on that point where a whole series of different developments in society and a set of related discourses intersect. Identity emerges as a kind of unsettled space, or an unresolved question in that space, between a number of intersecting discourses. My purpose is to mark some of those points of intersection, especially around questions of cultural identity, and to explore them in relation to the subject of ethnicity in politics.

Let me start by saying something about what seems to have been the logic of the way in which we have thought and talked about questions of identity until recently. The logic of the discourse of identity assumes a stable subject, i.e., we've assumed that there is something which we can call our identity which, in a rapidly shifting world, has the great advantage of staying still. Identities are a kind of guarantee that the world isn't falling apart quite as rapidly as it sometimes seems to be. It's a kind of fixed point of thought and being, a ground of action, a still point in the turning world. That's the kind of ultimate guarantee that identity seems to provide us with.

The logic of identity is the logic of something like a "true self." And the language of identity has often been related to the search for a kind or of authenticity to one's experience, something that tells me where I come from. The logic

Stuart Hall, "Ethnicity: Identity and Difference," *Radical America*, 23, 4 (October–December 1989), pp. 9–20. Edited version of a speech given at Hampshire College, Amherst, Massachusetts, in the Spring of 1989.

and language of identity is the logic of depth—in here, deep inside me, is my Self which I can reflect upon. It is an element of continuity. I think most of us do recognize that our identities have changed over time, but we have the hope or nostalgia that they change at the rate of a glacier. So, while we're not the fledglings that we were when we were one year old, we are the same sort of person.

DISRUPTION OF IDENTITY

So where does the recent disruption of identity come from? What is displacing this depth—the autonomous origin, point of reference, and guaranteed continuity that has been so long associated with the language of identity? What is it about the turbulence of the world we live in that is increasingly mirrored in the vicissitudes of identity?

While, historically, many things have displaced or decentered the stable sense of identity that I just described, I want to focus on four great decenterings in intellectual life and in Western thought that have helped to destabilize the question of identity. I'll attach particular names to three of them, just for convenience sake. I don't want to say they alone did it, but it is quite useful to summarize by hooking the ideas to a particular name. The fourth cannot be attached to a single name, but is just as important.

Marx begins the de-centering of that stable sense of identity by reminding us that there are always *conditions* to identity which the subject, cannot construct. Men and women make history but not under conditions of their own making. They are partly made by the histories that they make. We are always constructed in part by the practices and discourses that make us, such that we cannot find within ourselves as individual selves or subjects or identities the point of origin from which discourse or history or practice originates. History has to be understood as a continuous dialectic or dialogic relationship between that which is already made and that which is making the future. While Marx's argument deconstructed a lot of games, I'm particularly interested in his impact on the identity/language game. Marx interrupted that notion of the sovereign subject who opens his or her mouth and speaks, for the first time, the truth. Marx reminds us that we are always lodged and implicated in the practices and structures of everybody else's life.

Secondly, there is the very profound displacement which begins with Freud's discovery of the unconscious. If Marx displaced us from the past, Freud displaced us from below. Identity is itself grounded on the huge unknowns of our psychic lives, and we are unable, in any simple way, to reach through the barrier of the unconscious into the psychic life. We can't read the psychic *directly* into the social and the cultural. Nevertheless, social, cultural and political life cannot be understood except in relationship to the formations of the unconscious life. This in itself destabilizes the notion of the self, of identity, as a fully self-reflective entity. It is not possible for the self to reflect and know completely its own identity since it is formed not only in the line of the practice of other structures and discourses, but also in a complex relationship with unconscious life.

Thirdly, we must consider Saussure and his model of language and linguistics which has so transformed theoretical work. Saussurian linguistics suggests that speech—discourse, enunciation itself—is always placed within the relationships of language. In order to speak, in order to say anything new, we must first place ourselves within the existing relations of language. There is no utterance so novel and so creative that it does not already bear on it the traces of how that language has been spoken before we opened our mouths. Thus we are always within language. To say something new is first of all to reaffirm the traces of the past that are inscribed in the words we use. In part, to say something new is first of all to displace all the old things that the words mean—to fight an entire system of meanings. For example, think of how profound it has been in our world to say the word "Black" in a new way. In order to say "Black" in a new way, we have to fight off everything else that Black has always meant—all its connotations, all its negative and positive figurations, the entire metaphorical structure of Christian thought, for example. The whole history of Western imperial thought is condensed in the struggle to dislocate what Black used to mean in order to make it mean something new, in order to say "Black is Beautiful." I'm not talking about Saussure's specific theories of language only. I'm talking about what happens to one's conception of identity when one suddenly understands that one is always inside a system of languages that partly speak us, which we are always positioned within and against.

These are the great figures of modernism. We might say that if modernity unleashes the logic of identity I was talking about earlier, modernism is modernity experienced as trouble. In the face of modernity's promise of the great future: "I am, I am Western man, therefore I know everything. Everything begins with me," modernism says, "Hold on. What about the past? What about the languages you speak? What about the unconscious life you don't know about? What about all those other things that are speaking you?"

However, there's a fourth force of destabilization. This could be given a variety of names. If you wanted to stay within the episteme of Western knowledge, you could say Nietzsche. But I want to say something else. I want to talk about the de-centering of identity that arises as a consequence of the end of the notion of truth as having something directly to do with Western discourses of rationality. This is the great de-centering of identity that is a consequence of the relativization of the Western world—of the discovery of other worlds, other peoples, other cultures, and other languages. Western rational thought, despite its imperializing claim to be *the* form of universal knowledge, suddenly appears as just another episteme. To use Foucault's words, just another regime of truth. Or Nietzsche's, not absolute Knowledge, not total Truth, just another *particular* form of knowledge harnessed to particular forms of historical power. The linkage between knowledge and power is what made that regime True, what enabled that regime to claim to speak the truth about identity for everyone else across the globe.

When that installation of Western rationality begins to go and to be seen not as absolute, disinterested, objective, neutral, scientific, non-powerful truth, but dirty truth—truth implicated in the hard game of power—that is the fourth game that destabilizes the old logic of identity.

COLLECTIVE IDENTITIES

I've been talking so far about intellectual, theoretical, conceptual displacements of the notion of identity, but I want to talk about some of the displacements of identity that come from social and cultural life rather than from conceptual and theoretical thought. The great social collectivities which used to stabilize our identities—the great stable collectivities of class, race, gender and nation—have been, in our times, deeply undermined by social and political developments.

The whole adventure of the modern world was, for a long time, blocked out in terms of these great collective identities. As one knew one's class, one knew one's place in the social universe. As one knew one's race, one knew one's racial position within the great races of the world in their hierarchical relationship to one another. As one knew one's gender, one was able to locate oneself in the huge social divisions between men and women. As one knew one's national identity, one certainly knew about the pecking order of the universe. These collective identities stabilized and staged our sense of ourselves. That logic of identity that seemed so confident at the beginning of my talk, was in part held in place by these great collective social identities.

Now, it is not the best kept secret in the world that all sorts of things have rocked and shaken those great collective, stable, social identities of the past. I don't want to talk about any of those developments in detail, but if you think, for instance, of class, it certainly is not true that, in societies like yours and mine, questions of class—of social structure and of social inequality that are raised by the notion of class—have gone away. But, nevertheless, the way in which class identities were understood and experienced, the way in which people located themselves in relation to class identities, the way in which we understood those identities as organized politically—those stable forms of class identity are much more difficult to find at this point in the twentieth century than they were 100 years ago. In fact, looking backwards, we're not sure whether the great stable identities of class were ever quite as stable as we told ourselves they were. There's a kind of narrative of class that always makes the past look simpler than it probably was. If you go back into English nineteenth century life, you will find that class was a pretty complex formation even then. I think there is, nevertheless, some relative sense in which the nation-state, the great class formations of industrial capitalism, certainly the way in which gender was conceptualized, and, toward the end of the nineteenth century, the way in which the entire population of the world could be thought of in terms of the great family of races—I do think there is a way in which these great structuring principles did tie down the question of our social and cultural identities and that they have been very considerably fractured, fragmented, undermined, dispersed in the course of the last fifty years.

THE UNIVERSE IS COMING

Now, this fragmentation of social identity is very much a part of the modern and, indeed, if you believe in it, the postmodern experience. That sense of fragmentation has a peculiar and particular shape to it. Specifically, if I may say this metaphorically, the fragmentation goes local and global at one and the same time, while the great stable identities in the middle do not seem to hold.

Take "the nation." The nation-state is increasingly besieged from on top by the interdependence of the planet—by the interdependency of our ecological life, by the enormous interpenetration of capital as a global force, by the complex ways in which world markets link the economies of backward, developed, and overdeveloped nations. These enormous systems are increasingly undermining the stability of any national formation. Nation-states are in trouble, though I am not going to prophesy that the nation-state, that has dominated the history of the world for so long, is going to bow out gracefully.

So on the one hand, the nation and all the identities that go with it appear to have gone upwards—reabsorbed into larger communities that overreach and interconnect national identities. But at the same time there is also movement down below. Peoples and groups and tribes who were previously harnessed together in the entities called the nation-states begin to rediscover identities that they had forgotten. So for example if you come to England and hope to see some great stable cultural identity called "the English"—who represent everybody else—what you will find instead is that the Scots, for example, are about to fly off somewhere. They say "We are Scottish and we are European, but we certainly aren't British." And the Welsh say "We're not British either because you've forgotten us and we might as well go somewhere else." And at the same time the Northwest and the Northeast of England, that were left to rot by Mrs. Thatcher, are not truly British any longer either—they're sort of marginal to everybody else. Then the old trade unionists and all Blacks are somebody else, too. You're left with the English as a tight little island somewhere around London with about 25 souls and the Thatcher government hovering over it. And they are continually asking the question—not only about the rest of the world but about most of the people in their own society—"are you one of us?"

So at one and the same time people feel part of the world and part of their village. They have neighborhood identities and they are citizens of the world. Their bodies are endangered by Chernobyl, which didn't knock on the door and say "Can I float radiation over your sovereign territory?" Or another example, we had the warmest winter I've ever experienced in England, last year—the consequence in part of the destruction of rain forests thousands of miles away. An ecological understanding of the world is one that challenges the notion that the nation-state and the boundaries of sovereignty will keep things stable because they won't. The universe is coming!

So on the one hand, we have global identities because we have a stake in something global and, on the other hand, we can only know ourselves because we are part of some face-to-face communities. This brings me back to the question of the fate of cultural identity in this maelstrom. Given this theoretical and conceptual de-centering that I've just spoken about, given the relativization of the great stable identities that have allowed us to know who we are—how can we think about the question of cultural identity?

POST-IDENTITY? COVER STORIES

There is some language for the notion of doing without identity all together. That is my somewhat unfavorable reference to the extreme version of postmodernism. The argument is that the Self is simply a kind of *perpetual signifier* ever wandering the earth in search of a *transcendental signified* that it can never find—a sort of endless nomadic existence with utterly atomized individuals wandering in an endlessly pluralistic void. Yet, while there are certain conceptual and theoretical ways in which you can try to do without identity, I'm not yet convinced that you can. I think we have to try to reconceptualize what identities might mean in this more diverse and pluralized situation.

This takes us back to some of the very profound things that people have said about identity within recent forms of theorizing. First of all, we are reminded of the structure of "identification" itself. Identity, far from the simple thing that we think it is (ourselves always in the same place) understood properly is always a structure that is split; it always has ambivalence within it. The story of identity is a cover story. A cover story for making you think you stayed in the same place, though with another bit of your mind you do know that you've moved on. What we've learned about the structure of the way in which we identify suggests that identification is not one thing, one moment. We have now to reconceptualize identity as a *process of identification*, and that is a different matter. It is something that happens over time, that is never absolutely stable, that is subject to the play of history and the play of difference.

I don't want to bore you autobiographically, but I could tell you something about the process of my own identification. If I think about who I am, I have been—in my own much too long experience—several identities. And most of the identities that I have been I've only known about *not* because of something deep inside me—the real self—but because of how other people have recognized me.

So, I went to England in the 1950s, before the great wave of migration from the Caribbean and from the Asian subcontinent. I came from a highly respectable, lower middle class Jamaican family. When I went back home at the end of the 50s, my mother, who was very classically of that class and culture, said to me "I hope they don't think you're an immigrant over there! I had never thought of myself as an immigrant! And now I thought, well actually, I guess that's what I am. I migrated just at that moment. When she hailed me, when she said "Hello immigrant," she asked me to refuse it and in the moment of refusal—like almost everything my mother ever asked me to do—I said "That's who I am! I'm an immigrant" And I thought at last, I've come into my *real* self.

And then, at the end of the 60s and the early 70s, somebody said to me "These things are going on in the political world—I suppose you're really Black." Well, I'd never thought of myself as Black, either! And I'll tell you something, nobody in Jamaica ever did. Until the 1970s, that entire population experienced themselves as all sorts of other things, but they never called themselves Black. And in that sense, Black has a history as an identity that is partly *politically* formed. It's not the color of your skin. It's not given in nature.

Another example: at that very moment I said to my son, who is the result of a mixed marriage, "You're Black." "No," he said, "I'm brown." "You don't understand what I'm saying! You're looking to the wrong signifier! I'm not talking about what color you are . People are all sorts of colors. The question is whether you are *culturally, historically, politically* Black. *That's* who you are."

THE OTHER

So experience belies the notion that identification happens once and for all—life is not like that. It goes on changing and part of what is changing is not the nucleus of the "real you" inside, it is history that's changing. History changes your conception of yourself. Thus, another critical thing about identity is that it is partly the relationship between you and the Other. Only when there is an Other can you know who you are. To discover that fact is to discover and unlock the whole enormous history of nationalism and of racism. Racism is a structure of discourse and representation that tries to expel the Other symbolically—blot it out, put it over there in the Third World, at the margin.

The English are racist not because they hate the Blacks but because they don't know who they are without the Blacks. They have to know who they are *not* in order to know who they are. And the English language is absolutely replete with things that the English are not. They are not Black, they are not Indian or Asian, but they are not Europeans and they are not Frogs either and on and on. The Other. It is a fantastic moment in Fanon's *Black Skin, White Masks* when he talks of how the gaze of the Other fixes him in an identity. He knows what it is to be Black when the white child pulls the hand of her mother and says "Look momma, a Black man." And he says "I was fixed in that gaze." That is the gaze of Otherness. And there is no identity that is without the dialogic relationship to the Other. The Other is not outside, but also inside the Self, the identity. So identity is a process, identity is split. Identity is not a fixed point but an ambivalent point. Identity is also the relationship of the Other to oneself.

DIFFERENCE(S)

You could tell that story also in terms of a psychic conception of identity. Some of the most important work that modern psychoanalysts have done—Lacan and so forth—and that feminists have done in terms of sexual identity is to show the importance of the relationship of the Other. The *construction of difference* as a process, as something that goes on over time, is something that feminism has been showing us is never finished. The notion that identity is complete at some point—the notion that masculinity and femininity can view each other as a perfectly replicating mirror image of each another—is untenable after the slightest reading of any feminist text or after reading Freud's *Three Essays on Sexuality*.

So the notion that identity is outside representation—that there are our selves and then the language in which we describe ourselves—is untenable. Identity is within discourse, within representation. It is constituted in part by representation. Identity is a narrative of the self; it's the story we tell about the self in order to know who we are. We impose a structure on it. The most important effect of this reconceptualization of identity is the surreptitious return of difference. Identity is a game that ought to be played against difference. But now we have to think about identity *in relation to* difference. There are differences between the ways in which genders are socially and psychically constructed. But there is no fixity to those oppositions. It is a relational opposition, it is a relation of difference. So we're then in the difficult conceptual area of trying to think identity *and* difference.

There are two *different* notions of difference operating. There are the great differences of the discourse of racism—Black and white, civilized and primitive, them and us. But this new conception of difference is a conception much closer to that notion of difference one finds in Derrida. In Derrida you find a notion of *difference* that recognizes the endless, ongoing nature of the construction of meaning but that recognizes also that there is always the play of identity and difference and always the play of difference *across* identity. You can't think of them without each other.

You see, there has been in our lifetime—not in yours, but in mine—a *politics* of identity. There was a *politics* of identity in 1968 in which the various social movements tried to organize themselves politically within one identity. So the identity of being a woman was the subject of the feminist movement. The identity of being a Black person was the identity of the Black movement. And in that rather simpler universe, there was one identity to each movement. While you were in it, you had one identity. Of course, even then, all of us moved between these so-called stable identities. We were sampling these different identities, but we maintained the notion, the myth, the narrative that we were really all the same. That notion of essential forms of identity is no longer tenable.

THE THATCHER PROJECT

So, how can one think about identity in this new context? I want to say just a word about the way this has emerged politically in the United Kingdom in the last ten years. I referred a few moments ago to a very narrow and exclusive conception of Englishness that lies at the absolute center of the political project of Thatcherism. When I first started to write about Thatcherism in the early 70s, I thought it was largely an economic and political project. It is only more recently that I understood how profoundly it is rooted in a certain exclusive and essentialist conception of Englishness. Thatcherism is *in defense* of a certain definition of Englishness. England didn't go to the Falklands War inadvertently. It went because there was something there about the connection of the great imperial past, of the empire, of the lion whose tail cannot be tweaked, of the little country that stood up to the great dictator. It's a way of mythically living all the great moments of the English past again. Well, it happens that this time it had to be in the South Atlantic, miles away from anything—in a little corner of the globe that most

English people can't identify on the map. This is Marx's famous phrase "The first time is history, the second time is farce." And the third time is an extremely long trip to the South Atlantic. This is the moment of decline that is always a moment of danger in national cultures.

THE RETURN OF THE REPRESSED

So it's a very profound part of the Thatcher project to try to restore the identity that in their view *belongs* to Great Britain—Great Britain, Inc., Ltd.—a great firm, Great Britain restored to a world power. But in this very moment of the attempted symbolic restoration of the great English identities that have mastered and dominated the world over three or four centuries, there come home to roost in English society some *other* British folks. They come from Jamaica, Pakistan, Bangladesh, India—all that part of the colonial world that the English, just in the 1950s, decided they could do without. Just in the very moment when they decided they could do without us, we all took the banana boat and came right back home. We turned up saying "You said this was the mother country. Well, I just came home." We now stand as a permanent reminder of that forgotten, suppressed, hidden history. Every time they walk out on the street, some of us—some of the Other—are there. There we are, *inside* the culture, going to their schools, speaking their language, playing their music, walking down their streets, looking like we own a part of the turf, looking like we belong. Some third generation Blacks are starting to say "We are the Black British." After all, who are we? We're not Jamaicans any more. We have a relationship to that past, but we can't be that entirely any more. You can see that debates around questions of identity are at the center of political life in England today.

ETHNICITIES: OLD AND NEW

What does all that I've been saying have to do with ethnicity? I've left the question of ethnicity to the last because ethnicity is the way in which I want to rethink the relationships between identity and difference. I want to argue that ethnicity is what we all require in order to think the relationship between identity and difference. What do I mean by that? There is no way, it seems to me, in which people of the world can act, can speak, can create, can come in from the margins and talk, can begin to reflect on their own experience unless they come from some *place*, they come from some history, they inherit certain cultural traditions. What we've learned about the theory of enunciation is that there's no enunciation without positionality. You have to position yourself *somewhere* in order to say anything at all. Thus, we cannot do without that sense of our own positioning that is connoted by the term ethnicity. And the relation that peoples of the world now have to their own past is, of course, part of the discovery of their own ethnicity. They need to honor the hidden histories from which they come. They need to understand the languages which they've been not taught to speak. They need to understand and revalue the traditions and inheritances of cultural expression and creativity. And in that sense, the past is not only a position from which to speak, but it is also an absolutely necessary resource in what one has to say. There is no way, in my view, in which those elements of ethnicity that depend on understanding the past, understanding one's roots, can be done without.

But, on the other hand, there comes the play of difference. This is the recognition that our relationship to that past is quite a complex one, we can't pluck it up out of where it was and simply restore it to ourselves. If you ask my son, who is seventeen and who was born in London, where he comes from, he cannot tell you he comes from Jamaica. Part of his identity is there, but he has to *discover* that identity. He can't just take it out of a suitcase and plop it on the table and say "That's mine." It's not an essence like that. He has to learn to tell himself the story of his past. He has to interrogate his own history, he has to relearn that part of him that has an investment in that culture. For example, he's learning wood sculpture, and in order to do that he has had to discover the traditions of sculpturing of a society in which he has never lived.

So the relationship of the kind of ethnicity I'm talking about to the past is not a simple, essential one—it is a constructed one. It is constructed in history, it is constructed politically in part. It is part of narrative. We tell ourselves the stories of the parts of our roots in order to come into contact, creatively, with it. So this new kind of ethnicity—the emergent ethnicities—has a relationship to the past, but it is a relationship that is partly through memory, partly through narrative, one that has to be recovered. It is an act of cultural recovery.

Yet it is also an ethnicity that has to recognize its position in relation to the importance of difference. It is an ethnicity that cannot deny the role of difference in discovering itself. And I'll tell you a simple, quick story to show you what I mean. About two years ago I was involved in a photographic exhibition that was organized by the Commonwealth Institute in England, and the idea behind it was very simple. Photography is one of the languages in which people speak about their own past and their own experience and construct their own identity. Large numbers of people in the marginal societies of the British Commonwealth have been the *objects* of someone else's representation, not the *subject* of their own representations. The purpose of this exhibition was to enable some people in those regions to use the creative medium of photography to speak and address their own experience—to empower their ethnicities.

When we came to look at the exhibition, one saw two things at one and the same time. First of all, we saw the enormous excitement of people who are able for the first time to speak about what they have always known—to speak about their culture, their languages, their people, their childhood, about the topography in which they grew up. The arts in our society are being transformed hourly by the new discourses of subjects who have been marginalized coming into representation for the first time. But we also saw something else that we were not prepared for. From those local ethnic enclaves, what they want to speak about as well is the entire world. They want to tell you how they went from the village to Manhattan. They are not prepared to be ethnic archivists for the rest of their lives. They are not prepared only to have something to say of marginalization forever.

They have a stake in the whole dominant history of the world, they want to rewrite the history of the world, not just tell my little story. So they use photography to tell us about the enormous migrations of the world and how people now move— of how all our identities are constructed out of a variety of different discourses. We need a place to speak from, but we no longer speak about ethnicity in a narrow and essentialist way.

That is the new ethnicity. It is a new conception of our identities because it has not lost hold of the place and the ground from which we can speak, yet it is no longer contained within that place as an essence. It wants to address a much wider variety of experience. It is part of the enormous cultural relativization of the entire globe that is the historical accomplishment—horrendous as it has been in part—of the twentieth century. Those are the new ethnicities, the new voices. They are neither locked into the past nor able to forget the past. Neither all the same nor entirely different. Identity *and* difference. It is a new settlement between identity and difference.

Of course, alongside the new ethnicities are the *old* ethnicities and the coupling of the old essentialist identities to power. The old ethnicities still have dominance, they still govern. Indeed, as I tried to suggest when I referred to Thatcherism, as they are relativized their propensity to eat everything else increases. They can only be sure that they really exist at all if they consume everyone else. The notion of an identity that knows where it came from, where home is, but also lives in the symbolic—in the Lacanian sense—knows you can't really go home again. You can't be something else than who you are. You've got to find out who you are in the flux of the past and the present. That new conception of ethnicity is now struggling in different ways across the globe against the present danger and the threat of the dangerous old ethnicity. That's the stake of the game.

Paul Gilroy

Paul Gilroy worked at the Birmingham Centre for Contemporary Cultural Studies (CCCS), and has taught at Goldsmith's College of the University of London, the University of Essex, and Yale University. He was part of the CCCS collective that produced *The Empire Strikes Back: Race and Racism in 70s Britain* (London: Hutchinson, 1982), which in one way can be seen as a continuation of the analysis in Stuart Hall et al., *Policing the Crisis: Mugging, the State, and Law and Order* (London: Hutchinson, 1978), which anticipated much of the work influenced by CCCS in the 1980s. But although the "race text" runs right through the center of this earlier analysis (in its origins and formal focus, *Policing the Crisis* was about the moral panic surrounding an instance of "racial" mugging), in another way race recedes into a broader argument about the state, hegemony, and class in the British past and present. *The Empire Strikes Back* was an angry protest at this effacement of race, and a sustained argument for making it central to our understanding of British politics. More specifically, Gilroy and his co-authors insisted that notions of British identity—and of the "Englishness" at their heart— are structured around powerful assertions of racial difference, transmitted partly from the imperial past, and coming partly from the postimperial social antagonisms of Britain's decline, which both center national identity around an unspoken "whiteness," and marginalize and silence the presence of blacks. Even the radical reworking of British traditions in the thought of Raymond Williams, Edward Thompson, and the New Left, they charged, inscribed the same latent ethnocentrism. One aim of *The Empire Strikes Back* was to bring these assumptions into the open, to force the "Britishness" or "Englishness" of cultural studies into self-consciousness.

The essay reprinted here is a detailed exposition of this case. It reflects the movement away from older habits of class-centered analysis toward a recognition that consciousness, identity, and subjectivity are formed in other ways too. As Gilroy says: "It challenges theories that assert the primacy of structural contradictions, economic classes, and crises in determining political consciousness and collective action." Moreover, as well as exploring the close articulation with ideas of race in contemporary nationalist discourse, Gilroy subjects the former to a powerful antiessentialist critique, which is quite continuous with the deconstructive or constructionist approach to national differences this volume has been trying to stress. British racism is conceived in cultural and not biological terms, he argues, as a kind of "ethnic absolutism," which asserts the immutable nature of racial characteristics, with roots deep in the unconscious, and visible via customs, family forms, cuisine, music, sociability, and of course unchangeable pathologies (in the racist's view) such as criminal and other behaviors that don't "belong" with the British way. On the other hand, Black culture exhibits forms of autonomy and resistance, which are drawn elsewhere, beyond the boundaries of the territorialized British nation, to the Caribbean, the United States, Africa, and South Asia. Thus "race," as a historically specific field of cultural relations in Britain, has come to organize collective identities into strongly centered and marginalized constructions of the nation. Gilroy has developed these arguments more extensively in two books, *"There Ain't No Black in the Union Jack": The Cultural Politics of Race and Nation* (Chicago: University of Chicago Press, 1987), and *The Black Atlantic: Modernity and Double-Consciousness* (Cambridge, Mass.: Harvard University Press, 1993), and a collection of essays, *Small Acts: Thoughts on the Politics of Black Cultures* (London: Serpent's Tail, 1993).

One Nation under a Groove: The Cultural Politics of "Race" and Racism in Britain

> How much is here embraced by the term *culture*. It includes all the characteristic activities and interests of a people; Derby Day, Henley Regatta, Cowes, the twelfth of August, a cup final, the dog races, the pin table, the dart board, Wensleydale cheese, boiled cabbage cut into sections, beetroot in vinegar, nineteenth century Gothic churches and the music of Elgar.
>
> T. S. ELIOT

> While there is some community of interest called Britain and common institutions and historical experiences called British, and indeed a nationality on a passport called British, it is not an identity which is self contained. . . . Britain is a state rather than a nation. The British state imposed upon the English, Scottish, Welsh and part of the Irish peoples and then imposed world wide, is an inherently imperial and colonial concept at home and abroad. The British state cannot and should not be an object of affection, save for those who want to live in a form of authoritarian dependency.
>
> DAFYDD ELIS THOMAS

Studying the politics of "race"[1] necessitates tracing at least two separate yet intertwined threads of history. The first involves mapping the changing contours of racist ideologies, the semantic fields in which they operate, their special rhetoric, and their internal fractures, as well as their continuities. The second centers on the history of social groups, both dominant and subordinate, that recognize themselves in terms of "race" and act accordingly. Neither of these histories is reducible to the other, and they reciprocate in a complex manner over time bringing together the myths of descent with the management of conquest and the negotiation of consent. The groups we learn to know as "races" are not, of course,

Paul Gilroy, "One Nation under a Groove: The Cultural Politics of 'Race' and Racism in Britain," *Anatomy of Racism*, ed. David Theo Goldberg (Minneapolis: University of Minnesota Press, 1990), pp. 263–82.

Author's note: I would like to thank Vron Ware and Mandy Rose for their help with this essay (which was completed in December 1987).

formed simply and exclusively by the power of racial discourses. The intimate association between ideas about race and the employment of unfree labor in plantation slavery, "debt peonage," apartheid, or the coercive use of migrant labor should be a constant warning against conceptualizing racial ideologies as if they are wholly autonomous. Race may provide literary critics with "the ultimate trope of difference," but the brain-teasing perplexities of theorizing about race cannot be allowed to obscure the fact that the play of difference in which racial taxonomy appears has extradiscursive referents. At different times, economic, political, and cultural factors all play a determining role in shaping the character of "races." The power of race politics can be used as a general argument for realist conceptions of ideology that emphasize referential conceptions of meaning and defend a problematic of relative or partial autonomy.[2]

Races are not, then, simple expressions of either biological or cultural sameness. They are imagined—socially and politically constructed—and the contingent processes from which they emerge may be tied to equally uneven patterns of class formation to which they, in turn, contribute. Thus ideas about race may articulate political and economic relations in a particular society that go beyond the distinct experiences or interests of racial groups to symbolize wider identities and conflicts. Discussion of racial domination cannot therefore be falsely separated from wider considerations of social sovereignty such as the conflict between men and women, the antagonism between capital and labor, or the manner in which modes of production develop and combine. Nor can the complexities of racial politics be reduced to the effect of these other relations. Dealing with these issues in their specificity and in their articulation with other relations and practices constitutes a profound and urgent theoretical and political challenge. It requires a theory of racisms that does not depend on an essentialist theory of races themselves.

These methodological observations help to negotiate a critical distance from positivist and productivist Marxian and neo-Marxian approaches that risk the reduction of race to a mystical conception of class as well as those that have buried the specific qualities of racism in the difficulties surrounding the analysis of ideology in general. Pursuing a radical analysis of race and racism within the broad framework supplied by historical materialism requires a frank and open acknowledgment of its limitations. Yet Marxism understood in Richard Wright's phrase as a "transitory makeshift pending a more accurate diagnosis"[3] can provide some valuable points of departure. If the capacity of race and racism to slide between the realm of "phenomenal forms" and the world of "real relations" means that they have baffled and perplexed Marxian orthodoxy,[4] there is much to learn from the radically historical approach that has emerged from some of the more sophisticated applications of Marx's insights. Working from an explicitly Marxian perspective. Stuart Hall puts it like this:

> Racism is always historically specific. Though it may draw on the cultural traces deposited by previous historical phases, it always takes on specific forms. It arises out of present—not past—conditions. Its effects are specific to the present organisation of society, to the present unfolding of its dynamic political and cultural processes—not simply to its repressed past.[5]

This important observation points squarely at the plurality of forms in which racism has developed, not simply between societies but within them also. It underlines the idea that there is no racism in general and consequently there can be no general theory of race relations or race and politics. More important, a perspective that emphasizes the need to deal with racisms rather than a single ahistorical racism also implicitly attacks the fashionable overidentification of race and ethnicity with tradition, allowing instead the opportunity to develop a view of contemporary racisms as responses to the flux of modernity itself.[6]

This perspective places severe limitations on analysis of particular local racisms. It demands that the development of racist discourses must be periodized very carefully and that the fluidity and inherent instability of racial categories is constantly appreciated. With these qualifications in mind, I want to examine some aspects of recent race politics in Britain, by looking, first, at the particular contemporary forms of racist discourse and, second, at the distinctive political outlook articulated by the expressive cultures of England's black settlers.

The starting point for this inquiry must be an acknowledgment of Britain's postcolonial decline and crisis. Although this crisis originates in the economic sphere,[7] it has a variety of features—economic, political, ideological, and cultural. They are not wholly discrete and although they are definitely discontinuous, they are experienced as a complex unity of many unsynchronized determinations. How then is this unity constructed? I want to suggest that ideas about race that are produced by a new and historically specific form of racism play a primary role in securing it. This crisis is thus *lived* through a sense of race. A volatile populist racism has become an obvious political feature of this crisis. But racism is more than simply an increasingly important component of a morbid political culture. It has also become part of how the different elements of this protracted "organic" crisis have become articulated together.[8]

The centrality of racism to this crisis does not, however, mean that the word "race" is on everybody's lips. It bears repetition that racism changes and varies historically. It is essential to remember that we are not talking about racism in general but British crisis racism in particular. One of the ways in which this form or variety of racism is specific is that it frequently operates without any overt reference to either race itself or the biological notions of difference that still give the term its commonsense meaning. Before the rise of modern scientific racism in the nineteenth century the term "race" did duty for the term "culture."[9] No surprise, then, that in its postwar retreat from racism the term has once again acquired an explicitly cultural rather than a biological inflection.

The stress and turbulence of crisis have induced Britons to clarify their national identity by asking themselves a question first posed by Enoch Powell: "What kind of people are we?" Their self-scrutiny has prompted a fascination with primary, ascribed identities that is manifested in an increasingly decadent preoccupation with the metaphysics of national belonging. Examining contemporary British ideas about race and their relationship to notions of nationhood and national belonging in particular can therefore tell us something about the crisis as a whole.

It would appear that the uncertainty the crisis has created requires that lines of inclusion and exclusion that mark out the national community be redrawn. Britons are invited to put on their tin hats and climb back down into their World War II air raid shelters. There, they can be comforted by the rustic glow of the homogeneous national culture that has been steadily diluted by black settlement in the postwar years. That unsullied culture can be mystically reconstituted, particularly amidst national adversity when distinctively British qualities supposedly emerge with the greatest force and clarity. The analogy of war is extensively employed, not just in attempts to represent black immigration and settlement as the encroachment of aliens but around the politics of crime and domestic political dissent. Industrial militants and black settlers have come to share the designation "The Enemy Within." In 1982, real war off the coast of Argentina provided, in the words of one New Right ideologue, an opportunity for the nation to discover "what truly turns it on." From this perspective, which has provided a cornerstone for popular, commonsense racism, blacks, trapped by the biology of their skin shade into a form of symbolic treason, are excluded from the national community because their cultures have obstructed the acquisition of that special hallmark of a true patriotism: the willingness to lay down one's life for one's country.

The culturalism of the new racism has gone hand in hand with a definition of race as a matter of difference rather than a question of hierarchy. In another context Fanon refers to a similar shift as a progression from vulgar to cultural racism.[10] The same process is clearly seen in the cultural focus that marked the inauguration of the apartheid system in 1948.

Culture is conceived along ethnically absolute lines, not as something intrinsically fluid, changing, unstable, and dynamic, but as a fixed property of social groups rather than a relational field in which they encounter one another and live out social, historical relationships. When culture is brought into contact with race it is transformed into a pseudobiological property of communal life.

Thus England's black settlers are forever locked in the bastard culture of their enslaved ancestors, unable to break out into the "mainstream" alternative. Their presence in the ancient territory of the "Island Race" becomes a problem precisely because of their difference and distance from the standards of civilized behavior that are second nature to authentic (white) Britons. The most vocal ideologists of the English New Right[11]—Powell himself, John Casey, and Ray Honeyford—stress not only that they are not racists but that they have no sense whatever of the innate superiority of whites or the congenital inferiority of blacks. They profess allegiance to the nation rather than the race and identify the problems of contemporary black settlement in terms of cultural conflict between the same groups that were once misrecognized as biologically distinct races. This cultural sense of race has posed key problems for antiracist strategy and tactics.

As the distance from crude biologism has increased, the question of law has become more important as a marker for the cultural processes involved. English law is presented as the summit of the national civilization, the pinnacle of Britain's historic achievements. An unwritten constitution distills the finest qualities of the national community and enshrines them in a historic compact to which blacks are

unable to adhere. Black violations of the law supply the final proof of their incompatibility with Britain. Their "illegal immigration" and a propensity to street
crime confirm their alien status. These specific forms of lawbreaking, as I have
shown elsewhere, are gradually defined as a cultural attribute of the black population as a whole.

One significant continuity with the colonial setting can be identified in the way
that the most potent symbols of the national culture are not merely racialized but
gendered too. Once-proud Britannia has, like her declining nation, fallen on hard
times. A resurgent nativist politics has recast her as an aged white woman. Initially
violated by Powell's demons, the "widegrinning picaninnies" who chase her
through the streets chanting "racialist," she is, with the onset of their adoles-
cence, terrorized by them again when they turn to more financially remunerative
forms of harassment like mugging. The predatory figure of the black rapist also
makes an appearance here, demonstrating the failure of the civilizing process and
the resistance of black culture to its evangelical imperatives.[12]

For a long while, the question of black criminality provided the principal
means to underscore the *cultural* concerns of this new racism. Its dominance
helped to locate precisely where the new racism began—in the bloody nightmare
of the old woman pursued through the streets by black children. However, crime
has been displaced recently at the center of race politics by another issue that
points equally effectively to the supposed incompatibility of different cultures
sealed off from one another forever along ethnic lines. This too uses images of
the black child to make its point. It seems that the cultural sins of the immigrant
parents will be visited on their British-born children. Where once it was the mean
streets of the decaying inner city that hosted the most fearsome encounter between
white Britons and their most improbable and intimidating other—black youth—
now it is the classrooms and staffrooms of the nation's inner-city schools that
frame the same conflict and provide the most potent terms with which to make
sense of racial difference.

The recent publication of *Anti-racism: An Assault on Education and Value*[13]
confirmed that the school has become the principal element in the ideology with
which the English New Right has sought to attack antiracism. It is essential to
understand *why* its burgeoning anti-antiracism has shifted the emphasis from
crime to education. Although it poses a range of different strategic difficulties,
the change may be less significant than it may first appear. Schools are defined
by the Right as repositories of the authentic national culture that they transmit
between generations. They mediate the relation of the national community to its
youthful future citizens. Decaying school buildings provide a ready image for the
nation in microcosm. The hard-fought changes that antiracists and multicultur-
alists have wrought on the curriculum come to exemplify the debasement of all
genuine British culture. Antiracist initiatives that supposedly denigrate educational standards are identified as an assault on the "traditional virtues" of British
education. This cultural conflict is a means through which the dynamics of power
are transposed and whites become a voiceless ethnic minority oppressed by the
antiracist policies of totalitarian Labour local authorities. In the same ideological
movement, the racists are redefined as the blacks and their allies, and Mr.

Honeyford becomes a tenacious defender of freedom who is invited into the inner sanctums of government as a consultant.

If the importance of culture rather than biology is the first quality that marks this form of racism as something different and new, the special ties it discovers between race, culture, and nation provide further evidence of its novelty. The expansive ideology of the Commonwealth and the Imperial family of nations bonded in common citizenship has given way to a more parochial and embittered perspective that sees culture in neat and tidy national formations. The family remains a key motif, but the multiracial family of nations has been displaced by the racially homogeneous nation of families. The nation is composed of even, symmetrical family units that, like Mr. Honeyford's beleaguered inner-city school, transmit folk traditions between generations. The emphasis on culture allows nation and race to fuse. Nationalism and racism become so closely identified that to speak of the nation is to speak automatically in racially exclusive terms. Blackness and Englishness are constructed as incompatible, mutually exclusive identities. To speak of the British or English people is to speak of the *white* people.

Brief consideration of the British general election of summer 1987 allows us to see these themes and conflicts played out with a special clarity. The theme of patriotism was well to the fore and a tussle over the national flag was a major feature of the campaign. The Labour party pleaded for Britain to heal its deep internal divisions and become "one nation again," whereas the Conservatives underlined their success in "putting the Great back into Britain" by urging the electorate not to let the Socialists take this crucial adjective out again. Significantly, this language made no overt reference to race, but it acquired racial referents. Everyone knows what is at stake when patriotism and deference to the law are being spoken about. The seamless manner in which the themes of race, culture, and nation came together was conveyed by a racist leaflet issued in the north London constituency of Bernie Grant, a black Labour candidate who had achieved national prominence in the aftermath of the 1985 riots as an apologist for the rioters. It was illustrated by a picture of his head grafted on to the hairy body of a gorilla. It read:

> Swing along with Bernie, it's the very natural thing
> he's been doing it for centuries and now he thinks he's king
> He's got a little empire and he doesn't give a jot
> But then the British are a bloody tolerant lot
> They'll let him swing and holler hetero—Homo—Gay
> And then just up and shoot him in the good old British way.

These lines signify a powerful appropriation of the rights and liberties of the freeborn Briton once so beloved of the New Left. The rhyme's historical references demonstrate how completely blackness and Britishness have been made into mutually exclusive categories, incompatible identities. It would appear that the problems Bernie represents are most clearly visible against the patterned backdrop of the Union Jack. The picture of him as a gorilla is necessary on the leaflet because its words make no overt mention of his inferior biology. The crime for which he may be justifiably lynched is a form of treason, not the transgression involved in mere racial inferiority. The poem knits together images invoking empire, sovereignty, and sexuality (an allusion to the local council's progressive policy on lesbian and gay rights), with its exhortation to violence. There is nothing about this combination of themes that marks it out as the exclusive preserve of the Right. The leaflet provides a striking example of how the racism that ties national cultures to ethnic essences, which sees custom, law and constitution, schools and courts of justice beset by corrosive alien forces has moved beyond the grasp of the old Left/Right distinction. The populist character of the new racism is crucial. It works across the lines of formal politics as well as within them. It can link together disparate and antagonistic groups leading them to discover the morbid pleasures of seeing themselves as "one nation," inviting them to draw comfort from a mythic sense of the past[14] as it is reconstructed as historical memory in the present.

As a political issue, concern with the erosion of the national culture is perhaps spontaneously identified with the self-consciously conservative postures of the Right. The emphasis on crime and the law that identified the early stages of the new cultural racism also emerged from that quarter. However, many of the same ideas about what race, nation, and culture mean and how they fit together are held more broadly. Sections of the Left have recently stressed the issues of crime and patriotism without regard for any of their racial connotations. More significantly and ironically, some vocal factions inside the black communities have also sought to emphasize the cultural incompatibility of Afro-Caribbean and Asian settlers with Britain and Britishness. Ultra-Right, New Left, and black nationalists can accept variations of the idea that Britain may be a multiracial society but is not yet and may never be a multiracial nation.

The convergence between the Left and Right over what race means in contemporary Britain can be illustrated by looking at Raymond Williams's brief discussion of race in *Towards 2000*.[15] In this passage, Williams not only proved himself unable to address the issue of racism, he unwittingly echoed Powell in arguing that there was far more to authentic "lived and formed" national identity than the rights conferred by the "alienated superficialities" of formal citizenship. For blacks denied access to meaningful citizenship by the operation of a "grandfather clause" these legal rights are rather more than superficial. Indeed, they have constituted the substance of a protracted political conflict with which Williams is clearly unfamiliar. I am not suggesting that Conservative and Socialist positions are the same but rather that a significant measure of overlap now exists between them. An absolutist definition of culture tied to a resolute defense of the idea of the national community appears uncompromisingly in both.

Themes and concepts that parallel the outpourings of the new racists have appeared in the political pronouncements of many of Britain's black cultural nationalists. Often, the theories and preoccupations of the white racists have simply been inverted to form a thoroughly pastoral account of black culture. This has been combined with an extreme version of cultural relativism that relies for its effect on a *volkish* ethnic absolutism. Here too the family is the key unit out of which nationality is built and the central means of cultural reproduction.

Where the racists have measured black households against the idealized nuclear family form and found them wanting,[16] this black politics has viewed black children as the primary resource of the race with predictable consequences particularly in terms of the continued subordination of women. Where this tendency is strongest, particularly in local government agencies where black professionals have been able to consolidate their power, a special concern with black fostering and adoption policy has emerged as the primary vehicle for black cultural nationalism. This issue has precipitated a debate over the capacity of white families to provide an environment in which black culture and identity can be nurtured. It has achieved a symbolic currency far beyond its immediate institutional context. An absolutist conception of cultural or ethnic difference appears here to underpin the fear that new forms of slavery are being created in the placement of black children in white families for adoption or fostering and the consequent belief that racial identity necessarily overrides all other considerations. The class character of the political formation organized around this ideology cannot be elaborated here. It would appear, however, that these potent symbols of a racial community and its beleaguered boundaries play an important role in securing the unity of an emergent black petite bourgeoisie and in mystifying their intrinsically problematic relationship to those they are supposed to serve, particularly in a social work setting. Belief in the transcendental racial essence capable of uniting the black professionals with their dispossessed black clients conjures away awkward economic and historical complexities and occludes the conspicuous divergence of interests between the never employed and the cadre of black bureaucrats employed by the local state to salve their misery.

This divergence within the black communities is significant because the logic of Britain's crisis is itself a logic of cultural and political fragmentation. The recent history of race politics can be identified by the decomposition of open, inclusive definitions of "blackness" that facilitated political alliances by accommodating the discontinuous histories of Afro-Caribbean and Asian-descended people. The more restrictive definitions that emerged to take their place and restrict the term "black" to those of Afro-Caribbean ancestry betoken a general retreat into the dubious comfort of ethnic particularity. However, this fracturing process is far more extensive than its intraethnic dimensions suggest. The economic effects of the crisis are, for example, unevenly developed in the most radical manner; they are unevenly distributed even within the same city. It has become commonplace to speak of Britain as two nations—an exploited and immiserated north bearing the brunt of deindustrialization and a more affluent south. These definitions of the nation are more than competing metaphors. They correspond to important changes in the mode of production itself and the geography of class formation and political representation. The Labour party presides over the north and the inner cities almost without challenge. The Conservatives enjoy a similar monopoly of power in the more prosperous and suburban areas. Amidst these divisions, to answer the pleas for aid from the ailing north, where notions of region and locality have provided an important axis of political organization, with the language of nationalism and patriotism, is fundamentally misguided. The racial connotations that emerge with this rhetoric work actively to distance black citizens from the system of formal politics as a whole. The counterposition of local and national identities makes nonsense of the idea of a homogeneous national culture. The intensity with which it has emerged as a political problem suggests a deeper crisis of the nation-state.

Elsewhere in *Towards 2000* Williams has suggestively described the nation-state as being simultaneously both too large and too small a unit for the necessary forms of political interaction required by the advancement of radical democracy during the years ahead. Seeing the nation as a totality of different societies constructed for different purposes allows us to ask how these may learn to coexist; and in particular, what role the cultural politics of Britain's black settlers and their British-born children may play in creating the pluralistic ambience in which people are able to discover positive pleasure in their inescapable diversity.

An understanding of the limitations of the nation-state as a form is central to the sense of the African diaspora as a cultural and political unit that anchors black English political culture. The majority of Britain's blacks are postwar settlers, but their refined diaspora awareness is more than a reflection of the proximity of migration. It corresponds directly to the subordinate position Britain's small and diverse black population has occupied within the vast network of cultural and political exchange that links blacks in Africa, the Caribbean, the United States, and Europe. Until very recently, this country's identifiably black culture has been created from the raw materials supplied by blacks elsewhere, particularly in America and the Caribbean.

In one sense, the political network that made this cultural relationship possible was a direct product of the commercial traffic in slaves. The activities of eighteenth- and nineteenth-century abolitionists, the transnational and international organization of antislavery activities and Pan-African initiatives[17] prepared the way for the great gains of the Garvey movement. Each of these phases of black self-organization consolidated independent means of communication between the different locations within the diaspora. What principally concerns us here is the cultural character of these developments: the special premium they have placed on expressive culture—music, song, and dance. Artistic forms have produced and sustained an interpretive community outside the orbit of formal politics in a long sequence of struggles that has been irreducibly and simultaneously both cultural and political. The internationalization of the leisure industries and the growth of important markets for cultural commodities outside the overdeveloped world have provided new opportunities for the consolidation of diaspora awareness. The popular Pan-Africanist and Ethiopianist visions inherent in reggae were, for example, carried to all the corners of the world as an unforeseen consequence of selling the music of Jamaica beyond the area in which it was created. The ideologies and sign systems of Afro-American Black Power, in part, traveled by a similar route. The narrow nationalism we saw in the politics of the emergent black petite bourgeoisie contrasts sharply with the voice of the social movement that has been articulated through the language, styles, and symbols of the diaspora. Britain's black population is comparatively small and heterogeneous. Britain has no ghettos along the American model or any residential communities comparable to the Bantustans and squatter camps of South Africa. The blackest areas of the inner city are, for example, between 30 and 50 percent white. Here, the idea of the black community necessarily expresses something more than just the physical concentration of black people. The term has a special moral valency and refers above all to a community of interpretation whose cultural cohesion has sometimes enabled it to act politically. This is a community bounded by language and by cultural forms that play an ethical and educative role. Although the collapse of certainties once provided by class identity, class politics, and class theory has been a pronounced feature of the recent period in Britain, it is also a community that has been articulated, at a number of points, with the contemporary structures of class relations. In the encounter between black settlers and their white inner-city neighbors, black culture has become a class culture. There is more to this transformation and adaptation than the fact that blacks are among the most economically exploited and politically marginal sections of the society, overrepresented in the surplus population, the prison population, and among the poor. From the dawn of postwar settlement, diaspora culture has been an ambiguous presence in the autonomous institutions of the working class. Two generations of whites have appropriated it, discovering in its seductive forms meanings of their own. It is now impossible to speak coherently of black culture in Britain in isolation from the culture of Britain as a whole. This is particularly true as far as leisure is concerned. Black expressive culture has decisively shaped youth culture, pop culture, and the culture of city life in Britain's metropolitan centers. The white working class has danced for forty years to its syncopated rhythms. There is, of course, no contradiction between using black culture and loathing real live black people, yet the informal, long-term processes through which different groups have negotiated each other have intermittently created a "two-tone" sensibility that celebrates its hybrid origins and has provided a significant opposition to "commonsense" racialism.

It is often argued that the spontaneity of black musical forms, their performance aesthetic, and commitment to improvisation have made them into something of a magnet for other social groups. Certainly the centrality that issues of sexuality, eroticism, and gender conflict enjoy within black folk cultures has given them a wide constituency. Their Rabelaisian power to carnivalize and disperse the dominant order through an intimate yet public discourse on sexuality and the body has drawn many outsiders into a dense and complex network of black cultural symbols. These aspects of black forms mark out a distinct field of political antagonisms that I do not intend to examine here. Instead, I want to explore the equally distinctive *political* character of these forms and the urban social movement they have helped to create and extend.

The politics of this movement are manifested in the confluence of three critical, anticapitalist themes that have a historic resonance in diaspora culture and can be traced directly and indirectly back to the formative experience of slavery. Together they form a whole but nonprogrammatic politics that has sustained Britain's black settler populations and their white inner-city associates. The first theme deals with the experience of work, the labor process, and the division of labor under capitalism. It amounts to a critique of productivism—the ideology that sees the expansion of productive forces as an indispensable precondition of the attainment of freedom. In opposition to this view of production, an argument is made that sees waged work as itself a form of servitude. At best, it is viewed as a necessary evil and is sharply counterposed to the more authentic freedoms that can only be enjoyed in nonwork time. The black body is here celebrated as an instrument of pleasure rather than an instrument of labor. The nighttime becomes the right time, and the space allocated for recovery and recuperation is assertively and provocatively occupied by the pursuit of leisure and pleasure.

The second theme focuses on the state. It addresses the role of law in particular and, in challenging capitalist legality to live up to the expansive promises of its democratic rhetoric, articulates a plea for the dissociation of law from the processes of domination. The legal institutions on which Babylon's order of public authority rest do not provide equal rights for all. The version of justice they peddle is partial and inseparable from the system of economic interests that capitalist legality simply guarantees. The coercive brutality of the state is seen as an intrinsic property of these institutions. The exterminism and militarism that characterize them are denounced, not only where they reach into people's lives as the police or army but for the way that they symbolize the illegitimate nature of the capitalist state in general. This mystified form of rule is unfavorably compared to two quite different standards of justice: first, a divine version that will ultimately redress the miscarriages of earthly "man-made" law and, second, an alternative secular moral standard—truth and right—that derives its legitimate power from popular sovereignty. It is significant that capitalist legality is understood to have denied blacks the status of legal subjects during the slave period.

The third theme concentrates on the importance of history understood as a discontinuous process of struggle. An affirmation of history and the place of blacks within it are advanced as an antidote to the suppression of temporal perception under capitalism. This theme also answers the way in which racism works to suppress the historical dimensions of black life offering a mode of existence locked permanently into a recurrent present where social existence is confined to the roles of being either a problem or a victim.

The contemporary musical forms of the African diaspora work within an aesthetic and political framework that demands that they ceaselessly reconstruct their own histories, folding back on themselves time and again to celebrate and validate the simple, unassailable fact of their survival. This is particularly evident in jazz, where quotes from earlier styles and performers make the past actually audible in the present. This process of recovery should not be misunderstood. It does not amount to either straightforward parody or pastiche. The stylistic voices of the past are valued for the distinct register of address each offers. The same playful process is evident in the less abstract performances that define Washington's "Go-Go" dance funk. This style consists of a continuous segue from one tune to the next. The popular black musics of different eras and continents are wedded together by a heavy percussive rhythm and an apparently instinctive antiphony. A recent concert in London by Chuck Brown, the kingpin of the Go-Go, saw him stitch together tunes by Louis Jordan, Sly Stone, Lionel Hampton, Melle Mel, and T-Bone Walker into a single epic statement. Reggae's endless repetition of "versions" and the tradition of answer records in rhythm and blues betray a similar historical impulse.

The core themes I have identified overlap and interact to generate a cohesive but essentially defensive politics and a corresponding aesthetic of redemption from racial subordination. The critique of productivism is reinforced and extended by the structural location of black labor power in Britain and the other overdeveloped countries. It is also tied to the movement among young blacks that actively rejects the menial and highly exploitative forms in which work is made available. The concern with history demands that the experience of slavery is also recovered and rendered vivid and immediate. It becomes a powerful metaphor for the injustice and exploitation of contemporary waged work in general.

The anticapitalist politics that animate the social movement against racial subordination is not confined to the lyrical content of these musical cultures. The poetics involved recurrently deals with these themes, but the critique of capitalism is simultaneously revealed in the forms this expressive culture takes and in the performance aesthetic that governs them. There is here an immanent challenge to the commodity form to which black expressive culture is reduced in order to be sold. It is a challenge that is practiced rather than simply talked or sung about. The artifacts of a pop industry premised on the individual act of purchase and consumption are hijacked and taken over into the heart of collective rituals of protest and affirmation, which in turn define the boundaries of the interpretive community. Music is heard socially and its deepest meanings revealed only in the heat of this collective, affirmative consumption. Struggles over the commodification of black music are reflected in a dialectical conflict between the technology of reproduction and the subcultural needs of its primary consumers in the "race market." Here, the pioneering use of live recordings occupying the whole side of a long-playing disk, issuing the same song in two parts on different sides of a forty-five, and putting out various mixes of a song on one twelve-inch disk to facilitate scratch mixing are all part of the story. Musicians and producers for whom the "race market" is the primary constituency are reluctant to compromise with the commercial formats on which the music business relies. Where they are able to exercise control over the form in which their music is issued, black artists anticipate this specific mode of consumption and privilege it. Records are issued in an open, participative form that invites further artistic input. The Toaster or MC (rapper) adds rhymes and comments to the wordless version of a tune that is routinely issued on the reverse of the vocal version. Several different versions of the same piece are issued on a single record. Twelve-inch disks that allow for extended playing time are favored. Thus the original artifact negotiates the supplementary input of other artists unseen and unknown yet anticipated by the original creator of the music.

The clubs, parties, and dances where these creative negotiations between original and supplementary performances take place are governed by a dramaturgy that prizes the local, immediate, and seemingly spontaneous input above all. Leaving behind the passive role of spectator to which they would be assigned by

Western convention, these audiences become instead active participants. In this metaphysics of intimacy, race mediates the social relation between internal pain and its externalization in cathartic performance. The audience's association with the performer dissolves Eurocentric notions of the disjunction between art and life, inside and outside, in the interplay of personal and public histories for which the traditions of the black church serve as a model and an inspiration.[18] The complex, dialogic rituals involved become sources of profound pleasure in their own right, particularly where singers and musicians encounter a crowd directly. The musical countercultures of black Britain are primarily based on records rather than live performances, but the same aesthetic of performance applies. Music recorded on disks loses its preordained authority as it is transformed and adapted. In reggae, soul, and hip-hop subcultures the disk that appears in the dominant culture as a fixed and final product is extended and reconstructed as it becomes the raw material in a new creative process born in the dialogue between the DJ, the rapper or MC, and the dancing crowd. A range of de- and reconstructive procedures—scratch mixing, dubbing, toasting, rapping, and beatboxing—contribute to new layers of local meaning. The original performance trapped in plastic is supplemented by new contributions at every stage. Performer and audience alike strive to create pleasures that can evade capture and sale as cultural commodities. A hostility to commercial trafficking in black music has grown so steadily that the majority of black clubs and leisure spaces are actively disinterested in the latest new records, forsaking them in favor of old and hard-to-obtain disks in an antiaesthetic cult known as the "Rare Groove" scene. Popularized by the illegal pirate radio stations that deal exclusively in the various styles of black music, this fashion has placed a special premium on politically articulate American dance-funk recordings from the Black Power period. Because it cannot be bought, the pleasures in hearing a particular tune are severed from the commercial relations of pop. Dislocated from the time and place in which they were created, disks like Hank Ballard's 1968 "How You Gonna Get Respect? You Haven't Cut Your Process Yet"[19] become abstract metaphysical statements on the nature of blackness. The same process applies to music imported into Britain's black communities from the Caribbean. Again, for both reggae and soul-based traditions, the polysemic qualities of black speech add to the subversive potency of the DJ's and MC's language games.

These issues can be examined further by considering the impact of "I Know You Got Soul," an American hip-hop record that was the most popular item in London's black clubs for several months at the beginning of 1987. The record was a new version of Bobby Byrd's sixteen-year-old Black Power anthem. Snatches of his original version were still clearly audible, but it had been transformed by the addition of a drum machine and an unusually clever and poetic rap. Eric B. and Rakim, the creators of the new version, declared themselves emphatically committed to a ghetto constituency, people who, as Rakim put it when I spoke to him, "turn to music because they got nothin' else." The record affirms this commitment by celebrating the concept of soul that is thought to be fundamental to black experience. "You listen to it . . . the concept might break you." Its dense, dizzy sound privileges and anticipates a public hearing: "Sit by the radio hand on the dial, soon as you hear it pump up the volume." But the public sphere to which it is addressed is defined against the dominant alternative to which blacks enjoy only restricted access. This is an altogether different forum bounded by the strictures of race and community and marked out by the naming process that gave these young men their identity as performers. The Soul Power the record manifests is also the force that binds their listeners together into a moral, even a political community. For black Britain constructing its own distinct culture from material supplied by the United States and the Caribbean, "I Know You Got Soul" brilliantly tied a sense of exclusive contemporary style to an older, positive message of self-respect and political autonomy that derives its power from the American black movement of the 1960s. The disk, an adaptation and transformation of an earlier piece that retained the original within its own fractured form, was scratched, dubbed, and made over time and time again in the dancehalls, parties, and other leisure spaces of Britain's black community. Its consumption by Afro-Caribbean and Asian-descended Britons and their white friends, lovers, and associates defines the boundaries of a utopian social movement. This movement aims to defend and extend spaces for social autonomy and meets the oppressive power of racial capitalism with the radical aspiration that one day work will no longer be servitude and law no longer equated with domination. Thus the territoriality of identity is counterposed to the territoriality of control. An immediate, nonnegotiable politics is infused with a powerful sense of locality and a rootedness in tradition. "It ain't where you're from," intones Rakim, "its where you're at."

It is interesting to note that at the very moment when celebrated Euro-American cultural theorists have pronounced the collapse of "grand narratives" the expressive culture of Britain's black poor is dominated by the need to construct them as narratives of redemption and emancipation. This expressive culture, like others elsewhere in the African diaspora, produces a potent historical memory and an authoritative analytic and historical account of racial capitalism and its overcoming. There are of course many problems in trying to hold the term "postmodernism" together. It refers simultaneously and contradictorily to modernization, to a cognitive theory, to a change in the cultural climate in the overdeveloped countries, and to an aspect of the logic of late capitalism. The concept may have some value as a purely heuristic device, but it seems often simply to serve to validate another equally Eurocentric master narrative from which the history and experiences of blacks remain emphatically absent. Fredric Jameson, for example, views postmodernism as "the cultural dominant."[20] However, all the constitutive features of the postmodern that he identifies—the new depthlessness, the weakening of historicity, the waning of affect—are not merely absent from black expressive cultures but are explicitly contradicted by their repertoire of complete "hermeneutic gestures." These cultural forms use the new technological means at their disposal, not to flee from depth but to revel in it, not to abjure public history but to proclaim it! They have created their own thoroughly subversive means to inhabit what Jameson calls "the bewildering new world space of late multi-national capital."

There is, in the history of these forms, a suggestion that the grand narrative of reason is not being brought to an end but is itself transformed, democratized, and extended. This transformation that sees the center of ethical gravity shift away

from "the West" is mistakenly identified as the end of reason. Forms of rationality are being created endlessly. The postmodernists' claim that the present
moment is *the* moment of rupture contains echoes of earlier European obsessions
with the precise timing of the new dawn. Rather than seek to substitute an aesthetic radicalism for a moral one as the spokespersons for postmodernism have
implicitly and explicitly suggested, the expressive culture shows how these two
dimensions can be aligned in a complex sensibility sometimes utopian, sometimes
fiercely pragmatic.

The movement it articulates has coalesced somewhere between what Jean Cohen has called the "identity-oriented" and "resource-mobilisation" paradigms
for comprehending social action.[21] It is neither a class nor, of course, a racially
homogeneous grouping. Its identity is a product of immediate local circumstances
but is apprehended through a syncretic culture for which the history of the African
diaspora supplies the decisive symbolic core. Partly because religious language
conveys an intensity of aspiration for which there is no secular alternative, this
culture has a spiritual component. As we have already seen, it views the body as
itself an important locus of resistance and desire. The body is therefore reclaimed
from its subordination to the labor process, recognized as part of the natural world,
and enjoyed on that basis. Third, and most important, this movement can be
identified by its antipathy to the institutions of formal politics and the fact that it
is not principally oriented toward instrumental objectives. Rather than aim at the
conquest of political power or apparatuses, its objective centers on the control of
a field of autonomy or independence from the system.

The distinctive political perspective that emerges from this movement can lead
us to a more scrupulous and detailed periodization of modernity itself. The modernizing processes in which commodification and industrialization come together
with the political institutions of formal democracy have had *regional* as well as
temporal characteristics. It is therefore useful to reconceptualize the struggles of
African diaspora populations not simply as anticapitalist but as a product of one
of modernity's most significant and enduring countercultures. Capitalism, industrialization, and their political counterparts are differentiated and then analyzed
in their articulation. The social movement that is the contemporary heir to a non-
European radical tradition[22] has a more total critique of them than that currently
spoken in furtherance of the struggle to emancipate labor from capital.

Identifying this radical tradition unburdened by the dream of progress and a
positivistic faith in the easy certainties of Marxian science returns us to the question of whose master narratives are collapsing and whose growing stronger? This
inquiry in turn provides a further cue to shift the center of debate away from
Europe, and to explore other encounters with modernity that a dogmatic postmodern perspective ignores or dismisses as peripheral. As C. L. R. James argued
long ago, the history of communism ought to reckon with political communities
for whom the "enthusiasm of 1789" relates to Port-au-Prince before it relates to
Paris.[23] Why is it so difficult to think through the relationship between them? To
put it another way, it is not, as J.-F. Lyotard puts it in *Le Differend*, only the
"annihilation named Auschwitz" that now requires a formal transformation of
what counts as history and as reality, of our understanding of reference and the

function of the proper name.[24] These problems have been the substance of diaspora culture through slavery and since. The people whom June Jordan has elo-
quently called "the stubborn majority of this world"[25] have had a variety of
complex and problematic relationships to "modernity." This has been true from
the moment when Africans, detached from an identifiable location in space and
time, became Negroes—in the West but not organically of it—and acquired the
"double vision" that a subordinate position entails. As slaves, their exclusion
from universal human categories demanded the acquisition and validation of an
authentic humanity. It is also relevant that their experiences as unfree working
populations engaged in industrial capitalist production have been accorded secondary status behind those of the industrial proletariat by four generations of
Marxist theoreticians.

Questions of political economy aside, studying the distinct "intertextual"
traditions of the African diaspora alone demands extensive adjustments to the
conceptualization of modernization, modernity, and aesthetic modernism. The
idea of a "Populist" modernism is a useful preliminary means to comprehend
the cultural and political strategies that have evolved not only where European
philosophy and letters have been bent to other purposes by Nella Larsen, Richard
Wright, James Baldwin, David Bradley, Alice Walker, or most self-consciously
in Amiri Baraka's black Baudelaire, but also to make sense of the secular and
spiritual *popular* forms—music and dance—that have handled the anxieties and
dilemmas involved in a response to the flux of modern life.

The cultural politics of race can be more accurately described as the cultural
politics of racism's overcoming. It challenges theories that assert the primacy of
structural contradictions, economic classes, and crises in determining political
consciousness and collective action. Traditions of radical politics arising from
groups whose enduring jeopardy dictates that the premises of their social existence are threatened may, in our postindustrial era, be more radical than more
obviously class-based modes of political action. The high level of support for the
striking miners and their families inside Britain's black communities during the
recent coal dispute seems to indicate that these different varieties of radicalism
can be brought together. During that industrial dispute, highly dissimilar groups
were able to connect their fates across the divisions of "race," ethnicity, region,
and language. For a brief period, inner-city populations and the supposed vanguard of the orthodox industrial proletariat shrank the world to the size of their
immediate communities and began, in concert, to act politically on that basis. In
doing so, they supplied a preliminary but nonetheless concrete answer to the
decisive political questions of our age: how do we act locally and yet think globally? How do we connect the local and the immediate across the earthworks
erecte d by the division of labor?

NOTES

1. The themes and problems discussed in this essay have been elaborated in my book
There Ain't No Black in the Union Jack: The Cultural Politics of Race and Nation (London:
Hutchinson, 1987).

2. One version of this problematic appears in the work of Stuart Hall, particularly his 1980 paper "Race, Articulation and Societies Structured in Dominance," published in the UNESCO reader, *Sociological Theories: Race and Colonialism*. See also his "Signification, Representation, Ideology: Althusser and the Post-Structuralist Debates," in *Critical Studies in Mass Communication*, 2 (June 1985). A similar position is sketched on somewhat different ground by Alex Callinicos in his "Postmodernism, Post-Structuralism and Post-Marxism?" *Theory Culture and Society*, 2 (1985). Both pieces draw heavily on the work of Volosinov and Bakhtin.

3. "The Voiceless Ones," *Saturday Review*, 16 (1960).

4. I am thinking here of Robert Miles's *Racism and Migrant Labour* (London: Routledge & Kegan Paul, 1982); and John Gabriel and Gideon Ben Tovim's essay "Marxism and The Concept of Racism," *Economy and Society*, 7 (May 1978).

5. Hall, "Racism and Moral Panics in Post-war Britain," in Commission for Racial Equality (ed.), *Five Views of Multi-racial Britain* (London: 1978).

6. *Shamanism, Colonialism and The Wild Man: A Study in Terror and Healing* (Chicago: University of Chicago Press, 1987). Michael Taussig's absolutely brilliant study of race and colonial terror is an excellent example of what can be achieved. Less inspiring but worth investigating nonetheless are Orlando Patterson's *Ethnic Chauvinism: The Reactionary Impulse* (New York: Stein & Day, 1977), and Anthony D. Smith's *Ethnic Revival in The Modern World* (Cambridge: Cambridge University Press, 1981).

7. Andrew Gamble, *Britain in Decline* (London: Macmillan, 1981).

8. Apart from *There Ain't No Black*, see Centre for Contemporary Cultural Studies (eds.), *The Empire Strikes Back* (London: Hutchinson, 1982); and S. Hall et al., *Policing the Crisis* (London: Macmillan, 1979).

9. Nancy Stepan, *The Idea of Race in Science: Great Britain 1800–1960* (London: Macmillan, 1982).

10. Frantz Fanon, *Toward the African Revolution* (Harmondsworth: Pelican, 1967).

11. A useful account of the development of the English New Right is provided in R. Levitas (ed.), *The Ideology of the New Right* (London: Polity, 1985). See also *The New Right Enlightenment: Young Writers on the Spectre Haunting the Left* (Sevenoaks: Economic and Literary Books, 1985). The men referred to here are part of an influential grouping around the journal *Salisbury Review*. Ray Honeyford in particular became something of a celebrity when he opposed the introduction of "antiracist and multicultural" teaching methods into the inner-city school where he was headmaster.

12. See Vron Ware and Mandy Rose, *The White Woman's Burden: In Search of a Feminist Antiracism* (London: Verso, forthcoming).

13. Frank Palmer (ed.), *Anti-racism: An Assault on Education and Value* (London: Sherwood Press, 1986).

14. See Patrick Wright's *On Living in an Old Country* (London: Verso, 1985).

15. Raymond Williams, *Towards 2000* (London: Chatto, 1983).

16. A concern with the supposedly pathological forms in which black family life develops is shared by Lord Scarman's report into the 1981 riots in London and Daniel Moynihan's report *The Negro Family and the Case for National Action*. This convergence and the image of family breakdown in racist ideology is discussed by Errol Lawrence in the CCCS volume, *The Empire Strikes Back*.

17. I am thinking here of the settlement of Sierra Leone and of the travels of black abolitionists in Britain and Europe. On the latter see C. Peter Ripley (ed.), *The Black Abolitionist Papers*, vol. 1 (Chapel Hill: University of North Carolina Press, 1985), and Clare Taylor (ed.), *British and American Abolitionists* (Edinburgh: Edinburgh University

Press, 1974). For Sierra Leone see Immanuel Geiss, *The Pan-African Movement* (London: Methuen, 1974).

18. Gerald L. Davis, *I Got the World in Me and I Can Sing It, You Know: A Study of the Performed African-American Sermon* (Philadelphia: University of Pennsylvania Press, 1985).

19. Hank Ballard and the Dapps, "How You Gonna Get Respect?" (King Records, K6196). The cut is also included on the 1969 album "You Can't Keep a Good Man Down" (King, K1052).

20. Fredric Jameson, "Postmodernism or the Cultural Logic of Late Capitalism," *New Left Review*, 146 (July–August 1984).

21. Jean Cohen, "Strategy or Identity: New Theoretical Paradigms and Contemporary Social Movements," *Social Research*, 52 (Winter 1985).

22. Cedric J. Robinson, *Black Marxism: The Making of the Black Radical Tradition* (London: Zed Press, 1982).

23. C. L. R. James, *The Black Jacobins* (London: Allison & Busby, 1985).

24. J.-F. Lyotard, *Le Différend* (Paris: Minuit, 1983). See also Meaghan Morris, "Postmodernity and Lyotard's Sublime," *Art and Text*, 16 (Summer 1984).

25. June Jordan, *Civil Wars* (Boston: Beacon Press, 1981).

Julie Skurski

Educated at Stanford University and the University of Chicago, Julie Skurski did field work in Venezuela and Cuba, combining research on multinationals, the state, and popular religion with her interests in nationalism. Integrating approaches from history and anthropology and drawing on theoretical contributions from cultural studies, gender theory, and postcolonial studies, she is completing a book on competing constructions of national identity and culture in Venezuela at various political conjunctures in the nineteenth and twentieth centuries. Along with Fernando Coronil and Valentine E. Daniel, she is also co-editing a volume about political violence entitled *States of Violence*.

Skurski holds that "nationalism is a relational and a contested construct which builds on contradiction and abiguity even as it unwaveringly proclaims essential truths." She exposes the paradox in the harmonizing goal of nationalists. "While nationalism represents itself as an equalizing project, it is engendered by and constitutive of social hierarchies." National unity, she reveals, remains unstable and ambiguous, and the idealization of the nation in liberal ideology, as a finite, autonomous, and homogeneous community, conceals this complexity.

Using the novel *Doña Bárbara* (1929) by Romulo Gallegos as a social and cultural mirror, Skurski argues that anticolonial nationalism seeks recovery of an authentic communal past, but in Latin America the Creole elite, born in Spanish domination, is unable to claim the precolonial past as its own. The elite in Venezuela elaborated a discourse in which Spain and colonialism were defined as degenerate and Venezuelan authenticity is found in its rebelliousness. Extending an insight from Partha Chatterjee, Skurski shows how the anticolonials accepted the very intellectual premises of modernity on which colonialism is based. The nation was conceived as an Enlightenment project of establishing the rule of reason and citizens' rights, but in the postcolonial period, a gap grew between the state's unifying claims and its exclusionary practices and beliefs. In the story she tells in this essay, the Creole elite is caught between its ties to colonialism (and its need to express its difference with the colonizing power) and its difficulty with being an authentic part of the national community. One of the solutions to social distance, proposed by no one less than Simón Bolívar himself, was racial mixing and the creation of a new authentic Latin American, the *mestizo*.

Noting that earlier theorists, like Benedict Anderson, had ignored "the foundational exclusion of women" from the national community, Skurski brings gender to the center of the study of nationalism. The struggle against colonialism was coded masculine, and women were seen as forces to be tamed and protected. While the family is used as a metaphor for unification of the nation, patriarchy was conceived as parallel to the power in the state, and women were imagined as dependent, not sovereign, and reproducers, the "mothers of the nation."

The Ambiguities of Authenticity in Latin America: *Doña Bárbara* and the Construction of National Identity

> We ... do not even retain the vestiges of our original being. We are but a mixed species of aborigines and Spaniards. Americans by birth and Europeans by law, we find ourselves engaged in a dual conflict: we are disputing with the natives for titles of ownership, and at the same time we are struggling to maintain ourselves in the country that gave us birth against the opposition of the invaders.
>
> SIMÓN BOLÍVAR, CONGRESS OF ANGOSTURA, 1819

In the turbulent period following World War I, a powerful strand of nationalist discourse contributed to the reconfiguration of political possibilities in Latin America. Claiming that the region could help revitalize world civilization through its fusion of disparate cultures, the discourse of authenticity defined a position from which ascending middle-class elites sought to reformulate the basis of national identity. Fashioned in response to both imperial and domestic pressures, it drew on idealist and "irrationalist" currents of thought which made a strong intellectual impact on the metropolitan centers in this period. These currents challenged the determinist evolutionary concepts that guided ruling groups in much of Latin America while valorizing the spiritual and instinctual dimensions of life, which had long been disdained by liberal republicanism.

The broad appeal of the discourse of authenticity lay in its dual thrust: it criticized the mimetic upper-class elites for divorcing themselves from the *pueblo*

Julie Skurski, "The Ambiguities of Authenticity: *Doña Bárbara* and the Construction of National Identity," *Poetics Today*, 15, 4 (Winter 1994), pp. 605–42. Copyright © 1994 by The Porter Institute for Poetics and Semiotics.

Author's note: Aspects of this research formed part of a joint project, undertaken with Fernando Coronil, which was partly supported by the Spencer Foundation. The Centro de Estudios Latinoamericanos Rómulo Gallegos (CELARG) in Venezuela offered me its hospitality while I was working on this project. For their insightful suggestions concerning the issues I develop here, I would like especially to thank Lauren Berlant, Fernando Coronil, Geoff Eley, Roger Rouse, and David Scobey. I have also benefited greatly from discussions with Crisca Bierwert, Raymond Grew, Yolanda Lecuna, Roberto da Matta, Sabine MacCormack, Sherry Ortner, Doris Sommer, Ann Stoler, Rebecca Scott, and the members of the women's history discussion group at the University of Michigan.

(people), and it promoted the formation of a nationally grounded elite which could channel popular energies. From this perspective, the hybrid racial makeup of Latin America was both a source of creative energy and a threat to civilized order. The emerging middle-class elite sought to negotiate conflicting claims to authority across class and national borders, consolidating yet concealing the ambiguity at the center of the nationalist project.

The discourse of authenticity constructed the figure of the spiritually elevated leader as a solution to the problem of authority in societies fractured by colonial relations. Rómulo Gallegos (1884–1969), Venezuelan novelist and political leader, had a leading role in weaving this solution. His classic 1929 novel *Doña Bárbara* imagined the peaceful unification of Venezuela's land and people in the wake of civil strife and turned a newly hopeful gaze upon the terrain and customs of the cattle-savanna frontier, the *Hanos*. This novel of national origins has been identified by its commentators primarily with the Enlightenment ideals that have guided modernity. Yet critical analyses of *Doña Bárbara* have directed little attention to the undercurrent of metaphysical beliefs that sustain it or to the relational notions of identity and authority that it proposes.

I discuss in this essay the emergence of a discourse of national identity which involved the redefinition of the elite's link to the pueblo. Continuing to express the historical concern of Latin American thinkers with the unresolved issue of identity for a continent shaped by conquest, colonization, and neocolonialism, the discourse of authenticity sought to present the nation's geography and untutored population as sources of untapped energy for resolving the opposition between the forces of "civilization" and of "barbarism." According to Gallegos's influential vision of this conflict in *Doña Bárbara*, the nation could achieve the synthesis of forces promised by Latin America's *mestizaje* (racial mixing) only if its elite became morally and culturally transformed through its efforts to redeem and reshape the pueblo.

AMBIGUOUS FOUNDATIONS

Doña Bárbara addresses the expansion of the polity and the legitimacy of authority in a nation ruled by regional caudillos and prey to foreign incursions. As Doris Sommer argues in her innovative analysis, this novel is a populist version of the national romance. It allegorically depicts the political union between the state and the popular classes as simultaneously reflected in and dependent on the achievement of a romantic union between lovers of disparate class and racial origins. By bridging vertical class differences to create a bond based on love, the couple ultimately legitimizes the "nation-family." While sharing the concerns and narrative structure of the nineteenth-century national romance, which addressed the problem of fissures within the elite and depicted the union of lovers who had relatively equal status and flexible gender roles, the populist romance reinforces gender boundaries and reiterates social hierarchies. Concerned with legitimating an expanded state and pacifying an unruly populace, it seeks to establish closure and hierarchy and to impose boundaries from a position of authority (see Sommer 1991: 286–89). Sommer's earlier analysis explored how the populist narrative helped to prepare the culture of populism by fixing categories and heroizing male authority (see Sommer 1990: 90). This focus highlights an important dimension of the novel's effectiveness: its naturalization of the nation as a bounded unit that inspires passionate attachments.

On this unstable postcolonial terrain, however, neither unity nor authority could be secured. My discussion here foregrounds the ambiguity underlying this unity which at once destabilizes authority and authorizes its renewal through the ongoing need to assert fluid boundaries.[1] This process recreates the appeal of authority, making it seem both desirable and necessary. It thus establishes a model for legitimate rule which rests on the power to negotiate the contradictory allegiances and claims of the populist elite.

Literary commentary on *Doña Bárbara* reflects the growth and demise of the promise of progress for Latin America. During the rise of economic nationalism and of modernization theory, critics praised the novel's epic depiction of an "optimistic" resolution to the problem of backwardness in Latin America. But economic decline and political reaction fundamentally challenged the modernization project's premise of linear progress, and with it the ordering intent of nation-building literature. Latin America's literary Boom of the 1960s and 1970s, which was linked to the critique of modernization's homogenizing assumptions and marginalizing consequences, brought with it a rejection of *Doña Bárbara* on the part of many writers. They saw its depiction of a harmonious path to national unity by means of "love" rather than violence as an effect of a totalizing voice, one that echoed the state's effort to construct itself as the locus of truth (ibid.: 72–74). Critics contrasted it to contemporary novels that imaginatively rendered the indeterminacy of meaning and the arbitrariness of authority that nation-building novels suppressed.

The conflicting claims for *Doña Bárbara* as either an expression of Latin America's authentic nature or a homogenizing construct that conceals Latin America's actual play of reality and illusion tend to reproduce an assumption of authenticity rather than analyzing the novel in relation to the historical construction of authenticity as a concept.[2] My examination of the historical conditions of this novel's production and reception addresses the continuities between elite republican discourse and populist ideology, highlighting the interplay between representations of unity and of subordination in the construction of national community.[3]

THE POLITICS OF FRATERNAL COMMUNITY

Benedict Anderson (1991), in an unusual step that has received little attention, raises the issue of Latin America's role in formulating nationalism as a cultural construct. He credits the Creole elite, which played a leading role in the foundation of the Latin American republics, with having pioneered the formulation of modern nationalism in its fullest form. As exemplified by Simón Bolívar's proposals, this formulation asserted an unequivocal relationship between the nation-state and the bond of citizenship that linked all those born within the national territory. This conceptualization of a horizontal and undifferentiated unity among the people who shared the birthplace of a given bounded land was transformative for the history of nationalism. It set the parameters for the construction of what Anderson defines, "in an anthropological spirit," as an "imagined political community." The national community, he argues, is not a fabrication or a falsehood, but a particular kind of cultural creation: an imagining of an abstract common tie of citizenship that extends uniformly across the territory, uniting the members of "even the smallest nation." Although most members of a nation remain unknown to each other, "in the minds of each lives the image of their communion" (ibid.: 5–7). Through a myriad of regulatory techniques and standardizing concepts, national belonging becomes constructed as a natural attribute of identity. Above all, the construct of the nation is built on an abstract and decontextualized foundation from which it derives its modular character. Buttressed by regulatory technologies that represent citizens and nations as identical to their respective peers and that collectively construct them as a "fraternity of equals," nationalism reorders identities and experiences on the basis of a disjunction between representation and social practice. For the "fraternal" bond that unites the national community, Anderson argues, is achieved *apart from* existing practices of domination: "Regardless of the actual inequality and exploitation that may prevail in each, the nation is always conceived as a deep, horizontal comradeship" (ibid.: 6–7).

Anderson's argument asks us to make the leap from an elite construct whose content is highly contested to a belief that is collectively held across social divisions. In his view, the equalizing concept of nationhood and the printed word that disseminated it were so compelling that the memory of the elite's effort to control the feared masses during the nation-state's foundation was quickly "washed away." Cleansed of these memories, the independent nation soon became a model available for "pirating" by aspiring or threatened elites in other regions of the world (ibid.: 81). Yet this assertion ignores the constitutive relationship between the model and its conditions of production and reproduction. The Creole elite's struggle for independence was inseparable from its efforts to resist both royal and popular pressure for reform and to maintain control over land and labor. Violent conflicts over citizenship, including civil wars inflected by class and race and campaigns to suppress indigenous peoples, rent Latin American republics during their independence struggles and up to the end of the century. While Anderson notes the elite's defensive stance, he nevertheless presents the concept of the nation as inclusive and as capable of equally motivating masses and elites to fight on its behalf.[4]

In analyzing the nation's universalizing form apart from the full range of its conceptual and institutional foundations, he also ignores the foundational exclusion of women from the national fraternity, uncritically utilizing "fraternity," associated with male bonds, as an image of inclusive and equalizing secular community. Anderson thus continues what Carol Pateman (1989) argues is the contemporary embrace of fraternity as the favored model of freely undertaken communal civic bonds. As a result, fraternity has become the emblem of cooperative association, with little attention given to the historical exclusions that have shaped its development (ibid.: 78–81). Commenting on the unremarked exclusion of women from Anderson's model, Mary Louise Pratt (1987) has argued that his "community approach" reproduces certain assumptions of liberal ideology. This type of analysis treats "communities" in an idealized fashion, as if they were finite, autonomous, and homogeneous. Consequently, it either ignores relations of hierarchy or examines the dominant and the dominated as separate groups rather than as mutually constituted sectors, each with an "identity" that is bound up with the other's.[5]

The disjunction in Anderson's analysis between the form of dominant belief and the conditions and meanings which inform its construction and appropriation poses the question of the relationship between representation and power. Can we fruitfully analyze nationalism as a cultural artifact if it is severed from the hierarchical field of relations within which it is constituted and toward which it is addressed? How are its seemingly immutable features related to the contested field of meanings within which it is locally elaborated? Does nationalism as an anticolonial construct set within neocolonial relations take form and develop in specific ways?

While the concept of the nation represents itself in abstract terms, representations of national belonging weave together images that promise collective unity as well as collective exclusions and thus interlock, in Jameson's (1981) terms, the utopian and the ideological dimensions of national consciousness. Without reducing nationalism to its expressive or instrumental functions, I wish to examine the construction of conceptions of unity and exclusion, of equality and hierarchy, as they address and encode historical practices and political projects.

DOUBLE DISCOURSE AND AUTHENTICITY

Anticolonial nationalism frequently claims as its goal the recovery of an authentic communal past. It assumes that a colonized people share an original identity which can be liberated or restored through the rejection of colonialism's pervasive influence. This assumption links authenticity to ideas of undisputed origins, original creation, and sustained tradition rather than to notions of imitation, appropriation, and syncretism. It evokes the image of a unified past from which the present is derived, in contrast to the ruptures and fragmentation induced by colonizing powers. In this guise, authenticity is called on to impart certainty and wholeness to collective existence.

However, in Venezuela, as in much of Latin America, anticolonial nationalist discourse was based on an ambiguous relationship to the past and thus to the notion of authenticity as regards origins and purity. The Creole elite could not claim the precolonial past as its own, for its power rested on the Spanish Empire's domination of indigenous peoples and suppression of their past. Compounding the rupture was the elite's view of Venezuela's native cultures as of a lower order than the acknowledged great civilizations of ancient Mexico and Peru. They

lacked the visible signs of institutionalized state, religious, and intellectual authority to which the elite could lay claim as heirs.[6] Paradoxically, the elite claimed
that the indigenous resistance to conquest which characterized the nation's colonial past was central to Venezuela's authentic character, the origin of the re-
bellious spirit that runs through "Venezuelan blood." Rebelliousness was transformed from a sign of savagery to a mark of national independence.

The elite, in its quest for legitimacy, repudiated declining Spain and saw its
legacy as a colonial power as one of social degeneration rather than of community.
Officially, the nation was conceptualized in terms of the Enlightenment promise
that national unity could be achieved by eschewing the past and embracing the
rule of reason and citizens' rights.[7] Yet the elite resisted the transformation of
colonial economic and social relations required by these principles. Thus abstract
liberal rhetoric and law preceded the establishment of effective state authority in
the new republic, and successive strong-man regimes utilized these abstractions
as instruments of legitimation and concealment. As a result, a divorce between
the state's unifying claims and the exclusionary practices and beliefs they sustained became institutionalized in the post-Independence period.[8]

Duality and ambiguity as regards the bases of collective authority thus characterized the formation of the elite-led nationalist project, giving rise to a double
discourse of national identity. Reflecting and effecting divisions in the source of
authority as well as concealing and recreating the fractures of a colonial legacy,
this discourse has negotiated the shifting meanings attached to seemingly opposed
social categories. The Creole elite was constituted by these divisions. Under colonialism, this elite had been simultaneously defined as a "colonial community
and an upper class," and thus was subject to imperial domination, but also ruled
as part of the colonial system (Anderson 1991: 59). In the postcolonial project of
nation-building, the elite could be located within what Homi Bhabha (1990) calls
a "doubly shifting field of categories." Belonging to a nation at the periphery of
the metropolitan centers made the elite the object of ambiguous colonizing notions
of the colonial other. Caught between the need to deny and the need to assert its
difference from the metropolitan power, the elite remained unable to establish its
authority through the authenticity of its origins (Bhabha 1985: 162).[9]

Nationalist discourse reflects these contradictory impulses: on the one hand, it
presents itself as expressing a challenge to colonial and imperial domination,
while, on the other, it promotes the goal of remaking society in the image of
international progress. As Partha Chatterjee (1986:30) has argued, the foundational principles legitimizing the domestic elite's rule are split between a commitment to national autonomy and an acceptance of "the very intellectual premises of 'modernity' on which colonial domination was based."[10] This split has
characterized the elite's efforts to assert authority in Latin America, as its nationalist discourse embraced metropolitan models in the name of independence. In
response to demands for reforms which would have challenged oligarchic control
and imperial expansion, the discourse of authenticity offered a new narrative of
the nation's origins. Turning the national landscape into a domestic space, it made
authenticity the offspring of the relationship between elite and pueblo on the
national soil.[11]

FRATERNITY AND MATRIMONY

The concept of the nation as the source of collective authority and identity was only marginally related to the political practices and beliefs that prevailed during the founding period of the Venezuelan republic. Political independence from Spain, achieved after a long, devastating war (1811–1821), raised the issue of the arbitrary colonial divisions among the empire's territories and foregrounded the fragility of the local state and the lack of attachment by the populace to the nation.[12] While the ruling elites elaborated a rhetoric of national progress and popular sovereignty, they nevertheless continued to implement and defend an exclusionary system of class and ethnic relations throughout the nineteenth century. The symbols and regulatory practices of nationhood emerged more as a result of their internal conflicts and efforts to attract foreign capital than from the establishment of promised reforms.

By the post–World War I period, civil order and state consolidation had been achieved under the autocratic rule of General Juan Vicente Gómez (1908–35). Political demands for the removal of Gómez and for the modernization of the state then arose, with implications at the ideological level of a need to endow the nation's past and its pueblo with positive cultural content. In the context of domestic as well as hemispheric challenges to oligarchic control, the effort made by some sectors of the intelligentsia to find value and promise in the racially mixed population had great political significance.

This quest for national identity did not entail validating Venezuela's cultural origins, but rather forging a synthesis of elite reason and popular energy through the taming of the nation's social and physical terrain. The discourse of authenticity posited a distinct Latin American path to civilization marked by the ascendancy of spiritual and telluric forces, guided by reason, over mere rationalist determinism. Central to the effort to renegotiate the relationship between Latin America and the metropolitan powers, this discourse inverted the terms of dominant ideology, aligning materialist progress with spiritual debasement and coercion, and spiritualism with universality and humanism.

Gender was to play a crucial role in configuring this project. During the independence struggle, patriarchal family metaphors were used to justify revolt and to image political union with appeals to a son's justified rebellion against a stunting or tyrannical parent and to the fraternal right of male independence leaders to claim their patrimony (Felstiner 1983). At this time, the male military hero, the virile defender of abused national honor and territory, became the sacred icon of independent nationhood. In the subsequent period of national integration, however, the gendered configuration of nationalist discourse became more complex. Women were closely associated with the forces of the land to be tamed and protected, for example, while the family unit became a metaphor for the unification of the fatherland under a central authority which could defend it. The married couple, bound by a natural hierarchy that included the wife's dependence and the husband's enlightened authority, metaphorically imaged the education of subordinate sectors of the population by the modernizing elite in a mutually energizing relationship. A metaphor that blurred class and ethnic divisions, the image of the nation as a family unit in which opposing principles were synthesized and productively channeled embodied the promise of civilizing reforms.

Doña Bárbara represents the primitive pueblo in ambiguous terms. The pueblo's barbarism, at once alluring and repellent, is intimately linked to women and to female forces. And, like the incomplete domestication of women, its disorderliness is never fully resolved by the project of reform. With the argument that national identity could be constructed through the synthesis of contradictory forces, ambiguity would no longer be banished as a legacy of colonialism, but would be incorporated into the ordering of evolving social relations. *Doña Bárbara* offered a symbolic model for this synthesis within a familial union bound by emotional ties of love and desire. This widely disseminated model has become an element in the "National Symbolic," which, Lauren Berlant (1991) argues, operates as "the order of discursive practices" that makes those born within a national terrain "subjects of a collectively-held history." This order, providing "a common language of a common space," is deployed in nationalist discourse "to produce a fantasy of national integration" (ibid.: 20–22).

BOLÍVAR: SPIRITUAL GUIDE

In order to understand the ideological foundations of the discourse of authenticity, it is helpful to examine the early Republican leadership's debates, for they shaped the commonsense beliefs that the discourse reelaborated. In this respect, Bolívar's thought is central. Although his efforts to advance social reform in the republics were defeated by the landed elite during his lifetime, his thought later became canonized as Republican scripture.[13] Considered the manifest expression of an already accomplished political emancipation, Bolívar's thought was invoked by contending forces to validate their respective claims.[14]

Bolívar's address to the Congress of Angostura in 1819, near the end of the War of Independence, was pivotal to the subsequent formulation of nationalist ideology. His utopian vision of the Republic; his conviction that popular upheaval and the elite's divided identity threatened the Republic's survival; his assertion that racial mixing was the only equalizing solution to social divisions; and his conviction that the political leadership was responsible for the moral elevation of the masses framed nationalist doctrine. Bolívar's concluding injunction to the Republic to achieve racial, and thus class, unity reflected the on-going effort to contain revolt and to establish the foundations of an ideology of mestizaje:

> All our moral powers will not suffice to save our infant republic from this chaos unless we fuse the mass of the people, the government, the legislation, and the national spirit into a single united body. Unity, unity, unity must be our motto in all things. The blood of our citizens is varied: let it be mixed for the sake of unity. (Bolívar 1951: 191)

Bolívar offered the leaders of the divisive War of Independence an image of the Creole elite's split identity. On the one hand, the elite was heir to Europe's civilization and its beliefs and rules should rightfully be adhered to by the re-

fractory population. Yet the Creole elite, like the popular masses, had been oppressed by Spain and should rightfully lead the masses in the struggle for freedom
and independence. Thus Bolívar acknowledged the elite's conflicting allegiances
to the colonizer and the colonized.

As a result of the elite's role as an agent of domination, however, the popular
masses did not recognize it as their rightful leader. Faced with the threatened
dissolution of the Republic, Bolívar argued for the creation of a strong central
government to control popular anarchic tendencies. Although citizens enjoyed
"complete political equality" under the Constitution, most of them had been
corrupted by Spain's degrading system of rule and their full political participation
would produce only a dangerous illusion of democracy.[15] The state had to "re-
educate men" degraded by this "pernicious teacher" (ibid.: 176–77). With the
creation of hereditary seats in a Senate composed of select men, the citizenry
could be educated in the "love of country" and "love of law" that they lacked.[16]
Through a distinction between elevated and degraded spirits, this solution naturalized a division between the tutelary elite and the untutored people.

Bolívar closed his speech with a utopian flight "to the ages to come," in which
he imagined the nascent nation as part of a united continent, a paragon of civilized
life. This image laid the ground for his later efforts to promote a conception of
the Americas as a cultural whole and to invert the existing hierarchy of world
civilization. Marveling at "the prosperity, the splendor, the fullness of life which
will then flourish in this vast region," Bolívar envisioned a future when the new
Republic, no longer a backward colony, would be located at the very "heart of
the universe," a source of mineral treasures, healing plants, and secret knowledge
with which it would supply the rest of the world. "I can see her crowned by
glory, seated upon the throne of liberty with the sceptre of Justice in her hand,
disclosing to the Old World the majesty of the New" (ibid.: 197).

In this address, Bolívar renounced his military title, "The Liberator," and
asked to be called "The Good Citizen" (*El Buen Ciudadano*), for he felt that the
nation's leaders should attend to the formation of an enlightened citizenry, the
basis for which was civic education. With his passage from military defender of
liberty to civil tutor of fraternity, Bolívar established the opposing poles between
which the construction of nationalist discourse was to oscillate.

THE MAKING OF A NATIONALIST MYTH

A mythic battle between the spirits of two leaders structures *Doña Bárbara*.
Simón Bolívar and Juan Vicente Gómez, Venezuelan leaders almost one hundred
years apart, both became woven into political discourse and popular imagery as
figures of extraordinary powers. They are juxtaposed in the novel through their
incarnations, the morally principled reformer Santos Luzardo and the voracious
tyrant Doña Bárbara.

An epic tale of combat on the cattle plains between the forces of civilization
and barbarism, *Doña Bárbara* depicts the triumph of the cultivated urban lawyer
Santos Luzardo, a seeker of political reform, over Doña Bárbara, a personification

of rural despotism.[17] In Luzardo's quest to bring peace and legal order to the plains, he must expel from the region the primitive mestiza Doña Bárbara, who devours land and men, as well as her predatory Yankee ally, Mr. Danger, an adventurer who laughs at the nation's feeble laws. In an undertaking that parallels this battle, Luzardo instructs the lovely, innocent Marisela in correct speech and good manners. She is the untutored daughter of Doña Bárbara, who abandoned her, and Luzardo's cousin, Lorenzo Barquero, a former law student who sank into moral decay. Luzardo succeeds in vanquishing Doña Bárbara through legal means rather than by violence, likewise domesticating Marisela through "education" and "love." The marriage between Luzardo and Marisela announced at the novel's end represents the promise of the nation's harmonious and productive future under the direction of the benevolent liberal state. The family will become orderly and productive, just as the llanos will be fenced and the cattle domesticated.

Gómez had governed Venezuela for twenty-one years by the time *Doña Bárbara* was written.[18] A rural strong man from the Andean region who had little formal education, he occupied high government positions after 1899 and became president in 1908 by deposing the man who had brought him to power. Ruling during the years when Gallegos began to teach and write, Gómez came to embody for the author the defeat of the Bolivarian promise to elevate the pueblo. Much of the propertied and professional elite allied themselves with Gómez, for he ended civil conflict among regional caudillos. Civil peace and the suppression of dissent allowed the agrarian export economy to recover and provided a favorable climate for attracting foreign petroleum companies. In the 1920s, these companies established the oil export industry which was to transform the country.[19]

In Gómez's handpicked Senate sat intellectuals who drew on European geographic and racially determinist theories to argue that the autocratic Gómez was the "necessary gendarme" for Venezuela's unruly people. The writings of his leading ideologue, Laureano Vallenilla Lanz, a conservative thinker whose critique of liberal institutions as unsuited to Latin American reality was influential outside Venezuela, defined the Gómez regime as "Democratic Caesarism," the form of government appropriate to overseeing the evolution of an anarchic, mixed-race society.[20] This doctrine, he claimed, derived from the ideas of Bolívar, who had proclaimed himself dictator for life in the wake of strife within the new Republic. Gómez was indifferent to these theories, but revered Bolívar as a military leader and an advocate of strong central rule. Rejecting the language of abstractly equal subjects, Gómez constructed an image of the national community on the model of an orderly and productive cattle hacienda under his patriarchal rule.[21]

Opponents of Gómez also drew on Bolívar's legacy to construct a critique of the regime. In 1928, the first mass protest against Gómez, which began as a celebration of the university, linked the leaders of Independence to popular struggles against oppression. Student speeches rhetorically identified the university's Queen of the Students with the spirit of liberty and called on Bolívar's spirit to lead the people in her defense against domestic and foreign oppressors.[22] They revived a suppressed Bolivarian image of the national community as a fraternal member of a Latin American union formed to repel colonizing assaults. In this vision, the repositories of national value, that is, liberty and the land, were imaged as female.

The demonstrations and subsequent arrests were pivotal to the formation of a new opposition leadership and consciousness. They drew broad expressions of support from across social classes, and the imprisonment of sons of the middle and upper class disturbed even the regime's allies. Out of this experience the nuclei of future political parties were conceived, led by those who became collectively known as the "Generation of '28."

Rómulo Gallegos wrote *Doña Bárbara* in dialogue with these protests and with the suppressed dissent to the regime that they revealed. Many of the students who were arrested had studied with him at the Caracas high school where he not only taught, but was the director, and regarded him as their mentor. Throughout his career as an essayist, fiction writer, and educator, Gallegos expressed his belief in the need to govern the pueblo by law rather than by force. In a political culture characterized by violent competition for power, he sought to construct a model of the virile reformer of nonviolent means.

Following the protests, Gallegos revised the manuscript of his latest novel, which concerned a female rural boss on the llanos.[23] With these changes, it became a tightly structured mythic tale, an allegory of the nation's rule by despotism and of the projected triumph of the liberal, modernizing state. Uncertain as to the reaction of the repressive Gómez regime, Gallegos published *Doña Bárbara* in Spain, at his own expense, while he was in Europe. It won a literary prize, and Spanish critics hailed it as an authentic expression of Latin America's human drama. This recognition by Europe at once validated the work in the view of the Venezuelan public and defined it as an expression of a Latin American reality for readers elsewhere. Critics in Latin America hailed *Doña Bárbara* as a work of "universal literature," deeming it "classic" in style, resonant of Cervantes and Tolstoy, and free of the "parochial descriptions" (*costumbrismo*) found in much of the region's literature. These critics in Spain and Latin America accorded *Doña Bárbara* literary greatness because it had turned its gaze inward toward the rural heart of the nation, yet had adopted a narrative position of distance from and mastery over the scenes it presented.[24] It was identifiably local and yet abstract, it avoided implicating the national elite directly in its denunciation, and it was thus accessible to different political sectors in diverse countries.

Written in visibly symbolic terms and in the familiar form of a romance, *Doña Bárbara* was intended to reach an audience beyond literary circles. Eschewing the era's literary conventions, Gallegos sought to incorporate both elite and popular speech and practices within a narrative structure that would model the principles of social and individual transformation that he promoted.[25] This ambitious intent, which is often misread by today's critics and readers, transformed the descriptive material about life on the llanos into symbolic expressions of archetypal cosmic and psychic forces. In doing so, the novel addressed Venezuelan and Latin American readers as participants in the world of "universal" literary works and historical processes.

This populist national romance dressed in positivist clothing appeared at a time when the social basis of the regime was beginning to shift. Given Gómez's monopolization of power and wealth in the context of the nation's increasing incorporation into the international economy, discontent with the regime's restrictions was growing within the elite and among foreign powers. While the Gómez regime had long employed a conservative rhetoric of progress, it then began to refashion its image to convey an appearance of reform.

Doña Bárbara lent itself to a variety of political interpretations, including those consistent with dominant evolutionary assumptions. In an incident which is not included in contemporary official discourse, for it suggests dangerous continuities with the present, Gómez made a striking effort to appropriate *Doña Bárbara* as an expression of his regime's civilizing vision. As the story goes, Gómez, who closely monitored suspected critics of his regime, heard conflicting reports about Gallegos's novel and its intent. While many praised its optimistic vision of orderly progress, others warned Gómez that the novel criticized his rule through the figure of the brutal Doña Bárbara, a landowner who ruled the llanos by means of magic, seduction, and force. Ordering his secretary to read the novel out loud to him at his hacienda, from which he governed, Gómez was transfixed by the story, insisting that his secretary finish reading the book by the light of car headlights. This book, Gómez allegedly declared with satisfaction, was not against him. Indeed, writing such books was what all writers should be doing, instead of fomenting foolish revolutions (Liscano 1969: 117). Gómez then sought to align Gallegos with his regime and thus to intervene in the novel's reception by casting it as a tribute to his pacification of the countryside. He appointed Gallegos Senator from Apure, the llanos state in which the novel was set and which had been a source of troops for the War of Independence. With one gesture, then, Gómez attempted to incorporate author, novel, and region, along with their respective associations of Independence, into his centralizing project.[26]

In an effort to establish himself and his novel as a voice and an expression of opposition, Gallegos left Venezuela for exile in Spain until Gómez's death.[27] There he wrote novels and became an adviser for and emblem of non-Marxist reform movements in Latin America. With his return to Venezuela in 1936, he moved from emblem to active leader of the democratic opposition, working to found a multi-class reformist party which would be neither Marxist nor conservative. This mass party, "Acción Democrática" (Democratic Action), was founded in 1941, with Gallegos as its president, and *Doña Bárbara*'s elevation to the status of national novel accompanied the rise of the party. When AD held power from 1945 to 1948, it launched a capitalist reform project that party followers believed mirrored the novel's vision.[28] Gallegos, who had become publicly identified with the redemptive figure of Santos Luzardo, won an overwhelming victory in 1947 as the nation's first president to be elected under universal suffrage. However, he was overthrown by the military and was exiled again nine months after taking office. With AD's return to power in 1959 and with the consolidation of oil rent-based democracy in the following decades, *Doña Bárbara* became institutionalized as the mythic charter for the modern state, a representation of unity that elided and concealed class differences.[29]

FLUID IDENTITIES

Beneath *Doña Bárbara*'s didactic narrative voice, which persistently seeks to establish unambiguous categories, lies an unsettling recognition of the instability of meanings. Opposing forces traverse land and people, dissolving moral boundaries and awakening transgressive desires, thereby revealing the arbitrary marks of colonizing authority. In what Maya Scharer-Nussberger (1979a: 509–17) terms a pendular movement between subject and object, characters interact with their externalized self-reflection, become puppets of their mythic creations, and merge fantasy with reality.[30]

This relational model of identity formation, which draws on Romantic subject/object paradigms, gives subjective content to a hierarchical model of spiritual evolution and moral authority. Shifting categories interact with the normative framework in a movement of reciprocal construction. The result is neither the fixing of unambiguous categories nor the deconstruction of categories by the indeterminacy of meaning. Instead, new authority is constituted through the negotiation of ambiguity. Santos Luzardo and Doña Bárbara exemplify this relational model of self-realization. Luzardo's sense of identity is both renewed and threatened by his immersion in a land which is primitive but not pristine. The land was taken from the natives by conquerors, yet the land conquered the invaders, in turn, by making them mixed-race, semi-barbarians who plague the embattled cities. The violence of llanos life is rendered both as authentically Venezuelan and as a sign of the nonviability of Venezuela's nationhood.[31]

Luzardo is split into opposing selves which reflect the fractures of his class. Upon reencountering his cousin, Lorenzo Barquero, who is the helpless discard of despotism, he "sees" what he himself could become under the seductive influence of life on the lawless llanos. His cousin had also once been a brilliant lawyer in the capital, a glittering orator among the imitative urban elite who had argued for political reform. But when Barquero realized that his knowledge of the law was a meaningless artifice, an illusion of rhetoric, he had become consumed with self-loathing and had returned to the llanos. There, he succumbed to his obsession with Doña Bárbara, "bewitched by the insatiable woman and victim of the aphrodisiac potion she made him drink" (Gallegos 1959 [1929]: 578, 519). Luzardo recognizes in his cousin, a figure of "enlightened barbarism," the elite's failure to conquer and domesticate rural barbarism and thus its failure to establish its authority by anchoring meaning to moral action.[32]

Yet the conquest of barbarism implies the need for Luzardo to control his own potential for barbarism, the "Centaur" he carries within him. He almost succumbs to the lure of lawlessness and self-gratification, strongly attracted as he is to its unbounded freedom and its seeming inescapability. In the process of proving himself as a man, by meeting challenges to his leadership and physical prowess, he begins to become despotic and violent. He is only redeemed through Marisela's love, with her domestication rendered as the product of his benevolent instruction.[33] Luzardo's formation as a truly masculine leader, ruled by rationality, requires that he develop a spiritual, feminine side.

Doña Bárbara is also split into opposing selves—in her case, as a consequence of colonialism's predatory violence. In the past she had been simply Bárbara, an innocent, untutored girl who yearned for love and whose youthful self is later mirrored in her daughter, Marisela. Now she has become the feared Doña Bárbara, a destructive figure of undifferentiated sexual energy, with male and female impulses mixing in a "monstrous hybrid combination," driven to conquer men in revenge for her own conquest. She is the creation of a monstrous act, for she was raped as an adolescent by men who also murdered the young man from whom she had learned to read and who had aroused feelings of love and respect in her. Thus Doña Bárbara's encounter with Luzardo unexpectedly transforms her, as she responds to him unconsciously as the incarnation of her murdered love and, correspondingly, as the enlightened "law" that she desires. Aware that she is becoming domesticated and feminine, Doña Bárbara reflects upon herself in a rare moment of introspection. She acknowledges the destabilizing effect on her identity of her desire for Luzardo, telling him, "If I had encountered men like you in my path before,my story would be a different one" (ibid.: 654). From this insight follows her attempt to undo her life of despotism. Her spirit familiar tells her, in what the narrator calls "Kabbalistic" words, "Things return to the place from whence they came" (ibid.: 709). She rids herself of her henchmen, her stolen lands, and her masculine demeanor, and she grants her abandoned daughter the inheritance due her. Yet she cannot become another in the eyes of Luzardo, for he regards her transformation as but a change in appearance.

With an act in which she returns to her origins as the hate-filled Doña Bárbara, she achieves authentic change. Upon seeing Marisela and Santos Luzardo in affectionate conversation, Doña Bárbara is seized by an impulse to shoot Marisela and eliminate her rival. But she suddenly "sees," as in a vision, her former self incarnated in the person of Marisela and decides instead to leave the llanos. By renouncing her desire to possess through violence, she makes it possible for the parallel domestication of the llanos to begin. As she recedes downriver to her place of origin, the barbarous currents within Luzardo and Marisela subside as well, and they agree to marry. But as the ambiguous ending suggests, with its evocation of indigenous beliefs in hidden water spirits, Doña Bárbara remains as a submerged presence. She lives on in legend and fantasy, a symbol of seductive primal instincts within leader and pueblo alike. As she returns to her riverbed, in the novel's last line, she leaves behind the llanos, where "a good race [raza] loves, suffers and hopes."

METAPHYSICAL NATIONALISM

This relational construct of identities mediated by mythic forces and intuitive comprehension draws on the critique of rationalism and determinism that gained acceptance among the intelligentsia during the interwar period. However, largely because of their modernizing assumptions, accounts of nationalism's consolidation in Latin America tend to present a genealogy of ideas divorced from their social context and from their role in the production of the social order. Such accounts devote little attention to nationalism's cultural dimension, abstracting it from the religious beliefs and historical memories that inflected political concepts derived from European contexts. Secularizing assumptions and reductionist notions of power have thus been projected onto nationalist movements and projects, obscuring dimensions of meaning that have been refracted through the experience of colonialism.

The prevailing currents of nationalist thought in Latin America after World War I involved a critique of determinist theories of racial evolution and the assertion of mestizaje as a uniquely Latin American contribution to the advancement of world civilization.[34] Prior to this period, the European-oriented domestic elites, allied with foreign interests, had promoted positivist evolutionism. Based on a biologically defined notion of race and a belief in the superiority of the racially pure, then modified by Comtean notions of geographic determinism, this theory closely accorded with the imperial division of the world.[35] Latin America's mixed-race societies were relegated to the bottom rung of the social-evolutionary ladder, justifying their consignment to the margins of world civilization and their passive role as suppliers of materials and recipients of material progress.[36]

Those intellectuals who employed the discourse of authenticity sought to counter this Eurocentric model, which threatened to eventually destroy national culture and autonomy. Rejecting biological determinants in relation to national potential, they built on a geocultural concept of the pueblo as a product of evolution on a shared terrain. The theory that geography and people interacted historically to produce a collective soul became the basis of the notion of race, or "raza," as people. The environment was a factor that both conditioned and expressed a people's character. Raza became the defining term in the effort to cast Latin America as a site of historical agency and source of cultural originality. While the land-based notion of raza originated in positivist geographic determinism and retained some of its essentializing assumptions, it was combined with relativizing anthropological findings on non-Western cultures and neo-Romantic concepts of spiritual forces in order to call into question unilinear notions of progress.

This rejection of a biological concept of race was accordingly part of an epistemological critique of the rationalist premises that sustained evolutionary determinism. The postulation of industrial progress as the highest form of civilization, critics argued, rested on a dichotomy between mind and spirit, a dichotomy that permitted the unchecked advance of materialism and that valorized a notion of progress divorced from moral and spiritual development. Anglo-American capitalism, they claimed, promoted material progress at the cost of human spiritual impoverishment.[37] This "civilized barbarism" had been unleashed upon the world, displacing older forms of civilization. Its mimicry by the Latin American elite was an expression of "enlightened barbarism" (la barbarie ilustrada), the nation's worst enemy.[38] This critique, which focused on capitalism's imperialist manifestations and on Anglo-American control, sought to center a humane capitalism within the domestic elite's domain.

The articulation of these ideas involved the intelligentsia in direct engagement with social and political issues, for a central tenet of this philosophical reorientation was that the nation's leadership must have an intimate knowledge of the pueblo in order to uplift it.[39] This effort to reverse colonialist conceptions of backwardness was crucial for the political elite's assumption of a position of authority within the context of national political reform. If the intellectual leadership turned to an exploration of the national terrain, it did so not in order to give a voice to the pueblo, but to discover and synthesize popular elements in its construction of an authentic national identity.

The goal of seeking new sources of creativity within the nation accorded new value to the spiritual and religious dimensions of life that were important to both pueblo and elite. This intersection in Latin America between religious beliefs and a political nationalism infused with mystical notions has been largely overlooked. Yet many were concerned with these issues, and their concepts were familiar among broad sectors of the political and intellectual elite in Europe and Latin America during the late nineteenth and early twentieth centuries. The impulse to link nationalism with metaphysical or mystical beliefs received strong support from the European thinkers who identified with the challenge to positivism and the turn toward the "irrational." Public interest centered on two, closely interrelated areas: scholarly theories that affirmed the priority of the nonrational in the development and perception of the world; and the popularization of Eastern thought, the Kabbalah, Freemasonry, spiritualism, and the occult.

Latin American thinkers applied the European challenge to positivism toward the revaluation of Latin American culture's spiritual character. The formulation of a nationalist critique of dominant materialist theories drew heavily on Hegel, especially on his concept of history as a dialectic of self-realizing spirit, and on Nietzsche, particularly his concept of the spiritually elite as capable of attaining free will.[40] Bergson's and Sorel's theories concerning the intuitive apprehension of reality, the central role of symbols and myth in history, and the relativity of time also had a strong impact on arguments for Latin America's nonmaterialist culture.

European self-questionings became implicated in the redefinition of Latin America's identity. After World War I, which had provoked a broad challenge to the belief in progress, many influential European thinkers began to express a conviction that Western civilization had become dangerously ossified and that "barbarism" could provide a revitalizing infusion of primal energy. Rather than being viewed as a threatening source of anarchy, societies and peoples associated with barbarism were regarded from this perspective as sources of creative power and imagination waiting to be tapped. The quest by social thinkers for these sources, the turn toward the primitive occurring in the European arts, and the search by mystical thinkers for terrains that would be receptive to the development of esoteric knowledge converged to reconfigure Latin America as a privileged site of spiritual revitalization.

For the intelligentsia in Latin America, the leading source for these views was an influential journal published in Spain, *Revista de Occidente* (Journal of the Occident), founded in 1923 by the Spanish philosopher José Ortega y Gasset. This journal, which featured articles by German idealist and phenomenological philosophers, tended to problematize rationalism.[41] The journal grew out of

Spain's identity crisis following its final defeat as an imperial power by the United States in 1898. Ortega y Gasset asked how Spain could join, yet not be marginalized by, Europe's stifling civilization. Influenced by Hegel and Nietzsche, he argued that an enlightened elite must guide the impulses of the masses in order to develop a nation's vitality. Latin America, he concluded, offered the vigorous barbarism that Europe needed, one that promised to restore Europe's greatness.[42]

The journal also published Spanish translations of major books on these subjects, which circulated widely in Latin America. Two of these are relevant to this discussion: Oswald Spengler's (1926 [1918]) *Decline of the West*, in 1923, and Count Hermann Keyserling's 1932 *South American Meditations*, in 1933.[43] Spengler, who was read avidly by a broad public, drew on theorists of the unconscious and historical idealists to inform his argument that cultures follow independent paths of growth in cyclical rhythms and evolve through unique racial syntheses of cosmic and psychic forces. Like Nietzsche before him, Spengler believed that only an injection of energy from primitive sources could halt the decline of the materially advanced West. His influential work not only inspired the Latin American intelligentsia to explore autochthonous cultural expressions, but his ideas, appropriated from the margins of the metropolitan West, were seen as ratifying Latin America's identity as an original, synthetic civilization derived from the mixing of different races on American soil.

Count Keyserling synthesized the diverse currents of Eastern, spiritualist, and esoteric thought, which were enjoying a widespread revival at that time in Europe. A member of the German aristocracy in Estonia, he wrote for and lectured to a largely elite audience in Western Europe on the future of civilization, the nature of cosmic order, and the path to enlightenment. More optimistic than Spengler, Keyserling predicted the birth of a vigorous civilization on the South American continent, although at present, he noted, this region had reached only "the third day of creation." The continent was still at a primordial stage, he declared, as shown by the Andean people, who were "mineraloid men," and life there was driven purely by telluric energy and was still devoid of spirituality (Keyserling 1933 [1932]: 14–41).[44]

While Latin America provided for European intellectuals a revitalizing encounter with the primitive Other, the Latin American intellectual elite defined its own encounter with the internal Other as a recognition of Self. Three influential works by leading intellectuals celebrated mestizaje as Latin America's indigenous cultural contribution to world civilization: José Vasconcelos's (1948 [1926]) *La raza cósmica*; Ricardo Rojas's (1924) "Eurindia"; and Raúl Haya de la Torre's (1936) *A dónde va Indoamérica?* By "indigenous," Vasconcelos and Rojas meant the people who had settled the American lands, not the "Indians," whom they regarded as conquered and broken.[45] For them, the idea of mixing, or synthesis, was part of an evolutionary movement toward "white," understood as modern, culture.[46] "Perhaps among all the characters of the fifth race those of the white one will predominate, but this supremacy should be the fruit of the free elevation of choice" (Vasconcelos 1948 [1925]: 37). Through a spiritually guided process of mestizaje, argued Vasconcelos, in terms resonant with mystical references, evolution toward a final "cosmic race" would occur.

Haya de la Torre, a leading Peruvian political figure whose nationalist doctrine was influential across the continent, asserted that the Indian rather than the Hispanic past provided an image of communal unity and a promise of the future equality that would be attained by the region's new raza.[47] Drawing on Inca culture and steeped in mysticism, Eastern philosophy, and occult beliefs derived from his studies in Europe, particularly of Count Keyserling's work, Haya formulated a theory of "historical space-time" on which he based his vision of civilization's regeneration in the Americas. This rebirth would depend on the intervention of spiritually prepared leaders who, through their access to special sources of knowledge, would be able to synthesize the forces associated with the different civilizations then at odds in the hemisphere: the Anglo-European, and the Indo-American. This task could be accomplished only by leaders who had attained the highest levels of consciousness.[48]

These thinkers all assumed that the unformed pueblo could attain consciousness as a historical subject through the mediation of its enlightened leadership. Yet they offered no explanation of how either of these subjects would emerge. Their discourse exemplified what Terry Eagleton (1990: 28) refers to as "the metaphysics of nationalism," which speaks of "the entry into full self-realization of a unitary subject known as the people." This monadic subject, curiously, is assumed to "preexist its own process of materialization," to be equipped with "determinate needs and desires, on the model of the autonomous human personality." And it was to the human personality that this discourse turned.

THE AUTHENTIC LEADER

In light of this discussion, we can better locate *Doña Bárbara* within the intersecting currents of social and intellectual life that framed its production. During the forced quiescence of political and cultural life under Gómez, buttressed by elite support for his project as well as by his effective system of repression, opposition discourse slowly developed between the lines of official political discourse. It incorporated the language and assumptions of positivist evolutionism into a revised framework that was informed by idealist and neo-Romantic beliefs.

This emergent opposition discourse, while reflecting an evolutionary framework and an emphasis on geographic determinism, effected important transformations as well: the spiritually elevated individual became an agent of free will; the pueblo was endowed with a capacity for redemption; and the land was infused with a positive force. Together, these concepts sustained the opposition to autocracy and support for a constitutional regime.

Gallegos was particularly critical of the imitative traditional elite, the "barbarie ilustrada," and of its failure to provide an enlightened leadership that could wrest control from the backward caudillos. In the context of political repression and elite complicity, his self-constructed persona of an authentic civic leader, one who brought word and deed together in active unity, had a broad political purpose. We may see Gallegos's assertion of the link between his life and his writings as a practical critique of rationalist assumptions through which he established his "locus of enunciation" (Mignolo [in press]). Identity, Gallegos argued in his writings and in the classroom, was the product of one's acting upon one's surroundings, a process through which self-recognition and moral development were achieved. This position, which refused to set artistic creation apart from collective concerns, aligned him with Ortega y Gasset's influential philosophy of "circumstantialism."

Gallegos regarded his life as a text of his own making, and his texts, in turn, as actors in his life. His biographer and friend, the author Juan Liscano (1969: 9) wrote that his "life and work so complemented each other that one could compose a novel in his own style using his biography." Furthermore, "Gallegos created himself in contrast to the dictatorship and the dictator," as if they embodied conflicting principles. "For Gallegos, public and political action was the opportunity to identify himself with the figures of his books, to embody them" (Liscano 1985: 117, 202).[49] He sought to constitute the nation's history and himself through his writing and his actions; his life and his writing, the nation's history and his representations of it, interpenetrated. Through his own actions, the script he wrote for his characters took on new life.

His central concern in his writing was the creation of a Bolivarian vision of social reform that was rooted in the nation's origins and incarnated in heroic figures, a cultural foundation for the populist project whose language spoke to broad social sectors. The parallels between the personas of Gallegos and Bolívar are striking. Both leaders represented themselves as educators of the unformed pueblo. They spoke as moral guides from an elevated plane of existence who sought to channel the people's unruly spirit toward a higher degree of development. For Gallegos, Bolívar the civic reformer and moral educator, rather than the military leader, was his model and the source of his reformist ideas. He wrote extensively on educational reform and on the role of the leader as an educator in terms that resembled Bolívar's writings on these subjects. Publicly known as "El Maestro" ("The Teacher") until his death, he played the role of a moral leader, not a politician, and found in Santos Luzardo the literary representation of this role. Through his conduct and his literary characterization, he made the exemplary individual his Bolivarian answer to the problem of authority on a postcolonial terrain.[50]

In an early essay of 1912, "La Necesidad de Valores Culturales," Gallegos defined the intellectual as a product of a superior culture who helps bring about the evolution of the masses by channeling their "vital energies," which are "instinctual forces like rivers overflowing their bed" (Gallegos 1954: I, 95–97). For in Venezuela, he argued in 1931, strikingly foreshadowing Count Keyserling, the "sixth day of creation" had not yet ended; in this unfinished, seething land, satanic forces shaped souls into barbarism, and men hastily formed from the residue of creation emerged from the earth to don uniforms and exert their rule (ibid.: 116–19). As a writer, he explained in 1954, he did not seek to depict this landscape for purely creative purposes, but to symbolize through his characters the "intellectual or moral forms of [his] concerns with regard to the problems of the Venezuelan reality within which [he had] lived." He grounded his symbols in his experience and created them to help alter his society, he explained, for the nation needed myths through which to recognize and represent itself. He created the figure of Doña Bárbara so that through her "a dramatic aspect of the Venezuela in which [he had] lived [might] become visible, and so that in some fashion her imposing character [might] help us remove from our souls that part of her that resides in us" (ibid.: II, 116–17).[51]

Gallegos's concern for the spiritual was grounded in the earthly construction of a harmonious society governed by moral and aesthetic principles.[52] Yet his creation of archetypal characters through whom vital forces could manifest themselves and his belief in the redemptive capacity of spiritually elevated individuals to direct these forces were informed by the Romantic, phenomenological, and idealist thought of the period, as inflected by elements of mysticism.[53]

With its international success, *Doña Bárbara* came to rewrite Gallegos's life, as the novel constructed him as a voice of the continent. Mexico's José Vasconcelos, himself a founding figure of mestizaje as an ideology and political program, lauded *Doña Bárbara* in 1931; it was, he asserted, an expression of Hispanic America's soul, "the best novel in America, without excluding the good novels that have been written in English, in the North" (Vasconcelos 1982 [1931]: 50).[54] During the interwar period, Gallegos spoke not as a political party leader or officeholder, both of which he would later become, but as that imagined ideal, the voice of a single, unified pueblo.

TRANSFORMATIVE IMAGES

Keeping in mind the novel's role as a charter of Venezuelan nationalism, we may now turn to *Doña Bárbara*'s reception in Venezuela, focusing on the upper- and middle-class reading public.[55] Changes brought about by the impact of the oil export industry helped create a desire among the conservative elite for a constitutional regime, while demands for democracy and reform arose primarily from the nascent middle class. The incipient organization of labor in cities and among petroleum workers also brought a new class component to the project of political change.[56]

Doña Bárbara presented a mythic construct in which presumably all sectors of the population could see themselves reflected. This symbolic construct at once imaged their present existence and envisioned their future transformation within a hierarchical yet integrative social order. It portrayed the demise of the elite in its role as an adjunct to military and foreign interests and its rebirth as an enlightened, civilizing force. The middle class's servility toward corrupt power was exposed, but its future as a virile, conquering bourgeoisie was also proposed. The popular sectors were depicted as the passive and degraded subjects of despotism, but also projected as productive and devoted citizens who would energize the nation. And the novel offered a vision of men and women as no longer driven by untamed instinct under barbarism's rule, but becoming fruitfully joined in familial union by the forces of civilization.

Male leaders of the middle-class opposition explicitly identified with the novel. For many, from both the center and the left, Santos Luzardo became their unquestioned model. As Juan Bautista Fuenmayor, a petroleum union organizer of elite origins and founder of the Communist Party, recalled in a personal interview (June 1989): "We all wanted to be Santos Luzardo and to defeat tyranny." Similarly, Domingo A. Coronil, son of a Gómez government official, student of Gallegos, and a Supreme Court justice, stated that in that era, "We saw in Santos Luzardo the future of the nation, and Marisela was like the pueblo, a diamond in the rough" (personal interview, July 1989). Mariano Picón Salas, author and leader of the AD, recalled that opponents of Gómez read *Doña Bárbara* in jail and "planned to act against the disastrous mess of the dictatorship just as Santos Luzardo had done upon the ruins of Altamira," his abandoned hacienda (Karsen 1979: 501). And Raul Roa (1985 [1954]: 68–69), Cuban author and political leader, recalled that, while jailed in Cuba in 1930 for opposition to the dictator Machado, the prisoners read *Doña Bárbara* aloud: "It was a revelation . . . a faithful image of a conflict which was our own, but in a different setting."[57]

The conservative elite had a more ambivalent response to this novel. Yet *Doña Bárbara* drew on and reproduced hierarchical conceptualizations of unity and mystical beliefs which resonated with those of the elite.[58] The noted novelist Teresa de la Parra, a member of the elite, was critical of Gómez, but she also rejected the modernizing project of his liberal opponents. Her ambivalence reflected the attitude of an intelligentsia dissatisfied with its subordination to dictatorial rule. Writing from Europe in 1931 to an upper-class biographer of Bolívar, Vicente Lecuna, de la Parra imagined an ideal Venezuela of the colonial past: "Like the Far East, it is a land where mysticism grows spontaneously . . . . I see Bolívar as a yogi; the result of three hundred years in the valleys of Aragua." This land, where feminine values of beauty and love reigned and people of all stations lived in harmony, had been ruined by materialist, Europeanizing liberalism after Independence.[59] Now, she lamented, people accept Gobineau's racial determinism. In a statement which reveals how, for its own elites, Latin America had become a terrain on which alternative visions of civilization contended, de la Parra wondered, with anguish: "Will we really one day be truly superior nations? Is it true that from that terrible mixture of races there will be created a homogeneous one with true qualities of a superior race? . . . I believe that Vasconcelos, the Mexican, maintains the opposite position [to Gobineau's]; I am going to read him, and Keyserling as well" (De la Parra 1951: 71).[60] Her own attempt to construct a counter-notion of Venezuelan identity based on beauty and harmony of the spirit drew on the same intellectual currents which informed Gallegos and his public. This convergence suggests how different social sectors saw themselves reflected in and reconfigured by *Doña Bárbara*'s allegory of national integration.

The appropriation and reconfiguration of this mythic national charter has continued over time and across media. A film version of the novel, produced in Mexico in 1945, spread the story to popular sectors of the rural as well as the urban regions, while subsequent dramatizations in radio and television serializa-

tions have continued to disseminate the story and to refract it through contemporary lenses.[61] A continuing presence in popular speech and religion, Gallegos's
characters are familiar figures who reappear, under different names, in contemporary dramas and are believed to populate the political scene.

CONCLUSION

Returning to Benedict Anderson's assertion that *regardless* of actual conditions
of inequality and exploitation the nation is conceived as a horizontal comradeship,
we may well ask whether it is precisely in the *context* of structures and notions
of inequality that this abstract conception of fraternity is most insistently sustained
and given meaning. If we regard relations of domination as formative of conceptions of community rather than as external to them, we may better understand the
complex ways that the nation is constructed and in which it mediates identities.
Seen in this light, nationalism is a relational and a contested construct which
builds on contradiction and ambiguity even as it unwaveringly proclaims essential
truths.

While nationalism represents itself as an equalizing project, it is engendered
by and constitutive of social hierarchies. Thus if our analyses attend only to
nationalism's self-representation, we will overlook its ties to both the practices
and the representations of inequality. Central to these is the gender hierarchy
which, as Pratt (1991: 51) asserts, creates a "deep cleavage in the horizontal
fraternity." For from the outset of Republican life, women have been "produced"
in "permanent instability with respect to the imagined community," defined by
their reproductive capacity as mothers of the nation, and "imagined as dependent
rather than sovereign." My discussion has sought to show the lines of connection
between the gendered representation of Latin American nations' ambiguous
claims to Republican statehood and the identification of women with the natural
and the metaphysical, the instinctive and the dependent.

Produced in an unstable relationship to "nation," "woman" has served as a
sign of postcolonial national identities. As a marker of otherness and dependency,
"woman" has been multiply constructed by being articulated with class, ethnic,
and regional hierarchies and given content by a linear narrative of history. From
the perspective of determinist evolutionary theories of history, "woman" config-
ures the lowest elements in these hierarchies, to be understood as a sign of anach-
ronism or backwardness and as an obstacle to Western progress. From the perspective of the discourse of authenticity, "woman" also embodies the authentic
and the universal, a force to be tamed in the service of civilization. "Woman"
thus validates the role of the male elite as an agent of progress within the nation
and stands for the nation's subaltern position in relation to metropolitan progress.

The discourse of authenticity sought to open up and reconfigure conceptions
of history based on Enlightenment assumptions that were inextricably tied to the
foundation of Latin American nations. By bringing to the fore nationalism's metaphysics and by embracing Romantic and mystical conceptions of spiritual evolution and cosmic unity, the discourse of authenticity located Latin American

nationhood on a distinct course of civilizing evolution, one claimed to be authentically its own. Elaborating a narrative of history which countered but did not fundamentally challenge the dominant construct, this discourse construed Latin American nations as contributors to the flow of world history while it continued to accept dominant temporal and hierarchical premises. Ambiguity and authenticity were closely intertwined. They were linked to female forces and to control over women's reproductive powers. Within this transcendental scheme of historical evolution, what had once been construed as unambiguous signs of backwardness could be ambivalently construed as sources of originality and creativity, provided that these constructs were reworked and contained within a male elite project.

My focus here has been on the moment of *Doña Bárbara*'s production and early reception, when ambiguity was negotiated as a defining force in the configuration of Latin America's synthetic identity. *Doña Bárbara* has since been incorporated into the nationalist development project as a paradigmatic narrative of history which shaped the language of national belonging. In this movement from the textual to the political, from the emergent to the paradigmatic, ambiguity as a mode of imagining and expressing the resolution of colonial schisms has become, like Doña Bárbara herself, a submerged yet still living presence.

NOTES

1. See Carlos J. Alonso (1990) for discussion of allegorical excess and fluid meanings in *Doña Bárbara*.

2. Roberto González Echevarría (1985) takes an alternative position, making the interesting argument that contemporary Latin American literature is characterized by its deconstructive stance toward writing. However, at one level his argument continues the search for an authentic Latin American identity. He places *Doña Bárbara* within this deconstructive current and, in so doing, severs it from the social relations to which it was addressed.

3. See Raymond Williams (1979) on the historical analysis of literary works. My discussion also draws on Stuart Hall's (1986) interpretation of Gramsci; Fredric Jameson's (1981) analysis of the political unconscious; and Lauren Berlant's (1991) analysis of national subjects.

4. See Guha's (1985) critical comments on Anderson's attention to elite nationalism at the expense of popular-sector initiatives.

5. Pratt cites examples from studies of linguistic communities in which Black English is essentialized as authentic and the impact of power differentials on gendered differences in speech behavior is ignored.

6. Venezuela lacked a major indigenous civilization, such as Mexico had in the Aztecs, which could serve as a corresponding source of past greatness for the Creole elite (Pagden 1990). The native population was viewed largely as the degraded product of conquest and thus as a threat to progress.

7. Anthony Pagden (1990) has stressed the abstract character of liberal discourse in Latin America, while Ernesto Laclau (1979: 178–79) has emphasized its antidemocratic, elitist character.

8. Echoing a widely held conviction, Octavio Paz (1980: 111) has decried the divisive and oppressive effects of liberal rhetoric in Mexico: "Liberal democratic ideology, far

from expressing our concrete historical situation, concealed it. *The political lie* was virtually constitutionally installed among our peoples" (his emphases).

9. Bhabha (1985: 150) links this division within the colonized to that within the colonizer: "The colonial presence is always ambivalent, split between its appearance as original and authoritative and its articulation as repetition and difference."

10. Chatterjee elaborates here on the contradictory dynamics of nationalist discourse, which, in its quest to deny the alleged inferiority of the colonized people, asserts the nation's ability to undertake modernization on its own and thus endorses the premises of "modernity" on which colonial domination was based.

11. See Berlant's (1991) innovative analysis of national fantasy and the state-mediated construction of identities.

12. Venezuela was not a separate administrative unit during most of the colonial period. Simón Bolívar, leader of the independence struggle in Venezuela and northern South America, attempted to reunite the territories that had once been joined to create a new nation, Gran Colombia, composed of Venezuela, Colombia (including Panama), and Ecuador. The union disintegrated in 1830, along with Bolívar's dream of Pan-American unity, at the time of his death. See Arturo Ardao (1978) on the idea of Gran Colombia.

13. Bolívar's persistent efforts to abolish slavery and to redistribute the land, in particular, met with failure. See Miguel Izard's (1979) discussion of the conservative Creole elite's resistance to reform and the popular rebellion that it provoked.

14. For a pathbreaking discussion of the virtual deification of Bolívar, see Germán Carrera Damas (1969).

15. Pagden (1990) underlines Rousseau's influence on Bolívar, as regards his concept of democracy and the popular will, so that by "the people" Bolívar meant those who had sufficient standing and education to engage in the political process as citizens.

16. Bolívar proposed a hereditary Senate divided into two chambers: Morality and Education. He claimed as models for this entity the British Parliament and the governing bodies of antiquity to be found in Athens, Sparta, and Rome (Bolívar 1951: 192). An electoral division between "active" and "passive" citizens, which was not based on clear class distinctions, would allow the select few to check the "popular will" and promote "popular enlightenment." This proposal was rejected by Congress. Bolívar feared the divisive actions of a conservative elite that wielded power but was unprepared for leadership, so he sought a structure that would educate the elite as well as the masses.

17. The civilization/barbarism opposition structured nineteenth-century liberal discourse, and the names of *Doña Bárbara*'s main characters locate them in relation to this conflict. Santos Luzardo's name suggests "Holy Light," while Doña Bárbara means "Madam Barbarian." The title "Doña," reserved in colonial times for the white elite woman, signifies her status as a landowner (*dueña*) and powerful local figure. As Roberto da Matta (1991) points out in his pioneering work on ambiguity and figures of power, Doña Bárbara, like other female literary figures of Latin America, is able to exercise power from within the strictures of patriarchal relations.

18. Gómez ruled from 1908 until his death in 1935. He secured political power through his monopolistic hold over land, industry, and trade, which brought him enormous wealth. He allowed no political organizations and repressed all opposition, asserting that Venezuela's political parties were but fronts for the privileged pursuit of financial gain and incitement of civil strife.

19. See Fernando Coronil (in press) for an analysis of the transformations that occurred in the definitions of value and national identity with the rise of the petroleum industry.

20. Vallenilla Lanz, positivist sociologist, president of the Senate, and editor of the regime's newspaper, wrote articles on social evolution and history that were collected in

his influential *Cesarismo Democrático* (Vallenilla Lanz 1952 [1919]). See Charles A. Hale (1986: 413) on the intellectual context of Vallenilla's thought.

21. On the still inadequately studied Gómez regime, see B. S. McBeth (1983), Elias Pino Iturrieta (1988), Tomás Polanco Alcántara (1990). Yolanda Segnini (1982), Arturo Sosa (1985), and William Roseberry (1986).

22. See Mario Torrealba Lossi (1979: 63–94) for an account of these events, and Skurski (1993) for an analysis of the actions taken and speeches made at the student demonstrations.

23. Gallegos began to write essays on civic affairs and public morality in 1908, with Gómez's ascent, for a journal optimistically titled *La Alborada* (The Dawn), which was soon closed down by the regime. See Rafael Fauquie Bescos (1985), on Gallegos's early writings. For an account of the circumstances under which he wrote—and revised—*Doña Bárbara*, see Juan Liscano (1969), D. L. Shaw (1972), and John E. Englekirk (1948).

24. Critics widely viewed *Doña Bárbara* as a nationalist reworking of prevailing positivist notions of progress and regarded it as a descendant of Domingo Sarmiento's 1845 denunciation of rural caudillismo, *Facundo*. Sarmiento, an Argentine reformer and statesman, had also promoted popular education and was once president of his country. However, he sought to imitate and import European and U.S. models of progress and disparaged the rural population (see Sarmiento 1985 [1845]).

25. On the trends that were popular among the literary vanguard of this period, see T. Nelson Osorio (1985).

26. See S. R. D. Baretta and John Markoff (1978) for an innovative study of the cattle plains' associations with Independence and with violence.

27. In a public letter from his preliminary exile in New York, Gallegos refused his appointment to the puppet Senate and denounced the Gómez regime as unconstitutional (see Liscano 1969: 120).

28. Acción Democrática came to power in a contradictory fashion, namely, through a military coup against the elite-controlled but reformist Medina regime. See Steve Ellner (1980) on AD's expansion during this period.

29. For discussion of *Doña Bárbara*'s appropriation by official and opposition discourse and the populist project's construction of authority, see Coronil and Skurski (1991), and Skurski and Coronil (1993).

30. Scharer-Nussberger (1979a, 1979b) provides a compelling analysis of the deconstructive interchange between the subject and its fetishized reflection. However, in treating the power of ambiguity as the novel's actual but unintended meaning, she contradicts Gallegos's didactic purpose. In doing so, she ignores the link between the dissolution of identities and the reassertion of them within a relationship of power.

31. *Doña Bárbara* presents the plainsmen as the indigenous people of this land, while the Indians, reduced to a miserable residual population, live at the margins of even this frontier. The novel regards Indians with repugnance. They embody gross superstition and unsocialized behavior; jungle Indians taught the young Bárbara evil spells and sexual magic so that she could enslave men, for example, while Marisela chases Indian beggars from Luzardo's door, calling them pigs. The Indian of the national landscape exists only as a curse on the land left by the vanquished and as living proof that certain character traits, such as indolence and cruelty, are inherited, carried within the blood from generation to generation (Gallegos 1959 [1929]: 517, 570, 646, 661).

32. González Echevarría (1985: 54–55) regards Barquero as having "the final authority in the novel," for his insight into the nonreferentiality of language deconstructs signification. However, the dissolution of meaning that Barquero enacts can be seen alternatively as the sterile response of an imitative elite that refuses to ground its knowledge in en-

gagement with social reality. Luzardo is ratified in the novel as a creator of meaning through his efforts to link word and deed.

33. For an illuminating discussion of the formation of the bourgeois subject through the differentiation and mutual constitution of high and low, see Peter Stallybrass and Allon White (1986).

34. For discussions about the diverse thinkers who contributed to the cultural nationalist critique, see Martin S. Stabb (1967), H. E. Davis (1963), Nicolas Shumway (1991), Leopoldo Zea (1944), Ofelia Schutte (1993), Richard M. Morse (1989), and Charles A. Hale (1986).

35. Positivist evolutionism was built on the theories of Darwin and Spencer, which dominated Anglo-American scientific discourse of the late nineteenth century. See Nancy Stepan (1982) on the British development of theories of racial determinism.

36. Ann Stoler (1992) offers an insightful analysis of the politically charged process by which those of mixed race are defined.

37. These ideas, although common to many, became closely associated with José Enrique Rodó. This Uruguayan writer's influential 1900 essay *Ariel* defined an elitist brand of idealism in which Anglo-Saxon culture was regarded as lacking in the aesthetics and vision that characterized Latin culture and which posited the rightful leadership by a natural meritocracy composed of the intellectual elite (Stabb 1967: 35–42).

38. Many of these ideas had been developing since the mid-nineteenth century. Argentine thinkers and political leaders in particular formulated conflicting theories of the civilization/barbarism opposition with reference to the clash between centralists and federalists. For example, Alberdi lauded regional life and attacked the artificial "barbarie ilustrada" in writings with which Gallegos was familiar. See José Luis Gómez-Martínez (1980: 492), and Shumway (1991).

39. For examples in relation to Mexico, see Zea (1944); for those pertaining to Argentina, see Shumway (1991). Mabel Moraña (1984) discusses the impact of changing center/periphery and class relations on political thought during the period. On the continuing engagement with authenticity in Latin American thought, see Mario Samborino (1980).

40. On the impact of the Kabbalah on Hegel and other European thinkers, see Bruce F. Campbell (1980: 13), and Gershom Scholem (1941: 203; 1974: 200).

41. See González Echevarría's (1977: 52–61) discussion of the journal's impact and its influence on the rise of the Afro-Cuban movement in the arts. "Despite its name the *Revista de Occidente* disseminated in the twenties theories of culture in which Western civilization no longer occupied a privileged place." He cites references to the Kabbalah in the writings of Alejo Carpentier, a leading Cuban novelist active in the European avant-garde, as an expression of this period's strong interest in the hidden dimension of reality.

42. Ortega y Gasset expressed these ideas in his 1926 essay "Hegel and America" (Ortega y Gasset (1957 [1926]). He first visited Latin America in 1914 (Stabb 1967: 70–71).

43. Keyserling's (1927) *World in the Making* was well-known in European intellectual circles. Essays by these authors appeared in the journal as well (see, e.g., Spengler [1924] on "race" and "people").

44. According to Keyserling (1933 [1932]: 238), "It is possible and even probable that the next rebirth of that spirit which made possible in ancient times the Greek miracle . . . will arise in South America, for the salvation of all men and to redeem them from savagery." One of Keyserling's followers noted with surprise that South American readers were not alienated by this book despite its unflattering portrayal of the people there. Because South America had "a continental inferiority complex," she reasoned, readers there

were "extremely flattered to have Keyserling write a whole thick volume about it, declaring it to be the most important and significant continent in the world, even if only in a creepy, slimy, reptilian sort of way" (Parks 1934: 272).

45. Rojas, a leading Argentinian literary critic, made nativism a metaphor for domestic culture, which he associated with the aesthetic, the land, and freedom, and called for its integration with cosmopolitan culture, which he associated with material advancement and political organization. Their synthesis would create a national culture, "Eurindia."

46. Vasconcelos, Mexico's Minister of Education in the post-Revolutionary period, influenced the turn in the arts and education toward the glorification of indigenous elements in Mexican culture. In his Spenglerian work *la raza cósmica* (Vasconcelos 1948 [1925]), he envisioned the development of a cosmic race in the tropics, near the site of the lost continent of Atlantis, that would revive the ancient Egyptian ideal of harmony among three states: the intellectual, the aesthetic, and the material. See Ronald Stutzman (1981) for a discussion of mestizaje as an ideology of cultural "whitening." On the promotion of cultural "whitening" in Venezuela, see Winthrop Wright (1990) and, in Brazil and Mexico, see Richard Graham (1990).

47. Haya de la Torre was the founder of Peru's Alianza Popular Revolucionaria Americana (APRA) movement and a major voice in the reconfigured nationalist discourse of Latin America, a region which he renamed "Indo-America" in 1924. He helped chart a centrist program for nationalism, at once anti-imperialist and developmentalist, to be directed by a populist party with middle-class leaders. His writings influenced the evolution of Venezuela's Acción Democrática party; see Fredrick B. Pike (1986) for an innovative discussion of the sources and development of Haya's mystical beliefs.

48. Augusto Sandino, the Nicaraguan revolutionary leader of the 1920s, was of a similar persuasion, although the content of his politics was quite different. He became a radical Freemason in Mexico and was an adherent of anarcho-syndicalism as well as a spiritualist, and he joined the Magnetic-Spiritual School of the Universal Commune. As a student of the occult, Sandino situated the Mexican Revolution and his battle in Nicaragua against the United States within a cosmology of an earthly redemptive struggle between the forces of good and evil. Bolívar was a central figure in his system of belief. For a discussion of the origins of his thought, see Donald C. Hodges (1986).

49. For Liscano (1985: 202), Gallegos became the incarnation of Santos Luzardo when in 1948, while serving as Venezuela's president, he refused to compromise with the military and was overthrown. Humberto García Arocha (1985), a close associate and friend of Gallegos, has claimed that Gallegos identified with Luzardo (an assertion that García Arocha repeated in a personal interview, June 1989).

50. There is a common perception that Gallegos and Santos Luzardo are Bolívarian figures. The spirit of Bolívar is considered in popular belief and religious practice to inspire national and popular struggles and to work through the medium of superior individuals.

51. Liscano has argued that Gallegos had a mystical relationship to the land, which he regarded as a site of cosmic forces and primordial creation. His symbols were created to perform a kind of "exorcism" of this land, banishing destructive forces from it (see Liscano 1969: 101–17; 1985: 207). This account has parallels to certain concepts in popular religious beliefs.

52. Gallegos regarded the human imaginative capacity to create art and science as the highest expression of its spirit, while imagination placed at the service of commercial ends or industrial production was a lower expression (see Gallegos 1954: I, 123).

53. While a university student in 1905, Gallegos read widely in European and Latin American thought. As a result, he left the Catholic Church, the faith in which he had been a "mystical" believer, to become a "free thinker." His readings centered on Tolstoy,

Nietzsche, and classical and contemporary Spanish writers, especially Cervantes and Unamuno, and he participated in a literary group that read Ortega y Gasset's *Revista de Occidente* (Liscano 1985: 203).

54. Vasconcelos's review was mainly taken up with two other novels, *Ifigenia* and *Las Memorias de Mamá Blanca*, by the Venezuelan author Teresa de la Parra (1981 [1926], 1985 [1929]). It is striking that these novels by writers of opposing literary styles and political outlooks were equally well received by the author of *La raza cósmica*. For excellent discussions of de la Parra, see Garrels (1986) and Sommer (1991).

55. At the time of *Doña Bárbara*'s publication in 1929, Venezuela's population was approximately 75 percent rural and had a very low literacy rate (estimates range from 20–30 percent). See John Beverley (1987) for an informative discussion of Venezuela's literary history.

56. See Charles Bergquist (1986: 205–42) for a helpful discussion of labor organization and class relations during this period.

57. Torrealba Lossi (1979: 179) reported that the novel had a great impact on young opponents of Gómez; they even began to reformulate reality in terms of the novel's cosmic forces and symbolic characters. Although he noted the participation of young women in the 1928 protests, he did not indicate with whom they identified.

58. Since the mid-nineteenth century, spiritualism (known as "metaphysics") had been popular among some sectors of the Venezuelan elite, particularly the writings of Kardec, who incorporated some teachings from Indian philosophy and theories of the occult (Yolanda Lecuna, personal interview, August 1990). Another source of occult teachings was Freemasonry. Bolívar, like many other leading intellectual figures of Independence and national consolidation, was a Freemason, which helped to legitimize metaphysical thought as scientific and as relevant for national construction. For a list of prominent Venezuelan Freemasons, see Hello Castellón (1985).

59. De la Parra (1985 [1929]) affectionately depicted this ideal world of the hacienda in *Las Memorias de Mamá Blanca*. See Garrels (1986) for an illuminating discussion of her conservative feminism.

60. She had already attended lectures by Keyserling and was very enthusiastic about them, promising to send Lecuna the collected volume of Keyserling's lectures when it was published (De la Parra 1951: 34).

61. On his visit to the llanos in 1947, Englekirk (1948: 270) was struck by the impact that the film version of *Doña Bárbara* had on the rural population, many of whom regarded its characters as real.

REFERENCES

Alonso, Carlos J. 1990. *The Spanish-American Regional Novel: Modernity and Autochthony* (Cambridge: Cambridge University Press).

Anderson, Benedict. 1991. *Imagined Communities: Reflections on the Origin and Spread of Nationalism*. Rev. and exp. ed. (London: Verso).

Ardao, Arturo. 1978. *Estudios Latinoamericanos: Historia de las Ideas* (Caracas: Monte Avila Editores).

Baretta, Silvio R. Duncan, and John Markoff. 1978. "Civilization and Barbarism: Cattle Frontiers in Latin America," *Comparative Studies in Society and History* 20(4): 587–605.

Bergquist, Charles. 1986. *Labor in Latin America: Comparative Essays on Chile, Argentina, Venezuela, and Colombia* (Stanford: Stanford University Press).

Berlant, Lauren. 1991. *The Anatomy of National Fantasy: Hawthorne, Utopia, and Everyday Life* (Chicago: University of Chicago Press).

Betancourt, Rómulo. 1982. *Rómulo Betancourt, 1928–1935: Contra la dictadura de Juan Vicente Gómez* (Caracas: Ediciones Centauro).

Beverley, John. 1987. "Venezuela," in *Handbook of Latin American Literature*, compiled by David William Foster (New York: Garland Press).

Bhabha, Homi K. 1985. "Signs Taken for Wonders: Questions of Ambivalence and Authority under a Tree outside Delhi, May 1817," *Critical Inquiry* 12(1): 144–65.

———. 1990. "DissemiNation: Time, Narrative, and the Margins of the Modern Nation," in *Nation and Narration*, edited by Homi K. Bhabha, 291–322 (New York: Routledge).

Bolívar, Simón. 1951. *Selected Writings of Bolívar*, vol. 1, compiled by Vicente Lecuna, edited by Harold A. Bierck, Jr., translated by Lewis Bertrand (New York: Colonial Press).

Campbell, Bruce F. 1980. *Ancient Wisdom Revived: A History of the Theosophical Movement* (Berkeley: University of California Press).

Carrera Damas, Germán. 1969. *El Culto a Bolívar* (Caracas: Universidad Central de Venezuela).

Castellón, Hello. 1985. *Guia Histórica de la Masoneria Venezolana* (Caracas: Lito-Jet C.A.).

Chatterjee, Partha. 1986. *Nationalist Thought and the Colonial World: A Derivative Discourse?* (Avon: Zed Books).

Coronil, Fernando. In press. *The Magical State: Money Fetishism, Democracy, and Capitalism in Venezuela* (Chicago: University of Chicago Press).

Coronil, Fernando, and Julie Skurski. 1991. "Dismembering and Remembering the Nation: The Semantics of Political Violence in Venezuela," *Comparative Studies in Society and History* 33(2): 288–335.

Davis, Harold Eugene. 1963. *Latin American Social Thought* (Washington, DC: The University Press of Washington).

De la Parra, Teresa. 1951. *Cartas* (Caracas: Cruz del Sur).

———. 1981/1926. *Ifigenia* (Caracas: Alfadil, S.A.).

———. 1985/1929. *Las Memorias de Mamá Blanca* (Caracas: Monte Avila Editores).

Eagleton, Terry. 1990. "Nationalism: Irony and Commitment," in *Nationalism, Colonialism, and Literature*, edited by Terry Eagleton, Fredric Jameson, and Edward W. Said, 23–39 (Minneapolis: University of Minnesota Press).

Ellner, Steve. 1980. *Los partidos politicos y su disputa por el control del movimiento sindical en Venezuela, 1936–1948* (Caracas: Universidad Católica Andrés Bello).

Englekirk, John E. 1948. "Doña Bárbara, Legend of the Llano," *Hispania* 31 (August): 259–70.

Fauquie Bescos, Rafael. 1985. *Rómulo Gallegos: La Realidad, La Ficcion, El Símbolo* (Caracas: Biblioteca de la Academia Nacional de la Historia).

Felstiner, Mary Lowenthal. 1983. "Family Metaphors: The Language of an Independence Revolution." *Comparative Studies in Society and History* 25(1): 154–80.

Gallegos, Rómulo. 1954. *Una posición en la vida* (Mexico: Ediciones Humanismo).

———. 1959/1929. *Doña Bárbara, Obras Completas*, 1:493–799 (Madrid: Aguilar, S.A.).

García Arocha, Humberto. 1985. "Rómulo Gallegos: Concordancia cabal entre el escritor y el pueblo," in *Rómulo Gallegos a la luz de cuatro discursos conmemorativos*, 25–31 (Caracas: Comisión Ejecutiva Nacional para la Celebración Centenario del Natalicio de Rómulo Gallegos).

Garrels, Elizabeth. 1986. *Las grietas de la ternura* (Caracas: Monte Avila Editores).

Gómez-Martinez, José Luis. 1980. "De Sarmiento a Rangel: Nueva Lectura de *Doña Bárbara,*" in *Relectura de Rómulo Gallegos,* 491–98. Instituto Internacional de Literatura Iberoamericana (Caracas: Centro de Estudios Latinoamericanos Rómulo Gallegos).

González Echevarría, Roberto. 1977. *Alejo Carpentier: The Pilgrim at Home* (Austin: University of Texas Press).

———. 1985. *The Voice of the Masters: Writing and Authority in Modern Latin American Literature* (Austin: University of Texas Press).

Guha, Ranajit. 1985. "Nationalism Reduced to Official Nationalism," *ASAA Review* 9(1): 103–8.

Hale, Charles A. 1986. "Political and Social Ideas in Latin America, 1870–1930," in *The Cambridge History of Latin America,* edited by Leslie Bethell, 4: 367–441 (Cambridge: Cambridge University Press.).

Hall, Stuart. 1986. "Gramsci's Relevance for the Study of Race and Ethnicity," *Journal of Communication Inquiry* 10(2): 5–27.

Haya de la Torre, Raúl. 1936. *A dónde va indoamérica?* 3d ed. (Santiago: Biblioteca América).

Hodges, Donald C. 1986. *Intellectual Foundations of the Nicaraguan Revolution* (Austin: University of Texas Press).

Howard, Harrison Sabin. 1976. *Rómulo Gallegos y la Revolución Burguesa en Venezuela* (Caracas: Monte Avila Editores).

Hughes, H. Stuart. 1958. *Consciousness and Society: The Reorientation of European Social Thought, 1890–1930* (New York: Vintage Books).

Izard, Miguel. 1979. *El miedo de la revolución: La lucha por la libertad en Venezuela, 1777–1830* (Madrid: Tecnos).

Jameson, Fredric. 1981. *The Political Unconscious: Narrative as a Socially Symbolic Act* (Ithaca: Cornell University Press).

Kaplan, Amy. 1990. "Romancing the Empire: The Embodiment of American Masculinity in the Popular Historical Novel of the 1890s," *American Literary History* 2(4): 659–90.

Karsen, Sonja. 1979. "*Doña Bárbara*: Cincuenta años de crítica," in *Relectura de Rómulo Gallegos,* 499–507. Instituto Internacional de Literatura Iberoamericana (Caracas: Centro de Estudios Latinoamericanos Rómulo Gallegos).

Keyserling, Count Hermann. 1927. *The World in the Making,* translated by Maurice Samuel (London: Jonathan Cape).

———. 1933/1932. *Meditaciones Suramericanas,* translated by Luis-López-Ballesteros y de Torres (Madrid: Espasa-Calpe, S.A.).

Laclau, Ernesto. 1979. *Politics and Ideology in Marxist Thought* (London: Verso).

Liscano, Juan. 1969. *Rómulo Gallegos y su Tiempo* (Caracas: Monte Avila).

———. 1985. "Encuentro con Rómulo Gallegos," in *Homenaje Continental a Rómulo Gallegos,* edited by Ricardo Montilla, 197–212 (Caracas: Ediciones del Congreso de la República).

Matta, Roberto da. 1991. *Carnival, Rogues, and Heroes* (Notre Dame: University of Notre Dame Press).

McBeth, B. S. 1983. *Juan Vicente Gómez and the Oil Companies in Venezuela, 1908–1935* (Cambridge: Cambridge University Press).

Mignolo, Walter. In press. *A Darker Side of the Renaissance: Literacy, Territoriality and Colonization* (Ann Arbor: University of Michigan Press).

Moraña, Mabel. 1984. *Literatura y Cultura Nacional en Hispanoamérica (1910–1940)* (Minneapolis: Institute for the Study of Ideologies and Literatures).

Morse, Richard M. 1989. *New World Soundings: Culture and Ideology in the Americas* (Baltimore: Johns Hopkins University Press).

Ortega y Gasset, José. 1957/1926. "Hegel y América," *Obras completas*, 2: 566–72 (Madrid: Revista de Occidente).

Osorio, T. Nelson. 1985. *La Formación de la vanguardia literaria en Venezuela* (Caracas: Biblioteca de la Academia Nacional de la Historia).

Pagden, Anthony. 1990. *Spanish Imperialism and the Political Imagination* (New Haven: Yale University Press).

Parks, Mercedes Gallagher. 1934. *Introduction to Keyserling* (London: Jonathan Cape).

Pateman, Carol. 1989. *The Disorder of Women: Democracy, Feminism and Political Theory* (Stanford: Stanford University Press).

Paz, Octavio. 1980. *The Labyrinth of Solitude* (New York: Pantheon).

Pike, Fredrick B. 1986. *The Politics of the Miraculous in Peru: Haya de la Torre and the Spiritualist Tradition* (Lincoln: University of Nebraska Press).

Pino Iturrieta, Elias, ed. 1988. *Juan Vicente Gómez y su época* (Caracas: Monte Avila Editores).

Polanco Alcántara, Tomás. 1990. *Juan Vicente Gómez: Aproximación a una biografía* (Caracas: Grijalbo).

Pratt, Mary Louise. 1987. "Linguistic Utopias," in *The Linguistics of Writing: Arguments Between Language and Literature*, edited by Nigel Fabb, Derek Attridge, Alan Durant, and Colin MacCabe, 29–38 (New York: Methuen).

———. 1991. "Women, Literature, and National Brotherhood," in *Women, Culture, and Politics in Latin America*, compiled by the Seminar on Feminism and Culture in Latin America, 66–89 (Berkeley: University of California Press).

Roa, Raul. 1985/1954. "Discurso de Raul Roa," in *Homenaje Continental a Rómulo Gallegos*, edited by Ricardo Montilla, 67–75 (Caracas: Ediciones del Congreso de la República).

Rojas, Ricardo. 1924. "Eurindia," *Obras*, 5: 217–39 (Buenos Aires: Juan Roldán y Cía).

Roseberry, William. 1986. "Images of the Peasant in the Consciousness of the Venezuelan Proletariat," in *Proletarians and Protest*, edited by Michael Hanagan and Charles Stephenson, 149–69 (Wesport, CT: Greenwood Press).

Samborino, Mario. 1980. *Identidad, Tradición, Autenticidad: Tres problemas de América Latina* (Caracas: Centro de Estudios Latinoamericanos Rómulo Gallegos).

Sarmiento, Domingo F. 1985/1845. *Facundo: Civilización y Barbarie* (Mexico City: Editorial Porrua).

Scharer-Nussberger, Maya. 1979a. "La Figura del Vaivén," in *Relecturn de Rómulo Gallegos*, 509–20. Instituto Internacional de Literatura Iberoamericana (Caracas: Centro de Estudios Latinoamericanos Rómulo Gallegos).

———. 1979b. *Rómulo Gallegos: El Mundo Inconcluso* (Caracas: Monte Avila).

Scholem, Gershom G. 1941. *Major Trends in Jewish Mysticism* (Jerusalem: Schocken).

———. 1974. *Kabbalah* (Jerusalem: Keter).

Schutte, Ofelia. 1993. *Cultural Identity and Social Liberation in Latin American Thought* (Albany: State University of New York Press).

Segnini, Yolanda. 1982. *La consolidación del régimen de Juan Vicente Gómez* (Caracas: Biblioteca de la Academia Nacional de la Historia).

Shaw, D. L. 1972. *Gallegos: Doña Bárbara* (London: Grant and Cutler).

Shumway, Nicolas. 1991. *The Invention of Argentina* (Berkeley: University of California Press).

Skurski, Julie. 1993. "The Leader and the 'People': Representing the Nation in Postcolonial Venezuela." Ph.D. dissertation, University of Chicago.

Skurski, Julie, and Fernando Coronil. 1993. "Country and City in a Postcolonial Land-
    scape: Double Discourse and the Geopolitics of Truth in Latin America," in *View
    from the Border: Essays in Honor of Raymond Williams*, edited by Dennis Dworkin
    and Leslie Roman, 231–59 (New York: Routledge).
Sommer, Doris. 1990. "Irresistible Romance: The Foundational Fictions of Latin Amer-
    ica," in *Nation and Narration*, edited by Homi K. Bhabha, 71–98 (New York:
    Routledge).
———. 1991. *Foundational Fictions: The National Romances of Latin America* (Berke-
    ley: University of California Press).
Sosa, Arturo A. 1985. *El pensamiento político positivista venezolano* (Caracas: Ediciones
    Centauro, S.A.).
Spengler, Otto. 1924. "Pueblos y Razas," *Revista de Occidente* 2(15): 351–74.
———. 1926/1918. *The Decline of the West*, translated by Charles Francis Atkinson (New
    York: Alfred A. Knopf).
Stabb, Martin S. 1967. *In Quest of Identity* (Chapel Hill: University of North Carolina
    Press).
Stallybrass, Peter, and Allon White. 1986. *The Politics and Poetics of Transgression* (Ith-
    aca: Cornell University Press).
Stepan, Nancy. 1982. *The Idea of Race in Science: Great Britain 1800–1960* (London:
    Macmillan).
———. 1991. *The Hour of Eugenics* (Ithaca: Cornell University Press).
Stoler, Ann. 1992. "Sexual Affronts and Racial Frontiers: National Identity, 'Mixed
    Bloods' and the Cultural Genealogies of Europeans in Colonial Southeast Asia,"
    Comparative Studies in Society and History 33(3): 514–51.
Stutzman, Ronald. 1981. "El Mestizaje: An All-Inclusive Ideology of Exclusion," in
    Cultural Transformation and Ethnicity in Ecuador, edited by Norman E. Whitten,
    49–76 (Urbana: University of Illinois Press).
Torrealba Lossi, Mario. 1979. *Los Años de la Ira* (Caracas: Editorial Atenco de Caracas).
Vallenilla Lanz, Laureano. 1952/1919. *Cesarismo Democrático* (Caracas: Tipografia Gar-
    rido).
Vasconcelos, José. 1948/1925. *La raza cósmica: Misión de la raza ibervoamericana* (Bue-
    nos Aires: Espasa-Calpe Argentina, S.A.).
———. 1980/1931 " 'Doña Bárbara' e Ifigenia,' " in *Teresa de la Parra Ante la Crítica*,
    edited by Velia Bosch, 116–25 (Caracas: Monte Avila Editores).
Williams, Raymond. 1979. *Politics and Letters* (London: New Left Books).
Wright, Winthrop. 1990. *Café con Leche* (Austin: University of Texas Press).
Zea, Leopoldo. 1944. *Apogeo y Decadencia del Positivismo en México* (Mexico City: El
    Colegio de México).
———. 1988. *Discurso desde la marginación y la barbarie* (Barcelona: Editorial An-
    thropos).

IV
BEYOND THE NATION

David Held

Contemporary processes of globalization in the economy, and the growing prevalence of transnational communication flows, with the astonishing growth of new media and information technologies, have dramatically reconfigured the cross-cutting relations among local, regional, national, supraregional, and global contexts of thought and action during the last twenty-five years, shrinking and reordering the world more accessibly than ever before. Whether in terms of international finance and commodity markets, labor mobility (both highly qualified, professional, specialized on the one hand, and menial, unskilled, illegal on the other), mass entertainment cultures, fashions and style, or the movement of refugees, transnational mobility has become a commonplace of late twentieth-century life. The diminishment of the nation-state as the dominant framework of social, political, and cultural identity and the expanding reach of American, European, and new supraregional influences are matched by profound changes in the international state system. Most dramatically, Communism has collapsed, leading to the Eastern European democratic revolutions and the disintegration of the Soviet Union, not to mention the regional catastrophe of former Yugoslavia. While this fragments previous federalisms and removes one important supraregional bloc (the USSR and the Warsaw Pact), it also facilitates over the longer run the reintegration of the East into "Europe." Moreover, in the same period, between the mid-1980s and the end of 1992, we have seen a major strengthening of the Common Market, now known as the European Union, expanding from twelve to fifteen states and laying the ground for further accessions, while the graduation of its strengthened economic institutions into political federation was interrupted only by the fallout from the unification of Germany in 1990. These changes are decisively compromising the strong model of national state sovereignty on which the international system has been founded since the French Revolution. The weakening of the nation-state and the growing permeability of national frontiers have countervailing effects. On the one hand, these logics change the terms on which politics have to be conducted, directing energies and imagination outward to the new transnational centers of decision making—Brussels, Strasbourg, and elsewhere. On the other hand, they throw conservatives of all stripes onto the defensive, and the permeability of all boundaries can also be the source of powerful anxieties about life as it has been lived. In this latter sense, transnational changes can inflame and agitate national differences rather than making them less severe, and the resurgence of xenophobic violence and neofascist forms of nationalist belief during the 1990s, in various parts of Europe, is one depressing result.

   David Held's essay provides a succinct reflection on this new logic of transnational political development. Held, who teaches social sciences at the Open University, is well known for his writings on critical theory. This present essay grows more immediately out of his work on the state and the forms of contemporary democracy, including *Models of Democracy* (Stanford, Calif.: Stanford University Press, 1987), and *Political Theory and the Modern State. Essays on State, Power, and Democracy* (Stanford, Calif.: Stanford University Press, 1989). Its argument concerns the changing global context in which specifically national forms of political identification and action have to occur.

The Decline of the Nation State

Mrs. Thatcher's recent expression of concern about sovereignty has—in some sense—missed the boat. Britain today is already enmeshed in a tight network of international relations and organisations which infringes upon its sovereignty. The lessons to be drawn from this, however, not only affect Thatcher's Conservatives but also the Left. The Left's traditional anti-European stance is almost as anachronistic as Thatcher's position. Surprisingly perhaps, the Right and Left have a lot in common when it comes to raising the flag and putting—or hoping to put—Britain first. In what follows I shall focus on some of the ways in which the sovereignty of the state has been eroded and on some of the consequences of this.

The concept of "sovereignty" is usually taken to mean that a nation state has power and control over its own future: that it has, in other words, the ability to take final decisions and to make and enforce the law in a given community or territory. A loss of sovereignty implies a loss of legal and actual control over the determination of the direction of national policy.

Sovereignty must be distinguished from "autonomy." The idea of autonomy refers to the capacity of nation states, not to set goals, but to achieve goals and policies once they have been set, because in an interdependent world all instruments of national policy may be less effective. It is a diminution of the capacity to achieve national policies—a loss of national autonomy—which may alone be behind the anxieties about a loss of "sovereignty." The question to pose is: has sovereignty remained intact while the autonomy of the state has diminished, or has the modern state actually faced a loss of sovereignty?

In raising questions about sovereignty and autonomy in the modern world, I do not mean to imply that the problems posed by the international order for the individual nation state are entirely new. On the contrary, it seems to be the case that a dense pattern of global interconnections began to emerge with the initial expansion of the world economy and the rise of the modern state from the late 16th century. Nevertheless, there are many new dimensions to patterns of global interdependence, for example, the growth of international organisations, which have developed especially rapidly since 1945 and which have major consequences for the future of sovereignty.

David Held, "The Decline of the Nation State," in *New Times: The Changing Face of Politics in the 1990s*, eds. Stuart Hall and Martin Jacques (London: Lawrence & Wishart, 1990), pp. 191–204.

The analysis below concentrates on a number of dimensions of globalisation which highlight "disjunctures" or "gaps" between, on the one hand, the power of the nation state as in principle capable of determining its own future and, on the other, the actual practices and structures of the state and economic system at the global level. In mapping out these disjunctures, I shall draw most of the examples from the processes and relations which impinge most directly on the states of Europe. It is the fate of the states of Europe which will be uppermost, although I will return to some issues facing British socialists in particular at the end.

DISJUNCTURE 1: THE WORLD ECONOMY

There is a disjuncture between the formal authority of the state and the actual system of production, distribution and exchange which in many ways serves to limit or undermine the power or scope of national political authorities.

When Marx studied capitalism he concentrated on relations and forces largely internal to society. Change was presumed to occur with mechanisms "built in" to the very structure of a given society, and governing its transformation. The relevance of such a perspective has been thrown into doubt by the rapid development in the postwar years of global economic relations—relations which operate in a broad international, multinational and transnational context.

The emergence of a complex international divison of labour is one mark of this new age. There has been a steady expansion of industrial capitalism at the so-called "periphery" of the international economy—South Korea, Taiwan, Singapore and the other newly industrialising countries. If post-Fordism is a growing element of Western economies "assembly-line production" exploiting cheap labour power is a growing characteristic of many Third World countries. If new systems of flexible production and control are developing in the West, then they are connected directly to a worldwide division of labour which has shifted some of the routine, monotonous and dangerous work to countries in which it can be carried out all too often without political regulation and trade-union challenge.

Two aspects of the new international economic processes are central: the internationalisation of production and the internationalisation of financial transactions, organised in part by fast-growing multinational companies. Multinational corporations plan and execute their production, marketing and distribution with the world economy firmly in mind. Even when multinationals have a clear national base, their interest is above all in global profitability, and their country of origin may count little in their overall corporate strategy: the "national loyalty" of multinationals is of an instrumental rather than a sentimental kind. Financial organisations such as banks are also progressively more global in orientation. They are able to monitor and respond to developments in London, Tokyo and New York at the touch of a button. New information technology has radically increased the mobility of economic units—currencies, stocks, shares, "futures" and so on—for financial and commercial organisations of all kinds.

There is considerable evidence to support the claim that technological advances in communication and transportation are eroding the boundaries between hitherto separate markets—boundaries which were a necessary condition for independent national economic policies. Markets and societies are becoming more sensitive to one another even when their distinctive identities are preserved. The October stock-market crash of 1987 is one obvious example of this. The very possibility of a national economic policy is, accordingly, reduced. The monetary and fiscal policies of individual national governments are frequently dominated by movements in the international financial markets. Likewise, the levels of employment, investment and revenue within a country are often subordinated to the decisions of multinationals about where they will locate their production and administrative facilities, among other things.[1]

The loss of control of national economic programmes is, of course, not uniform across economic sectors or societies more generally: some markets and some countries can isolate themselves from transnational economic networks by, among other things, attempts to restore the boundaries or "separateness" of markets and/or to extend national laws to cover internationally mobile factors and/or to adopt co-operative policies with other countries for the co-ordination of policy. The particular tensions between political and economic structures are likely to be different in different spheres, and between them: West-West, North-South, East-West. It cannot, therefore, simply be said that the very idea of a national economy is superseded: there is still insufficient evidence to support such a view.

However, the internationalisation of production finance and other economic resources is unquestionably eroding the capacity of the state to control its own economic future. At the very least, there appears to be a diminution of state autonomy, and a disjuncture between the idea of a sovereign state determining its own future and the conditions of modern economies, marked as they are by the intersection of national and international economic processes. 1992—the date set for the establishment of the single European market—will be a further major impetus to these developments.

DISJUNCTURE 2: HEGEMONIC POWERS AND POWER BLOCS

Connected to changes in the world economy, there is a disjuncture between the idea of the state as an autonomous strategic, military actor and the development of the global system of states, characterised by the existence of hegemonic powers and power blocs, which sometimes operate to undercut a state's authority and integrity. The dominance of the USA and USSR as world powers, and the operation of alliances like Nato and the Warsaw Pact, clearly constrains decision-making for many nations. A state's capacity to initiate particular foreign policies, pursue certain strategic concerns, choose between alternative military technologies and control certain weapon systems located on its own territory may be restricted by its place in the international system of power relations.

Within Nato, for example, clear evidence of what might be called the "internationalisation of security" can be found in its joint and integrated military command structure. When Nato was originally established in the late 1940s, the US sought to limit (if not undercut) the political sovereignty of the European states by the introduction of a clause in the founding treaty which would have allowed Nato forces to intervene in a Nato country in cases of "indirect aggression," that is, "an internal *coup d'état* or political change favourable to an aggressor." The clause was successfully resisted by European states, but ever since then Nato's concern with collective security has trodden a fine line between, on the one hand, maintaining an organisation of sovereign states (which permits, in principle, an individual member state not to act if it judges this appropriate) and, on the other, developing an international organisation which *de facto*, if not *de jure*, operates according to its own logic and decision-making procedures. The existence of an integrated supranational command structure—headed by the supreme allied commander in Europe, who has always been an American general appointed by the US president—ensures that, in a situation of war, Nato's national armies would operate within the the framework of Nato's strategies and decisions.[2] The sovereignty of a national state is decisively qualified once its armed forces are committed to a Nato conflict.

But even without such a commitment, state autonomy as well as sovereignty can be limited and checked; for the routine conduct of Nato affairs involves the integration of national defence bureaucracies into international defence organisations; these, in turn, create transgovernmental decision-making systems which can escape the control of any single member state. Such systems can lead, moreover, to the establishment of informal, but none the less powerful, transgovernmental personnel networks or coalitions which are difficult to monitor by national mechanisms of accountability and control. Having said this, no brief account of Nato would be complete without emphasising also that its members are rivals competing for scarce resources, arms contracts, international prestige and other means of national enhancement. Membership of Nato does not annul sovereignty; rather, it qualifies sovereignty for each state in different ways. Aspects of sovereignty are negotiated and renegotiated through the Nato alliance.

DISJUNCTURE 3: INTERNATIONAL ORGANISATIONS

A third major area of disjuncture between the political theory of the sovereign state and the contemporary global system lies in the vast array of international regimes and organisations (of which Nato is only one type) which have been established to manage whole areas of transnational activity (trade, the oceans, space, and so on). The growth in the number of these new forms of political association (see the table below) reflects the general expansion of transnational links.

Date	Intergovernmental organisations	International non-governmental organisations
1905	37	176
1951	123	832
1972	280	2173
1984	365	4615

The development of international and transnational organisations has led to important changes in the decision-making structure of world politics. New forms of multinational politics have been established and with them new forms of collective decision-making, involving states, intergovernmental organisations and a variety of transnational pressure groups. The International Monetary Fund, for example, pursuing a particular line of economic policy, may insist as a condition of its loan to a government, that the latter cut public expenditure, devalue its currency and cut back on subsidised welfare programmes. In a Third World country, for instance, this may create hunger amongst many people, trigger bread riots and perhaps the fall of a government, or it might contribute directly to the imposition of martial law. It has to be borne in mind that IMF intervention is routinely at the request of governmental authorities or particular political factions within a state and, therefore, cannot straightforwardly be interpreted as a threat to sovereignty. Nonetheless, a striking tension has emerged, between the idea of the sovereign state—centred on national politics and political institutions—and the nature of decison-making at the international level. The latter raises serious questions about the conditions under which a country is able to determine its own policies and directions.

The European Community is an important illustration of these issues. Its significance, however, perhaps reaches further than any other kind of international organisation due to its right to make laws which can be imposed on member states. Within Community institutions, the Council of Ministers has a unique position; for it has at its disposal powerful legal instruments (above all, "regulations," "directives" and "decisions") which allow it to make and enact policy. Of all these instruments, "regulations" are the most notable because they have the status of law independently of any further negotiation or action on the part of member states. Moreover, the Community's extensive range of activities makes it a form of "public power" at the intersection of relatively new types of politics. For the Community's command over resources and capacity to adjudicate between conflicting national interests are of intense concern now to, among others, individual governments, transgovernmental coalitions of ministers and officials, and an array of transnational interest groups, from the European steel producers to environmentalists.

The member states of the European Community are no longer the sole centres of power within their own borders.[3] On the other hand, it is important to bear in mind that the Community's powers are limited powers when considered in relation to a typical European state; for the Community does not possess, for instance, coercive powers of its own—an army, a police force and other institutions of direct law enforcement. The Community's powers were gained by the "willing surrender" of aspects of sovereignty by member states—a "surrender" which, arguably, has actually helped the survival of the European nation state faced, on the one hand, with the dominance of the USA in the first three decades following the second world war and, on the other, with the rise of the Japanese economic challenge. In certain respects, the European Community has strengthened the national state's ability to act at home and abroad.

In short, the European Community provides opportunities and restraints. The states of the Community retain the final and most general power in most areas of their domestic and foreign affairs—and the Community itself seems to have strengthened their options in some of these domains. However, within the Community sovereignty is now also clearly divided: any conception of sovereignty which assumes that it is an indivisible, illimitable, exclusive and perpetual form of public power—embodied within an individual state—is defunct.

DISJUNCTURE 4: INTERNATIONAL LAW

There is a fourth significant disjuncture to note—a gap between the idea of membership of a national political community, ie, citizenship, which bestows upon individuals both rights and duties, and the development of international law which subjects individuals, governments and non-governmental organisations to new systems of regulation. Rights and duties are recognised in international law which transcend the claims of nation states and which, while they may not be backed by institutions with coercive powers of enforcement, have far-reaching consequences. For example, the International Tribunal at Nuremburg laid down, for the first time in history, that when *international rules* that protect basic humanitarian values are in conflict with *state* laws every individual must transgress the state laws (except where there is no room for "moral choice").[4] The legal framework of the Nuremburg Tribunal marked a highly significant change in the legal direction of the modern state; for the new rules challenged the principle of military discipline and subverted national sovereignty at one of its most sensitive points: the hierarchical relations within the military.

Of all the international declarations of rights which were made in the postwar years, the European Convention for the Protection of Human Rights and Fundamental Freedoms (1950) is especially noteworthy. In marked contrast to the United Nations' Universal Declaration of Human Rights (1947) and subsequent UN charters of rights, the European convention was concerned, as its preamble indicates, "to take the first steps for the *collective enforcement* of certain of the Rights of the UN Declaration" (emphasis added). The European initiative was committed to a most remarkable and radical legal innovation: an innovation which in principal would allow individual citizens to initiate proceedings against their own governments. Nearly all European countries have now accepted an (optional) clause of the Convention which permits citizens to petition directly the European

Commission on Human Rights, which can take cases to the Committee of Ministers of the Council of Europe and then (given a two-thirds majority on the Council) to the European Court of Human Rights. While the system is far from straightforward and is problematic in many respects, it has been claimed that, alongside legal change introduced by the European Community, it no longer leaves the state "free to treat its own citizens as it thinks fit." In Britain alone, for example, telephone tapping laws have been altered after intervention by the European Commission and findings of the European Court of Justice have led to changes in British law on issues as far-reaching as sexual discrimination and equal pay.

Within international law more generally, there are two legal rules which, since the very beginnings of the international community, have been taken to uphold national sovereignty: "immunity from jurisdiction" and "immunity of state agencies." The former prescribes that "no state can be sued in courts of another state for acts performed in its sovereign capacity," and the latter stipulates that "should an individual break the law of another state while acting as an agent for his country of origin and be brought before that state's courts, he is not held 'guilty' because he did not act as a private individual but as the representative of the state."

The underlying purpose of these rules is to protect a government's autonomy in all matters of foreign policy and to prevent domestic courts from ruling on the behaviour of foreign states (on the understanding that all domestic courts everywhere will be so prevented). And the upshot has traditionally been that governments have been left free to pursue their interests subject only to the constraints of the "art of politics." It is notable, however, that these internationally recognised legal mainstays of sovereignty have been progressively questioned by Western courts. And while it is the case that national sovereignty has most often been the victor when put to the test, the tension between national sovereignty and international law is now marked, and it is by no means clear how it will be resolved.

Against this background of "disjunctures," the limits of a politics that derives its terms of reference exclusively from the nation state become apparent. This point is reinforced by a consideration of the principle of "majority rule." The application of this principle is, of course, at the centre of Western democracy: it is at the root of the claim of political decisions to be regarded as worthy or legitimate. Problems arise, however, not only because decisions made by *other* states, or by quasi-supranational organisations such as the EC, Nato, or the World Bank, diminish the range of decisions open to a given "majority" but also because *decisions of a nation do not only affect (or potentially affect) its citizens.*

For example, a decision made against the siting of an international airport near a capital city for fear of upsetting the local rural vote may have disadvantageous consequences for airline passengers throughout the world who are without direct means of representation. Or a decision to build a nuclear plant near the borders of a neighbouring country is likely to be a decison taken without considering whether those in the nearby country (or countries) ought to be among those who are consulted (reflect on the French decision to build large numbers of nuclear reactors in northern France). Or a decision to suspend food aid to a country may stimulate the sudden escalation of food prices in that country and contribute directly to the outbreak of famine among the urban and rural poor (as happened in Bangladesh when the US temporarily suspended aid). Or the decision by a government in West or East to suspend or step up military aid to one side or another in a political struggle in a distant country may decisively influence the outcome of that conflict, or fan it into a further vortex of violence (Central America).

The modern theory of the sovereign state presupposes the idea of a "national community of fate"—a community which rightly governs itself and determines its own future. This idea is certainly challenged by the nature of the pattern of global interconnections and the issues that have to be confronted by a modern state.[5] National communities by no means exclusively "programme" the actions, decisions and policies of their governments and the latter by no means simply determine what is right or appropriate for their own citizens.

While a complex pattern of global interconnections has been evident for a long time, there is little doubt that there has recently been a further "multinationalisation" of domestic activities and an intensification of decision-making in multinational frameworks. The evidence that transnational relations have eroded the powers of the modern sovereign state is certainly strong. From considerations such as these some observers have concluded that sovereignty is fundamentally undermined and that the democratic system of Western states is progressively less viable: a national system of accountability and control risks obsolescence in the face of international forces and relations. The conclusion, however, requires some qualification.

While I have mapped some of the common challenges to the sovereign state in the modern postwar world, it is important to stress that the effect of these challenges is likely to vary under different international and national conditions— for instance, a nation's location in the international division of labour, its place in particular power blocs, its position with respect to the international legal system, its relation to major international organisations. Not all states, for example, are equally integrated into the world economy (compare the USA, Portugal and Bulgaria) and, thus, while national political outcomes will be heavily influenced by global processes in some countries, in others regional or national forces might well remain supreme.

Further states remain unready on the whole to submit their disputes with other states to arbitration by a "superior authority," be it the United Nations, an international court or any other international body. At the heart of this "great refusal" is the protection of the right of states to go to war.[6] Despite the fact that states today operate in a world of international political economy, military alliances, international law and so on, it remains that the modern state is still able to determine the most fundamental aspect of people's life chances—the question of life and death. In a complex interdependent world, this element of sovereignty remains a powerful moment.

Moreover, one way in which states continue to exercise their sovereignty is— as indicated by the EC in particular—by participating in the creation of organisations which might better monitor and regulate transnational forces and relations beyond their control. While such organisations frequently create new restraints upon national states, they also create new forms of political participation and intervention. At issue here is the active renewal of the rights of states in and through the international system itself.

It is misleading simply to conclude, then, that sovereignty is wholly undermined in contemporary circumstances. On the other hand, this discussion of the four disjunctures between the sovereign state and the late 20th century economic and political world does reveal a set of forces which combine to restrict the freedom of action of governments and states by blurring the boundaries of domestic politics; transforming the conditions of political decision-making; changing the institutional and organisational context of national politics; altering the legal framework and administrative practices of governments; and obscuring the lines of responsibility and accountability of nation states themselves. From these processes alone one can say that *the operation of states, in an ever more complex international system, both limits their autonomy and infringes ever more upon their sovereignty.* Any conception of sovereignty which interprets it as an illimitable and indivisible form of public power is undermined. Sovereignty itself has to be conceived today as already divided among a number of agencies—national, international and transnational—and limited by the very nature of this plurality.

What are the implications of this for British politics? As the sun set over Britain's empire, and competition among industrial nations intensified throughout the postwar years, politicians of nearly all persuasions placed hopes in general political and economic rejuvenation on strategies geared to the maintenance of Britain's international status either as an independent power or in junior partnership with the United States. These strategies helped sustain the illusion that the decline in Britain's world position could be checked. Symbols of these strategies included the maintenance of a strong pound (the status of which was often regarded as more important than the health of manufacturing industry) and high expenditure on arms and military materials (relative to Britain's industrial competitors). Of course, these strategies have been continued to the present day in one form or other, and have received their most forceful articulation in Thatcherism's dubious mix of patriotism and free market economics.

The aspirations, values and beliefs which formed the culture in support of a great and independent Britain have profoundly affected the Labour Party in and out of office and the Left more generally. It is a culture which contributed to the Left's misunderstanding of the changing pattern of global relations and to its misreading of the political importance of the new institutions and options developing in the postwar world. The "England right or wrong" mentality led to a naive belief that Britain could either once again lead world politics or, if not, cut itself adrift and live in splendid isolation. The reluctance to participate in the European Community during its formation, and the continuing reluctance to participate fully in its organisations, must be understood in this context. The Left has been as tenacious as the Right, albeit for different reasons, in its anti-Europeanism.

The issue the Left needs to consider more and more is how it should participate in, and seek to shape, the new international order that is emerging. This order cannot be run away from; it cannot be pretended that it doesn't exist. Nor can it be pretended that Britain will again ever enjoy pre-eminence on the world stage. The question is: what is the appropriate form of national and international politics for the Left to develop now? How can democratic and socialist theory accommodate the new reality?

In my view, the Left needs firstly to accept and think through the meaning of Britain's "second division" status and secondly to examine how it can participate in the development of the international institutions and forces moulding global politics today. High on this agenda must be rethinking the nature of European unity. For Europe presents the Left with a unique opportunity to create a new set of alliances around a concern for greater accountability, extended rights, and a new independence in world politics—concerns which only a *European-wide movement* has any real chance of sustaining in contemporary circumstances.

A European Left could pursue—and perhaps even deliver—three vital things.

Firstly, the extension and deepening of mechanisms of democratic accountability across Europe to cover resources and forces which are already beyond the control of national democratic mechanisms and movements. One issue here is bolstering the role of the European parliament so that it has the capacity to legislate on central transnational issues—then environment, health, new forms of communication and so on.

Secondly, the protection and strengthening of the European human rights programme, and the further development of the role of the European courts system, in order that groups and individuals have an effective means of suing their governments for the enactment and enforcement of key civic, political, economic and social rights.

Thirdly, the establishment of Europe as a major independent voice in world politics. At the centre of this objective must be the pursuit—as a matter of urgency—of a non-aligned European foreign policy and a non-aligned European armed force: a "Nato" without the USA. Such a development would contribute decisively to breaking up the current division of the world by the two hegemonic powers and would help create the conditions for greater political diversity and choice on the world stage.

If these issues were to be given more priority it would be one step toward creating a politics beyond the sovereign nation state—a new international politics for new times.

NOTES

1. R. Smith, "Political Economy and Britain's External Position," *Britain in the World*, ESRC Compilation 1987.

2. D. Smith, "States and Military Blocs: Nato," *The State and Society* 6, The Open University Press 1984.

3. A. Whickham, "States and Political Blocs: the EEC," *The State and Society* 6, The Open University Press 1984.

4. A. Cassesa, *Violence and Law in the Modern Age*, Polity Press 1988.

5. C. Offe, *Disorganised Capitalism*, Polity Press 1985.

6. F. H. Hinsley, *Sovereignty*, 2nd ed., Cambridge University Press 1986.

Renata Salecl

A sociologist and philosopher from the Institute of Criminology at the University of Ljubljana School of Law in Slovenia, Renata Salecl has brought the insights of Lacanian psychology to the problem of nationalism and political violence in the Balkans. Her dissertation, "The Notion of Power in the Work of Michael Foucault," and her subsequent investigations have been examples of the power of French postmodernist thought in illuminating social and political problems. She is the author of *The Dark Side of Eastern Europe: Antifeminism and the Politics of Fantasy.*

The end of the securities and certainties of Communism and the bipolar world have, in Salecl's words, "dismantled most traditional points of social identification" and left, most powerfully, in its wake "national identity." She envisions the nation as "the traumatic element around which fantasies are interlaced," now ominous fantasies of enemies, aliens, and threats to the nation. But the locus of hatred is not clearly the Other outside of us, but "always the other within us" that ultimately reveals itself as "hatred of one's own enjoyment." In postsocialist societies a new form of the "moral majority" has arisen, more socialist than conservative, but now promoting an organic national ideology overlaid with Christian and socialist values. The socialist moral majority is at one and the same time anticapitalist and nationalist, embracing an "authoritarian populism" and a renewed reliance on the national state.

National Identity and Socialist Moral Majority

The present outbursts of nationalism in East European socialist countries are a reaction to the fact that long years of (Communist) Party rule, by destroying the traditional fabric of society, have dismantled most traditional points of social identification, so that when people now attempt to distance themselves from the official ideological universe, the only positive reference point at their disposal is their national identity. In the new struggles for ideological hegemony, national identification is used by the opposition as well as by the old Party forces. On the one hand, national identity serves as a support for the formation of a specific version of the "moral majority" (in Poland, Slovenia and Croatia, etc.) which conceives Christian values as the ideological "cement" holding together the Nation, demands the prohibition of abortion and other regressive measures; on the other hand, the Communist party in some countries (Serbia, for example) has assumed an authoritarian populist—nationalist discourse, thus producing a specific mixture of orthodox Communist elements and elements usually associated with fascism (violent mass movements structured around a charismatic leader and directed towards an external-internal enemy, etc.).

The use of psychoanalysis to analyse these developments enables us to avoid simple condemnations of nationalism, as well as the false solution of its division into "good" (progressive, anti-imperialist . . .) versus "bad" (chauvinist, colonizing . . .) elements; it enables us to conceive the nation as something that "always returns" as the traumatic element around which fantasies are interlaced[1], and thus to articulate the fantasy structure which serves as a support for ethnic hatred. Both nationalist movements—the opposition moral majorities and the authoritarian-populist Communist parties—have built their power by creating specific fantasies of a threat to the nation and so put themselves forward as the protector of "what is in us more than ourselves"—our being a part of the nation.

It is first necessary to emphasize that with all nationalism, national identification with "our kind" is based on the fantasy of an enemy, an alien who has insinuated himself into our society and constantly threatens us with habits, discourse and rituals which are not "our kind." No matter what this Other "does,"

Renata Salecl, "National Identity and Socialist Moral Majority," *New Formations*, 12 (Winter 1990), pp. 25–31.

his very existence is perceived as threatening. The fantasy of how the Other lives on our account, is lazy, exploits us etc. is repeatedly recreated in accordance with our desire. For example, there is the criticism that immigrants are lazy, lacking in the work habit, etc. with the simultaneous accusation that they steal our jobs. The Other who works enthusiastically is especially dangerous—it is only his way of deceiving us and becoming incorporated into "our" community. Similarly with their assimilation: they are usually accused of retaining their strange habits, of being uncivilized, etc. If however they adopt our customs, then we assume that they want to steal "our thing"—the nation.

We are disturbed precisely by the fact that the Other *is* Other and that he has his own customs, by which we feel threatened. As Jacques Alain Miller says, hatred of the Other is hatred of the Other's enjoyment, of the particular way the Other enjoys. For example, when Germans are irritated by Turkish workers eating garlic, or when the English find unbearable the way blacks enjoy themselves, what they are identifying is the threat of the Other not finding enjoyment in the same way as we do.

> I am willing to see my neighbour in the Other but only on condition that he is not my neighbour. I am prepared to love him as myself only if he is far away, if he is removed . . . . When the Other comes too near, when it mingles with you, as Lacan says, new fantasies emerge which concern above all the surplus of enjoyment with the Other.
>
> What is at stake is of course the imputation of an excessive enjoyment. Something of that kind could consist, for example, in the fact that we ascribe to the Other an enjoyment in money exceeding every limit. The question of tolerance or intolerance is not at all concerned with the subject of science and its human rights. It is located on the level of tolerance or intolerance toward the enjoyment of the Other, the Other as he who essentially steals my own enjoyment . . . . When we are considering whether the Other will have to abandon his language, his convictions, his way of dressing and talking, we would actually like to know the extent to which he is willing to abandon or not abandon his Other enjoyment.[2]

The conservative English writer John Casey says of West Indians: "they simply cannot form part of 'our' group or belong to 'our' kind, for their behaviour outrages 'our' sense of what English life should be like and how the English should behave towards a duly constituted authority."[3] The Other outrages our sense of the kind of nation ours should be in so far as s/he steals our enjoyment— to which we must add that this Other is always an Other in my interior, i.e. that my hatred of the Other is really the hatred of the part (the surplus) of *my own* enjoyment which I find unbearable and cannot acknowledge, and which I therefore transpose ("project") into the Other *via* a fantasy of the "Other's enjoyment."

Before the disintegration of really existing socialism, democracy was popularly conceived as a charge which would explode when the lid of Communist party terror was lifted. Today the countries of Eastern Europe are confronted with nationalist conflict, anti-semitism, anti-feminism and fascist populist movements. It appears that the present free nations of Eastern Europe in some way don't want to enjoy freedom: as if some kind of internal blockade obstructs their path to democracy, as if they are afraid to confront the fact that democracy (democratic freedom) is no more than a *form* and does not immediately procure positive material welfare. It is for this reason that they are forced—at the very moment of acquiring their long-desired freedom—to invent again and again a figure of an Enemy which prevents them enjoying "effective freedom" (i.e. the welfare associated with the notion of "western democracy"). Here, of course, we find a precise demonstration of hatred of one's own enjoyment—the fact that the nations of Eastern Europe are seeking new enemies, obsessively reviving old national hatreds, demonstrates quite clearly that the Other is always the Other within us and that hatred of the Other is in the final analysis hatred of one's own enjoyment. Intolerance of Others' pleasure, whether Jews, immigrants or even members of the same nation, bureaucrats, for example, produces the fantasies by which members of particular nations organize their own enjoyment.

Serbian authoritarian populism, for example, has produced an entire mythology of the fight against internal and external enemies. The first enemies are Albanians who are perceived as threatening to cut off the Serbian autonomous province of Kosovo, and thus to steal Serbian land and culture. The second enemy is an alienated bureaucracy which threatens the power of the people: alienated from the nation, it is said to be devouring Serbian national identity from within. Both images of the enemy are based on specific fantasies. In Serbian mythology, the Albanians are understood as pure Evil, unimaginable, subjects who cannot be subjectivized—made people from—because they are so radically Other. The Albanian population is constantly presented as immigrant, although immigration took place in the Middle Ages and the Albanians are arguably the successors of much earlier Illyrian inhabitants of the region. The Serbs describe their conflict with the Albanians as a fight of "people with non-people." The only exception to the rule is the "honest Albanian" who accepts the Serbian view and is held up as an example of one who has broken with his natural national environment—unlike the "dishonest Albanian," who, in contrast with his "honest" counterpart, appears all the more clearly "Other." Lacan says that jealousy as a pathological condition has nothing to do with real causes: my wife can deceive me, all my forebodings can be more than legitimate, but my jealousy is, nevertheless, no less pathological. We can thus say that the very real Albanian pressure on the Serbs in Kosovo does not legitimize the way that the Serbs react to it, the form in which they have made monsters of their opponents. The Serbs do not even begin to allow the Albanians a public voice—to appear as political subjects, thus making democratic dialogue possible.

The second enemy—the bureaucrat—is presented as a non-Serb, as a traitor to his own nation and as effeminate. The revolt against the bureaucracy doesn't take place because of its actual economic errors but because of its estrangement from tradition, its primarily spiritual, rather than material, betrayal of the people.

Both enemies are portrayed, importantly, as impotent. Just as English conservatives describe the danger to Britain from immigrants, especially blacks, as "the rape of the English race" so the Serbs portray Albanians as rapists of the Serbian nation, as those who steal Serbian national identity, imposing their own culture. However, this figurative picture of rape is reinforced by the Serbs with stories of supposed actual attempts at the rape of Serbian girls by Albanians. What is important here is that it is always only attempted rape. A picture of the enemy is created, an Albanian who tries to rape Serbian girls but is actually unable to do so. This fantasy is based on portraying the enemy's impotence—the enemy tries to attack, to rape, but is confounded, is impotent, in absolute contrast to the heroic Serb.

The mythology of the new Serbian populism constantly stresses the difference between real men—workers, men of the people—and bureaucrats—effeminates. The bureaucrat in this mythology is portrayed as a middle-class feudal master, a kid-gloved capitalist with top hat and tie, "clean outside and dirty within," in real contrast to the worker, the man of the nation, "dirty on the outside but pure within."[4] The essence of the argument is that the bureaucrat is not a real man— he is effeminate, slug-like, fat, drinking whiskey and eating pineapples—as opposed to the macho worker who eats traditional national food and dresses in worker's dungarees or national costume. Bureaucrats are not men because of their alienation from tradition and their betrayal of the heroic Serbian people.

To demonstrate its link to the nation, Serbian populism uses the dead bodies of national heroes. In the new Serbian populist mythology, those who are fighting today for Serbian sovereignty are constantly compared to the Serbian heroes who fought the Turks six hundred years ago.[5] Bones have a special role in this heroic identification with Serbian history. Serbian populism has rediscovered the old Orthodox custom by which the mortal remains of a ruler were carried through all the monasteries of the country before burial. The restoration of real Serbian identity was thus confirmed in 1989 by the transfer to Kosovo after more than six hundred years, of the bones of the famous Serbian hero King Lazar, who had been killed in battle with the Turks. The old Orthodox ritual of carrying the bones around the monasteries designated the new birth of the symbolic community. The bones can be seen here in Lacanian terms as the Real, that "something more" which designates the symbolic community of the Serbian nation—the national thing comes out precisely in the bones. So Lazar's bones are the Real which has returned to its place—his return to Kosovo is symbolic confirmation that Kosovo has always been the cradle of "that which is Serbian."

As Lacan says, race is established in the way in which a particular discourse preserves the symbolic order. The same can also be said of national community— in the case of Serbia, the ridiculous ritual of transferring bones also functions in preserving the symbolic order. On the rational level, it involves only a pile of trivial bones, which may or may not be the king's, which may have some archaeological or anthropological value but which act in the symbolic community of society as a little piece of the Real. In the case of Serbia, the bones also represent what the enemy has always wanted to deprive us of, that which we must guard with special care. The national conflict between the Serbs and the Albanians, as well as that between Serbs and Macedonians has always used the symbolism of stealing bones from Serbian graves. A mythology has even been created by which Albanians are supposed to dig up the graves of Serbian children, and Macedonians are supposed to have used the bones of Serbian soldiers who fell in the First World War for anatomical studies in their medical faculties.

Intolerance of the Other's enjoyment, linked as it is to national identification, is also connected to the fantasies put into circulation by the newly created socialist moral majority in the countries of Eastern Europe. The socialist moral majority cannot be said to have the same significance as in the west. In view of its structural role, the moral majority in socialism is democratic and anti-totalitarian—its voice is an oppositional one. Moral revolt against a real socialist regime predominates in its criticism of the authorities. It thus articulates a distinction between civil society (in the name of which it speaks) and the totalitarian state, as a distinction between morality and corruption. A return to Christian values, the family, the "right to life" etc. is presented as a rebellion against immoral real socialist authority which, in the name of the concept of communism, permits all sorts of state intervention into the privacy of the citizen.

Paradoxically, the moral majority in the east, in spite of its oppositional role is comparatively more socialist than conservative in relation to its western counterpart. Where the latter is characterized by an anti-socialist market ideology in which each person answers first for himself and the state is not the guardian of his well-being, the new socialist moral majority, in the name of an organic national ideology, reforges a link with the socialist heritage. When it calls for the reinforcement of national affiliation and Christian values, it simultaneously stresses that we must not surrender to soulless capitalism, that we must create a state-supported national programme, etc.

The difference between western and socialist moral majorities can also be seen in their different perspectives on the problem of abortion. First, we must point out that in Yugoslavia, as well as in the majority of other Eastern European countries (with the exception of countries practising extreme forms of nationalistic Communism, such as Ceaucescu's Rumania), abortion was legalized and within easy reach of every woman; indeed often, it has been the only available form of contraception. It was the catholic-nationalist opposition that first raised the question of its restriction; but it did so in terms unfamiliar in western anti-abortion movements. The traditional "moral majority," as known in western countries, does not oppose abortion on the grounds of the threat it poses to the nation, but in the name of the Christian values of sanctity of life, the sacred significance of conception, etc., from which it derives the thesis that abortion is murder. Objections to abortion from the moral majority in Slovenia and in Croatia are connected with their thesis of the threat it poses to the nation. The linkage of images of abortion as a crime against humanity to the image of a threat to the nation produces an ideology by which support for Slovenes or Croats becomes synonymous with opposition to abortion. When the Croatian opposition writes that "a foetus is also a Croatian" it clearly demonstrates that any opinion about abortion will also be an opinion about the future of the nation. The production of these kinds of fantasies of a national threat must of course be seen in terms of the political struggle they engender. The strategy is to transfer the political threat of totalitarianism into a national menace which can only be averted by an increase in the birthrate—in other words, by limiting the right to abortion. This produces the hypothesis that to be a good Slovene or a good Croat means primarily to be a good Christian, since the national menace can only be averted by Christian morals.

In the ideology of national threat, women are simultaneously pronounced culprit and victim. The strongest opposition party in Croatia, the Croatian Democratic Community (which won the elections), has gone so far in this that it has publicly blamed the tragedy of the Croatian nation on women, pornography and abortion. "This trinity murders, or rather hinders, the birth of little Croats, that 'sacred thing which God has given society and the homeland.' "[6] The Croatian moral majority regards women who have not borne at least four children, not as women, but as "female exhibitionists," since they have not fulfilled "their unique sacred duty." Women who, for whatever reason, decide on abortion have been proclaimed murderers and mortal enemies of the nation, while gynaecologists who have assisted them in this murderous act are pronounced butchers.

Women, then, are pronounced guilty; yet at the same time, they are depicted as victims of overly liberal abortion laws. Ideologists of the socialist moral majority take as their starting point the notion that a free decision about how many children a person will have is an inalienable human right, and that society is obliged to maintain population policies which enable them to have the desired number of children. They believe therefore that a state which prioritizes the right to abortion is refusing its citizens access to this second inalienable right—that of having the desired number of children. Here the real victims, in their opinion, are women.

> To insist only on free abortion . . . means not only disregarding medical, ethical, religious, demographic, national and parent-human reasons, as well as the feelings of individuals, but also transforming women into victims, sacrificing their health, spiritual peace and maternal feelings, allowing them to be subjected to mortal danger in order to satisfy the instincts and demands of others. Essentially, it involves seeing woman only as a resource which man can use and abuse, who is irresponsibly fertilized and then allowed to be subjected to bodily and spiritual maltreatment. The interruption of conception, the violent removal of a child from a woman's body and heart, amounts to a suppression of her ethical and religious beliefs and her maternal feelings, and a violation of her conscience.[7]

This fantasy of the woman victim is based on the hypothesis that the woman's wish and the desire of the nation are one—to give birth. If a woman is defined by maternity then abortion is an attack on her very essence; yet it is also an attack on the essence of the nation, since the national community, according to this ideology, is defined by the national maternal wish for expansion.

The arguments of ideologists of national threat have the same logic as Ceaucescu's answer to one journalist's question as to whether the ban on Romanians travelling abroad was not a violation of human rights. Ceaucescu's answer was: Since the most important human right is to be able to live in one's own country, the ban on travelling abroad simply guarantees this right. So, too, the ideologists of national threat represent their desire to limit the right to free abortion as simply reinforcing the human right to have the desired number of children. Just as Ceaucescu "helped" people not to violate the right of living in their own country and not to suppress their deepest desire by banning them from travelling abroad, so the ideologists of the new moral majority protect human, national and maternal feelings. If for Communists, the capitalist and "bourgeois" right are those who steal their enjoyment, then for the ideologists of national threat, these are women. For them, woman is an enemy in so far as her enjoyment threatens "our kind."

The meeting point of the two ideologies presented—official "authoritarian populism" and the oppositional ideology of the national moral majority—can be located in their common offer of a collective fantasy whose message reads, between the lines, "we are the sole defenders of the nation." A real democratic transformation in the countries of socialism can only be expected when the driving force becomes the motto "to each his/her fantasy." This does not mean a refusal to admit national identity, only the removal of the Subject presented as the nation's only protector—as the only one who acts in the name of "our kind."

NOTES

1. See Jacques Lacan, *The Four Fundamental Concepts of Psycho-Analysis* (Harmondsworth: Penguin Books 1979).

2. Jacques-Alain Miller: Unpublished seminar 1985–86—*Extimite*.

3. Bhikhu Parekh: "The 'New Right' and the Politics of Nationhood," in *The New Right* (London: The Runnymede Trust 1986), 36.

4. Ivo Zanic, "Bukvar 'antibirokratske revolucije,' " *Start*, 30.9.1989.

5. The Battle of Kosovo, where in 1389 the Serbs lost a battle with the Turks has become the source of a whole series of associations in the contemporary struggle of the Serbian nation with the Albanians; the Serbian leader, Milošević, for example, is compared to the former hero Oblič, the Albanian leader Vllasi with the hated Turkish Sultan Murat. Symbolic identification with the place popular heroes have in Serbian mythology has given the new leadership a special position: not only have they been given an aura of sanctity as folk heroes, they have also been enabled to repair the historical damage which occurred with the loss of the battle of Kosovo. The discourse of the anti-bureaucratic revolution returned to the time of the Turkish struggle in so far as it wanted to stress that Milošević's warriors are the only ones who can end the six-hundred-year vasselage of the Serbian nation.

6. *Dnevnik*, Ljubljana, 26.2.1990.

7. Ante Vukasovic: "Zavaravanje zena," *Danas*, Zagreb, 27.3.1990.

Khachig Tölölyan

A literary critic, specialist in the writing of Thomas Pynchon, and editor of *Diaspora: A Journal of Transnational Studies*, Khachig Tölölyan combines teaching in the Department of English at Wesleyan University with writing and research on problems of diasporic communities, Armenian intellectual history and politics, and modern literary theory. His mobility in the intellectual worlds of Europe and the United States and between history and literary and cultural studies, as well as his particular interests in Armenian affairs, is evident in his Armenian-language study, *Spiriuki mech* (In the diaspora). Tölölyan has written extensively on terrorism, the Armenian Church, and the origins of Armenian nationalism, but his greatest influence has come from his theorizing the transnational communities known as diasporas and editing the major venue for writing in this new field of study.

Students of nationalism and the origins of nations have long been intrigued by the formative influences of exiles and diasporas in the early generation of nationalist ideas and movements. A major impetus for modern Greek nationalism came from the *Filike Eteria*, which was founded in the Russian port of Odessa. Armenians are indebted to the Catholic monks of the Mekhitarist order, like the poet and historian Father Alishan, who never visited Armenia proper but knew it best from his cell on the island of San Lazzaro in the Venetian archipelago. We are reprinting here the opening editorial statement by Tölölyan for *Diaspora* in which he presented a vision of the new transnational communities that depended on the ways in which nations were constructed and envisioned. Diasporas are "sometimes the paradigmatic Other of the nation-state and at other times its ally, lobby, or even, as in the case of Israel, its precursor."

The Nation-State and Its Others: In Lieu of a Preface

"What ish my nation?" asks the Scots officer Macmorris, speaking a foreign tongue, of his Welsh colleague Fluellen, who also serves in Henry the Fifth's polyglot "English" army in Shakespeare's *Henry V* (III.ii.121). The question focuses the spectrum of issues this journal will address as it considers the Nation and its Others. We find the query useful, as Shakespeare did when he set out in 1599 to instruct his audience about its fiction of "England" in 1415. He wrote from within a barely secure new nation about a time when English kings still viewed Normandy, Anjou, Aquitaine, and the inhabitants thereof as their land and their people, though not yet their nation(-state).

Writing *Ulysses* between 1914 and 1921, James Joyce has a Dublin citizen of 1904 ask the ambiguously Jewish Leopold Bloom: *"What is your nation[?]"* Bloom answers by indirection, defining "a nation [as] the same people living in the same place" (Joyce 331; emphasis added). This fails to satisfy the questioner, a nationalist who bristles at the rule of the British Empire and envisions liberation through a coming struggle in which a "greater Ireland" that includes the Irish diaspora will participate: "We'll put force against force . . . . We have our greater Ireland beyond the sea. They were driven out of house and home in the black [18]47 . . . . Ay, they drove out the peasants in hordes. Twenty thousand of them died in the coffinships. But those that came to the land of the free remember the land of bondage" (Joyce 329–30). To the citizen, Irish emigrants in America are part of the Irish nation, and so Bloom's answer has unacceptable implications. Throughout *Ulysses*, written as the Irish fought Britain and each other to make the Irish Free State between 1916 and 1921, Joyce uses the story of Odysseus's homeward journey to question the meanings of "home" and "nation," and of keeping faith with a national culture while living elsewhere, in individual or communal exile. *Ulysses* examines the idea of longed-for but exigent home that the nation-state would become.[1]

The conviction underpinning this manifesto disguised as a "Preface" is that *Diaspora* must pursue, in texts literary and visual, canonical and vernacular, indeed in all cultural productions and throughout history, the traces of

Khachig Tölölyan, "The Nation and Its Others," *Diaspora*, 1, 1 (Spring 1991), pp. 3–7.

struggles over and contradictions within ideas and practices of collective identity, of homeland and nation. *Diaspora* is concerned with the ways in which nations, real yet imagined communities (Anderson), are fabulated, brought into being, made and unmade, in culture and politics, both on land people call their own and in exile. Above all, this journal will focus on such processes as they shape and are shaped by the infranational and transnational Others of the nation-state.

Shakespeare's and Joyce's queries about nationhood bracket the centuries in which European nations forged themselves and their state apparatuses, even as they acquired colonies and empires. These projects were intertwined; both employed military, technological, political, and commercial strategies that extracted an extraordinary human toll, violently expelling some conquered populations while confining others to fractions of their land: the reservation "nations" of Native Americans and the ethnonational republics of the Soviet Union are among some of the products of such actions. Elsewhere, the most monstrous and sustained efforts of the western empires uprooted, killed, or transported millions into slavery, creating the African diasporas. Combinations of economic coercion and incentive encouraged the formation of overseas communities such as those of the Japanese, Indians, and Chinese, which, like the African-descended collectivities, now increasingly represent themselves to themselves and to others as diasporas (Pan).[2]

Some of the entities this history has shaped remain purely infranational: they endure within a particular state and resist the cohesion imposed by it (e.g., the Navajo, the Inuit, the Québecois, the Georgians of the USSR). Others are both infra- and transnational, living disadvantaged lives within reduced territory while reaching out to kindred people elsewhere (e.g., Moldavians, Armenians, Crimean Tatars, Palestinians, Iroquois, Magyars in Romania). Today, the processes of uprooting and dispersion continue, but already by 1916, the Irish subjects of Britain and the subjugated Arabs of the Ottoman Empire had launched uprisings that heralded the possibility of remaking old collectivities into new nations, while challenging the claims of existing states. What has emerged in the past two decades, under the impact of new transnational, global forces, is the view that nation-states may not always be the most effective or legitimate units of collective organization.

Of course, multicultural colonial empires—Hellenic and Roman, Persian and Ottoman—have existed since antiquity, and some of the phenomena characteristic of our transnational moment are as old as history: individual exile like Ovid's, collective dispersion like that of the Jews by the waters of Babylon. This journal will address that history. But the past five centuries have been a time of fragmentation, heterogeneity, and unparalleled mass dispersion; additionally, the past five decades have been a time of cultural and political regrouping, of renewed confidence for ethnonations existing across the boundaries of established nation-states. In fact, migrations have led to a proliferation of diasporas and to a redefinition of their importance and roles. Crucially, these dispersions, while not altogether new in form, acquired a different meaning by the nineteenth century, in the context of the triumphant nation-state, which as a polity claims special political and emotional legitimacy, representing a homogeneous people, speaking one language, in a united territory, under the rule of one law, and, until recently, constituting one market.

In naming this publication *Diaspora: A Journal of Transnational Studies*, we give equal emphasis to both sides of the colon. We use "diaspora" provisionally to indicate our belief that the term that once described Jewish, Greek, and Armenian dispersion now shares meanings with a larger semantic domain that includes words like immigrant, expatriate, refugee, guest-worker, exile community, overseas community, ethnic community. This is the vocabulary of transnationalism, and any of its terms can usefully be considered under more than one of its rubrics. For example, Cubans outside Cuba are in certain ways a diaspora that stretches from Madrid to Miami and beyond, the result of both coerced and voluntary departure. The US media refer to them as an exile community, particularly when underscoring the ambitions of some leaders to overthrow Castro. And "Cuban" is of course an ethnic designation. Thus, Cubans are a transnational collectivity, broken apart by, and woven together across, the borders of their own and other nation-states, maintaining cultural and political institutions; the study of their specificity, their interpenetration and articulation with others is part of our enterprise.

To affirm that diasporas are the exemplary communities of the transnational moment is not to write the premature obituary of the nation-state, which remains a privileged form of polity. Conflicts like the Gulf War revive and reaffirm the nation-state's legitimacy even as new forms of economic and political interaction, communication, and migration combine to erode its sharply defined borders, increasingly turning even the mightiest and most ocean-buffered polities, like the United States, into "penetrated" (Brown)[3] and "plural" societies (Smith). Yet, as these incursions multiply and many nation-states confront the extent to which their boundaries are porous and their ostensible homogeneity a multicultural heterogeneity, other collectivities strive for nationhood through struggles conducted in both homeland and diaspora (e.g., Eritreans, Kurds, Palestinians, Sikhs, Tibetans, Armenians).

In such a context, transnational communities are sometimes the paradigmatic Other of the nation-state and at other times its ally, lobby, or even, as in the case of Israel, its precursor (Sheffer). Diasporas are sometimes the source of ideological, financial, and political support for national movements that aim at a renewal of the homeland (Sun Yat Sen, Yasser Arafat). In the cases of the now only nominally "Soviet" republics of Armenia and Lithuania, diasporan organizations operate across the boundaries of the multiethnic empire and bring to their kindred ethnonations new ideas, new money, even new languages. Elsewhere, it becomes impossible to comprehend the new shape of certain polities—Los Angeles, the European Community—without taking into account the effects of massive movements of Hispanic, North African, or Turkish migrations of "guest-workers"; similar claims apply to states as diverse as South Africa and Germany, Nigeria and Sweden. In these and other places, transnational forces are intervening in ways whose consequences are not yet clear.

Diaspora is concerned as well with all of the other forces and phenomena that constitute the transnational moment. These include massive and instantaneous movements of capital; the introduction of previously "alien" cultures through the practice of "media imperialism"; issues of the double allegiance of populations and the plural affiliations of transnational corporations. All these developments point to the need to interrogate the national context in which certain assumptions about collective identity once prevailed; they also raise questions about the global context.

Of the making and unmaking of nations and exile communities there is no end in sight. The recent Iraqi invasion of Kuwait was born of a tangle of motives, some less problematic than others, many comprehensible only from the transnational perspective. One was the impulse to enlarge the Iraqi "nation" of Kurds and Arabs; another was to make a united Iraq and Kuwait that would serve as a prototype of the Arab nation. The invader wanted to destroy the emerging territorial state of Kuwait, which was not quite a nation in August of 1990, though doubtless it will become one in the war's aftermath. The flood of refugees the invasion triggered (Indians and Pakistanis, Egyptians and Palestinians, Sri Lankans and Filipinos) reminds us that 60% of the population of Kuwait was not Kuwaiti, that in fact "before [Kuwait was] a nation, [it was] a business" (Kramer). In fact, many nations began as businesses, a fact concealed by mythologies of national origin but disclosed by the movements and histories of diasporas. It is not accidental that USA, like IBM, is an acronym for an establishment (as in Est. 1766) that was founded fairly abruptly, not in the intimate coevolution of a people and nation over centuries, like France and the French, say. The United States began, in part, as a set of commercial enterprises, as did British Canada: tracts for real-estate development and fur-trapping, units of the transatlantic economy. International commerce initiated the development of many nations; in some ways, it is now supplanting them, which is why "sovereignty," like "nation," is one of the concepts this journal will interrogate.

Diasporas are emblems of transnationalism because they embody the question of borders, which is at the heart of any adequate definition of the Others of the nation-state. The latter always imagines and represents itself as a land, a territory, a place that functions as the site of homogeneity, equilibrium, integration; this is the domestic tranquility that hegemony-seeking national elites always desire and sometimes achieve. In such a territory, differences are assimilated, destroyed, or assigned to ghettoes, to enclaves demarcated by boundaries so sharp that they enable the nation to acknowledge the apparently singular and clearly fenced-off differences *within* itself, while simultaneously reaffirming the privileged homogeneity of the rest, as well as the difference *between* itself and what lies over its frontiers.

In the past, diasporan communities confined in this way have remained self-protectively silent about their own view of themselves; their self-representations and assignments of meaning to their collective existence have been carefully policed. Stated too loudly and clearly, these representations would inevitably blur difference, even while pointing to an endemic doubleness, or multiplicity, of identities and loyalties, taboo topics both within and outside the diaspora community. Such silence long seemed necessary to the maintenance of the nation-state, whose frontiers were ideally absolute limits, crossed only in heavily regulated economic, cultural, and demographic interactions. This vision of a homogeneous nation is now being replaced by a vision of the world as a "space" continually reshaped by forces—cultural, political, technological, demographic, and above all economic—whose varying intersections in real estate constitute every "place" as a heterogeneous and disequilibriated site of production, appropriation, and consumption, of negotiated identity and affect.

Admittedly, this is an abstract description. On the one hand, it points to what we celebrate as the reinvigorated diversity of a plural society woven out of diasporas and ethnicities. But even the nation-states most receptive to this pluralism—Canada, the United States, Australia, as well as the somewhat more reluctant members of the European Community—must increasingly acknowledge the way in which few of the old "general" interests continue successfully to claim nationwide legitimacy and consent, except in the guise of hypocritical fictions of hegemony. Meanwhile, new and forcefully asserted concerns and claims, like those of transnational communities, perhaps anachronistically continue to be regarded as "special" interests. This changed state of affairs affects nearly every area of cultural, political, and scholarly endeavor; it is welcomed by some and detested by others. At any rate, the chain of analogies that once joined the image of the safely enveloped individual body (the site of unique personal identity) to the homogeneous territorial community (the site of national identity) is no longer plausible. The image of the ideal world as a League of (sovereign and united) Nations is under pressure, beset by what is seen as the threat or promise of what Roger Rouse calls, in his article in this issue, "an alternative cartography of social space." Such a cartography does not wager on the end of nationalism; in fact, it assumes that, precisely because the proliferation of infranational and transnational alternatives to the nation-state has led to a realignment of collective emotional investments, nationalism and other forms of loyalty will compete for a long time. *Diaspora* is a forum for debates about those concrete and theoretical remappings of global "order" that take both the nation-state and its transnational Others into account.

NOTES

1. Conversations with James Fairhall and Edna Duffy helped me to formulate my thoughts about *Ulysses*.

2. Most overseas Chinese do not yet think of their communities as diasporan, but this is beginning to change, as Pan's title suggests. Until the late 1960s, most African-Americans did not use the term either. It was first applied by a handful of intellectuals to the group for which they sought to speak; the term has now gained currency, both in the community and among scholars writing about it. In at least two communities, the Jewish and the Armenian, in North America and elsewhere, the vocabulary of "diaspora" and "galut" (*spurk* and *gaghut* in Armenian) is traditional and widespread, as it is in certain Greek communities.

3. I am deviating slightly from Brown's use of the term. He writes solely of Middle Eastern states and societies as "a penetrated subsystem of international relations"(4).

REFERENCES

Anderson, Benedict. *Imagined Communities: Reflections on the Origin and Spread of Nationalism*. London: Verso, 1983.

Brown, Leo Carl. *International Politics and the Middle East*. Princeton, Princeton UP, 1984.

Joyce, James. *Ulysses*. 1922. New York: Random, 1961.

Kramer, Michael. "Towards a New Kuwait." *Time* 24 Dec. 1990: 28.

Pan, Lynn. *Sons of the Yellow Emperor: A History of the Chinese Diaspora*. Boston: Little, 1990.

Sheffer, Gabriel, ed. *Modern Diasporas in International Politics*. New York: St. Martin's, 1986.

Smith, M. G. *The Plural Society in the British West Indies*. Berkeley: U of California P, 1965.

Liisa Malkki

Liisa Malkki, whose own biography mirrors the argument of her essay (raised in Finland and Iran, before coming to the United States, where she now teaches in the Anthropology Department at the University of California, Irvine), presents an eloquent reflection on the "homelessness" which has come to characterize contemporary life for so many people in all parts of the world. In the late twentieth century, she argues, there is a striking field of contradiction between the established tropes of "rootedness," "nativeness," and "territorialization" through which people voice their identity, and on the other hand the actual conditions of displacement, mobility, and uprootedness, both voluntary and enforced, which increasingly characterize their lives. She follows Nairn, Anderson, and others, in seeing nationalism as a generalized condition of the modern political world, proposing the term "the national order of things" for this purpose. But at the same time, she points to the formation of nationality beyond the confines of the nation-state and explores the ways in which specific national identities are often dissociated from the very fixities of place, history, and "purity" of culture which their bearers insist they possess. Continuities of belonging and traditions of culture and community seem far more deep and fixed than they actually are, particularly in times of crisis, danger, and threat, when such securities become a valuable shield against dispossession and loss.

"Diaspora" has become a common description for homes and homelands of all kinds we have left behind, offering ways of securing a relationship to a past and of imagining a community beyond our immediate experience, beyond our everydayness, and often beyond the states that claim our immediate citizenly allegiance. Narratives of exile and expatriation become more and more common in the present world of transnational and globalized economic and cultural communication and exchange. How we understand our cultural identity, and how we make ourselves a "home," is being increasingly complicated by the restructuring of the material world. As large-scale examples of what we mean here, we might cite the massive importance of labor mobility in and to North America and Europe (the enormous flows of transnational labor migration in the economies of southern California, the American south-west, or New York City; and the restructuring of the integrated economy of the European Union); the shrinkage of the world into new systems of globalized electronic communications; and the ease of passage of intellectuals between different parts of the world.

After exploring the general relationship of identity and territory in discourses of nation and nationalism, in both scholarly and commonsense terms, Malkki focuses on a huge example of a mobile or uprooted population, namely, refugees, using the specific case of the Hutus living in Western Tanzania since the Burundi massacres of 1972, both in a rural refugee encampment and in the township of Kigoma. As a kind of liminal category, refugees allow the impact of the above changes on the bases of national identification to be clarified, for "trying to understand the circumstances of particular groups of refugees illuminates the complexity of the ways in which people construct, remember, and lay claim to particular places as 'homelands' or 'nations.' " She finds strong differences between the "camp refugees," who constructed their national belonging in pure and heroic forms as a vital "moral community," and the "town refugees," who celebrated a kind of rootless and mobile cosmopolitan "impurity." Moreover, both forms of displacement are counterposed to the "sedentarism" through which national identity is still normally conceptualized. In laying this out, Malkki adds beautifully to the argument regarding identity's "constructed" and "processual" qualities, while simultaneously pointing to the complex ways, via history, memory, and experience, through which it is nonetheless emplaced.

National Geographic: The Rooting of Peoples and the Territorialization of National Identity among Scholars and Refugees

"To be rooted is perhaps the most important and least recognized need of the human soul," wrote Simone Weil (1987:41) in wartime England in 1942. In our day, new conjunctures of theoretical enquiry in anthropology and other fields are making it possible and necessary to rethink the question of roots in relation—if not to the soul—to identity, and to the forms of its territorialization. The meta-phorical concept of having roots involves intimate linkages between people and place—linkages that are increasingly recognized in anthropology as areas to be denatured and explored afresh.

As Appadurai (1988, 1990), Said (1979, 1986), Clifford (1988:10–11, 275), Rosaldo (1989:196 ff.), Hannerz (1987), Hebdige (1987), Robertson (1988), and others have recently suggested, notions of nativeness and native places become very complex as more and more people identify themselves, or are categorized, in reference to deterritorialized "homelands," "cultures," and "origins." There has emerged a new awareness of the global social fact that, now more than perhaps ever before, people are chronically mobile and routinely displaced, and invent homes and homelands in the absence of territorial, national bases—not in situ, but through memories of, and claims on, places that they can or will no longer corporeally inhabit.

Liisa Malkki, "National Geographic: The Rooting of Peoples and the Territorialization of National Identity among Scholars and Refugees," *Cultural Anthropology*, 7, 1 (February 1992), pp. 24–44. Copyright © 1992 American Anthropological Association.

Author's note: I would like to thank the following friends and colleagues for their valued comments on this article: Jim Ferguson, Laurie Kain Hart, Ann Stoler, Karen Leonard, Jane Guyer, Fernando Coronil, David Scobey, Mihalis Fotiadis, the faculty and students at the Departments of Anthropology at Stanford, Princeton, and Columbia, and at the Department of Ethnic Studies at the University of California, San Diego. My colleagues at the Michigan Society of Fellows, the University of Michigan, Ann Arbor, provided an exciting intellectual environment during the writing of this article. The Society of Fellows and a Grant for Advanced Area Research from the Social Science Research Council provided funding that made this work possible.

Exile and other forms of territorial displacement are not, of course, exclusively "postmodern" phenomena. People have always moved—whether through desire or through violence. Scholars have also written about these movements for a long time and from diverse perspectives (Arendt 1973; Fustel de Coulanges 1980:190–193; Heller and Feher 1988:90; Marrus 1985; Mauss 1969:573–639; Moore 1989; Zolberg 1983). What is interesting is that now particular theoretical shifts have arranged themselves into new conjunctures that give these phenomena greater analytic visibility than perhaps ever before. Thus, we (anthropologists) have old questions, but also something very new.

The recognition that people are increasingly "moving targets" (Breckenridge and Appadurai 1989:i) of anthropological enquiry is associated with the placing of boundaries and borderlands at the center of our analytical frameworks, as opposed to relegating them to invisible peripheries or anomalous danger zones (cf. Balibar 1991:10; Comaroff and Comaroff 1987; van Binsbergen 1981). Often, the concern with boundaries and their transgression reflects not so much corporeal movements of specific groups of people, but, rather, a broad concern with the "cultural displacement" of people, things, and cultural products (e.g., Clifford 1988; Goytisolo 1987; Hannerz 1987; Torgovnick 1990). Thus, what Said, for example, calls a "generalized condition of homelessness" (1979:18) is seen to characterize contemporary life everywhere.[1]

In this new theoretical crossroads, examining the place of refugees in the national order of things becomes a clarifying exercise. On the one hand, trying to understand the circumstances of particular groups of refugees illuminates the complexity of the ways in which people construct, remember, and lay claim to particular places as "homelands" or "nations." On the other, examining how refugees become an object of knowledge and management suggests that the displacement of refugees is constituted differently from other kinds of deterritorialization by those states, organizations, and scholars who are concerned with refugees. Here, the contemporary category of refugees is a particularly informative one in the study of the sociopolitical construction of space and place.

The major part of this article is a schematic exploration of taken-for-granted ways of thinking about identity and territory that are reflected in ordinary language, in nationalist discourses, and in scholarly studies of nations, nationalism, and refugees. The purpose here is to draw attention to the analytical consequences of such deeply territorializing concepts of identity for those categories of people classified as "displaced" and "uprooted." These scholarly views will then be juxtaposed very briefly with two other cases. The first of these derives from ethnographic research among Hutu refugees who have lived in a refugee camp in rural Western Tanzania since fleeing the massacres of 1972 in Burundi. It will be traced how the camp refugees' narrative construction of homeland, refugeeness, and exile challenges scholarly constructions and common sense. In the second case, the ethnography moves among those Hutu refugees in Tanzania who have lived (also since 1972) outside of a refugee camp, in and around the township of Kigoma on Lake Tanganyika. These "town refugees" present a third, different conceptual constellation of links between people, place, and displacement—one that stands in antagonistic opposition to views from the camp, and challenges from yet another direction scholarly maps of the national order of things.

MAPS AND SOILS

To begin to understand the meanings commonly attached to displacement and "uprootedness" in the contemporary national order of things, it is necessary to lay down some groundwork. This means exploring widely shared commonsense ideas about countries and roots, nations and national identities. It means asking, in other words, what it means to be rooted in a place (cf. Appadurai 1988:37). Such commonsense ideas of soils, roots, and territory are built into everyday language and often also into scholarly work, but their very obviousness makes them elusive as objects of study. Common sense, as Geertz has said (1983:92), "lies so artlessly before our eyes it is almost impossible to see."

That the world should be composed of sovereign, spatially discontinuous units is a sometimes implicit, sometimes stated premise in much of the literature on nations and nationalism (e.g., Gellner 1983; Giddens 1987:116, 119; Hobsbawm 1990:9–10).[2] To take one example, Gellner sees nations as recent phenomena, functional for industrial capitalism,[3] but he also conceptualizes them as discrete ethnological units unambiguously segmented on the ground, thereby naturalizing them along a spatial axis. He invites us to examine two kinds of world maps.

> Consider the history of the national principle; or consider two ethnographic maps, one drawn up before the age of nationalism, and the other after the principle of nationalism has done much of its work. The first map resembles a painting by Kokoschka. The riot of diverse points of colour is such that no clear pattern can be discerned in any detail . . . . Look now instead at the ethnographic and political map of an area of the modern world. It resembles not Kokoschka, but, say, Modigliani. There is very little shading; neat flat surfaces are clearly separated from each other, it is generally plain where one begins and another ends, and there is little if any ambiguity or overlap. [1983:139–140]

The Modigliani described by Gellner (*pace* Modigliani) is much like any school atlas with yellow, green, pink, orange, and blue countries composing a truly global map with no vague or "fuzzy spaces" and no bleeding boundaries (Tambiah 1985:4; Trinh 1989:94). The national order of things, as presented by Gellner, usually also passes as the normal or natural order of things. For it is self-evident that "real"[4] nations are fixed in space and "recognizable" on a map (Smith 1986:1). One country cannot at the same time be another country. The world of nations is thus conceived as a discrete spatial partitioning of territory; it is territorialized in the segmentary fashion of the multicolored school atlas.

The territorialization expressed in the conceptual, visual device of the map is also (and perhaps especially) evident on the level of ordinary language. The term "the nation" is commonly referred to in English (and many other languages) by such metaphoric synonyms as "the country," "the land," and "the soil." For example, the phrase "the whole country" could denote all the citizens of the country or its entire territorial expanse. And "land" is a frequent suffix, not only in "homeland," but also in the names of countries (Thailand, Switzerland, England) and in the old colonial designations of "peoples and cultures" (Nuerland, Basutoland, Nyasaland). One dictionary definition for "land" is "the people of a country," as in, "the land rose in rebellion."[5] Similarly, soil is often "national soil."[6] Here, the territory itself is made more human (cf. Handler 1988:34).

This naturalized identity between people and place is also reflected and created in the course of other, nondiscursive practices. It is not uncommon for a person going into exile to take along a handful of the soil (or a sapling, or seeds) from his or her country, just as it is not unheard of for a returning national hero or other politician to kiss the ground upon setting foot once again on the "national soil." Demonstrations of emotional ties to the soil act as evidence of loyalty to the nation. Likewise, the ashes or bodies of persons who have died on foreign soil are routinely transported back to their "homelands," to the land where the genealogical tree of their ancestors grows. Ashes to ashes, dust to dust: in death, too, native or national soils are important.

The powerful metaphoric practices that so commonly link people to place are also deployed to understand and act upon the categorically aberrant condition of people whose claims on, and ties to, national soils are regarded as tenuous, spurious, or nonexistent. It is in this context, perhaps, that the recent events in Carpentras, Southern France, should be placed (Dahlburg et al. 1990:H1; Plenel 1990:16; cf. Balibar 1990:286). On the night of 9 May 1990, 37 graves in an old Jewish cemetery were desecrated, and the body of a man newly buried was disinterred and impaled with an umbrella (Dahlburg et al. 1990:H1). One is compelled to see in this abhorrent act of violence a connection to "love of country" in the ugliest sense of the term. The old man's membership in the French nation was denied because he was of the category "Jew." He was a person in the "wrong" soil, and was therefore taken out of the soil (cf. Balibar 1990:285).

ROOTS AND ARBORESCENT CULTURE

The foregoing examples already suggest that the widely held commonsense assumptions linking people to place, nation to territory, are not simply territorializing, but deeply metaphysical. To begin to understand the meaning of displacement in this order of things, however, it is necessary to explore further aspects of the metaphysic. The intent in this section is to show that the naturalizing of the links between people and place is routinely conceived in specifically botanical metaphors.[7] That is, people are often thought of, and think of themselves, as being rooted in place and as deriving their identity from that rootedness. The roots in question here are not just any kind of roots; very often they are specifically arborescent in form.

Even a brief excursion into nationalist discourses and imagery shows them to be a particularly rich field for the exploration of such arborescent root metaphors. Examples are easy to find: Keith Thomas has traced the history of the British oak as "an emblem of the British people" (1983:220, 223; cf. Daniels 1988:47 ff.;

Graves 1966). Edmund Burke combined "the great oaks that shade a country" with metaphors of "roots" and "stock" (cited in Thomas 1983:218). A Quebecois nationalist likened the consequences of tampering with the national heritage to the withering of a tree (Handler 1988:44–45). An old Basque nationalist document links nation, race, blood, and tree (Heiberg 1989:51).

But more broadly, metaphors of kinship (motherland, fatherland, *Vaterland*, *patria, isänmaa*) and of home (homeland, *Heimat, kotimaa*) are also territorializing in this same sense; for these metaphors are thought to "denote something to which one is naturally tied" (Anderson 1983:131). Motherland and fatherland, aside from their other historical connotations, suggest that each nation is a grand genealogical tree, rooted in the soil that nourishes it. By implication, it is impossible to be a part of more than one tree. Such a tree evokes both temporal continuity of essence and territorial rootedness.

Thinking in terms of arborescent roots is, of course, in no way the exclusive province of nationalists. Scholars, too, often conceptualize identity and nationness in precisely such terms. Smith's *The Ethnic Origins of Nations* (1986) provides one example of the centrality of root metaphors in this intellectual domain. In an effort to find constructive middle ground between "primordialist"[8] and "modernist" versions of the emergence of nations, he sets out "to trace the ethnic foundations and roots of modern nations" (1986:15), and states: "No enduring world order can be created which ignores the ubiquitous yearnings of nations in search of roots in an ethnic past, and no study of nations and nationalism that completely ignores the past can bear fruit" (Smith 1986:5).[9]

Thinking about nations and national identities may take the form of roots, trees, origins, ancestries, racial lines, autochthonism, evolutions, developments, or any number of other familiar, essentializing images; what they share is a genealogical form of thought, which, as Deleuze and Guattari have pointed out, is peculiarly arborescent.

> It is odd how the tree has dominated Western reality and all of Western thought, from botany to biology and anatomy, but also gnosiology, theology, ontology, all of philosophy . . . : the root-foundation, *Grund, racine, fondement*. The West has a special relation to the forest, and deforestation . . . . [1987:18]

THE NEED FOR ROOTS AND THE SPATIAL
INCARCERATION OF THE NATIVE

Two kinds of connection between the concept of the nation and the anthropological concept of culture are relevant here. First, the conceptual order of the "national geographic" map (elucidated above by Gellner) is comparable to the manner in which anthropologists have often conceptualized the spatial arrangement of "peoples and cultures." This similarity has to do with the ways in which we tend to conceptualize space in general. As Gupta points out:

> Our concepts of space have always fundamentally rested on . . . images of break, rupture, and disjunction. The recognition of cultures, societies, nations, all in the *plural*, is unproblematic exactly because there appears an unquestionable division, an intrinsic discontinuity, *between* cultures, *between* societies, etc. [Gupta 1988: 1–2]

This spatial segmentation is also built into "the lens of cultural relativity that, as Johannes Fabian points out, made the world appear as culture gardens separated by boundary-maintaining values—as posited essences" (Prakash 1990:394). The conceptual practice of spatial segmentation is reflected not only in narratives of "cultural diversity," but also in the internationalist celebration of diversity in the "family of nations."

A second, related set of connections between nation and culture is more overtly metaphysical. It has to do with the fact that, like the nation, culture has for long been conceived as something existing in "soil." Terms like "native," "indigenous," and "autochthonous" have all served to root cultures in soils; and it is, of course, a well-worn observation that the term culture derives from the Latin for cultivation (see, e.g., Wagner 1981:21). "The idea of culture carries with it an expectation of roots, of a stable, territorialized existence" (Clifford 1988:338). Here, culture and nation are kindred concepts: they are not only spatializing but territorializing; they both depend on a cultural essentialism that readily takes on arborescent forms.[10]

A powerful means of understanding how "cultures" are territorialized can be found in Appadurai's (1988:37) account of the ways in which anthropologists have tended to tie people to places through ascriptions of native status: "natives are not only persons who are from certain places, and belong to those places, but they are also those who are somehow *incarcerated*, or confined, in those places." The spatial incarceration of the native operates, he argues, through the attribution not only of physical immobility, but also of a distinctly ecological immobility (1988:37). Natives are thought to be ideally adapted to their environments— admirable scientists of the concrete mutely and deftly unfolding the hidden innards of their particular ecosystems, PBS-style (1988:38). As Appadurai observes, these ways of confining people to places have deeply metaphysical and moral dimensions (1988:37).

The ecological immobility of the native, so convincingly argued by Appadurai, can be considered in the context of a broader conflation of culture and people, nation and nature—a conflation that is incarcerating but also heroizing and extremely romantic. Two ethnographic examples will perhaps suffice here.[11]

On a certain North American university campus, anthropology faculty were requested by the Rainforest Action Movement (RAM) Committee on Indigenous Peoples to announce in their classes that "October 21st through the 28th is World Rainforest Week. The Rainforest Action Movement will be kicking the week off with a candlelight vigil for Indigenous Peoples." (The flyer also lists other activities: a march through downtown, a lecture "on Indigenous Peoples," and a film.) One is, of course, sympathetic with the project of defending the rainforests and the people who live in them, in the face of tremendous threats. The intent is not to belittle or to deny the necessity of supranational political organizing around these issues. However, these activities on behalf of "The Indigenous," in the *specific* cultural forms that they take, raise a number of questions: Why should the rights of "Indigenous People" be seen as an "environmental" issue? Are people "rooted" in their native soil somehow more natural, their rights somehow more sacred, than those of other exploited and oppressed people? And one wonders, if an "Indigenous Person" wanted to move away, to a city, would his or her candle be extinguished? The dictates of ecological immobility weigh heavily here.

But something more is going on with the "Indigenous Peoples' Day." That people would gather in a small town in North America to hold a vigil by candlelight for other people known only by the name of "Indigenous" suggests that being indigenous, native, autochthonous, or otherwise rooted in place is, indeed, powerfully heroized.[12] At the same time, it is hard not to see that this very heroization—fusing the faraway people with their forest—may have the effect of subtly animalizing while it spiritualizes. Like "the wildlife," the indigenous are an object of enquiry and imagination not only for the anthropologist but also for the naturalist, the environmentalist, and the tourist.[13]

The romantic vision of the rooting of peoples has recently been amplified in new strands of "green politics" that literally sacralize the fusion of people, culture, and soil on "Mother Earth." A recent article in *The Nation*, "How Paradise Was Lost: What Columbus Discovered," by Kirkpatrick Sale (1990), is a case in point. Starting from the worthwhile observation that the history of the "discovery" of the Americas needs to be rewritten, Sale proceeds to lay out a political program that might be described as magical naturalism. The discovery, he writes, "began the process by which the culture of Europe, aptly represented by this captain [Columbus], implanted its diseased and dangerous seeds in the soils of the continents . . . . " (1990:445). The captain, we are told, is best thought of as "a man *without place* . . . always rootless and restless" (1990:445). By contrast, "the cultures" discovered and destroyed are best thought of as originally "*rooted in place*" (1990:445). They had "an exquisite sense of . . . the bioregions" (1990:445). Sale is not content with mere nostalgia; he distills moral lessons and a new form of devotional politics from this history.

> The only political vision that offers any hope of salvation is one based on an understanding of, a rootedness in, a deep commitment to, and a resacralization of, *place* . . . . It is the only way we can build a politics that can spread the message that Western civilization itself, *shot through with the denial of place* and a utilitarian concept of nature, must be transformed . . . .
> Such a politics, based, as the original peoples of the Americas had it, upon love of place, also implies the place of love. For ultimately love is the true cradle of politics, the love of the earth and its systems, the love of the particular bioregion we inhabit, the love of those who share it with us in our communities, and the love of that unnameable essence that binds us together with the earth, and provides the water for the roots we sink. [Sale 1990:446, emphasis added]

The "natives" are indeed incarcerated in primordial bioregions and thereby retrospectively recolonized in Sale's argument. But a moral lesson is drawn from this: the restless, rootless "civilization" of the colonizing "West," too, urgently needs to root itself. In sum, the spatial incarceration of the native is conceived as a highly valued rooting of "peoples" and "cultures"—a rooting that is simultaneously moral and literally botanical, or ecological.

It is when the native is a national native that the metaphysical and moral valuation of roots in the soil becomes especially apparent. In the national order of things, the rooting of peoples is not only normal; it is also perceived as a moral and spiritual need.

> Just as there are certain culture-beds for certain microscopic animals, certain types of soil for certain plants, so there is a certain part of the soul in every one and certain ways of thought and action communicated from one person to another which can only exist in a national setting, and disappear when a country is destroyed. [Weil 1987:151–152]

A SEDENTARIST METAPHYSICS

The territorializing, often arborescent conceptions of nation and culture explored here are associated with a powerful sedentarism in our thinking. Were we to imagine an otherworldly ethnographer studying us, we might well hear that scholar observe, in Tuan's (1977:156) words: "Rootedness in the soil and the growth of pious feeling toward it seem natural to sedentary agricultural peoples." This is a sedentarism that is peculiarly enabling of the elaboration and consolidation of a national geography that reaffirms the segmentation of the world into prismatic, mutually exclusive units of "world order" (Smith 1986:5). This is also a sedentarism that is taken for granted to such an extent that it is nearly invisible. And, finally, this is a sedentarism that is deeply metaphysical and deeply moral, sinking "peoples" and "cultures" into "national soils," and the "family of nations" into Mother Earth. It is this transnational cultural context that makes intelligible the linkages between contemporary celebratory internationalisms and environmentalisms.

The *effects* of this sedentarism are the focus of the following section on refugees. Refugees are not nomads, but Deleuze and Guattari's comments on allegorical nomads are relevant to them:

> History is always written from a sedentary point of view and in the name of a unitary State apparatus, at least a possible one, even when the topic is nomads. What is lacking is a Nomadology, the opposite of a history. [1987:23]

UPROOTEDNESS: SOME IMPLICATIONS OF
SEDENTARISM FOR CONCEPTUALIZING DISPLACEMENT

Conceiving the relationships that people have to places in the naturalizing and botanical terms described above leads, then, to a peculiar sedentarism that is reflected in language and in social practice. This sedentarism is not inert. It actively territorializes our identities, whether cultural or national. And as this section will attempt to show, it also directly enables a vision of territorial displacement as pathological. The broader intent here is to suggest that it is in confronting displacement that the sedentarist metaphysic embedded in the national order of things is at its most visible.

That displacement is subject to botanical thought is evident from the contrast between two everyday terms for it: transplantation and uprootedness. The notion of transplantation is less specific a term than the latter, but it may be agreed that it generally evokes live, viable roots. It strongly suggests, for example, the colonial and postcolonial, usually privileged, category of "expatriates" who pick up their roots in an orderly manner from the "mother country," the originative culture-bed, and set about their "acclimatization"[14] in the "foreign environment" or on "foreign soil"—again, in an orderly manner. Uprootedness is another matter. Even a brief overview of the literature on refugees as uprooted people shows that in uprooting, the orderliness of the transplantation disappears. Instead, broken and dangling roots predominate—roots that threaten to wither, along with the ordinary loyalties of citizenship in a homeland (Heller and Feher 1988:89; Malkki 1985:24–25).

The pathologization of uprootedness in the national order of things can take several different (but often conflated) forms, among them political, medical, and moral. After the Second World War, and also in the interwar period, the loss of national homeland embodied by refugees was often defined by policymakers and scholars of the time as a politico-moral problem. For example, a prominent 1939 historical survey of refugees states, "Politically uprooted, he [the refugee] may sink into the underworld of terrorism and political crime; and in any case he is suspected of political irresponsibility that endangers national security" (Simpson 1939:9).[15]

It is, however, the moral axis that has proven to command the greatest longevity in the problematization of refugees. A particularly clear, if extreme, statement of the perceived moral consequences of loss of homeland is to be found in the following passage from a postwar study of the mental and moral characteristics of the "typical refugee":

> Homelessness is a serious threat to moral behavior . . . . At the moment the refugee crosses the frontiers of his own world, his whole moral outlook, his attitude toward the divine order of life changes . . . . [The refugees'] conduct makes it obvious that we are dealing with individuals who are basically amoral, without any sense of personal or social responsibility . . . . They no longer feel themselves bound by ethical precepts which every honest citizen . . . respects. They become a menace, dangerous characters who will stop at nothing. [Cirtautas 1957:70, 73]

The particular historical circumstances under which the pathologization of the World War II refugees occurred has been discussed elsewhere (Malkki 1985). The point to be underscored here is that these refugees' loss of bodily connection to their national homelands came to be treated as *a loss of moral bearings*. Rootless, they were no longer trustworthy as "honest citizens."

The theme of moral breakdown has not disappeared from the study of exile and displacement (Kristeva 1991; Tabori 1972). Pellizzi (1988:170), for instance, speaks of the "inner destruction" visited upon the exile "by the full awareness of his condition." Suggesting that most of us are today "in varying degrees of exile, removed from our roots," he warns: "1984 is near" (1988:168). Another observer likens the therapeutic treatment of refugees to military surgery; in both cases, time is of the essence.

> Unless treated quickly, the refugee almost inevitably develops either apathy or a reckless attitude that "the world owes me a living," which later proves almost ineradicable. There is a slow, prostrating and agonizing death—of the hopes, the idealism and the feeling of solidarity with which the refugees began. [Aall 1967:26][16]

The more contemporary field of "refugee studies" is quite different in spirit from the postwar literature. However, it shares with earlier texts the premise that refugees are necessarily "a problem." They are not ordinary people, but represent, rather, an anomaly requiring specialized correctives and therapeutic interventions. It is striking how often the abundant literature claiming refugees as its object of study locates "the problem" not in the political conditions or processes that produce massive territorial displacements of people, but, rather, within the bodies and minds (and even souls) of people categorized as refugees.

The internalization of the problem within "the refugee" in the more contemporary study of refugees now occurs most often along a medicalizing, psychological axis. Harrell-Bond, for instance, cites evidence of the breakdown of families and the erosion of "normative social behaviour" (1986:150), of mental illness (1986:152, 283 ff.), of "psychological stress" (1986:286), and of "clinical levels of depression and anxiety" (1986:287 ff.).[17]

The point here is obviously not to deny that displacement can be a shattering experience. It is rather this: Our sedentarist assumptions about attachment to place lead us to define displacement not as a fact about sociopolitical context, but rather as an inner, pathological condition of the displaced.

THE "FAMILY OF NATIONS" AND THE EXTERNALITY OF "THE REFUGEE"

These different texts on the mental and moral characteristics of refugees first of all create the effect of a generalized, even generic, figure: "the refugee." But the generalization and problematization of "the refugee" may be linked to a third process, that of the discursive externalization of the refugee from the national (read: natural) order of things. Three examples may clarify this process.

In a study of the post–World War II refugees, Stoessinger (1956:189) notes the importance of studying "the peculiar psychological effects arising from prolonged refugee status," and stresses that "such psychological probings constitute an excursion into what is still largely *terra incognita*." The title of a more recent article reflects a comparable perception of the strangeness and unfamiliarity of the world peopled by refugees: "A Tourist in the Refugee World" (Shawcross 1989:28–30). The article is a commentary in a photographic essay on refugees around the world entitled *Forced Out: The Agony of the Refugee in Our Time* (Kismaric 1989). Excursions into *terra incognita*, guided tours in "the refugee world," and the last image of being "forced out"—all three point to the externality of "the refugee" in the national order of things.

Hannah Arendt outlined these relations of strangeness and externality very clearly when writing about the post–World War II refugees and other displaced peoples in Europe. The world map she saw was very different from the school atlas considered earlier.

> Mankind, for so long a time considered under the image of a family of nations, had reached the stage where whoever was thrown out of one of these tightly organized closed communities found himself thrown out of the family of nations altogether ... the abstract nakedness of being nothing but human was their greatest danger. [1973:294, 300][18]

Refugees, liminal in the categorical order of nation-states, thus fit Turner's famous characterization of liminal personae as "naked unaccommodated man" or "undifferentiated raw material" (1967:98–99). The objectification to which Arendt's and Turner's observations refer is very evident in the scholarly and policy discourse on refugees. The term "refugees" denotes an objectified, undifferentiated mass that is meaningful primarily as an aberration of categories and an object of "therapeutic interventions" (cf. Foucault 1979). One of the social and analytical consequences of the school atlas, then, is the political sensitivity and symbolic danger of people who do not fit, who represent "matter out of place" (Douglas 1966).

These relations of order and aberration also raise questions for anthropological practice: If "the refugee" is "naked unaccommodated man," naked and not clothed in culture, why should the anthropologist study him? The heroizing concept of the "family of nations" is comparable to another naturalistic term: the "family of man" (cf. Haraway 1986:9, 11). Thus does the nakedness of the ideal-typical refugee suggest another link: that between nationlessness and culturelessness. That is, territorially "uprooted" people are easily seen as "torn loose from their culture" (Marrus 1985:8),[19] because culture is itself a territorialized (and even a botanical and quasi-ecological) concept in so many contexts. As Clifford (1988:338) observes: "Common notions of culture" are biased "toward rooting rather than travel." Violated, broken roots signal an ailing cultural identity and a damaged nationality. The ideal-typical refugee is like a native gone amok (cf. Arendt 1973:302). It is not illogical in this cultural context that one of the first therapies routinely directed at refugees is a spatial one. The refugee camp is a technology of "care and control" (Malkki 1985:51; Proudfoot 1957)—a technology of power entailing the management of space and movement—for "peoples out of place."

In the foregoing, an attempt has been made to clarify the following points: (1) The world of nations tends to be conceived as discrete spatial partitionings of territory. (2) The relations of people to place tend to be naturalized in discursive and other practices. This naturalization is often specifically conceived in plant metaphors. (3) The concept of culture has many points of connection with that of the nation, and is likewise thought to be rooted in concrete localities. These botanical concepts reflect a metaphysical sedentarism in scholarly and other contexts. (4) The naturalization of the links between people and place leads to a vision of displacement as pathological, and this, too, is conceived in botanical terms, as uprootedness. Uprootedness comes to signal a loss of moral and, later, emotional bearings. Since both cultural and national identities are conceived in territorialized terms, uprootedness also threatens to denature and spoil these.

In the next section, these often taken-for-granted ways of thinking and two different conceptions of the links between people and place will be juxtaposed.

NATIONALS AND COSMOPOLITANS IN EXILE

The two very condensed ethnographic examples to be given are drawn from detailed accounts presented elsewhere (Malkki 1989, 1990). Based on one year of anthropological field research in rural western Tanzania among Hutu refugees who fled the genocidal massacres of 1972 in Burundi, this work explores how the lived experiences of exile shape the construction of national identity and historicity among two groups of Hutu refugees inhabiting two very different settings in Tanzania. One group was settled in a rigorously organized, isolated refugee camp, and the other lived in the more fluid setting of Kigoma Township on Lake Tanganyika. Living outside of any camp context, these "town refugees" were dispersed in non-refugee neighborhoods. Comparison of the camp and town settings revealed radical differences in the meanings ascribed to national identity and homeland, and exile and refugee-ness.

The most striking social fact about the camp was that its inhabitants were continually engaged in an impassioned construction and reconstruction of their history as "a people." Ranging from the "autochthonous" origins of Burundi as a "nation" to the coming of the pastoral Tutsi "foreigners from the North" to the Tutsi capture of power from the autochthons by ruse to, finally, the culminating massacres of Hutu by Tutsi in 1972, which have been termed a "selective genocide" (Lemarchand and Martin 1974), the Hutu refugees' narratives formed an overarching historical trajectory that was fundamentally also a national trajectory of the "rightful natives" of Burundi. The camp refugees saw themselves as a nation in exile, and defined exile, in turn, as a moral trajectory of trials and tribulations that would ultimately empower them to reclaim (or create anew) the "Homeland" in Burundi.

Refugee-ness had a central place in these narrative processes (cf. Malkki 1990:44 ff.). Far from being a "spoiled identity," refugee status was valued and protected as a sign of the ultimate temporariness of exile and of the refusal to become naturalized, to put down roots in a place to which one did not belong. Insisting on one's liminality and displacement as a refugee was also to have a legitimate claim to the attention of "international opinion" and to international assistance. Displacement is usually defined by those who study refugees as a subversion of (national) categories, as an international problem (Malkki 1985, 1989). Here, in contrast, displacement had become a form of categorical purity. Being a refugee, a person was no longer a citizen of Burundi, and not yet an immigrant in Tanzania. One's purity as a refugee had become a way of becoming purer and more powerful as a Hutu.

The "true nation" was imagined as a "moral community" being formed centrally by the "natives" in exile (Malkki 1990:34; cf. Anderson 1983:15). The territorial expanse named Burundi was a mere state. The camp refugees' narratives agree with Renan: "A nation is a soul, a spiritual principle" (1990:19). Here, then, would seem to be a deterritorialized nation without roots sunk directly into the national soil. Indeed, the territory is not yet a national soil, because the nation has not yet been reclaimed by its "true members" and is instead governed by "impostors" (Malkki 1989:133). If "anything can serve as a reterritorialization, in other words, 'stand for' the lost territory," then the Hutu nation has reterritorialized itself precisely in displacement, in a refugee camp (Deleuze and Guattari 1987:508). The homeland here is not so much a territorial or topographic entity as a moral destination. And the collective, idealized return to the homeland is not a mere matter of traveling. The real return can come only at the culmination of the trials and tribulations in exile.

These visions of nation, identity, and displacement challenge the common-sense and scholarly views discussed in the first section of this article, not by refuting the national order of things, but, rather, by constructing an alternative, competing nationalist metaphysic. It is being claimed that state and territory are not sufficient to make a nation, and that citizenship does not amount to a true nativeness. Thus, present-day Burundi is an "impostor" in the "family of nations."

In contrast, the town refugees had not constructed such a categorically distinct, collective identity. Rather than defining themselves collectively as "the Hutu refugees," they tended to seek ways of assimilating and of manipulating multiple identities—identities derived or "borrowed" from the social context of the township. The town refugees were not *essentially* "Hutu" or "refugees" or "Tanzanians" or "Burundians," but rather just "broad persons" (Hebdige 1987:159). Theirs were creolized, rhizomatic identities—changing and situational rather than essential and moral (Deleuze and Guattari 1987:6 ff., 21; Hannerz 1987). In the process of managing these "rootless" identities in township life, they were creating not a heroized national identity, but a lively cosmopolitanism—a worldliness that caused the camp refugees to see them as an "impure," problematic element in the "total community" of the Hutu refugees as "a people" in exile.

For many in town, returning to the homeland meant traveling to Burundi, to a spatially demarcated place. Exile was not a moral trajectory, and homeland was not a moral destination, but simply a place. Indeed, it often seemed inappropriate to think of the town refugees as being in exile at all. Many among them were unsure about whether they would ever return to Burundi, even if political changes were to permit it in the future. But more important, they had created lives that were located in the present circumstances of Kigoma, not in the past in Burundi.

The town refugees' constructions of their lived circumstances were different from *both* the national metaphysic of the camp refu of scholarly common sense. Indeed, they dismantled the national mo refusing a mapping and spurning origin queries altogether. They mou a robust challenge to cultural and national essentialisms; they denatur scholarly, touristic, and other quests for "authenticity" that imply a n ___ traffic in "fake" and "adulterated" identities; and, finally, they trivialized the necessity of living by radical nationalisms. They might well agree with Deleuze and Guattari.

> To be rhizomorphous is to produce stems and filaments that seem to be roots, or better yet connect with them by penetrating the trunk, but put them to strange new uses. We're tired of trees. We should stop believing in trees, roots, and radicles. They've made us suffer too much. All of arborescent culture is founded on them, from biology to linguistics. [1987:15]

CONCLUSION

Anderson (1983:19) proposes that "nationalism has to be understood by aligning it, not with self-consciously held political ideologies, but with the large cultural systems that preceded it, out of which—as well as against which—it came into being" (cf. Bhabha 1990:1 ff.; Kapferer 1988; Orwell 1968:362). It is in this spirit that the phrase "the national order of things" has been used here (in preference to "nationalism"). Its intent has been to describe a class of phenomena that is deeply cultural and yet global in its significance. That is, the nation—having powerful associations with particular localities and territories—is simultaneously a supralocal, transnational cultural form (Appadurai and Breckenridge 1988:1 ff.).

In this order of things, conceptualizations of the relations between people and place readily take on aspects of the metaphysical sedentarism described here. It is these naturalized relations that this article has tried to illuminate and decompose through the three-way comparison of sedentarist common sense, of the Hutu in the refugee camp, and of the cosmopolitan refugees in Kigoma. These ethnographic examples underscore what a troubled conceptual vehicle "identity" still is, even when the more obvious essentialisms have been leached out of it. Time and again, it reappears as a "root essence," as that "pure product" (Clifford 1988:1 ff.) of the cultural, and of the national, soil from which it is thought to draw its nature and its sustenance. That many people (scholars included) see identity through this lens of essentialism is a cultural and political fact to be recognized. But this does not mean that our analytical tools must take this form. The two main oppositions in this article—first, that between sedentarism and displacement in general, and, second, that between "the nationals" and "the cosmopolitans" in exile in Tanzania—suggest alternative conceptualizations.

They suggest that identity is always mobile and processual, partly self-construction, partly categorization by others, partly a condition, a status, a label, a weapon, a shield, a fund of memories, et cetera. It is a creolized aggregate composed through bricolage. The camp refugees celebrated a categorical "purity," the town refugees a cosmopolitan "impurity." But both kinds of identity were rhizomatic, as indeed is any identity, and it would not be ethnographically accurate to study these as mere approximations or distortions of some ideal "true roots."[20]

What Deleuze and Guattari (1987:3 ff.) somewhat abstractly describe as rhizomatic is very succinctly stated by Hebdige in his study of Caribbean music and cultural identity. Defining the terms of his project, he says:

> Rather than tracing back the roots . . . to their source, I've tried to show how the roots themselves are in a state of constant flux and change. *The roots don't stay in one place.* They change shape. They change colour. And they grow. There is *no such thing as a pure point of origin* . . . but *that doesn't mean there isn't history.* [1987:10, emphasis added]

Observing that more and more of the world lives in a "generalized condition of homelessness"—or that there is truly an intellectual need for a new "sociology of displacement," a new "nomadology"—is not to deny the importance of place in the construction of identities.[21] On the contrary, as this article has attempted to show, and as Hebdige suggests above, deterritorialization and identity are intimately linked. "Diasporas always leave a trail of collective memory about another place and time and create new maps of desire and of attachment" (Breckenridge and Appadurai 1989:i).[22] To plot only "places of birth" and degrees of nativeness is to blind oneself to the multiplicity of attachments that people form to places through living in, remembering, and imagining them.

NOTES

1. Kristeva (1991) arrives at similar observations along quite different theoretical trajectories.

2. A more detailed discussion of the literature on nations and nationalism can be located in Malkki (1989: 11 ff.).

3. A recent critique of Gellner's position has been done by Moore (1989).

4. The "real" nation is implied in such terms as Giddens's "classical form" (1987:269) and Smith's "standard or 'classic' European 'nation' " (1986:8). See also Smith (1986:17) on "dubious" forms.

5. *Webster's New Collegiate Dictionary*, 9th ed., s.v. "land."

6. Extracted and translated from a 1950s South Tyrolean almanac by Doob, cited in Tuan (1977:156): "Heimat is first of all the mother earth who has given birth to our folk and race, who is the holy soil, and who gulps down God's clouds, sun, and storms . . . . But more than all this, our Heimat is the land which has become fruitful through the sweat of our ancestors. For this Heimat our ancestors have fought and suffered, for this Heimat our fathers have died."

7. Clearly, the other great metaphor for community is blood, or stock. But the tree more closely reveals the territorialization of identity, and is thus given primacy here. Frequently, these dominating metaphors are also combined, of course, as in the family

tree. My understanding of the politico-symbolic significance of blood has been enriched by conversations with Ann Stoler.

8. One variety of primordialism is to be found in Mazzini's view that God "divided Humanity into distinct groups upon the face of our globe, and thus planted the seeds of nations" (cited in Emerson 1960:91).

9. Cf. Kapferer (1988:1) on cultures as the "root essence" of nations and national identities in discourses of nationalism.

10. Elsewhere (Malkki 1989:16) it has been examined how Durkheimian views of the nation seem to rest on metaphors of the organism and the body (the female body, in particular).

11. The first example raises the issue of rainforests and the people who live in them. Here it is necessary to emphasize that it is not being suggested that the political efforts converging on these forests are futile or trivial. Similarly, in the case of the second example of environmentalism and green politics, the intent is not to advocate a cynically agnostic stance toward environmental politics, or to echo the unfortunate relativism of a book like Douglas and Wildavsky's *Risk and Culture* (1982). The purpose is to sharpen the focus on these phenomena so as to better study their place and effects in the contemporary transnational context.

12. Verhelst's study *No Life Without Roots* (1990) is an example of such heroization. Looking to Third World "grass-roots communities" (1990:4) for a "spiritual message" (1990:87) for the West, he states: "Indigenous cultures contain within them the seeds necessary to give birth to societies which differ from the standardized and devitalized model that has spread over the world" (1990:24).

13. This postcolonial relationship was powerfully portrayed in the fine ethnographic film *Cannibal Tours* (O'Rourke 1987).

14. Notably, not "acculturation."

15. A more detailed study of European refugees at the end of the Second World War has been done elsewhere (Malkki 1985).

16. Cf. Vernant (1953:17) on the "refugee complex"; and also Robert Neumann on "emigré life" as a "highly contagious" "corrosive disease" (cited in Tabori 1972:398–399).

17. See also Harrell-Bond (1989:63). Cf. further Godkin (1980:73–85), a study of "rootedness" and "uprootedness" among alcoholics, which finds that belonging to a place fosters psychological well-being.

18. This is discussed in Malkki (1989:57–58).

19. Shawcross (1989:29) echoes this sense of the loss of culture: "the poignant voices of refugees recall their lost homes, their precious rituals forcibly abandoned . . . . "

20. Deleuze and Guattari write: "Unlike trees or their roots, the rhizome connects any point to any other point, and its traits are not necessarily linked to traits of the same nature; it brings into play very different regimes of signs, and even nonsign states . . . . It is composed not of units but of dimensions, or rather directions in motion. It has neither beginning nor end, but always middle *(milieu)* from which it grows and which it overspills . . . . The tree is filiation but the rhizome is alliance . . . the fabric of the rhizome is the conjunction" "and . . . and . . . and . . ." [1987:21, 25]

21. On the question of a new sociology of displacement, see Breckenridge and Appadurai (1989:iv). On the concept of a new nomadology, see Deleuze and Guattari (1987:23).

22. It is also worth considering why "to some people the very 'state of movement' is being 'at home' " (Marianne Forró, cited in Tabori 1972:399).

REFERENCES

Aall, Cato. 1967. Refugee Problems in Southern Africa. In *Refugee Problems in Africa*. Sven Hamrell, ed. Pp. 26–44. Uppsala, Sweden: The Scandinavian Institute of African Studies.

Anderson, Benedict. 1983. *Imagined Communities: Reflections on the Origin and Spread of Nationalism*. London: Verso.

Appadurai, Arjun. 1988. Putting Hierarchy in Its Place. *Cultural Anthropology* 3(1):36–49.

———. 1990. Disjuncture and Difference in the Global Cultural Economy. *Public Culture* 2(2):1–24.

Appadurai, Arjun, and Carol Breckenridge. 1988. Why Public Culture? Public Culture. *Bulletin of the Project for Transnational Cultural Studies* 1(1):5–9.

Arendt, Hannah. 1973. *The Origins of Totalitarianism*. New York: Harcourt Brace Jovanovich.

Balibar, Étienne. 1990. Paradoxes of Universality. In *Anatomy of Racism*. David T. Goldberg, ed. Pp. 283–294. Minneapolis: University of Minnesota Press.

———. 1991. Es Gibt Keinen Staat in Europa: Racism and Politics in Europe Today. *New Left Review* 186:5–19.

Bhabha, Homi K. 1990. Introduction: Narrating the Nation. In *Nation and Narration*. Homi K. Bhabha, ed. Pp. 1–7. New York: Routledge.

Breckenridge, Carol, and Arjun Appadurai. 1989. On Moving Targets. *Public Culture* 2(1):i–iv.

Cirtautas, Claudius Kazys. 1957. *The Refugee: A Psychological Study*. Boston, Mass.: Meador.

Clifford, James. 1988. *The Predicament of Culture: Twentieth-Century Ethnography, Literature, and Art*. Cambridge, Mass.: Harvard University Press.

Comaroff, John, and Jean Comaroff. 1987. The Madman and the Migrant: Work and Labor in the Historical Consciousness of a South African People. *American Ethnologist* 14(2):191–209.

Dahlburg, John-Thor, et al. 1990. Hate Survives a Holocaust: Anti-Semitism Resurfaces. *Los Angeles Times*, June 12:H1, H7.

Daniels, Stephen. 1988. The Political Iconography of Woodland in Later Georgian England. In *The Iconography of Landscape*. Denis Cosgrove and Stephen Daniels, eds. Pp. 43–82. Cambridge: Cambridge University Press.

Deleuze, Gilles, and Felix Guattari. 1987. *A Thousand Plateaus: Capitalism and Schizophrenia*. Minneapolis: University of Minnesota Press.

Douglas, Mary. 1966. *Purity and Danger. An Analysis of the Concepts of Pollution and Taboo*. London: Routledge.

Douglas, Mary, and Aaron Wildavsky. 1982. *Risk and Culture: An Essay on the Selection of Technological and Environmental Dangers*. Berkeley: University of California Press.

Emerson, Rupert. 1960. *From Empire to Nation: The Rise to Self-Assertion of Asian and African Peoples*. Cambridge, Mass.: Harvard University Press.

Foucault, Michel. 1979. *Discipline and Punish: The Birth of the Prison*. New York: Vintage.

Fustel de Coulanges, Numa Denis. 1980. *The Ancient City: A Study on the Religion, Laws, and Institutions of Greece and Rome*. Baltimore, Md.: Johns Hopkins University Press.

Geertz, Clifford. 1983. *Local Knowledge: Further Essays in Interpretive Anthropology.* New York: Basic Books.

Gellner, Ernest. 1983. *Nations and Nationalism.* Ithaca, N.Y.: Cornell University Press.

Giddens, Anthony. 1987. *The Nation-State and Violence.* Berkeley: University of California Press.

Godkin, Michael A. 1980. Identity and Place: Clinical Applications Based on Notions of Rootedness and Uprootedness. In *The Human Experience of Space and Place.* Anne Buttimer and David Deamon, eds. Pp. 73–85. New York: St. Martin's Press.

Goytisolo, Juan. 1987. *Landscapes after the Battle.* New York: Seaver Books.

Graves, Robert. 1966. *The White Goddess.* New York: Farrar, Straus and Giroux.

Gupta, Akhil. 1988. Space and Time in the Politics of Culture. Paper presented at the 87th Annual Meeting of the American Anthropological Association, Phoenix, Arizona.

Handler, Richard. 1988. *Nationalism and the Politics of Culture in Quebec.* Madison: University of Wisconsin Press.

Hannerz, Ulf. 1987. The World in Creolisation. *Africa* 57(4):546–559.

Haraway, Donna. 1986. The Heart of Africa: Nations, Dreams, and Apes. *Inscriptions* 2:9–/001193/

Harrell-Bond, Barbara. 1986. *Imposing Aid: Emergency Assistance to Refugees.* Oxford: Oxford University Press.

———. 1989. Repatriation: Under What Conditions Is It the Most Desirable Solution for Refugees? *African Studies Review* 32(1):41–69.

Hebdige, Dick. 1987. *Cut 'n' Mix: Culture, Identity and Caribbean Music.* London: Methuen.

Heiberg, Marianne. 1989. *The Making of the Basque Nation.* Cambridge: Cambridge University Press.

Heller, Agnes, and Ferenc Feher. 1988. *The Postmodern Political Condition.* New York: Columbia University Press.

Hobsbawm, Eric. 1990. *Nations and Nationalism Since 1780: Programme, Myths, Reality.* Cambridge: Cambridge University Press.

Kapferer, Bruce. 1988. *Legends of People, Myths of State, Violence, Intolerance, and Political Culture in Sri Lanka and Australia.* Washington, D.C.: Smithsonian Institution Press.

Kismaric, Carole. 1989. *Forced Out: The Agony of the Refugee in Our Time.* New York: Random House.

Kristeva, Julia. 1991. *Strangers to Ourselves.* New York: Columbia University Press.

Lemarchand, René, and David Martin. 1974. Selective Genocide in Burundi. Report No. 20. London: The Minority Rights Group.

Malkki, Liisa. 1985. The Origin of a Device of Power: The Refugee Camp in Post-War Europe. Anthropology Department, Harvard University, unpublished MS.

———. 1989. Purity and Exile: Transformations in Historical-National Consciousness among Hutu Refugees in Tanzania. Ph.D. dissertation, Anthropology Department, Harvard University.

———. 1990. Context and Consciousness: Local Conditions for the Production of Historical and National Thought among Hutu Refugees in Tanzania. In *Nationalist Ideologies and the Production of National Cultures.* Richard G. Fox, ed. Pp. 32–62. American Ethnological Society Monograph Series, 2. Washington, D.C.: American Anthropological Association.

Marrus, Michael. 1985. *The Unwanted: European Refugees in the Twentieth Century.* New York: Oxford University Press.

Mauss, Marcel. 1969. *La nation et l'internationalisme*. Oeuvres III: *Cohesion sociale et divisions de la sociologie*. Pp. 573–639. Paris: Minuit.

Moore, Sally Falk. 1989. The Production of Cultural Pluralism as a Process. *Public Culture* 1(2):26–48.

O'Rourke, Dennis. 1987. *Cannibal Tours*. Canberra, Australia: O'Rourke and Associates Filmmakers.

Orwell, George. 1968. *As I Please: 1943–1945: The Collected Essays, Journalism, and Letters of George Orwell*. vol. III. Sonia Orwell and Ian Angus, eds. New York: Harcourt Brace Jovanovich.

Pellizzi, Francesco. 1988. To Seek Refuge: Nation and Ethnicity in Exile. In *Ethnicities and Nations: Processes of Interethnic Relations in Latin America, Southeast Asia, and the Pacific*. Remo Guidieri, Francesco Pellizzi, and Stanley J. Tambiah, eds. Pp. 154–171. Austin: University of Texas Press.

Plenel, Edwy. 1990. "Words Are Weapons" and Le Pen's Army Knows How to Pull the Trigger. *Manchester Guardian Weekly* 142(21):16.

Prakash, Gyan. 1990. Writing Post-Orientalist Histories of the Third World: Perspectives from Indian Historiography. *Comparative Studies in Society and History* 32(2):383–408.

Proudfoot, Malcolm. 1957. *European Refugees: 1939–1952*. London: Faber and Faber.

Renan, Ernest. 1990. What Is a Nation? In *Nation and Narration*. Homi K. Bhabha, ed. Pp. 8–22. New York: Routledge.

Robertson, Jennifer. 1988. Furusato Japan: The Culture and Politics of Nostalgia. *Politics, Culture, and Society* 1(4):494–518.

Rosaldo, Renato. 1989. *Culture and Truth: The Remaking of Social Analysis*. Boston, Mass.: Beacon Press.

Said, Edward. 1979. Zionism from the Standpoint of Its Victims. *Social Text* 1:7–58.

——— . 1986. *After the Last Sky. Palestinian Lives*. New York: Pantheon.

Sale, Kirkpatrick. 1990. How Paradise Was Lost: What Columbus Discovered. *The Nation* 251(13):444–446.

Shawcross, William. 1989. A Tourist in the Refugee World. In *Forced Out: The Agony of the Refugee in Our Time*. Carole Kismaric, ed. Pp. 28–30. New York: Random House.

Simpson, John. 1939. *The Refugee Problem: Report of a Survey*. London: Oxford University Press.

Smith, Anthony. 1986. *The Ethnic Origins of Nations*. New York: Blackwell.

Stoessinger, John. 1956. *The Refugee and the World Community*. Minneapolis: University of Minnesota Press.

Tabori, Paul. 1972. *The Anatomy of Exile: A Semantic and Historical Study*. London: Harrap.

Tambiah, Stanley J. 1985. *Culture, Thought, and Social Action. An Anthropological Perspective*. Cambridge, Mass.: Harvard University Press.

Thomas, Keith. 1983. *Man and the Natural World: A History of the Modern Sensibility*. New York: Pantheon.

Torgovnick, Marianna. 1990. *Gone Primitive: Savage Intellects, Modern Lives*. Chicago, Ill.: University of Chicago Press.

Trinh, T. Minh-Ha. 1989. *Woman, Native, Other: Writing Postcoloniality and Feminism*. Bloomington: Indiana University Press.

Tuan, Yi-Fu. 1977. *Space and Place: The Perspective of Experience*. Minneapolis: University of Minnesota Press.

National Geographic   **453**

Turner, Victor. 1967. *The Forest of Symbols. Aspects of Ndembu Ritual.* Ithaca, N.Y.:
    Cornell University Press.
Van Binsbergen, Wim. 1981. The Unit of Study and the Interpretation of Ethnicity. *Journal
    of Southern African Studies* 8(1):51–81.
Verhelst, Thierry. 1990. *No Life Without Roots: Culture and Development.* London: Zed.
Vernant, Jacques.
———1953. *The Refugee in the Post-War World.* London: Allen & Unwin.
Wagner, Roy. 1981. *The Invention of Culture.* Chicago, Ill.; University of Chicago Press.
Weil, Simone. 1987[1952]. *The Need for Roots: Prelude to a Declaration of Duties To-
    wards Mankind.* New York: Ark.
Zolberg, Aristide. 1983. The Formation of New States as a Refugee-Generating Process.
    In *The Global Refugee Problem.* Gilburt Loescher and John Scanlan, eds. Pp. 24–
    38. The Annals of the American Academy of Political and Social Science (special
    issue). Beverly Hills, Calif.: Sage.

David Morley and Kevin Robins

Globalization requires a rethinking of the categories through which political economy, the international division of labor, sovereignty, interstate relations, and the complex interconnectedness of states and societies can be grasped. As David Held's essay signals, such processes change the overall institutional environment in which political thought and action, at the most general of levels, have to occur. The definition of vast free-trade areas, like the European Union (EU) and the North American Free Trade Agreement (NAFTA), are only the most obvious of these geopolitical reconfigurings, which necessarily reframe the terms on which political identities are being formed. The nation, nationalism, national identity are all affected in this sense. But these contemporary changes present themselves not only as new regimes of regulation; new fields of meaning are being generated as well. The changes in Eastern Europe, and the cancellation of half a century of complex history in the region, not to speak of the disappearance of the Soviet Union and its regional imperium, remove a massive impediment from the imagining of a common European identity, even as the continuing expansion of the EU entails fresh systems of distinction inside this overall European scene. The unification of Germany in 1990 further complicates this dialectic of coalescence and fracture, reinstating a strong territorial presence in the center of the continent, realigning the interstate configuration of Eastern Europe, and constraining the previously persuasive logic of the EU's political federation. Meanwhile, the mobility of populations, through the post-Fordist labor markets, the gathering-in of German diasporas, and the huge refugee movements associated with the collapse of Yugoslavia and other instabilities, provides massive material incitement for discourses of homelessness, migration, and exile.

In other words, economic and political restructuring beyond the nation-state is producing instabilities of European identity, which in turn affect how national identities can be understood. The upheaval in the former Soviet Union, the East European revolutions, the unification of Germany, the civil war in the Balkans, the enhancement of the EU—all these call existing conceptions of Europe into question, and in so doing agitate given assumptions about the distinctiveness and sufficiency of national culture. David Morley and Kevin Robins engage these questions via Edgar Reitz's TV film *Heimat* (1984), which by its counterposition with the U.S.-produced TV series *Holocaust* (shown in Germany in 1979) directly implicated questions of cultural americanization. They ask how the borders of "Europe" are being constructed, imaginatively speaking, now that the old verities of the cold war no longer run, using the trope of "home" to highlight the importance of history and memory to this fraught and contested process. The appeals and anathemas of americanization provide one edge of this discourse, while the disappearance of the Iron Curtain (and the Berlin Wall) has problematized the borderlands to the east. While older notions of *Mitteleuropa* (Central Europe) have been resuscitated in Germany as part of this flux, the flaring of hostilities to "foreigners" (refugees and immigrant workers, especially Turks) inside German society resonate with another European borderline between "Western Christendom" and "Islam," which, in the words of one Turkish German poet, "runs right through my tongue." In their rich and wide-ranging analysis, Morley and Robins explore the centrality of media like film and TV to the process of imagining the nation, and of the vital role of history and memory for this purpose. The authors bring an impressive set of backgrounds in cultural studies and communications, and as such call attention once again to the impact on approaches to nationalism by these fields.

No Place like *Heimat:* Images of Home(land) in European Culture

Our story is the old clash between history and home. Or to put it another way, the immeasurable, impossible space that seems to divide the hearth from the quest.

JEANETTE WINTERSON, "ORION"

Every country is home to one man
And exile to another.

T. S. ELIOT, "TO THE INDIANS WHO DIED IN AFRICA"

Everybody needs a home, so at least you can have some place to leave, which is where most folks will say you must be coming from.

JUNE JORDAN, "LIVING ROOM"

Our concern here is with questions of identity and memory in the construction of definitions of "Europe" and "European Culture." It is in this context that we address the centrality of the metaphor of Heimat ("home/land"). We take as a particular instance the debates opened up in the Federal Republic of Germany by Edgar Reitz's *Heimat*, with its focus on the opposition of Heimat:Fremde ("homeland"/"foreignness"). Our specific focus is on the relations between European and "other" cultures in the post-war period and, more particularly, on the question of the representation of the European past as constructed through the American and the German media. Our argument is that we see played out here, in these debates over who holds the franchise on the representation of the past, an illuminating pre-echo of contemporary debates as to who (the Germans? the Allies?) has the right to determine Germany's future. This is, of course, no local matter, but is crucial to the future of Europe as a whole, as the franchise rights on the past are clearly intermeshed with the franchise on the future. We take the "German story" to be both a symbolic condensation of many of the most problematic themes of the European past and to be clearly a central issue in the contemporary *realpolitik* of Europe.

David Morley and Kevin Robins, "No Place like *Heimat*: Images of Home(land) in European Culture," *New Formations*, 12 (Winter 1990), pp. 1–23.

If Germany, the past (somehow) reconciled, is to be united, and Europe no longer divided by the "iron curtain" then the question arises, inescapably, as to where "Europe" ends (what is the status of "Mitteleuropa" or "Eastern Europe"?) and against what "other" (besides America) "Europe" and "European Culture" is to be defined, if not against Communism. Our argument is that, if America continues to supply one symbolic boundary, to the "west," there is also, implicit in much recent debate, a reworking of a rather ancient definition of Europe—as what used to be referred to as "Christendom"—to which Islam, rather than Communism, is now seen to supply the "eastern" boundary. Our concern is with identifying some of the threads from which this pattern is being woven—the better, hopefully, to unravel it.

BRINGING IT ALL BACK HOME

"Modern man," Peter Berger and his colleagues argue, "has suffered from a deepening condition of 'homelessness' ": "The correlate of the migratory character of his experience of society and of self has been what might be called a metaphysical loss of 'home'."[1] To be modern, writes Marshall Berman,

> is to find ourselves in an environment that promises adventure, power, joy, growth, transformation of ourselves and the world—and, at the same time, that threatens to destroy everything we have, everything we know, everything we are. Modern environments and experiences cut across all boundaries of geography and ethnicity, of class and nationality, of religion and ideology; in this sense, modernity can be said to unite all mankind. But it is a paradoxical unity, a unity of disunity; it pours us all into a maelstrom of perpetual disintegration and renewal, of struggle and contradiction, of ambiguity and anguish.

The project of modernity is then "to make oneself somehow at home in the maelstrom."[2]

It is this image of home that interests us. Home in a world of expanding horizons and dissolving boundaries. Anthony Giddens draws attention to the implications of modernity for ontological security, for the confidence we have "in the continuity of [our] self identity and in the constancy of the surrounding social and material environments of action."[3] In pre-modern times, he argues, this sense of trust and security was rooted in kinship systems, in local community, in religious beliefs, and in the continuity of tradition. The effect of the great dynamic forces of modernity—what Giddens calls the separation of time and space, disembedding mechanisms, and institutional reflexivity— has been to "disengage some basic forms of trust relation from the attributes of local contexts."[4] Places are no longer the clear supports of our identity.

If anything, this process of transformation has become accelerated, and time-space distanciation has come to be ever more intense.[5] It is through the logic of globalization that this dynamic of modernization is most powerfully articulated. Through proliferating information and communications flows and through mass human migration, it has progressively eroded territorial frontiers and boundaries and provoked ever more immediate confrontations of culture and identity.[6] Where once it was the case that cultures were demarcated and differentiated in time and space, now "the concept of a fixed, unitary, and bounded culture must give way to a sense of the fluidity and permeability of cultural sets."[7] Through this inter-mixture and hybridization of cultures, older certainties and foundations of identity are continuously and necessarily undermined. The continuity of identity is broken too. "There are *lieux de mémoire*, sites of memory," writes Pierre Nora, "because there are no longer *milieux de mémoire*, real environments of memory .... We speak so much of memory because there is so little of it left."[8] Indeed, we speak so much of memory, and also of place and community. As Michael Rustin argues, there is an increasingly felt need for "some expressive relationship to the past" and for attachment to particular territorial locations as "nodes of association and continuity, bounding cultures and communities."[9] There is a need to be "at home" in the new and disorientating global space.

Home, homeland, Heimat. It is around the meaning of European culture and identity in the new global context that this image—this nostalgia, this aspiration—has become polemically activated. It is associated, particularly, with Gorbachev's appeal to a "common European home":

> Europe is indeed a common home where geography and history have closely inter-woven the destinies of dozens of countries and nations. Of course, each of them has its own problems, and each wants to live its own life, to follow its own traditions. Therefore, developing the metaphor, one may say: the home is common, that is true, but each family has its own apartment, and there are different entrances, too.[10]

This notion of a single Europe, from the Atlantic to the Urals, has an obvious appeal. But what does it really amount to? What kind of community does it offer? Perhaps Susan Sontag is right. Where once Europe symbolized empire and ex-pansionism, the new idea of Europe is about retrenchment: "the Europeanisation, not of the rest of the world, but . . . of Europe itself."[11] This is a defensive identity, a fortress identity, defined against the threat of other cultures and identities (Amer-ican, Japanese, Islamic, African, or whatever). What this reassertion of European cultural identity amounts to is a refusal to confront the fact of a fundamental population shift that is undermining "the little white 'Christian' Europe" of the nineteenth century. As Neal Ascherson argues, "we are living in a new America which is reluctant to admit the fact; in a continent which the poor of the outside world are beginning to choose as a destination."[12] The European Heimat invokes the past grandeur of Europe as a bastion against future uncertainties. This is a Europe that divides those who are of the Community from those who are *extra-communitari* and, effectively, extraterrestrial.[13]

There are those, however, who are less committed to this vision of a European home.[14] They are, to appropriate Gorbachev's metaphor, more interested in the different apartments than in the common home. For them, a faceless Europeanism is inimical to the rich diversity of national cultures and identities that are, sup-posedly, the basis of a more authentic sense of belonging: it is only in the sense of nationhood that one can feel truly "at home." Throughout Europe, we can now see the rekindling of national and nationalist sentiments. It is more apparent in central and eastern Europe where national aspirations of sixty or seventy years ago are currently being reactivated through the reassertion of ethnic, religious and cultural differences. But also in western Europe, particularly in the context of German reunification (*Deutschland, einig Vaterland*), national allegiance is a powerful way of belonging. As Ian Davidson argues, "western reactions to the prospect of German unification show that the civilized advances of European integration are very recent compared with the old reflexes of nationalism; and that despite 45 years of reconciliation, there are primitive national feelings which lie only millimetres below the skin."[15]

As an alternative to continental Europeanism and to nation-statism, there is yet another kind of "homely" belonging. This is the identity rooted in the Heimat of regions and small nations. According to Neal Ascherson, the "melting away" of the European nation states "may allow other entities, smaller but more durable, to replace them." He evokes the rich pluralism of regional traditions, languages, dialects and cultures as the true basis for authentic identities. The European community, Ascherson argues, "will travel from the western Europe of nation-states via the Brussels superstate to the Europe of Heimats."[16] This "small is beautiful" ideal of a Europe of the regions clearly seems to offer a richer and more radical way to belong. There is a romantic utopianism in this celebration of small nationalism and regionalism, a utopianism of the underdog. "The Irish, the Basques, the Corsicans, the Kurds, the Kosovans, the Azerbaijanis, the Puerto Ricans, the Latvians," writes John Berger, "have little in common culturally or historically, but all of them want to be free of distant, foreign centres which, through long bitter experience, they have come to know as soulless." All of them "insist upon their identity being recognized, insist upon their continuity—their links with their dead and the unborn."[17]

Yet Heimat is an ominous utopia. Whether "home" is imagined as the community of Europe or of the national state or of the region, it is drenched in the longing for wholeness, unity, integrity. It is about community centred on shared traditions and memories. As the German film director Edgar Reitz puts it:

> The word is always linked to strong feelings, mostly remembrances and longing. Heimat always evokes in me the feeling of something lost or very far away, something which one cannot easily find or find again . . . . It seems to me that one has a more precise idea of Heimat the further one is away from it.[18]

Heimat is a mythical bond rooted in a lost past, a past that has already disintegrated: "we yearn to grasp it, but it is baseless and elusive; we look back for something solid to lean on, only to find ourselves embracing ghosts."[19] It is about conserving the "fundamentals" of culture and identity. And, as such, it is about sustaining cultural boundaries and boundedness. To belong in this way is to protect exclusive, and therefore, excluding, identities against those who are seen as aliens and "foreigners." The "other" is always and continuously a threat to the security and integrity of those who share a common home. Xenophobia and fundamentalism are opposite sides of the same coin.[20] For, indeed, Heimat-seeking is a form of fundamentalism. And, like all fundamentalist beliefs, it is built around what Salman Rushdie calls "the absolutism of the Pure." The "apostles of purity,'' he argues, are always moved by the fear ''that intermingling with a different culture will inevitably weaken and ruin their own.''[21] In contemporary European culture, the longing for home is not an innocent utopia.

COMMUNICATIONS, MEMORY AND IDENTITY

In our view these questions—of identity, memory and nostalgia—are inextricably interlinked with patterns and flows of communication. The ''memory banks'' of our times are in some part built out of the materials supplied by the film and television industries. It is to the role of these industries in the construction of memory and identity that we now turn.

Elsewhere[22] we have directly addressed the debates concerning the role of new communications technologies (satellite, cable, etc.) in the creation of ''electronic spaces'' transcending established national boundaries and in the reconfiguration of European culture. As argued there, that dynamic involves two poles—pressures both towards globalization and centralization and towards the localization and regionalization of cultures. We take the position that most current perspectives on these issues are inadequate in so far as they operate with a (technologically) determinist model of the communication process. Within this prevailing framework cultural identities can only ever be responsive and reactive to the controlling stimulus of communications technologies. What is needed is a better formulation of the problem, one that takes questions of cultural and national identity as problematical and central categories.

One of the first questions concerns how we are to understand the ''national''—as a process of ''remembering, a pulling together and reassemblage of its members''[23] and what the role of institutions such as television and cinema is in the construction of national identities. To take first the institution of cinema: as Andrew Higson notes, the concept of national cinema has almost invariably been mobilized ''as a strategy of cultural (and economic) resistance; a means of asserting national autonomy in the face of . . . Hollywood's international domination.''[24] In that context, *art* cinema has played a central role ''in the attempts made by a number of European countries both to counter American domination of their indigenous markets in film and also to foster a film industry and film culture of their own.''[25] The discourses of ''art,'' ''culture,'' ''quality'' and ''national identity/nationhood'' have thus been mobilized against ''Hollywood'' and used to justify various nationally specific economic systems of support and protection for indigenous cinema-making.

The role of the state is crucial in this respect, in so far as state policies have often determined the parameters and possibilities of various ''national cinemas,'' in the context of governmental recognition of ''the potential ideological power of cinema . . . as a national cultural form, an institution with a 'nationalizing' function.''[26] Given that nationhood is always an image constructed under particular conditions, and drawing on Benedict Anderson's concept of history as ''the necessary basis of national narrative,''[27] Stephen Heath has suggested that, just as nationhood is not a given but ''always something to be gained'' so ''cinema

needs to be understood as one of the means by which it is 'gained' . . . . "[28] The
same points would apply in relation to EEC policies designed to mobilize television in the production of European identities. This is, necessarily, a contentious
business. Thus definitions of British cinema always involve the construction of
an "imaginary homogeneity of identity and culture . . . apparently shared by all
British subjects"; a process of inclusion and exclusion whereby one definition of
"British" is centralised and others are marginalised, in a process which Higson
refers to as one of "internal cultural colonialism."[29]

It is a question of recognizing the role of the stories we tell ourselves about
our past in constructing our identities in the present. One key issue concerns the
power of the idea of the "nation" to involve people in a common sense of identity
and its capacity to work as an inclusive symbol which provides "integration"
and "meaning" as it constructs and conscripts public images and interpretations
of the past "to re-enchant a disenchanted everyday life."[30] In this fashion "the
rags and tatters of everyday life take on the lustre of the idealised nation when
they are touched by its symbolism. There is therefore no simple replacement of
'community' by 'nation' . . . but rather a constant . . . redemption of its unhappy
remains,"[31] as the idea of the national past is constantly reworked and represented
within the historical experience of a particular nation-state.[32]

The "struggle for the past" has been a central issue at different stages in a
number of European countries in recent years. Thus, in France in particular, the
mid-1970s saw the emergence in the cinema of the "retro style" (*Lacombe Lucien*, etc.) with films aiming to articulate a new, post-Gaullist concept of French
history and French identity, specifically with reference to the role of the French
Resistance movement (the "emblem" of French identity at that point) under
Fascism.[33] As Foucault noted at the time these films represented an attempt to
"re-programme popular memory" through film and television, to recover "lost,
unheard memories" which had been denied (or buried) by the dominant representations of that past. So identity, it seems, is also a question of memory, and
memories of "home" in particular.

It is in this context that we address the centrality of the metaphor of Heimat
(or "home"): principally with reference to the specific debates opened up in the
Federal Republic of Germany by Edgar Reitz's film/TV series of that name. The
"Heimatfilm" is, of course, a well established genre in Germany. One obvious
question concerns whether one *can* work within this traditionally reactionary
genre and yet give the material new and different meanings. Reitz's attempt to
do so has to be seen in the context of the political revitalization of the rural
"Heimat" tradition in West Germany in the 1970s—as an attempt by a coalition
of ecological and anti-nuclear groupings to reclaim these traditions for the left,
via the rediscovery/revaluation of regional/folk traditions, dialect poetry, etc. in
an anti-centralist (and anti-urban) political movement.[34] This turn to ecology represents an important shift, and in this context Adolf Muschg has noted that "in
the face of the steady destruction of the environment "homeland" has ceased to
be a dirty word."[35] More cynically perhaps, just as Raphael Samuel[36] has noted
the resurgence of a concern with "roots" and "tradition" in contemporary Britain, Baudrillard observes that "when the real is no longer what it used to be,

nostalgia assumes its full meaning. There is a proliferation of myths of origin . . . and authenticity."[37] Heimat then is a place no one has yet attained, but for which everyone yearns. Reitz notes that "Heimat, the place where you were born, is for every person the centre of the world" and yet recognizes that the concept is not simply territorial, but rather invokes a "memory of origin" and inevitably involves a notion of an "impossible return" to (imaginary or real) roots or origins.[38] The question is *which* "roots" and to whom they, and their "heritage" are seen to "belong."

TELEVISION, FILM AND POPULAR MEMORY

An ABC Network newspaper advertisement boasted in February 1983 "more people relived the war than fought it" when its eighteen-hour mini series *The Winds of War* achieved the distinction of becoming one of the highest rated programmes in television history, reaching, according to ABC projections, virtually every American over twelve.[39] In much the same way, millions of Europeans have "experienced" the Vietnam War through the lens of films such as *Apocalypse Now* or *The Deer Hunter* (see below). As Anton Kaes argues, "these films interpret national history for the broad public and thus produce, organise and homogenise public memory . . . swiftly spreading identical memories over the earth."[40]

This is no new process. As Anthony Smith pointed out in his review of Koppes and Black's *Hollywood Goes to War*,[41] at times, the role of national cinema in the representation of others (as allies, enemies, good, bad, etc.) is quite transparent. Koppes and Black quote the head of the US War Department's public relations section (Office of War Information) in this period as reporting that "No matter what we want from Hollywood, we get it—and quick. We do not even have to ask—Hollywood comes to us," in a context where the Hollywood chieftains were revelling in the new role they had acquired, of orchestrating and manipulating popular images of the participants in the drama of World War Two. As Koppes and Black demonstrate, the content and scripts of movies were explicitly manipulated so as to mobilize American public opinion, firstly to support the war, and secondly to accept each changing situation and shifting military alliance, as the war proceeded. Thus the Office of War Information prevailed on the studios to tone down their mockery of the English class system expressed in their "castles and caste" picture of Britain and to stress the country's "stubborn resistance" after Dunkirk. More problematically, but with a notable degree of success, the studios were also prevailed on, when it became politically necessary, to transform their depiction of the Soviet Union. As Smith notes "here a whole history had to be turned around and a series of pro-Soviet films created, to explain how Russians came to be fighting alongside Americans and their Allies in a just war"[42]—a process which involved "humanising" the representations of Russians in general, presenting Stalin as a normal and balanced personality, and turning Russia into the perfect ally.

Our sense of "others" has long been mediated by such processes. When the American-produced TV series *Holocaust* was shown in West Germany in 1979 it was watched by more than 20 million Germans, who were confronted with this version of their history in their own living rooms. Very large proportions of the West German TV audience (25 to 50 per cent) watched both *Holocaust* and, later, *Heimat* and both these series acquired the status of "TV events"—a "critical mass" at which it was simply necessary for people to watch the programme if they were to be able to participate effectively in the public debates that were generated in daily conversation. Thus when *Heimat* was shown in the Federal Republic of Germany, in the autumn of 1984, it was much more than a TV series—it was a "media event" which provided the focus and stimulus for a wide-ranging debate on German identity and history, with the popular press proclaiming, for instance, that "Germany's theme this fall is Heimat."[43] As Thomas Elsaesser puts it:

> The move of some filmmakers (Reitz, Lanzmann) . . . to undertake projects whose scale can generate TV events can be seen as an attempt to use film and cinema as release mechanisms for a discursive activity that crosses the boundaries of entertainment, and even of the arts. When a documentary film makes it from the review pages to the front of newspapers or becomes the subject for late night talk shows it demonstrates television's potential for creating something like an instant public sphere.[44]

The question then, is that of who has the power to construct the discourses which structure and dominate this "instant public sphere."

In this connection Heinz Hone argued in *Der Spiegel* that:

> an American TV series, made in a trivial style, produced more for commercial than for moral reasons, more for entertainment than for enlightenment, accomplished what hundreds of books, plays, films . . . documents and the concentration camp trials themselves have failed to do in the three decades since the end of the war: to inform Germans about crimes against Jews committed in their name so that millions were emotionally touched and moved.[45]

Reitz, of course, explicitly conceived *Heimat* as the German "answer" to this American series. For Reitz, *Holocaust* was a "glaring example (of an) international aesthetics of commercialism (for which) the misery produced by the Nazis is nothing but a welcome background spectacle for a sentimental family story."[46] Reitz was concerned that German filmmakers should establish their right to their own history, reclaiming it from the hands of the Americans. For Reitz the real scandal was "German history—Made in Hollywood" (hence his subtitle to *Heimat*: "Made in Germany"). In Reitz's view the issue was that the Americans, with *Holocaust* "have stolen our history . . . taken narrative possession of our past . . . . I watched the crocodile tears of our nation and I saw how it was all taken seriously and how the question of guilt in German history was being discussed by all the great German intellectuals on the basis of this travesty."[47] The further point is that, when shown in America, many critics responded negatively, deeming the series to be a dangerous whitewash of German history. Clearly, a history that unleashed a world war does not belong to any single nation. Our argument, as stated in the introduction to this article, is that we see played out here, in these debates over the politics of the representation of the German past, a pre-echo of the contemporary political debates as to who (the Germans? the Allies? the EEC?) has the "right" to determine Germany's future.

HOW GERMAN IS IT? AN IMPOSSIBLE HISTORY

> Everyone is passionately in love with outdoors, in love with what they refer to as Natur, and the splendid weather is an added inducement to put on their Lederhosen and spend several hours serenely tramping through the woods.
>
> (WALTER ABISH, *How German Is It?*)

In his commentary on Adorno's essay "On the question: What is German," Thomas Levin notes that "In order to say just what is the German language, one must be able to establish the identity, limits and character of a natural idiom."[48] Adorno argues that the character or specificity of a natural idiom can best be ascertained by reference to those of its terms which cannot successfully be translated. Thus:

> Every language draws a circle around the people to which it belongs, a circle from which we can only escape in so far as one at the same time enters another one.[49]

The very form of the question "What is German?," argues Adorno, "presupposes an autonomous collective entity—'German'—whose characteristics are then determined after the fact." However, he argues, in reality, it is quite "uncertain whether there even is such a thing as the German person or specifically German quality or anything analogous in other nations."[50] These concerns inevitably take us back into questions of stereotyping and collective narcissism. In this process the central dynamic is one in which "the qualities with which one identifies oneself—the essence of one's own group—imperceptibly become the Good; the foreign group, the others, the Bad. The same thing then happens, in reverse, with the image the others have of the German."[51] For our present purposes, the key issue concerns the way in which the images and identities of "Germany" and "America" have been (and continue to be) defined in relation to each other. Our initial stress is on the distinction between the signifier and the signified, in each case.

As Wim Wenders notes, "America always means two things: a country, geographically, the USA, and an 'idea' of that country which goes with it. (The) 'American Dream,' then, is a dream of a country in a different country that is located where the dream takes place . . . . 'I want to be in America,' the Jets sing, in that famous song from West Side Story. They are in America already and yet still wanting to get there."[52] Similarly, Buruma notes the necessity to distinguish between "Germany as a legal and political entity, a Reichstaat, and 'Germany' as a romantic ideal, a 'Heimat,' devoid of politics, a land of pine forests, lonely mountain tops and dreamy Wandervogel anxiously searching for identity."[53]

Moving to the central term in our argument, Heimat, Wenders notes a crucial difference between the meanings of the term "home" in American, as opposed to German culture.

> They have that in America: "Mobile Homes." "Mobile" is said with pride and means the opposite of "bogged down" ... (or) "stuck." "Home" means "at home," "where you belong" ... (whereas) ... what *makes* it a home in the German language is the fact that it's fixed somewhere.[54]

In the context of the German debate, one of the crucial dimensions along which the term "Heimat" is defined is by contrast to all that is foreign or distant: "America" in particular, becomes the very antithesis of "Heimat." Thus the characteristics of the traditional Heimat film genre, according to Rentschler, include "a conflict between the stable world of the 'Heimat' and the threatening assault of the 'Fremde' (foreign) . . . . "[55]

Reitz's film *Heimat* follows exactly this pattern, in so far as it is structured around a central contrast between those (principally women) who stay in the village (*die Dableiber*) and those (men) who represent a culture of emigrants, who left home (*die Weggegangenen*). As Anton Kaes notes,[56] a pervasive anti-Americanism recurs in *Heimat*, from the first mention of the United States as the "land of the electric chair" (*sic*). In Reitz's own production notes for the series, one of the central characters, Paul, is described as having "become a real American ... a man without a home, without roots, a sentimental globetrotter."[57] To this extent, Reitz seems to fall into what Duncan Webster has described as a "standard image of Americanisation ... drawn from American horror films, the invasion of the alien, the replacement/transformation of the local, the community (viewers, consumers) becoming mindless zombies."[58]

Throughout the series, Kaes argues, *Heimat's* sympathetic treatment of the pre-war period and the focus on the destruction of "Heimat" in the post-war period, means that the weight of its critique falls on the Federal Republic of Germany which, the film implies, has lost all trace of its identity—in the course of its Americanization. Thus as Michael Geisler puts it:

> With *Heimat* working to reconcile the German left . . . with its own country, "America" seems to have taken the place formerly occupied by "Deutschland" . . . Reitz . . . is projecting . . . a mythical "America," country of the perennially homeless . . . a land of loneliness, without history, without culture . . . . As the German left is trying to renegotiate their traditional stance towards their "Heimat," the exclusionary mechanisms find a new target in "America."[59]

Against this kind of perspective, Webster[60] points out that when one of Wenders' characters, in *Kings of the Road* says that the "Americans have colonised our subconscious" it should be noted that the "our" in question has a double resonance—"we Germans" and "we post-war consumers of popular culture"— and these resonances mark the site of intersection of generational, cultural and national identities. What is at stake here is something more than any simple "invasion" of other cultures by America: what Wenders poses is, rather, the *specific* appeal of American culture to a generation growing up in post-war Germany (Wenders was born in 1945), with what Webster describes as a "schizophrenic response to history, a double bind of remembering and forgetting fascism ... (where) ... one way of dealing with this was an involvement with other cultures."[61]

In similar vein, Gabriele Kreutzner[62] argues that, as a result of this history, intellectuals on the German left have taken on the heritage of an overdetermined hostility toward popular phenomena of German culture. At the same time, she notes that it is common practice for the German left to supply its public events with music from the third world (South America, Africa, etc.). Kreutzner suggests that this "celebration of traditional music not only signifies a (romantic) desire for an 'authentic' popular culture. It also suggests that the search for popular phenomena with which they can identify leads the German intellectual outside of her or his immediate cultural context."[63] It is only the "popular" phenomena of other lands which are thus felt to be free of an ideological taint.

Thus the appeal of American culture has to be seen in the context of Germany's "profound mistrust of sounds and images about itself," its post-war greed for foreign images: "I don't think that any other country has had such a loss of faith in its own images, stories and myths as we have."[64] As Wenders puts it:

> In the early Fifties or even the Sixties, it was always American culture .... In other words, the need to forget 20 years created a hole, and people tried to cover this, in both senses, by assimilating American culture much more than French or Italian or British people did. The only radio I listened to was American Forces Network. But the fact that US imperialism was so effective over here was highly favoured by the Germans' own difficulties with their past. One way of forgetting it, and one way of regression, was to accept (or indeed, embrace—DM/KR) the American imperialism.[65]

Rock 'n' roll might have been "foreign" but at least it had nothing to do with fascism.

A close parallel can be made between this contemporary analysis and Adorno's comments on the significance of "foreign words" (*Fremdwörter*) in the German language. Adorno recounts how, as a child, he delighted in the "exterritorial and aggressive" character of these terms, which provided, for him, a refuge from the increasingly unavoidable German chauvinism of the period. Thus, for him "the *Fremdwörter* formed tiny cells of resistance against the nationalism in the First World War."[66] The Nazis, not surprisingly, systematically eliminated the *Fremdwörter* from the culture, in so far as they were able, in order to protect the "purity" of the mother-tongue.[67] In a similar way, Kaes notes that the term "Heimat" was a synonym for race (blood) and territory (soil)—a deadly combination that led to the exile or annihilation of anyone who did not "belong." Under the National Socialists "Heimat" meant the murderous exclusion of anything "un-German."[68]

Reitz has argued that "The problem with us, in Germany, is that our stories are blocked by ... history. In 1945 everything started happening from scratch, erasing all that had gone before. It's like a gaping hole in people's memories and feelings.''[69] As he puts it:

> It is our own history that is in our way. In 1945 the nation's "zero hour" wiped out and created a gap in people's ability to remember ... an entire people has been "unable to mourn" ... unable to tell stories, because our memories are obstructed ... we are still afraid that our personal stories could recall our Nazi past and remind us of our mass participation in the Reich .... [70]

Thus, it is argued, "Deutschland" became, in the post-war period, an entity which it was impossible to represent:

> Nazism, the war ... the defeat and its aftermath ... produced a homelessness ... in the feeling of a loss of "right" to a homeland ... even language no longer provided a "home." Even the image of Germany in the post war period was part of this uprootedness. America (was) represented, for example, by the White House, England by Buckingham Palace ... France by the Arc de Triomphe ... Germany, however, (was always) represented by its division, above all by the Berlin Wall, marking the absence of certainty about home: separation, expulsion, exile.[71]

Prior to the success of *Heimat*, it could be argued that the West German audience for art cinema (in its enthusiasm for Bertolucci's *1900* or the Tavianis' *Padre Padrone*, for example) had compensated for the lack of an acceptable image of its own history and peasant culture by over-identifying in a plainly nostalgic way with that of its neighbours.[72] The other side of this coin was that:

> Hollywood had a wonderful time after 1945, because they had limitless possibilities for showing evil Nazis, whereas before they'd had to content themselves with a limited repertoire of (stereotypical) villains. But in reality, the personification of evil doesn't exist. The Nazi people were as ordinary as everyone else: in special moments ... they acted as Nazis.[73]
>
> In this process "Nazi Germany" or "Deutschland" readily becomes a cipher for an undefined, only superficially historicized evil—a diabolical entity: thus the real horror of the war was "contained" and, in a sense, defused.[74] As Enzensberger has noted, this is "yet another transfiguration of the attribute 'German' into a metaphysical entity—only this time it carries a negative charge (i.e. simply the inversion of a Nazi ideology—DM/KR) .... Instead of Good, as before, it is now the absolute Evil, which is defined along biological or racial parameters.''[75]

WHERE IS EUROPE ANYWAY?

The debates around the concept of "home" and "homeland" occasioned by *Heimat* have now, of course, also to be seen in the transformed context of President Gorbachev's call for the construction of a "common European home" to transcend the cold war division of Europe which found its most dramatic expression in the division of Germany. As argued above, the debates around the question of who should hold the franchise rights over the telling of the story of the German past have many parallels in the debates as to who should have the right to determine Germany's future. Current debates concerning the reunification of Germany have a necessary centrality to our argument: not least in so far as in the context of *perestroika* and *glasnost* the very concept of "Europe" now becomes geographically less distinct. If Europe no longer has a de facto boundary at the "Iron Curtain," where does it end? What is the status of "Mitteleuropa" or of "Eastern Europe"? And if this boundary has fallen, what is to replace it? As argued below, it would seem that, implicitly, religion may be becoming the new criterion—or rather, that what is implicit in much recent debate is, in fact, a rather ancient definition of Europe—as what used to be referred to as "Christendom," to which Islam supplies the boundary.

As argued in an earlier paper,[76] we are committed to a perspective in which identities are understood to be necessarily constructed as relational, through processes of boundary-drawing and exclusion, where the "I" or "we" can only be defined in relation to the Other, from whom it is distinguished. Given this premise, one part of our concern is with tracing the processes through which these boundaries have been drawn and thus with the various others (Americans, Soviets, Muslims, Blacks) against whom Europe has been, and is being defined.

"Mitteleuropa" has recently asserted itself as the true repository for European civilization: "they are desperately trying to restore the past, the past of culture, the past of the modern era. It is only in that period, only in a world that maintains a cultural dimension, that Central Europe can still defend its identity, still be seen for what it is."[77] The drama of Central European identity, with its "long meditations on the possible end of European humanity," evokes a fundamental insecurity:

> Thus it was in this region of small nations who have "not yet perished" that Europe's vulnerability, all of Europe's vulnerability, was more clearly visible before anywhere else. Actually, in our modern world where power has a tendency to become more and more concentrated in the hands of a few big countries, *all* European nations run the risk of becoming small nations and of sharing their fate. In this sense the destiny of Central Europe anticipates the destiny of Europe in general, and its culture assumes an enormous relevance.[78]

The same vulnerability is apparent in the responses of the European nations to the great America (Satan) of anti-culture. Here, too, there is a fight against "the subtle, relentless pressure of time, which is leaving the era of culture in its wake."[79] America, the future, is counterposed to the values and traditions by which Europeans have understood themselves and identified themselves as European. Here, too, European identity must come to terms with the sense of threat and loss.

The real issues concern European identity in a changing world, and "America" can be a vehicle for defensively containing, rather than resolving, these issues. Change and disruption are projected onto an imaginary America[80] and, in the process, tradition and conservative ideals of European and national identity are reinforced. This strategy is akin to what is described by psychoanalysts as projective identification. An aspect of European identity is split off and projected outwards. This can take the form of a "benign defence which simply wishes to postpone confrontation with some experience that cannot yet be tolerated," or it can take a more trenchant form that "aims really to *disavow* identification, and perhaps would be better called projective *dis*identification."[81] The consequence is that the crisis of European culture is never directly confronted. And "America," as the container of that "experience that cannot be tolerated," assumes a fantasy dimension as that which always threatens to "contaminate" or overwhelm European cultural integrity.

THE LOUDEST SILENCE: QUESTIONS OF RACE AND RELIGION

A number of useful parallels can be drawn between the debates surrounding Heimat and the filmic representation of "Vietnam" in the USA. Here again we see the pertinence of Patrick Wright's[82] argument that the representation of the past is very much a question of active processes in the present—as the Vietnam war continues to be waged symbolically on television, in bookshops and at a cinema near you.[83] The historical Vietnam war, a specific set of conflictual events, policies and conditions, has been transformed into a symbolic "Vietnam" just as with the German (and thus the European) past: *Holocaust/Heimat*. In the case both of *Heimat* and of the Vietnam films we have the questions not only of loss and of mourning but, more problematically, the blockage created by questions of guilt and how *that* is to be represented. In both cases we also have the question of the (im)possibility of attempts to construct a progressive reappropriation of patriotic sentiment and the further issue of the potential usurpation of the role of victim by the perpetrators of the initial violence.[84] And then, of course, we have the question of the silences in these discourses—on the one hand, the marginalization of the Holocaust itself in *Heimat's* sixteen hours, on the other, the almost total absence of anything other than caricature representations of the Vietnamese themselves in Hollywood's "Vietnam" films.[85]

The subtext of both *Heimat* and the "Vietnam" films is, of course, the question of race and racism: it is precisely in relation to this question that the metaphor of "home" and "homeland" (*for whom*? cf. Lanzmann, quoted earlier) acquires such power. The question of race is of course central to the definition of "Europe" and "European culture."[86] Our primary concern here is with a differently focused question—that is the centrality of Christianity in the definition of European culture, as the Iron Curtain crumbles and the boundary of Europe shifts from the east to the south. If Germany, the past (somehow) reconciled, is to be united, and Europe is no longer to be divided as it has been since the end of World War II, then the question arises, inescapably, as to where "Europe" ends and against what "Other" European culture is to be defined, if not against Communism.

In this context the debates generated by Turkey's application to join the EEC offer a number of interesting insights into the issues at stake. At one level, the issue is simple. On the one hand Turkey, on account of its membership of NATO, its possession of a small but important triangle of land on the European side of the Bosphorus, and the modern secular framework of institutions bequeathed by Kemal Atatürk has a strong *prima facie* case for membership of the EEC. On the other hand, there is a complex set of questions concerning trade barriers, the potential impact of cheap Turkish agricultural (and increasingly, electrical) products on existing EEC countries, and, of course, the continuing question of Turkey's record on human rights.

However, we would want to suggest that, at base, something far more fundamental is at stake: and that is the question of whether in contemporary debates "Europe" is being defined as coextensive with what used to be called Christendom. Or, to put it the other way round, can an Islamic (albeit a partially secularized) state be fully accepted as part of Europe, given that historically (through the Crusades, and the Moorish and Ottoman empires' invasions of Southern Europe) "The Turk" and "The Moor" have always provided key figures of difference, or "threat" (and indeed, dread) *against* which "Europe" has defined itself? Edward Mortimer reminds us that today's EEC was founded by Christian bureaucrats (indeed, Catholics) across Europe; historically it was the fact that they professed Christianity and saw themselves as threatened by "the Turk" that first gave European nations a sense of common purpose and identity.

The point is that if "Europe" as a concept really is another word for "Christendom," then the maintenance of the distinction between it and the world of Islam (or in Muslim terms, the continuing division of the world in to Dar-el-Islam—the realm of the true faith—and Dar-el-Harb—the realm of war) is central to its identity, and the Sword of Islam will remain Europe's (not so) private nightmare.

Certainly, in recent years there has been a marked increase in the anxiety and suspicion with which many Europeans view the Islamic world. Across Europe we can see an emerging pattern of racial hostility towards Islamic peoples— dramatized in complex ways by the Rushdie affair in Britain, by violence and hostility to Turkish immigrant workers in Germany,[87] and to North African immigrants in France and in Italy. One could argue that the oil crisis of the 1970s, images of PLO terrorists and Lebanese hostage-takers and the growth of Islamic fundamentalism throughout the Middle East have been aggregated in the popular media to produce a greater sense of an "Islamic threat" to Europe than at any time since the seventeenth century. The French mass circulation news magazine *Le Point* recently headlined a story about Islamic fundamentalism in Algeria— "The Holy War at our Gates"—a story full of references to the Muslim "danger" and its "threat" to French national identity.[88] Jean-Marie le Pen, the French far-right National Front leader, claims Joan of Arc as his inspiration. Sefyi Tashan, director of the Turkish Foreign Policy Institute in Ankara, puts it quite simply: "In Europe, many people see us as a new version of the Ottoman empire, attacking this time in the form of guest workers and terrorists."[89]

Certainly it can be argued that Islam (in the shape of the Muslim populations of North Africa, Turkey and the Indian subcontinent) is now the primary form in which the Third World presents itself to Europe and that the North–South divide, in the European context, has been largely inscribed onto a pre-existing Christian– Muslim division. However, there is more to it than that, in so far as the relation between these two terms, or rather, the significance of this relation, has itself been shifted by the current transformation of East–West relations.

As Mortimer argues,[90] the deep-seated anxieties about "European identity" (and the centrality of Christianity to that definition) were, for a long period driven underground by the Cold War, during which Stalin's empire provided Europe with a de facto eastern frontier: whatever was not "communist" was, by contra-distinction "western" (i.e. European). To this extent, as a member of NATO (and a strategically crucial one, at that) the "European" credentials of Turkey were therefore long accepted, without much question. Certainly many Turks now re-gard their membership of NATO as "proof" of their "western" status. But now, suddenly, it seems the Iron Curtain has gone (or is crumbling) and Eastern Europe is reasserting its identity, in large part, as a Christian one—which means that Europe has now to re-establish its boundaries anew (and especially its eastern one). In this process of redefinition, it is of course the question of who is to be excluded (and in contra-distinction to whom or what "European" identity is to be defined) which moves to the centre of the contemporary historical stage.

There is it seems, after all, no place like home—or rather, perhaps, no place in that home for some who wish to dwell there. Our common European home remains to be built: but the stories we tell ourselves about our common (and uncommon) past are already shaping our understanding of how it should be con-structed, how many floors it should have (a basement for the servants?), which way it should face (what price a south-facing garden?) and who should have the keys to the door.

Our discussion has, at various points, focused on Germany because of its particular strategic and symbolic importance in the contemporary transformation of Europe. Germany, once again the question mark of Europe. Germany has been divided against itself, and this divide has also marked the separation of the eastern and western halves of Europe. Now the dividing wall has been deconstructed: what was protectively solid has apparently melted into air. "Germany is stretching its limbs," wrote Jens Reich shortly before the 9 November:

> The Federal Republic is shedding its geopolitical hair-shirt like a dried skin. The GDR is bursting its ideological corset, supposedly all that can give its existence legitimacy. Reunification or confederation, annexation or single cultural nation?— it is all equally alarming. The neighbours are on the qui vive and look for ways to keep the two components of the poison in their separate vessels. The pressure on the valves grows.[91]

Now the two components have come into direct contact. What compound mixture is being distilled in the process? If Germany had until recently been seen as a kind of "post-national" society, questions of national culture and identity are once again on the political agenda. What does it mean to be German today, after forty years of division? What is "German" now? The border ran right through German identity and now it has been dissolved and Germany re-encoun-ters itself, across space and also across time. Ralf Dahrendorf describes a kind of historical "doppelgänger" effect; West Germans must now see their past, their history, reflected back at them; and East Germans have the dislocating and dis-orientating experience of confronting their future.[92] Who now are "we the peo-ple"?

The tragedy will be if reunification provokes a defensive and exclusivist form of nationalism. The defeat will be if German identity is refounded in terms of a closed community, with boundaries drawn between those who belong and those who do not. "Germany is one" and "we are one people" were the slogans chanted outside the opera house in Karl Marx Square. One people. One homeland. For Edgar Morin, nationalist sentiments are akin to infantile attachments to the family. The nation, he argues, is both mother and father: "It is maternal-feminine as the motherland (mère patrie) that its sons should cherish and protect. It is paternal and virile as the just and commanding authority that calls them to arms and to duty." This complex allegiance, this "matri-patriotism," expresses itself, Morin argues, in a strong sense of rootedness, of belonging to a home and a homeland ("un sentiment très fort de la patrie-foyer (*Heimat, home*), toit, maison").[93] One people, one family, one homeland: belonging together, with common origins. "We the people" defined against the "others" who do not belong, and have different origins.

The question of a German home, as we have argued at length, has been a central motif in recent cultural debates in the Federal Republic. At the heart of the New German Cinema the problem of identity and the quest for origins have centred on the theme of the family, the damaged relation to the (absent) father, and the fixation on the mother figure.[94] For many, this has been about trying to find a way home. It has been about becoming reconciled to German culture and identity. The romantic utopia of Heimat, with all its connotations of remembrance and longing has been about reconnecting with a national heritage and history. For others, however, the issue is far more complex. National integrity is a vain ideal; one people, a false utopia. The cinema of Wim Wenders, particularly, has been about the state of homelessness that seems to be a necessary expression of the condition of modernity. Wenders evokes "a world of surfaces increasingly deprived of memory or self-reflection, where fantasy and reality have become so confused and the notion of self-identity so diluted that it no longer seems possible to tell one's story."[95] In his films there is no easy recourse to the security of origins, rootedness and authenticity. As Thomas Elsaesser has argued, Wenders is concerned with journeys, with crossing borders, with exile, with the relation between inside and outside. What he seeks to explore, particularly through his relationship to "America," are the realities of difference, otherness and estrangement. For Wenders, there is no utopia of home and homeland:

> The idea is that, not being at home [my heroes] are nevertheless at home with themselves. In other words, not being at home means being more at home than anywhere else .... Maybe the idea of being more oneself when one's away is a very personal idea .... Identity means not having to have a home. Awareness, for me, has something to do with not being at home. Awareness of anything.[96]

Being away, not being at home, is what Wenders aspires to. Not being at home is, of course, the permanent destiny of so many people and peoples ("involuntary cosmopolitans") in the modern world. It is the condition of those millions of *Ausländer* or *Gastarbeiter* who live precarious and unsettled lives in the German homeland itself. As Ruth Mandel emphasizes, "Germany has a long history of confronting a salient other. The incorporation of 'others' into the German *Volks-*

gemeinschaft has long been troublesome, as it has challenged the underpinnings of German notions of identity'': *Überfremdung* (over-foreignization) has been perceived as a threat to national integrity and culture.[97] Now it is the 1.5 million Turks living in Germany who have become the salient and disturbing "other." "We the people" are now defined, in Germany, against the Islamic "other." The question is whether Germany can come to terms with this "Islam within," or whether the new nation will be imagined on the basis of an exclusive and excluding racism. The question is whether Germany can understand that it is not one, can never be one, because it is multiple, because it contains many peoples, Germans of different ethnicities.

What must be seen is that, if Germany is a home for some, then it is at the same time exile for others. What must be understood is the relation between Heimat and Fremde. If Heimat is about security and belonging, Fremde evokes feelings of isolation and alienation. Fremde is a "synonym for separation, hardship, privation, homesickness, and the loss of a sense of belonging."[98] Germany—the real, rather than the imaginary, Germany—is at once Heimat and Fremde. Is it possible to come to terms with this relational truth, rather than taking refuge in the comforting absolute of Heimat? Is it possible to live with this complexity and ambivalence? In his poem "Doppelmann," Zafer Senocak writes of his Germany:

> I carry two worlds within me
> but neither one whole
> they're constantly bleeding
> the border runs
> right through my tongue.[99]

It is this experience that is fundamental to questions of German—and also European—culture and identity today. It is out of this tension—between homelessness and home—that we might begin to construct more meaningful, more complex, identities. As Zafer Senocak writes: "The split can give rise to a double identity. This identity lives on the tension. One's feet learn to walk on both banks of the river at the same time."[100]

Our discussion has been about images of home and homeland, and it has arrived at the reality of homelessness. If it has focused particularly on the idea of a German home, it has done so to illuminate the powerful appeal of Heimat throughout a changing Europe. Whether it is in terms of a national home, a regional home, or a common European home, the motivating force is a felt need for a rooted, bounded, whole and authentic identity. And yet Heimat is a mirage, a delusion. As Edgar Reitz recognizes, "Heimat is such that if one would go closer and closer to it, one would discover that at the moment of arrival it is gone, it has dissolved into nothingness."[101] It is a dangerous delusion. Heimat is rooted in that intolerance of difference, that fear of the "other," which is at the heart of racism and xenophobia.[102]

The crucial issue that now confronts European culture, we would argue, is whether it can be open to the condition and experience of homelessness. The questions posed by Wim Wenders are at the heart of the matter. Can we imagine an identity, an awareness, grounded in the experience of not having a home, or of not having to have a home? Can we see home as a necessarily provisional, always relative, truth? Writing of modern Irish culture and identity, Richard Kearney describes its multiple complexities and paradoxes:

> It is striking how many modern Irish authors have spoken of being in transit between two worlds, divided between opposing allegiances. They often write as *émigrés* of the imagination, conveying the feeling of being both part and not part of their culture, of being estranged from the very traditions to which they belong, of being in exile even while at home.[103]

It is this experience of transit that is fundamental to the culture. "The contemporary sense of 'homelessness,' " Kearney argues, "which revivalism sought to remedy by the reinstatement of a lost homeland, becomes for modernism the irrevocable condition not only of Irish culture but of world culture."[104]

There can be no recovery of an authentic cultural homeland. In a world that is increasingly characterized by exile, migration and Diaspora, with all the consequences of unsettling and hybridization, there can be no place for such absolutism of the pure and authentic.[105] In this world, there is no longer any place like Heimat. More significant, for European cultures and identities now, is the experience of displacement and transition. "Sometimes we feel that we straddle two cultures," writes Salman Rushdie of his own experience, "at other times we fall between two stools."[106] What is most important is to live and work with this disjuncture, what Paul Willemen calls "this in-between position."[107] Identity must live out of this tension. Our feet must learn to walk on both banks of the river at the same time.

NOTES

1. Peter L. Berger, Brigitte Berger and Hansfried Kellner, *The Homeless Mind: Modernisation and Consciousness* (Harmondsworth: Penguin 1974), 77.

2. Marshall Berman, *All that Is Solid Melts into Air: The Experience of Modernity* (London: Verso 1983), 15, 345.

3. Anthony Giddens, *The Consequences of Modernity* (Cambridge: Polity 1990), 92.

4. Ibid., 108.

5. Peter Emberley, "Places and stories: the challenge of technology," *Social Research*, 56, 3 (Autumn 1989), 755–6.

6. Kevin Robins, "Global Times," *Marxism Today* (December 1989).

7. Eric R. Wolf, *Europe and the People Without History* (Berkeley: University of California Press 1982), 387.

8. Pierre Nora, "Between memory and history: *Les lieux de memoire*" *Representations*, no. 26 (Spring 1989), 7.

9. Michael Rustin, "Place and time in socialist theory," *Radical Philosophy* no. 47 (Autumn 1987), 33–4.

10. Mikhail Gorbachev, *Perestroika: New Thinking for Our Country and the World* (London: Collins 1987), 195.

11. Susan Sontag, "L'idée d'Europe (une élégie de plus)," *Les Temps Modernes*, no. 510 (January 1989), 80.

12. Neal Ascherson, "Europe 2000," *Marxism Today* (January 1990), 17.

13. See Ed Vulliamy, "Carnival 'joke' turns out to be a nation's tragedy," *Guardian* (13 April 1990).

14. For example, Enoch Powell, "My view of a Common European Home," *New European*, 2, 4 (Winter 1989/90); Ferry Hoogendijk, "There is no 'European House,' " *European Affairs*, 4, 1 (Spring 1990).

15. Ian Davidson, "Old European ghosts return to haunt Germany," *Financial Times* (22 March 1990). See also, Richard Evans, "Promised Land?," *Marxism Today* (April 1990).

16. Neal Ascherson, "Little nations hang out their flags," *Observer* (1 October 1989).

17. John Berger, "Keeping a rendezvous," *Guardian* (22 March 1990).

18. Franz A. Birgel, "You can go home again: an interview with Edgar Reitz," *Film Quarterly* (Summer 1986), 5.

19. Berman, op. cit., 333.

20. See Eric Hobsbawm, *Nations and Nationalism since 1780* (Cambridge: Cambridge University Press 1990), 168.

21. Salman Rushdie, "In good faith," *Independent on Sunday* (4 February 1990).

22. See D. Morley and K. Robins, "Spaces of Identity," *Screen* vol. 30.4 (Autumn 1989); D. Morley and K. Robins, "Non-tariff barriers" in Gareth Locksley (ed.) *The Single European Market* (London: Belhaven Press 1990).

23. Sean Cubitt, "Over the borderlines," *Screen* vol. 30.4 (Autumn 1989), 2.

24. Andrew Higson, "The concept of national cinema," *Screen* vol. 30.4 (Autumn 1989), 37.

25. Steve Neale, "Art cinema as institution," *Screen* vol. 22.1 (Spring 1981), 11.

26. Higson, op. cit., 43.

27. Benedict Anderson, quoted in Higson, op. cit., 44.

28. Stephen Heath, quoted in Higson, op. cit., 44.

29. Higson, op. cit., 44.

30. Patrick Wright, *On Living in an Old Country* (London: Verso 1985), 24.

31. Wright, op. cit., 24.

32. In his review "The Age of Dead Statues" (*New Society*, 6 December 1985) of David Lowenthal's *The Past is a Foreign Country* (Cambridge University Press 1985) Patrick Wright argues that, far from being merely archival, the past exists as an accomplished social and cultural presence—a *modern* phenomenon which owes its shape and meaning largely to the present society which saves, evokes and retrieves it. Memory, of course, is the guarantor of identity, and ideas (indeed celebrations) of our past (vide the present debate over the content of the "A" level history syllabus) have played a vital role in the last few years of British politics.

33. See, for example, "History/Production/Memory" *Edinburgh TV Festival Magazine* no. 2, 1977.

34. See Richard Gott, "The Green March" (*Guardian* 17 March 1989) for a review of Anna Bramwell's *Ecology in the Twentieth Century* (New Haven, Conn.: Yale University Press 1989) which identifies the extent to which, in Gott's words "In Germany the Greens are clearly a German nationalist movement. They fill the vacuum inevitably left blank since 1945."

35. Adolf Muschg, quoted in Martin Chalmers, "Heimat: Approaches to a Word and a Film," *Framework*, no. 26–7 (1984), 91.

36. Raphael Samuels, "Exciting to be English" in R. Samuels (ed.), *Patriotism: The Making and Unmaking of British National Identity* (London: Routledge 1989).

37. Jean Baudrillard, quoted in Martin Chalmers, op. cit., 91.

38. Reitz, quoted in Anton Kaes, *From Hitler to Heimat* (Massachusetts and London: Harvard University Press 1989), 163.

39. Kaes, op. cit., 195.

40. Ibid., 196.

41. Anthony Smith, "In wartime the movie is the message" (*Sunday Times* 7 February 1988), review of Clayton R. Koppes and Gregory Black, *Hollywood Goes to War* (London: I. B. Tauris, 1988).

42. Smith, op. cit.

43. Quoted in Kaes, op. cit., 183.

44. Thomas Elsaesser, "National Cinema and International Television: the death of New German Cinema," in Cynthia Schneider and Brian Wallis (eds), *Global Television* (New York: Wedge Press 1988) 133.

45. Quoted in Ian Buruma, "From Hirohito to Heimat," *New York Review of Books,* 26 October 1989, 40.

46. Quoted in Kaes, op. cit., 184.

47. Miriam Hansen, "Dossier on Heimat," *New German Critique* no. 36 (Fall 1985), 9.

48. Thomas Y. Levin, "Nationalities of Language," *New German Critique* no. 36 (Fall 1985), 111.

49. Theodor Adorno, "On the Question: 'What is German?,' " *New German Critique* no. 36 (Fall 1985), 117.

50. Adorno, op. cit., 121.

51. Ibid., 121.

52. Wim Wenders, "The American Dream" in his *Emotion Pictures* (London: Faber, 1989), 117–18.

53. Buruma, op. cit., 43.

54. Wenders, op. cit., 144.

55. Quoted in Hansen, op. cit., 10.

56. Kaes, op. cit., 190.

57. Michael Geisler, "*Heimat* and the German Left," *New German Critique* no. 36 (Fall 1985), 63.

58. Duncan Webster, "Coca-Colonization and National Cultures," *Over here* vol. 9, no. 2 (Winter 1989), 65.

59. Geisler, op. cit., 65.

60. Webster, op. cit., 65.

61. Webster, op. cit., 67.

62. Gabrielle Kreutzner, "On doing Cultural Studies in Western Germany," *Cultural Studies* vol. 3, no. 2 (May 1989).

63. Kreutzner, op. cit., 245.

64. Quoted in Webster, op. cit., 69.

65. Ibid., 67.

66. Levin, op. cit., 115.

67. Ibid., 118–19. Thus Adorno's chilling aphorism: "*Fremdwörter* are the Jews of language."

68. Kaes, op. cit., 166. The point is made most forcibly by Claude Lanzmann, in his discussion of the history of European anti-semitism, as documented in his film *Shoah*. As

Lanzmann puts it "Initially it was 'you cannot live among us as Jews'; then it was 'you cannot live among us'; then it was 'you cannot live'."

69. Reitz, quoted in Don Ranvaud, "Edgar Reitz at Venice," *Sight and Sound* vol. 54.2 (Spring 1985).

70. Reitz, quoted in *City Limits*, no. 176 (15 February 1985), 12.

71. Chalmers, op. cit., 93.

72. Cf. Hansen, op. cit.

73. Reitz, quoted in *City Limits*, no. 176 (15 February 1985).

74. Cf. Geisler, op. cit.

75. Hans Magnus Enzensberger, quoted in Geisler, op. cit., 32.

76. Morley and Robins, 1989, op. cit.

77. Milan Kundera, "A kidnapped West—or—Culture bows Out," *Granta* no. 11, 1984, 119.

78. Kundera, op. cit., 109.

79. Ibid., 118.

80. See Duncan Webster, *Looka Yonder: The Imaginary America of Populist Culture* (London: Comedia 1988).

81. J. Grotstein, *Splitting and Projective Identification* (New York: Jason Aronson 1981).

82. Wright, 1985, op. cit.

83. Webster, 1990, op. cit.

84. See Webster, 1990, op. cit., on Richard Nixon's view of the USA as a "pitiful, helpless giant" in South East Asia. See also Webster's comments on Stallone's representation of that "beefcake vulnerability" in his film roles; cf. also some of the debates in Germany about the post-war generation as "victims" of the Nazi past.

85. Cf. conversely, the telling detail in Michael Herr's *Dispatches*, of a map of the Western United States with the shape of Vietnam reversed and fitted over California. It is also, finally, a question of the difficulty of "bringing it all back home" (the experience of the returning "Vets," their sense of rejection "at home," the impossibility of their reassimilation) and of the difficulty of representing any post-traumatic "Heimat." On this see Walter Benjamin (quoted in Kaes, op. cit., 257): "Didn't we notice at the end of the . . . (first world) . . . war that people came back from the front mute? Not richer, but poorer in their ability to communicate their experience." Similarly, see Bobbie Ann Mason's *In Country*, where the "Vet" explains to his niece, desperate to understand "what happened"—"You can't learn from the past. The main thing you learn from history is that you can't learn from history. That's what history is."

86. See, *inter alia*, Yasmin Alibhai, "Community whitewash," *Guardian* (23 January 1989); Paul Gilroy, *There Ain't No Black in the Union Jack* (London: Hutchinson 1987); Edward Said, *Orientalism* (Harmondsworth: Penguin 1985) and "Identity, Negation and Violence," *New Left Review* no. 171, 1988; S. Sassen-Koob, "Issues of core and periphery" in J. Henderson and M. Castells (eds), *Global Restructuring and Territorial Development* (London: Sage 1987); A. Sivanandan, "The new racism," *New Statesman and Society* (4 November 1988); M. Walker, "A pigsty without frontiers," *Guardian* (15 November 1988).

87. See *New German Critique* no. 46 (Winter 1989), for a collection of articles addressing this issue.

88. R. W. Johnson, in *Independent on Sunday* (20 May 1990).

89. *Newsweek* (21 May 1990).

90. Edward Mortimer, "Is this our frontier?," *Financial Times* (3 April 1990).

91. Jens Reich, "Germany—a binary poison," *New Left Review*, no. 179 (January–February 1990), 122.

92. Ralf Dahrendorf, "Europe's vale of tears," *Marxism Today* (May 1990), 23.

93. Edgar Morin, "Formation et composantes du sentiment national," *Cosmopolitiques*, no. 16 (May 1990), 30.

94. See Thomas Elsaesser, *New German Cinema: A History* (London: British Film Institute/Macmillan 1989), ch. 8.

95. Richard Kearney, *The Wake of Imagination* (London: Hutchinson 1988), 324.

96. Wim Wenders, quoted in Thomas Elsaesser, "Germany's Imaginery America: Wim Wenders and Peter Handke," in Susan Hayward (ed.), *European Cinema* (Modern Languages Department, Aston University 1985), 48.

97. Ruth Mandel, "Turkish headscarves and the 'foreigner problem': constructing difference through emblems of identity," *New German Critique*, no. 46 (Winter 1989), 37.

98. Heidrun Suhr, "*Ausländerliteratur*: minority literature in the Federal Republic of Germany," *New German Critique*, no. 46 (Winter 1989), 72.

99. Quoted in ibid., 102.

100. Ibid., 103.

101. Birgel, op. cit., 5.

102. See Stephen Frosh, "Psychoanalysis and racism," in Barry Richards (ed.), *Crises of the Self* (London: Free Association Books 1989).

103. Richard Kearney, *Transitions: Narratives in Modern Irish Culture* (Dublin: Wolfhound Press 1988), 14.

104. Ibid.

105. See Stuart Hall, "New ethnicities," in *Black Film, British Cinema* (London: Institute of Contemporary Arts 1988); Paul Gilroy, *There Ain't No Black in the Union Jack* (London: Hutchinson 1987), ch. 5.

106. Salman Rushdie, "Imaginary homelands," *London Review of Books* (7–20 October 1982), 19.

107. Paul Willeman, "The third cinema question: notes and reflections," in Jim Pines and Paul Willemen (eds), *Questions of Third Cinema* (London: British Film Institute 1989), 28.

Jeffrey M. Peck

Jeffrey Peck (who teaches German literature at Georgetown University) takes up the questions explored by Morley and Robins, bringing them more pointedly to bear on the current discourse around "foreigners" in Germany since unification. The resurgence of Germans' belief in the strength and legitimacy of their own nationhood, after almost half a century of doubt, guilt, and disablement (as the advocates of Germany's new-found self-assertiveness see it) cast by the shadow of Nazism, has translated into a nationalism which has caught many of its critics, inside and outside Germany, by surprise. Germany's growing preponderance in Europe—both within the European Union and in relation to Eastern Europe—was already the source of much discussion in the 1980s. But the stability of West Germany's political institutions and its secure location in the democratic community of the West counteracted potential anxieties provoked by Germany's large population and cultural dominance, and especially by the nightmare of Germany's imperialist and Nazi pasts, so that the Federal Republic's growing economic power seemed more a force for stability in Europe than a cause for far-reaching concern. The combination of economic strength and constitutional liberalism, reinforced by the democratic upsurge of the late 1960s and early 1970s, and by a continuing public vigilance around issues of coming to terms with the past and acceptance of responsibility for Nazism, encouraged benign readings of a "constitutional patriotism," a form of nationalism oriented toward toleration, pluralism, and peaceful coexistence with other nationalities, rather than the aggressive hostility to difference associated with the Third Reich and earlier nationalisms in German history.

Events in Germany since unification, and the main lines of public discussion in response, have badly damaged the confidence of this judgment. The rise of rhetorical and physical violence against "foreigners" has severely strained the democratic credibility of Germany's political culture. In the ensuing debate, the numerical presence of international refugees thanks to West Germany's exceptionally liberal law of asylum (since changed) and the longer-standing problem of the host society's attitude to its immigrant workers (*Gastarbeiter*) became the immediate focus of attention. But the definition of German citizenship by "blood" as opposed to residence provides the underlying context of this crisis, for at a time when German public opinion has been agitated against the unwanted presence of "foreigners," the German constitution has positively welcomed the arrival of vast numbers of "ethnic Germans" from the former Soviet Union, Poland, Romania, and elsewhere, most of whom have little realistic relation to "Germanness" in its instituted postwar forms, beyond the bloodlines allowed by the constitution, sometimes verified by completely dubious Nazi documentation. This recentering of German identity around notions of blood, history, and homeland, by which the faculty of democratic citizenship is ideologically displaced from the dominant languages of national belonging, is crudely divisive, for the gathering-in of "Germans" on the basis of heredity means the keeping-out of others, namely, dark-skinned people from Turkey, the Mediterranean, South Asia, and Africa, as well as the inevitable Sinti and Roma. Moreover, in this situation the connotations of the rhetoric of home are not only exclusionary and xenophobic, Peck argues, but also evoke the most disturbing of continuities with the Third Reich. The late twentieth-century discourse of German nationalism has become reinscribed with a racism, which is no less disturbing for its convergencies with similar racisms in Britain and France, where the common referent is increasingly the dangerous and sinister Islamic Other.

Rac(e)ing the Nation: Is There A German "Home"?

The fall of the Wall (November 1989) and subsequent German unification that subsumed the German Democratic Republic eleven months later (October 1990) occurred at breakneck speed. Another year passed and attacks on foreigners, especially those from Southern Europe, Turkey, the Middle East, Africa, the Subcontinent, and Vietnam rose dramatically, notably in the eastern regions of the new Germany. Racism and xenophobia (Ausländerfeindlichkeit) accompanied and in some cases was encouraged by the nationalistic fervour of some Germans for their new-found unity and national identity. The latter was reinforced by Germany's already established economic power, larger population, capacity for growth, and the strength of its image.

While I do not want to overdraw the connection between the haste with which Germany "healed" its divisions and the outbreak of divisive racial and ethnic tensions, it is striking that a unification that moved so quickly to include all Germans, at least in a reshaped political structure, left so many "others" out. While some of these peoples have found a home, even a new German "*Heimat*" (homeland), others are homeless. The united Germany has not made room in its house for the black, brown, and yellow people (7.2 per cent of the population[1]) who live there. Former Soviet President Gorbachev's call for a "common European home" went unheeded not only in Germany, but, as recent events have shown, in his own disintegrating union.

Within a few weeks of the reunited Germany's first anniversary, the country was to re-experience events that it had not known since the Nazis' systematic attack on Jews began in 1938. The impact of race on the definition of who is foreign and who is German emerged again as a central issue in German life. Hoyerswerda, a small town in Saxony (in the former GDR), became the first city to announce it would make itself "*ausländerfrei*" (free of foreigners). Fifty years before, Hitler had convinced the Germans that the Jews, who thought themselves integrated into the German population, should be considered "foreigners," aliens who would destroy the "purity" of German blood, the German race and the German nation. When Hitler called all Germans "*Heim [home] ins Reich,*" he

Jeffrey M. Peck, "Rac(e)ing the Nation: Is There a German "Home"?," *New Formations*, 17 (Summer 1992), pp. 75–84.

was establishing within the bounds of an imperial(istic) nation state a community of people (*Volksgemeinschaft*) based on a racial identity. Race was elided with nation and linked it to a Romantic notion of *Heimat*: a quasi-mythical realm called the Thousand Year Reich, but realized for only a brief twelve years in a real political entity—a Germany whose theories of racial purity and homogeneity provided the basis for its practices of domination of other peoples in Europe.

With too many parallels to those terrible years, many people, including the Germans themselves, wondered what was to come. Fears of a dominant and dominating Germany remain, even two years after the *Wende* (the change), as Germany assumes *de facto* leadership in the developing European Community and challenges the authority of its former patrons.[2] Memories of the Nazi past revive as comparisons are drawn between its practice and this recent wave of attacks on foreigners, asylum seekers, and other immigrants by self-styled neo-Nazi groups and proto-fascist skin-heads.

While the parallels between Nazi racism against the Jews and other "foreign" peoples have been correctly acknowledged, it is important to recognize that this new version of racism is not exactly the same. Skin colour figures much more prominently by marking both difference and sameness, and targeting certain populations for attack. Unlike in the 1930s, for example, no symbiosis to speak of exists between the Germans and the foreigner populations as there was thought to be between the Germans and the Jews.

Therefore, I want to examine the homologous, yet opposing notions of German and *Ausländer* (foreigner) and the hierarchies in the latter.[3] In fact, the latter term itself collapses distinctions among the many kinds of non-Germans and distracts attention from the racial underpinnings of xenophobia, while simultaneously reifying the notion of the German. This binary opposition continues to be propagated in a variety of cultural discourses such as official taxonomies and public representations (like political and commercial advertisements) that fix as normative, and naturalize, negative and repressive roles, and set standards for behaviour that are always one-sided and asymmetrical.

If one believes that culture is a process, always emergent and contested, then only through a constantly shifting cultural dialogic can new meanings emanating from words and images about "being German" and "being foreign" be generated and then deployed. Even the well meant efforts of liberals and leftists to ameliorate the situation seems to falter at this level where culture and discursive analysis coincide, since by continuing to use the term *Ausländer*, overdetermined by conservative politicians, they perpetuate the reification of an opposition that needs to be deconstructed from within, no matter how severely it has been questioned from without.

Let us start with the literal etymology of the word *Ausländer* and its relation to home(land), the German *Heimat*. *Aus-länd* means very simply from outside the country and is associated with the related German word *fremd* meaning strange. Whoever comes from outside of the country is "strange": a foreigner.

But in Germany, unlike other European countries, the classification of who is German and who is foreign is more complicated because of laws of consanguinity for citizenship and the continued political, historical, and territorial impact of the collapse of the Nazi regime. The division and reunification of Germany, the Germans' responsibility towards foreigners living among them (as in the 1930s), and the status of those "Germans"[4] displaced by the war in Eastern regions still impinge on whether those are fortunate to be designated as "Germans" or those who can receive political asylum (4.4 per cent in 1990)[5] can at least try to make Germany their home. Most foreigners in Germany who are not naturalized or able to be granted political asylum live in a very insecure and tenuous state. There is, in short, a hierarchy on both sides of the racial and ethnic divide and it is the fulcrum around which immigration and asylum policy turns.

If *Heimat* is defined "by contrast to all that is foreign or distant,"[6], as two British cultural critics suggest, then those outsiders desiring Germany as a *Heimat* can never hope to achieve this status, whether they become citizens or not. This would imply that the entire debate around citizenship is misplaced, since such a notion of belonging in the political realm does not suffice at the subjective and emotional level where people "feel" as if they have trust and security in their new identity—in short, that they feel at home. According to Andrea Klimt, an anthropologist who has done fieldwork with Portuguese guestworkers:

> None of the migrants I knew, regardless of class, generation, or degree of "integration," considered the prospect of "becoming German" to be desirable, realistic, or even imaginable. They, along with most Germans, understand that "being German" does not rest on such mutable characteristics as legal status, political loyalty, or acquired knowledge. "Germanness" is not perceived to be an open or permeable category, and Portuguese migrants feel that neither the colour of their passport nor the degree of their cultural and linguistic fluency will ensure respect of acceptance.[7]

That the debate around asylum seekers and immigration is misdirected is reinforced by the racial issue which itself is ignored. Trapped in their own nationalistic discourses, both the German government and many progressives cannot see how they are reinforcing racial stereotypes. Even the well meaning attitudes expressed in the liberal newspaper *Die Zeit*—"Buy your fruit at a Turkish store (if you don't already do that)" or "the next time you are in the subway, sit next to an African,"[8]—cannot break down objectified notions of the foreign since they reinscribe paternalistic and patronizing attitudes of one group over the other. It is clear who sets the terms of the debate. Even the German magazine *Der Spiegel* has entered this discussion by criticizing what they term "bipolar thinking"[9] and by drawing attention to the exaggerated positive reaction of some Germans towards foreigners. Everyone has their pet foreigner, (their favourite "darkie," as the article puts it) through whom they can demonstrate goodwill and openness. Even in Germany, the "some of my best friends are foreigners" defence works to ward off suspicion of xenophobia.

This particular response to the attacks on foreigners illustrates the inflation of terminology on both sides of the political spectrum—*ausländerfreundlich* (friendly to foreigners) on the left, *ausländerfeindlich* (hostile to foreigners) on the right—which allows the left to take the moral high ground and the right to continue to objectify the foreigner as an Other. It is a response that also makes it impossible for foreigners to individualize an identity based on criteria of their own choice, to construct an identity that can accommodate both what they once were and are now supposed to be; an identity that is somewhere in-between. The spatial metaphor situates the discussion of the foreigner in "the locality of national culture [that] is neither unified nor unitary in relation to itself, nor . . . seen simply as 'other' in relation to what is outside or beyond it."[10] Homi Bhabha, extrapolating from Derrida's notion of "incomplete signification," emphasizes what he calls the "Janus-faced" nature of hybridity: "the turning of boundaries and limits into the *in-between* spaces through which the meanings of cultural and political authority are negotiated." These boundaries and limits that re-emerge constantly to define who belongs and who is excluded set the borders for a particular notion of home, one that cannot be singularly captured in this mythical term *Heimat*.

The English word home does not capture the overflow of meanings and values connoted in this peculiarly German concept. "There are no satisfactory English equivalents for '*Heimat*' or '*Fremde*,' " notes Heidrun Suhr. "Both terms imply far more than simply 'homeland' or 'a foreign place.' '*Heimat*' also connotes belonging and security, while '*Fremde*' can refer to isolation and alienation. This is not simply a problem of translation."[11] I would go so far as to say that as a word without equivalent, *Heimat belongs* to the Germans, to a specific past and tradition that are linked to common values, ideals, customs, and locations. To be able to participate in this *Heimat* requires an identification that is at least ethnic, if not racial. The immigration of the so-called "ethnic Germans," their acceptance not as foreigners, but (in official parlance) as "*Aussiedler*" (those literally "moving out," from the lands where they do not "belong" such as Poland, the Soviet Union, and Romania), their legitimacy based on racial notions of Germanness (German parents or grandparents) and the frequent, grotesque establishment of their identities by Nazi documents all constitute a complex system of establishing foreignness or Germanness in the German legal system. Even Barbara John, the Christian Democrat *Ausländerbeautagte* (person in charge of foreigners) in Berlin and a member of the government's Special Commission on Integration "argues that Germany needs to change its asylum practices, its immigration laws and its attitudes. She wants Germany to restrict the entry of ethnic Germans and to change its outmoded, some would argue racist, definition of nationality."[12]

The presence of these "Germans" next to the top of the scale of immigrants (not foreigners) foregrounds the inconsistencies in German laws around immigrants, asylum seekers, and refugees. Because of German blood lines, these people are "officially" German, although they and their families may not have lived in Germany for generations, and in some cases, can neither speak German nor know very much, if anything, about the country to which they are "returning."

Above these ethnic Germans are the officially sanctioned *Übersiedler* (refugees who "moved over" from the former GDR) and below these privileged immigrants are a whole series of "real" foreigners categorized hierarchically: guestworkers (*Gastarbeiter*), homeless foreigners (*heimatlose Ausländer*), contingent refugees (*Kontingentenfüchtling*), recognised asylum seekers (*Asylber-echtigte*), asylum seekers (*Asylbewerber*), Eastern block refugees (*Ostblockflüch-tling*), *de facto* refugees (*Defacto-Flüchtling*), illegals (*Illegale*).[13] The criteria on which these distinctions are founded are confusing and unsystematic, with "finely hierarchized privileges and murky borders that are characterized by coincidences and arbitrary actions."[14]

Conditioned by politics, contradictory and ambiguous terms govern the lives of foreigners and rule the chaos of legal decisions in Germany as to who can stay, who can work, and ultimately who may "become a German." However, an unofficial, though more forceful set of criteria also determines who finds a home in Germany. Thus I would propose a different classification system, also stratified, also moving hierarchically through the same groups of people: the criterion that I would like to add is "race" and differentiations by skin colour. I suggest the following classification:

1. The Germans: GDR citizens in the West and now all citizens of the former GDR. They look like West Germans racially and physically. They were welcomed in the years after the Wall, up until the collapse of the GDR, but are now disdained and resented, because of their financial drain. The resentment has spawned increasing awareness of distinctions of habitus, dress and language.

2. Almost Germans: Ethnic Germans. They resemble the Germans physically, i.e. they are Caucasians, with light skin and blond hair. They are generally welcomed but economic stress has strained their integration.

2a. The German-Jews: Clearly below the ethnic Germans, these "almost Germans" are similar in that they are indistinguishable from the Germans, except perhaps for their names. (The old Nazi "racial" designations of hooked nose, black stringy hair, weak chin, etc. was already unreliable in Nazi Germany—a fact that precipitated the wearing of the yellow star to mark them.)[15] Some German-Jews survived the war, and remained, and others returned from exile after the war. Most, of course, were killed and the majority of those who left or survived never returned. This is an anomalous category since *German*-Jews make up a very small percentage of Jews living in Germany today. The majority of Jews (85 per cent or more) are of other "nationalities" and would be categorized along with that national group.

3. "Noble foreigners":[16] This category was established by the sociologist Dieter Thränhardt and denotes West Europeans (British, French, Swedes etc.); I would add all Scandinavians and the Dutch, and selected North Americans. While they may be called "foreigners," they are not really *Ausländer*, since that word has a pejorative connotation and they are treated as equals by the German population. One must also mention here that the members of the European Community also have special legal privileges that Americans, for example, do not have—the right to work and remain in the country without registration.

4. Ausländer: Turks, guestworkers, and other Mediterraneans, *Südländer*

(people from the south), *Roma* and *Sinti* (Gypsies), Indians, Pakistanis, Tamils and Black Africans. They are the people with dark skins and hair; not white, although in almost all cases they are "Caucasians." They are considered greasy and dirty. Finer racial and ethnic distinctions are subsumed by colour.[17]

5. Asian Ausländer: These are simply Vietnamese from the former GDR.

These categories, which are not homologous with legal criteria, emphasize the discrepancy between public discourse and legal terminology and the lived, subjective experience of Germans. On the one hand, laws are made by politicians to classify, categorize and organize. Ultimately such statements can also neutralize people from over thirty countries into an undistinguishable and anonymous mass whose objectification reduces them to a manageable and unthreatening lot. On the other hand, the Germans experience these people according to how they look, the racial or ethnic group with which they identify, not their nationality or their asylum or immigration status.[18]

Based on a notion of foreignness founded in displacement, transience and literal movement, only those immigrants (*Übersiedler* and *Aussiedler*) who are not legally considered foreigners (*Ausländer*) can call Germany home. For as Morley and Robins state:

> It (*Heimat*) is drenched in the longing for wholeness, unity, integrity. It is about community centred on shared traditions and memories ... *Heimat* is a mystical bond rooted in a lost past, a past that has already disintegrated ... It is about conserving the "fundamentals" of culture and identity. And, as such, it is about sustaining cultural boundaries and boundedness. To belong in this way is to protect exclusive, and therefore, excluding, identities against those who are seen as aliens and "foreigners." The "other" is always and continuously a threat to the security and integrity of those who share a common home.[19]

The "coloured" markings of race and ethnicity make it impossible for those who look different or alien or strange to belong. To be acceptable, and even appealing, racial or ethnic differentiations may be upgraded by money, class, and status: foreignness is unthreatening when colour is whitewashed by social standing, equalizing differences between different racial or ethnic groups. The legal and racial hierarchies of foreignness I allude to above are erased when their "looks" are adjusted to fit commercial needs, when they are commodified in representations in the public sphere.

Let me offer only one such example (less well-known than the now infamous, "multicultural" Benetton clothing adverts): a popular advert by the cigarette manufacturer Peter Stuyvesant found in magazines and newspapers, as well as on billboards in Germany. The images of white, black and Asian faces smiling broadly at each other and at the spectator give the impression of racial harmony and ethnic equality. In these ads, the beautiful people tell us how wonderful the world could be if we could. As the ad states in English, "Come together, and learn to live as friends." Multiculturalism is palatable as long as "coloured" peoples normalize their habitats and lifestyle by smoking the right cigarette and smiling. In the internationalism of the marketplace their ethnic and racial markers, those signs that make them exotic, are reduced to a marketing ploy. The English language of the advert invokes (especially in Germany) America—the land of the "melting pot" and multiculturalism, the country that while representing the ideal heterogeneous society, likewise connotes ironically "all that is foreign or distant."[20] The implicit reference to America (and not the American who is accepted to Germany) the place "imagined" by many Germans, reminds us simultaneously that this kind of equality is appealing yet definitively American and not German. It may sell cigarettes, like the popular Marlboro ads set in an unspecified American Western frontier locale, but it cannot represent what multicultural life in Germany is all about. The slippage attracts, however, a particular class of smoker to a product and to a "multicultural" world that she or he finds desirable, one that is different from everyday life and the relationship of foreigners and Germans on the streets of Frankfurt, Berlin, or Hoyerswerda.[21]

While *Ausländer* of all categories are clearly visible and displaced in Germany (except perhaps for the international capital Bonn-Bad Godesberg with its diplomatic community of "high-class" foreigners), the kind of scenes in these ads do not reflect German life. These ads with their happy, smiling faces represent a multiracial, multiethnic and multicultural paradise that does not exist, certainly not in Germany. These imaginary scenarios do not represent the German's sense of *Heimat*, which the filmmaker Wim Wenders takes up when he talks about America:

> They have that in America: "Mobile Homes," "Mobile" is said with pride and means the opposite of "bogged down" . . . (or) "stuck." "Home" means "at home," "where you belong" . . . (whereas) what *makes* it a home in the German language is the fact that it is fixed somewhere.[22]

By addressing the issue of movement and place, Wenders reminds us again of the significance of the in-between position that Homi Bhabha emphasizes. He draws our attention to the fact that as long as the discursive and mutually exclusive positioning of *Ausländer* and German remains polarized and imbedded in stereotypes on both sides, it will not be possible to open up Germany as an *Einwanderungsland (land of immigration)* in everyday experience. In short, the notion of German must become more porous; it must be possible to be a German who is from Turkey, Sri Lanka or Nigeria. Black, brown and yellow Germans will have to be fully accepted, although not necessarily "assimilated" or "integrated" into the German body politic.

My reference to the body and the indelible boundaries with which human beings are marked by colour (signifying race or ethnic identification) reminds us that a new notion of home in Germany will have to undo these rigid boundaries, be mixed and hybrid, heterogeneous and fluid, not fixed, static, and normative. It will have to make a place for hyphenated identities, shifting identities that, when they settle down, do so only tentatively and temporarily on the borders of the in-between. A redefined notion of home (rather than *Heimat*) in Germany would have to put up with the indeterminacy of borders, would have to see the border as a "liminal" and "transitional sphere"[23] where a new identity has constantly to be constructed, to be "up for grabs," on both sides—the German and the foreign. Since the Germans have power through legal, economic and territorial means, the responsibility lies on those who find themselves in the dominant position to create an environment where a place can be made for the foreigner to feel "at home" without a "*Heimat*." The context within which *Heimat* and exile (no home), German and foreigner, can find themselves therefore has to be relational and open for debate.[24]

The conflation of foreigners with exiles attests to the fact that all *Ausländer* in Germany are to some degree exiles or homeless. Again the in-between space of hyphenated identities needs to be constructed for those who settle in Germany, whether refugees, immigrants, exiled persons, or asylum seekers. It must be possible to live in a non-absolute, non-utopian home. As Morley and Robbins state, "The crucial issue that now confronts European culture, we would argue, is whether it can be open to the condition and experience of homelessness . . . Can we imagine an identity, an awareness, grounded in the experience of not having a home, or of not having to have a home?"[25]

The new Germany may have to give up the Romantic notion of *Heimat* literally grounded in a genealogically rooted common past and a country (the remnants of the old Nazi *Blut und Boden* [blood and soil] concept) that is used to confirm a present fixed in a particular place. What results, according to Nora Räthzel, is a reunited Germany based on a common-sensical notion of cultural and biological homogeneity and articulated in a West German state reinforced and reaffirmed by the inclusion of the former GDR.[26] The conservative forces that continue to substantiate this notion have to recognize Germany's status as an immigration state that necessarily contains both a plethora of identities as well as racism. In Räthzel's terms:

> [W]hile the Federal Republic claims not to be a country of immigration, no less than 15 per cent of its workforce are immigrants. Consequently, concern focuses mainly on "integrating" migrants to keep in place the homogeneity of the *Kultur-nation*, while racism itself is untackled; indeed, racism does not exist, only *Ausländ-erfeindlichkeit*. It is within this logic, of the German nation as having a homogeneous population of German citizens, that battles are fought between those wanting to preserve such homogeneity, and those on the left who challenge this notion by rejecting any notion of national identity at all, because they see it as so closely bound up with the form of the state.[27]

Thus, leftists are equally to blame for the polarization "German/foreigner" that encourages racism and xenophobia. As part of their 1960s' heritage, they reject any notion of national identity, incorporated into a nation state they saw as inheriting the guilt and responsibility of the Third Reich. According to Gabriele Kreutzner, they seek "authentic" popular culture, for example, by "supply[ing] their public events with music from South America, from Greece, Turkey, etc." that "signifies a (romantic desire)"[28] for such authenticity outside of Germany. By reifying the foreign as exotic, as that which can only be experienced elsewhere, they contribute to a simple-minded celebration of otherness: only that which is not-German is "free of an ideological taint,"[29] worthy of admiration.

Unfortunately, the German discussion is so embedded in both the right's nationalist or common-sensical anti-immigrant discourses and the left's analogues
that the reevaluation of immigration laws as well as popular conceptions of otherness have been impeded. The association of German with white and Christian[30]
excludes the *Ausländer* ("coloured" and Muslim) and the Jew as well, it is not
surprising that the Turks have been called the "new Jews." Without a large and
visible Jewish community to provide a focus for any widespread anti-Semitic
movement (although anti-Semitism clearly exists without Jews), racism and xenophobia are displaced onto those people of colour who bear the brunt of anti-
foreign attacks. Obviously these discourses of hate circulate and transcend the
temporal or national political boundaries of the Third Reich of the two "new"
Germanies (after the so-called "*Stunde Null*" (Zero Hour) of 1945 that supposedly erased past evils and now of the newer reunited Germany.

As the literature I have cited reveals, critiques of racism, xenophobia and the
relationship to "home," seems to come apparently from outside of Germany or
from Germans such as Räthzel or Kreutzner writing in English for American or
British journals and audiences. Kreutzner's own discussion about cultural studies
in West Germany develops a thesis about why this displacement takes place. The
construction of a discourse in German in Germany has not yet been achieved and
may well still be the victim of the same bipolar thinking as that which constructs
absolute categories about Germans and *Ausländer*.

In a country that has invested so much of its identity as a *Kulturnation*, even
when divided into two German states, it may be time to go "beyond culture."[31]
Beyond the boundaries of a unified national "*Kultur*" (a German invention often
contrasted with French *civilisation*), it is the *multiplicity* of "cultures" (*Kulturen*)
that much more accurately represents contemporary German life. Even within a
narrowly German-defined concept of culture there are considerable differences
between and among "Germans" themselves, as the *de facto* continuing existence
of two Germanies within one newly (re)united Germany demonstrates. If unification has proved anything, it has shown that wholeness, totality, and harmony
is very much a romantic utopian notion not realizable in the political entities
peoples use as reference points for defining themselves. The breaks and disjunctures in Germany today attest to the "unachievability" of such myths in everyday
life. *Heimat*, the territorial vision of such an ideology, also remains unattainable,
at least in its present form. Today, in fact, the opposite is true, since the refugee
more appropriately represents the universal man or woman, since displacement,
fragmentation, transcience, as oxymoronic as it may be, seem to have become
rather permanent states.

The attention focused on foreigners, immigrants, asylum seekers, refugees and
on the attendant problems of xenophobia and racism have increased since Hoyerswerda. While this town became a symbol of hate and represented the frightening beginnings of a new phase in German social relations, it no longer resonates
so strongly, as attacks have spread all over Germany. Hardly a day has gone by
without some report, no matter how minor, of hostility towards foreigners. As
attacks increase in Germany and elsewhere in the new Europe, now on its way

towards "unity," we might take the German situation as a warning against the danger of reifying people and places, making neo-Nazis and Hoyerswerda emblematic for racism and thereby dismissing it from our everyday experience and our participation in such practices. Then we can be alerted to the limits and possible perils of seeking out "homes" that claim "to being people together" in the false dreams of wholeness, totality, and uniformity fixed in a specific place. The well-worn homily "There's No Place like Home"[32] takes on new import when place and location can no longer anchor people and identities constantly on the move. Perhaps we should learn to cope with the diasporic nature of European and American life in this future decades, and leave more space for coming and going.

NOTES

1. Exact figures are: "5.7 million foreign residents in all of Germany at present, comprising 7.2 per cent of the population. In some densely populated urban areas they account for well over 20 per cent. The largest ethnic group are Turks, with 1.7 million; Yugoslavs, slightly under 700,000 (excluding those who fled the war and are thus only temporarily in Germany); some 500,000 Italians; 330,000 Greeks; and 270,000 Portuguese." "Focus on Foreigners in Germany: Guest Workers, Asylum Seekers, Refugees and Ethnic Germans," German Information Centre, XI/91, p 3. The wording of the brochure and the descriptions accompanying the figures reinforce the distinctions and hierarchies that I address in this article among different kinds of foreigners. These figures appear to include only migrants and "guest" workers rather than white Westerners permanently residing in Germany.

2. "Das haßliche deutsche Haupt," Der Spiegel no. 6, 1992, pp 18–24. This recent article is only one of many in the German press about European fears and resentment towards reunified Germany's increasing political and economic power. Germany's position during the Yugoslavian conflict was one of the first examples of their new leadership position.

3. I am aware here as throughout this paper that while I am trying to distinguish hierarchies among "foreigners." I generalize about "the Germans." A similar differentiation is needed about "Germans" as well, especially today as regional identities in Germany become stronger.

4. These people, known as "ethnic Germans" (or "Volksdeutsche"), in official terms "Aussledler," designate those Germans in Western Poland who were part of Germany until the end of the Second World War. In a broader sense, they also refer to the descendants of those Germans who settled in Russia, Romania, Czechoslovakia and Hungary (German Information Centre brochure, p 5).

5. Figure from German Information Centre brochure, p 4: "During the first ten months of 1991, 203,320 persons sought asylum, already more than in all of last year and an increase of 25 per cent over the same period one year before. At present, most asylum seekers come from Eastern and Southeastern Europe." Since the Federal Republic has traditionally had one of Europe's most liberal asylum policies, many people who seek asylum are "no longer fleeing from individual political persecution, but from war and poverty in Third World countries and from economic chaos in Eastern Europe. This observation is borne out by the small percentage of those who are ultimately granted political asylum."

6. David Morley and Kevin Robins, "No Place Like *Heimat*: Images of Home(land) in European Culture." *New Formations*, no. 12, Winter 1990, p 10. This excellent article was indispensable in writing this piece and I am grateful to the authors for putting the *Heimat* debate into a broader European context.

7. Andrea C. Klimt, "Returning 'Home.' Portuguese Migrant Notions of Temporariness, Permanence, and Commitment," *New German Critique*, no. 46, Winter 1989, pp 69–70. This volume focuses on the topic "Minorities in German Culture."

8. Frank Drieschner, Kuno Kruse, and Ulrich Stock, "*Das Deutsche und das Fremde*," *Die Zeit*, no. 45, 8 November 1991, p 8.

9. "*Böse Deutsche, gute Ausländer, Rechte und linke Denkblokaden verhindern eine neue Einwanderungspolitik.*" *Der Spiegel*, no. 47, 1991, pp 112–23. The article refers to a discussion of this problem in a recently published book by Ute Knight and Wolfgang Kowalsky, *Deutschland nur den Deutschen.*

10. Homi K. Bhabha, "Introduction," *Nation and Narration*, Routledge, London and New York 1990, p 4.

11. Heidrun Suhr, "*Ausländerliteratur*: Minority Literature in the Federal Republic of Germany," *New German Critique*, no. 46, Winter 1989, pp 71–2.

12. Judith Miller, "Strangers at the Gate," *New York Times Magazine*, 15 September, 1991, p 81.

13. Roland Tichy, *Ausländer rein! Warum es kein "Ausländerproblem" gibt*, Piper, Munich and Zurich 1990, p 38.

14. Ibid., p 39.

15. I thank John Efron for drawing my attention to this important point. For further elaboration on Jews and racial policy see his dissertation, "Defining the Jewish Race: The Self-Perception and Responses of Jewish Scientists to Scientific Racism in Europe 1882–1993," Columbia University, New York 1991.

16. Dieter Thränhardt, "Patterns of Organization among Different Ethnic Minorities." *New German Critique*, no. 46, Winter 1989, p 13.

17. Thränhardt distinguishes between noble foreigners, foreigners (Spaniards, Yugoslavs and Greeks), strange foreigners (Portuguese, Italians and Vietnamese), and rejected foreigners (North Africans, Black Africans, Pakistanis, Persians and Turks). The two former categories require these people to be recognizable "nationally," for example, as an Italian or a Spaniard, rather than an Arab or an African.

18. Ruth Mandel, an anthropologist working with Turkish guestworkers in Germany, recounts a story about some of these ethnic Turks from Western Thrace, the northeastern-most region of Greece, who, while they carry Greek passports and are Greek citizens, identify themselves as " 'Turks from Western Thrace,' never as Greeks." This is an interesting twist to the questions of the presentation of self, construction of identity, and the permeability of ethnic boundaries . . . (pp 70–1). "Ethnicity and Identity Among Migrant Guestworkers in West Berlin," in *Conflict, Migration, and the Expression of Ethnicity*, Nance L. Gonzalez and Carolyn S. McCommon (eds), Westview Press, Boulder 1989.

19. Morley and Robins, op. cit., pp 4–5.

20. Morley and Robins, op. cit., p 10. Citing critics like Anton Kaes, Michael Geisler, Eric Rentschler and Duncan Webster on *Heimat*, the authors reinforce the central point that America, represented in Edgar Reitz's controversial film *Heimat*, is foreign, antithetical to Germany and has colonized the German's consciousness.

21. I pursue this topic in greater detail as it represents the problem of foreigners in Germany in a forthcoming article. "Refugees as Foreigners: The Problem of Becoming German and Finding Home." This will be published in a volume from the United Nations/

WIDER Conference "Trust and the Refugee Experience," held in June 1992 in Bergen, Norway.

22. Cited in Morley and Robins, op. cit., p 10.

23. I refer here to the terms used by Michael Kearney in an excellent article, "Borders and Boundaries of State and Self at the End of Empire," *Journal of Historical Sociology*, vol. 4, no. 1, March 1991, pp 52–74.

24. Morley and Robins, op. cit., p 13.

25. Ibid., p 19.

26. Nora Räthzel, "Germany: One Race, One Nation?." *Race & Class*, vol. 32, no. 3, 1991, pp 31–48. Aside from a penetrating analysis of German national identity and foreigners, Räthzel provides important demographic figures as part of her study.

27. Ibid., p 45.

28. Gabriele Kreutzner, "On Doing Cultural Studies in West Germany," *Cultural Studies*, vol. 3, no. 2, May 1989, p 245.

29. Morley and Robins, op. cit., referring to Kreutzner, p 11.

30. I am grateful to the work of Ruth Frankenberg on the construction of whiteness. See, for example, "Whiteness and Americanness: Discursive Constructions of Race, Culture, and Nation in White Women's Life Narratives," conference paper, American Ethnological Society, March 1991.

31. Edited by James Ferguson and Akhil Gupta. This is precisely the point made in the introduction to a recent volume of *Cultural Anthropology* on "Space, Identity, and the Politics of Difference."

32. See my article "There's No Place Like Home? Remapping the Topography of German Studies," *The German Quarterly*, vol. 62, no. 2, Spring 1989, pp 178–87.

Lauren Berlant

Lauren Berlant teaches English at the University of Chicago. She is the author of *The Anatomy of National Fantasy: Hawthorne, Utopia, and Everyday Life* (Chicago: University of Chicago Press, 1991), which uses the work of Nathaniel Hawthorne to explore the relationship between the "local" and the "national" in the public sphere and imagined community of nineteenth-century America, while abstracting a more general argument about the "political space of the nation." Her definition of the "National Symbolic," which we also use in our own introduction, is worth citing in full:

> the order of discursive practices whose reign within a national space produces, and also refers to, the 'law' in which the accident of birth within a geographic/political boundary transforms individuals into subjects of a collectively-held history. Its traditional icons, its metaphors, its heroes, its rituals, and its narratives provide an alphabet for a collective consciousness or national subjectivity; through the National Symbolic the historical nation aspires to achieve the inevitability of the status of natural law, a birthright. (p. 20)

By "national fantasy" in this context, Berlant means the process by which the complex and variegated imagery of the nation—its claims and incitements, and its broad and imposing array of representations—become meaningful and enter into the lives of its people, whether citizens or no. This process is particularly important to understand for those categories of the people who are not admitted to citizenship, but who nonetheless find themselves in the nation's promise and appeal, whether African-Americans before and after slavery, diverse minority cultures, outsiders of all sorts, women, or children.

Elsewhere in her work, Berlant explores histories of subalternity since the American Civil War, focusing both on women and the politics of sex and sexual privilege in the public sphere, and on African-Americans and the expropriating of their public history for the purposes of the dominant culture. She shows race working intricately with ideas and representations of gender and sexuality in the commodity and entertainment cultures of twentieth-century America, constructing elements of a national public sphere, which denies and affirms different promises of freedom and citizenship. This speaks to a specific set of histories, located in the conjunction of Hollywood and popular literature and commodification of culture between the 1920s and the 1950s, which are crucial to the power of the "national" in the modern United States. Berlant's essays expose both a key site of twentieth-century domination and the possibilities for survival within it. They show how cultural power is produced, instated, and secured; how its claims are naturalized; and how an appropriate representational repertoire is worked out and fashioned into place. They give us access to the making of hegemony in the Gramscian sense, in the double sense of power and resistance, imposition and consent. See "National Brands/National Body: *Imitation of Life*," in Bruce Robbins (ed.), *The Phantom Public Sphere* (Minneapolis: University of Minnesota Press, 1993), pp. 173–208; "The Queen of America Goes to Washington City: Harriet Jacobs, Frances Harper, Anita Hill," *American Literature*, 65, 3 (September 1993), pp. 549–74; "Race, Gender, and Nation in *The Color Purple*," *Critical Inquiry*, 14 (Summer 1988), pp. 831–59.

In this current essay she extends this analysis into a contemporary televisual text, an episode of the hugely popular cartoon show "The Simpsons," in which one of the characters, a daughter of the family, retraces a generic pilgrimage to the capital city, familiar from countless films, TV shows, fictions, and autobiographies, to experience "the nation in its totality." Many of Berlant's themes are brilliantly present in this essay—the centrality of mass-entertainment cultures in constructing the scene of national desire and identification; the rich and dense landscape of national iconography (buildings, monuments, heroes and personalities, regionalisms, physical geography, events and narratives of old and recent history, the general archive of national memory), which textures the visual culture of contemporary America; the innocence of citizenship; narratives of corruption and correction; forms of national pedagogy; the passages from everydayness to grandiosity, in which the national and the local meet. The essay demonstrates the importance of taking popular culture seriously, and is a splendid example of the new interdisciplinarity of cultural studies in motion.

The Theory of Infantile Citizenship

When Americans make the pilgrimage to Washington they are trying to grasp the nation in its totality. Yet the totality of the nation in its capital city is a jumble of historical modalities, a transitional space between local and national cultures, private and public property, archaic and living artifacts, processes of nation making that bridge the national history that marks the monumental landscape and the everyday life temporalities of federal and metropolitan cultures. That is to say, it is a place of national *mediation*, where a variety of nationally inflected media come into visible and sometimes incommensurate contact. As a borderland between these domains, Washington tests the very capacity of anyone who visits there: this test is a test of citizenship competence. Usually made in tandem with families or classes of students, the trip to the capital makes pedagogy a patriotic performance, one in which the tourist "playing at being American" is called on to coordinate the multiple domains of time, space, sensation, exchange, knowledge, and power that represent the scene of what we might call "total" citizenship.[1] To live fully both the ordinariness and the sublimity of national identity, one must be capable not just of imagining but of managing being American.

To be able to feel less fractured than the nation itself would be, indeed, a privilege. Audre Lorde tells a story of her family's one visit to Washington in 1947.[2] Lorde's parents claim to be making the trip to commemorate their two daughters' educational triumphs, in an eighth grade and a high school graduation. The truth is, though, that Lorde's sister Phyllis was barred from accompanying her graduating class on its celebratory visit to Washington because Washington was a southern, segregated city, not at all "national" in the juridical or patriotic sense. The Lorde family refuses to acknowledge racism as the impetus for its own private journey: rather, the very denial that racism is a national system motivates their performance as American tourists. For at every moment the family encounters its unfreedom to enter certain spaces of private property, the parents refuse to acknowledge the irony that, although "public" monuments like the Lincoln Memorial allow African-Americans like Audre Lorde and Marian An-

Lauren Berlant, "The Theory of Infantile Citizenship," *Public Culture*, 5, 3 (Spring 1993), pp. 395–410. Copyright © 1993 by The University of Chicago. All rights reserved.

Author's note: Much thanks to Michael Warner and the great audience at the Society for Cinema Studies for their critical engagement with this paper/project.

derson access to a public sphere of symbolic national identification, the very ordinary arrangements of life in America, eating and sleeping, are as forbidden to the Lorde family in Washington as America itself is to those without passports. This is to say that in Washington the bar of blackness effectively splits the national symbolic from the possessive logics of capitalist culture, even as each nonetheless dominates the American public sphere.

Still, they schedule their visit to Washington on Independence Day, and when Lorde bitterly remarks on her patriotic exile from America, symbolized in the apartheid of its most local abridgment, and in particular in a waitress's refusal of the family's desire to celebrate the nation's birthday by eating ice cream they had paid for *inside* of a restaurant, she describes it as the line she steps over from childhood to something else, a different political, corporeal, sensational, and aesthetic "adulthood": "[T]he waitress was white, and the counter was white, and the ice cream I never ate in Washington D.C. that summer I left childhood was white, and the white heat and the white pavement and the white stone monuments of my first Washington summer made me sick to my stomach."[3] Lorde's "education" in national culture provoked a nauseated unlearning of her patriotism— "Hadn't I written poems about Bataan?" she complains, while resolving, again, to write the president, to give the nation another chance to not betray her desire for it—and this unlearning, which is never complete, as it involves leaving behind the political faith of childhood, cleaves her permanently from and to the nation whose promises drew her parents to immigrate there and drew herself to identify as a child with a horizon of national identity she was sure she would fulfill as an adult citizen.

That was 1947. Stephen Heath has argued recently that transformations in the production of political consciousness that have taken place in the context of developments in global media culture have made the category "citizen" archaic, and many worthy theorists of television in particular agree that the ruptural force of its technologies and logics of capital has unsettled norms of signifying national culture and political agency.[4] It is now a commonplace in television criticism that television promotes the annihilation of memory and, in particular, of historical knowledge and political self-understanding. It may be an ontology and ideology of "liveness," common sense, banality, distraction, catastrophe, interminable "flow": it may be the implicitness of capital in generating an ideology of "free" entertainment (which makes the consumption of commercial, "free/floating" anxieties about power, history, and identity the metaproblem *and* the critical promise of the medium), it may be the global lexicon of images that has come to dominate the pseudomulticultural scene of consumption, or—perhaps— some combination of these.[5] But because in all areas of its mode of production television encounters, engages, and represents citizenship, and because it underscores the activity of animating and reflecting on as well as simply having a national identity, the problem of generating memory and knowledge in general becomes fraught with issues of national pedagogy, of representing what counts as patriotism and what counts as criticism to the public sphere of consumers itself.[6]

If, as I have described, the pilgrimage to Washington is already all about the activity of national pedagogy, the production of national culture, and the constitution of competent citizens, then the specificity of mass mediation in the dissemination of national knowledges redoubles and loops around the formation of national identity. There is nothing archaic about citizenship—its signs and cadences are changing. Margaret Morse (1990) argues that television enters history by annexing older forms of national self-identity, cultural literacy, and leisure. It does this to reacclimate continuously consumer identifications during transitions in media-saturated national and international public spheres: in these conditions of specifically uneven development, the work of media in redefining citizenship and framing what can legitimately be read as national pedagogy becomes more, not less, central to any analysis of political identity in postmodern American culture.

This is to say that the definitional field of citizenship—denoting either simple membership in a political identity category or a reflexive operation of agency and criticism—is precisely what is under contestation, as the norms of signifying in what we might call "mass nationality" change the face of power in America (e.g., in the public discussion over town halls versus other modes of national "expert" culture). In addition, the problem of harnessing publicity to struggles within national culture predates the televisual moment—just as *Mr. Smith Goes to Washington* predates *Adventure in Washington, Born Yesterday*, and more recent narratives like *The Distinguished Gentleman*. These intertexts and many others structured by pilgrimages to Washington all foreground the problem, place, and promise of media in the business of making nationality; they all contain montages and plots that show both the potential for agentive citizenship and the costs of the mediated dispersal of critical national identifications. Television's role in constructing the hegemony of the national must thus be understood as a partial, not a determining, moment in a genealogy of crises about publicity and the production of "national" subjects.[7]

This essay explores the genre of the pilgrimage to Washington, focusing not on a news or a biographical event but on an episode of the popular weekly cartoon television show "The Simpsons," entitled "Mr. Lisa Goes to Washington." This project is about how different modes of national and mass cultural memory specifically intersect in America. As intertexts to this episode, the essay will gesture toward the other tourist/citizenship pilgrimages this episode revises, notably *Mr. Smith Goes to Washington*. Deploying the typical codes of the narrative trope, they hold that the state of America can be read in the manifestations of infantile citizenship and in the centrality to national culture of an imaginary children's public sphere.[8]

Lisa Simpson wins a trip to Washington ("all expenses paid") by writing a "fiercely pro-American" patriotic essay for a contest that her father, Homer Simpson, discovers in a complementary copy he receives of *Reading Digest*. The family stays at the Watergate, encounters Barbara Bush in the bathtub at the White House, visits the mint, and generates commentary on national monuments. Then Lisa accidentally witnesses graft (securing the destruction of her beloved hometown national park by logging interests—signaling the realpolitik, the will-to-dominate-nature of the Reagan-Bush era). Lisa then tears up her prizewinning essay, substituting for it a new essay about how Washington "stinks." Losing her patriotic simplicity, she loses the national jingoism contest. A Senate page, seeing her loss of faith in democracy, calls his senator for help, and within two hours the FBI has the crooked congressman in jail: he rapidly becomes a born-again Christian. On witnessing the evidence of the effects of her muckraking, Lisa exclaims, at the end of the show, "The system works!" We will return to the question of systems later.

I have described the aspects of this plot that are repeated in the other pilgrimage-to-Washington narratives. Someone, either a child or an innocent adult described as an "infant," goes to Washington: the crisis of her/his innocence/illiteracy emerges from an ambivalent encounter between America as a theoretical ideality and America as a site of practical politics, mapped onto Washington, D.C. All of the "children" disrupt the norms of the national locale: their "infantile citizenship" operates the way Oskar Negt and Alexander Kluge (1992) predict it would, eliciting scorn and cynicism from "knowing" adults who try to humiliate them and admiration from these same adults, who can remember with nostalgia the time that they were "unknowing" and thus believed in the capacity of the nation to be practically utopian.

As it is, citizen adults have learned to "forget" or to render as impractical, naive, or childish their utopian political aspirations, in order to be politically happy and economically functional. Confronting the tension between utopia and history, the infantile citizen's insistent stupidity thus gives her/him enormous power to unsettle, expose, and reframe the machinery of national life. Thus the potential catastrophe of all visits to Washington: can national identification survive the practical habitation of everyday life in the national locale? Can the citizen/tourist gain the skills for living nationally without losing faith in nationality to provide the wisdom and justice in promises? Is the utopian horizon of national identity itself a paramnesia or a Zizekian "fantasy" that covers over impossible contradictions and lacks in national culture?[9] The stakes in a text's answer to these questions have everything to do with the scene of "adult" or "full" citizenship in its historical imaginary.

The transition in Audre Lorde's life from patriotic childhood to a less defined but powerful rage at the travesty everyday life makes of national promises for justice indeed marks a moment in the education of an American citizen that marks both personal and fictional narratives of the pilgrimage to Washington whose intertextual topography will be the subject of this essay. When cinematic, literary, and televisual texts fictively represent "Washington" as "America," they thus both theorize the conditions of political subjectivity in the United States and reflect on the popular media's ways of constructing political knowledge in a dialectic of infantile citizenship and cynical reason. To extricate the politics of this dialectic on behalf of a history of citizenship, my strategy here will be to work from the negative pedagogical to the utopian, mass-mediated horizons of national identity practice.

INCOMPETENT CITIZENS AND JUNK KNOWLEDGES, AMERICAN-STYLE

"Mr. Lisa Goes to Washington" shares with *Born Yesterday, The Distinguished Gentleman*, and other "Washington" narratives a rhetoric of citizenship that locates the utopian possibilities of national identity in terroristic, anarchic, and/or comic spectacles of someone's personal *failure* to be national. The "scene" of citizenship is revealed by way of events that humiliate a citizen, disclosing him/her as someone incapable of negotiating the semiotic, economic and political conditions of his/her existence in civil society. And just as the dirty work of representing the detritus of a white, bourgeois national culture will almost inevitably go to the citizens whose shameful bodies signify a seemingly natural incapacity to become (masters of the) abstract, the plot of "Mr. Lisa Goes to Washington" is embedded not in Lisa's story but in the gross activities of the failed father, Homer Simpson.

The show opens with Homer opening his junk mail. He is reading what the mail says and yelling at the letters in minor sarcastic outrage at their mistakes (e.g., one is addressed to "Homer Simpsoy") and their pseudopromises of wealth with no risk or labor. Yet, for all of his cynical knowledge, he also makes a grave optimistic reading error. Rapacious and desiring to the point of senselessness, Homer takes a representation of a "check" in a Publisher's Clearing House–like contest as a real representation of money. He goes to the bank to cash the million-dollar pseudocheck—that says phrases like "void void void" and "This is not a check"—and is devastated to find the "deal" "queered." Homer continues, throughout the episode, to show himself incompetent in the face of money—indeed, in a scene toward the end, he makes the very same error with another check. When the eventual winner of the patriotism contest symbolically shares his prize with Lisa, a prize represented by what the young man calls an "oversized novelty check," Homer yells from the audience, "Give her the check!" and then, amidst everyone's laughter, protests, "I wasn't kidding." Though at every moment money appears in the show Homer has no control over the differences between its symbolic and exchange value—unlike Bart, who understands and exploits to his great pleasure the ambiguity of the word "expense" in "all expenses paid"—Homer is constantly surprised and betrayed at his constant "discovery" that even in Washington money is not "free."

What Homer does well instead is to drool and moan and expose himself compulsively like an idiot relegated to his insipid appetites. Immediately after his humiliation by the advertising check, he becomes, literally, the "butt" of more jokes about freedom and about money: having proved his inadequacy to owning money in late capitalism by miscasting the contest check as a negotiable one, he stands up and shows the "Simpsons" audience the top, cracked part of his exposed rear. Like a bald spot or an unzipped fly, the crack of the butt winks at the cruel superior public that knows how to use money, knows how to distinguish between real and false checks, and can stick to a decorous hierarchy of desires, needs, and appetites, while regulating its body. Homer has no capacity to think abstractly, or to think: as when he drools on the head of a worker at the mint and then sputters "lousy, cheap country!" when they refuse to give out free samples of money.

There are many other instances of Homer's humiliation by the tacit text of bourgeois nationalism in this episode, as he tries to enter as a master public language and knowledges. His working-class brutishness is disclosed, for example, in the scene of Lisa's triumph at the "Veterans of Popular Wars" contest. When a contest judge feels suspicious of young Lisa having written such a beautiful essay, she opines, "Methinks I smell the sickly scent of the daddy," and decides to interview Homer, who becomes entirely aphonic and grunting in the face of her series of questions. Lisa gets extra points for having survived descending from such a brute. Later, snorting down "free" food at the convention in Washington, Homer again loses language at a moment when he explicitly attests to his love of the vocabulary-builder sections of *Reading Digest*: he asks but is unable to retain the information clarifying this chain of signs: "V (Very) I (Important) P (Person)." Why should he? for he is none of these things. With none of the social competences of a person who has knowledge about money or the world, he demonstrates what George Lipsitz has called the "infantile narcissism" of consumer self-addiction: "Who would have thought," he says to Lisa, "that reading or writing would pay off!"[10]

"HAVE . . . YOU EVER RUN INTO ANY PROBLEMS BECAUSE OF YOUR SUPERIOR ABILITY?"

When Homer "loses" the million dollars, his wife, Marge, consoles him by showing him the "free" *Reading Digest* they have received in the mail. Like Billie Dawn learning to negotiate the topography of power through print and other national media in *Born Yesterday*, Homer becomes a regular public intellectual while he reads the magazine: he pulls the children away from a "period" film they are watching on television about the Anglo-American theft of land from Native-American nations (which depicts a white preacher telling an "Indian chief" that the tribe's homeland will be more valuable if they abandon and irrigate it) and reads them a true-life adventure story; he is caught reading on the job at the nuclear power plant by Mr. Burns, who asks his assistant, "Who is that bookworm, Smithers? . . . His job description clearly specifies an illiterate!"; and he reads "Quotable Notables" as a substitute for eating lunch. But when Homer reads that the patriotic essay contest is for children, he loses interest in the magazine and throws it out. This is when "Mr. Lisa" takes over the plot: fishing as usual through the garbage of her family's affections to gain some emotional capital, she becomes, as Bart says, ". . . the pony to bet on."

In what does Lisa's smartness and competence consist? When she first attempts the patriotic essay, she tries dutifully to quote Ben Franklin or to extract inspiration from a diagram showing how a bill becomes law. But, quoting *Mr. Smith*, "Mr. Lisa" comes to derive her power from association with a kind of "natural" national property whose value is in its noncirculation in a system of exploitation and profit: the public domain called Springfield National Park. "America, inspire me," she says to the park, and a bald eagle straight from the national seal alights in front of her. This collaboration of the national symbolic and nature enkindles Lisa, and the show provides a montage of such speeches by our "patriots of tomorrow" in which her speech takes top honors.

As a backdrop to this little speech-making montage, the "nation" imagined by its youth is visually signified by a pastel national map marked by the kinds of local-color images that airport postcards often sport, by some regional accents, and by the homely spun-out puns and metaphors of American children:

1. Nelson Muntz ("Springfield"), "Burn, Baby Burn": So burn that flag if you must! But before you do, you'd better burn a few other things! You'd better burn your shirt and your pants! Be sure to burn your TV and your car! Oh yeah, and don't forget to burn your house! Because none of those things would exist without six red stripes, seven white stripes, and a helluva lotta stars!!

2. Anonymous girl (Rosemount, Minnesota), "Recipe for a Free Country": Recipe for a Free Country: Mix one cup liberty, with three teaspoons of justice. Add one informed electorate. Baste well with veto power . . . . Stir in two cups of checks, sprinkle liberally with balances.

3. Anonymous boy (Mobile, Alabama), "The American Nonvoter": My back is spineless. My stomach is yellow. I am the American non-voter.

4. Anonymous boy (Queens, New York), "Ding-Dong": Ding dong. The sound of the Liberty Bell. Ding. Freedom. Dong. Opportunity. Ding. Excellent Schools. Dong. Quality Hospitals.

5. Lisa Simpson (Springfield, T.A.): "The Roots of Democracy": When America was born on that hot July day in 1776, the trees in Springfield Forest were tiny saplings, trembling towards the sun, and as they were nourished by Mother Earth, so too did our fledgling nation find strength in the simple ideals of equality and justice. Who would have thought such mighty oaks or such a powerful nation could grow out of something so fragile, so pure. Thank you.

There is a certain regularity to what counts as a patriotic essay: the range of tonalities and rhetorical modes notwithstanding, fiercely patriotic citizenship always requires the deployment of analogies that represent the threat of imaginary violence to the national body—of the biosphere; the citizen; the conceptual, mappable nation. Even the feminine essay, "Recipe for a Nation," carries the implied warning that bad citizenship together with bad government is a form of bad nutrition that threatens the body politic. The national stakes of keeping these domains of the social in at least linguistic conjunction are comically telegraphed throughout the episode: the ultimate contest winner, Vietnamese immigrant Trong Van Din, says, "That's why, whenever I see the Stars and Stripes, I will always be reminded of that wonderful word: flag!"

But why does Lisa win? Is she simply smarter or more creative than the other kids? She wins with her essay, "The Roots of Democracy," because she uses not just analogy but a national allegory that links organically the nation's natural growth to the emergence of its political facticity. In addition, her speech is itself an allegory of infantile citizenship, for the nation grows out of "something so fragile, so pure," so young. No secular or human power has yet affected its course: apparently, in the national/world "system" natural value prevails, assuring that in the infinite "tomorrow" all systems will exist in the space of America. In this, her "intelligence" is articulated in excess to the jingoism of ordinary Americans—in this episode, these are figured by white, decorous persons carrying protest-style placards bearing messages like "Everything's A-OK," "No Complaints Here," and "Things Are Fine" in front of the White House.

Thus, when Lisa gets to Washington, she feels supremely national, symbolic, invulnerable, intellectual. Although her superiority to other kids derives simply from her capacity to sustain a metaphor, and although in Washington she makes pranks and acts like a kid, she also seeks there an affirmation of her idealized self-image: learning early that the reason people go to national conferences is to find confirming images of their ideal selves, she asks the other kid finalists, "Have either of you ever run into any problems because of your superior ability?" and hugs them when they confirm, saying plaintively, "Me, too!" Her capacity to reflect on language and power marks her as the national Simpson in this episode, even as the public surely knows that it is Bart, not Lisa, who has captured the minds and money of consumers who identify with his bratty tactical disruptions and exploitations of the bourgeois public sphere. Her already-confirmed failure as a commodity outside of the show surely follows her around every episode in which she imagines that she might find a place for her "superior talents" in the national system. In this regard, she is Homer's twin, not his opposite: their excesses to the norms of body and language mark them each precisely as American failures, citizens unfit to profit from their drives and talents in a national symbolic and capitalist system.

THE END OF NATIONAL FANTASY:
"THE SYSTEM WORKS!"

However, while each of the Simpsons is finding and revelling in her/his level of national competence, the federal nation is itself operating and corrupting both the natural and the capital forms that inspire the Simpson family. National corruption is tacitly everywhere in the show: the family stays at the Watergate; their bank advertises itself as "not a savings and loan"; Homer scoffs, "Yeah, right," at a sign in the White House bowling alley that claims Nixon bowled back-to-back 300 games there; Teddy Kennedy sits quietly at the Kennedy Center award ceremony, looking formless and dissipated; Lisa's congressman is shown cynically exploiting her for a photo opportunity (a form of presidential mass mediation invented, naturally, by Nixon).

But when Lisa witnesses graft that threatens to despoil the natural beauty of Springfield National Park, the tacit knowledge of national corruption the show figures via "Nixonia" becomes itself the ground of a new figuration of nationality that she produces. This requires, in two stages, recourse to a genealogy of national forms through which criticism and patriotism have been traditionally routed and

mediated. The transformation of consciousness, sensuality, causality, and aesthetics she experiences is, again, typical of this genre, in which the revelation of
the practical impossibility of utopian nationalism produces gothic, uncanny, mir-
aculating effects in the affects of the persons whose minds are being transformed
by "true," not idealized, national knowledges.

In stage one of Lisa's transfiguration, she immerses herself in the national
symbolic, preparing to give her patriotic speech by visiting a constellation of
Washington monuments. The payoff she sees takes place at the "Winnifred Bee-
cher Howe" memorial, raised in fictive tribute to "an early crusader for women's
rights [who] led the Floor Mop Rebellion of 1910," who later "appeared on the
highly unpopular 75 cent piece." Howe's motto, I Will Iron Your Sheets When
You Iron Out the Inequities in Your Labor Laws, marks the overdetermined and
absurd space of Lisa's imaginary relation to American nationality. It is not only
the absurd notion that America would honor a labor activist who foregrounds the
exploitation of women as workers, not the incommensurateness of sheets/labor
laws, nor, merely, the wild ungoverned state of Howe's statuesque body, in its
messy housewife regalia, nor Lisa's sighing adoration of this spectacle. The violent, nationally authored insult this absurdity hides in sarcasm is reduced, finally,
to mere sexual grossness: in the afterglow of the congressman's sale of his favors
to the lobbyist at the memorial, they look at Howe and say, on parting, "Woof
woof!" and "What a pooch!"

Lisa is heartbroken: "How can I read my essay now, if I don't believe my
own words?" She looks up from the reflecting pool at the Lincoln Memorial and
feels that "Honest Abe" will "show me the way." But the memorial is over-
crowded with Americans obsessed with the same possibility. They crowd around,
projecting questions to Lincoln's stony, wise, iconic face; the questions range
from, "What can I do to make this a better country?" to "How can I make my
kid brush more?" and "Would I look good with a mustache?" Lisa, crowded
out in the cacophony of national-popular need, goes to Jefferson's memorial,
where the statue yells at her in ressentiment that his own accomplishments are
underappreciated by the American people. She leaves quickly and goes to sit on
the Capitol steps. There, magically, federal workers in their white-collar suits are
transformed into pigs with skins engraved in the mode of dollar bills, sitting at
troughs gorging themselves on dollar bills, wiping their mouths on the flag. This
mutation of the cartoon places this episode in a genealogy of critical editorial
cartooning, especially where national criticism takes the form of petty sarcasm;
moreover, the gluttonous snorting of the pigs refers to Homer's own grotesque
greedy excesses, thus reframing the class hierarchies and incompetences of national culture that the Simpsons embody into translations of the patriarchal corruptions of the national symbolic and the federal system themselves.

It turns out, in short, that Lisa was not that smart. I have described how America is split into a national and a capitalist system in "Mr. Lisa Goes to Washington." But this simple description is for infants, just as Bart's opening punishment
on the blackboard, "Spitballs are not free speech," reduces the problem of protecting costly speech to a joke, a joke that once again allegorizes the conceptual

problematic of freedom and its media by locating politics in a disgusting body. Lisa's response to the revelation of graft is to not become an adult, that is, to disidentify with the horizon of the politically-taken-for-granted whom the nation seeks to dominate. Her first response is to become abjected to America, by visiting Lincoln and soliciting his pedagogy. We have seen there, comedically, how the overidentification with national icons evacuates people's wisdom from the simplest judgments of everyday life; failing this identification, Lisa next invents a countercartoon aesthetic: she changes her title from "The Roots of Democracy" to "Cesspool of the Potomic."

But this first explosion of the affect, causal norms, monumental time, vision, sensation, and aesthetics of American citizenship is followed by yet another dislocation. This montage sequence takes place at the moment the Senate page beholds Lisa's crisis of faith in democracy. He telephones a senator; the FBI entraps the corrupt congressman, on videotape; the Senate meets and expels him; George Bush signs the bill; a newspaper almost instantly reports the congressman's imprisonment and conversion to a born-again consciousness. Lisa says, "The system works!"

As in the telephone, telegraph, newspaper popular media montage sequence of *Mr. Smith Goes to Washington*, "The Simpsons" produces national criticism through another countertransformation of time, space, and media that involves shifting from the lexicon of patriotic monumentality and classical national representation to accelerating postmodern media forms: video, microchip bugs, cameras, late-edition daily newspapers. In addition, here the FBI's mastery of the media establishes it as the guardian of America, much as in the extraordinary 1933 film *Gabriel over the White House*: in contrast to the corrupt and lazy print media of *Mr. Smith*, "The Simpsons," and dozens of other pilgrimage-to-Washington films, global media formations are the real citizen-heroes here. Televisual technology itself becomes the representative of the "average man" who rises above his station, protected by FBI agents who seek to clean out and preserve all sorts of purity: of language (the FBI agent uses a southern drawl in his criminal guise and reverts to a television announcer's pure generic intonations in his "real" persona as the police), of region, and of the purity of the stream of faith that connects residents of the "mythical" Springfield, T.A., to the nation that represents America in Washington.

In two minutes of television time, and two hours of accelerated chronological time, then, the system cleans itself out, and the cesspool itself becomes born again, returns "home" to the discourse of national growth. Nothing complicated about this. The performance of mass media–dominated national political culture reveals a system of national meaning in which *allegory is the aesthetic of political realism* at every moment of successful national discourse, one in which the narrative of that discourse itself, at a certain point of metarepresentation, becomes a conceit that erases aggregate memory as it produces knowledge of the nation as a thing in itself. The competent citizen knows this and learns how conveniently and flexibly to read between the lines, thus preserving both domains of utopian national identification and cynical practical citizenship. This temporalizing mode of resolving questions about the way power dominates bodies, value, exchanges, dreams in the national public sphere is typical of the pilgrimage genre: for the resolution in time takes over what might slowly and unevenly happen in space were the system to be publicly engaged and remarked on in its own incoherence and unevenness. As it is, when Lisa says, "The system works!" she embodies the "patriot of tomorrow," because through the randomness we have witnessed she continues to believe a system exists, that "bills" motivated by democratic virtue do, indeed, become law. But to which system does she refer?

"SPITBALLS ARE NOT FREE SPEECH"

In "Mr. Lisa," as in every fictive pilgrimage to Washington, national monuments, traditional symbolic narratives, print, radio, and television news coexist with other popular phenomena: here the right-wing cultural agenda of the Reagan-Bush era is everywhere in the narrative, including in its recourse to sarcasm as a form of criticism and in the tacitness of the Nixon intertext, which "reminds" without interfering with the pleasure of the narrative of a televisual moment when the nation thought it possible to imagine a patriotic mass-mediated *criticism*. It is not just that television histories, children's textbooks, *Reader's Digest*, FBI surveillance video, national parks, and national spaces are here brought into conjunction, constituted as the means of production of modern citizenship. It is not even just that the Bushes themselves are portrayed here as benign patriarchs—for this might be coded as the text's return to the modality of wishful resolution that seems to mark the crisis of *having* national knowledge inevitably produced by the pilgrimage.

But the very multiplicity of media forms raises the question of the genres of patriotism itself, modes of collective identification that have become the opposite of "protest" or "criticism" for a generation of youths who have been drafted to vitalize a national fantasy politics unsupported by a utopian or even respectable domestic political agenda. The construction of a patriotic youth culture must be coded here as a postmodern nationalist mode of production: in this light, Bill Clinton's recent appearances on "Mister Rogers' Neighborhood," MTV, and so on involve merely one more extension of the national aura to the infant citizens of the United States, who are asked to identify with a "youthful" idealism untempered by an even loving critical distance.

This is to say that Lisa's assertion that the system works counts as even a parodic resolution to her epistemic murk because consciousness that a system exists at all has become what counts as the ideal pedagogical outcome of contemporary American politics: thus, in the chain that links the fetus, the wounded, the dead, and the "children" as the true American "people," the linkage is made through the elevation of a zero-sum mnemonic, a consciousness of the nation with no imagination of agency—apart perhaps from voting, here coded as a form of consumption. In other words, national knowledge has itself become a modality of national amnesia, an incitement to forgetting that leaves simply the patriotic trace, for real and metaphorically infantilized citizens, that confirms that the nation exists and that we are in it. Television is not the cause of this substitution of the fact (that the nation exists) for the thing (political agency) but is one of many vehicles where the distilling operation takes place and where the medium itself is installed as a necessary switch point between any locales and any national situation.

Let me demonstrate this by contrasting the finales of *Mr. Smith* and "Mr. Lisa": It is a crucial and curious structure of infantile citizenship plots that the accumulation of plot leads to an acceleration and a crisis of knowledge relieved not by modes of sustained criticism but by amnesia and unconsciousness. At the end of *Mr. Smith*, Jefferson Smith, played by Jimmy Stewart, is defeated by capitalists' manipulation of the law, property rights, and the media: Smith, who has been filibustering and improving on what discursive virtue might look like in the Senate, is confronted by a wagon load of telegrams embodying a manufactured public opinion mobilized against Smith and his cause; Smith, dispirited and depleted, faints on the Senate floor. His loss of spirit drives a senator (Claude Rains) to attempt suicide and to confess everything: in the film's final moments, a hubbub lead by Jean Arthur claims victory over corruption, and the mob dances out of the chambers into, presumably, the streets. The film, in other words, leaves Mr. Smith lying there on the Senate floor, unconscious. It might be interesting to speculate about what he would think when he awoke: would he think the system had worked? How could he, when so many systems were at play?

In contrast, it might seem that Lisa's violation by capital logic produces consciousness: but her belief in the "system" is renewed by the condensation of time and power the television-style media produce for her. By the end the field of waste and excess that has dominated the scene of patriotism makes her forget not just what she knew but what she did not know: and we realize, on thinking back to her speech, that at no point did Lisa know anything about America. She could be inspired by the national symbolic and by the corruptions of capital; she is moved aesthetically by nature's nation and also by the boorish appetites of both professional and ordinary men; she is not at all transformed by her experience of Washington, though she remembers she had experiences there.

The infantile citizen has a memory of the nation and a tactical relation to its operation. But no version of sustained agency accompanies the national system here. It provides information but no memory-driven access to its transformative use: it is not surprising, in this context, that the two commercials between the opening credits and the narrative proper—for the U.S. Army and for an episode of "In Living Color" that featured the violent heterosexualization of a gay film critic—promote the military life and the Cold War, to the suppression of American gay identity on behalf of national boyhood and heterosexual national manhood; it is not surprising, in this context, that I could pull the script of this episode from a "Simpsons" bulletin board using Internet, a computer network derived from a U.S. Defense Department system that currently frames much of the information about scientific and military culture across the telephone lines daily. Just as every pilgrimage-to-Washington narrative deploys information and scientific technologies to link the abstract national to the situated local, underinformed, abjected, and idealistic citizen, so too this system confirms its necessity at every moment for the production of the knowledge that American media perform for the child/consumer who has no "interests" but is touring Washington in order to feel occasionally "free."

Yet a distinguished tradition of collective popular resistance to national policy has taken the form of marches on Washington: dispossessed workers, African-Americans, gays, lesbians, queers, pro- and antichoice activists, feminists, veterans of popular and unpopular wars, for example. These collective activities invert the small-town and metropolitan spectacle of the "parade" honoring local citizens into national acts, performances of citizenship that predict votes and make metonymic "the people" whom representatives represent, but they also claim a kind of legitimate mass political voice uniquely performed outside of the voting booth. On the one hand, mass political marches resist, without overcoming, the spectacular forms of identification that dominate mass national culture—through individualizing codes of celebrity, heroism, and their underside, scandal—for only in times of crisis are Americans solicited to act en masse as citizens whose private patriotic identifications are indeed *not enough* to sustain national culture at a particular moment. On the other hand, we might note as well the problem mass political movements face in translating their activities into the monumentalizing currency of national culture: in this light, we witness how an impersonation or an icon of political struggle can eclipse the movement it represents, for instance in the image of Martin Luther King on the mall; in the image of the subaltern citizen in the body of the fetus; or in the image, dominating national culture as we speak, of the infantile citizen, too helpless to do anything but know, without understanding, what it means that the "system" of the nation "freely" exists, like "free" television itself.

NOTES

1. See Anderson (1983) and Caughie (1990).
2. See Lorde (1982:68–71).
3. Ibid., 71.
4. See Heath (1990:278–79).
5. For the main arguments for the pervasiveness of televisual amnesia or information fatigue, see Mellencamp, ed. (1990:222–39). See also Feuer (1983).
6. The ongoing pedagogic/civic activity of television is more widely appreciated on the right, and the saturated moral domination of the medium by conservatives has been central to the right-wing cultural agenda of the Reagan-Bush era. What counts as "public" access "public" television has undergone massive restrictive redefinition under the pressure of a certain pseudorepresentative form of "public" opinion, whose virtue is established by reference to a supposedly nonideological or noninterest group–based politics of transcendence that must be understood as fundamentalist in its imagination of a nation of pure, opinionated minds. For overviews and thoughtful reconsiderations on the left, see Lipsitz (1990); Morse (1990); Rasula (1990); Schwoch, White, and Reilly, eds. (1992).
7. This essay is a much shortened version of a longer investigation of pilgrimages to Washington in history/narrative, as one relay into thinking through whether there is, in fantasy or in instrumental practice, something called a "national" culture. The texts mentioned in this paragraph are crucial intertexts to the theory of infantile citizenship.
8. See Negt and Kluge (1992).

9. See Zizek (1989:87–129).
10. Lipsitz (1990:70–71).

REFERENCES

Anderson, Benedict. 1983. *Imagined Communities: Reflections on the Origins and Spread of Nationalism.* London: Verso.

Caughie, John. 1990. "Playing at Being American." Pages 44–58 in Mellencamp, ed.

Feuer, Jane. 1983. "The Concept of Life Television: Ontology as Ideology." Pages 12–21 in E. Ann Kaplan, ed., *Regarding Television: Critical Approaches—an Anthology.* Washington, D.C.: University Publications of America.

Heath, Stephen. 1990. "Representing Television." Pages 278–79 in Mellencamp, ed.

Lipsitz, George. 1990. *Time Passages: Collective Memory and American Popular Culture.* Minneapolis: University of Minnesota Press.

Lorde, Audre. 1982. *Zami: A New Spelling of My Name.* Trumansburg, N.Y.: Crossing Press.

Mellencamp, Patricia, ed. 1990. *Logics of Television: Essays in Cultural Criticism.* Bloomington: Indiana University Press.

Morse, Margaret. 1990. "An Ontology of Everyday Distraction: The Freeway, the Mall, and Television." Pages 193–221 in Mellencamp, ed.

Negt, Oskar, and Alexander Kluge. 1992. "Selections from *The Proletariat Public Sphere.*" *Social Text* 35/36:28–32.

Rasula, Jed. 1990. "Nietzsche in the Nursery: Naive Classics and Surrogate Parents in Postwar American Cultural Debates." *Representations* 29 (Winter): 50–77.

Schwoch, James, Mimi White, and Susan Reilly, eds. 1992. *Media Knowledge: Readings in Popular Culture, Pedagogy, and Critical Citizenship.* Albany, N.Y.: SUNY Press.

Zizek, Slavej. 1989. *The Sublime Object of Ideology.* New York: Verso.

Index

CPSIA information can be obtained at www.ICGtesting.com
Printed in the USA
BVOW020716291111

276945BV00002B/4/P